9th edition

fundamentals of selling

John W. Wingate

Professor Emeritus of Marketing
Bernard M. Baruch College
City University of New York

Carroll A. Nolan

Professor of Marketing
Chairman, Department of Business Education
Syracuse University

SOUTH-WESTERN PUBLISHING COMPANY

Cincinnati / Chicago / Burlingame, Calif. / Dallas / New Rochelle, N. Y.

S16

Library of Congress Catalog Card No.: 70-78527

45678H65432

Printed in the United States of America

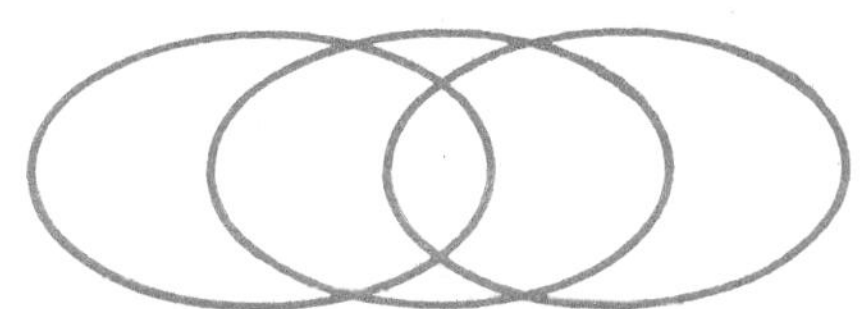

preface

In the 40-year span between the first edition of *Fundamentals of Selling* and this, the Ninth Edition, there have been extensive changes in the business world that have changed the very nature of selling. Years ago, when communication facilities were practically nonexistent, business customers and ultimate consumers could not afford the time nor expense for trips to central markets. The market had to be brought to them. Thus, the conduct and expansion of trade was dependent largely upon traveling salesmen who called upon far-distant customers at long intervals. During their visits, these salesmen used every trick of persuasion to force their customers to place orders. Their goal was to overcome customer resistance and to bring home the order.

This situation no longer exists. Today's competitive marketplace and today's sophisticated consumers call for a new kind of selling: creative selling. Today's salesman wants to sell—he must sell—what is best for the customer. He has a continuing interest in his customers' problems. He cultivates long-term relationships and does not look to each immediate order as his only source of income. The manufacturer's or wholesaler's salesman looks to his customers' healthy growth for his own growth and profits. His primary job is to help his customers sell. The retail salesman of today is not merely an order taker but rather is expected to be a merchandise authority who can give sound advice to the consumer with a buying problem.

During the years that have elapsed between the Eighth and Ninth Editions of *Fundamentals of Selling,* the greatest change in selling has been the giving of increased emphasis to the study of consumer behavior. Experts in marketing and selling have come to realize that for a salesman to sell most effectively, he must thoroughly understand why the consumer acts as he does. To help understand consumer buying behavior, progressive sellers are coming more and more to draw upon the principles of the behavioral sciences. In this Ninth Edition, *Fundamentals of Selling* has been completely revised to reflect this new attitude and to make the textbook more suitable for modern teaching approaches.

The Ninth Edition contains 16 chapters grouped into five units. Each chapter is divided into five parts, and each part is suitable for one day's reading assignment. The arrangement of supplementary activities has been completely changed in this edition. Each part is followed by vocabulary exercises, review questions, and discussion questions which enable students to review and amplify the knowledge they have gained from reading the part. Each chapter is followed by skill-building activities in English and arithmetic, research activities related to the chapter's content, case problems, and a continuing project which allows the student to develop an occupation manual in a chosen area of selling. For students in need of additional work, extra credit assignments are also provided at the end of each chapter.

Unit I presents fundamental business and economic information which serves as a background for the remainder of the book. Before he can hope to become a good salesman, a student must understand the economic framework in which he will be working. Part B, "Characteristics of the American Economy," and Part D, "Economic Trends," are two new parts which give essential economic information that has great implication for tomorrow's salesmen.

The content of Chapter 2, "Selling Organizations and Selling Jobs," has been completely reorganized; and one new part has been added. This part, "Theories of Selling," discusses the various selling theories commonly used today and emphasizes the importance of using depth selling and creative salesmanship to adequately satisfy customer needs and wants. Throughout the book, and particularly in this chapter, the duties and responsibilities of the contact salesman and the retail salesman have been clearly separated.

Chapters 4 and 5 in Unit II are the two basic chapters dealing with the importance of understanding consumer buying behavior, although the relationship between the behavioral sciences and selling is a continuing thread throughout the book. Chapter 4 discusses consumer needs, wants, and buying motives in considerable detail. Part E of this chapter is of special interest to sellers and marketers, since it deals with market segmentation—a new and important tool for virtually every modern selling firm. Chapter 5, "Communicating with Customers," is entirely new. It describes both the basic communication process and the operation of the communication process in selling. Many of the principles discussed in this chapter can be applied to any kind of communication, whether selling-oriented or not.

Unit III, "Personal Selling Techniques," is the heart of the text. This unit contains five chapters, and these five chapters give students detailed and specific guidelines for handling face-to-face customer contacts. The activity of personal selling is described in a logical sequence: prospecting, the preapproach, the appointment, the approach, the sales talk, demonstrating, handling objections, closing the sale.

Chapter 11 within Unit III, "Special Skills in Contact Selling," is an entirely new chapter. Most students using this text will enter retail selling, and the primary emphasis throughout the text is upon retail selling. Yet, to get a broad picture of the total selling activity, students should understand the specialized duties of the manufacturer's or wholesaler's salesman. Chapter 12, "Special Skills in Retail Selling," is a companion to Chapter 11 and contains two new parts on stockkeeping and on handling complaints and guarding store security.

In this Ninth Edition, the treatment of nonpersonal selling techniques has been expanded. Today, mass media of communication—many of which reach buyers all over the country—perform much of the selling job. By nonpersonal means, the customer is made aware of merchandise and services offered for sale and of their points of superiority. Three new parts dealing with printed advertising media have been added to the text in Chapter 13. In Chapter 14, three new parts on radio and television advertising have been included.

The content of Chapter 15, "Activities in Sales Management," has been reorganized and expanded. The principal addition in this chapter is Part E, "Data Processing in Selling," which discusses important applications of electronic data processing techniques in sales management decision making.

The format of *Fundamentals of Selling* has been completely changed in this Ninth Edition to give a more modern, open appearance. Chapters are organized so that different levels of headings, each in a different type face or type size, are used. Thus, each chapter is easy to outline and review. Color is used throughout the book to improve its teaching effectiveness and its appearance. Virtually all illustrations in this edition are new.

With the intensification of competition in the business world, businessmen are recognizing that their chief problem is not to create products and services but rather to sell them. To achieve this goal, they welcome all the assistance they can get from trained, competent salespeople. Selling is one of the oldest professions in existence and one of the most rewarding. A young person may enter the field of selling with the knowledge that it is a worthy profession with tremendous possibilities for serving other people.

John W. Wingate
Carroll A. Nolan

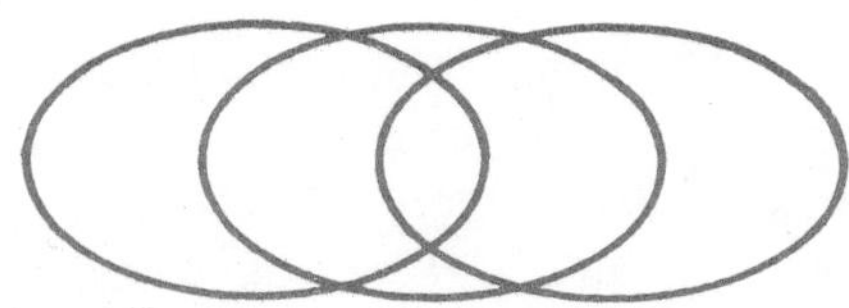

contents

UNIT I
THE WORLD OF SELLING

UNIT II

THE CUSTOMER, THE PRODUCT, THE FIRM

UNIT V

SALES MANAGEMENT

Selling in the 1920's . . .

The decade began with Prohibition and a wild, frustrated generation that hurled itself into what appeared to be postwar prosperity. Lindbergh and Byrd were its heroes, Jolson and that crazy jazz, its soul. It was an age of overnight miracles. Radio stations sprang up one after the other. Insulin was discovered in 1922. The Eskimo Pie was patented along with dry ice and the household gas refrigerator. In 1928, men finally had electric shavers, and women had a home permanent wave. Throughout the decade, the car changed the whole pattern of the real estate market and sparked new methods of consumer finance. It was an age of excess, but many a spirit crumbled under the likes of Tammany Hall. Most remarkably, the 1920's made real the automobile philosophy of producing more for less.

UNIT I

The World of Selling

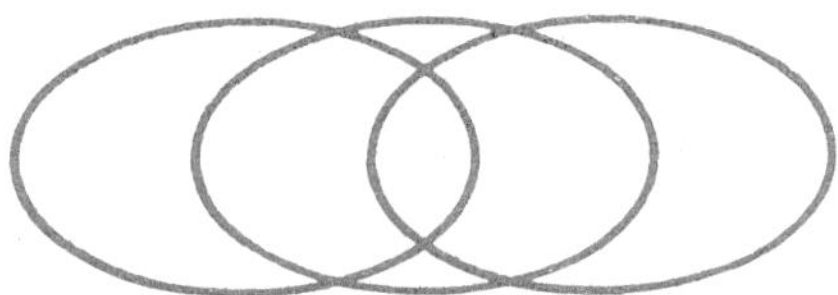

chapter 1

foundations of modern selling

KEY QUESTIONS

A In what respects are we all salesmen, even though we may not make selling our career?

B How does selling contribute to the national prosperity of this country?

C If the marketing concept had never been developed, what effect would this have had on selling?

D What might it be like to be selling goods and services in the year 2000?

E Can a salesperson successfully pretend to be interested in his customer if his true interest is the money he will make on the sale?

part A

the changing nature of selling

Of all occupations, selling is perhaps the most far-reaching and the most permanent. Salesmen have existed in every society, in every part of the world, in every century since one primitive man swapped an animal skin for a stone chisel. And at some time in his life—whether or not he is conscious of it—every person is a salesman.

WHAT IS SELLING?

Ask someone what "selling" means, and the answer is likely to go something like this: "The activity in which goods and services are transmitted from a seller to a customer in return for money from the customer." This definition is accurate enough, but it is too limited. *Selling* is the specialized business of assisting and persuading prospective customers to obtain goods and services to the mutual satisfaction of both buyer and seller. Within this broad definition, one can think of many instances in which he himself has been a salesman.

Everyone has something to sell. Friends are people to whom one has "sold" the idea that they would like to know him. In getting a job, one "sells" his services to an employer, and the employer continues to pay for the services so long as they are performed satisfactorily. Either goods or services may be sold; goods are called *tangibles*, and services are called *intangibles*. The manufacturer must sell the products that he makes, and the farmer must sell the agricultural products that he grows. These goods are tangibles. Banks sell many types of financial services; theaters sell entertainment services. These services are intangibles.

A GLIMPSE OF SELLING'S HISTORY

Selling—a crude form of it—began when one enlightened caveman discovered that another caveman had an article that he wanted and that there was a better way to get the article than clubbing its owner over the head. That first caveman looked around for something he owned that the other caveman might want, then he tried to talk the second caveman into exchanging one article for the other. Trading was the first kind of selling; it still exists in some situations in our economy and is still a major selling method in other less advanced societies. No money was involved in early sales transactions. The introduction of money to the selling process has been attributed to the Phoenicians.

Throughout the early history of selling, sales activities were confined to limited areas. Transportation and communication between populated areas were practically nonexistent. Also, each family made or grew most of the goods it needed to survive and required relatively few exchanges of goods. The Middle Ages gave a sudden boost to the activity of selling. Transportation had improved; so had communication; and there were simply more people who were potential users of goods. In this era, certain persons began to specialize in making certain kinds of goods. Shops of craftsmen in metal, leather, and textiles appeared in the growing towns. These craftsmen soon began to travel from town to town to peddle their merchandise, and selling became more firmly planted in people's lives.

Many people think that only goods and services can be sold, yet many other activities are really selling activities. What might this radio disc jockey be selling?

The event which most stimulated the development of modern selling was the Industrial Revolution, which began in England in 1760. Machines replaced hand labor; and goods could be made in greater quantities, in less time, and at lower prices than ever before. Hundreds of new products were introduced by new manufacturers, and selling became a critical skill. Businessmen could no longer wait for the customer to come to them when a product was needed. To make a profit, these businessmen had to seek out customers and convince them to buy their products. Without the skills of salesmen, few of the businesses could have stayed in operation.

SELLING IN AMERICA

In the early days of America's existence, the population was, of course, clustered on the Atlantic coast. People made many of the household products they needed and depended primarily on European manufacturers for the goods they could not make. As people moved westward after the American Revolution, they had to have contact with the sources of goods on the eastern coast; and this need resulted in the appearance of the *peddler*. He traveled on horseback or by wagon, selling to frontier families and to trading posts the goods that could not be produced in wilderness regions. These goods included food products such as spices that could not be raised on the farm, simple manufactured household goods and tools, and some clothing supplies. The peddler did little creative selling; his customers were anxious to get the items he brought, so he assisted—rather than persuaded—them to buy.

As trading posts and crossroads stores grew into villages and towns, larger merchants began to make semiannual trips to the central buying markets. At first these centers were located in eastern seaports; later Chicago and other midwestern cities became buyers' markets. In these centers, merchants were often wined and dined by high-pressure salesmen of specialized lines who frequently banded together to monopolize all of a visiting merchant's patronage.

With the railroad in the 19th Century came a new kind of traveling salesman—the *drummer*. Merchants with expanding merchandise assortments found that they could not visit the buying centers often enough to purchase the goods they needed, and manufacturers in the buying centers found that they would lose business if they waited for buyers to come to them. So the manufacturers hired representatives—drummers—to travel to the buyers' places of business.

The drummer usually depended on a fast-talking approach, a dominating personality, and plenty of selling gimmicks. His arrival in a town was exciting, because he was the chief news-bearer from the "civilized" world. To the drummer, making a substantial sale on the spot was more important than building a loyal clientele. He generally made a quick sale and caught the next train out of town.

THE RISE OF MODERN SELLING

By the early part of the 20th Century, selling had progressed greatly in the development of its techniques and in making its place in the world's economies. However, the basic strategy of selling—from the seller's point of view—had changed little since primitive times: Sell your product to the customer any way you can; the purpose of selling is to benefit *you*, not the customer. Few salesmen considered either the customer's potential satisfaction in making a sale or the building of long-term selling relationships. Selling tactics were often unethical, and the gullible customer had little chance of not being fleeced by a glib-tongued salesman.

As America progressed into the second and third decades of the 20th Century, however, the old era of selling began to die. Certain economic developments made a new kind of salesmanship necessary. Production increased, more and more new products were introduced, the purchasing power of consumers increased, communication and transportation improved. But perhaps the most important developments pointing toward the need for creative selling were the growing education and sophistication of consumers and the protection of consumer interests by government regulations. The consumer no longer had to come to a particular seller every time a particular item was needed. He could choose from among a number of sellers and a number of similar products. He was becoming knowledgeable enough to demand honesty in selling and to demand that selling efforts be directed toward his, not the seller's, satisfaction.

In our present economic environment, a salesman can no longer be just a high-pressure order taker. He must be a creative salesman. *Creative salesmanship* involves both assisting and persuading customers to buy the products or services which best fit the customer's needs and wants.

The need for creative salesmanship has never been more critical than it is now. The modern salesman must concentrate on satisfying his customers and his employer in the best possible way. Today the

Montgomery Ward

The person who sells furniture must be a creative salesman. He must not only be an expert on furniture styles, upholstery fabrics, and workmanship, but must also have considerable knowledge about interior decorating to make sure that the furniture he sells will best fit the customer's needs and wants.

salesman must have a continuing interest in customer problems. He must cultivate long-term relationships and not look to each immediate order as his only source of income. A young person may enter the field of selling with confidence that he can become a skilled merchandise advisor to his customers and that he can occupy a useful, respected place in society.

CHECKING YOUR KNOWLEDGE

Vocabulary:

The following terms are commonly used in selling. Study these words and make them a permanent part of your vocabulary by using them often.

(1) selling	(4) peddler
(2) tangibles	(5) drummer
(3) intangibles	(6) creative salesmanship

Review questions:

1. Why is it said that everyone has something to sell?
2. What contribution did the Middle Ages make to the selling process?

3. How did the Industrial Revolution affect modern selling?
4. Compare today's selling in this country with the selling that existed in the 18th and 19th Centuries.
5. Why does successful selling now involve more than just taking orders?

For discussion:

1. Goods are sold by some businesses, and services are sold by other businesses. Do you think goods or services are more important to today's consumer? Why?
2. Successful selling depends on obtaining customer satisfaction and repeat sales instead of forcing merchandise on a customer with no regard for repeat business. Do you think today's salesman should be trained differently than the drummer of past years? Why?
3. What do you think is the greatest challenge faced by salesmen today?

part B
characteristics of the American economy

America's economic system is a *private*, or *free, enterprise system*. Under this system, persons are free to go into business, produce whatever they desire, and distribute the products as they choose. The theory behind the system is that the businessmen who best serve customers will succeed and the inefficient businessmen will fail. Another name for this economic system is *capitalism*. It has been found that we need some government regulation to insure fairness in business dealings for both businessmen and consumers, so the term *modified capitalism* more accurately describes our economic system today.

Because of the freedom inherent in our economic system, the role of selling is perhaps more important here than in any other type of economic system. Consumers are free to buy or not to buy, and creative selling is necessary to persuade them that one seller's product will better fit their needs than will a competitor's product. Good selling intensifies the tempo of business activity. It can help raise the standard of living and make it possible for consumers to match their needs and wants with the merchandise and services the marketplace provides. In economics, the only substitute for selling is compulsion.

BASIC ECONOMIC CHARACTERISTICS

The economic system of this country has been defined. The importance of the selling activity in this economy has been discussed. But what factors make the private enterprise system like other economic systems, and what factors make it like no other? A knowledge of how our economic system operates is essential to good selling. The next few paragraphs discuss the economic concepts our private enterprise system shares with certain other systems. Later in the part there will be a discussion of the factors that make our system unique.

Needs and Wants of Consumers

Everyone who uses goods and services is a *consumer*. Those persons who use goods and services for their own satisfaction are called *ultimate consumers;* those who use goods and services in their businesses to produce other goods or to operate public institutions are known as *industrial, commercial,* or *institutional users.*

To survive, ultimate consumers must have food, clothing, shelter, and rest. These things need not be elaborate nor expensive, but the consumer must have certain quantities of each. To survive, the industrial, commercial, or institutional user must have basic materials, equipment, and supplies to manufacture his products or provide his services. The necessities of both types of consumers are called *needs*.

Ultimate consumers also desire goods and services that provide a sense of well-being beyond that resulting from the satisfaction of needs. Membership in a country club, a wardrobe purchased at the most exclusive store in town, and a new sports car can contribute to a consumer's sense of well-being; but they are not needs. An industrial consumer may desire furniture to make his office more attractive, lounges to make his employees more comfortable, and a new imposing building to keep up his image in the community. The desires for products which fulfill a function other than that of satisfying needs are called *wants*.

It is sometimes difficult to draw a line between needs and wants, mostly because consumers are not always logical in their choice of whether to satisfy a particular need or a particular want. Each consumer has a scale of needs and wants. The needs are generally satisfied first, and the wants are satisfied to the extent that the consumer's economic situation allows. One undisputed point can be made, however, about needs and wants: they are endless. Needs must constantly be satisfied if a consumer is to exist; and once a particular want has been satisfied, a different want generally takes its place.

Production

Without production, there could be no goods and services to satisfy consumer needs and wants. *Production* in its broadest sense means the creation of utility. *Utility* is the economic value in goods which makes them useful to consumers. Four different kinds of utility are added to goods during the production cycle. When the form or shape of an item is altered to make the item more useful to consumers, the product acquires *form utility*. When a product is available at the place where it is needed or wanted, it acquires *place utility*. When a product or service is available at the time it is needed or wanted, it acquires *time utility*. When the ownership of a good or service is transferred to the person who will use it, the product acquires *possession utility*. From the point of view of most consumers, a product must have all four utilities before it can satisfy a need or want.

To carry on the production cycle, four basic *factors of production* are necessary: natural resources, labor, capital goods, and management. Natural resources are, of course, such things as minerals, water, and soil. Labor is the human effort which is responsible for the production of goods and services. *Capital goods* are things such as tools and machines which do not directly satisfy wants but which are used to produce other goods and services that can satisfy wants. Management, in the form of a person or a group, brings together the other three factors and allocates them so as to maximize production. Our technology and its utilization of the factors of production is more advanced than that of any other country in the world, and a significant aspect of this technology is *mass production*—the use of machinery to manufacture great numbers of the same kind of article.

Consumption

When consumers use goods and services to satisfy needs and wants, this activity is called *consumption*. Two different types of goods may be consumed—industrial goods and consumer goods. *Industrial goods* are those commodities used to produce other goods or that are consumed in business operation. Examples are raw materials, parts, machinery, and supplies used by manufacturers and other types of businesses. *Consumer goods* include all merchandise destined to be sold to and consumed by the ultimate consumer. An example is an automatic washer for household use. For general classification purposes, industrial and consumer services are usually included in the category of "goods."

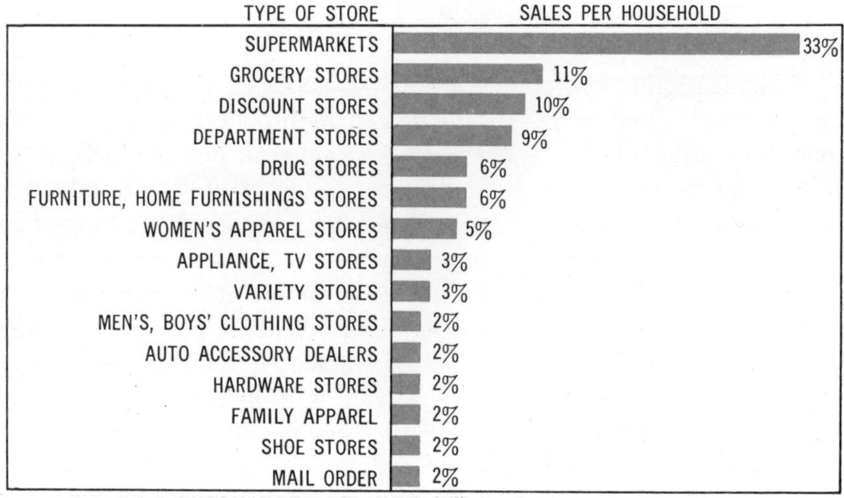

The Discount Merchandiser

Most consumer goods are bought in retail stores. The chart above shows how annual consumer expenditures for a recent year were distributed among the major types of retail stores (exclusive of service businesses).

UNIQUE CHARACTERISTICS OF OUR ECONOMY

Certain elements make the private enterprise system different from economic systems in other countries. The most important of these elements are private property, competition, supply and demand, and distribution of income.

Private Property

Basically, persons go into business to earn an income for themselves. They also want to perform a service or provide a product that they think is necessary or desirable, but the profit motive is the most important reason. *Profit* is the difference between costs of operation and receipts from sales. To make a profit, businessmen must be able to own, use, and sell articles of value; the ability to do this is called the right of *private property*.

Competition

The lifeblood of our economic system is *competition*—the rivalry among businesses for buyers. This rivalry exists at every level of business: manufacturers compete with one another for resale of their products to wholesalers and retailers; wholesalers compete with each other for resale to retailers; retailers compete with each other for resale to ultimate consumers. Primarily, it is competition—coupled with the element of consumer freedom of choice—that makes selling such an essential function in our economy. The salesman must differentiate between competing products similar to his own and show the consumer how his product can satisfy the consumer's needs and wants.

Supply and Demand

Supply refers to the quantity of a product that will be offered for sale at a particular time and at a particular price. *Demand* refers to the quantity of a certain product that will be bought at a particular time and at a particular price. Before demand is said to exist, the consumer must have not only the need or want for the product but also the money with which to buy the product and the willingness to part with that money.

In other economic systems, such as communism, the government determines the supply and the price of a product. In the private enterprise system, with its freedom of buying choice and its competition,

American Airlines

From a seller's point of view, a major problem in meeting competition is differentiating between his product or service and the similar product or service of a competitor. The first airline companies to install television sets in their planes did so to differentiate their basic services of travel convenience and safety from the services of competitors. Now virtually all major airline companies have television sets on coast-to-coast flights.

supply and demand forces constantly interact to determine the price at which an item will be sold. Generally, the more demand for a product, the higher is its price. Thus, an item in short supply for which there is great demand can be sold at a rather high price. If the supply of the product were greater than the demand for it, the price would drop.

Distribution of Income

A decision that must be made by all societies is how to use the factors of production (natural resources, labor, and so on) and how to divide the resulting production among the people in the society. In some economies, the production may be divided equally among all people, regardless of each person's contribution to the total production effort. In our economy, an individual's share of the production is determined by how much money he has to buy goods and services; and the amount of money he has to buy goods and services is determined by the amount and quality of his production effort. Essentially, money that he acquires is based on his skill in his occupation, for which he is rewarded in wages. This is not necessarily an individual's only source of income, but it is the major source for most people.

CHECKING YOUR KNOWLEDGE

Vocabulary:

(1) private, or free, enterprise system
(2) capitalism
(3) modified capitalism
(4) consumer
(5) ultimate consumers
(6) industrial, commercial, or institutional users
(7) needs
(8) wants
(9) production
(10) utility
(11) form utility
(12) place utility
(13) time utility
(14) possession utility
(15) factors of production
(16) capital goods
(17) mass production
(18) consumption
(19) industrial goods
(20) consumer goods
(21) profit
(22) private property
(23) competition
(24) supply
(25) demand

Review questions:

1. Why does selling have such an important role in our economic system?
2. Is it always possible to classify the needs and wants of consumers? Why?
3. Name the four kinds of utility added to goods during the production cycle.
4. What specific elements of our free enterprise system make it different from economic systems of other countries?
5. How do supply and demand determine the price at which an article will be sold?

For discussion:

1. Why do other economic systems possess some concepts that are common to our free enterprise system?
2. How does selling help to determine what is produced?
3. How can a product be improved through competition?
4. Is profit basically a return to the businessman for his services, or is it a toll he is able to exact from his customers?

part C
the marketing process

Production and consumption are the most important forces behind our whole economic structure. Without production, there can be no consumption; without consumption, no production. But how are the two brought together? Shoes at the end of a production line do no one any good. They are of no use to the manufacturer until they are sold; they are of no use to the consumer until he buys and wears them. How do these shoes in an Illinois factory reach the feet of a customer in New Jersey? How do Florida oranges get to the refrigerator of a Detroit family? The answer is: through marketing.

Marketing includes all the activities of moving goods from producer to consumer and of changing the goods' ownership. The term *distribution* is often used interchangeably with the term "marketing." The marketing process adds place, time, and possession utilities to goods; and, as you have learned, these utilities make goods valuable and desirable for consumption.

MARKETING ACTIVITIES

Many different businesses help carry out the marketing activities. Some businesses perform the basic marketing activities; others perform the subsidiary activities. Both types of activities are essential to the smooth operation of the marketing process.

Basic Marketing Activities

Merchandising, buying, and selling are the basic marketing activities. Merchandising involves planning to provide the right goods, at the right time, in the right quantities, at the right place, at the right price. Buying involves obtaining goods from producers or suppliers. Selling includes the activities of personal salesmanship and nonpersonal salesmanship, such as advertising and display.

Subsidiary Marketing Activities

Performing the basic activities of merchandising, buying, and selling is still not enough to move goods from producer to consumer. A number of other activities are necessary: (1) storing, (2) financing, (3) traffic management, (4) accounting, (5) risk management, (6) marketing research, and (7) standardization and grading.

The storing activity involves keeping an adequate supply of goods on hand and in a proper order for easy use. Financing involves providing the needed capital for business operation and granting credit to customers in return for their promises to pay in the future. Traffic management means the determination of methods and routes of shipment. Accounting, an essential activity in every business, concerns the keeping of adequate records. In risk management, businesses assume or shift the risk of loss through insurance in order to serve customers promptly. Marketing research, an area of extreme importance today, is the collection and analysis of information about customers, suppliers, and merchandise. Standardization and grading involve the establishment of uniform specifications for varieties of merchandise and sorting the merchandise according to these standards and grades.

CHANNELS OF DISTRIBUTION

In the marketing process, the path that a product takes on its way from producer to consumer is called the *channel of distribution*. Sometimes a producer may choose to sell goods directly to the consumer; this is called *direct marketing*. At other times he may choose to distribute his goods through other businesses in order to reach the consumer; this is called *indirect marketing*.

Direct Marketing

Both industrial and consumer goods are moved by direct marketing. Industrial goods, however, are most commonly distributed by this method because it is the simplest way for producers to move their products to those businesses which will use them in making other consumer goods or in operating public institutions. Thus, manufacturers of automobile

Chas. Pfizer & Co., Inc.

International marketing is becoming increasingly important for many American businesses. Complicated marketing installations and large sales forces are often established in foreign countries to effectively distribute goods from the manufacturer in this country to a consumer in another country. In this illustration, a sales representative for an American manufacturer of pharmaceuticals is discussing his products with a doctor in Nagoya, Japan.

tires sell their tires directly to the automobile factory. Consumer goods distributed by direct marketing are generally perishable items such as farm products. However, manufacturers of such items as household supplies and cosmetics also find direct marketing effective.

Indirect Marketing

With indirect marketing, one or more businesses are placed in the channel of distribution between producer and consumer. These businesses are called *middlemen*—dealers who assist in the distribution of goods from producer to consumer. The channel chosen may have one, two, or more middlemen; and sometimes a combination of channels is used. Indirect marketing is the most common method for distributing consumer goods.

Channels with One Middleman. When a producer of consumer goods decides to sell to a retail store, which will then resell to the ultimate consumer, he has added one middleman to the channel of distribution. Merchandise which has a distinct fashion appeal or which is quite expensive is frequently distributed through one middleman. Some industrial goods may be distributed through channels with one middleman, a *wholesaler*. This is a dealer who buys from producers or other wholesalers and sells to retailers or to industrial, commercial, or institutional users.

Channels with Two Middlemen. For some consumer-goods items, manufacturers find it more efficient to distribute their products through both wholesalers and retailers. Staple goods, such as canned foods, are frequently bought by the wholesaler and then resold to the retailer, who eventually resells to the ultimate consumer. Seldom are industrial goods distributed through two middlemen.

Channels with More Than Two Middlemen. When more than two middlemen are added to a channel of distribution, these middlemen may be agent middlemen, commission merchants, or brokers. You will learn more about their activities in Chapter 2. Some consumer goods are distributed through more than two middlemen; but industrial goods are not distributed in this way, because the large quantities involved make repeated handling costly.

THE MARKETING CONCEPT

It is impossible to separate selling activities from the marketing process; selling is involved in every marketing activity. Manufacturers must sell their products to wholesalers or to other manufacturers; wholesalers must sell their products to retailers, to other middlemen, or to industrial consumers; retailers must sell their goods to ultimate consumers; producers of services must sell their services to manufacturers, middlemen, and ultimate consumers.

In Part A you learned about the "new" selling attitude. The change in selling's attitude toward its own functions is part of the revision of the overall attitude of businesses engaged in marketing. As a result of changes in the economic environment, businesses found that they needed to take a hard look at their approach to the marketing process and at their attitudes toward the consumer's role in marketing. The scrutiny many of these businesses gave their old marketing doctrines resulted in the adoption of the *marketing concept*. Briefly defined, this concept is the idea that all business activities should be focused on the needs and wants of the consumer and that all marketing functions should be organized into one major division of the business. All businesses engaged in marketing—and, thus, all businesses engaged in selling—should be customer-oriented.

A number of economic developments stimulated the formulation of the marketing concept, but the most significant developments were these:

1. *Increased product competition.* Today the marketplace offers thousands of new products and services that did not exist a decade ago. The success of new products and services hinges on the flexibility, effectiveness, and speed with which new techniques of moving these goods can be developed.
2. *Increased consumer purchasing power.* In the early years of this century, consumers had barely enough money to purchase necessities. Now, however, as our economy flourishes, the amount of discretionary income continues to increase. *Discretionary income* is the difference between a person's total disposable income and what he has to spend

Whirlpool Corporation

To effectively utilize the marketing concept, firms must constantly evaluate their marketing efforts. Many businesses periodically conduct training seminars at which salesmen can exchange experiences, learn about new and improved products, and sharpen their selling techniques.

for a minimum standard of living. Businesses must plan how to market their goods effectively so as to obtain their proper share of this discretionary spending.

3. *Increased consumer sophistication.* Today's consumer is better educated and more sophisticated than the consumer of 30 years ago. He has more leisure time, more mobility, and more income to buy the luxuries he wants; he is protected by government legislation from buying products that might be deceptive in content or that might be harmful to him. Sellers have learned that to get the consumer to buy their products, they must study him carefully and anticipate his needs.
4. *Dependence on mass communication.* Many different kinds of advertising media are now available to businesses, and by nonpersonal means consumers are made aware of merchandise and services offered for sale. In planning advertising, businesses must consider the particular consumer to whom their advertising should be directed and the appeals they will use for this consumer.

When a firm fully utilizes the marketing concept, there are certain obvious characteristics of its operation:

1. The firm has a long-range view of its marketing activities, rather than a short-run view.
2. The firm emphasizes the interdependence of all its marketing activities.
3. Products are analyzed in terms of the value they have for the consumer.
4. The firm is primarily concerned with satisfying the consumer and believes that its profits are the necessary result of giving the consumer quality products at a fair price.
5. The firm continually seeks to develop new and improved products and to increase its share of the consumer market.

CHECKING YOUR KNOWLEDGE

Vocabulary:

(1) marketing
(2) distribution
(3) channel of distribution
(4) direct marketing
(5) indirect marketing
(6) middlemen
(7) wholesaler
(8) marketing concept
(9) discretionary income

Review questions:

1. Name and define the three basic marketing activities.
2. Name and define the seven subsidiary marketing activities necessary to move goods from producer to consumer.

3. Explain the basic differences between direct and indirect marketing channels.
4. Trace briefly the four major economic developments which stimulated the formulation of the marketing concept.
5. Why is the marketing concept essential to modern selling?

For discussion:

1. Some consumers feel that the marketing process would be more efficient if certain middlemen were eliminated. Do you agree? Why?
2. What should salesmen do to bring about effective application of the marketing concept?
3. As our economy grows and more products are available to the consumer, do you think the marketing concept will be as important as it is today?

part D

economic trends

At no time have selling and marketing been more important—and more difficult—than they are today. Because of the nature of our private enterprise system, our economy is a dynamic one. By the minute, changes occur in economic characteristics. What exists today may not exist tomorrow, and the change a marketer least expects may be a reality a week from now. Identifying the changes—and even anticipating them—is critical; but the most important implication of flux in the economy, from the seller's point of view, is how to meet change effectively. It can be met by scientific marketing techniques and by creative salesmanship.

CURRENT ECONOMIC DEVELOPMENTS

The trends with which today's sellers and marketers are most concerned are those involving population, mobility, the youth movement, income, education, leisure time, and automation.

Population

It is predicted that by 1975, there will be more than 225 million ultimate consumers in this country. In addition to this figure, industrial, commercial, and institutional users consume over half the dollar value of all manufactured goods. Since the end of World War II, the population has been growing at the rate of 1½% per year. This growth obviously means that there is a greater market for goods and services than ever before, but the very size of the population also makes marketing and selling tasks more difficult. Once a people's living standard rises above that of providing the minimum necessities, the presence of more people does not automatically mean greater sales. Sales efforts must be expanded to cope with the population increase. Without increased consumption, there cannot be increased production; and in order to increase consumption, it is necessary to create more buyers and more buying.

The location of the population is also of significance to marketers. The West and Southwest are growing faster than other parts of the country, and more and more people are moving to the suburbs. The farm population now accounts for less than 10% of the total population. These figures are of particular importance to new retailing businesses trying to decide where to locate their firms. Obviously they will want to choose the location which has the most potential customers. The most noticeable result of the flight to the suburbs is the growth of the shopping center, which was practically unheard of several decades ago. These centers now account for about 25% of U. S. retail trade.

Mobility

Americans are a nation of travelers. Tourism is a major industry and has resulted in the establishment of hundreds of new businesses, particularly service businesses such as travel agencies, motels, and roadside restaurants. Estimates also show that about 25% of the total population will change residence in any given year. This, of course, means business for such firms as moving companies, storage firms, and real estate agencies. The mobility of our population also means that marketing organizations must continually study their markets to make sure their selling efforts are still directed to the proper consumer group.

Youth Movement

The age group showing the greatest increase in number since World War II is the young-adult group. Today about 40% of our population is under 20; about 50% is between 20 and 64; and about 10% is over 64. Gaining in importance is the teenage market, partly because many of these persons have part-time jobs and thus have their own money to spend and partly because they greatly influence the spending

Mobile Homes Manufacturers Association

The tremendous sales increase in mobile homes can be traced to Americans' freedom of mobility. Today there are more than 22,000 mobile home parks in this country, and nearly 5 million people live in mobile homes. Of the mobile home households, 25% have incomes over $7,000; and 10% are headed by professional and managerial people.

habits of their families. Much marketing effort in product development, in advertising, and in personal selling must be directed to this youth market and to the young adults setting up their own households.

Income

Most consumers today have more money to spend than they have ever had before. The median family income has more than doubled since 1947, and a large portion of this income is discretionary income. All businessmen struggle to get their share of this discretionary income, and most advertising is aimed at attracting this income rather than at attracting the consumer's expenditures for necessities. The middle class—those persons earning $5,000 to $15,000 per year—is the most important market for most selling organizations. This class accounts for about 60% of the total consumer income.

Education

College enrollment should double between 1960 and 1970, and there is no sign of a decrease in the desire of young people to go to college. Such trends have implication for marketing businesses because

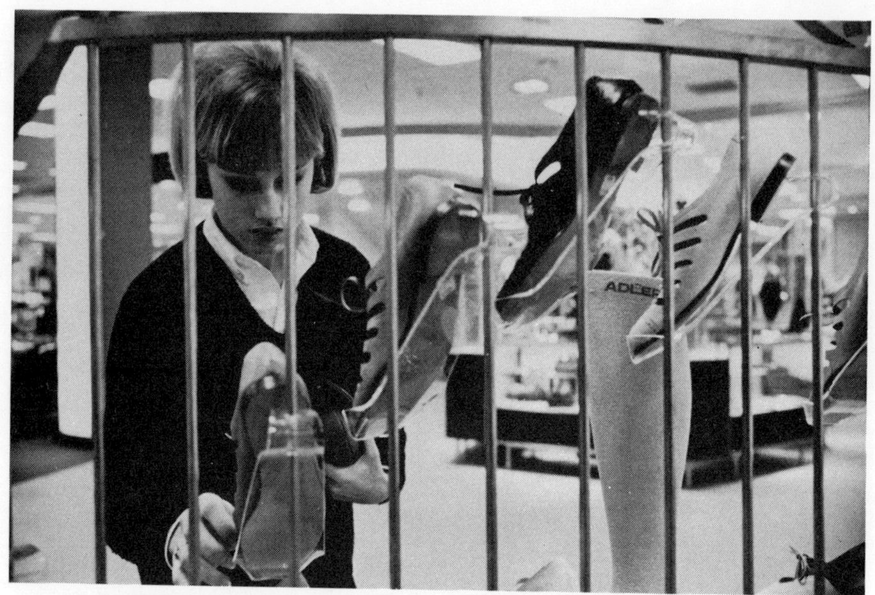

I. Howard Spivak, ASMP

Today's sellers are paying much attention to meeting the demands of the youth movement. The influence of young people is especially strong in the selling of clothing and recreational goods and services.

as education increases, income tends to increase. Also, the tastes of people change as they become better educated. This change may give rise to the development of new products and will also certainly affect the selling appeals that are used.

Leisure Time

Hundreds of labor-saving devices are available to consumers; the work week has been shortened; and consumers have leisure time on their hands. This leisure time which consumers want to devote to recreation has stimulated the growth of many service businesses and the introduction of new products designed to entertain the consumer. This trend is certain to continue and will have important implications for the product development policies of marketing firms.

Automation

Today many business operations are performed by *automation*—the process of handling work by machines with a minimum of human effort. The advances made through automation have greatly increased our ability to produce. Therefore, it becomes necessary for us to improve our ability to distribute the goods and services that result from increased production. The increase in productivity through automation must be matched with an equal or greater increase in consumption.

THE SALESMAN'S ROLE IN ADAPTING TO ECONOMIC TRENDS

The individual salesman is in an ideal position to help his company keep up with current economic trends. He stands at a critical point between consumer and producer. He should know his consumers better than anyone else, and he can funnel marketing data back to the selling firm so that policies and procedures can be adapted accordingly.

In an economy as complex as ours, the work of every individual is important. One never knows when something he does or fails to do may set off a chain of events or influence a situation with far more important results than he might imagine. The countdowns in our space flights dramatize this point. The work of each of hundreds of individuals plays a particular part in the success or failure of the ultimate launching. In the business world today, there will always be a series of countdowns. If a poor job is done or someone fails to get his assignment completed on time, the impact can be a chain reaction involving many people. Like our space programs which are based on 100% performance, persons working in selling must render high-level performance.

CHECKING YOUR KNOWLEDGE

Vocabulary:

automation

Review questions:

1. Name the trends with which today's marketers are most concerned.
2. How does the standard of living affect sales volume?
3. Why is the youth movement so important to today's marketers?
4. How can education give rise to the development of new products?
5. Why has increased leisure time stimulated the development of new products?

For discussion:

1. Why must a successful retailer be aware of economic trends?
2. Is it possible to be a successful salesman and yet ignore economic trends? Why?
3. Can you think of any current economic trends other than those discussed in this part?

part E

goals of good selling

Good selling is not easy, but to maintain prosperity in our country, salesmen working at all levels must perform their functions to the best of their abilities. The primary goal of good selling is the mutual satisfaction of both buyer and seller. Only when this goal is achieved can a good business relationship be established, one that has a chance to continue beyond the first purchase.

Good selling means that the product or service being sold will fully meet the requirements of the customer and that the customer will be treated with courtesy and respect. The retail customer is interested in gaining personal satisfaction from his purchases, and the retail salesperson who is doing a good job makes sure that the article or service sold will best fit the immediate needs of the customer. When this is done with courtesy and a sincere desire to be of help, the successful retail salesman finds that he has made a permanent customer for himself and for the store.

The wholesale salesman should help his customer, usually a retailer, to order merchandise that can be readily resold. He must not forget that he is in a unique position to operate as a merchandising specialist. In the many calls he makes in a given territory, he contacts dealers who are not competing for the same business but who are faced with similar problems. He sees good and poor merchandising taking place, and he may have ideas for merchandising that will be of value to the retailer. As a specialist, he can pass this information on to noncompeting merchants so that each may do a better job of promoting the sale of his product. By recognizing the customers' interests in this way, he aids them and at the same time helps his own firm.

The salesman who sells raw materials or services to a manufacturer will help him buy materials or services that will make a better product, decrease the costs of manufacturing, or increase his sales.

ASSISTANCE AND PERSUASION

Selling involves both assistance and persuasion. Much retail selling is primarily a matter of assisting the customer to purchase wisely. The customer often needs no persuasion but simply must be given the facts and shown their application to his particular needs.

All customers should be considered as guests of the salesman, not as persons to be exploited. Customers have a right to expect courteous and pleasant treatment from the salesman and to expect their needs to take precedence over the salesman's desire to sell. Courtesy and a "you" attitude typify good selling.

Salesmen of industrial goods must be able to furnish the manufacturer with a product that meets his exact specifications. So that his customers may buy wisely, it is imperative that the industrial salesman have exhaustive information about his product. Among the most expert of all salespeople in helping their customers are those who handle machinery and special installations. Preliminary contacts with prospective buyers are necessary for these salespeople to become intimately acquainted with the manufacturing processes and special problems of their potential customers. In situations of this kind, it is possible that the salesman will know the customer's needs before the customer himself is fully aware of them.

"This is the phantom. If you know what's good for you, you'll withdraw all your money from your regular bank and deposit it in Superba Savings where you get 5¼% compounded quarterly!"

Changing Times

Creative selling involves the sale of goods or services that won't come back to people who will come back. This idea is of paramount importance in all selling. Where there is no mutuality of interest, selling becomes a racket.

Although selling is becoming more and more a matter of helping the customer to buy, one must not believe that persuasion is never to be used. There is often a need to prevail upon the buyer to make a positive buying decision rather than to hesitate and either defer buying or make an inferior choice.

At the retail level, for example, one finds many customers who are indecisive, who have difficulty making up their minds. Even customers who are able to make their own decisions often go through the mental process of weighing objections to immediate purchase, although it may be in their best interests to act at once. If the salesperson is confident that the product meets his customer's needs, it is in the customer's best interest that the salesman persuade him to buy.

In selling to businessmen rather than to ultimate consumers, persuasion is more frequently needed. When a businessman is approached by a salesman, he expects the salesman to try to persuade him to buy. Usually he listens to the presentations of a number of competing salesmen and then reaches a buying decision. The businessman knows that each salesman represents a single product or merchandise line and expects the salesman to persuade him that the product or line best fits his needs.

REQUIREMENTS OF A SELLING CAREER

The major qualifications for selling include:

1. A recognition of the importance of the selling job and of the dignity attached to it.
2. A liking and understanding of people, coupled with the ability to involve oneself in the problems and decisions of others.
3. A thorough knowledge of the product, merchandise line, or service.
4. The ability to use sound selling techniques.

This book is designed to broaden your knowledge about these requirements. The old belief that "salesmen are born, not made" is false. There are certain basic principles of selling, just as there are certain principles of chemistry, law, and medicine. The basic principles of selling can be taught; they can be learned; and they can be practiced. Properly taught, almost anyone can learn how to sell and sell well.

In this book you will have a chance to apply the principles of selling, under the supervision of your instructor, by working on the projects at the end of each chapter. You should consider securing practical experience either in a part-time selling job while in school or in a full-time job after completion of the course. It is important for you not to

Attributes of a Selling Career

Income		At the start of a selling career, you will probably be paid at the same starting rate as in many other types of jobs. As you progress, your income can rise as fast as—and in direct proportion to—what you produce in sales volume. You have the satisfaction of knowing that there is no ceiling on what you can earn.
Security		Security in a selling career is based on the salesman's ability to produce business at a profit. Since all business operation is based on sales, there is always a need for high-caliber salesmen. No other employee group is less subject to layoffs since most companies must look to their salesmen to keep business going.
Interesting Work		If you like new challenges daily, selling will never be a dull career. Aiding consumers in making buying decisions adds variety to your job.
Self-Development		In a selling career, you will find the need for continuous study and development of new sales techniques as well as for learning to profit by the know-how of others more experienced than you.
Satisfaction of Serving Others		Every sale made to the mutual satisfaction of both parties provides ample opportunity to be of great service to all concerned. Good salesmen take pride in contributing to the well-being of their customers.
Advancement		In few other careers does the opportunity for advancement exist in so sure a way as in selling. There is always room at the top for those persons with proper qualifications, training, and experience. The yardstick for measuring the rate of advancement is the ability to produce.

The career that an individual chooses for himself should have certain attributes that can give him a rich, happy life. Listed above are some of the attributes of a selling career. Which of these attributes are most important to you?

wait for a formal job before you try your hand at selling. Opportunities to sell are all around you, in school and at home. You should be on the lookout for these opportunities; when they come, use the selling principles you study from day to day.

CHECKING YOUR KNOWLEDGE

Review questions:

1. What is the primary goal of good selling?
2. How does selling involve both assistance and persuasion?
3. Why is more persuasion used in selling to businessmen than in selling to ultimate consumers?
4. Should all customers be considered guests of the salesman? Why?
5. Why is the belief false that "salesmen are born, not made"?

For discussion:

1. Is it necessary that all salesmen have an equal amount of technical training regarding the different products they are to sell? Why?
2. How can persuasion be an essential part of the selling process if the underlying purpose of selling is to match the product with the customer's needs?

BUILDING YOUR SKILLS

Improving your English:

Each of the following sentences contains two verbs in parentheses. Only one of the verbs may be used correctly in the sentence. On a separate sheet of paper, write the number of each sentence and the correct verb to be used in each sentence.

1. Seven managers (was, were) preparing the report.
2. Henry and John have (went, gone) to the exhibit.
3. In the files (was, were) located his itinerary and a record of his expenses.
4. You, not he, (is, are) to meet Mr. Johnson for lunch.
5. Neither Mr. Marshall nor the salesmen (was, were) expecting the larger order.
6. Each supervisor and each salesman (is, are) to attend the seminar.
7. Either the manager or the vice-president (is, are) to arrange the sales meeting.
8. You, not she, (is, are) to meet Sue at the bank.
9. Either Bill or Ed (is, are) to give the demonstration.
10. Neither Bill nor the ladies (was, were) able to reach the quota.

Improving your arithmetic:

Perform the required calculations in the following exercises.

1. The weekly salaries of the employees in the A-1 Discount House receiving department are:

Bill Jones	\$96.00	Clyde Rowe	\$89.00
Frank Grant	91.00	Jim Samuels	97.00
Ben Smith	94.00	Mike Sherman	85.00

Determine the yearly earnings of each employee, the total weekly payroll for the receiving department, and the average monthly wage of receiving department employees.

2. The dollar value of the toy department inventories in the Frankow Chain is:

Store A	$2,448.64
Store B	1,226.00
Store C	4,686.28
Store D	2,204.15

What is the total dollar value of the toy department inventories? What is the average inventory value for the departments in the chain?

3. The following items can be obtained at a 25% price reduction in a local discount store:

Hair dressing	$ 1.60	Pipe rack	$ 4.64
Clothes brush	2.36	Dictionary	10.40
Ice skates	12.68	Stationery	5.28

Compute the discount store's net price for each item and the total price for all items.

4. The Frazier Shop purchased a group of 50 dresses of various sizes and styles. The store sold 10 of the dresses at $12.95 each, 15 at $17.95 each, 15 at $19.95 each, and 10 at $24.95 each. What was the average selling price for the dresses?

5. John Finney's sales in the men's furnishings department were $2,700, $4,100, $3,100, $3,050, $4,200, and $4,800 respectively for the first six months of the year. What were his average monthly sales? What must his total sales be for the next six months in order to average sales of $4,000 per month for the year?

Improving your research skills:

1. Talk to an experienced retailer and determine the changes in selling that have taken place in his business during the past 20 years. Prepare a brief report of your findings.
2. Select three products that are distributed in your community and trace the channels of distribution from manufacturer to consumer.
3. Suggest new products that may be very important to ultimate consumers in the next few years. Justify your selections.

APPLYING YOUR KNOWLEDGE

Case problem:

The Hallmart Shop, a local sewing machine outlet, has always practiced high-pressure selling tactics. Newspaper advertising has never been dishonest, but complete facts have not always been disclosed. The salesmen push machines that produce the highest commission per sale. The store has always made a reasonable profit; but the new manager, Mr. Evans, has statistics proving that a large part of the potential market has not been reached. Mr. Evans places much confidence in the marketing concept and plans to organize training sessions for his salesmen to acquaint them with this concept.

1. Do you think Mr. Evans is wise in pushing the marketing concept when his salesmen have not generally been accustomed to this broader application of selling? Why?
2. What specific actions would Mr. Evans take in modernizing the efforts of his sales force to emphasize the marketing concept?
3. Will the marketing concept necessarily apply to all selling situations? Why?

Continuing project:

The project you are about to begin will continue throughout the entire course. For this project, you are to select a specific selling occupation that you might like to enter upon completion of your education. This project will enable you to apply to a specific sales occupation of your choice the principles and methods of selling discussed in each chapter. Directions for each section of the project will be found at the end of each chapter. The projects will be devoted to the preparation of a Sales Occupation Manual for the particular sales job you have selected.

In selecting a sales occupation in which you would like to engage, you may choose to sell a service, such as insurance, or a product, such as an automobile. You may choose any sales job that involves sales effort on your part, as distinct from a sales job in which a customer may buy with little sales effort from you as the salesperson. Examples of sales occupations that would not be acceptable for this project are the selling of candy or school supplies from a variety store, the selling of medications and cosmetics from a drugstore, and the selling of merchandise indirectly through a vending machine. After you have chosen a selling occupation, your instructor will approve your selection.

For your Sales Occupation Manual, it is recommended that you use a notebook 8½ by 11 inches in size. Prepare a cover and a title page for your manual. On the title page, place a phrase or statement that adequately describes the sales occupation you have chosen.

Extra credit:

Select one of the economic trends discussed in Part D and write an essay of about 1,000 words relating the topic to present-day salesmanship. Do research on the chosen topic in your library, conduct interviews, and draw on your own observations and experience.

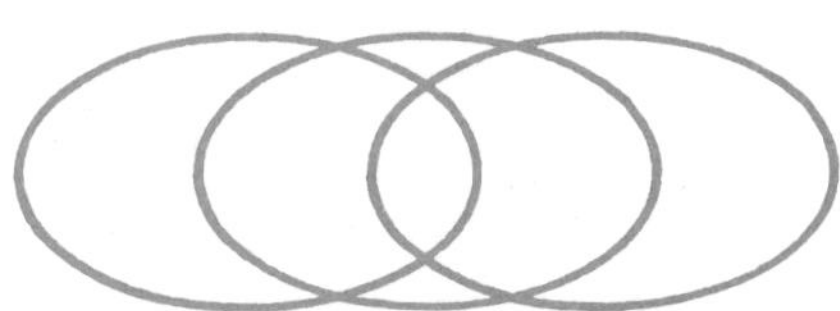

chapter 2

selling organizations and selling jobs

KEY QUESTIONS

A Into what major categories may selling organizations be classified?

B What are the kinds of retail businesses, classified according to type of operation?

C Which salesmen usually work for manufacturers and which salesmen usually work for wholesalers?

D What are some responsibilities of retail salespeople?

E Is the need-satisfaction theory of selling more effective and thorough than the stimulus-response theory?

part A

sellers—producers and middlemen

A wheat farmer, a manufacturer of conveyor belts, a wholesaler of hardware supplies, a grocer—what do they have in common? They are all sellers. Each must sell his products to someone else—to a manufacturer, to a middleman, to an ultimate consumer—if he hopes to make a profit and stay in business.

Few ultimate consumers realize how many times an item has been sold before they buy the product in a retail store. Consider a power lawn mower. Before a customer bought it at a garden-supplies store, someone—probably a wholesaler—had sold it to the retailer. Before that, someone sold it to the wholesaler. Before that, someone sold the manufacturer such components as an engine for the mower, paint, wheels, spark plugs, rubber handles, and machinery to build the mower. The factory in which the mower was made was either owned or rented, and a real estate salesman probably helped the manufacturer find the factory. There is more to selling than just writing out a sales check for a purchase; involved in the selling process are industrial salesmen, wholesale salesmen, retail salesmen, and salesmen of services. In this chapter you will learn about the kinds of selling organizations and the different kinds of individual selling jobs in these organizations.

THE PRODUCER

Production, as you have learned, means the creation of utility. This is a broad definition, and within it almost every business could be termed a "producer." However, a *producer* is more commonly defined as someone who extracts natural resources or raises products for consumption or who manufactures articles for consumption. A producer is someone who creates form utility. Manufacturers, farmers, canneries, fisheries, mining operations, and lumber mills are producers. Producers sell to other producers (in the case of materials and supplies), to middlemen, and to ultimate consumers.

Major Kinds of Manufactured Products

- Primary metals
- Fabricated metal products
- Machinery
- Transportation equipment
- Instruments and related products
- Clay, glass, and stone products
- Lumber and products
- Furniture and fixtures
- Textile mill and apparel products
- Leather and products
- Paper and products
- Chemicals and products
- Rubber and plastic products
- Petroleum products
- Foods and beverages
- Tobacco products

The major kinds of manufactured products can be separated into two general categories: durable goods and nondurable goods. Durable goods—listed in the left column—can be used over and over again for a relatively long time. Nondurable goods—listed in the right column—are quickly consumed.

THE MIDDLEMAN

All people or businesses that operate in the channel of distribution between producer and consumer are middlemen. Middlemen do not manufacture or process goods; but they do analyze demand, obtain suitable merchandise, and effect its sale. They add place, time, and possession utilities to the goods they handle; and they must practice creative selling if they are to add these utilities to the goods.

Merchant Middlemen

The *merchant middleman* owns the goods he sells. He generally performs all the marketing activities, but he may omit one or more of them. For example, a *drop shipper* does not store goods but rather asks the producer to ship the goods directly to his customers. A *cash-and-carry middleman* eliminates the financing and delivery activities so that he can reduce prices for his customers. Merchant middlemen operate on both wholesale and retail levels.

Wholesale Merchants. Wholesale merchant middlemen are usually called simply "wholesalers." This type of middleman performs the various marketing functions for the retailer, just as the retailer performs the functions for the ultimate consumer. The wholesaler assembles goods, stores them, breaks shipments into smaller quantities, and bears the risk of price change, style change, and credit loss. He may advise both the retailer and the manufacturer about goods to buy and to produce. The manufacturer looks to him for information about customer demand for certain goods, and the retailer looks to him for help in buying and promoting goods.

There are many kinds of wholesalers. Based on sales volume, the most important are those that handle (1) groceries and farm products; (2) automotive goods (cars, supplies, and fuel); (3) dry goods and wearing apparel; and (4) machinery, equipment, and supplies. Wholesalers are generally classified according to the variety of merchandise they handle. These are the most common classifications:

1. *General merchandise wholesalers* stock a wide variety of unrelated goods.
2. *General line wholesalers* handle a complete line of merchandise in one field.
3. *Specialty wholesalers* handle a single commodity.

Retail Merchants. The retailer performs the last step in the marketing process and usually takes title to the goods he sells. He is the merchant with whom most people are familiar, and his selling activities will be a topic of major importance throughout this book. Because of his important role in selling, the types of retail selling organizations will be discussed in detail in Part B.

Modern wholesale establishments are often located in the suburbs of a community rather than in the downtown area. Plenty of parking space is provided for employees, transportation workers, and customers.

Agent Middlemen

Agent middlemen do not own the goods with which they deal. They help bring about a transfer of goods from one person to another, but they avoid such risks of ownership as merchandise depreciation and change in market price. The major kinds of agent middlemen are commission merchants, brokers, and assemblers. Agent middlemen operate mainly on the wholesale level, although some retailers are also agents.

Commission Merchants. A *commission merchant* receives goods, stores them, and sells them. He then deducts a commission for his services and gives the balance from the sale to the person who supplied the goods to him. The most important commission merchants are those who deal in agricultural products and textiles.

Closely related in function to the commission merchant and sometimes regarded as types of commission merchants are manufacturers' agents and sales agents. The *manufacturer's agent* is the exclusive agent for the distribution of a manufacturer's product in a given region. He may sell noncompeting lines of merchandise or specialize in one product. In the food field, manufacturers' agents may represent certain noncompeting national brands in a geographical area and may sell to supermarkets, wholesalers, hotels, and other institutional buyers.

The activities of a *sales agent* are much the same as those of a manufacturer's agent; the main difference between the two is in the authority given to the sales agent. The manufacturer's agent is rather limited in authority concerning the setting of prices and terms of sale, but the sales agent is given considerable authority in these areas and may take complete responsibility for the selling of a product nationally. Unlike the true commission merchant, manufacturers' and sales agents do not necessarily handle the goods in which they deal. Merchandise may be shipped from the manufacturer directly to the agents' customers.

Brokers. Like the commission merchant, the *broker* sells goods without holding title to them. However, unlike the commission merchant, the broker does not have physical possession of the goods in which he deals. He acts as a go-between to bring buyers and sellers together, and he receives a commission for his services.

Brokers may represent either the seller or the buyer. Many brokers deal in agricultural commodities, and large grocery chains frequently buy goods through a broker. In the dry goods and clothing fields, many stores employ brokers—called resident buyers—to help them find the best sources of merchandise.

Assemblers. For farm products, there is a special kind of middleman called the *assembler*. He obtains relatively small lots of agricultural products from individual farmers; then he assembles these goods at a central point, grades them, and sells them to manufacturers, wholesalers, and large retailers. The assembler allows farmers to specialize in production without assuming the responsibilities related to the ultimate distribution of a product.

An assembling organization is frequently owned by the farmers themselves, and it is then called a *cooperative marketing association.* This arrangement relieves farmers of the responsibility of grading their products and maintaining a warehouse and also assures them that they will have a representative who will get the best prices for their products.

CHECKING YOUR KNOWLEDGE

Vocabulary:

(1) producer
(2) merchant middleman
(3) drop shipper
(4) cash-and-carry middleman
(5) general merchandise wholesaler
(6) general line wholesaler
(7) specialty wholesaler
(8) agent middlemen
(9) commission merchant
(10) manufacturer's agent
(11) sales agent
(12) broker
(13) assembler
(14) cooperative marketing association

Review questions:

1. To whom do producers sell their output? Give some examples of producers.
2. What are the two major types of middleman? How do they differ?
3. Describe the functions of the wholesale merchant.
4. What is the main difference between a commission merchant and a broker?
5. Describe the functions of the assembler. What kind of goods does he usually handle?

For discussion:

1. In what ways would the job of selling for a producer differ from the job of selling for a middleman?
2. What are some of the duties of a resident buyer—a broker operating in the dry goods and clothing fields?
3. Would it be ethical for a broker to collect a commission from both the seller and the buyer of a specific quantity of goods?

part B

sellers—the retailer

The retailer is the only middleman whose primary concern is selling to the ultimate consumer. At times manufacturers may sell directly to the ultimate consumer, and certainly the activities of both manufacturers and wholesalers are greatly influenced by this consumer; but it is the retailer who must consider the ultimate consumer during every step of his buying and selling operations.

There are four principal methods of retail selling. The most important method of selling to the ultimate consumer is through *over-the-counter retailing*. With this method, the customer personally visits the retailer's place of business and selects and purchases what he wants from the retailer's stock. The second method is *mail-order selling*. The customer may shop from a catalog or printed advertisement and either mail an order to the retailer's place of business or telephone the order to him. The third method is *door-to-door selling,* or *direct retailing,* in which a retail salesman calls at a customer's house, shows merchandise samples, and solicits an order on the spot. The fourth method of retail selling is through *automatic vending,* in which a customer deposits money in a machine and receives the goods immediately from the machine.

For almost every consumer, his first contact with selling is in visiting a retail store. And probably everyone has more contacts with over-the-counter selling than with any other retail selling method. Thus, in this book our discussion of retail selling will center upon activities in retail stores using over-the-counter selling.

TYPES OF RETAIL STORE OPERATION

There are five general types of operation for a retail store, whether it is a large or a small establishment. A retail firm may be operated as: (1) an independent store, (2) part of a chain of stores, (3) a branch store, (4) a cooperative, or (5) a sideline store.

An *independent store* is owned and operated by the same person or persons. About 90 percent of the retailers in the country are classified as independents. Most independent stores are small and employ only one or two people in addition to the owner; however, many large stores, which may employ hundreds of people, are also independents. When an owner operates two or three stores located close enough together for him to visit each daily, the group is known as a *multi-independent*. To gain buying power and promotional aid, independents sometimes voluntarily affiliate with other stores or selling organizations. Today many independents are operating as *franchise stores*. For a fee, certain manufacturers and service establishments assign to independents the right to sell their products and/or standardized services. The franchisee is authorized to trade under the well-known name of the manufacturing or service establishment; is provided with a standardized store or office, usually rented from the franchisor; is given expert managerial, merchandising, and financial guidance; and is assured of a supply of suitable merchandise and equipment. Franchising gives the independent merchant a chance to concentrate almost exclusively on the selling activities of the business, since many other operating activities are handled by the franchisor. Important examples of franchise businesses are motels and hotels, roadside restaurants, and auto supply agencies.

Four or more stores, with central ownership and central control of operations, are commonly classified as a *chain*. A chain store system usually involves a local, regional, and/or national marketing area. Chains are found in the retailing of nearly all classes of goods; but they are generally associated with food, variety, drug, and discount stores.

With the growth of the shopping center and the population movement to the suburbs, many downtown department stores have found it necessary to open subsidiary stores in important shopping districts away from the downtown area. These smaller stores, called *branch stores*, carry narrower merchandise assortments than do the main stores and stock merchandise needed to take advantage of the local buying situation and to meet competition.

Cooperative stores are formed by consumers, who invest small sums of money in the cooperative and hire a manager to run it. Records of members' purchases are kept, and earnings of the cooperative are distributed to members on the basis of their purchases rather than on the basis of investment. Cooperatives are generally formed to handle agricultural products; but they may also handle such products as groceries, dry goods, apparel, meat, fuel, and lumber.

A *sideline store* is operated by businesses or groups that have other major interests. Such stores include utility-operated stores designed to increase the sale of equipment using electricity and gas, company stores operated for the benefit of the company's employees, and government commissaries run by branches of the armed services.

SMALL-SCALE RETAILING

A retailer is considered a small-scale retailer if he employs fewer than 10 people and does less than $300,000 worth of business a year. About four-fifths of all retail stores in this country are small-scale businesses, but they account for only about one-fourth the total retail sales volume.

General Stores

The *general store,* once found in virtually every town in the country, has served America for more than 200 years. Now these stores are usually found only in small towns and in rural areas. Such stores carry a highly diversified line of products, including foods, staple clothing, and housewares. There are no separate departments within the store.

H. Armstrong Roberts

In many small towns in the 18th and 19th Centuries, the general store was the center of activity. The store owner stocked most of the merchandise that families needed, sorted and distributed mail, and provided a place for people to socialize. Today a general store like the one above is hard to find.

Single-Line Stores

Single-line stores specialize in one merchandise line or in a few related lines. Bakeries, shoe stores, and drugstores are single-line stores. Such stores developed because the public demanded better merchandise assortments than general stores provided. There are two types of single-line stores: convenience-goods stores, or neighborhood stores, and shopping-goods stores, or specialty shops.

A *convenience-goods store,* sometimes called a *neighborhood store,* is located in or close to residential neighborhoods and sells primarily *convenience goods.* These are items which are bought frequently and for which customers do not want to make special shopping trips. Candy stores and newspaper stands are examples of convenience-goods stores. Convenience-goods stores are also found in business districts where they cater to persons going to or coming from work.

Shopping-goods stores are generally found in a central shopping district or suburban shopping center rather than in neighborhoods. *Shopping goods* are items which are more expensive than convenience goods and which customers usually wish to compare in several stores before buying; jewelry is a shopping good. When shopping-goods stores specialize in clothing, they are called *specialty shops.*

Service Businesses

The number of businesses selling services and the variety of services offered have increased tremendously in the last ten years. As consumers' discretionary incomes increase, the desire for services also increases. Thus, today there is a multitude of businesses offering services ranging from baby-sitting to window washing. There are almost as many opportunities for young salespeople in personal service businesses as there are in retail and wholesale establishments dealing primarily in merchandise. Most service businesses are small-scale, but some—such as travel agencies—are large-scale in nature and nationwide in scope.

LARGE-SCALE RETAILING

The most common large-scale retailers are department stores, variety stores, mail-order houses, supermarkets, and discount stores. Certain of these businesses may sometimes exist as small-scale establishments, but they are customarily quite large in size.

Franklin Simon

Although specialty shops cannot properly be called department stores, they are sometimes divided into departments. This division often occurs when store management wants to promote certain merchandise with a seasonal or fashion appeal and wants to set off this merchandise from surrounding goods. The department illustrated above displays different articles of leather clothing and leather accessories for women.

Department Store

The *department store* handles a wide variety of merchandise, is organized into separate departments, and operates under a central management. In recent years department stores have been confronted with the problems of overcrowding and lack of parking space in the downtown areas, the population movement to the suburbs, and the competition of the discount store. However, department store management is working to meet the problems, and the department store is certain to remain an important part of the retailing scene.

Variety Store

The *variety store,* like the department store, handles different merchandise lines. However, it concentrates on lower price lines than are offered in most department stores and, unlike most department stores, offers a minimum of customer services. Variety stores give little attention to selling such items as furniture and outer clothing; they stock toys, sewing notions, tableware, light hardware, cosmetics, candy, and similar articles. Newer variety stores are operated on a self-service basis.

Mail-Order House

Typically, a *mail-order house* contacts customers by sending them a merchandise catalog and sells goods by mail rather than over the counter. However, larger mail-order houses have established retail stores in many cities and now most of their sales volume comes from these stores. In smaller towns, there may be *order offices* where samples of key items and merchandise catalogs are available. Customers go to these stores, look at the samples, and order from the catalog.

There are two kinds of mail-order houses: the *general merchandise mail-order house,* which resembles a department store in the type of merchandise it handles, and the *specialty mail-order house,* which is more like a specialty shop.

Supermarket

The *supermarket* features primarily food products, is characterized by self-service in most departments, and generally operates on a cash-and-carry basis. The merchandise lines are usually classified as groceries, meats, baked goods, dairy products, fresh fruits and vegetables, and frozen foods. In order to increase their profit margins, many supermarkets also stock such nonfood items as health and beauty aids, staple housewares, and certain soft-goods lines such as hosiery. The supermarket has probably done more to promote the use of self-service in many retailing operations than has any other retailer.

Discount Store

Discount stores carry a wide variety of general merchandise, most of which is sold on a self-service basis at prices considerably below those of traditional stores selling the same goods. The low prices are made possible by the elimination of personal service, by concentration on best sellers when fashion appeal is not of great importance, by emphasis on a high average sale, by maximum use of store facilities, and by high stock turnover. There are two types of discount stores: the *closed-door discount store,* which sells only to persons who are members, and the *open-door discount store,* which sells to all persons and must use effective advertising to attract customers.

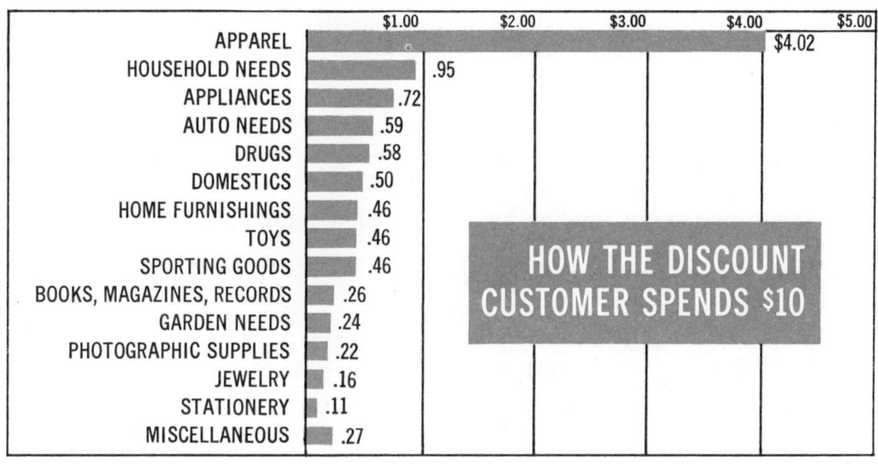

The Discount Merchandiser

Discount stores are continuously growing in number, size, and sales volume. Even persons who shop at elegant, exclusive specialty shops are going to discount stores to purchase everyday necessities. The chart above shows how an average customer with $10 to spend would divide his money among the various products in a discount store.

CHECKING YOUR KNOWLEDGE

Vocabulary:

(1) over-the-counter retailing
(2) mail-order selling
(3) door-to-door selling, or direct retailing
(4) automatic vending
(5) independent store
(6) multi-independent
(7) franchise store
(8) chain
(9) branch store
(10) cooperative store
(11) sideline store
(12) general store
(13) single-line store
(14) convenience-goods store, or neighborhood store
(15) convenience goods
(16) shopping-goods store
(17) shopping goods
(18) specialty shop
(19) department store
(20) variety store
(21) mail-order house
(22) order office
(23) general merchandise mail-order house
(24) specialty mail-order house
(25) supermarket
(26) discount store
(27) closed-door discount store
(28) open-door discount store

Review questions:

1. What are the four principal methods of retail selling?
2. Name the five general types of operation for a retail store.

3. What prompted the development of single-line stores?
4. What are the most common types of large-scale retailers?
5. How can discount stores offer prices that are considerably below those of traditional stores selling the same merchandise?

For discussion:

1. Should automatic vending be considered a retail selling method, since no salesperson is involved?
2. From the ultimate consumer's viewpoint, what advantage does the independent store have over the chain store?
3. With the trend toward large-scale business operation today, do you think there is any chance that small-scale retailing establishments will disappear in the future? Explain your answer.

part C

selling jobs—producers and middlemen

Within the selling organizations you have just read about, there are many different kinds of selling jobs. These jobs differ mainly because of the selling organization for whom the salesman is working, but they also differ because of the product sold, the customers to whom the product is sold, the location of the selling territory, and the abilities of the individual salesman. These variations among selling jobs make the classification of the jobs difficult. There is much overlapping of selling responsibilities from organization to organization and even within a single organization. And because of the complexity of selling activities, there is not always a clearly defined channel of distribution for a given product. Manufacturers do not always sell just to other manufacturers or to wholesalers, for instance. They may sell to retailers and sometimes even to ultimate consumers.

No matter how different the selling jobs and how complex their duties, though, each of them falls into one of two general categories: personal selling or nonpersonal selling. In *personal selling,* a salesman makes direct face-to-face or telephone contact with a customer. In *nonpersonal selling,* certain elements such as advertising, display, and special selling devices are used to sell merchandise. The coordination of these two general kinds of selling to produce the best sales results is called *sales promotion.*

The most important kind of selling is personal selling. It is the heart of every selling activity, and in the rest of the book we shall be primarily concerned with the kinds of personal selling jobs and the techniques of effective personal selling.

SELLING FOR PRODUCERS

When businessmen talk about selling for producers, they generally call this kind of selling *industrial selling.* It is the selling of commodities used to produce other goods or of commodities consumed in business operations. Products handled in industrial selling include: (1) raw materials, such as iron ore; (2) semi-finished articles, such as lumber; (3) finished parts, such as nuts and bolts; (4) installations, such as air conditioning systems; (5) equipment, such as accounting machines; (6) supplies, such as light bulbs; and (7) services, such as group insurance plans.

An important point that should be made about industrial selling is: all industrial selling is done between extractors and manufacturers, between industrial wholesalers and manufacturers, and between manufacturers and other manufacturers; but few manufacturers are engaged in industrial selling alone. Manufacturers of goods that will eventually be used by the ultimate consumer sell their output to wholesalers, to retailers, or to ultimate consumers; and when manufacturers engage in this kind of selling, it is not industrial selling—it is consumer-goods selling. The salesman who works for an extractor or a manufacturer can thus be involved in either industrial selling or consumer-goods selling.

The salesman who works for an extractor generally does not employ as much creative selling as do other salesmen. The market demand determines to a great extent what and how much he can sell. The price he can obtain for his products is usually also determined by the market structure; this is particularly true in the case of agricultural products. For raw materials such as minerals and lumber, the demand is generally fairly stable; and a salesman's efforts are directed largely toward just getting the buyer and seller together.

Manufacturers' salesmen, however, must employ creative selling techniques; and often they must do more than just sell their employers' products. They must be goodwill ambassadors for their companies, and this can involve many activities. The following selling jobs are most commonly found in manufacturing businesses: the sales engineer, manufacturer's representative, pioneer salesman, dealer-service salesman, missionary salesman, and direct salesman.

In Part B you learned about manufacturer's agents, sales agents, and brokers—all of whom sell the output of producers and manufacturers. These persons have not been included in the above list of manufacturers' salesmen because they are in business for themselves and may sell the output of several noncompeting manufacturers. Thus, they are really selling organizations rather than individual salesmen. Remember that the selling jobs to be discussed in the following paragraphs may not be found in every manufacturing organization. Some firms may combine the duties of several of these jobs into one selling job, and some may give different names to the various jobs. The classification that follows is intended to be a general one which will give you a guideline to understanding the various selling jobs in manufacturing.

Sales Engineer

The *sales engineer* is the true industrial salesman. He generally works for companies that make complex machinery to be used by other manufacturers, and he sells to other producers. Of all salesmen, he must be the most thoroughly trained in his field and must have the greatest knowledge of his product.

The sales engineer's job seldom starts with an attempt to sell his product to a customer. He may be asked to solve technical problems for the customer, design special equipment for the customer's production processes, prepare technical material for other salesmen, devise new ways of increasing his customer's production, and adapt old equipment to fit new processes. The sales engineer must be highly trained in the particular product line he is selling; and degrees in mechanical, electrical, or chemical engineering are common among sales engineers.

Manufacturer's Representative

Whereas the sales engineer is concerned with specific technical aspects of selling and customer relations, the *manufacturer's representative* is involved in virtually all aspects of selling and customer relations; his job is much wider in scope. The manufacturer's representative is a jack-of-all-trades; and to the persons he contacts, he *is* the manufacturer. He may sell to other manufacturers, to wholesalers, or to retailers. He is a goodwill ambassador for his company; he may be called upon to

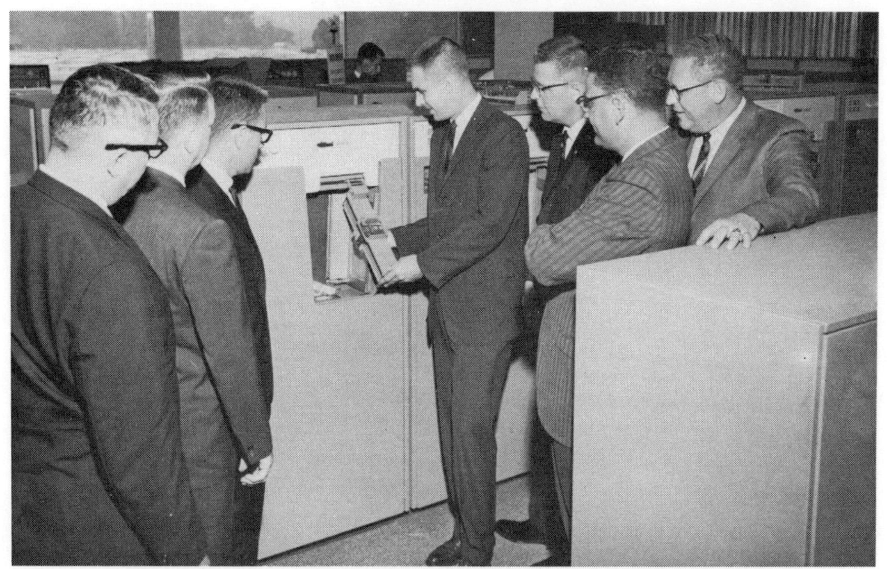

National Cash Register Company

To the manufacturer of electronic data processing equipment, the job of the sales engineer is particularly important. A primary responsibility of this sales engineer is to conduct thorough training sessions in which customers learn how to use the equipment they buy so that they can fully benefit from its purchase.

give advice on advertising and how to increase sales volume and may have to handle complaints. He must have in-depth knowledge about his company and its products, for he may be required to answer almost any type of question. He must be able to discuss new products, train middlemen to sell his products to other middlemen, and keep his employer informed about what is happening in his territory.

Pioneer Salesman

The *pioneer salesman* is responsible for promoting new products with which customers may not be familiar. He sells primarily to wholesalers but may sell to other manufacturers and also to retailers. His job is to persuade customers that it is to their advantage to add his products to their assortment of goods for resale. Such a salesman may call on new customers in his territory or may branch out into a new territory. He usually spends considerable time with each customer, suggesting new products, new uses for products, and new selling methods. The drug salesman who works for a manufacturer of pharmaceuticals is a highly skilled pioneer salesman.

Armstrong Cork Company

The duties of a manufacturer's representative may include everything from interpreting a blueprint to handling the complaint of an irate customer. Can you think of a job in retailing that would be comparable to the job of a manufacturer's representative?

Dealer-Service Salesman

After a pioneer salesman has convinced another manufacturer, wholesaler, or retailer that he should use the company's product, it is the job of the *dealer-service salesman* to make sure that the customer is kept adequately supplied with the product. His basic job is to see that the customer keeps reordering the merchandise. He checks the customer's inventory at regular intervals and writes up the necessary orders. Efficiency and thoroughness are necessary in this job, but there is less opportunity for creative selling than in other selling jobs with the manufacturer.

Missionary Salesman

Some manufacturers, and occasionally a wholesaler, employ salesmen to contact customers of the middleman who handles their product lines. For example, a garment manufacturer who distributes through wholesalers may send missionary salesmen to call on each wholesaler's retail customers to create demand and develop goodwill. The job of *missionary salesmen* is to help the retailer sell so that he will reorder from the wholesaler. At times they may approach a retailer before he places an order, but they are not really soliciting business directly for their own firms. Rather, they are soliciting business for their customer—the wholesaler.

Direct Salesman

A few manufacturers sell their products directly to the ultimate consumer. They may sell through a catalog mailed to the customer, through house-to-house selling by a *direct salesman,* or through a party plan. Manufacturers of such articles as unfinished furniture often sell through catalogs; the Fuller Brush Company and Avon Company are well known for their house-to-house selling; and the manufacturer of Tupperware plastic products is the most famous manufacturer using the party plan to sell to the ultimate consumer.

SELLING FOR WHOLESALERS

There are some wholesalers who sell industrial goods to manufacturers—mainly small, frequently used parts which are handled most efficiently through wholesaling organizations—but our concern in the following paragraphs will be with those wholesalers who sell to retailers. The activities of wholesale salesmen are quite similar to the activities of manufacturers' salesmen; the difference is that while a manufacturer's salesman will be handling only the output of his employer, the wholesaler's salesman may be handling the output of a number of competing and noncompeting lines.

The salesmen who are engaged primarily in selling for wholesalers to retailers are: the general wholesale salesman, merchandising salesman, detail salesman, rack salesman, and truck salesman. As with manufacturers' salesmen, this classification is not a rigid one and may vary from wholesaler to wholesaler.

General Wholesale Salesman

The duty of the *general wholesale salesman* is to persuade the retailer that he should buy part of his stock requirements from the wholesaler whom the salesman represents. Because a given wholesaler may stock many different kinds of items, the general wholesale salesman usually sells from a merchandise catalog which the retailer studies. The other duties of a general wholesale salesman are similar to those of a manufacturer's representative. The general wholesale salesman must create goodwill for his firm by making sure that the retailer is properly served and is kept satisfied.

Merchandising Salesman

A *merchandising salesman* is sometimes employed by a manufacturer; but in a manufacturing firm, his duties are more commonly handled by other salesmen, such as a manufacturer's representative. The merchandising salesman is, for all practical purposes, a sales promotion man. His job is to help his customers produce the maximum sales of the product they order from his wholesaler, thereby creating reorders. The merchandising salesman wants to sell his products to customers, but his chief duty is giving merchandising advice. He must encourage retailers to advertise and display his products, and he may supply certain advertising and display aids to the retailer.

Detail Salesman

Two different kinds of detail salesmen work for wholesalers—the straight detailer and the combination detailer. The duties of the *straight detailer* are quite similar to those of the dealer-service salesman who works for a manufacturer. The straight detailer checks the inventory in stores which handle his merchandise, takes orders, and may make suggestions to help increase sales volume.

The *combination detailer* is a mixture of missionary salesman, merchandising salesman, and straight detailer. The best example of the combination detailer is the wholesale drug salesman. Like the sales engineer, he must have a great deal of product knowledge and must be able to earn the respect of the pharmacists and physicians with whom he deals. His job is to acquaint physicians with the features of his products and to convince physicians that his products should be recommended for patients. He may also check the stock of his products in drugstores and advise the druggist on what and how much to stock. Sometimes the medical detailer turns the maintenance of his accounts over to a straight detailer once regular customers have been established.

Rack Salesman

The duties of a *rack salesman* are similar to those of the straight detailer; but the rack salesman is limited to handling nonfood items, such as beauty aids, in supermarkets. He regularly checks the store's supply of his products, replenishes stock as needed, and keeps displays in order. He is paid only for the amount of his goods the store sells.

Truck Salesman

The *truck salesman,* whose duties are comparable to those of a route salesman such as a milkman, combines the job of a salesman with that

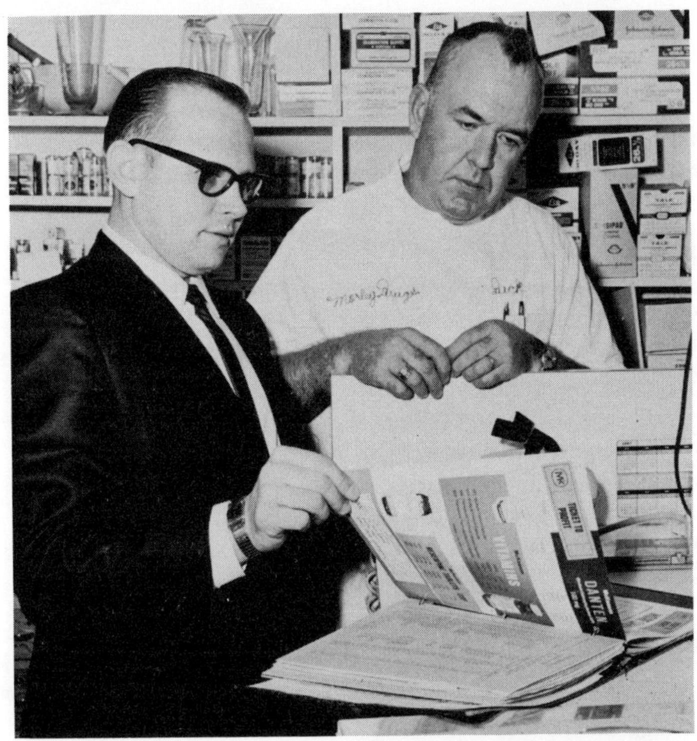

McKesson & Robbins Drug Company
and Wholesale Drugs Magazine

A wholesale drug salesman performs duties of the missionary salesman, the merchandising salesman, and the straight detailer. An exhaustive amount of product knowledge and an ethical approach to selling are requisites for his job of combination detailer.

of a deliveryman. He goes from store to store, making many calls during a selling day and selling for cash to various retailers. Items such as candy, soft drinks, dairy products, and fruit and vegetables are commonly handled by the truck salesman.

CHECKING YOUR KNOWLEDGE

Vocabulary:

(1) personal selling
(2) nonpersonal selling
(3) sales promotion
(4) industrial selling
(5) sales engineer
(6) manufacturer's representative
(7) pioneer salesman
(8) dealer-service salesman
(9) missionary salesman
(10) direct salesman
(11) general wholesale salesman
(12) merchandising salesman
(13) straight detailer
(14) combination detailer
(15) rack salesman
(16) truck salesman

Review questions:

1. What products are usually handled in industrial selling?
2. Describe the functions of the sales engineer. How does his job differ from that of the manufacturer's representative?
3. Which salesmen are engaged primarily in selling for wholesalers to retailers?
4. What is the difference between the pioneer salesman and the dealer-service salesman?
5. Describe the functions of the combination detailer who works in the wholesale drug field.

For discussion:

1. How does the value of merchandise handled by producers and middlemen affect the type of selling job required?
2. What are some qualities necessary for the salesman selling for a producer? For a wholesaler?

part D

selling jobs—retailers

Almost ten million persons are employed in this country's retail establishments—general merchandise stores, supermarkets, clothing stores, and furniture stores, among others. The majority of these persons are engaged in personal selling, either external or internal. As its name implies, *external personal selling* is carried on outside the retail store through such methods as direct selling, telephone selling, and demonstrations. *Internal personal selling* is carried on inside the store; it is over-the-counter selling in which a customer visits the store, and the retail seller helps him reach a purchasing decision on goods that will satisfy his needs and wants.

SELLING FOR A RETAIL STORE

Many of the persons who are studying this course will likely have their first selling jobs in retail stores, such as supermarkets, drugstores, and department stores. Therefore, in discussing the selling jobs available in retailing, we shall consider the selling jobs available in retail stores; we shall not discuss every specific job in selling to the ultimate consumer. The jobs most often found in retail stores are those of a salesclerk, a salesman or salesperson, an outside salesman, a demonstrator, and a telephone salesperson. The job titles and job duties described on the next pages may vary somewhat from store to store depending on the store's size, customer clientele, and merchandise sold.

Salesclerk

The *salesclerk* generally does not employ much creative selling. He sells goods to customers who have made up their minds to buy an item before coming to the store. He may use suggestion selling techniques, but there is little need to use in-depth analysis of the customer's needs and wants. Salesclerks frequently handle convenience goods which, as you have learned, are items that customers must buy frequently and for which they do not wish to make special shopping trips.

The salesclerk is required to do little presentation and demonstration of merchandise and to give little merchandise information. He must, however, have a thorough knowledge of merchandise location, the ability to show goods promptly and effectively, and the ability to handle the mechanics of a sales transaction efficiently. Speed in handling transactions is of critical importance.

Salesman or Salesperson

Many people think that the terms "salesclerk" and "salesman" or "salesperson" can be used interchangeably. This is not so. The duties of the salesman or salesperson are more difficult and more challenging than those of the salesclerk. The *salesman,* or *salesperson,* generally sells shopping goods, those items that the customer examines and compares in several stores before buying. When the customer meets the salesman, he has usually not made a complete decision on what to purchase; and the salesman must analyze the customer's needs and wants and the features of his merchandise to help the customer make a satisfactory choice. The salesman must know his merchandise thoroughly, must be able to employ the principles of creative selling, must be pleasant, and must speak with authority.

When the shopping goods are quite expensive or unusual—items such as furniture, custom-made goods, and hearing aids—the need for creative selling is even greater. The salesman must probe deeply into the customer's problem, with no outward sign of pressure and with the flexibility to suggest changes and adjustments in the product to make it wholly acceptable to the customer. The salesman sometimes does not make an immediate sale but continues his consultation over a number of customer contacts.

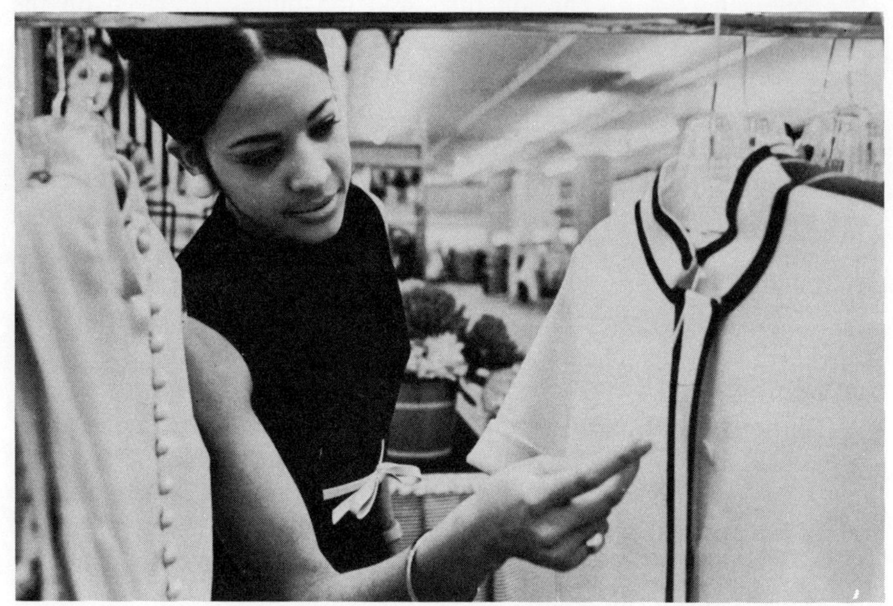

I. Howard Spivak, ASMP

Skilled salespeople are particularly important in the selling of women's clothing. The salesperson with a good deal of fashion knowledge and product information, a sense of what looks attractive on other people, and the ability to use creative selling techniques is an asset to the store.

Outside Salesman

The *outside salesman* for a retail store actually spends part of his working day in the store and part of the day calling on customers. He first obtains "leads" on prospective customers, either from persons who have visited or phoned his store and expressed interest in his products, from other salesmen, or from established customers. Then he calls the prospective customers on the telephone and tries to interest them in his product. He sets up an appointment to see a customer, then goes to the customer's home and makes his sales presentation. This method of direct selling is called the *appointment method*. Household appliances, food plans, house renovations, upholstery, storm windows, and other such goods are frequently sold by outside salesmen using this method.

The outside salesman is sometimes called a *specialty salesman,* because he concentrates on selling a particular item and must have a detailed knowledge of it. Actually, any salesman who concentrates on the repeated sale of a particular product can be called a specialty salesman, but this term is perhaps most often applied to the outside salesman of a retail store.

Demonstrators

The job of a *demonstrator* is somewhat similar to that of an outside salesman, but a demonstrator sells to groups of people whereas an outside salesman usually sells to only one customer at a time. The demonstrator talks to such groups as women's clubs and civic organizations. Sometimes he is not directly trying to sell a product but rather is trying to build goodwill for his firm, to encourage customers to remember the firm when they need a particular item. The demonstrator must be highly skilled in public speaking and must be familiar with the principles of group selling, which you will learn about in a later chapter.

Sometimes demonstrators are employed by manufacturers and work inside a retail store. They show the manufacturer's product in use and concentrate on promoting the sale of his product, but they may also be allowed to sell other goods in the store. Cosmetics, foods, and home furnishings are sometimes handled by manufacturers' demonstrators.

Telephone Salesperson

Selling by telephone is becoming an important part of the operations of many large retail stores. In telephone selling there are two quite different jobs. The *order taker* is comparable to a salesclerk. He takes orders over the telephone from customers who are selecting merchandise from a catalog or from an advertisement, and he has little opportunity for creative selling beyond suggestion selling. He is primarily concerned with accurately recording the customer's name and address, special delivery instructions, and an exact description of the article wanted.

A *telephone salesperson,* however, must employ the principles of creative selling and must have great tact. He obtains leads on prospective customers, much as an outside salesman does. Unlike the outside salesman, however, the telephone salesperson must try to make the sale over the telephone without presenting the merchandise visually to the customer.

Because of its limitations, telephone selling is used largely for staple merchandise. In some stores telephone salespeople call regular customers to tell them about special sales and to try to encourage the customers to place their orders over the telephone.

SELLING FOR SERVICE BUSINESSES

Persons employed in service businesses often do not think of themselves as salespeople, but they are. It is true that customers will often voluntarily come to a service business when they need a particular service, but the persons in the business must use creative salesmanship to satisfy customers and assure that the customers will come back to them when they again need the service. In selling services, the building of long-term customer goodwill is of great importance.

In many ways, selling services—intangibles—is more difficult than selling merchandise—tangibles. In fact, the selling of such intangibles as insurance is one of the most specialized and respected of selling jobs. Like the outside salesman, persons selling services such as insurance must have a great deal of knowledge about their particular service; and they also are often called specialty salesmen.

The most important service businesses in this country are those offering the following services: (1) personal services, such as barber shops and dry cleaners; (2) hospitality services, such as motels and restaurants; (3) financial services, such as banks and stockbrokers; (4) entertainment services, such as bowling alleys and theaters; (5) transportation services, such as airlines and car rental agencies; (6) insurance services, such as life and automobile insurance; and (7) repair services, such as watch and furniture repair shops.

All service businesses do not serve the ultimate consumer. Some service businesses, such as advertising agencies, are geared to helping the manufacturer, wholesaler, and retailer. However, the majority of service businesses in operation are designed to serve the ultimate consumer.

NONPERSONAL SELLERS

As was mentioned earlier, personal selling is the heart of the overall selling process; little selling could be carried on without it. Yet most successful businesses find it necessary to use both personal sellers and nonpersonal sellers. Selling that is done in a nonpersonal way by directing a sales message to a group rather than to individual customers is handled by people other than salesmen—advertising men, display men, sales promotion men, and public relations men.

Advertising Men

The advertising manager is responsible for developing and controlling the advertising program of his business. He must also weigh

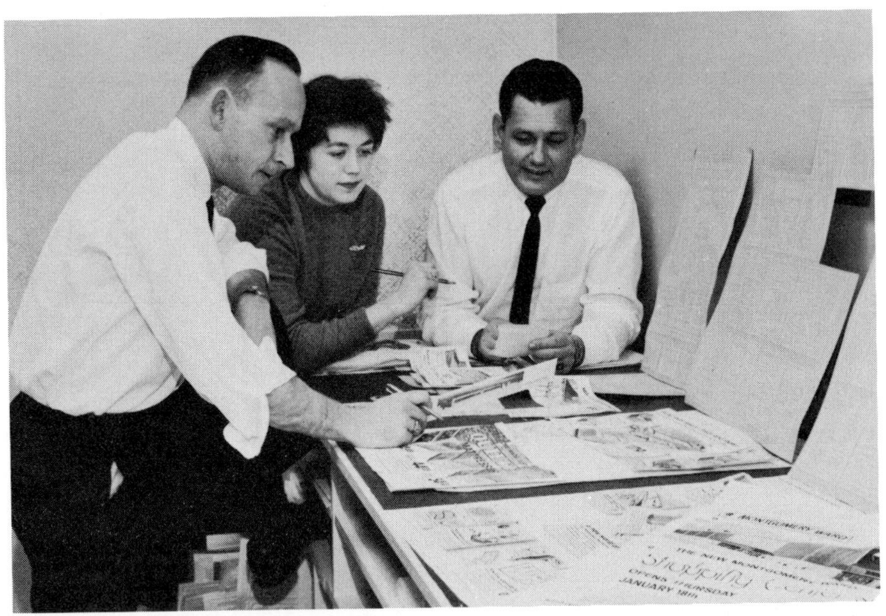

Montgomery Ward

Personal and nonpersonal sellers in the picture above are coordinating their plans for a special sales campaign. In a large-scale business operation, both types of sellers are necessary, although different businesses may depend more upon one type of seller than upon the other. Precise coordination of personal and nonpersonal sales effort is needed if sales volume is to be maximized.

carefully the budgeting of funds to the media used to present sales messages to the public. The most commonly used media are newspapers, magazines, direct mail, radio, and television.

Display Men

The person responsible for display of merchandise in store windows and inside the store must be a highly skilled technician if his business is to realize the greatest value from merchandise displays. The display manager schedules displays, selects merchandise to be displayed, and devises themes for displays, all the while keeping in mind the overall store image. Window dressers are responsible for the actual execution of the displays.

Sales Promotion Men

Sales promotion men plan and execute selling events that supplement advertising, display, and personal selling. They plan and develop such things as: (1) premium plans, in which the customer is offered something of value if he buys the product being promoted; (2) "deals" in which a number of items are grouped together and sold at a special price; (3) contests for both customers and employees; and (4) campaigns with samples that are distributed to potential customers. Sales promotion men also frequently conduct special sales, fashion shows, exhibits, and other newsworthy events.

Public Relations Men

One facet of the work of public relations men is their responsibility for publicity in various news media. These men see that news releases on new products, price changes, and other special events or promotions reach the press in order to gain mention of their products or services in newspapers and magazines and over the air.

Some public relations people might almost be considered personal salesmen since they contact individual editors and program directors in an effort to sell them on the idea of giving some form of publicity or promotion without charge. Public relations men also have the responsibility of creating a favorable public image for the firms they represent.

CHECKING YOUR KNOWLEDGE

Vocabulary:

(1) external personal selling
(2) internal personal selling
(3) salesclerk
(4) salesman, or salesperson
(5) outside salesman
(6) appointment method
(7) specialty salesman
(8) demonstrator
(9) order taker
(10) telephone salesperson

Review questions:

1. What are the requirements for a person employed as a salesclerk?
2. Name four merchandise items that are frequently sold by outside salesmen.
3. What are the two kinds of demonstrators? Describe the activities of each.
4. What is the difference between a telephone order taker and a telephone salesperson?
5. Name the most important service businesses in this country.

For discussion:

1. In what areas would the qualifications of a personal salesman differ from those of a nonpersonal seller?

2. What are some of the difficulties involved in selling a service that are not encountered in selling a product?
3. Would a salesclerk or a salesperson be needed in the following transactions? (a) A homeowner wants to buy permanent storm windows and screens; (b) a car owner needs new snow tires; (c) a man is interested in buying a color TV set; (d) a woman wants to buy a sport shirt for her husband; (e) a man wishes to buy automobile insurance.

part E

theories of selling

A *theory,* according to the dictionary, is the "general or abstract principles of a body of fact, a science, or an art." There are theories of philosophy, theories of political science, theories of history. And there are also theories of selling.

No matter who the salesman is, what merchandise he is selling, and what firm he is selling for, he uses one or more of the common theories of selling. Many salesmen do not realize they are using selling theories; but their sales presentations are invariably based on one or more of these theories: stimulus-response theory, formula theory, need-satisfaction theory, and depth theory.

Why study selling theories? There are two important reasons. First, understanding the theories of selling helps the salesman to steer his sales efforts in the most effective direction; the theories give him background information that he can use in dealing with customers. Knowledge of theories is particularly helpful when the salesman is inexperienced. Second, knowledge of the various theories can result in the formulation of a single, general selling theory. This general theory, if it is combined with truly creative selling, can help all salesmen to sell all products to all customers more effectively.

STIMULUS-RESPONSE THEORY

A *stimulus* is any element that produces an effect in an individual; a *response* is the effect produced. A person stubs his toe and it hurts; the stubbing is the stimulus, and the resulting "Ouch!" is the response. In selling with the *stimulus-response theory,* the salesman consciously uses certain predetermined stimuli—visual or oral—to produce a response—buying—from the customer. This theory is the simplest selling theory, and it is also the most limited in creative selling potential.

The stimulus-response theory requires that a salesman hold certain behavioral concepts in his mind, that he mentally develop certain stimuli and their hoped-for responses, and that he throw these stimuli at customers in a selling situation. If one stimulus does not produce a buying response, the salesman tries another. There is a tendency for the salesman to develop unyielding stimulus-response patterns for his product and then apply these patterns to all customers, without taking into account the individual differences of customers.

There are two major disadvantages of this theory. First, the theory is too simple to explain the differences in human behavior. All people behave differently, and chances are that no two people will respond to the same stimuli in exactly the same way. Thus, the predetermined stimulus-response patterns may work with some customers and may not work with others. It is a hit-and-miss kind of selling. Second, the theory does not allow for effective exchange of information between salesman and customer. The salesman must rigidly control the sales interview if he is to present his stimulus-response patterns, and there is little opportunity for the customer to enter the conversation. With the stimulus-response theory, there is little consideration of customer needs and wants.

FORMULA THEORY

The oldest and most widely used theory of selling is the AIDA formula theory, sometimes called just the *formula theory*. Its premise is that to effectively sell a product, the salesman must conduct the sales presentation in four definite steps: (1) attract the customer's attention, (2) secure his interest, (3) stimulate his desire for the product, and (4) induce action to buy. It is somewhat more scientific than the stimulus-response theory, but using it alone is not creative selling.

The most significant disadvantage of this theory is its rigidity. If a salesman believes firmly that he must take the customer through each of the steps to reach a buying decision, he will find it difficult to adjust his sales presentation if a customer balks at one of the steps or refuses to be receptive to the salesman's presentation. Many salesmen using this theory tend to become so involved in concentrating upon the various steps that they ignore customer reactions to the sales talk. There is a lack of the two-way communication which is so necessary to creative selling.

Montgomery Ward

The salesman in the picture above is attempting to sell a camera to a young married couple. If the salesman were to use the stimulus-response theory, what stimulus-response patterns might he employ? Would this be the most effective way of selling the camera?

The formula theory is not really customer-oriented in the sense of determining customer needs and wants and satisfying them as well as possible; this theory is mainly seller-oriented. Too often salesmen use gimmicks just for the sake of attracting attention, just for the sake of securing interest, and so on, without considering whether the product or service most satisfactorily meets the customer's needs and wants.

The main advantage of the formula theory is that it is simple to teach and to use; thus, it can be used easily by beginning salesmen.

NEED-SATISFACTION THEORY

When the *need-satisfaction theory* was developed, selling came a step closer to becoming a science. According to this theory, the salesman should analyze his product to find its particular selling points—features capable of satisfying customer needs and wants—and in the sales talk relate these points to the customer's needs. This approach is more customer-oriented than is either the stimulus-response theory or the formula theory; yet it still does not go far enough in analyzing customer needs and in analyzing customer behavior.

Once a salesman has analyzed his product's need-satisfaction features, he has a tendency to apply the results of this analysis to all customers. When this is done, there is no allowance for the differences in customer behavior. Salesmen also tend to list as many need-satisfaction points as possible and then to rattle off all of them in the sales presentation, even though some of them may not apply to the particular customer involved in the presentation.

DEPTH THEORY

Once an individual thoroughly understands the background of a subject, he is better qualified to discuss and make decisions concerning this subject. This is also true of selling, and the *depth theory* makes this possible. It is the newest and most comprehensive theory of selling, and it is the most effective. It is representative of the new attitude toward selling and of the need for creative salesmanship.

The principle recognized in depth selling is that often the buyer approaches a salesman with a need or want before it is expressed in terms of a specific product or service. Through conversation, the salesman can assist the buyer in exploring and focusing on his need and can also explore his own capacity—in terms of goods or services—to satisfy this need. The interchange of ideas leads to a clarification of the buyer's problem and to an understanding of how the salesman can help solve it. Such understanding leads to a buying decision favorable to both parties.

The other theories of selling essentially explain only the "how" of salesmanship, but depth theory explains both the "how" and the "why" of salesmanship. It explains not only how a customer will react in a certain situation but why a customer will react in a certain way in a certain situation. Depth theory combines the principles of the other selling theories, but it goes beyond them into the areas of *behavioral science*—the study of human actions—to draw on principles of education, sociology, and psychology. Depth theory does not offer only a how-to-do-it approach. It sees the selling process, not as a rigidly defined set of stimulus-response patterns, not as a set of psychological steps, not as a mechanical series of need-satisfaction points, but rather as a continuous, overlapping flow of ideas leading from the definition of customer wants to the satisfaction of these wants.

Depth theory recognizes that every customer and every selling situation are different; and it places a premium on the salesman's abilities in

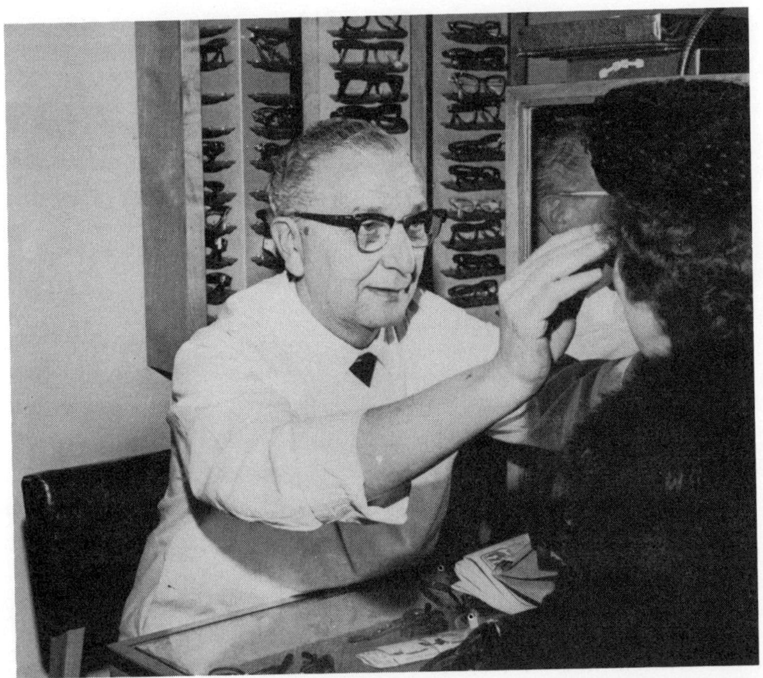

Macy's, New York City

The optometrist sells both a product and a special type of service. Which is more important—the product or the service? Does the optometrist need to employ depth selling?

customer analysis, problem solving, and decision making. It is both customer-oriented and seller-oriented; it not only considers the customer's needs and wants but also the seller's needs and wants. Communication between salesman and customer is an essential aspect of this theory. So is flexibility in approach, because as the salesman gains greater understanding of his customer, he is able to adjust his behavior and his sales presentation to the customer's behavior.

Depth selling utilizes the most valuable principles from the other selling theories and amplifies them with principles of behavioral science. The salesman who thoroughly understands and is able to implement depth theory can draw on all the principles of the other approaches in a selling situation. Depth selling accomplishes three major objectives of good selling: (1) it helps the seller to understand himself, and without this understanding he cannot solve the buying problems of others; (2) it helps him to understand the needs and wants of others; and (3) it helps develop the salesman's skill as a decision maker and problem solver.

CHECKING YOUR KNOWLEDGE

Vocabulary:

(1) theory
(2) stimulus
(3) response
(4) stimulus-response theory
(5) formula theory
(6) need-satisfaction theory
(7) depth theory
(8) behavioral science

Review questions:

1. Why is it important for salesmen to study the various selling theories?
2. Describe the operation of the stimulus-response theory of selling. What are its major disadvantages?
3. Describe the operation of the formula theory of selling. What is its major advantage?
4. Describe the operation of the need-satisfaction theory of selling.
5. Describe the operation of the depth theory of selling. What three major selling objectives does it accomplish?

For discussion:

1. For each of the major selling theories, name several products that could be effectively sold by following that theory. In what kinds of businesses could these selling theories be effectively used?
2. Is the depth theory of selling compatible with the traditional American desire to complete a sales transaction as quickly as possible?

BUILDING YOUR SKILLS

Improving your English:

Complete each of the following sentences by writing on a separate sheet of paper the correct form of the word given in parentheses.

1. The blue coat is the _______ of the two. (large)
2. The attractive collar is the _______ of the three. (small)
3. Harry's performance is the _______ of the five. (good)
4. This glass is the _______ of the two. (tall)
5. The salesman stated that "doeskin" was the _______ of the two shades and would complement most furnishings. (light)
6. Manmade fibers appear _______ than natural fibers. (heavy)
7. Of the three bicycles available, this is the _______. (fast)
8. Many customers believe that the four-cycle engine is the _______ of the two available. (strong)
9. Although three sizes are available, this one is actually the _______. (large)
10. The new fashions for fall are the _______ of the year. (good)

Improving your arithmetic:

Perform the following exercises involving subtraction.

1. Given below are the amounts of customer purchases and customer payments for a number of different sales transactions. For each transaction, how much change should be given to the customer?

Amount of Purchase	*Amount Tendered*
$ 6.78	$10.00
$13.14	$20.00
$ 1.33	$ 5.00
$ .22	$ 1.00
$ 8.39	$10.00

2. A salesman in Wrobel's Hardware Store sold an electric knife to a customer. The price of the knife was $32.50, and the customer chose to pay for the knife in installments of $5 a month for 6 months, plus a $5 down payment. How much would the customer have saved if he had paid cash?
3. A salesperson in a specialty shop buys for herself a handbag for $15.75, a compact for $5.50, and two scarfs for $4.25 each. She is entitled to a 3% employee discount. If the state sales tax is 4%, what is the total amount of her purchases?
4. Last week the gross salary of a salesman for Garson's Men's Store was $110.40. The following amounts were deducted from the gross salary: federal income tax, $10.00; social security taxes, $5.30; group insurance charge, 95¢. If there is also a city income withholding tax of 1% of the gross salary, what will be the salesman's take-home pay?
5. The Weaver Sporting Goods Company pays its salesmen a commission of 1% on all sales and an additional 2% on monthly sales in excess of $4,500. In June one salesman sold $8,000 worth of merchandise. What was his commission for the month?

Improving your research skills:

1. Identify the types of wholesale middlemen in your area and briefly discuss the duties performed by each.
2. Some products or services can be sold with a minimum of sales effort on the part of the salesperson. Other products or services require a great deal of sales effort. Name five products or services that require a minimum of sales effort and five products or services that require a great deal of sales effort. Give reasons for your selections.
3. Observe a salesman as he sells a particular item. Note the extent to which the selling theories discussed in this chapter are used. Prepare a brief report on the way he demonstrated or explained his product.
4. Examine magazine advertising and displays in several leading stores for a new article you have never seen before. Will it require a great deal of personal salesmanship? Why? Give your answers in class.

APPLYING YOUR KNOWLEDGE

Case problem:

The Capital Wholesale Company sells only to retail grocery stores and handles most items stocked by small and medium-sized grocers. Capital has been in business for over 50 years and has been very successful in maintaining existing accounts and in acquiring additional accounts when new stores opened. Management has supervised sales efforts rather closely and has insisted that all sales talks mention a certain feature of a product in order to get an initial response. If the response is unfavorable, another feature of the product is mentioned until a more favorable response is received. Competing wholesalers are apparently doing a more thorough job of selling, since Capital's sales volume has not increased at its normal rate this year while overall industry figures show a substantial increase.

1. Why do you think Capital's efforts have been so successful up to this time?
2. Of the selling theories discussed in this chapter, which did Capital probably use most frequently?
3. Discuss selling theories which other wholesalers may currently be using.
4. How might Capital improve its sales efforts?

Continuing project:

Based on the facts you have learned in Chapters 1 and 2 and in your research activities, start your Sales Occupation Manual by writing about each of the following topics:

1. The product or service you want to sell. Explain why you would like to sell the product or service.
2. If you choose to sell a product, tell how it will be produced and manufactured and the probable channel of distribution for the product.
3. The customers you plan to serve.
4. The selling organization you want to work for and the type of selling job you want to hold within this organization. You should spend considerable time in writing on this topic, since the choice you make here will influence the content of the rest of your manual.
5. The selling theories you will use in selling your product or service.

Extra credit:

Make an appointment with the personnel manager for a large seller in your community—a manufacturer, a wholesaler, a retailer, or a seller of some service. Determine what selling jobs the company offers, the qualifications required of applicants, the training provided by the firm, and the opportunities for advancement. Write an essay reporting your findings and indicating your reactions to the information you found. Ask for your instructor's assistance in planning your interview.

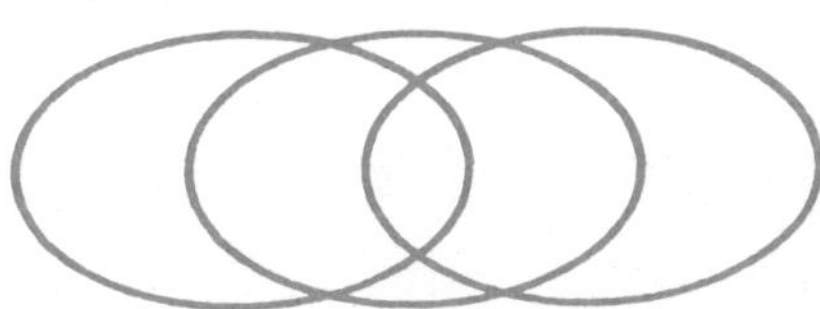

chapter 3

personality of the successful salesman

KEY QUESTIONS

A Why are the customer's first impressions of a salesman so important?

B Can a salesman who uses language carelessly in everyday conversation speak correctly when he makes a sales talk?

C If a salesman could see himself as others see him, would he be able to improve his moral and social characteristics?

D Why is self-analysis necessary before an individual begins the job-seeking process?

E What are the major ethical responsibilities of a salesman to his employer?

part A

physical characteristics

In the last chapter the role of the individual salesman in various selling organizations was emphasized, and you learned about the theories of selling that a salesman may employ. To be successful, a salesman must be thoroughly familiar with the products or services he is to sell, the buying motives and buying patterns of his customers, and the skills needed to adequately satisfy customers' buying needs and wants. Yet, important as these knowledges are, they are not enough to effectively carry out a sales transaction. Before the salesman can use these knowledges, he must make a favorable initial contact with the customer. In the space of a few seconds, he must convince the customer that he is someone with whom the customer would like to do business. This favorable initial contact depends upon the salesman's personality.

WHAT IS PERSONALITY?

Personality is the sum of a person's physique, character traits, attitudes, and habits; it is the sum of how a person appears and what he does in his relationships with others. Individuals who create impressions that attract other people are said to have pleasing personalities.

Based on their personality characteristics, persons are often classified as extroverts, introverts, or ambiverts. The *extrovert* has a great liking for people and feels at home in almost any social situation. The *introvert* is usually more comfortable when working alone. The *ambivert* falls between these two extremes and can find pleasure in solitary work and in work dealing with other people. A commonly held belief is that only the extrovert can be a good salesman. This is not true; the successful salesman is one who has a genuine interest in solving his customers' problems, and such a person can be an extrovert, introvert, or ambivert.

Probably everyone can improve his personality. By self-analysis he can eliminate characteristics that are objectionable to others and cultivate characteristics that are pleasing to others. Continual self-analysis is particularly important in selling jobs because a salesperson is constantly contacting new and different people. A business carries on a continual analysis of its operations; so must a salesman.

PHYSICAL ELEMENTS OF PERSONALITY

An important part of developing a successful personality is making a favorable physical impression on others. Making a favorable first impression is particularly important in selling. A customer reacts quickly to a salesman's physical appearance, especially if the salesman is a stranger. Often selling contacts are too short for the customer to discover what kind of person the salesman really is, so much of a customer's opinion is based on the salesman's physical appearance. Thus, a salesman should be quite careful about his physical appearance if he is to convey the impression of a pleasing personality.

Health

Good health is of great importance to individuals because it is the foundation upon which other physical and mental qualities are built. The chief factors that contribute to good health are proper diet, exercise, sleep, and medical and dental care.

Diet. Everyone must be careful of what he eats, where he eats, when he eats, and how he eats. In selling, the strain and bustle of the job often lead to irregular eating habits. Too many salespeople eat little for breakfast, gulp lunch hurriedly—often while trying to talk business with a customer—and eat a heavy dinner, followed by a midnight snack. A few rules for sensible eating are:

1. Eat nutritious, well-balanced meals.
2. Eat at regular hours and avoid snacks between meals.
3. Take an adequate amount of time for eating meals.
4. Don't eat when you are nervous or overtired.
5. Don't overeat.
6. Don't eat too much food or drink of any one kind.

Exercise. Most salesmen get some exercise in their jobs, but most of them need additional regular exercise to stay in good health. Sports that are recommended because they are not too tiring for persons in reasonably good health are volleyball, badminton, bowling, tennis, golf, swimming, baseball, bicycling, and skating. Jogging is becoming very popular and is an excellent form of exercise.

Sleep. Without adequate sleep, salesmen cannot be in prime condition to serve their customers. Eight hours' sleep each night is advisable for most persons. It is also wise for salesmen to relax for five or ten minutes several times during the day; a brief rest does much to restore waning energy and enthusiasm.

H. Armstrong Roberts

Pleasing personal appearance is not so much a matter of attractive face or figure as it is a matter of good taste and neatness.

Medical and Dental Care. Many business firms require physical examinations of all job applicants, and those applicants who would be expected to deal with the public are sometimes rejected because of a health defect that could be remedied. Bad teeth, diseased tonsils, poor eyesight, and overweight are common reasons for rejection. These factors may not immediately affect a person's working efficiency, but they are almost sure to lead to ill health and loss of working time later. Everyone should have regular physical and dental checkups.

Posture

A person's good health contributes considerably to his overall physical appearance, but poor posture can quickly detract from an otherwise attractive appearance. Failure to stand erect, with the body well balanced on the feet, makes a person look slouchy and awkward. A salesperson's good posture gives the impression that he is successful and has confidence in himself and his work.

Grooming

Cleanliness is important to everyone, but to a salesman it is critical. No one likes to buy from a person who has unclean hands, face, teeth, or body, or bad breath. Grooming, however, involves more than just keeping the face, hair, hands, and body clean. Grooming concerns all aspects of one's outward physical appearance, and good grooming is essential to a salesman's pleasing appearance. For instance, men should be careful that they are always clean-shaven and that their hair is neatly trimmed. Women should not overuse cosmetics and should wear their hair in simple, becoming styles.

Clothes

Good taste in clothing always avoids extremes of style; clothing should be viewed as an aid to a person's appearance rather than as existing for its own sake. For the salesperson, there are three simple rules of dress:

1. Wear clothes that are conservative and appropriate to the job.
2. Wear clothes that are in good repair.
3. Wear clothes that are clean and well pressed.

Businessmen have a right to demand that employees who contact the public must dress to suit the employer, not to suit themselves. Many customers will withhold their patronage if they feel that the employees they meet are consistently unconventional in appearance. A number of retail stores have established dress regulations so that salespeople will avoid extremes of dress. Some specialty shops and restaurants require their salespeople to wear uniforms, and many department stores require saleswomen to wear navy or black dresses with little or no jewelry.

Mannerisms

Too many salesmen have acquired or developed mannerisms that are distracting to customers. There are mannerisms of gesture, expression, voice, speech, posture, and so on. The salesman may consider such mannerisms unimportant; but if they irritate or distract a customer, they can result in lost sales. Mannerisms that should be avoided include drumming on furniture with one's fingers or a pencil, continually clearing one's throat, twirling one's hat, buttoning and unbuttoning one's coat, crossing and uncrossing one's legs, tapping on the floor with one's foot, constantly repeating such phrases as "I mean" and "you know," and using slang phrases too often.

Rules for Good Grooming

Men:

- Wear clean shirts; avoid dingy, frayed, or wrinkled cuffs and collars.
- Keep your clothes pressed; never let your trousers get baggy.
- Keep your hair trimmed, and shave every morning.
- Wear dark suits except where store regulations permit light ones.
- Wear clean and neatly pressed ties.
- Wear coats during selling hours on the selling floor, except at such seasons or days when your management permits exception. A lightweight service coat is permitted in hot weather. This includes men in offices where the public is received, and any others whose duties may occasionally bring them to the selling floor. Exceptions must be approved by your manager.

Women:

- Use good judgment in applying makeup; don't overdo it.
- If you wear nail polish, wear an appropriate shade and be sure it is not chipped.
- Use perfume sparingly.
- Wear appropriate dresses. Avoid printed, figured, lace, or other transparent dress fabrics except where store regulations permit otherwise.
- Avoid dresses or shoes designed for evening wear.
- Use good taste in selecting costume jewelry or other dress ornaments.

Men and Women:

- Keep your hands and nails clean. Wash your hands several times daily.
- Keep your shoes clean and well groomed.
- Avoid bad breath. Search out the cause and correct it.
- Avoid body perspiration odor by daily bathing and use of deodorants.

Cleanliness is the basis for building up a good personal appearance.

Sears, Roebuck & Company

In the Sears, Roebuck & Company retail stores, employees are given this set of rules pertaining to personal appearance. These rules may be adapted to all forms of selling. It is important to remember that the salesperson should make the maximum effort to achieve a pleasing physical appearance.

International Business Machines Corporation

In every selling situation—whether goods or services are being sold —the seller relies upon his voice to keep the prospect's attention centered on the sales message. The voice is the best index of a person's feelings, and the salesman should take great care to develop and use his voice properly.

Voice

For the salesman, it is not only what he says but how he says it that enables him to gain and hold customer attention. The functions of a good selling voice are: (1) to carry a message to the prospect, (2) to keep the prospect's attention centered on the sales message, and (3) to create a feeling of confidence in the salesman. Some principles of effective speaking are:

1. Speak distinctly.
2. Speak with moderate speed.
3. Speak reasonably loudly.
4. Emphasize key words and phrases.
5. Vary the pitch of the voice.
6. Speak in a conversational tone.
7. Speak sincerely.

CHECKING YOUR KNOWLEDGE

Vocabulary:

(1) personality
(2) extrovert
(3) introvert
(4) ambivert

Review questions:

1. Why is a pleasing personality so important in selling?
2. What are the physical elements of personality?
3. List ten rules for good grooming as formulated by Sears, Roebuck.
4. Give examples of undesirable mannerisms that would have an adverse effect on a salesman's success. How might they be overcome?
5. What seven principles should be followed in developing an effective selling voice?

For discussion:

1. Is there any difference between an effective sales personality and an effective personality in other occupations?
2. Give the advantages of a healthy appearance to each of these salesmen: (a) a retail meat salesman, (b) a wholesale drug salesman, (c) a wholesale salesman of sporting goods, (d) a house-to-house salesman of encyclopedias.
3. Describe the proper type of clothing for each of the following salesmen: (a) a salesman of men's high-grade clothing, (b) a salesman of textbooks who sells to high schools, (c) a wholesale salesman of groceries, (d) a soda clerk in a drugstore.

part B

verbal characteristics

Language is perhaps the salesman's most important tool, for it is the chief means of conveying to a prospective customer his thoughts about the product or service he is selling. If he cannot speak clearly and confidently, he cannot sell—no matter how fine his personality, how sincere his interest in his prospects, and how impressive his sales demonstration. The ability to use verbal language correctly and forcefully is one of the most necessary qualifications of the salesman. He must also be able to express himself clearly in written language; but because verbal skills are more important than written skills to most salesmen, we shall discuss some aspects of verbal skills in this part.

ELEMENTS OF VERBAL LANGUAGE

Verbal language consists of various mechanical elements combined to express the thoughts of the speaker as precisely as possible. The elements that a salesman should master include vocabulary, choice of effective words, grammar, and pronunciation and enunciation.

Building a Vocabulary

Words are symbols of ideas; a person's ability to convey his thoughts to others is limited by his mastery of words. Most people can understand many words they read but seldom use in writing and conversing, but a salesman should concentrate on enlarging his speaking vocabulary rather than on building a large reading vocabulary. By having a large speaking vocabulary, he can express thoughts about his products quickly and forcefully. A person is considered to have mastered a word when: (1) he knows its exact meaning; (2) he can pronounce it correctly; and (3) he is able to use the word correctly and without hesitation in conversation.

Vocabulary can be increased through reading and through personal contacts with well-educated people. Good reading for vocabulary building includes the literary classics, quality fiction and nonfiction, biographies of famous people, magazines, and newspapers.

Choosing Words for a Sales Talk

A large vocabulary will be of little value to a salesman unless he can choose the proper words to use in his sales talk. Words should be appropriate to the article being sold and should be selected with the customer in mind. If a salesman uses words that the prospective customer cannot understand, he will probably not convince the customer to buy.

The traveling salesman should avoid using local expressions because expressions commonly used in one part of the country may not be used in another part. For example, in some parts of the country green beans are called "snaps" while in other parts they are called "hullers."

A great problem in choosing the proper words is the use of technical terms. Words commonly used by members of one trade or profession may be unknown to members of other trades or professions. It is always dangerous to use technical terms in describing an article to someone who is not familiar with the terms. A salesman should use the precise vocabulary of a trade in talking with a person belonging to this trade, but the salesman should never try to show off his technical knowledge.

Stock Expressions To Be Avoided

gents	as per
your favor	recent date
near future	at all times
at this time	highest grade
in due course	unusual value
by return mail	state (for *say*)
buy (as a noun)	inform (for *tell*)
party (for *person*)	same (as a pronoun)
greatly in demand	an excellent value
advise (for *inform*)	at the present time
earliest convenience	only too happy (for *glad*)
according to our records	communication (for *letter*)
proposition (for *proposal*)	as of (referring to a date)
do not hesitate to write us	let me call your attention to
above mentioned (for *foregoing*)	guaranteed to give satisfaction
contact (for *get in touch with*)	per (when used with English noun)

Salespeople frequently make the mistake of using what they believe to be business English but which is merely a conglomeration of hackneyed words and phrases. These words and phrases have been used so much that they are dull and lifeless, and some are even grammatically incorrect.

Another problem in choosing words is the emotional impact and association of words. Words and phrases are often "loaded" because they create emotional responses in the listener that may be either favorable or unfavorable. For instance, most people associate the word "cheap" not only with low price but also with poor quality. So the wise salesman substitutes the word "inexpensive."

Salesmen should generally use short words rather than long words in the sales talk, because short words are more clearly understood and often more forceful than are longer words. Exclusive use of either long or short words, however, becomes monotonous. Clever speakers and writers vary their use of long and short words purely for the attention-getting results of an abrupt change.

In general, slang should be avoided. It is usually inexact and careless language that goes out of date quickly, and it often gives a bad impression of the speaker. The consistent use of slang decreases a salesman's command of effective verbal language.

The Importance of Correct Grammar

Some salesmen have sold big orders without using correct grammar, but these persons are rare. No one can escape the fact that he is judged by his correct use of grammar just as he is judged by his physical appearance.

The use of incorrect grammar is harmful for several reasons. First, poor grammar immediately lowers the salesman in the estimation of the customer, especially if the customer is well-educated. Second, incorrect grammar may give the prospect a poor impression of the firm that the salesman represents. Third, incorrect grammar is likely to draw the customer's attention from what the salesman is saying to how he is saying it; and anything that takes the customer's attention from the selling message reduces the chance of making a sale. Fourth, incorrect grammar may garble the intended idea and lead to misunderstanding.

Many handbooks on grammar have been published, some of which cost little and are easy to use. It is a good idea for the salesman or potential salesman to buy one of these handbooks and review the rules of grammar at his convenience. He should study the way he talks, list his own grammatical errors, and then try to correct them.

Pronunciation and Enunciation

People who are careful about the exact use of words and about the rules of grammar are sometimes careless about pronunciation. Yet, customers notice mistakes in pronunciation just as quickly as they notice mistakes in grammar and probably more quickly than they notice mistakes in word usage.

Words can be mispronounced in many different ways. The most common types of errors are: (1) a vowel is given the wrong sound ("deaf" is sometimes incorrectly pronounced as though it were spelled "deef"); (2) silent letters are sounded (the "t" in "often" is sometimes pronounced); (3) syllables that do not exist are sounded ("umbrella" is sometimes pronounced as though it were spelled "umberella"); (4) letters and syllables that should be sounded are omitted ("family" is sometimes pronounced as though it were spelled "famly").

Enunciation refers to the act of speaking distinctly. People often run words together or slur the first or last syllables. A common fault is dropping the "g" in "ing." A salesman's carelessness in enunciation is likely to be taken as an indication of carelessness in other areas, and poor enunciation is likely to result in the customer's misunderstanding what the salesman is saying.

Commonly Mispronounced Words

acclimate	exquisite	measure
appellate	February	patron
blatant	flaccid	positively
calliope	granary	precedent
candidate	hasten	radio
chastisement	height	research
column	ideology	respite
condolence	Illinois	robust
coupon	impious	romance
Detroit	indict	schism
diamond	insurance	senile
disruptive	italics	suite
Edinburgh	joust	temperament
engine	lamentable	Terre Haute
envoy	maintenance	vaudeville

The words listed above are commonly mispronounced in conversation. Can you pronounce them correctly? Can you define them? Use a dictionary, if you must, to determine the correct pronunciation and meaning of each word.

COMPOSING A SALES TALK

Mastery of the principles of correct word usage, grammar, and pronunciation and enunciation do not necessarily lead to an effective sales talk. The sales talk is an oral composition, and it should be planned and given in accordance with the principles of composition—unity, coherence, and emphasis.

Unity

The principle of *unity* requires that a speaker stay with one main topic in his spoken message. Thus, the salesman should concentrate on talking about only one article or group of related articles at one time. The average person cannot effectively grasp two different ideas at the same time.

Coherence

The salesman should organize his ideas so that they are presented logically. The principle of *coherence* involves more than a logical order of ideas, however; it also requires that the ideas be properly connected to each other. Expressions such as "in the first place" and "in the second place" clearly show the relation of one idea to another, but they should not be used too often because they are quite mechanical. It is better to use transitional words and phrases such as "therefore," "moreover," "notwithstanding," "for this reason," or "looking at it from another angle." The salesman should not depend too much upon one type of transitional word or phrase, because the talk may become monotonous.

Emphasis

The principle of *emphasis* requires that a speaker single out ideas in accordance with their importance. Methods of emphasizing important ideas in a sales talk are through position, proportion, repetition, and vocal techniques.

Emphasis Through Position. The beginning and the end of a sales talk are the most conspicuous parts and those a listener is most likely to remember. Thus, the salesman's most important selling points should be placed at the beginning and/or end of the talk.

Emphasis Through Proportion. Emphasis may be secured by devoting to each idea in the sales talk an amount of time proportionate to

Common Errors in Enunciation

Lazy Group: sumpin, generly, probly, praps, mebbee
Careless Group: fer, frum, wuz, kin, git, jest
Run In's: Whyavenchew astfort?
Slurred: Wydoncha teller?
One Worder's: Zatso?
What Is This: Wyancha letumalone?
Wrong Sounds or Syllables Added: umberella, rememberance, fillum, drownded, acrost, warsh
Wrong Vowels: ketch, wrastle, crick
Beginning and Ending Sounds: kep, slep, comin', 'ats, tackful
Omitting Consonants: reconize, goverment, temperment

Some of the words and phrases above look as though they were taken from a foreign language. Actually, they are English words and phrases that represent common errors in enunciation. What is the correct enunciation for each example given?

its importance. Thus, a successful salesman will fully develop his important sales points, merely touching lightly on minor points unless these points appear to be of special interest to the buyer.

Emphasis Through Repetition. A debate is generally won by the side that drives home one important point, rather than by the side that lists the greatest number of arguments. The wise salesman follows this principle. He repeats an important idea in slightly varied form throughout the sales talk or repeats the exact words of a slogan that often represents the chief selling point of an article.

Emphasis Through Vocal Techniques. Ideas may be emphasized by raising the voice, by lowering the voice, by pausing after an important statement, and by speaking slowly. These mechanical means are very effective in the sales talk if they are used sparingly. Overuse of mechanical methods, however, may annoy the prospect and take his attention from the sales talk itself. Mechanical methods must seem natural and spontaneous or they will appear insincere.

CHECKING YOUR KNOWLEDGE

Vocabulary:

(1) unity
(2) coherence
(3) emphasis

Review questions:

1. What elements of verbal language should a salesman master?
2. When is a person considered to have mastered a word?
3. What are some problems a salesman may encounter in choosing words for a sales talk?
4. Why is the use of incorrect grammar harmful to the salesman?
5. Name some common errors in pronunciation.
6. What are the methods of emphasizing important ideas in a sales talk?

For discussion:

1. Why is it difficult for one person to make his ideas understood by another person?
2. "The salesman should choose words that are in accord with the nature of the article being sold." Explain this statement.
3. How does the reading of good literature improve one's grammar, increase vocabulary, and result in a more fluent use of English?

part C

mental characteristics

In studying people, we recognize as many differences in mental characteristics as in physical characteristics. Thus, it is important to discuss some of the differences in mental characteristics as they apply to selling. Although an individual's physical characteristics largely determine the impression he conveys in an initial, face-to-face contact, his mental qualities reveal his true personality.

In this part, you will learn more about the moral qualities, the personality qualities determined primarily by intellectual capacity, and the social qualities that a successful salesman must have. No attempt will be made to explore all the desirable characteristics in each category; rather, those that are particularly important in selling will be discussed.

PERSONALITY AND MOODS

Man is both a physical and a mental being, and these two segments are interdependent. Together they determine an individual's success in his work, in his domestic and social life, and in his contribution to society. Experts in medical science now agree that prolonged mental stress—such as worry, fear, and anguish—are major contributors to many physical ills. Persons who have problems difficult to bear often turn to psychiatrists, clergymen, and other counsellors for help in self-understanding.

The key to sound mental development and a well-adjusted approach to life is the understanding and control of one's emotions. An *emotion* is a strong feeling which can produce other mental and physical responses; fear is an emotion.

When an emotion is strong or of long duration, it results in the creation of a *mood*. Everyone has moods, or prevailing emotional feelings. The main thing that psychologists know about moods is that they are constantly changing. Thus, a person may feel very happy in the morning and very depressed in the afternoon. Psychologists have even developed mood scales to measure changes in mood over short and long time periods. Mood changes generally follow a pattern such as this: a sharp drop from a peak of mental well-being to depression, followed by a more gradual rise to the peak again.

Characteristics of the Emotionally Mature Person

- He is aware of his capabilities and limitations.
- He shows his emotions in constructive, rather than destructive, ways.
- He can keep his emotions from dominating his common sense.
- He respects other people and is sensitive to their feelings.
- He is constantly aware of the effect his behavior has on others.
- He sets goals for himself and works toward those goals.
- He can follow directions, accept responsibility, and accept constructive criticism.
- He can adapt easily to almost any new situation.
- He has a sense of humor, even when that humor is directed toward himself.
- He can find equal pleasure in being by himself or in being with other people.

Some of the characteristics of an emotionally mature person are listed above. The person who exhibits these characteristics is the one most likely to succeed in his work, in his domestic and social life, and in his role as a useful member of society.

The salesman should recognize that moods exist and that they are always changing. He should attempt to plan his work around his moods as long as he can do this without harming his productivity. On some days he is better equipped mentally to take a long trip and call on a large number of customers, to deal with a difficult customer who has a problem that requires ingenuity to solve, or to calculate costs of a proposed installation involving a great many variable factors. If the salesman has little control over his varied activities—as in the case of a retail salesperson—he will not permit his depressed moods to interfere with his work, knowing that the temporary depression will pass and be replaced by a more positive mood.

MORAL CHARACTERISTICS

Every society in every age has had its *moral code*—its rules for acceptable conduct in interpersonal relationships. For a salesman to live up to his own moral code and the moral code of his society, he must possess five important moral qualities: honesty, responsibility, courage, loyalty, and industry.

Honesty

A salesman must be honest with himself, with his employer, and with his customers. *Honesty* is the fairness and straightforwardness of conduct. Being honest with oneself means putting forth one's best efforts in doing a full day's work every day; this honesty should bring personal satisfaction to the salesman. If he finds that his working environment will not give him satisfaction, it may mean that he is in the wrong job. There is a direct correlation between honesty with oneself and honesty with one's employer; honesty with the employer requires nothing less than one-hundred-percent integrity. Stealing from the employer or collecting payment for services not performed is flagrantly dishonest.

Honesty in dealing with customers is the foundation of long-term salesman-customer relationships, and you will learn more about this type of honesty in Part E, "Ethics in Selling."

Responsibility

Responsibility is the carrying out of promises one has made and the seeing through of a job. Sometimes salesmen make glib promises to close a sale and then later forget about these promises. Sometimes salesmen make appointments with customers and then fail to keep them. Such conduct shows lack of responsibility. An unreliable person disrupts sound business relationships almost as much as does a dishonest one. The unreliable person shows no respect for the interests and rights of others.

Courage

Courage is the mental and moral strength that causes one to withstand danger, fear, or difficulty. The salesman needs courage because he must continuously contact and influence other people, many of whom are strangers whose likes and dislikes are unknown to him. The courageous salesman will stick to his job even when everything seems to be going against him. Such courage depends upon the salesman's confidence in his products, his firm, and himself. It requires perseverance and foresight to realize that troubles are temporary and that one has within himself a strength reserve upon which he can draw.

Loyalty

Loyalty is a trait that concerns the faithfulness of an employee to other employees and to the firm. Unless the salesman associates his own personal well-being with that of his company, customers may question whether the firm's products and services are really best for their needs. Loyalty to one's fellow employees is essential because effective cooperation among salespeople is found only where there is mutual trust. Loyalty is shown when a salesman recognizes the good work of his fellow salesmen and speaks of that work to others.

Industry

Diligence in any pursuit is called *industry*. Industry is closely related to honesty with one's employer. Manufacturers' salesmen who do much traveling can easily waste time if they desire because it is not easy to check on the actual hours they have worked. However, the industrious salesman uses every selling opportunity to the fullest advantage to himself and his company. Retail salespeople must not only contact their fair share of the customers who come to the store but must also know how to occupy their time when there are no customers. The industrious salesman will perform such tasks as replenishing stock and rearranging merchandise displays when there are selling lulls.

PERSONALITY CHARACTERISTICS DETERMINED BY INTELLIGENCE

A person's intellectual capacity or intelligence determines the degree to which certain mental characteristics may be present in his makeup. *Intelligence* is the ability of an individual to understand facts and concepts and their relations to each other and to reason about these facts and concepts. Obviously, intelligence also influences the moral and social characteristics we are discussing in this part; but it appears to have the most influence on the development of a person's resourcefulness, imagination, ambition, and adaptability.

Resourcefulness

A person possesses *resourcefulness* when he has the capacity to take action quickly in new situations and to handle quickly unexpected difficulties. The constant flow of new customers and new selling situations requires that all salesmen be resourceful. Suggestion selling gives retail salesmen a chance to practice resourcefulness, to both serve the customer and increase the ultimate sale. For manufacturers' and wholesalers' salesmen, a major duty is to expand the market in their territories by finding new users for their products and by developing new ways to meet the needs of these nonusers. This requires a great amount of resourcefulness.

Imagination

Imagination is that power which enables a person to form mental images of things that are not before him. In selling, imagination is the ability to see an article in use and to visualize new uses for it and new ways to combine it with other articles. Selling really has more to do with selling the use of an article than with selling the article itself. Selling the use of an article requires that the salesman have a knowledge of the article and also a vivid imagination.

Showmanship is an applied form of imagination and is useful and sometimes very necessary in selling. It is a knack for dramatization—the ability to present merchandise in a manner exciting to the customer. For example, a floor sample washing machine might be so constructed that customers could watch it work through a cabinet made of glass instead of the usual porcelain.

Sales/Marketing Today

Showmanship will always attract customers. At a big housewares trade show, where many manufacturers exhibited their wares to retailers, this "Yankee Peddler" wagon proved to be a great attention-getter.

Ambition

Ambition is the ever-present desire to achieve something; it is the drive that makes us work to attain our goals. It asserts itself mainly in the achievement of small victories, because success usually comes not from one great achievement but from a multitude of small, well-done jobs. In a salesman, ambition may appear as an attempt to break previous sales records or to outdo the work of fellow salesmen. Unfortunately, a few salesmen are overly ambitious; and in their desires to set sales records or earn large commissions, they use unethical selling practices. They disregard the fact that such practices are never excusable and that the salesman who uses them will eventually be the loser. Ambition should always be subordinate to honesty.

Adaptability

Being able to adjust or conform to a new set of circumstances and to different types of people is known as *adaptability*. It can be both an intellectual and a social characteristic. Since selling situations never remain constant, salesmen must be able to adapt easily. Adaptability requires consideration of four points:

1. You cannot change people; they change only when they want to.
2. You must change what you can and accept what you cannot change.
3. You must try to change yourself first.
4. You must be positive in your mental outlook.

Many experienced and formerly successful salesmen fail when they try to sell a new product or when they sell for a new firm. Sometimes they think that, because of their experience, they know all the answers; and they do not try to adjust to the new selling situation. To prepare himself for possible future changes in position, a salesman should make every effort to retain flexibility of mind and action.

SOCIAL CHARACTERISTICS

Some mental characteristics involve the ability to get along with other people. Of all the personality qualities discussed in this part, the social characteristics are those which can be most easily developed through practice and through experience in contacts with other people. All salesmen would be wise to work on developing these social characteristics: observation, enthusiasm, confidence, courtesy and tact, and sympathy and empathy.

"Better check the air and look at the oil."
"Give me change for the Coke machine, please."
"Mister, I can't reach the ladies' room key!"
"Can I have a map?"
"Please give the dog a drink of water."
"Ha! You forgot to clean the windshield!"

Changing Times

The salesman who possesses the social characteristics of observation, enthusiasm, confidence, courtesy and tact, and sympathy and empathy should be able to serve well even the most difficult customer.

Observation

Observation is the mental ability concerned with recognizing and noting facts or occurrences. It is important for the salesman to develop a keen appreciation of the value of observing things that go on about him. An ability for observation can enable the salesman to size up customers quickly and prepare his sales talks accordingly. This alertness and attentiveness can prove profitable in the form of increased sales.

Enthusiasm

Enthusiasm is the zest or excitement felt in performing some activity; it is the quality that makes work a pleasure. Enthusiasm enables the seller to talk in such a manner that he lends belief to what he says and acts as though he would rather perform his job than do anything else in the world. Enthusiasm is catching, and the indifferent attitudes of many salespeople keep them from arousing any enthusiasm from customers for their products or themselves.

Confidence

If a person knows that he possesses most of the characteristics we have just discussed, he will probably also have *confidence*—faith or trust in his actions and abilities. When a salesman displays confidence in an acceptable manner, this confidence tends to rub off on the customer. A high-caliber salesman is considered a specialist, and there is no surer way to instill confidence in a prospective customer than for the salesman to have a comprehensive amount of information about the product or service he is selling.

Studies show that self-confidence in selling expresses itself as a form of customer dominance. This is not an attitude of "lording" it over others but is rather an attitude of prevailing on the customer to regard the salesman as a trusted authority.

Courtesy and Tact

The terms "courtesy" and "tact" are often used interchangeably but do not mean quite the same thing. *Courtesy* is concerned with politeness and polished manners, such as showing deference to the customer and treating him as an honored guest. Courtesy is regarded as the outward sign of good breeding. *Tact,* however, has a deeper significance. It is a keen sense of what to do and say in order to maintain good relationships with other people; it is more than the outward signs of behavior accepted as correct by society. The tactful person can appreciate delicate situations and act accordingly.

Sympathy and Empathy

Current studies of human behavior reveal that creative selling is impossible unless the salesman has both sympathy and empathy for his customer. *Sympathy* is the ability to understand how another person looks at other people and at situations with which he is faced. *Empathy* goes further; it is the ability actually to feel what another person feels and to create in his own mind the feelings of another. By listening carefully to others, by noting their gestures and other nonverbal signs of communication, by exposing oneself to a variety of human experiences, and by having consideration and respect for other people, one can certainly acquire sympathy and perhaps go further and experience empathy.

CHECKING YOUR KNOWLEDGE

Vocabulary:

(1) emotion	(8) industry	(15) observation
(2) mood	(9) intelligence	(16) enthusiasm
(3) moral code	(10) resourcefulness	(17) confidence
(4) honesty	(11) imagination	(18) courtesy
(5) responsibility	(12) showmanship	(19) tact
(6) courage	(13) ambition	(20) sympathy
(7) loyalty	(14) adaptability	(21) empathy

Review questions:

1. What are some characteristics of the emotionally well-adjusted person?
2. Why is honesty in dealing with customers a prime requisite for all businessmen to follow?
3. What personality characteristics are determined largely by intelligence?
4. Name the four points that a truly adaptable person must always consider.
5. How may a salesman improve his social characteristics?

For discussion:

1. From the customer's point of view, which of the characteristics discussed in this chapter are most important for the salesman to have?
2. "Enthusiasm is based on belief; and belief, in turn, is based on knowledge." How does this statement apply to selling?

part D

"selling" personality to an employer

Selling your personality and your abilities to an employer is probably the most important selling activity you will ever conduct. Persons who cannot get a job in normal business times but who are physically fit and possess salable business skills generally fail to gain employment because they cannot sell themselves. Selling your services to an employer is like selling a product to a customer, and many of the selling techniques you will learn later in the book can be applied to the job-seeking process.

IMPORTANCE OF SELF-ANALYSIS

The product to be sold in an employment interview is *you.* Some salespeople try to sell products without having enough product knowledge, and many persons try to get a job without a certain amount of personal self-analysis. Before applying for a job, a person should thoroughly appraise his abilities and review his past activities. He should analyze his qualities so that he knows both his strong and his weak points. An easy way to perform this self-analysis is to list in one column of a page all his strong features and to list in another column all the features that need improvement. An applicant should not show this analysis to an employer; but it can give him a better understanding of himself, help him to overcome his weaknesses, and enable him to make the best possible impression when being interviewed.

STEPS IN THE JOB-SEEKING PROCESS

A job seeker will generally follow a pattern of definite steps after he has made his self-analysis. First, he prepares a summary of his salable qualities. Second, he locates prospective employers for whom he would like to work. Third, he applies formally for one or more jobs. Fourth, he is interviewed by prospective employers.

Preparing a Résumé

A *résumé,* or *personal data sheet,* is a summary of the significant personal, educational, and occupational facts about a person. It is generally prepared on a single sheet of paper, in a style similar to that shown on page 94, and accompanies the letter of application when it is sent to a firm. If the applicant is hired, the résumé usually becomes part of his permanent file.

Most prospective employers want a résumé to contain the following information:

1. *Educational background.* Schools or colleges that the applicant attended, years of attendance, degrees earned, scholastic record, extracurricular activities (particularly if leadership duties were involved), and major courses studied (if they have bearing on the job in question) should be listed.
2. *Work experience.* Former jobs held, dates of employment, names of employers, types of businesses, their locations, and the specific nature of the applicant's jobs should be mentioned.
3. *References.* Three or four persons who are not members of the applicant's family and who can give information about the applicant's

character and business skills should be listed. Teachers, clergymen, and former employers are excellent references. No one's name should be used as a reference without asking permission.

4. *Personal information.* The applicant's age, height, weight, general health, marital status, and military status should be mentioned. Hobbies or special skills relating to the job in question could also be reported.

Locating Prospective Employers

Major sources of job information are: (1) friends and acquaintances of the applicant, (2) advertisements, (3) placement bureaus and employment agencies, (4) direct application to firms, and (5) previous contacts. An applicant may use one or more of these sources in locating firms who have job openings in his work field.

Friends and Acquaintances. Many people locate prospective employers simply by telling friends that they are looking for a job and by describing the kind of job they want. The more "feelers" a person puts out, the better are his chances of making contacts with employers. If a friend already works for a company in which the applicant is interested, he may ask the friend to recommend him to the employer. Most companies are interested in employee recommendations made by their current employees.

Advertisements. Most newspapers print columns of help-wanted advertisements in each issue, and many persons read these columns thoroughly when they are searching for jobs. Many help-wanted advertisements are *blind advertisements;* this means that the advertiser's name is not given. The ad gives a post office or newspaper box number to which the applicant can write. Usually, blind advertisements indicate the type of work for which employees are being sought.

Sometimes a person may make known his desire for a job by placing job-wanted advertisements in newspapers or magazines. This method may work well for experienced people, but beginners should not use it.

Placement Bureaus and Employment Agencies. Nearly all schools and colleges have placement bureaus which help graduates contact business firms, supply vocational information and data about businesses, and give recommendations and personal information about the graduates. It is impossible, of course, for placement bureaus to guarantee jobs for their graduates; but they can be extremely helpful in the job-seeking process.

Résumé of
Richard L. Shipman
3100 Lexington Place
Pulaski, TN 37121

237-9999 (9 a.m. - 5 p.m.)
371-2313 (after 5 p.m.)

March 16, 1969

EDUCATION

1963-65 Pulaski Junior College. Received Associate of Science degree in salesmanship, June, 1965.

Major Courses Studied
- Salesmanship
- Retailing Principles
- Principles of Marketing
- Marketing and Buying

Activities
- Swimming Team -- two years
- Yearbook Business Manager -- one year

Scholastic Record
- Graduated "With Honors"

EXPERIENCE

September, 1967 - Present — Assistant Manager, Cook's Furniture Store, Pulaski. Experience in retail selling, hiring and supervising personnel, and purchasing merchandise.

June, 1965 - September, 1967 — Research Interviewer for the Davis Corporation, Princeton, New Jersey. Assisted in interviewing housewives concerning the durability of certain appliances.

1963-65 (Part-time) — Checker-Cashier, Parker's Market.

1959-61 (Summers) — Lifeguard, James K. Polk State Park

PERSONAL

Age 26; height, 6'2"; weight, 195 pounds; health, excellent; married, two children; served U. S. Army 1961-63; hobbies, swimming, golfing, and fishing.

REFERENCES

Dr. Charles Daniel Jewell
Chairman, Department of Business
Pulaski Junior College
Pulaski, TN 37121

Mr. John Cook, Owner
Cook's Furniture Store
212 Main Street
Pulaski, TN 37121

Mr. William Russell, Principal
Pulaski City High School
Elm Street
Pulaski, TN 37121

There is no standard form for a résumé, and the applicant may want to experiment with several forms before deciding on the one he likes best. The résumé should appear well balanced, uncrowded, and neat on the page; it is preferable that it consume only one page. There should be plenty of white space in the margins, and the major topics of information should be set up as headings. Complete sentences or phrases may be used in the body of the résumé. It is important that the résumé be typed.

In most cities, there are employment agencies which try to place persons in available jobs. If a beginning worker registers with an employment agency, he should make sure that he understands the agency's placement methods and his own financial obligations to the agency. Beginning workers may prefer to go through their state's employment service, a public employment agency which performs the same functions as a private employment agency but which charges no fee for its services.

Direct Application. If the firm in which an applicant is interested has an employment department, he might call in person at that department or write to the employment manager to inquire about available jobs. If there is no employment department, he might contact the manager of the department in which he wants to work. If the firm has only a branch office, factory, or store in the applicant's community, he might visit the local manager and ask his advice about securing employment with the company.

Previous Contacts. Many young graduates secure jobs through contacts they made before graduation. A person might meet a businessman who is visiting his home or a friend's home. He might have a chance to talk with an employer who is speaking to his class. He might interview businessmen to gather information for a class project. It is important that an individual try to make a favorable impression upon businessmen whenever he meets them. A seemingly insignificant contact might lead to a job offer later.

Applying for the Job

Writing a letter of application is the most common method of applying formally for a job. A help-wanted advertisement usually requires that a letter of application be written. Also, sometimes an applicant may write letters to several different businessmen in the hope that one or more of them will call him for an interview. Occasionally an employer may ask the individual to write a letter of application after the interview. This is done partly to test the applicant's ability to express himself in written language.

The letter of application is typically only three or four paragraphs long, so that an employer can read it quickly. Detailed information need not be given, since the letter will be accompanied by a résumé. Later in the book you will learn some of the principles for writing a good sales letter, and many of these principles can be applied to the writing of a letter of application. The letter of application should be written in a straightforward style and should, of course, be neatly prepared. An example of a letter of application is given on page 97.

The Interview

Interviews give the prospective employer a better chance to appraise what he is "buying." A person should never underestimate the importance of his physical appearance when he is being interviewed for a job. A conservative business suit or business dress should be worn and should be neat and becoming. The principles of good grooming discussed earlier in this chapter should be followed. The applicant should be confident, friendly, and courteous. His speaking voice, his opening remarks, and his English should be correct and pleasing.

When the applicant enters the employer's office, he should stand until the employer asks him to sit down. He should not greet the employer with a glad-handing, breezy, too-clever manner. During the interview, the applicant should emphasize those qualifications that particularly meet the employer's needs; and he should be able to point out how he can be an asset to the business.

The applicant should not try to pressure the employer into hiring him by suggesting that he has other job offers, that the employer must act quickly to hire him, or that he will consider working only if satisfactory arrangements can be made. Neither should he beg for the job; this lowers him in the employer's eyes. The applicant should not show too much concern about his starting salary. An opportunity for future advancement is more important than his initial wage. Nor should the applicant be overly concerned about the hours he will work. Most employers appreciate an employee's willingness to work at unusual hours, but they consider this time part of the scheduled work week.

Sometimes the employer will not hire the applicant on the basis of the first interview. He may want to contact references or discuss the applicant's qualifications with other officials of the company. An applicant should not show disappointment if he is not hired at once. He does have a right, however, to ask the employer if he will telephone or write him when he has made up his mind.

When an employer shows signs of having finished the interview, the applicant should thank him for his consideration and express the hope that he may be employed by the firm. The applicant should then pleasantly bid the employer good-bye and leave promptly.

3100 Lexington Place
Pulaski, TN 37121
March 16, 1969

Mr. Paul E. Phillips
Personnel Director
The Nashville Chair Company
2100 Broadway
Nashville, TN 37131

Dear Mr. Phillips

I am applying for the position of West Tennessee District Sales Manager that you advertised in Sunday's Tennessean. I believe that my educational background in sales and marketing and my professional experience in retail furniture sales should qualify me for this position.

I received the Associate of Science degree in salesmanship from Pulaski Junior College in 1965. From 1965 to 1967, I was employed by the Davis Corporation of Princeton, New Jersey, as a research interviewer. This position involved interviewing housewives concerning the durability of certain appliances. Its results were compiled into a report for a major appliance company. Since 1967, I have been employed as the assistant manager of Cook's Furniture Store in Pulaski. My responsibilities have included selling, hiring and supervising personnel, and purchasing merchandise.

Enclosed is a résumé of my educational and professional qualifications for the position your advertisement described. May I have an interview with you to discuss any questions you may have concerning my qualifications? You may reach me at 237-9999 between 9 a.m. and 5 p.m. or at 371-2313 after 5 p.m.

Sincerely yours

Richard L. Shipman

Richard L. Shipman

In writing a letter of application, the individual should follow the principles of correct letter writing and correct letter placement. The letter should be addressed to the appropriate official within the firm, and it should be written with the "you" attitude in mind—the applicant should tell the prospective employer what he can do for the firm. A letter of application should always be an original, never a mimeographed or a carbon copy.

CHECKING YOUR KNOWLEDGE

Vocabulary:

(1) résumé, or personal data sheet (2) blind advertisement

Review questions:

1. What information should be included on a résumé?
2. Name the major sources of job information.
3. Describe the functions of placement bureaus and employment agencies.
4. Under what circumstances may a job seeker write a letter of application?
5. What are some things an applicant should remember to do when being interviewed for a job?

For discussion:

1. Describe the various ways in which applying for a job resembles other forms of selling.
2. To what extent would you follow the advice of friends in applying for a job?
3. What opportunities are open to you in your school to develop leadership qualities? Why might participation in these activities be helpful when applying for a selling job in the future?

part E

ethics in selling

Once you have been hired and launched on your job, your progress will depend not only on your creative selling skills but also on your ethical conduct with your business associates. In ancient selling, it was moral or ethical for the Greek merchant to fill with air the skins of the fowls he was selling. It was customary to use the temple as a money exchange, and 25 percent to 30 percent interest was the usual rate charged by the Greek moneylender. Throughout the Middle Ages, business was dependent almost entirely upon shrewdness and bargaining ability rather than upon good judgment, foresight, honesty, and service. But today in America and in most of the civilized world, businessmen recognize that they have certain obligations to the many individuals and groups with whom they deal. For the salesman, this means that he has an ethical obligation to his customers, competitors, suppliers, associates, employer and fellow citizens.

Ethics is the system of rules—determined by beliefs of what is right and what is wrong—that governs human duty and obligation. The foundation of a code of ethics is justice—the recognition that every person has rights, that he has certain qualities which give him dignity and importance as an individual. With these rights go obligations to others in the social group and obligations to conform to the laws of life.

In discussing the ethics of selling in this part, we shall discuss only the ethical situations most frequently encountered in customer relations, competitor relations, vendor relations, and employer relations. An entire book could be written on ethics in selling.

ETHICS IN CUSTOMER RELATIONS

Success in business is largely the outgrowth of sound judgment and continuous ethical treatment of customers. The rule of *caveat emptor*—let the buyer beware—prevailed in business for centuries. It probably represented the attitude of ancient Roman merchants and, to some extent, it is still a recognized principle of business law. Fortunately, most business firms realize that a permanent clientele cannot be built upon the principle of caveat emptor. Customers will not return to a store nor give repeat orders to a salesman if they know that they must constantly be on the lookout for defects in the goods they buy. In his dealings with customers, the salesman must be above using the principle of caveat emptor.

Fairness in Pricing

If the customer is to receive good merchandise value for his money, the seller must follow a fair policy in regard to the prices charged to different customers. Most retailers have adopted a *one-price policy,* which means that at any given time all customers will be charged the same price for the same merchandise and that the seller will not discriminate in favor of certain customers who may be his friends or who may ask for a reduction in price. A one-price policy does not mean that the price is necessarily the same to people who buy at different times; prices may have to be reduced or raised according to market conditions. The test of a one-price policy is whether all customers pay the same price at any one time.

A Code of Ethics

- The foundation of business is confidence, which springs from integrity, fair dealing, efficient service, and mutual benefit.
- Contracts and undertakings, written or oral, are to be performed in letter and in spirit. Changed conditions do not justify their cancellation without mutual consent.
- Unfair competition embracing all acts characterized by bad faith, deception, fraud, or oppression, including commercial bribery, is wasteful, despicable, and a public wrong. Business will rely for its success on the excellence of its own service.
- Business should render restrictive legislation unnecessary through so conducting itself as to deserve and inspire public confidence.

Probably the best single code of business ethics is that of the Chamber of Commerce of the United States, which has been adopted by hundreds of local chambers of commerce, business clubs, and boards of trade. Given above are four articles taken from this code that should be of special interest to salespeople.

Misrepresentation

Misrepresentation is the giving of false or misleading information about merchandise to make the merchandise more appealing and to lure customers into buying. Misrepresentation is one of the most common of unethical selling practices, and some types of misrepresentation are illegal. The most common types of misrepresentation concern:

1. *Kind of goods.* A salesman may describe a piece of furniture as being made of solid walnut when it actually has only a walnut veneer.
2. *Quality of goods.* A salesman may describe a suit as custom tailored when it actually was not made to the individual measurements of the customer.
3. *Quantity of goods.* A seller may "fill slack" a package so that almost a third of the package is empty.
4. *Use of goods.* A druggist may recommend a medicine for an ailment upon which it will have no effect.
5. *Value of goods.* A retailer may buy early in the fall a new style of coat to sell for $75. Later in the season he may buy similar coats of lesser quality to be sold at $49.75. In his advertising he describes the second coats as "$75 values for only $49.75."
6. *Service.* A salesman may promise a customer that, if she buys a new clothes dryer, he can have it installed within the week. However, he is fairly certain that it will be two or three weeks before the store's serviceman can install the dryer.

Standing Behind Sales

A rule for dealing ethically with customers is for the seller to stand behind every sale, even if there is no misrepresentation of merchandise at the time of sale. This is desirable because sometimes defects in goods cannot be detected until after the goods are in use. The seller has an ethical obligation to see that the items he sells are suited to the purpose for which they are intended, to make good their failure to do what he said they would do, and to instruct his customers in the proper use of the product so that accidents will not occur nor repairs prove necessary. A chief complaint of today's customers concerns the repair of appliances. Manufacturers' warranties and guarantees are often ambiguous, and customers may find it difficult to have repairs made at a reasonable cost.

ETHICS IN COMPETITOR RELATIONS

The scope of ethics is not limited to the seller's customers; it includes other groups, and one of these important groups consists of competitors. All businesses are competitive, and it is easy to forget that some actions are unfair to competitors. Although a seller has every right to try to win more customer patronage than his competitors do, he nevertheless has important obligations to these competitors.

"Knocking" Competitors

Many disgruntled salesmen cover up their lack of selling skill by downgrading competitors, often in front of a customer. This is an unethical practice which is distasteful to most people and certainly will never win any respect for the salesman. Good salesmen sell by emphasizing the excellence of their own products and services, not by tearing down—often unfairly—those of other businesses. From a purely practical point of view, salesmen should remember that making degrading remarks about a competitor merely calls customer attention to him. This attention, coupled with the customer's distaste for the unethical salesman's tactics, could be enough to make the customer switch his orders to the competitor.

Hiring a Competitor's Employees

If an employee wants to make a job change, he should be able to do so. However, there is some question as to whether it is ethical for one firm to bid for the services of a salesman employed by a competitor. A firm will ordinarily consider it ethical to hire an employee of a competitor if the employee makes direct application for the position; but it is often considered unethical to solicit the competitor's employees. There are some firms who have a policy of not hiring any of their competitors' employees. Deliberately raiding a competitor to win over a group of employees is discouraged by law.

Style Piracy

In the fashion trade, manufacturers employ highly paid designers to create new styles. As soon as these styles are presented to the trade, however, they are copied and reproduced using cheaper materials and a poorer quality of workmanship and are sold at half the original price. Many ideas have been suggested to curb style piracy, but most of them have been either impractical or illegal. Some merchants recognize the creator's rightful interest in his new styles, and they will not buy an original article merely to have it copied. Some dealers even avoid buying copies distributed by manufacturers of lower quality goods.

Some manufacturers have secret formulas or procedures for making their products which are not patentable but which give them a competitive advantage as long as they are unknown to competitors. It is unethical to try to discover such secrets by spying or bribery.

ETHICS IN VENDOR RELATIONS

Nearly every seller of merchandise must buy something from other organizations. If he manufactures the goods he sells, he buys the raw materials from which his goods are made. If he is a wholesaler, he buys his goods from a manufacturer. If he is a retailer, he buys his goods from a manufacturer or a wholesaler. In any case, he is a buyer as well as a seller. His relations with those who supply him with goods frequently present ethical difficulties.

Returns and Cancellations

There are times when it is entirely ethical to return goods to a supplier or to cancel an order for goods after it has been placed. The goods received may not be as ordered; they may not have been shipped on time; or the price charged for them may not be the one originally agreed upon. Frequently, however, buyers are tempted to return goods or cancel an order when the supplier is not at fault. Thus, a retailer may buy more goods than can readily be sold, may find similar goods at a lower price from another source, or may find that the styles he ordered are not salable; and he may want to minimize his losses by returning the goods to the supplier. A buyer should exercise great care in buying; but if he makes a mistake, he should be willing to bear the loss and should not try to shift it to his supplier.

Demands for Excessive Concessions

Buyers sometimes make unfair demands on their suppliers. They ask for low prices that might cause the suppliers a loss; they demand immediate delivery when it is impossible to make it; they try to force manufacturers to sell them goods already consigned to other buyers; they ask the suppliers to pay transportation charges; and they ask for excessive advertising allowances. Merely asking for a concession is not necessarily unethical. The supplier must decide whether it is to his best interests to grant it and whether the concession would be fair to his other customers. What is unethical is the use of pressure to force the supplier to make the concession—making threats to give the supplier no more business in the future and making threats to prevail on other buyers not to purchase from him.

ETHICAL RELATIONS WITH THE EMPLOYER

A salesman has ethical obligations to his employer that are distinct from his obligations to his customers, his competitors, and his suppliers.

Conservation of Time

Since the traveling salesman is not closely supervised, he may be tempted to waste his time, especially if he is paid on a straight salary basis. He may make several successful calls early in the day and may therefore feel that he can afford to take it easy during the afternoon. It is just as dishonest to waste part of a day when being paid for a full day's work as it is to steal money. Even if the salesman is paid on a commission basis, he is expected by his employer to devote his full time and energy to his work. Inactivity is not a fault of traveling salesmen alone; retail salespeople often spend much time gossiping or simply watching passersby when they might be rearranging and cleaning stock or studying stock so that they can be of greater service to customers.

Expense Accounts

The use of company funds for expenses incurred by traveling salesmen is a necessity in business. The amount of money available to salesmen for such purposes will vary from company to company, and it may well vary from one salesman to another within a given organization. All salesmen should present honest expense account reports to their company at intervals required by company policy. All expense accounts are carefully audited by the company's sales management team.

Bribery

One of the least excusable business practices is for a vendor to procure sales from a merchant by bribing the latter's employees. Purchasing agents and store buyers are sometimes offered bribes to buy certain products for their firms. A wholesaler may bribe retail salespeople to push his products rather than the products of others. No employee should accept a bribe, no matter how small. This is being disloyal both to one's employer and to oneself.

Pilferage

A serious problem faced by retail stores today is *pilferage*—the theft of a store's merchandise by its employees. Many people who would never steal money think it is a lark to take merchandise from the store where they work. They think that a pair of hose, a record, or a book will never be missed. Pilferage is, of course, unethical; but it is also a crime and is punishable by fine and/or imprisonment. Even if a pilferer is not fined or imprisoned, a record of his offense remains with the police and often with a merchants' protective association. In most stores, a person caught stealing merchandise is automatically discharged and will probably never be able to get a job in any other store that subscribes to a merchants' protective association.

CHECKING YOUR KNOWLEDGE

Vocabulary:

(1) ethics
(2) caveat emptor
(3) one-price policy
(4) misrepresentation
(5) pilferage

Review questions:

1. To what individuals and groups do salesmen have obligations?
2. What are the most common types of merchandise misrepresentation?
3. What activities concerning a seller's relations with his competitors are considered unethical?

4. Under what circumstances may a buyer ethically return goods to a supplier?
5. Why does a salesman have an ethical obligation to his employer to conserve his time?

For discussion:

1. How may a thorough knowledge of the goods that he sells help the salesman to maintain high ethical standards?
2. A common practice among some sellers is to raise the prices of their merchandise or services whenever there is an unusual demand for it or a shortage of supply. Thus, hotels may raise their rates when a convention is in town, and public golf courses may raise their rates on holidays. Under what conditions are such increases justified? When are they not justified?
3. Why are bribes in the form of gifts more dangerous than money bribes?

BUILDING YOUR SKILLS

Improving your English:

Some of the verbs in the following sentences are incorrect. On a separate sheet of paper, write the correct verb to be used in each sentence. Indicate with the letter "C" any sentence in which the verb is correct.

1. The manager and his assistants was planning a divisional training session.
2. Neither the assistant nor the buyers was able to explain the purchase orders.
3. Three salesmen and John Fritz has completed the survey.
4. Henry Montag, of all the salesmen, were most helpful in obtaining the Harris account.
5. Shirts and ties represents the major repeat sales of the store.
6. The orders you wrote are to be mailed this evening.
7. Wholesalers has given retailers the capability of replenishing stock rapidly.
8. Following a holiday sale, merchandise returns takes much of a salesperson's time.
9. Direct selling and taking orders from customers requires different sales approaches.
10. Handling objections is a challenging part of selling.

Improving your arithmetic:

Perform the following multiplication exercises.

1. John's Fashion Shop received an invoice showing the following purchases: 12 dozen handkerchiefs at 87¢ per dozen; 2 dozen ties at $1.75 each; and 17 sweaters at $7.75 each. Compute the total amount of the invoice.

2. Gray's Equipment Company operates four branch stores in suburban areas. Sales for the month of November average $75,445 for each branch. The cost price of merchandise is 60% of the retail price. Compute the total branch store sales for November. Determine the total cost of the merchandise sold.
3. During December, Mary White's weekly sales averaged $2,324. Mary receives a base salary of $43 per week, plus a commission of 5% on all sales. What is Mary's total sales income for December, assuming that December has a 4-week selling period?
4. The Harrison Manufacturing Company gives a 35% trade discount off the retail price to its customers. The Lockley Electric Shop has just ordered the following items:

Item	*Unit Retail Price*
12 continuous-run motors	$47.95
15 door chimes	8.75
8 crystal chandeliers	89.95

   Compute the net amount that Lockley must pay the Harrison Manufacturing Company.
5. During a recent week the Clothes Horse sold 75 children's dresses at $8.95 each; 120 teen dresses at $16.95 each; and 92 women's casual dresses at $14.95 each. What were the total dress sales of the shop?

Improving your research skills:

1. Visit five different stores in your community and observe how these stores regulate the type of clothing worn by salespeople. It may be necessary to interview store executives to find out this information. Write a report of your findings and tell why you think the dress regulations were formulated.
2. Write a report telling how you would use imagination in selling each of the following items: (a) a portable typewriter to a student; (b) a waffle iron to a housewife; (c) garden tools to an office worker; (d) an automobile to a city resident; (e) a handbag to a young woman.
3. In a newspaper, find a help-wanted ad for a selling job in which you are interested. Prepare a résumé and a letter of application for this job.
4. Your instructor will appoint a committee to research what the chamber of commerce or a service club, such as Rotary, is doing in your community to promote the ethical treatment of customers by local business firms. A written report should be prepared by the committee.

APPLYING YOUR KNOWLEDGE

Case problems:

1. A recent high-school graduate with an excellent scholastic record visited a department store's employment office to apply for a selling job. The

employment manager's first question was: "I see you've just graduated from Hunter High. What have you been doing in your spare time—afternoons and evenings?" The applicant answered that he played trombone in a band to earn spending money. The employment manager seemed interested and asked more questions about music. The applicant, since he loved music, talked fluently and at some length about it. Presently the employment manager closed the interview, saying: "I'll let you know in a few days whether we can use you." Nothing had been said in the interview about the job or the applicant's qualifications. The applicant left feeling that he had failed in the interview, since he had talked only about his hobby.

(a) Should the applicant have given brief answers to the questions on music and switched the conversation to his qualifications for the job?
(b) Why did the employment manager allow the applicant to devote the entire interview to the apparently irrelevant discussion?
(c) If the store had an opening, do you think the applicant would get the job?

2. Suppose that you are employed as a salesperson in a men's clothing store and have just spent considerable time showing suits to a customer. The customer finally says that he wants to postpone buying until he examines the suits sold by Hussian, a competitor of your store. You know that Hussian's suits average in price about $10 less than yours, but you also know that they sell for less because they are made with cheaper materials and lower quality workmanship. How can you retain the customer's interest in your suits without knocking your competitor?

Continuing project:

In your manual, you should now prepare a section on the personality characteristics necessary for the type of salesman selling the product or service you have chosen. Take into consideration the physical characteristics, verbal characteristics, and mental characteristics. Also, discuss the ethical problems that would probably arise in connection with your sales occupation.

Extra credit:

The list of common trait terms that appears on page 108 may be used to help an individual gain self-understanding through self-appraisal. For each of the 93 sets of words, copy the word which comes closer than the other to describing you. Some of the words may be unfamiliar; refer to the dictionary for the meanings of those terms you do not understand. After you have made your selections, ask an acquaintance whose judgment you respect to rate you using this list. Tell him that you want him to be fair even though some of his reactions may not be what you want to hear. Compare his selections with yours and discuss in writing the points where you and your friend disagree. Write out a program for your self-improvement.

Common Trait Terms To Help Size Up People

1. adaptable
   inflexible
2. affected
   natural
3. alert
   sluggish
4. apathetic
   enthusiastic
5. argumentative
   agreeable
6. autocratic
   democratic
7. benevolent
   malevolent
8. blundering
   tactful
9. boastful
   self-effacing
10. bold
    retiring
11. bungling
    clever
12. charming
    repugnant
13. cheerful
    gloomy
14. complacent
    ambitious
15. confused
    clear-thinking
16. considerate
    selfish
17. conventional
    nonconforming
18. cooperative
    obstructive
19. courageous
    cowardly
20. crude
    polished
21. cruel
    affectionate
22. defiant
    obedient
23. deliberate
    impulsive
24. depressing
    stimulating
25. derogatory
    complimentary
26. distant
    friendly
27. estranged
    sociable
28. evasive
    frank
29. excitable
    calm
30. extravagant
    thrifty
31. extreme
    temperate
32. fatalistic
    self-controlling
33. fluent
    inarticulate
34. forbearing
    complaining
35. foresighted
    hindsighted
36. formal
    informal
37. forgetful
    retentive
38. gay
    serious
39. generous
    stingy
40. grateful
    ungrateful
41. habit-bound
    venturesome
42. harsh
    mild
43. honest
    deceitful
44. humble
    overbearing
45. humorous
    somber
46. imaginative
    plodding
47. imitative
    original
48. inexperienced
    sophisticated
49. industrious
    indolent
50. interests-wide
    interests-narrow
51. intuitive
    logical
52. irreverent
    pious
53. jealous
    well-wishing
54. leisurely
    hurried
55. light-eater
    gluttonous
56. loyal
    unfaithful
57. mature
    childish
58. modest
    conceited
59. moody
    stable
60. naive
    shrewd
61. negativistic
    agreeable
62. open-minded
    opinionated
63. opportunistic
    non-exploiting
64. optimistic
    pessimistic
65. persuasive
    yes-man
66. pliant
    stubborn
67. practical
    theoretical
68. practical joker
    considerate
69. price-minded
    quality-minded
70. progressive
    reactionary
71. rash
    cautious
72. realistic
    self-deceiving
73. reliable
    undependable
74. remorseful
    conscience-less
75. rude
    courteous
76. sarcastic
    gentle
77. satisfied
    displeased
78. self-pitying
    Spartan
79. self-respecting
    shameless
80. self-sufficient
    dependent
81. sensitive
    callous
82. sincere
    hypocritical
83. strong-willed
    suggestible
84. talkative
    close-mouthed
85. treacherous
    trustworthy
86. trusting
    suspicious
87. unconcerned
    curious
88. unsure
    self-confident
89. vacillating
    decisive
90. vindictive
    forgiving
91. worrying
    indifferent
92. Special abilities
    (e.g., mechanical, mathematical, athletic)
93. Special interests
    e.g., musical, literary, financial)

Personnel Development, Inc., New York

Selling in the 1930's . . .

Great expectations of the 1920's ended in the depressed 1930's. For 13 million unemployed, out of a labor force of 48 million, it became a matter of survival. While Auguste Piccard ballooned his way into the stratosphere, the GNP shrank from $194 billion in 1929 to $59 billion in 1932. But government, labor, and business, working together, finally restored a measure of confidence in the free-enterprise system. Chemistry alone opened up an astonishing world of synthetics and plastics. Nylon stockings were introduced, and fiberglass was perfected. The destruction of the Hindenburg marked the end of the dirigible era, but automatic washing machines began a new one. The aircraft industry sprouted its wartime wings, and war finally put the remaining 9 million unemployed back to work.

UNIT II

The Customer, The Product, The Firm

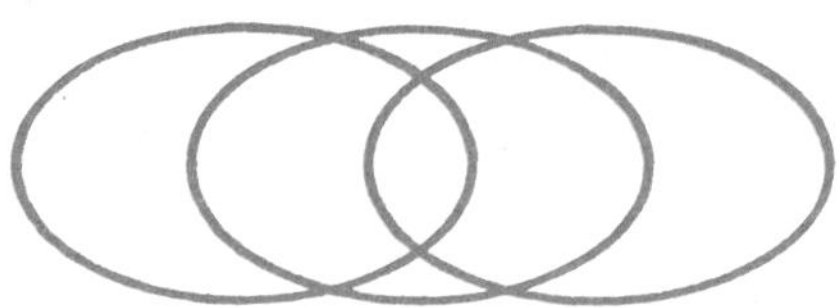

analyzing customer behavior

KEY QUESTIONS

A Why must every product or service that is sold satisfy a customer's need or want?

B Should sellers consider selective and patronage buying motives, or is it necessary to consider only primary motives?

C How can a salesman best determine the type of customer he is dealing with?

D Are today's customers more selective in their demands than were the customers of 20 and 30 years ago?

E Will market segmentation become more important in the future, or is it only a business fad of the moment?

part A

needs and wants

The American economy long ago passed the point where the consumer bought only according to his needs. Now consumers buy merchandise and services that they do not need for physical survival but that will enrich their lives. Our country's productive capacity allows producers to turn out many more products than are currently being absorbed in the marketplace. The big question facing these producers is: "Can the American consumer absorb all our production?" The answer lies mainly in the quality of this country's salesmanship. To maintain prosperity, all salesmen must perform to the best of their selling abilities; and the first step in achieving this goal is for them to understand why people buy.

The foundation of a customer's buying behavior is the recognition of a need or a want; and in this part you will learn about the customer needs and wants that are most important in selling.

KINDS OF NEEDS AND WANTS

As you learned in Chapter 1, both business consumers and ultimate consumers have unlimited needs and wants, and it is often difficult to determine whether a particular felt lack of something is a need or a want. Depending on a customer's basic personality, his scale of needs and wants, and his physical environment, the same "lack of something" may sometimes be a need and sometimes a want. A girl may want to buy a new winter coat because her old one is out of fashion. She may need to buy a new coat because her old one is worn out and no longer protects her from the cold.

Business consumers and ultimate consumers share a number of the same needs and wants. Many salespeople feel that a business consumer's needs and wants are easier to identify because they are generally based on the single desire to make a profitable sale. Also, sellers feel that the business consumer is usually more logical in his buying than is the ultimate consumer. These assumptions do not always hold true. The business consumer has two sets of needs and wants: those of his firm and his personal ones. When these two sets interact, a business consumer's needs and wants can be as complex and as emotional as those of the ultimate consumer.

All needs and wants do not result in the purchase of goods or services; those that do result in purchasing are called *buying motives.* You will learn more about the nature of buying motives in Part B. The needs and wants which are most important in selling and which generally represent customer buying motives are needs and wants for: (1) physical well-being, (2) relaxation, (3) recognition, (4) preservation of the self-image, (5) creation, (6) knowledge, (7) beauty, (8) order, and (9) money gain.

Physical Well-Being

Perhaps the strongest of all human needs is the need for self-preservation. Under this broad need are more specific needs which an

Ewing Galloway

Needs and wants influence every activity in which human beings engage. Even the achievements of our space program result from certain needs and wants. What do you think some of these needs and wants might be?

individual must satisfy to obtain physical well-being. From the salesman's point of view, the most important of these specific needs are those needs to satisfy appetite and to obtain rest, exercise, and self-protection.

Appetite. The main reason for buying food products is to satisfy hunger. However, most people want a variety of foods in order to achieve complete satisfaction. The variety of foods available today saves individuals from a diet that could sustain life but that would be monotonous. Sellers of food products buy for resale those products that have the attributes their customers want. Then they sell the products by describing and demonstrating the pleasure to be obtained from eating them.

Rest. A good mattress is sold because it makes restful sleep possible, but the physical need for rest also includes a secondary desire for comfort. Electric blankets are sold because they give not only rest but also comfort. Dishwashers, garbage disposals, and automatic blenders are sold because they reduce tedious labor and contribute to physical comfort.

Exercise. Although many jobs today still require muscular activity, labor-saving devices have reduced tremendously the amount of hard physical labor required of most people only a few decades ago. Now most individuals feel a need for exercise beyond that provided by their jobs. The growth of the sporting goods industry and of such service businesses as golf courses, driving ranges, and bowling alleys is due partly to the need for exercise.

Self-Protection. Because humans can anticipate future fears and dangers, they buy many goods and services to protect them from these fears and dangers. Some persons fear physical pain; others fear sickness, unemployment, or disability. Appeals to the need for self-protection are used extensively in selling such products as automobile seat belts, tire chains, home fire extinguishers, and insurance.

Relaxation

Closely related to the broad need to preserve physical well-being, and to the specific needs for rest and exercise, is the need for relaxation. Relaxation from regular work is needed to eliminate mental fatigue, and persons satisfy this need in different ways. Many people relax by attending football, basketball, and baseball games. The growth of the motion picture and television industries is due almost entirely to the desire for relaxation. Sometimes this desire is expressed as an urge to escape from everyday surroundings; a person who buys passage on a luxury vacation cruise is often expressing the escape urge. The purchase of novels often is a result of the same urge.

Recognition

Almost everyone feels the need or want to have friends and business associates think well of him. This desire for recognition takes many forms. Some people want to be recognized as being superior so that other people will respect and admire them. Persons may join country clubs to obtain prestige or may buy expensive cars to impress others.

One aspect of the desire for recognition is the desire to belong to a group and to feel needed by that group. This often results in imitation of group members' behavior. Fashion in clothing, particularly, is really the result of people's desires to conform to the standards of a group so that they can obtain the approval of this group.

The business consumer has just as much a personal desire for recognition as does the ultimate consumer. An order for lavish office furniture or a request for membership in an exclusive businessmen's club may reflect this desire. Or the businessman may install recreational equipment for his employees, not necessarily to improve employee morale but because he wants his employees to look upon him as a benefactor.

Preservation of Self-Image

The *self-image,* or *self-concept,* is the mental picture that an individual has of himself. Psychologists generally agree that the need to keep the self-image intact ranks along with the need for self-preservation as one of man's strongest needs, perhaps his second strongest need. For instance, a man who sees himself as a worldly, sophisticated person would never think of buying his clothes at a factory outlet store. This would not be in keeping with his self-image, so he shops at an exclusive men's apparel store.

It is not easy for a salesman to determine a customer's self-image, mainly because most sales contacts are brief. Also, people tend to make their self-images as favorable as possible, and the information they give the salesman concerning the self-image may not always be accurate. It takes practice and an understanding of human behavior to be able to determine a customer's self-image, but the salesman who can do this and show the customer merchandise that will enhance his self-image is more likely to persuade the customer to buy.

Creation

Many personal achievements result from the need or want to create something. This urge inspires inventors, painters, authors, and sculptors. In selling, the most significant result of this desire is the growth in sales of do-it-yourself supplies and hobby materials. Now people express the desire to create through a multitude of activities ranging from building model airplanes to taking pictures. Needlework departments, garden stores, hardware stores selling power tools, art supply shops, and hobby shops are all doing a thriving business because of the desire to create.

Knowledge

Everyone is curious—about health, about nature, about machinery, about other countries, about other people—and everyone wants knowledge of some kind. Most nonfiction books are bought because of the desire for knowledge, and such services as courses in sewing are also sold because of the desire for knowledge. Scientists buy laboratory equipment because of their desire to understand physical phenomena.

Beauty

Ideas about beauty differ greatly from person to person, but probably everyone has a desire to achieve some kind of beauty in his surroundings. Musical instruments, stereos, flowers and shrubs, furniture, works of art, and books can be sold by appealing to the customer's desire for beauty. Even the salesman of office furniture can direct his prospect's attention to the modern design or pleasing color of the furniture he is selling.

Order

Many people, particularly business consumers, have an acute desire for order in storing their possessions and running their everyday lives. Businessmen emphasize order because a standardized method of operation can greatly reduce operating expenses. They welcome equipment that will assure an orderly flow of work and give them easy access to necessary information. File cabinets, dividers, desks, and tool racks can be sold because of the human need for order.

Money Gain

From the salesman's point of view, the ultimate consumer does not have the need or want for money gain when he buys a product or

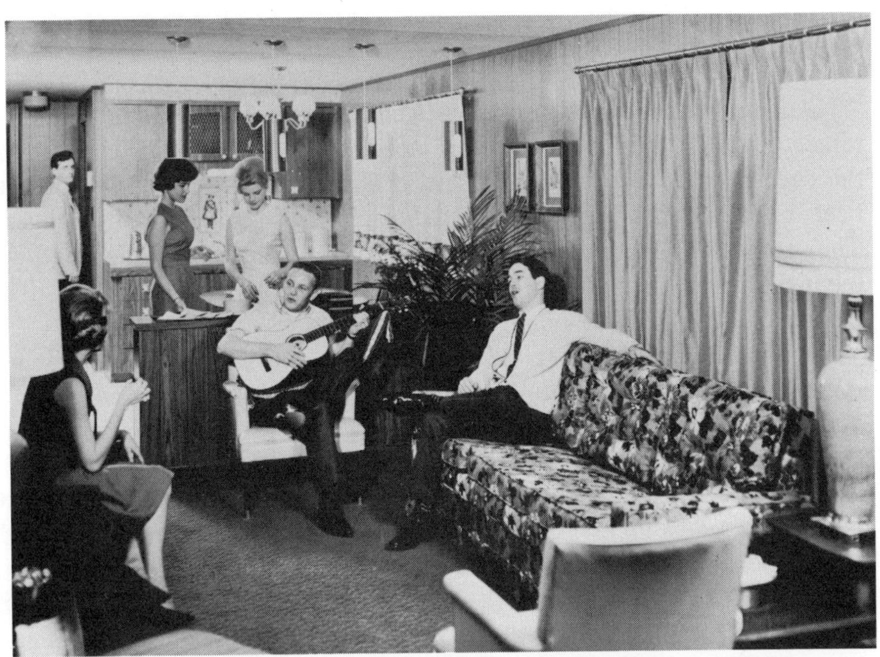

Mobile Home Manufacturers Association

All the merchandise items in this picture were bought because of a need or want. What needs and wants do you think might have influenced the purchase of the different items shown?

service, although the desire to get a bargain may sometimes lead the consumer to buy something that he does not really need or want. The need for money gain, however, is the basic need in all business consumers. This basic need can be achieved by: (1) increasing sales, (2) reducing costs and expenses, (3) protecting the business' assets, and (4) improving the business' products or services. Achieving these goals can satisfy the need for money gain. The successful salesman is a success partly because he appeals to these needs in his sales talks.

RECOGNIZING BASIC NEEDS AND WANTS

In determining the needs or wants of a particular customer, the salesman must consider many things. For example, when a manufacturer's salesman is selling to a wholesaler, he usually tries to help the wholesaler understand the product in relation to the needs or wants of the wholesaler's customer—the retailer. As a salesman becomes more experienced, he will find it easier to identify quickly his customers' needs and wants.

An important point for the salesman to remember is that the customer generally has an underlying need or want that is broader than the specific need or want mentioned. The customer who orders roast beef in a restaurant really wants a tasty meat dish to satisfy his hunger. The woman who asks for a particular style of dress is interested in buying a dress that will earn her the approval of others, whether it is the dress she asked for or another one.

A salesman can learn a customer's needs and wants by: (1) knowing what the basic needs and wants are; (2) observing the customer's actions and listening to what he says; (3) interpreting mentally what the customer says and does, sometimes "reading between the lines"; and (4) asking intelligent and probing questions. The salesman must always be ready to revise his first estimate of a customer's needs and wants. Sometimes he may have a carefully prepared sales presentation that he thinks will apply to the needs of a certain type of customer. However, if this presentation proves to be unsuitable, the salesman must be ready to discard it and formulate a more appropriate one.

CHECKING YOUR KNOWLEDGE

Vocabulary:

(1) buying motives (2) self-image, or self-concept

Review questions:

1. Name the nine needs and wants that are most important in selling and that generally represent customer buying motives.
2. What is perhaps the strongest of all human needs? What is probably the second strongest need?
3. Name five items that customers buy because of the desire for recognition.
4. How can business customers satisfy the basic need for money gain?
5. How can a salesman learn what a customer's needs and wants are?

For discussion:

1. Does a customer know his own needs and wants well enough to communicate them to a salesperson?
2. Describe what you would say if you wanted to appeal to a desire for money gain in selling each of these products: (a) stock in an electronics company to a business executive; (b) spray shoe polish to a grocer; (c) advertising space to a jeweler; (d) a course for a person planning to become a computer programmer.

part B

the nature of buying motives

After a salesman understands the customer needs and wants most important in selling, he next must learn how these needs and wants function as buying motives. Many people think that the terms "needs and wants" and "buying motives" have the same meaning, but there is a distinct difference between them. The needs and wants discussed in Part A are not the only needs and wants people have. Basic needs and wants cannot always be satisfied by obtaining goods and services and so, many basic needs and wants never become buying motives.

A need or want becomes a buying motive only when a person recognizes a need or want, realizes that it can be satisfied by purchasing goods or services, and is willing to exert effort to purchase the goods or services. For example, the desire for recognition is only a need or want. When a customer realizes that she can satisfy this desire by buying a mink coat and is willing to visit a furrier to look at mink coats, the desire for recognition has become a buying motive.

CLASSIFYING BUYING MOTIVES

For the salesman, a useful way of understanding buying motives is to classify them as primary, selective, or patronage motives. Classifying them in this manner can help the salesman decide which selling appeals to use with a certain customer. Of course, motives do not always fit neatly into one category or another. A desire for beauty, for instance, may sometimes be a primary motive and sometimes a selective motive. However, the following classification should give the prospective salesman some general guidelines for deciding whether a particular motive is a primary, selective, or patronage motive.

Primary Buying Motives

Buying motives that cause consumers to buy one class of goods rather than another are called *primary buying motives.* They are the broadest in scope of the three kinds of buying motives. Usually there are selective and patronage motives leading to satisfaction of a primary motive. Primary buying motives result directly from the needs and wants discussed in Part A. Thus, primary buying motives are generally the desires to achieve physical well-being, relaxation, recognition, preservation of the self-image, creation, knowledge, beauty, order, and money gain.

If he is to sell goods and services, every seller must differentiate his product from competitors' products; and knowing about motives other than the primary motives helps him do this. But the salesman must always be aware of the customer's primary reason for buying, because the primary motive must be satisfied if a sale is to be made. For example, an industrial air conditioner may have a number of variable controls and may be unusually quiet, but the buyer's primary motive for purchasing it is to raise production and thus increase profits by making his employees more comfortable. Sellers of new products, in particular, must emphasize the primary motives.

It might seem that primary motives would be easy to identify, since they are the most fundamental buying motives. This is not always true, though, because primary motives are often not expressed to the salesman. Sometimes the customer may not even be aware of his primary motives. Thus, it is up to the salesman to figure out the customer's primary motive and direct appropriate appeals to it.

Selective Buying Motives

Buying motives that cause consumers to buy a particular article within a class of goods are called *selective buying motives.* When a woman buys sheets, her primary motive may be to achieve comfort. This motive is strong enough to keep her from spending her money for another class of goods. But the customer chooses one sheet rather than another because of such selective motives as the desires for durability and economy. The most common selective buying motives are the desires for durability, dependability, convenience, versatility, and economy.

Durability. The desire for durability is an important selective buying motive in the purchase of such items as washers, ironers, refrigerators, freezers, and many items of furniture. Business consumers are extremely interested in obtaining durability in their equipment installations and office machines. In fact, sometimes this desire for durability becomes a primary motive, since it can relate directly to the desire for money gain.

Characteristics of Buying Motives

- ✓ All motives have direction.

  All buying motives are aimed at acquiring goods and services. Each buying motive has a definite goal, although the goals will differ from time to time and from customer to customer.

- ✓ One motive may have many buying effects.

  The desire to achieve recognition may result in joining a country club, buying a mink coat, or buying an expensive house.

- ✓ Different motives may lead to the same buying action.

  A person may buy a beautiful painting because he wants to achieve recognition, because he wants beauty to surround him, or because the painting represents a good investment and thus gives him security.

- ✓ Motives may operate together or opposite each other.

  A person may buy a book because he wants both knowledge and relaxation. An overweight person may want a box of chocolates to satisfy his appetite but may know that this purchase will be in conflict with the desire to achieve recognition because of an attractive physical appearance.

- ✓ Motives vary in intensity.

  A customer who lives in the suburbs and works downtown will have a much stronger motive for buying a new car than will a person who lives only a few blocks from his job.

- ✓ Motives must function in a physical environment.

  If a woman wants to have her hair set but finds that the beauty shops are closed, she cannot achieve her goal because of physical limitations.

- ✓ Motives may be conscious or unconscious.

  The desire to satisfy one's appetite is usually a conscious buying motive. The desire to buy a new dress may be unconscious; the consumer may not know she wants a new dress because it satisfies her desire for recognition.

- ✓ Motives operate somewhat because of habit.

  A person may stop to buy lunch in a restaurant, not necessarily because of a desire to satisfy appetite but because he has formed the habit of eating a meal in the middle of the day.

There are many different kinds of buying motives, but all motives have certain characteristics in common. Some of these characteristics are listed above.

Dependability. The desires for durability and dependability often go together in many purchases. Ultimate consumers, for instance, not only want durable appliances but also dependable appliances which will perform when needed and will require a minimum amount of repair. Business consumers must also have dependable equipment, for expenses increase if machines constantly break down and need repair.

Convenience. Ultimate consumers, particularly women, are always looking for articles which can make chores easier. Clothes made of permanent press fabrics were an instant success because they are easy to care for. Business consumers always want equipment that can be repaired easily, that requires a minimum amount of maintenance, and that employees can be quickly taught to use.

Versatility. Most consumers like to feel they are getting a lot for their money, even though price is not a prime buying consideration for the ultimate consumer. Thus, an ultimate consumer is pleased if he buys versatile items such as a sofa that makes into a bed or a candy container that can be used as a jewelry box. The desire for versatility in obtaining a product such as electronic data processing equipment is an important motive for business consumers. If one basic EDP installation can be adapted to process many different kinds of data, the business can be run more efficiently.

Economy and Price. For the ultimate consumer, getting a bargain price is often a selective motive for buying a specific product. The desire for economy, of course, is an important motive for business consumers, because this can help satisfy the primary motive of money gain. All middlemen, for instance, want to get the most favorable credit and shipping terms from their suppliers.

Patronage Buying Motives

Buying motives that cause consumers to select one seller over another are called *patronage buying motives.* The most important patronage motives are the desires for quality, large assortments, fashion, exclusiveness, service, convenience of location, price, self-affiliation with other patrons, and friendship or bias for the seller.

Quality. Many manufacturers, wholesalers, and retailers have established a reputation for quality. Thus, a housewife may buy all her meat from a particular supermarket because it has a reputation for selling

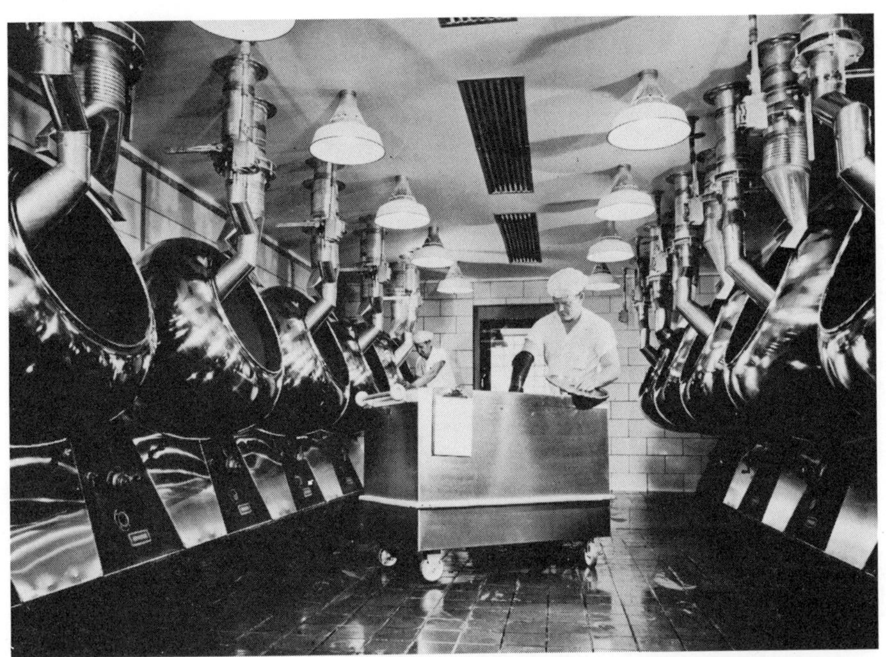

Chas. Pfizer & Co., Inc.

Business customers who purchase installations and supplies to be used in manufacturing want durability, dependability, convenience, versatility, and economy in the products they buy. Fulfilling these selective buying motives can fulfill the primary motive of money gain. This modern equipment is used to produce drugs in tablet form.

choice meat. A man may buy a house from a particular builder because of the builder's reputation for constructing quality homes. Textbooks may be purchased because of a publisher's reputation for excellence.

Large Assortments. Some firms put major emphasis on the wide variety of merchandise they have for sale. Ultimate consumers often shop at large department stores, for example, because the stores carry a wide variety of merchandise and offer many styles in each of the lines they carry. Business consumers want to buy from suppliers who handle a wide variety of merchandise, because it is more convenient to order different kinds of goods all at once.

Fashion. Ultimate consumers generally have either a desire to buy goods that are widely accepted as the current fashion or goods that represent new styles in advance of general acceptance. Thus, they will shop at a store, such as a specialty shop, which offers the latest fashions.

Business customers who buy for resale must buy from suppliers who have a reputation for being leaders in product design and for stocking fashion items.

Exclusiveness. Closely related to the desire for fashion is the desire for exclusiveness. Some stores specialize in stocking goods that are not available anywhere else, and they cater to the customer who wants "something different." The business customer is particularly interested in buying from suppliers who will confine certain styles to him and not sell the same item to competitors.

Service. Every seller provides some services, but some give more services than do others; and they may be patronized primarily because of these extra services. An insurance company, for example, may gain a reputation for settling claims promptly and may thus build up a large clientele. A wholesaler or manufacturer who offers generous credit terms and prompt deliveries will often earn the patronage of retailers.

Convenience of Location. Many sellers get customer orders, not necessarily because they appeal to other patronage motives, but simply because their locations are handy to the customer's home or place of business. For example, supermarkets are often located in suburban shopping centers where there is plenty of parking space.

Price. Price is generally a selective buying motive, but it can also be a patronage motive. A store's reputation for low prices—a discount store, for instance—can explain why customers patronize it rather than other stores. However, a business is not likely to be successful for long if low price is the only appeal. The business must satisfy some of the other patronage motives. Business consumers are extremely interested in getting the lowest possible prices from their suppliers, but only as low price is relative to the quality of merchandise and services provided.

Self-Affiliation with Other Patrons. For the ultimate consumer, an important patronage motive is self-affiliation with other people in his social set or in the set to which he would like to belong. A "social climber," for example, would shop in a store patronized by the town's socialites and eat only in restaurants patronized by this set.

Friendship or Bias for the Seller. Friendship for a certain seller or a belief in the importance of some cause that the seller is associated with is often a basis for patronage. However, friendship alone will not continue to draw trade indefinitely. The seller must cater to other patronage motives.

Rational and Emotional Buying Motives

The primary, selective, and patronage motives can be further classified as either rational or emotional motives. *Rational buying motives* are based on logical reasoning; *emotional buying motives* are based on personal feelings. The primary desires for physical well-being, knowledge, order, and money gain are usually rational motives. The desires for relaxation, recognition, preservation of the self-image, creation, and beauty are emotional motives. Selective motives are almost always rational motives. Of the patronage motives just discussed, the desires for quality, large assortments, service, convenience, and price are generally rational motives. The desires for fashion, exclusiveness, self-affiliation with other patrons, and friendship for the seller are generally emotional motives.

In determining a customer's buying motives and how best to satisfy them, it is helpful for the salesman to know whether primary, selective, and patronage motives are rational or emotional. Emotional buying motives are probably more fundamental than rational ones. However, most people pride themselves on being creatures of reason and logic, so they rationalize. This means that when they act mainly because of emotional motives, they try to justify their acts logically to themselves. A woman who buys a mink coat because it satisfies her desire for recognition may rationalize the purchase by emphasizing the durability of the coat, its sale price, its warmth, and its light weight. The alert salesman recognizes these considerations and is quick to provide the customer with rational motives, once it is clear that the customer feels an urge to buy.

Both rational and emotional buying motives are usually present in a single buying situation. For example, it is a rational motive to buy food expressly to provide a balanced diet and assure good health; but it is an emotional motive to buy a certain kind of food to satisfy a love for rich foods, spices, or sweets.

USING KNOWLEDGE OF BUYING MOTIVES

Patronage motives determine where a customer will go to satisfy the primary and selective buying motives, but the final decision to buy will be based on a consideration of how well the primary and selective motives will be satisfied by the purchase. The points of superiority of one product over another in the same class are usually related to selective motives, since all serve the same primary motive. Thus, the selling points of a product that the salesman emphasizes tend to be those related to selective motives.

Suppose that you are an automobile salesman. Quite often, a customer's primary motive for buying a new car is to acquire pleasure from driving it, pleasure which results in large part from receiving recognition from others. This is an emotional motive. You appeal to this motive by persuading the prospect to get behind the wheel in the showroom and perhaps even drive the car on the highway in order to get the feel of a new driving experience.

This appeal to an emotional motive will often outweigh other practical considerations, but you know that the final sale of a particular car depends almost entirely on the satisfaction of rational selective motives and rational or emotional patronage motives. Thus, you discuss and demonstrate features of the car that appeal to selective motives such as durability, dependability, economy, and safety.

Since new-car prospects do a good deal of shopping before they buy, you must appeal to the patronage motives. You may emphasize the workmanship provided by your agency's service department or the generous financing terms your agency can arrange. Certainly you will take advantage of every opportunity to build customer goodwill so that a patronage motive foremost in the customer's mind will be friendship for the seller.

CHECKING YOUR KNOWLEDGE

Vocabulary:

(1) primary buying motives
(2) selective buying motives
(3) patronage buying motives
(4) rational buying motives
(5) emotional buying motives

Review questions:

1. What are the primary buying motives?
2. Are primary buying motives easy to identify? Why?
3. Name the most common selective buying motives.
4. What are the most important patronage buying motives?

5. Which of the primary buying motives are rational motives? Which are emotional motives?
6. Are selective buying motives usually rational or emotional? Why?

For discussion:

1. Why is a buying motive a primary motive under certain conditions and a selective motive under other conditions? Give specific examples to support your answer.
2. What buying motives—primary, selective, or patronage, rational or emotional—might be the basis for the purchase of a car by (a) a society woman, (b) a man living in the suburbs, and (c) a college student?

part C

customer types

Talkative, silent, impulsive, suspicious, shrewd, timid—do these adjectives describe some of your friends? Probably. Every day you will most likely meet people whom these adjectives would accurately describe; and if you are a salesman, you are certain to meet such people often. These adjectives are commonly used by salesmanship instructors to classify types of customers.

You have learned about the basic customer needs and wants, and you have learned about the nature of buying motives. But you cannot effectively apply this knowledge until you learn something about the types of customers with whom you will have to deal in selling.

METHODS OF DETERMINING CUSTOMER TYPES

Perhaps the most practical methods of identifying customer types are (1) to classify a particular customer according to his stage of buying action and (2) to classify him according to his disposition of the moment. There is always a danger in "typing" a customer. Some salesmen cannot adjust their presentations quickly enough if and when they discover a prejudgment is wrong, and they may lose sales because of this. "Typing" customers, however, can give the salesman a foundation for his sales presentation; and a good salesman will be able to adjust his presentation to any customer response.

Stages of Buying Action

By observing a customer's actions and by carefully listening to what he says, a salesman can determine with reasonable accuracy the customer's stage of buying action. There are three customer types that can be classified using this method:

1. *Decided customer*. He has made up his mind about a purchase, knows exactly what he wants, and is the easiest customer for a salesman to serve if the product or service is available.
2. *Undecided customer*. He feels a need or want for something but does not know the exact product or service that will best satisfy his desires. Creative salesmanship, emphasizing the salesman's knowledge of buying motives, is definitely needed.
3. *Casual looker*. He does not intend to buy at the time of the initial sales contact but does have an interest in the product or service. The salesman must further stimulate his interest and must create goodwill for a future contact that can result in buying.

It is relatively easy for the alert salesman to identify these three customer types in retail stores. These types, though, are not confined to

A & P

Are customers in a self-service store typically decided, undecided, or just looking? Would they be at the same stage of buying action for all items they inspect?

retail stores but rather exist in all businesses that buy merchandise from other businesses. For instance, some manufacturers' purchasing agents are ready to buy and merely want the industrial salesman to work out specifications and terms of sale. Other purchasing agents are definitely in the market to buy but want to compare the offerings of various firms to get the best merchandise at the best price. Still other purchasing agents have no intention of buying immediately but want to learn about a salesman's goods and services in case they want to buy from him in the future.

Customers are not always at the same stage of buying action. Sometimes a retail customer may have his heart set on buying a certain article. At another time, he may be sure only of the general type of goods he wants. At other times, he may be merely looking around. Thus, the salesman must be able to tailor his presentation to meet the needs or wants of a particular customer at a particular stage of buying action.

Customer Dispositions

The second method of identifying customer types is to classify a customer according to his disposition, or temperament, during the sales contact. *Disposition* refers to the prevailing mood or emotions determined by a person's physical and mental makeup. Disposition is reflected in a customer's actions and speech. The types of customer dispositions which a salesman most frequently encounters are:

1. *Talkative customer.* He is friendly, wants to talk about many things, and often has a tendency to talk about things that are off the selling subject. The salesman can best handle him by showing interest in what he says while directing his enthusiasm as quickly as possible to the sale.
2. *Silent customer.* He has little to say and at times appears indifferent. He may be hesitant about asking questions. The salesman should never be impatient with him, for this will only cause him to withdraw. This customer can be drawn out by asking his opinions and by showing him facts and figures.
3. *Procrastinating customer.* He tends to put off action; although he is willing to listen to the salesman, he hesitates to make a decision. He can be induced to purchase by a salesman who is confident of himself and his product, will review key selling points, and can show logical objections to the customer's delaying action.
4. *Disagreeable customer.* He is perhaps the most difficult customer, for he may seem to go out of his way to make the sales transaction difficult for the salesman. The salesman can deal with the grouchy

customer successfully if he will patiently hear the customer out and retain an optimistic outlook in his presentation.

5. *Impulsive customer.* He tends to be impatient and to buy quickly goods that strike his fancy. With this customer, the salesman can speed up his sales talk and even omit secondary details about the product or service.
6. *Opinionated customer.* He tends to be inflexible and obstinate. Since he likes to feel important, the salesman should play up to his egotism and ask his advice on the product or service during the sales talk.
7. *Suspicious customer.* He is distrustful and does not always appear to believe what the salesman is saying. He may frequently be argumentative, but the salesman should never argue with him. Instead, he should use logic and present proven facts, admitting honestly the limitations of his product or service.
8. *Shrewd customer.* He evaluates carefully the merchandise and service features and is generally cautious in making decisions. By using subtle flattery, expressing respect for his judgment, and giving logical selling points, the salesman can win over the shrewd customer.
9. *Decisive customer.* He tends to be confident and positive. With him, the salesman should avoid a lengthy presentation and should give his sales talk clearly and quickly. A decisive customer should be allowed to express his conclusions more quickly than are other customers.
10. *Timid customer.* He tends to be shy, bashful, and cautious and must be guided in all the steps toward a purchasing decision. The salesman must show him that he has all the facts necessary for an intelligent decision. If the salesman cannot persuade this customer to act immediately, he might suggest that the customer consult with other persons. If the customer intends to return to the salesman, a specific appointment time could be set.

The creative salesman will adapt his sales presentation to the customer disposition he encounters. The same customer may be decisive at one time and procrastinating at another. He may be silent and even timid when he is unsure of his knowledge but opinionated and talkative when he is sure. Even in the same sales contact, a customer may be suspicious at the start and impulsive later. The salesman has to adjust himself to such changes in disposition and always maintain a sincere attitude of trying to be of service.

THE BUYING CYCLE

All customers go through a cycle in buying a particular item or service, although they may not be consciously aware of this cycle. Now that you have learned about the basic needs and wants, the functioning of buying motives, and the types of customers you may encounter, you have gone through four steps of this cycle.

First, a person feels a lack of something; he recognizes a need or want. Second, an uncomfortable feeling of deprivation is created by the need or want. Third, the person realizes that the unpleasantness might be eliminated by purchasing a product or service and is willing to exert force to purchase and to satisfy the need or want. At this point, the need or want becomes a buying motive. Fourth, the person engages in activities to purchase the goods or services: going to a selling organization, talking to a salesman, and so on. Since this step represents a salesman's first encounter with the customer, the salesman must be able to size up quickly the type of customer with whom he is dealing. Fifth, the customer buys the goods or services. Sixth, satisfaction results from having obtained the goods or services, and the unpleasant feeling of deprivation is eliminated.

The buying cycle for a particular good or service is not always completed. Sometimes a person may not be able to decide which product or service will satisfy his need or want. Sometimes he may substitute another goal for the original buying goal. For instance, if he wants relaxation but does not have enough money to go to a movie, he may borrow a book from the library and read it. Sometimes he may not know where to go to find the product or service that will satisfy his needs. Any successful purchasing action, however, will go through all the steps of the buying cycle.

The salesman meets the customer at the fourth stage of the buying cycle. If the salesman performs his task efficiently, the cycle will be completed to the mutual satisfaction of both parties.

CHECKING YOUR KNOWLEDGE

Vocabulary:

disposition

Review questions:

1. What are the most practical methods of identifying customer types? What is the danger in "typing" customers?
2. Describe the stages of buying action in which a salesman may encounter a customer.
3. Name the 10 types of customer dispositions that a salesman most frequently encounters.
4. What are the steps in the buying cycle for a particular good or service?
5. Why is the buying cycle for a particular item not always completed?

For discussion:

1. What behavior would you look for in a business consumer and in an ultimate consumer in order to "type" them according to their stages of buying action? What behavior would you look for in order to "type" them according to their dispositions?
2. Some selling experts feel that no attempt should be made to force the casual looker to buy. They feel that the main effort should be to gain the customer's goodwill so that he will come back to the firm to buy. Couldn't a salesman waste time following this rule? Explain.

part D

determining customer demand

Trying to satisfy customer needs and wants involves a series of searches. The customer searches mentally for the merchandise most likely to satisfy his needs and wants and for the selling organization most likely to stock this merchandise. The buyer in the selling organization searches his suppliers' stocks, trying to anticipate customer demand so as to have on hand the article which the customer is likely to want. The salesman searches his stock in the customer's presence to locate the one article that best fills the customer's need or want.

The searches are like three spotlights, each beamed at specific merchandise. If the customer, the buyer, and the salesman project their beams on the same merchandise, the marketing system operates smoothly. When each beam is projected at different merchandise, however, the market may provide goods the customer does not want, the salesman may show the wrong merchandise to the customer, and the customer may poorly select the business to visit for his needs.

An important part of keeping the spotlights and the marketing system working smoothly is providing the customer with goods that he wants. To do this, selling organizations must be skillful in determining customer demand.

IMPORTANCE OF PURCHASING POWER

The needs and wants of customers are not enough to create a market for goods and services; there must be effective demand. *Effective demand* is the ability of the buyer to pay for his needs and wants. Before effective demand can exist, the customer must have purchasing power. *Purchasing power* consists of both current income and savings in the customer's hands and the amount of credit he can command.

Discretionary Income

As you learned earlier, discretionary income is that part of the disposable personal income which is left after a person has paid for a minimum standard of living. Even with an adjustment for price changes, the disposable personal income has more than doubled since 1950, and the discretionary income figure has increased at an even greater rate. Discretionary income today is about 35% of the total disposable personal income, and this figure is likely to continue to increase. As the discretionary income increases, customer demand is also likely to increase; and all businesses must work constantly to obtain as much of this discretionary income as they profitably can.

Discretionary Fund

An important figure to most businesses is the amount of *discretionary fund*—discretionary income plus the amount that can be purchased on credit. The ability to get credit greatly increases an individual's purchasing power, and most retailers today offer credit. Firms that sell to business consumers would make few sales if they did not offer credit. Over 90% of all wholesale business, for instance, is conducted on credit.

In a recent year, the total consumer debt growing out of credit purchases (not including home mortgages) amounted to over $150 billion. A family with an annual income of $10,000 may owe about $2,000 for goods and services bought on credit.

ELEMENTS OF CUSTOMER DEMAND

Several years ago, a canner of fruit products began marketing a new brand of canned peaches. This product sold well in New England but remained on the grocers' shelves in the Midwest. The canner tried to analyze the causes of this difference in customer acceptance and found that in one region, a firm peach was preferred and that in the other region, a softer peach was preferred. Once these facts were discovered, the producer canned a firm peach for one region, a softer peach for the other region, and obtained good acceptance in both regions.

This example illustrates only one element of customer demand—selection factors. Customer demand for a particular item has a number of elements, and those with which sellers are most concerned are: (1) selection factors, (2) quantities demanded, (3) time demands, and (4) service and location demands.

Date *March 11, 19--* **WANT SLIP** Dept. No. *42* Employee No. *14*

Keep this slip in your salesbook. Whenever an item is called for that is not in stock, whether carried regularly or not, record that fact at once. Make certain that you record every call.

ITEMS CALLED FOR	WANTED				WHAT WAS SUBSTITUTED	BUYER'S DISPOSITION
	Style	Color	Size	Price		
Blouse	*chemise*	*White*	*34*	*3.98*	—	*On order*
Sweater	*crew-neck*	*Grey*	*36*	*7.98*	*V-neck*	*On order*
Flannel pajamas	*coat-style*	*Blue*	*10*	*2.98*	*Lounger*	*Discontinued*
Coat	*car-coat*	*Red*	*14*	*14.98*	—	*In reserve*
Gloves	*leather*	*White*	*6*	*4.98*	—	*On order*

Some retail stores determine customer demand, particularly for selection factors, by using want slips. A want slip is a record which is provided daily for each salesperson. On it are entered items that customers asked for but that were not in stock. These records are helpful in making future buying decisions.

Selection Factors

The specific factors customers look for in choosing goods include design, color, size, material, flavor, odor, feel, ease in care and use, durability, and price. Manufacturers and middlemen must make or select for resale those products that have the particular selection factors their customers want. Thus, if a shoe manufacturer finds that there is a demand for a red calf pump with squared toes, chunky heels, and brass trim, he will make such a shoe. Although planning an assortment for resale is mainly a buyer's duty, the salesman should know the most popular combinations of selection factors—particularly those factors for which customers tend to refuse substitutes.

Quantity Factors

One of the worst mistakes a retail store can make is to be out of goods that are in constant demand. However, few days pass in which a retail salesman does not lose at least one sale because his store does not have an article that should be in stock. Manufacturers also lose sales because they incorrectly estimate quantity demands and do not make enough goods to fill customer orders. Even sellers of services frequently cannot satisfy quantity demands. A dry-cleaning firm, for example, may lose business because its service is not fast enough.

Another mistake in selling operations is providing too much merchandise. For example, if a department store carries too large a stock of clothing, style changes may mean that the store cannot sell some of its stock. Stocking too large an assortment of goods may result in shopworn goods that have to be sold at a loss. Also, a too-large stock may make an unfavorable impression on customers. If customers continually see the same goods, they may think that the firm does not carry the latest items and may shop elsewhere.

Time Factors

Manufacturers, wholesalers, and retailers are all faced with the problem of making their assortments available to customers when the articles are wanted. A grocer who opens his store an hour after his competitors is bound to lose a number of sales. In retailing there is strong demand for evening shopping hours. Many downtown department stores that formerly closed at 5:30 p.m. now stay open one or two evenings a week until 9 p.m. Most stores in suburban shopping centers stay open until 9 or 10 p.m. every night except Saturday and Sunday.

Time demands also concern the seasons in which certain goods must be offered. In March, men are in the market to buy summer suits that they will need by April. If the retailer waits until after Easter to stock men's summer suits, he will lose sales. Producers, too, may lose sales because of failure to meet time demands. Suppose that a school wants to adopt a new economics textbook for use during the second semester. One publisher announces that it will publish such a textbook in March. Since this date is too late for the second semester, the school orders a book from another publisher.

Service and Location Factors

There are many variations in customers' service demands. In retail firms, some customers want to carry goods home with them while others want delivery service. Some pay cash; others prefer to charge their purchases. Service demands are generally easier to determine than are the other elements of customer demand, because customers will usually express their desires for certain services or their dissatisfaction with other services. An important point that should be made about service demands is that the seller must provide not only the type of service demanded but must also provide the service at the right time.

Convenience of location is an important element of customer demand. Suburban shopping centers draw many customers because they offer a concentration of stores in a convenient location. Manufacturers, too, locate their enterprises as conveniently to buyers as they can. For example, furniture marts in Chicago and in Jamestown, New York, house offices and showrooms for hundreds of manufacturers; and buyers can see the offerings of many manufacturers in a relatively short time.

METHODS OF ESTIMATING CUSTOMER DEMAND

The easiest way to determine certain elements of customer demand is simply to ask the customer what his requirements are at the time of purchase. This method is used mainly with tailor-made goods and services to be prepared after the customer has placed an order. Business consumers frequently buy tailor-made equipment and installations.

Whenever merchandise must be available at the time of purchase, however, the seller must have correctly anticipated customer demand and provided the right combination of demand elements. Otherwise, he is not likely to sell successfully. In estimating customer demand, sellers frequently use these methods: (1) study of past sales, (2) study of trade information, (3) consumer advisory committees, and (4) marketing research.

Study of Past Sales

Anyone who has sold for even a few years should know from experience a great deal about what customers will and will not buy. The owners of a relatively small men's clothing shop in Wilmington, Delaware, use the technique of keeping records of all customer purchases. For each purchase, the customer's name and address and the size, color, and style of article are recorded. The owners obviously must have a customer relationship that permits the use of such a technique; but when they do their buying, they know the recent demands of a reasonable percentage of their customers.

Such a method is not practical for most firms, so every selling organization must depend partly on the trial-and-error method in estimating demand on the basis of past sales. A news dealer stocks a variety of magazines; some are sold, and some are not. Those that move may be ordered in larger quantities, and those that do not move may be dropped. Manufacturers may stop making some products if customers do not buy them readily, and other products that sell well may be produced in greater quantity.

Study of Trade Information

Although customers are generally the most important source of demand information, a seller should not ignore other businesses who buy and sell goods similar to his. Businesses in other localities may reveal demand for a new article before the seller's customers have expressed a desire for this article. Retailers can learn of demand trends from their suppliers, trade papers, fashion magazines, and special market service bulletins. Manufacturers also get information from some of these resources and from designers and research bureaus that develop new products. By studying these sources of information, the seller can be ready with a supply of new goods by the time his customers express their demands.

Consumer Advisory Committees

Many retail stores have successfully estimated customer demand by establishing consumer advisory committees. These committees are made

October Selling News

and

Newspaper Advertising Work Sheet

October, 1968 | *Another Retail Service of Your Daily Newspaper* | 27 Selling Days

The Shirt

Photo courtesy of the National Shoe Retailers Association

NEW YORK–This is the year of the shirt. And the fall scene is packed with them.

"In" are: men's shirt classics . . . dramatic long-pointed collars . . . scarf ties . . . ruffled necks and bosoms . . . big full sleeves . . . nehru and stand-up collars . . . over-blouses with placket fronts, reports the *National Shoe Retailers Association.*

The look includes shirts with skirts, jumpers or vests . . . shirts with slacks . . . shirt/jacket combinations.

Richard Cole, president of Lady Manhattan, describes fall potential as "tremendous," reports *Women's Wear Daily.* A spokesman for Lady Van Heusen says, "We anticipate substantial gains over last year."

Lillian Wise of Malbe Blouse & Sportswear Co. sees great fall sales and notes that "blouses are now very much a part of the switch-around separates concept."

Color Brightens Profits of Appliances and Housewares

NEW YORK–Color has hit the appliance and housewares industries, reports *Merchandising Week.*

The reigning fashion colors for major appliances–avocado and coppertone–have been joined this year by harvest. Many retailers who have carried appliances in this new color report that their customers are reacting favorably to it.

In housewares, harvest is also moving in, joining the ranks of coppertone, avocado and flame as a standard color option.

In major appliances, most of the color activity is concentrated on built-in lines. One manufacturer estimates that about 80% of his built-in range sales are models in color (other than white), while only about 45% of his free-standing ranges are sold in color. This also holds true for dishwashers.

The reason, says one industry source, is that the free-standing or portable appliance is probably going to be taken along when the owner moves. Newlyweds who are just getting started might shy away from color because they face the prospect of moving around. But once they settle down in their permanent home, they're ready for colored appliances to give the kitchen a more customized, decorator look.

Color can help retailers brighten both their stores and their profit pictures. These appliances offer the merchant a chance to create an over-all color mood: pop, psychedelic, etc.

Color in housewares lends itself to bright "happening" promotions. Color can liven up a slow traffic area, can rejuvenate a tired table-setting display or function as an attention-getter in store windows.

A retailer might choose a "Who says a good pot has to be dull?" promotion theme and offer his customers a "paintbox of colored cookware" so they can create their own kitchen theme.

Merchandising Week suggests that the retailer coordinate his advertising with the new, colorful look of his stock. If he has a large stock of appliances in avocado, he can use this particular color in newspaper advertisements to show customers exactly what he is offering. And a special cookware sale certainly calls for a bright, cheerful ad in fashion colors.

Textures: Best of Fall Fabrics

NEW YORK–The fall fabric picture for women's wear focuses on textures. Be they gregarious, ropy plaids, brushed-up glens or simulated skins, it's what's on the surface that counts, reports *Women's Wear Daily.*

The Stars:

• Tweeds lead. Many textures are based on their nubby weaves.

• Classic Tartans are presented best in authentic colorings that reveal their rich heritage.

• Men's wear patterns are used in tailored yet softened shapes, so the feminine upstages the masculine.

• Knits adapt to the woolen texture picture with great mobility. They go tweed, plaid, textured, soft — in more directions than ever before.

• The swingers mold, drape, pleat and flare. Crepes, flannels, challis, surahs, velvets and voiles are strong.

• The rustlers add crispness to the multitude of textures. Taffeta and moire are back in favor.

• Prints are scaled down on darker ground.

• Color runs the spectrum, but it's toned down. Red—orangy, browned. Blue—royal, midnight and navy. Green — browned. Gold—burnished or bright. And the big neutrals—gray (in all hues), seal brown, camel, pale stone tones, black (in small amounts).

Bureau of Advertising, ANPA

This is part of a monthly bulletin that many retailers study for information on future customer demand. The bulletin reports fashion trends and mentions merchandise that is selling well.

up of persons who are representative of the store's clientele and who are alert to new trends in customer demand. The committees meet periodically with store management and make recommendations on future purchases.

Specialty shops and clothing departments have found consumer advisory committees especially helpful. For example, one store buyer intended to buy a large quantity of novelty hosiery; but the store's advisory committee of girls from well-known area colleges indicated that the hosiery would probably not be accepted for campus wear. The committee recommended buying another type of hosiery; this hosiery was bought and proved to be very popular.

Marketing Research

An extremely important tool for today's businessmen is *marketing research*—the study of product acceptance and of functions performed in the movement of goods from producer to consumer. Within this broad field are a number of specific research areas. Marketing research techniques are useful in determining customer demand; and from the seller's viewpoint, the most commonly used techniques are those employing questionnaires, consumer panels, and test marketing.

Questionnaires. A questionnaire is like an objective test you might take in school, except that there are no right or wrong answers. Any question may be asked, and answers are tabulated to give the firm the information it wants. Questionnaires are constructed so that a consumer can easily fill them out and so that answers can easily be tabulated. Questionnaires are generally sent by mail to selected consumers, but they may also be read to the consumer over the telephone or read by a door-to-door survey taker. Sometimes a retail store will survey customers currently shopping in the store and ask them to indicate preferences for certain products or services.

Consumer Panels. Manufacturers sometimes set up consumer panels which objectively evaluate merchandise before it is placed on the market. Product samples are prepared in different designs, colors, and sizes; and panel members express their preferences and their opinions during a group discussion. Based on the opinions of the panel members, the manufacturer may decide whether any changes should be made in the product before marketing it. Usually an advertising agency or research

Questionnaire

Section 1. CANNED OR BOTTLED GROCERY PRODUCTS INSTRUCTIONS:

COLUMN "A": Please draw a **circle** around the number which will tell us **about** how often you (or anyone in your home) have bought each product shown at a grocery store within the past twelve months. If you have not bought the product at the grocers **at all** during the past twelve months, circle the zero ⓪. If once, circle the one ①, if twice, circle the ②, and so on. If you have bought the product at the grocers **more than twelve** times, circle the ⑫. The ⑫ means "twelve **or more** times".

COLUMN "B": Please draw a circle around either the word "no" or the word "yes". Circle (no) if you do **not usually** buy a **specific brand** at the grocers, in other words circle (no) if you do not look for a particular brand when shopping. Circle (yes) if you usually buy (or look for) a specific brand name.

COLUMN "C": If your answer to Column "B" was (yes) please **write** the name of the brand you usually buy or look for on the blank space provided. If your answer to Column "B" was (no) please leave the space under Column "C" blank.

PRODUCT (Canned or Bottled)	COLUMN "A" Please circle the approximate number of times you have bought each product within the past twelve months at the grocers.	COLUMN "B" Please circle the word "no" or the word "yes" to tell whether or not you usually buy a specific brand.	COLUMN "C" If you do usually buy a specific brand, please PRINT the name of the brand you usually buy at the grocers.
HOT DOG CHILI	0 1 2 3 4 5 6 7 8 9 10 11 12	no yes	________
CHILI WITHOUT BEANS	0 1 2 3 4 5 6 7 8 9 10 11 12	no yes	________
CHILI WITH BEANS	0 1 2 3 4 5 6 7 8 9 10 11 12	no yes	________
BRUNSWICK STEW	0 1 2 3 4 5 6 7 8 9 10 11 12	no yes	________
BEEF STEW	0 1 2 3 4 5 6 7 8 9 10 11 12	no yes	________
BARBECUED PORK	0 1 2 3 4 5 6 7 8 9 10 11 12	no yes	________
PORK WITH BARBECUE SAUCE	0 1 2 3 4 5 6 7 8 9 10 11 12	no yes	________
BARBECUED BEEF	0 1 2 3 4 5 6 7 8 9 10 11 12	no yes	________
BEEF WITH BARBECUE SAUCE	0 1 2 3 4 5 6 7 8 9 10 11 12	no yes	________
BARBECUE TYPE HASH	0 1 2 3 4 5 6 7 8 9 10 11 12	no yes	________
SPAGHETTI WITH MEAT SAUCE	0 1 2 3 4 5 6 7 8 9 10 11 12	no yes	________
BARBECUE BEANS	0 1 2 3 4 5 6 7 8 9 10 11 12	no yes	________
BARBECUE SAUCE	0 1 2 3 4 5 6 7 8 9 10 11 12	no yes	________
STEAK AND MEAT SAUCE	0 1 2 3 4 5 6 7 8 9 10 11 12	no yes	________
WORCESTERSHIRE SAUCE	0 1 2 3 4 5 6 7 8 9 10 11 12	no yes	________
SEAFOOD AND COCKTAIL SAUCE	0 1 2 3 4 5 6 7 8 9 10 11 12	no yes	________

The Marketing Services Company, Decatur, Georgia

This is the first section of a questionnaire used by a manufacturer of meat products to determine which meat products homemakers buy, how often the products are purchased, and what brand names homemakers look for in grocery stores.

agency is hired to handle the operation of such a panel. It is important that the panel members represent a cross-section of the potential customers for the product being considered.

Test Marketing. When manufacturers try to estimate customer demand for a product by marketing it in a limited geographical area before marketing it nationally, they are using a technique called *test marketing*. The new or improved product is designed with great care, sometimes drawing on the demand-estimation techniques just discussed, and is offered for sale in a small geographical area. Resulting sales figures can be an index to the degree of customer demand the manufacturer might expect with broader distribution. New foods are frequently test marketed before being distributed regionally or nationally. Like the consumer panel, the chosen test area must contain a cross-section of potential customers with regard to such characteristics as age, income, and education.

CHECKING YOUR KNOWLEDGE

Vocabulary:

(1) effective demand
(2) purchasing power
(3) discretionary fund
(4) marketing research
(5) test marketing

Review questions:

1. Why is the amount of a customer's purchasing power so important to sellers?
2. Name the elements of customer demand with which sellers are most concerned.
3. Why is it important that the salesman understand the selection factors customers demand in goods?
4. Describe the methods that sellers often use to estimate customer demand.
5. From the seller's point of view, what are the most important marketing research techniques used to estimate customer demand?

For discussion:

1. Why do today's consumers have more spending power than ever before in spite of the rising cost of living and rising taxes?
2. Are the store buyer and the salesperson in a handbag department equally responsible for providing the customer with the exact article she is looking for?
3. In some small towns, all stores close one afternoon a week, frequently on Wednesday. Is it advisable for all kinds of stores and service businesses to be closed on the same afternoon; or should some close one day, some another? Why?

part E

market segmentation

"These suits are the latest style; I'm sure you'll like them." With this opening remark, a salesman of men's clothing tried to sell suits to three customers: a grandfather with his grandson, a farmer dressed in work clothing, and a conservatively dressed businessman. Each customer left the store without buying. Then the salesman waited on a young man his own age, used the same opening remark, and eventually made a sale. The salesman lost the first three sales because he talked to the different customers as though they were his own age and had his own interests.

Such a mistake was once common. Sellers tended to think of all consumers as a single unit, a mass of people having essentially the same characteristics. Finally it was realized that this approach was inaccurate and often misleading, and the technique of market segmentation was developed. *Market segmentation* is the process of dividing a total market into small parts so that the buying characteristics of each part can be easily studied and satisfied.

AN EXAMPLE OF MARKET SEGMENTATION

For Seneca, a New York apple grower, it started with too many McIntoshes. The company had a choice: to make all its apples into juice and cider and risk an oversupply of these products or to make the McIntoshes into applesauce. Research had shown that the McIntosh was the most popular "eating" apple in the northeastern states, but apple growers and processors regarded as inferior an applesauce made only from McIntoshes. A competing firm, the makers of Mott's applesauce, controlled the regional market for applesauce; and its appeal was that the applesauce was made from five different kinds of apples.

Seneca management believed—in spite of the trade people—that an all-McIntosh applesauce made for and sold only to the McIntosh lovers in the northeastern states would be welcomed. Seneca made the applesauce, conducted taste tests, and developed a distinctive container. The company gained the cooperation of middlemen by giving them special introductory allowances for providing shelf space, and it formulated an effective advertising campaign. Before long Seneca's all-McIntosh applesauce had captured eight percent of the metropolitan New York City market, and selling efforts had been extended as far west as Cleveland and as far south as Washington, D. C.

Seneca's market segmentation was successful. The company took its total consumer market, isolated one group of consumers—those people in the northeastern states who love McIntosh apples—and directed all its selling efforts toward that group. The company did not try to sell its McIntosh applesauce in another region, because consumers there might prefer Jonathan or Winesap apples.

Now Seneca intends to segment its general consumer market even further. The company has discovered that on the West Coast, the Delicious apple is favored; so Seneca plans to market in that area an applesauce made only from Delicious apples.

USES OF MARKET SEGMENTATION

The biggest advantage of market segmentation is that it allows a seller to direct his selling efforts at a definite group of consumers rather than using a shotgun selling approach. The seller who uses market segmentation becomes a specialist not only in selling his product or service but also in selling the product to a particular group of customers.

Sellers use market segmentation in the following ways:

1. In developing products that truly fit the needs of the most profitable segments of the total market.
2. In directing sales promotion campaigns to the potentially most profitable consumer groups.
3. In determining the appeals that will be most effective in selling to a particular group.
4. In choosing the proper timing for selling efforts and the best form of selling.
5. In choosing the best advertising media and determining advertising budgets.

Manufacturers and producers use market segmentation more frequently than do other sellers. In developing new products and devising advertising campaigns, they must have detailed knowledge of the consumer groups they will serve. Wholesalers use market segmentation less frequently than do other selling organizations. The number of retailers who might stock the wholesaler's products, within the wholesaler's geographical territory, will be relatively limited. Retailers use market segmentation in establishing new stores and deciding on the type of customer they will serve. They may also use segmentation for planning purposes, to decide what merchandise to stock and services to provide.

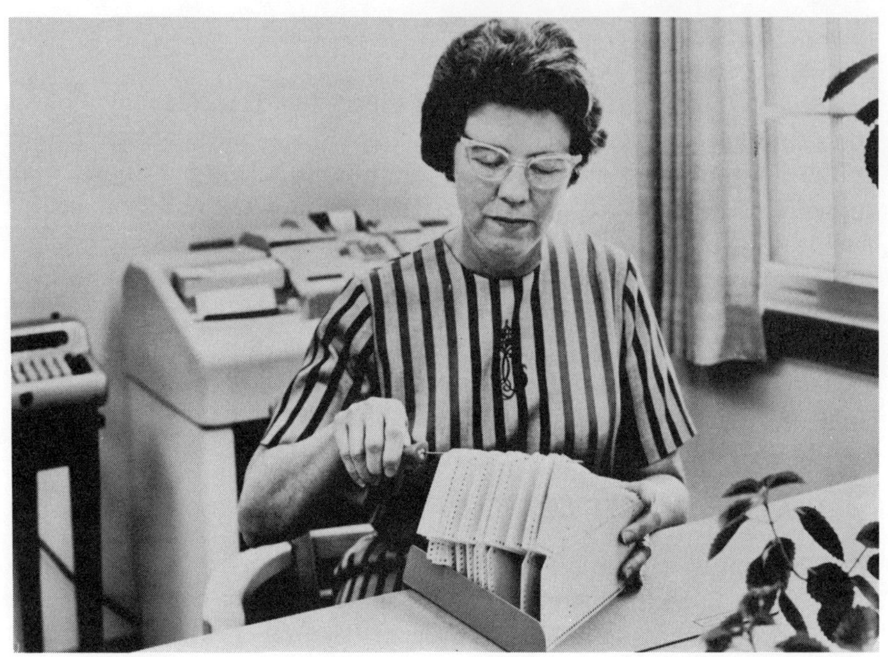

John Vogeler Associates

Most businesses need a huge amount of data to segment their markets, and a computer is generally used to handle the data efficiently. However, some businessmen may not need such vast quantities of data and so may use a simpler method of organizing customer information. Here, a special card record is prepared for each customer and is punched to indicate certain characteristics about the customer. By using a special needle, cards indicating similar characteristics can be readily separated from the other cards. When the separation is completed, one segment of the market has been isolated.

METHODS OF SEGMENTING MARKETS

Few selling organizations use the same methods of segmenting their total markets. Methods vary because of the products the firm handles, the extent of product distribution, and the size of the firm. The method chosen will depend on the business' particular needs, and the same method may not be used for every product handled by the firm.

First Steps in Segmenting Markets

Perhaps the first step in segmenting markets is to distinguish the domestic market from the foreign market. All businesses do not sell to foreign markets, but those that do will direct separate selling efforts to this market. Another step is to separate the government market from the private market. All governmental agencies who purchase goods receive special selling attention.

The most important segmentation for most sellers is the separation of the industrial goods market from the consumer goods market. Many sellers, as you have learned, concentrate on selling to only one of these markets. Firms that make materials, parts, equipment, and supplies will be concerned only with the industrial market. Some sellers sell both to industrial, institutional, or commercial users and to the ultimate consumer. Thus, a manufacturer of sheets may have sales efforts directed to hospitals and separate sales efforts directed to retail stores. A wholesaler of stationery may have one sales division to sell to office users and another to sell to retail stationery stores. There are, of course, still other firms who sell their products only to the ultimate consumer.

Segmenting the Ultimate Consumer Market

Segmentation techniques are most complex when they are used to divide the ultimate consumer market. The huge number of ultimate consumers and the many differences in consumer buying behavior make it necessary to isolate the appropriate consumer groups. Sellers often use one or more of the factors below in segmenting the ultimate consumer market:

1. Geography.
2. Income.
3. Occupation.
4. Education.
5. Age.
6. Sex.
7. Marital status.
8. Composition of household (number of adults and children).
9. Social class (upper, middle, lower).
10. Group membership (ethnic groups, religious groups, etc.).
11. Type of residence (home, apartment, etc.).
12. Political affiliation.
13. Special interests (sports, travel, etc.).

The seller must find data on these factors that would best characterize the consumers likely to buy his product. He may conduct his own research surveys or study published data to find the information he needs. If he were a seller of cheese, for example, he might learn that most cheese is bought by people who live in large cities and who have no children. The seller would choose these people as his prime market target and would direct his selling efforts to them.

your
lesson for
TODAY IS:
WHAT LOOKS AND FEELS LIKE LEATHER BUT ISN'T??? That's simple! "Cuir Sauvage" by Russ. You don't have to be a scientist to know that 100% virgin vinyl backed by 100% cotton has been scientifically treated to look and feel like fine imported leather. What's more, its special finish resists hard wear, scuffs, stains, rain spots and fading. Sturdy as it is supple. Completely washable. Antique brown, sizes 7 to 14. A. A-line skirt with two pockets . . . 6.98 Vest . . . 5.98 Maize body shirt . . . 3.98 B. Zipper front body jumper . . . 9.98 Maize body shirt . . . 3.98 Young World, Fifth Floor, all 5 stores, mail or phone Norma Fay, 381-2030
Mabley & Carew
CINCINNATI, OHIO

Mabley & Carew, Cincinnati

Geography is such an important standard for segmenting the ultimate consumer market that several nationally-circulated magazines publish regional editions. The basic content of the magazine is the same in all editions, but advertisements vary from edition to edition. For instance, the same advertisements will not appear in both the Northeastern edition and the Midwestern edition. This ad, taken from a regional edition of a national magazine, has a quite specific appeal for the residents of a single city.

Likewise, a manufacturer of yachts would certainly not regard everyone as a potential customer. He would probably concentrate on men in high-income brackets who have shown an interest in boating. Then he would find out where people with these characteristics live, what magazines they read, what events they attend, and what appeals they might respond to. A combination of personal and nonpersonal selling techniques would then be used to sell the yachts.

The ultimate consumer market is in a state of constant change. Conclusions that are valid today may not be valid tomorrow. Everyone learns patterns of buying behavior from his parents, but he is quickly influenced by friends' opinions and by communications media. Behavior patterns change rapidly. Thus, it is essential that a business continually evaluate its efforts in market segmentation and keep its consumer information up-to-date.

CHECKING YOUR KNOWLEDGE

Vocabulary:

market segmentation

Review questions:

1. What is the biggest advantage of market segmentation?
2. In what specific ways may sellers use market segmentation?
3. Why do methods of segmenting total markets differ from firm to firm?
4. What is the most important market segmentation for most sellers?
5. Name ten factors used in segmenting the ultimate consumer market.

For discussion:

1. Manufacturers make more use of market segmentation than do any other sellers. Why is this so?
2. The factors of geography, income, occupation, and education are often used in segmenting the ultimate consumer market. For each of these factors, name several products whose manufacturers would place great emphasis on that factor in segmenting their total markets. Give reasons for your answers.

BUILDING YOUR SKILLS

Improving your English:

On a separate sheet of paper, write the correct pronoun(s) to be used in each of the following sentences.

1. Bill and (I, me) will deliver the package.
2. The manager obtained the information for (she, her) and (me, I).

3. Please give the applications to (she, her) or (he, him).
4. The materials you requested are for (she, her) and Mr. Trenton.
5. Harry gave the messages to (he, him) and (she, her).
6. Send anyone but (he, him) to deliver the order.
7. That was (I, me) (who, whom) you saw.
8. He evaluated the supervisor more closely than (I, me).
9. The conference with Mr. Brown and (she, her) was successful.
10. Everyone but (he, him) responded to the challenge.

Improving your arithmetic:

Perform the division exercises given below.

1. Troy Buchanan's firewood sales to 18 homes on Iris Street totaled $504. What was the average sale per home?
2. Henry Banks delivers newspapers. If he collected $546 in November subscriptions from 195 regular customers, what is the monthly subscription rate?
3. If 4 dozen ties cost $74.40, what will one tie cost?
4. If head lettuce is on sale at 2 heads for 39¢, how many heads can be bought for $2.34?
5. Total November sales in the shoe department of a men's clothing store were $5,268, and the average price paid per pair was $21.95. How many pairs of shoes were sold?

Improving your research skills:

1. Select an article with which you are somewhat familiar and which is commonly sold in your community. Get the approval of your instructor before deciding definitely on the article. Ask ten students for their two main reasons for having bought such an article. If they have not bought the article, ask for the reasons that would most influence them if they were to buy the article. Then interview ten other persons who are not students and ask them the same questions. List all the buying motives of each group. Which motives were strongest among the students? Among other people? Among both groups? What explanation can you give for the differences in buying motives?
2. Listed below are ten products. Write a report describing the buying motive or motives that you think would be most influential in the purchase of each item. Where you feel that different people would have different buying motives for the same article, indicate the various motives and briefly describe the people who would be influenced by each motive you suggest.

(a) Oriental rug
(b) Microscope
(c) Barbells
(d) Golf clubs
(e) Motion picture projector
(f) Evening dress
(g) Pizza
(h) Mattress
(i) Vitamins
(j) Life insurance policy

3. The three situations described below represent failure to accurately estimate customer demand. In a report, tell what the result of each situation might be and give some probable causes for each firm's failure to determine customer demand.

   (a) A dress manufacturer produces a certain style of dress that does not sell.
   (b) A clothing store has not sold a large portion of its winter coats by the end of the season.
   (c) A candy store has hundreds of Easter eggs left over every year.

4. From such sources as your local chamber of commerce, merchants' association, local office of the U.S. Department of Commerce, or local office of the Small Business Administration, find out what statistical data are available on the population in your town or city. Use the factors listed on page 145 as guidelines for obtaining these data. Determine what segmentation of the local consumer market is made possible by these statistics. Indicate the information that is not available and whether there is any way that such information could be obtained.

APPLYING YOUR KNOWLEDGE

Case problems:

1. In the men's department of your store, there are many excellent imported suits on sale. There are also some medium-quality, classically styled, less expensive suits on sale. A well-dressed businessman walks into your department and briskly says that he wants a "plain, no-nonsense suit at a fair price and that will wear well." What buying motives could be influencing this customer? How might you persuade him to buy the more expensive imported suits?
2. A manufacturer is considering putting on the market a new type of motorized surfboard for "surfing" in inland lakes and rivers where there are no big waves. Although the surfboard is moderately expensive, it is made of high-quality, durable fiberglass and comes in a wide range of colors. The motor is simple and economical to operate and can be repaired easily. What segment of the total consumer market would be most likely to buy this product? What techniques of segmenting the total market and of determining customer demand might the manufacturer use?

Continuing project:

In your manual, you should now prepare a section on the behavior likely to characterize the consumers who will buy your product or service. You will probably want to write on the following topics:

1. The buying motives that will influence customers who buy your product or service.

2. The specific elements of customer demand for your product and the techniques you will use to determine customer demand.
3. The characteristics of the specific market segment to which your product or service will be sold.

Extra credit:

The salesman presents merchandise facts to his customer for the purpose of influencing the customer to act favorably—to buy the product offered for sale. Similarly, the good educator is not content to present only facts to his students; he attempts to influence their reactions to the subject matter and to influence their behavior.

Observe one of your instructors carefully for a week and note what techniques he uses to "sell" an idea to you, to influence your conduct rather than simply add to your store of knowledge. Prepare a report describing his techniques and indicate whether you think he would be a successful salesman. Give reasons for your evaluation.

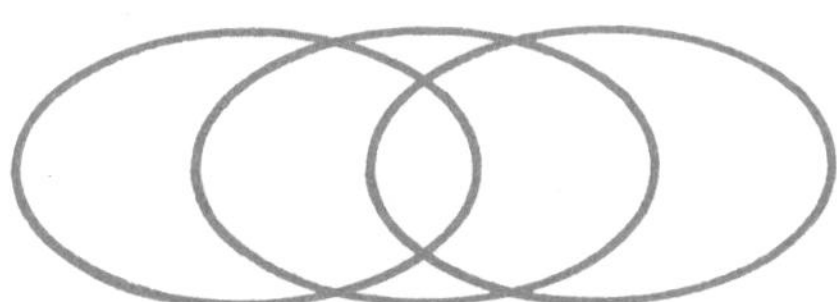

communicating with customers

KEY QUESTIONS

A In the communication process, what are the functions of the encoder and the decoder?

B Does a customer's image of a business affect his patronage of that business?

C Why are buying and selling increasingly becoming exercises in decision making?

D What determines whether a business will rely on personal or nonpersonal channels of communication?

E Is it possible for the sender of a message to control the receiver's decoding process?

part A

the communication process

Without communication, no activity in this world could take place. *Communication* is the process of transferring ideas from one mind to another. Animals communicate by smell, touch, and sound. Humans also communicate through these senses, but they communicate mainly through language. Selling is a special kind of communication because of the relationship between the sender and the receiver of the selling message. Unlike many forms of communication, the sender (seller) wants to persuade the receiver (customer) to do something: to buy the seller's product or engage his services. Thus, selling is often called persuasive communication.

HOW PEOPLE COMMUNICATE

Any act of communication is a partnership; one person must transmit a message, another person must receive it. The communication process consists of a sender, or source, a message, a message carrier (called a *channel,* or *medium, of communication*), and a receiver.

The first step in the communication process is an idea. Any person or group of persons can be a sender if they have ideas and information that they want to transmit to others. A salesman can be a sender, and so can a retailer, wholesaler, or manufacturer. Whoever the sender, he must have a reason for communicating; this reason results in the message.

Before a message can leave the sender's mind, it must be put into a symbol or language form that another person can understand. This process is called *encoding;* speaking, writing, and illustrating are forms of encoding. Next, the encoded message must be sent through a channel. If a sales message is encoded through speaking, the channel is the personal salesman or some form of broadcast media. If the message is encoded through illustrating or writing, the channel is some form of printed or broadcast media.

Through one or more of his senses, the receiver picks up the transmitted message. This message must be decoded before it means anything to him, so the message travels to his *decoder*—a mechanism that retranslates the message sent by the source. The nervous system and brain work together as a decoder.

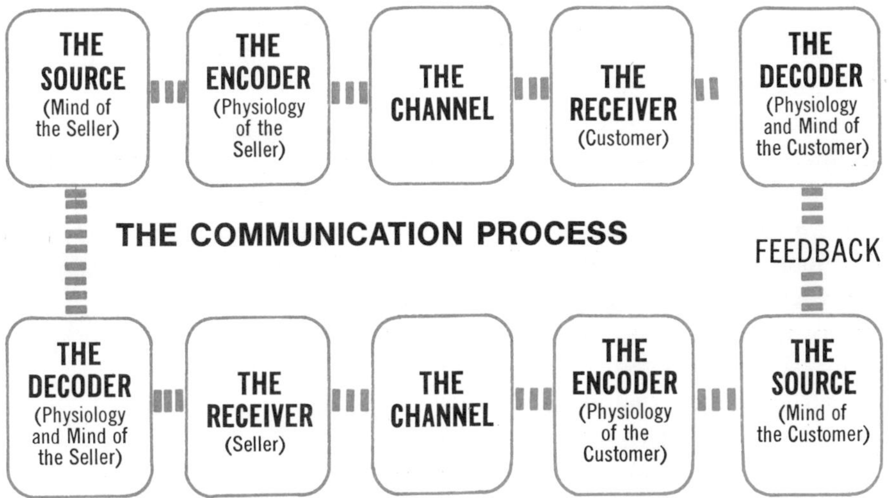

Shown above are the basic elements of the communication process. A breakdown of communication can occur at any step in the process; and if such a breakdown occurs, the cycle will not be completed.

Retranslation of a message is more than a mechanical process. Probably no message is decoded in the exact way the sender intended. For one thing, the receiver may not be listening or may listen only to the portions of the message that he wants to hear. Also, the message is modified by the receiver's attitudes, memories, and beliefs; and he may read into the message emotional overtones that the sender never intended. Thus, a symbol that has one meaning for the sender may have a very different meaning for the receiver. For instance, a real estate salesman may use blooming goldenrod as a symbol of the early autumn beauty of country living. To the receiver, the goldenrod may be a symbol of nothing but hay fever.

BARRIERS TO COMMUNICATION

To communicate effectively, the salesman must understand three things: (1) the purpose of his message, (2) the person for whom the message is intended, and (3) the art of speaking and listening effectively. If he understands these things thoroughly, he should be able to deal with any barriers to communication that he might encounter. The communication barriers most commonly met in selling are: (1) the receiver's mental set, (2) the different meanings of signals, and (3) the receiver's resistance to new stimuli.

Receiver's Mental Set

Perception is the receiver's awareness of a transmitted message. *Set* is the receiver's readiness to react automatically to a stimulus, and set influences not only what a person will perceive but also how he will perceive it. Mental set is like a runner's stance just before the signal to start a race. The runner is ready to go—without consciously thinking—the moment the gun sounds; he is "set." With mental set, the brain and nervous system are ready to respond before any reasoning takes place. Thus, the description "handmade" may quickly trigger in one customer the response that the product must be good. To another sensitive customer, however, "handmade" may trigger the response that laborers have been exploited. The mental set of each person determines how he will react to the stimulus "handmade."

Set also affects a person's expectations. A retail customer is "set" for a salesperson to greet him at the beginning of the sale and say farewell at the end of the sale. The reader of a teaser headline in an advertisement is "set" for the copy to tell him the headline's meaning in relation to buying something. If a customer doesn't receive what he is set to receive, he is upset; and this may ruin the salesman-customer relationship.

Mental set is due partly to the presence of old beliefs, and a salesman should not deny the truth of these beliefs. For example, if a customer firmly believes that an all-wool rug is the only kind to buy, the salesman should probably concentrate on selling the customer all-wool rugs. However, if nylon has been added to wool to provide greater strength and durability, the salesman should tactfully point this out. When a salesman respectfully recognizes the customer's beliefs, he reinforces the customer's self-image.

Different Meanings of Signals

One of the problems in selling—or any other kind of communication—is the uncertainty of what communication signals will mean to the receiver. Words actually have two meanings—denotative and connotative. The *denotative meaning* is the literal meaning of a word as it could be found in a dictionary. The *connotative meaning* is the emotional meaning that a receiver attaches to a word. A salesman must determine the connotative meanings that customers may attach to a sales message. For instance, you learned earlier that "cheap" and "inexpensive" have the same denotative meaning. However, "cheap" is far more likely to have unpleasant connotative meanings than is "inexpensive," so a salesman should not use "cheap" in describing merchandise.

In selling a tailored suit to a woman, one salesman emphasized the suit's businesslike, efficient appearance. This appeal resulted in unpleasant connotations. The customer associated the description "businesslike, efficient" with a loss of femininity and so did not buy the suit. Every salesman must be aware of the possible emotional impact and association of words. He must be careful not to use terms which, although they seem harmless to him, may offend others.

Receiver's Resistance to New Stimuli

One trait of human nature is the tendency to resist change. A customer's mental set often results in a quick resistance to new stimuli transmitted by the salesman. Resistance to new stimuli usually results in an expressed objection to buying, but sometimes the resistances are not encoded by the customer. Salesmen must be able to anticipate a customer's resistance to new stimuli, sometimes through a flash of intuition rather than through any physical communication. As a salesman becomes more experienced, he will find that he can often guess accurately what a customer's mental resistances are.

Suppose that a salesman is trying to sell a portable color TV set to a man who wants to buy it for his married daughter. As the man hesitates in his buying decision, questions such as the following—representing resistance to the sales stimuli—may be going through his mind:

1. Is it really portable? It seems very heavy.
2. The guarantee says that the set must be brought into this shop for free service. Won't that be too much for my daughter to handle?
3. Is buying a color set really wise? It has become a status symbol, and my daughter doesn't like to feel that she buys anything just to keep up with her neighbors.
4. The price seems reasonable, but I've only shopped in two other stores so far. Maybe I can do better.

The alert salesman will sense the major resistances and will adjust his part of the dialogue to eliminate the customer's negative thoughts.

IMPROVING SALES COMMUNICATION

An excellent means of improving salesman-customer communication is to make full use of feedback. From the salesman's point of view, *feedback* is a reversal of the communication process discussed earlier.

Sales Management

Every salesman must be able to communicate effectively with customers. If he can't, he will soon find himself out of a job.

After the customer has decoded the message, he becomes the sender and encodes a message in response to the first message. Only by this process can both parties understand each other's needs and wants. Feedback allows the salesman to adapt his presentation to the customer's behavior.

If the sender's and receiver's fields of experience overlap, the sender's message is likely to be decoded as he intends. If the two persons have a common background of experience, chances are good that they will interpret messages in the same way. The seller tries to get these fields of experience to overlap by learning in advance all he can about the prospect and by gaining a sense of empathy with him.

To improve communication, the salesman must also use symbols that the customer associates with a worthwhile goal. In selling a winter trip to Florida, a salesman might picture either a couple relaxing on the beach or a couple engaged in deep-sea fishing. He selects the symbol that he believes would appeal to the people receiving the message. An older couple would probably be stimulated by the first image, while a young couple would respond to the second image.

CHECKING YOUR KNOWLEDGE

Vocabulary:

(1) communication
(2) channel, or medium, of communication
(3) encoding
(4) decoder
(5) perception
(6) set
(7) denotative meaning
(8) connotative meaning
(9) feedback

Review questions:

1. Describe the process by which people communicate.
2. Are messages always retranslated by the receiver in the exact way that the sender intended? Why or why not?
3. What are the communication barriers most commonly met in selling?
4. How does a receiver's mental set influence the way he will retranslate a message?
5. Describe several means of improving salesman-customer communication.

For discussion:

1. Have you had an experience where an idea that you tried to communicate to another person was understood in a way very different from what you intended? Explain.
2. When people are considering the purchase of an expensive article, do many questions usually run through their minds? Does the seller have any satisfactory means of determining what these questions are?

part B

source of the message

Part A discussed the personal salesman as the sender in the sales communication process. The sender or source of a message can also be a manufacturer, wholesaler, retailer, service business, or nonprofit organization. In face-to-face contacts, the customer thinks of the salesman as the sender of the message. Yet, from the viewpoint of the salesman's employer, the salesman and his voice presentation actually make up the channel through which the employer transmits his message. In the overall view of the sales communication process, the selling organization is actually the sender; and in this part we shall think mainly of the selling organization as the sender, or source, of the message.

CREDIBILITY AND IMAGE OF THE SOURCE

The chief requirement of the source of a selling message is *credibility*. This means that if the source is to communicate effectively, its sales messages must be believable and customers must have confidence in the source. How is such credibility achieved? It is achieved mainly through developing and maintaining a favorable image. One retailer may have earned credibility because of a reputation for stocking unusually wide merchandise assortments; another, for maintaining high standards of quality through product testing; and another, for exceptionally good personal service to customers.

Definition of an Image

All people have distinct personalities, and so do all selling organizations. An *image* is the mental impression that customers have of a seller's personality. Today every firm that sells a product or service tries to create a pleasing public image. Every firm hopes that customers will attribute to it certain favorable characteristics so that a loyal clientele can be built. A personal salesman has a great responsibility for understanding his firm's image and for enhancing that image in all his customer contacts.

I. Howard Spivak, ASMP

A store's physical appearance influences greatly the store image that a customer will have. After studying the interior layout of this store, what image do you have of the store and its merchandise?

Creating an Image

To create an image, a firm must establish certain policies that it will follow consistently in offering goods and services for sale. No seller can hope to capture every segment of the total market. He cannot be all things to all customers. Rather, he must develop a set of special characteristics that will appeal to a significant portion of the market.

A manufacturer might choose to build his image around several of the following elements:

1. Quality of his products.
2. Leadership in introducing new products.
3. Variety of products.
4. Low prices in relation to quality.
5. Promotional aids to dealers.
6. Prompt and accurate filling of orders.
7. Quick and fair adjustment of customer complaints.

The middleman, whether wholesaler or retailer, might choose to build his image around several of these elements:

1. Large stock assortments.
2. Bargain prices.
3. Quality of merchandise.
4. Fashion leadership.
5. Original sales promotion campaigns.
6. Personal service to customers.
7. Dependability in keeping promises and making adjustments of complaints.

Maintaining the Image

Once a favorable image has been created, the seller is faced with the task of maintaining that image. His policies of operation and his communication efforts must all be planned to keep the desired image intact. Selling organizations carefully select and train their salesmen and continually evaluate salesmen's performances to make sure they are projecting the desired image. Sellers prepare all advertising and display campaigns so that they are consistent with the image. They introduce systems and procedures that insure prompt attention to the affairs of individual customers.

Many selling organizations believe that they can maintain a favorable image and lend credibility to their sales messages partly by using *endorsements*—expressions of approval for a product. There are three important kinds of individuals who give endorsements: paid endorsers, created endorsers, and unbiased endorsers.

Paid Endorsers. Selling organizations which advertise nationally on television and in magazines often use celebrities from the sports and entertainment fields to endorse their products. Even though the receiver of the sales message knows that the endorser is paid, he is likely to believe that the product is superior if the endorser's sales talk is convincingly delivered. Because Arnold Palmer is a famous golfer, he adds credibility to the seller's message and enhances the seller's image when he endorses a brand of golfing equipment.

Created Endorsers. Many retailers and manufacturers have created their own endorsers. They endow a fictitious person with characteristics that enhance the firm's image and lend credibility to the sales message. Betty Crocker was created by General Mills Corporation many years ago to build a favorable and long-lasting image for the company's food products. Created endorsers often make appearances on radio, television, and at social events, and address letters to customers over their signatures. Sometimes the real person behind the image changes, but the basic image remains the same.

Unbiased Endorsers. Obtaining source credibility from an unpaid, unbiased endorser is not easy to do. Professional testing organizations, such as Consumers' Research, Inc., can add credibility to sales messages and enhance a firm's image if they approve a firm's product. Procter & Gamble added to the credibility of their sales messages and to their image when the Council on Dental Therapeutics of the American Dental Association endorsed Crest toothpaste as an effective decay-preventing dentifrice.

Some publications, such as *Good Housekeeping,* issue seals of approval to certain products as a result of product tests they have made. A few publications have been accused of giving preference to products made by firms who advertise in the publications. However, there is no doubt that earning a seal of approval can greatly enhance a firm's sales messages and image.

STUDYING THE CURRENT IMAGE

Most selling organizations conduct research studies periodically to make sure that they are projecting the desired image to customers. One such research study was undertaken by a group of affiliated department stores. The group chose to poll one group of customers: young married couples with charge accounts. It was recognized that today the young married group is the most rapidly growing segment of the population and that spending power is greater for those persons who have charge accounts than for those who do not. Also, credit customers are more likely to have clear-cut ideas about the stores in which they have accounts. What this small group thought about each store's image was very important in planning for the future.

It was found that the image of one store in the group was negative. Customers felt that shopping at the store was a waste of time, that management was interested only in making a profit, that displays were little more than mediocre, and that advertising was misleading and full of half-truths. These comments told management that drastic operational changes were needed if the store's image was to be improved.

In contrast, another store was found to be doing a good job of projecting the desired image. Customers felt that shopping in the store was a pleasure and that management was progressive and interested in customer welfare. Displays were regarded as being original and an aid to shopping. Virtually all customers had a favorable impression of the store's advertising. Thus, the store's management could be reasonably sure that they were projecting a favorable image.

THE SOURCE AND THE OPINION LEADER

Much of a seller's communication will be directed toward *opinion leaders*—persons who influence greatly the buying decisions of others. An opinion leader and his verbal expressions can confirm or oppose a source's credibility and image. Sometimes an opinion leader can make or break all that a seller is trying to achieve in communication. Thus, it is important that the source win the opinion leader's endorsement of his product or service.

It is estimated that in any social group of about 15 people, there will be one opinion leader with tremendous influence over the other members' buying decisions for at least one broad class of products. Every community has its opinion leaders; and some opinion leaders, such as celebrities, are nationally known.

In general, opinion leaders have these characteristics:

1. They have a strong interest in the product field in which they are influential.
2. They hold jobs or positions that are believed to give them special competence.
3. They are accessible to the members of the group to which they belong.
4. They have contacts with outside sources not generally available to other group members.

5. They express their opinions freely.
6. They often have a slightly higher social status than their fellow group members, but the difference is not great enough to cut them off from free communication with the group.

The seller who can influence opinion leaders with his communications can often sell his product or service to the entire group. However, identifying opinion leaders is not easy; it takes considerable experience in selling and also considerable research effort.

CHECKING YOUR KNOWLEDGE

Vocabulary:

(1) credibility
(2) image
(3) endorsements
(4) opinion leaders

Review questions:

1. What is the chief requirement of a selling message? How can this requirement be achieved?
2. Around what elements might a manufacturer choose to build his image?
3. Around what elements might a middleman choose to build his image?
4. Describe the three kinds of endorsers that can lend credibility to a sales message.
5. What are the characteristics of opinion leaders?

For discussion:

1. Does your attitude toward a particular TV announcer, who describes a product for a manufacturer or middleman, have an effect on your attitude toward the product? Give examples.
2. Is there a business in your community that is trying to improve its image? Is it making changes in operations, sales messages, or both?

part C

the message

The message that a seller transmits when he communicates is simply this: the news that, in return for a price, he can contribute to the satisfaction of the potential customer's need or want. An effective sales message—whether it is transmitted through a salesman's voice or through a printed or broadcast advertisement—must convince the customer that he has something to gain by accepting the message, thinking about it, and responding favorably to it.

THE SELLER'S GOALS

From the seller's point of view, his message will have one or more of the following goals:

1. To persuade customers to try a new product or service.
2. To encourage customers to switch from a product or service they are currently buying to his product or service.
3. To move customers to buy more of his offerings.
4. To maintain his present sales volume in the face of such factors as strong competition, changes in customer buying habits, and decline in total customer purchasing power.
5. To develop and maintain an image for his products and his company that will sustain his sales over the long run.

To accomplish any one of these goals, the seller must decide which kind of message he will use: a primary message or a selective message.

Primary Message

A *primary selling message* is most often aimed at persuading the customer to try something new. It tries to sell the benefits of a general type of product rather than the benefits of one seller's product over a competitor's similar product. Sellers of new products recognize that potential customers tend to resist change and that considerable persuasion may be needed to get them to experiment with something new. Customers must be convinced that an experiment is in their own best interests. When the electric toothbrush was first put on the market, for instance, a sales message that stressed the qualities of Brand A over Brand B would have been ineffective. No electric toothbrushes could be sold until the customer was shown that the device was worth trying.

Primary messages are also important when a product's current acceptance is challenged by some new technological development. The market now offers a water sprayer that will remove hard-to-reach food particles. To maintain sales, a manufacturer of electric toothbrushes might have to resell the advantages of electric toothbrushes in general rather than selling the advantages of his product over another brand.

Selective Message

A *selective selling message* stresses the points of distinction between one seller's product or service and another seller's similar product or service. When he chooses to use a selective message, the seller assumes that the potential customer is familiar with the general nature of the product and its uses and benefits. A selective message is also used to encourage customers to remain loyal to a seller's product in the face of competition or to buy more of the seller's product than they have been buying.

There may be many different points of distinction between products. One seller's product may be more reliable, serviceable, and durable than a competitor's product. It may be safer to use. It may have features that make it visually attractive. It may be more versatile than a competing product. It may be less expensive. The point of distinction is sometimes just an attractive package or even a brand name that the customer has come to associate with desirable product qualities.

ECONOMIC AND SOCIAL ACHIEVEMENTS OF SELLING MESSAGES

Some people today question the necessity of selling communication. They feel that consumers know their own needs and wants and should require no persuasion to buy. They think it is an economic and social waste for someone else to try to direct a consumer's buying decisions.

In this country, the annual expenditure for advertising is now over $15 billion. Although there are no reliable estimates of expenditures for personal selling, this figure is probably three to four times the expenditure for advertising—perhaps as much as $50 billion. So-called "free" publicity may actually account for another $4 to $6 billion, making the total yearly cost of selling and selling communication over $70 billion. The fact that so much money is spent each year on selling indicates that most people are convinced of its value. However, there are some definite justifications for sales communication, and these justifications will be discussed in the following paragraphs.

Educating Consumers to Product or Service Values

Ultimate consumers as a group are slow to act in their own best interests. They tend to resist spending even for goods and services that would make their lives much more pleasant. Many persons would never buy insurance—which everyone needs—unless someone urged them to do so.

Each of the new products and services appearing on the market is intended to satisfy a human need or want, but often this need or want

If you've got a customer relations problem, it may be your air conditioning.

If the weather's hot and business is sagging, take a look at your air conditioning.

If it isn't cooling like it should be, let General Electric get things straightened out. And cooled off. Maybe you need to replace a worn out cooling system.

In some cases, GE's Weathertron® Heat Pump is best. It heats as well as cools and comes in ratings up to 20 tons. Other buildings may need GE's "Zoneline" system for perimeter-type area-by-area cooling and heating.

Whatever system you buy, you can count on it to hold up. For example, the exclusive General Electric Climatuff compressor is now quietly chalking up a 99% reliability record in 70,000 installations. What else do you know that's 99% reliable?

You may need some application engineering help and your GE Central Air Conditioning contractor can provide it. Just look him up in the Yellow Pages and call. He has what it takes.

GENERAL ELECTRIC

General Electric

Does this advertisement contain a primary message or a selective message? What do you think the goals of this message might be, from the seller's point of view?

is latent. This means that it is not recognized by the consumer. The qualities inherent in a new product cannot always be seen by casual inspection, and it may not be easy to place some products in locations where everyone can inspect them. The qualities of the new goods must be communicated by sellers through various channels.

For example, women who had always slaved in trying to remove baked-on grease from ovens had to be told that an oven can now be cleaned electronically with no work and bother. Telling, however, was not enough; the customer had to be shown that the process really worked quickly and effectively, that it was safe to use, and that it was free from mechanical failure. The customer also had to be convinced that the extra price for this feature was well worth it in view of the time that was saved and the inconvenience that was avoided. Only through sales communication could this have been accomplished.

Stimulating Production

The urge to buy and consume, stimulated by selling communication, tends to make consumers more productive than they would otherwise be. They know they must work harder and make a greater contribution to others so that they can earn money to satisfy their own expanding needs.

Some years ago, in a New England mill town, young working women had few urgent wants for new clothes and finery. The stores in the community stocked only standard convenience goods. But when one of the large mail-order houses distributed its catalogs in the textile mill and opened an order office, the attractive clothes presented and described stimulated the women to want them. This meant that they had to increase their production to earn money to pay for what they wanted.

Helping Consumers To Buy Wisely

The variety of goods and services available has never been greater than it is today. Wise buying requires knowledge of product features and benefits. By seeing and listening to the messages of different sellers, the consumer can set up a scale of product and service values best suited to himself. He can weigh, for example, the worth to himself of buying a new shirt in comparison with buying a fine meal at a leading restaurant.

Buying and selling are increasingly becoming exercises in decision making. This is particularly true when a business consumer rather than

American Airlines

A salesperson must adjust his message to fit the intended receiver. This airline consultant knows that a message directed to these young people must have a different structure and content than a message directed to businessmen traveling by air.

an ultimate consumer is the recipient of the selling message. Producers, wholesalers, and retailers look to sales communication for help in buying goods and services that will produce better goods and services, reduce expenses, improve profit margins, eliminate some hazards and insure against others, and improve their public images.

PREPARING THE MESSAGE

At this point in our discussion of communication, we will not go into detail on how to prepare the sales message. Later in the book you will learn techniques of preparing sales messages to be delivered by personal salesmen and to be transmitted via broadcast or printed media. There are, however, some basic principles of preparing sales messages that you should consider now. A great amount of research on sales messages has been done, and some important findings of this research were set down by the chairman of the board of the Equitable Life Assurance Society:

1. The more trusted the source of the message, the more readily the message will be accepted.
2. The more balanced the message, the more likely it is to be effective.
3. The higher the educational level of the audience, the more important it is for the communicator to be completely fair and to give all sides of the argument.
4. The more threatening the message, the less likely it is to be believed.
5. The greater the involvement of the audience in the topic of the message, the more receptive the audience is likely to be.
6. The greater the acceptance of a message, the stronger is the tendency to receive additional messages which support the new position.
7. The lower the self-esteem of the audience, the more resistant to messages it tends to be.

Every person involved in formulating a sales message should keep these points in mind.

CHECKING YOUR KNOWLEDGE

Vocabulary:

(1) primary selling message (2) selective selling message

Review questions:

1. From the seller's point of view, what are the goals of a selling message?
2. With what products are primary selling messages generally used? With what products are selective messages used?
3. What are some points of distinction between products that a selective message may emphasize?
4. Describe some of the economic and social achievements of selling messages.
5. List five important findings of recent research on sales messages.

For discussion:

1. Can you think of a well-known convenience item that seems to be losing popularity and sales to a newer brand? How should the businesses handling the first brand adjust their sales messages to the situation?
2. For each of the following products, tell whether you think sales messages would be effective in influencing present customers to buy the products more often or in greater quantities: TV dinners, detergent, children's shoes, gasoline, and floor coverings. Justify your answers.

part D

the channel of communication

For centuries, sales communication has taken place on a face-to-face basis. As written language was developed, letters were added to the available channels of communication. With the invention of the printing press, communicating through newspapers and direct-mail announcements became possible. In the late 19th Century, radio was invented; and in the 1930's, television.

It was not until the last 100 years that selling through nonpersonal channels was more than an announcement of where and when goods were available. Today, however, nonpersonal channels of communication are valuable aspects of sales communication. For many sellers, the decision on which communication channel to use—personal or nonpersonal—is not always an easy one to make.

PERSONAL VERSUS NONPERSONAL CHANNELS

Whether to rely on personal or on nonpersonal channels depends upon the nature of the product being sold, the nature of the market segment to be reached, and the size of the firm. In the following paragraphs, you will learn about some of the advantages and disadvantages of the two types of communication channels.

Personal Channels

The most important personal channel is, of course, the salesman. You have learned that from the customer's viewpoint, the salesman is the sender of the message; but from the viewpoint of the selling organization, the salesman is a channel. Another personal channel is, oddly enough, the customer. Customers who spread favorable product and service information to other customers are not consciously employed as channels by the seller, but their word-of-mouth advertising sometimes is more effective than the seller's prepared message.

When Personal Channels Are Used. Sellers of industrial goods must rely largely on salesmen because their firms may have to solve the

New York Telephone Company

The telephone is an important aid to effective communication. Research is constantly being conducted to find new ways in which telephones can be used. These exhibits were part of a medical convention and demonstrated new uses for telephones in the medical profession.

problems of business consumers. Industrial and institutional buyers may require special equipment adapted to their needs, assured sources of supply for a specific quality of material, and the engineering know-how that a salesman's firm is best able to provide. Such situations could not be handled through nonpersonal channels. Among the consumer goods for which personal channels are required are clothing, home furnishings, sporting goods, eyeglasses and hearing aids, major automotive equipment, home utilities, special cuts of meat, and homes and apartments.

Generally speaking, selling organizations rely on personal channels in the following situations:

1. When the product being sold must be demonstrated.
2. When the product must be tailor-made to a customer's needs.
3. When the sale involves a trade-in.
4. When the selling organization is small and cannot afford much advertising.
5. When the market segment is small.
6. When the product is expensive or is bought infrequently.

Advantages and Disadvantages of Personal Channels. Most sellers do not consciously think of the advantages or disadvantages of personal channels. They look upon personal selling as a necessity. Our marketing system is extremely complex. Although some goods and services may move directly from the producer to the consumer, merchandise generally passes through a number of hands. A manufacturer of small electric light bulbs, for example, might sell them to a toy manufacturer who needs the bulbs for his toys. The toy manufacturer might use the services of an advertising agency to help his salesmen sell the toys to a wholesale distributor. The wholesale distributor might sell to local wholesalers or to large retail stores. The local wholesaler might sell to hobby shops, department stores, or variety stores; and these firms sell to the ultimate consumer.

Each of these sellers needs personal salesmen to help move the toys toward the children who will play with them. Nonpersonal channels alone could not do the job. The efforts of persons working in nonpersonal channels of communication are often unsuccessful because of poor personal selling. Advertising and other nonpersonal channels cannot and should not be expected to do the entire job of moving goods into the hands of the ultimate consumer.

From the selling organization's viewpoint, a major disadvantage of relying on personal channels is finding qualified salespeople. Even if such persons can be found, training them is costly. For example, a survey by the Sales Manpower Division of the Sales Executives Club of New York estimated that in 1969, the cost of training 152,000 salesmen for personal selling in the 15 major manufacturing industries should average about $6,500 per man—not including salaries.

Keeping qualified salespeople can also be a problem. One of the most common causes of discontent—and one which the seller can do nothing about—is inherent in the job. The salesman must produce sales, yet he has no direct control over his customers. He has responsibility but, essentially, no authority. In other fields, a person who supervises others or works with materials and ideas generally has control over the elements upon which his success depends. No one controls today's customer.

Nonpersonal Channels

The nonpersonal channels of communication include printed media, display, broadcast media, "free" publicity, and special promotions. There are two major differences between personal and nonpersonal selling. First, nonpersonal selling is a one-way communication from seller to potential customer while personal selling—because it is a face-to-face encounter between salesman and customer—is a two-way communication. The other difference is that nonpersonal selling is directed toward groups rather than individuals.

When Nonpersonal Channels Are Used. Few sellers will rely solely on nonpersonal channels to transmit their sales messages, but nonpersonal channels could be relied upon to perform almost all the communication job in the following situations:

1. When the product being sold is well known, but the customer must be periodically reminded of its availability.
2. When the difference between one brand and a competing brand is small.
3. When the statement of a single point of distinction will influence the buying decisions of many customers.
4. When the price of the product is low and the product is new and intriguing.
5. When a special price concession is being provided for a limited time.

Advantages and Disadvantages of Nonpersonal Channels. There are certain distinct advantages of nonpersonal channels, and every seller should be aware of them:

1. Nonpersonal channels quickly gain customer attention. A prospect may refuse to talk to a salesman, but it is hard for him to ignore all the sales messages in newspapers, magazines, and direct mail, and on radio and television.
2. Nonpersonal channels can reach customers at much less cost per contact than can personal channels.
3. The content of nonpersonal sales messages can be controlled by the seller. The seller, however, cannot always control the statements of his salesmen.

Nonpersonal channels also have some disadvantages, and sellers should recognize them:

1. A message transmitted through a nonpersonal channel is less compelling than is a personal message.
2. Since nonpersonal sales messages are projected to a mass audience, they cannot be adjusted to the specific needs of each prospect.
3. In the sale of many products, the nonpersonal channel cannot answer all the questions or objections a potential customer may have. It might attempt to anticipate such questions and objections, but it cannot deal specifically with each one.

THE PROMOTIONAL MIX

Seldom is one communication channel used by a seller; he usually combines a number of channels for best results. The combination of selling tools used for any given purpose is called the *promotional mix.* For most sellers, personal channels are the primary means of communicating with customers; and these channels are supplemented by nonpersonal channels such as advertising and display. Sellers know that a customer is more likely to be influenced to buy if sales messages strike at him through several channels and appeal to all his senses.

A great deal of research is now being done to compare the effectiveness of certain nonpersonal channels with other nonpersonal channels and to compare the effectiveness of nonpersonal channels with personal channels. It has been found, for example, that newspapers are best suited for communicating messages about new products, current sales events, where to buy specific goods, and what prices are being asked. They stimulate customers who are almost ready to buy. Magazines, since they have more permanence than daily newspapers, are better suited for carrying messages involving specialized knowledge which must reach narrower segments of the total consumer market. They are better suited to the evaluative phase of buying where a customer must "try on" the goods mentally to see if they will satisfy him.

The messages transmitted through broadcast media last only for a moment. Thus, sellers using these channels must depend on a considerable amount of repetition if customers are to grasp the message. A broadcast medium generally has more control over its audience than does a printed medium. It is easier to flick a page than to turn off a set, especially if there is danger of missing part of an interesting program. For many listeners, the radio is a friendly and steady companion; thus, it is suited to repeated advertising of well-established products. Television, since it stimulates both sight and hearing, has much wider possibilities for carrying selling messages.

CHECKING YOUR KNOWLEDGE

Vocabulary:

promotional mix

Review questions:

1. What is the most important personal channel of communication? In what situations do selling firms rely almost entirely on personal channels?

2. What are some advantages and disadvantages of personal channels?
3. Name the nonpersonal channels of communication that are most often used in selling. In what situations can these channels perform virtually all the communication job?
4. What are some advantages and disadvantages of nonpersonal channels?
5. In what selling situations are newspapers more effective than other nonpersonal channels?

For discussion:

1. Do customers seem to place more reliance on what salespeople tell them about a product or on the advertising of the product?
2. Would a manufacturer of automobile seat covers be more likely to use personal or nonpersonal channels of communication?

part E

receiver of the message

Before an act of communication can be completed, the receiver must pick up the message that has been encoded by the sender and transmitted through a channel of communication. The message must travel to the receiver's decoder—nervous system and brain together—where it is retranslated into a form the receiver can understand.

How will the receiver decode my message? This is perhaps the most difficult question that the sender of a sales message must answer. As you learned in Part A, probably no message is decoded in the exact way the sender intended. But it is possible to control the decoding process to some extent by: (1) gaining a thorough understanding of customer behavior; (2) structuring the sales message so that it is in line with a customer's buying motives; and (3) being aware of the denotative and connotative meanings of the symbols used in the sales message.

DECODING THE MESSAGE

The entire decoding process takes place within a few seconds, and often the customer is not consciously aware of it. The process is, however, a quite complex one; and scientific knowledge of exactly how a message is received and retranslated is still incomplete. It is known, though, that every individual has a perceptual field, that a message must enter this field and become "in figure," and that certain cues must be taken from the total message and used to formulate thoughts about the message.

The Perceptual Field

In Part A, you learned that perception is the receiver's awareness of a transmitted message. Before perception can occur, however, a sales message must enter the receiver's *perceptual field*. This includes everything that an individual sees or knows about his world. What is included in an individual's perceptual field depends upon: (1) his past experiences, (2) his needs and wants, (3) his emotional makeup, (4) his mental set, (5) his membership in a particular social class, (6) his membership in a particular group within a social class, and (7) his physical environment.

The total perceptual field has two parts—the figure and the ground. The *figure* is the portion of the perceptual field that is in focus at any given time; it is the portion upon which the receiver is concentrating. The *ground* is the portion of the field that is not in focus. The sender of a sales message must make sure that his message becomes the figure of a customer's perceptual field. He can do this by capturing the customer's attention and showing how his product or service can satisfy the customer's need or want.

The activity of separating figure from ground in a perceptual field is similar to the activity of taking a picture. If someone wants to photograph a pretty girl standing in a field of wildflowers, he will focus the camera on the girl's features; and she becomes the figure of the camera's perceptual field. The wildflowers, trees, and sky become the ground.

Formulating Thoughts

After the sales message has become the figure of the receiver's perceptual field, the receiver's decoder is ready to take different symbols, or cues, from the message and organize these cues into thoughts. Suppose that a saleswoman is showing a dress to a customer and has phrased her sales message so that it is the figure of the customer's perceptual field. The saleswoman makes the statement, "This shade of blue and the flared skirt are quite popular this season." This statement, particularly the word "blue," can be a cue. This cue can lead to the customer's forming the thought, "Blue is my best color."

For the salesman of an intangible, such as insurance, it is often difficult to get his message into the receiver's perceptual field. Potential receivers often have a mental set against buying insurance, even though they may need it. Of all salesmen, those selling intangibles must be perhaps the most skilled in communication.

After cues have been organized into thoughts or concepts, positive or negative values are attached to the concepts. These values help the customer decide what action to take. The concept that "The dress is blue, and blue is my most becoming color" might have considerable positive value. However, the concept that "The flared skirt wouldn't be at all flattering to me" might have considerable negative value and might cancel out the earlier positive concept.

As you have learned, a customer's mental set is extremely important in organizing cues into thoughts. In our example, for instance, the customer's mental set might make her unwilling to buy any new dress, no matter whether she liked it or not. Thus, she would probably tell the saleswoman immediately that she was not interested in buying, even before other thoughts had been formulated.

MANIPULATING THE DECODING PROCESS

No seller can hope to control the decoding process, but he can manipulate it by the way he phrases his sales message. In a face-to-face contact, the salesman should be able to determine at least four elements of a customer's perceptual field: (1) the customer's needs and wants, (2) his membership in a particular social class, (3) his membership in a particular group within a social class, and (4) his physical environment. Feedback and a knowledge of customer buying behavior can help the salesman identify customer needs and wants. Through such physical factors as dress, speech, and actions, it is possible to determine the social class and possibly the social group to which an individual belongs. And the salesman and the selling organization exercise direct control over physical environment when the customer is in the seller's place of business.

Influence of Social Class Membership

Almost all societies tend to have layers of social classes, such as upper, middle, and lower. Persons fall into a particular class because of differences in such elements as income, education, occupation, and style of living. Each social class has certain distinct characteristics, many of which are evidenced in buying behavior. Knowledge of the behavior of social classes is helpful in choosing effective communication symbols. Generally speaking, a person in the middle class has interests extending well into the past and the future, while the person in the lower class lives more from day to day. The middle-class person tends to have broader interests, while the lower-class person is almost entirely concerned with his immediate surroundings. The middle-class person is more rational in his thinking, while the lower-class person tends to be emotional.

The seller should consider the social class membership of his customer in phrasing the sales message. For instance, a message about a dishwasher would probably be accepted by both the middle-class and the lower-class person. But the middle-class person would tend to concentrate upon the cues dealing with how the dishwasher would look in the kitchen; and the lower-class person would concentrate on the cues dealing with the dishwasher's labor-saving features.

Influence of Group Membership

In every social class, there are groups to which consumers belong. A *group* is defined as two or more persons who have common interests and who interact on a continuing basis. There are two general kinds of groups—primary groups and secondary groups. A *primary group* is a small, intimate group that is usually an extension of the individual and his self-image. The most important primary group for the majority of people is the family, and the family has a great influence on a person's buying behavior. A new bride, for instance, usually continues to use the household products her mother uses.

Secondary groups are larger and more formal; they often consist of a number of primary groups. A large corporation is an example of a secondary group. Although secondary groups have less of an influence on buying behavior than do primary groups, they are still of considerable importance to sellers. In a large corporation, for instance, employees may want to buy clothing that conforms to the standards set by company executives; and their buying actions may reflect the spending patterns of these executives.

BEHAVIORAL SCIENCES AND SELLING COMMUNICATION

It is hard for a seller to find out about the perceptual field elements of past experiences, emotional makeup, and mental set. However, a seller can gain some general understanding of these elements by learning as much as he can about customer behavior. To explain the "why" of customer behavior, creative sellers have adopted the principles of certain social sciences. These social sciences are called behavioral sciences because they study the actions of human beings and try to explain how people behave, why they behave as they do, and what the relationship is between an individual's behavior and his total environment.

The two behavioral sciences upon which sellers depend most are psychology and sociology. *Psychology* is the study of individual mental processes and behavior. It concentrates on the individual and his actions. The concepts dealing with needs, wants, and motivation which you learned about in Chapter 4 are drawn from psychology. *Sociology* is the study of the development, structure, and function of human groups within a society. Whereas psychology is concerned with explaining why an individual behaves as he does, sociology is concerned with groups of individuals and with explaining how they behave within the framework of their society. The concepts of social class and group membership are drawn from sociology.

No salesman has to be an expert in the behavioral sciences. The field is a fascinating one to study, however, and any potential salesman who wants to do research in this area will find that the extra knowledge will benefit him. The salesman who understands why customers behave as

Aldens, Inc.

In the future, sellers and customers may communicate by using this Picturephone. Both sender and receiver would have access to Picturephone units. The two parties can see and talk to each other, and merchandise can be demonstrated much as it would be shown on television.

they do is generally the salesman who can communicate his message most effectively. The more knowledge a seller has about his customers. the better equipped he is to make a sale to the mutual satisfaction of both parties.

CHECKING YOUR KNOWLEDGE

Vocabulary:

(1) perceptual field
(2) figure
(3) ground
(4) group
(5) primary group
(6) secondary group
(7) psychology
(8) sociology

Review questions:

1. What are three ways for a sender to control, at least in part, the decoding process?
2. List the seven elements that influence the makeup of an individual's perceptual field.
3. Briefly describe the process of decoding a message.
4. What four elements of a customer's perceptual field can a salesman generally determine in a face-to-face contact?
5. Why are social class and group membership important in selling and sales communication?
6. How can a salesman benefit from studying the behavioral sciences as they relate to selling?

For discussion:

1. Will it ever be possible for a sender to control the decoding process of a receiver? Why or why not?
2. Would social class membership or group membership probably have more influence on a customer's buying behavior?

BUILDING YOUR SKILLS

Improving your English:

Complete each of the following sentences by writing on a separate sheet of paper the correct form of the word given in parentheses.

1. Of the two departments, the displays of men's furnishings were ______. (good)
2. Peggy's modeling of the evening dress was the ______ of all. (beautiful)
3. David produced the ______ sales record in the entire store. (large)
4. The receiving department is the ______ of all departments in the store. (busy)
5. The performance of this engine is ______ than that of the Hermedes. (poor)
6. The first cashier was the ______ of the group. (slow)
7. Of the two figurines, the gold one appeared ______. (tall)
8. Jack's method of dividing the commissions is the ______ of the three suggested. (fair)

9. The Casual suit is ______ than the Rigby suit. (small)
10. Although the automobile has a short wheelbase, it is the ______ in its class. (long)

Improving your arithmetic:

Perform the addition exercises given below.

1. Ruth Jones sold to one customer 3¾ yards of bonded wool, 1⅞ yards of dacron-cotton, ⅜ yard of organdy, 2¼ yards of corduroy, 1⅓ yards of velveteen, and 3½ yards of dotted swiss. How many yards did the customer buy?
2. Gary White sold the following amounts of grass rope during one day: 21½ feet; 4⅔ yards; 3¾ feet; 8⅓ feet; 9⅓ yards; and 10½ yards. How many feet of grass rope did Gary sell?
3. A customer of Ferguson's Hardware Store wants to fence the back and both sides of a lot that measures 103 feet, 8 inches wide by 204 feet, 6 inches deep. How many feet of fencing will the customer need?
4. The Newton Distributing Company used the following quantities of paint in remodeling its offices:

   20½ gallons flat white latex
   10¾ gallons honeysuckle latex
   12¼ gallons seamist green latex
   1¼ gallons white enamel
   ½ gallon honeysuckle enamel
   ¾ gallon seamist green enamel

   How many gallons of latex paint were used? How many gallons of enamel paint were used?
5. The Howard Construction Company has just ordered the following quantities of nails:

   75¼ lb. #10 common nails
   50½ lb. #8 common nails
   41¾ lb. #8 finishing nails
   20¼ lb. #6 finishing nails
   50¾ lb. roofing nails
   10¼ lb. wire nails

   How many pounds of nails were ordered?

Improving your research skills:

1. Prepare a list of words and phrases commonly used in selling that might have disagreeable connotative meanings to some people and not to others.
2. Prepare a list of words and phrases commonly used in selling that are likely to trigger a predetermined response from a customer.
3. Six compact automobiles seem to be in direct competition: Dodge Dart, Plymouth Valiant, Rambler American, Ford Falcon, Chevrolet Nova, and Volkswagen. Determine how the public images and the selling

messages of these cars differ. Try to find out whether manufacturers of the six cars are trying to communicate with the same customers or whether different customers respond to different cars because of characteristics each group associates with the car of his choice. Present your findings in report form.

APPLYING YOUR KNOWLEDGE

Case problem:

Hunt's Department Store carries lines of inexpensive to average-priced merchandise. Although sales of the inexpensive merchandise have been high, the overall profit resulting from these sales has been so low that management is considering dropping the inexpensive lines. Sales of average-priced merchandise are good, and profits resulting from these sales contribute substantially to the store's earnings. If Hunt's drops its inexpensive lines and stocks average-priced to above-average-priced goods, different communication techniques must be used. Suggest a comprehensive communication campaign the store might employ to successfully upgrade its image and promote its merchandise.

Continuing project:

In your manual, you should prepare a section describing the techniques you will use in communicating with your customers. Discuss the image you want to create for your business and your product, the channels of communication you would most likely use, and the kinds of messages you would use. Describe the problems you might encounter in communicating with your customers, and tell how you would overcome these problems.

Extra credit:

There is growing evidence that communication takes place among individuals without use of the five senses. This kind of communication is called telepathy. Research this subject in your library, looking for references to parapsychology and psychical research as well as to telepathy. A large encyclopedia should give you some information, and the *Readers' Guide to Periodical Literature* will refer you to magazine articles on the subject. Several books which may prove helpful are: *Beyond the Reach of Sense* by Rosalind Hayward, *Challenge of Psychical Research* by Gardner Murphy, and *Hidden Channels of the Mind* by Louise Rhine.

Write a report of your findings, and discuss whether this kind of communication might ever be used in selling.

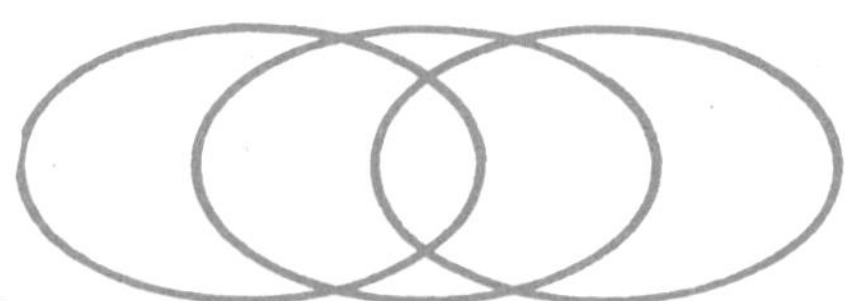

chapter 6

studying the product

KEY QUESTIONS

A Why is the salesman's task of product differentiation more difficult today than ever before?

B What are the benefits of product branding to the selling firm, to the salesman, and to the ultimate consumer?

C Who derives the most value from good packaging and labeling: the consumer or the seller?

D Which of the sources of product information are readily available to virtually every salesman?

E In communicating product information, why do salesmen generally emphasize product benefits rather than product features?

part A

differentiating the product

One large retail chain reports that during a recent year it carried 5,685 different items in stock and that in the following year it was offered 3,696 new items. A considerable number of items had to be dropped from stock periodically to make room for new or improved products. It has also been said that 50 percent of the items carried in the 1950 Sears catalog are no longer listed. They have been replaced by new and better products that were unknown even a few years ago. Some consumer-goods items that weren't marketed until after World War II are stereo phonographs, portable transistor radios, tape recorders, prepared food mixes, frozen baked goods, portable electric hair dryers, color television sets, self-cleaning ovens, and permanent-press clothing. Business consumers have seen hundreds of product innovations in the last 20 years, particularly in the field of automation.

What does all this mean to the salesman? It means that he is charged with the major responsibility of telling customers about new or improved products and about the particular advantages of his products. If he is to sell successfully, he must make his products stand out over competing products in the customer's mind.

REASONS FOR STUDYING PRODUCT INFORMATION

Many of the "new" items produced by manufacturers today are simply adaptations of established merchandise, and intense competition results in a number of almost identical products. Of the producers with nearly equal product-designing skills, success goes to those few who have the best salesmen. The "best salesmen" are those who can communicate to prospective customers the values of their products or services. To communicate effectively, the salesman must know his product inside out.

From the salesman's viewpoint, there are four main reasons for studying his product carefully:

1. To provide goods that will best fill customers' needs and wants.
2. To single out the right selling points in presenting the right goods to customers.
3. To answer customers' questions.
4. To gain self-confidence so that confidence on the part of the customer can be inspired.

Because of the need for technical product information, some selling firms employ specially trained people as their salesmen. For example, wholesale drug houses often hire former druggists to sell to retail pharmacies. Textbook publishers often employ former teachers to sell textbooks, particularly at the high-school level. Machinery manufacturers often hire college graduates who have majored in mechanical engineering.

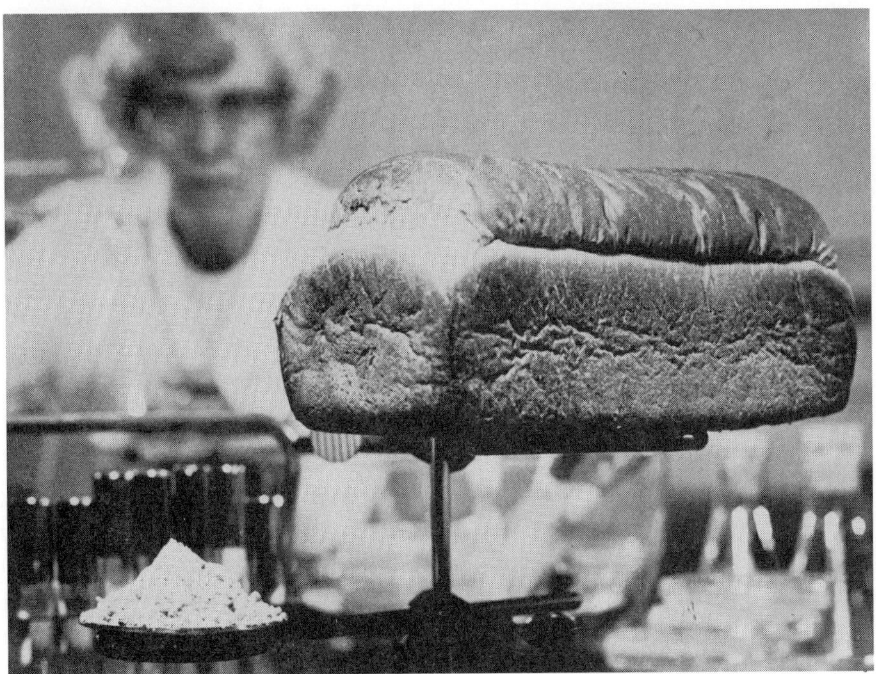

Esso Research and Engineering Co.

New products—often, amazing products—are continually being developed, and the salesman interprets the features of these products into consumer benefits. A leading oil company has developed this laboratory-made bread enriched with synthetic protein derived from petroleum products. How might a salesman sell this food-from-oil to the consumer?

The expert salesman should have more product information than he needs for any one sales presentation. A person can never know too much about the product or service that he sells, but he must be careful to present only the important selling points. Some salesmen actually talk themselves out of sales. They feel that the customer must be given all the product information they have, and they bore the customer with a long sales monologue.

ANALYZING PRODUCT FEATURES AND BENEFITS

The technique of creating, selecting, and stressing the points of superiority of a specific product is called *product differentiation.* It is one of the most important techniques salesmen use. For example, when General Mills first marketed its Wondra brand of flour, the chief point of differentiation was that the flour need not be sifted before use. The point of differentiation may be either a product feature or a product benefit; but salesmen generally choose to emphasize a product's benefits.

Many persons confuse the terms "product feature" and "product benefit." *Product features* are the physical elements of a product, such as size, color, and composition. *Product benefits* are the positive values that a customer will receive when he uses a product that has certain product features.

Product Features

There are really two kinds of product features. The first kind includes those factors contained in the product and which can readily be seen or otherwise sensed. For nearly all consumer goods and industrial goods, these features are: (1) size; (2) weight; (3) shape; (4) design; (5) pattern; (6) color; (7) material of composition; (8) construction; (9) finish or texture; (10) odor or taste; and (11) packaging.

The second kind of product feature is not contained in the product itself but rather reveals associations that may be important to the customer. Some of these features are: (1) price; (2) brand or designer; (3) fashion significance; (4) exclusiveness; (5) conditions of manufacture (quality control, sanitary conditions, etc.); (6) competing products and comparative features; (7) origin; (8) history or background of the product; (9) availability; (10) advertising; (11) special services (terms of sale, repair and servicing, etc.); (12) how to use; and (13) how to care for.

"And here's a great new safety feature! This bit isn't cardboard anymore!"

Changing Times

Construction is a product feature that can usually be seen readily by a salesman and customer. Often, it is one of the first features a salesman mentions.

Product Benefits

The benefits that a product can provide customers—because of both its inherent features and its associations—comprise the most important product information to be conveyed in a sales talk. From the viewpoint of the ultimate consumer, some important product benefits are: (1) pleasing to the senses (appearance, taste, sound, etc.); (2) comfort (warmth, coolness, softness, etc.); (3) protection and contribution to health; (4) prestige or importance resulting from possession of the product; (5) relaxation and escape from routine; (6) contribution to knowledge and satisfaction of curiosity; (7) versatility; (8) serviceability and durability; (9) ease of use, operation, and upkeep; and (10) savings in cost of operation and upkeep.

Some of these benefits may also be important to business consumers. However, product benefits that will apply mainly to business consumers include: (1) rate of sale; (2) markup; (3) stock turnover; (4) space required for storage; (5) lack of danger from obsolescence and depreciation; (6) little sales effort required; (7) savings in man-hours of labor; (8) low changeover and installation costs and minimum disruption of morale and work schedules; (9) increased production; and (10) improvements that will make the product more salable.

Example of Analyzing Features and Benefits

Let us see how a salesman might determine features and benefits of a specific product—a woman's scarf. The features inherent in the scarf might be: large; lightweight; square; finely detailed floral design; attractive color; made of pure silk; firm, plain weave with a hand-rolled hem; preshrunk; glossy finish; smooth and soft to the touch; and individually gift-wrapped in vellum envelope.

The features revealing associations to the customer might be: price, $5; scarf of this type is currently in fashion; will coordinate with many articles of clothing; pattern is exclusive with the store; guaranteed against fading; fabric is imported from Italy; and design is authentic copy of 18th Century French tapestry.

Benefits to the ultimate consumer might be: eye-catching and becoming; soft and comfortable against the skin; provides protection and warmth; will be admired by friends; can be used as a neckpiece or as a belt; will last for a long time without shrinking, fading, or fraying; easy to wash; and needs no special care.

All this information would not be communicated to each customer. Rather, the salesman must decide which features and benefits would be most meaningful to each particular customer. In later chapters you will see how this decision is made. Other features and benefits should be held in reserve to be used when the occasion warrants. Even if some information is never used, the knowledge that it is there if needed gives the salesman self-confidence.

STUDYING COMPETING PRODUCTS

A salesman's product knowledge is incomplete until he has compared the features and benefits of his product with those of competitors. He needs a detailed knowledge of competing goods to determine the chief selling points of his own merchandise and to meet customers' objections.

Ordinarily it is unwise to talk about a competitor or his goods unless the subject is introduced by the customer. This is a good rule to follow in order to avoid focusing attention upon a competitor and what he has to sell. However, a salesman should always be prepared to discuss the relative merits of his goods and those of his competitors, for customers sometimes ask questions about the features and benefits of competing products. Occasionally a salesman may even recommend a competitor's product if it is clearly more suited to the customer's needs than is his own. This evidence of the salesman's desire to serve the customer can build goodwill and result in many future sales.

In nearly every line, there is one product that outsells all others. Salesmen of brands other than the leading ones sometimes get inferiority complexes about their selling contributions. But if these salesmen would compare their products with the leading product, they would probably find that their products have certain features that make them more suitable than the leading product to certain customers. In fact, their products may be better in many respects but may not have been given the same selling effort that the leader received. There are some poor products on the market with which a good salesman should not associate himself; but in every line there are excellent products that deserve a salesman's loyalty, even though they are not top sellers.

CHECKING YOUR KNOWLEDGE

Vocabulary:

(1) product differentiation
(2) product features
(3) product benefits

Review questions:

1. What are the four main reasons why a salesman should know his merchandise?
2. Name at least eight readily seen features that may be contained in a product.
3. Name at least eight product features that may reveal associations to a customer.
4. Name at least eight product benefits that ultimate consumers may derive from a product.
5. Why is it important to know facts about competing products?

For discussion:

1. What product features and benefits will most customers insist upon in buying the following products? (a) men's suits, (b) hosiery, (c) kitchen carpeting, (d) breakfast cereal, and (e) occasional chairs. Justify your answers.
2. Since the customer is not required to care for goods until after he has purchased them, why should the salesman discuss the care of the product in his sales talk?
3. Should a salesman know as much about competing products as he does about his own? Explain your answer.

part B

product brands

What do customers first look for to distinguish one product from another? For many products, the first mark of identification is a brand. The term *brand* designates a word, letter, name, or design element that differentiates the goods or services of one seller from those of his competitors.

Virtually every consumer product sold in this country bears some kind of brand. The advantages of branding were discovered long ago, and patent-medicine manufacturers were among the first sellers in this country to use brand names. Some brands that were developed in the 19th Century can still be bought in stores. Quaker Oats and Ivory soap are two examples.

IMPORTANCE OF BRANDS

Branding is the most practical way for a seller to assure repeated demand for his goods. If a customer is pleased with an article that he has bought, he can get the same item again merely by requesting the same brand. The brand assures the customer of consistent product quality. From the viewpoints of both seller and customer, an established and respected brand adds value to merchandise. Many customers are not expert enough to determine the quality of goods by mere inspection. They must depend upon some symbol that assures merchandise values not apparent on the surface; a brand is such a symbol. When two articles are identical in appearance but one bears a recognized brand and the other does not, the first article has greater value to the customer because of the quality assurance the brand gives.

The manufacturer of specialty goods, particularly, relies on brands to build repeat business. He wants to create a situation in which a customer will not accept a substitute item but rather will insist upon buying his brand. Manufacturers of convenience goods, such as food products, use brands because they can easily create brand preference through advertising. It is true that a customer may accept a substitute for a convenience-goods brand; but a retailer can make shopping easier for the customer and can create goodwill by carrying recognized brands. With shopping goods, brands are probably less important. Customers want to compare assortments before buying, and they are guided more by the appearance of the articles than by hidden values.

CREATING BRANDS

Customers may hold any one of three different attitudes toward a particular brand—brand recognition, brand preference, and brand insistence. *Brand recognition* means that the customer has seen or heard about the brand but that he has no strong feelings about buying or not buying the branded product. *Brand preference* means that the customer or a person whose judgment he respects has bought the brand before and has been pleased with it. The customer would like to buy the same brand again but is willing to accept a substitute if he cannot find that brand. *Brand insistence* means that the customer will accept no substitutes for the brand he or his "authority" has previously bought. If he cannot find that brand, he will actually do without the product.

Every seller obviously would like to build brand insistence for the branded products he handles. Manufacturers and middlemen give careful attention to branding policies, choosing brand names, and protecting their brands.

Branding Policies

Both manufacturers and middlemen may put distinctive brand names and brand marks on the merchandise they produce or stock. A *brand name* is the portion of the total brand that can be written or spoken; "Dutch Boy" is a brand name for paint made by the National Lead Company. A *brand mark* is an illustrative design element which often accompanies a brand name. The brand mark for "Dutch Boy" paint is a tow-headed boy in Dutch costume, seated on a painter's ladder. Not every branded product will have a brand mark, but every branded product will have a brand name.

In formulating general policies on branding, businesses may choose from several alternatives:

1. *The business may use its own name on all the products it makes or stocks.* All "57 varieties" of products made by Heinz, for example, bear that company's name.
2. *The business may use a different brand name for each product line.* Sears, Roebuck uses the brand name "Craftsman" for its tools and the brand name "Kenmore" for its appliances.

3. *The business may use a different brand name for each product.* Procter & Gamble, which makes products in a number of varied lines, assigns a brand name to each different product in each product line. "Tide," "Bold," and "Cheer" detergents, "Duncan Hines" cake mix, and "Jif" peanut butter are examples.
4. *A business may use a different brand name for each price range.* American Motors manufactures, among other cars, the "Rebel," the "Javelin," and the "Ambassador." Each of these brand names represents a different price line.

It is important that the salesman understand his firm's branding policies. He may have to explain to a customer the relationship between his firm's brands or the differences between his firm's branding policies and those of another firm.

Choosing a Brand Name

Firms often sift through thousands of suggested brand names before they make a final selection for a new product. When a product is first introduced to the public, an effective brand name is extremely important. An intriguing name is often the sole factor that influences a customer to make the initial purchase of a product.

A good brand name meets the following requirements:

1. It is short and easy to spell and pronounce.
2. It is easy to recognize and remember.
3. It is versatile enough to be applied to new products that the business may introduce.
4. It is timely and will not become quickly outdated.
5. It has pleasant associations for customers and suggests some of the product's benefits.
6. It is not used with any similar product on the market.

Protecting a Brand

Because branding is so valuable in selling, businesses naturally want to keep their brands from being used by other businesses—particularly competitors. The Trademark Act is a federal law that permits a businessman to register his brand with the U. S. Patent Office in the Department of Commerce. Once a brand has been registered, it cannot be legally used later by another firm. A brand can be registered for a 20-year period, and the registration is renewable for 20-year periods.

Many persons think that the term trademark refers only to the illustrative design element that often accompanies a brand name. This

Here are some well-known brand marks. How many of them can you identify?

is not true. As you have learned, the design element is called the brand mark. A registered design element can be part of the trademark, but a registered brand name can also be part of the trademark. "Coca-Cola," for instance, is a trademark. A *trademark* is the legal term for the part of a brand that has been registered with the U.S. Patent Office. Elements of a brand that may be registered include: (1) a design element or picture; (2) the name of the product or producer; (3) letters, words, phrases, or numbers; and (4) distinctive type. A registered brand is identified in printed advertising or in packaging by either the letters "T.M." (for "trademark") or the letter "R" inside a circle (meaning "Registered"). These identifying marks are usually placed next to the brand name or brand mark.

NATIONAL BRANDS AND PRIVATE BRANDS

Sometimes a manufacturer will market all his production under his own brand. Sometimes he will place his own brand on products that are used in making other products. And sometimes a manufacturer will make goods and allow middlemen to sell these goods under their own brand names. Some manufacturers follow only one of these policies; some follow all three. Tire manufacturers, for instance, market their tires under their own brand names in their own retail outlets, produce for automobile manufacturers tires bearing their own brands, and produce for retailers tires that are sold under the retailers' brand names.

When a manufacturer markets his products under his own brand name, these products are called *national brands*. Appliances manufactured by the Whirlpool Corporation and bearing the brand name "Whirlpool" are national brands. When a manufacturer allows his products to be sold under a middleman's brand name, the products are called *private brands*. Whirlpool manufactures appliances that are sold by Sears, Roebuck under the brand name "Kenmore"; these appliances represent private brands.

Advantages of Private Brands to Retailers

There is a trend toward the sale of private brands by retailers. It is estimated that large retailers, such as Sears, Roebuck and J. C. Penney, sell about 90 percent of their volume in their own private brands. These private brands are comparable in quality to national brands and must meet rigid specifications set up by the retailer.

Many retailers feel that national brands may not bring customers back to their particular stores because these brands can be bought in competing stores. If retailers stock their own brands, they can build up repeat patronage. Moreover, the prices of national brands are often lowered by discount houses; and other retailers may be forced to cut their prices on national brands in order to compete. Thus, it becomes unprofitable to carry certain well-known brands. If the retailer uses his own brand, he is freed from direct price competition.

Often a retailer can buy unbranded goods for less than he would pay for identical goods bearing a national brand. This is especially true if the manufacturer's cost of advertising his own brand has been added to the price the retailer must pay. By purchasing identical or similar goods that the manufacturer has not had to advertise, the retailer can pass his savings on to the customer without sacrificing product quality.

Disadvantages of Private Brands to Retailers

The biggest problem in selling private brands is winning customer acceptance. Because national brands usually have the weight of a large advertising budget behind them, customers quickly become familiar with national brands. They read about them in magazines, hear about them on radio and television. In many cases, a customer has made up his mind to buy a national brand before he ever enters the store that carries it. He may never have heard of the retailer's private brand and will probably resist buying an unknown product.

Promoting private brands may result in higher local advertising costs than would be encountered in advertising national brands locally. Personal selling costs are higher, too. Creative selling by trained salespeople is needed to move private brands. Salesmen must be able to point out with authority and in detail the merits of their private brands. A salesman's product knowledge must often be greater to sell private brands than to sell national brands. Generally speaking, small retailers cannot afford to stock private brands because of the high development and selling costs they incur. They can, however, join a group of retailers which develops private brands for its member stores.

CHECKING YOUR KNOWLEDGE

Vocabulary:

(1) brand
(2) brand recognition
(3) brand preference
(4) brand insistence
(5) brand name
(6) brand mark
(7) trademark
(8) national brands
(9) private brands

Review questions:

1. Why is branding of products so important to selling organizations and to consumers?
2. Is branding more important for convenience goods or for shopping goods? Why?
3. From what alternatives may a businessman choose in formulating policies on branding?
4. List five requirements of a good brand name.
5. How can a businessman protect his product brand from being used by other businesses?
6. What are some advantages and disadvantages of private brands to retailers?

For discussion:

1. For the following items, would you recommend that a retailer use a national brand or a private brand? (a) filing cabinets, (b) sheets and pillowcases, (c) gift wrapping paper, (d) canned peaches, (e) women's dresses, and (f) transistor radios. Justify your answers.
2. What unusual method of branding goods have you seen recently?

part C

packaging and labeling

Today, customer preference is no longer limited to the merchandise itself; it includes the package in which the merchandise is contained. In buying breakfast cereal, for example, a housewife is influenced perhaps as much by an attractive package as she is by the flavor and nourishment of the cereal. Thus, to market products effectively the seller must determine not only what goods consumers want but also how they want these goods packaged.

FUNCTIONS OF PACKAGING

Packaging is the use of containers or wrapping materials to encase a product. For the consumer, packaging adds value to a product by: (1) protecting the product, (2) increasing the convenience of a product, (3) giving the product "eye appeal," (4) making the product easy to identify, and (5) adding versatility through reusable containers.

Packaging adds to the cost of merchandise, but most businessmen feel that the extra cost is justified. For the merchant, good packaging helps merchandise to be sold with a minimum of personal selling. Good packaging keeps merchandise from becoming shopworn and allows it to be easily advertised and displayed. A package can also describe the product inside and explain its uses and benefits; this information often gives the salesperson pertinent selling points that he can use in his sales talk. Another point in favor of proper packaging is that it tends to promote multiple selling of items. For example, if tennis balls are packed three to a carton, the customer will buy three balls rather than one ball, which he might buy if the balls were not packaged together.

Reasons for Increased Use of Packaging

Packaging America's products is now a $30-billion-a-year business. There are several important reasons why packaging is more important today than ever before. One reason is the trend toward self-service merchandising. Supermarkets, discount stores, variety stores, and even department stores allow customers to select the goods they want with a minimum of selling help and to pay for the goods at a central checkout station. Self-selection requires packaging that will keep products from becoming shopworn and that will attract customers' attention.

Another reason for the increased emphasis on good packaging is the demand for convenience in products. Today, more people are employed than at any other time in our country's history; and about 40 percent of the work force is made up of women. With their busy lives, working women demand products—particularly foods—packaged so that they can be quickly and conveniently used. Working women also want packages that give them product information at the point of purchase.

The growth of mass communications and the great increase in sales of color television sets have also contributed to the increased use of packaging. Now a seller can expose his product visually to millions of people in a single telecast. Many articles, such as detergents and beauty aids, have little eye appeal in themselves; but a colorful, well-designed package can make the product seem more dramatic. Through television, customers are often presold on articles. To keep preselling customers, sellers must continually search for the best packaging they can afford.

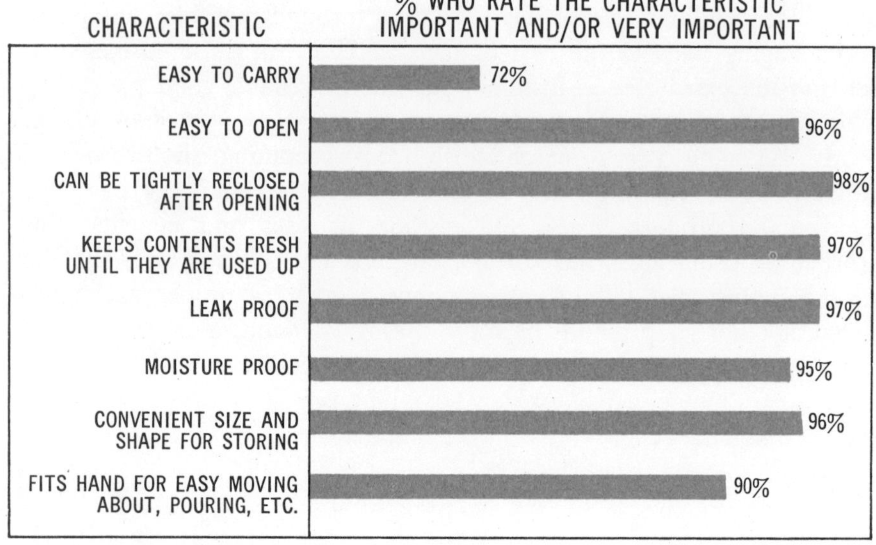

Sales Management

Sales Management *recently conducted a survey to discover what characteristics homemakers want most in product packaging. The eight most important demands are shown in the graph above, along with the percentages of homemakers surveyed who rated each characteristic as important or very important.*

Trends in Packaging

Each year at the National Packaging Exposition, some 400 different companies present the latest techniques in packaging. The packaging industry's most recent improvements have resulted in: (1) packaging of quantities acceptable to the consumer in a package that has utility; (2) improving visual description of the package's contents; and (3) increasing eye appeal of packages, so important when the customer makes his own merchandise selection without a salesperson's help.

The packaging industry is becoming concerned with the great accumulation of waste from used packaging materials. It is estimated that in one year the average American will pile up 1,600 pounds of waste in the form of used bottles, cans, plastic containers, and paper bags. The total cost of disposing of all this rubbish is some $3 billion a year. Attempts are being made to develop containers that can be consumed rather than being discarded. Some companies are even experimenting with edible envelopes as a means of packaging.

PRODUCING THE RIGHT PACKAGE

In general, packaging must be suited to the ultimate consumer's requirements. Packages must be available in a variety of sizes, shapes, and colors—often imprinted with pictures, cartoons, premium offers, and written messages. Packages often must contain a specific number of servings and must provide information on the care and use of the product. They must be convenient to store. They must be attractive. Sometmes packages are expected to have secondary uses. A glass containing peanut butter, for instance, may be used as a drinking glass after the peanut butter has been eaten. These packaging demands are especially important for food and drug products.

Packaging Materials

The most commonly used packaging materials are paper and related materials such as cardboard and cellophane, glass, wood, metal and metallic foil, and plastic. These materials may be used to make crates and boxes, bottles and jars, bags and wrapping paper, cans, and plastic sheets and bubbles.

Two of the most recent packaging developments are pull-tab tops and shrink-film packaging. The pull-tab top was first introduced on beverage cans, and it is now being used with many other kinds of canned products. Tape seals that can be whisked off easily are also being used on cans. Shrink-film packaging is currently used for both industrial and consumer goods. Plastic sheets are wrapped around a stack of items, then shrunk to the measurements of the stack under great heat. The items are thus protected from dirt and can be moved and stored easily. Since the individual items are held rigid, the danger of damage to items is greatly reduced.

The Middleman's Packaging Needs

Manufacturers must also consider the middleman's needs in selecting the best packaging methods, and they conduct a great amount of research on their middlemen's packaging requirements. Based on research findings, packaging may be designed by the manufacturer's packaging department, by an advertising agency, by an independent package designer, or by a supplier of packaging materials.

Manufacturers used to package their goods in bulk quantities, then distribute them to middlemen who either broke down the bulk quantities or sold the goods directly to the consumer from the bulk quantities. Crackers, for instance, used to come in huge barrels instead of in

Continental Can Company, Inc.

The packaging industry is the fourth largest industry in this country —led only by steel, automobiles, and petroleum. Huge quantities of packaging materials roll off production lines daily. This background wall of five thousand cans represents just 2.5 seconds production from the can lines of an important packaging manufacturer.

neat cardboard cartons. Customers bought the crackers they needed right from the barrel. Now, however, manufacturers pack merchandise in advance of sale in *unit prepacks* (individual packages) ready for sale and delivery to the customer.

The number of units to be included in a prepack is a major packaging consideration for the manufacturer. If a drug manufacturer, for example, were to sell his product only in gross lots, he would lose many potential sales to drugstores that needed only a dozen or so items. Drug manufacturers have solved this special problem by selling their drugs in large lots to wholesalers, who then sell in small lots to drugstores.

Some unit prepacks, on the other hand, may be too small. A hosiery manufacturer might be unwise to package each pair of women's hosiery in a separate box. Even small stores buy boxes containing three pairs each of a given style, size, and color; and many women buy a full box at one time. Packages of various sizes can help solve the problem of what quantity to place in prepacks, but the number of package variations increases the total stock that a middleman must carry.

LABELING THE PRODUCT

Closely related to the problem of selecting the proper package is the problem of labeling the product. Years ago, labels were used only for purposes of identification. They carried only the product's name or the name of the manufacturer or distributor. It soon became apparent, however, that labels had the potential for being "silent salesmen"; and product information began to appear on labels.

Types of Labels

There are three types of labels that may now be attached to goods or imprinted on the package: descriptive labels, informative labels, and grade labels.

A *descriptive label* reveals facts about the product's physical composition: what it is made of, how it is made, the weight or number of articles in the package, and so on.

An *informative label* not only describes the product but also gives facts about its special uses and about how to care for it. It sometimes carries information on how to assemble, install, and use the product. A reasonably complete informative label will give the following facts: (1) what the product will do; (2) what it is made of; (3) how it is made; (4) how to care for it, including assembly and installation; (5) recommended uses; (6) name of the manufacturer or distributor; (7) country of origin, if it is imported; and (8) warnings or cautions, if there is any possibility that the product might cause physical injury to consumers.

A *grade label* provides a measure of quality so that the customer can relate product quality to price. Without a grade label, the customer has no way—short of testing or prolonged use—to know whether a product is of good or poor quality. The earliest grade labeling identified goods as standard or substandard; as perfects, seconds, or irregulars; or as rejects or thirds. These grades are still used with some products, but for items such as canned foods, the grading process is more complex.

Labeling Regulations

The content of labels is strictly regulated by the federal government, and you will learn about this regulation in Chapter 16. Labeling regulations place a big responsibility on the salesman. First, he should notify his employer if any articles he sells fail to carry the required labels. Second, he should acquaint himself with the significance of all ingredients

NET WEIGHT
ACTIVE INGREDIENTS

Captan (N-trichloromethylthio-4-cyclohexene-1, 2-dicarboximide) 12.50%
Methoxychlor, technical 12.50%
Malathion (0, 0-dimethyl dithiophosphate of diethyl mercapto-succinate) 6.25%
1, 1-bis (p-chlorophenyl)-2, 2, 2-trichloro-ethanol ** 1.73%
INERT INGREDIENTS 67.02%
* Equivalent to 11.0% of 2, 2-bis (p-methoxy-phenyl)-1, 1, 1-trichloroethane and 1.50% other isomers and reaction products.

** From Kelthane.
USDA Reg No. 0000-00

Multi-Purpose Wettable Powder
FRUIT SPRAY

READ ENTIRE LABEL. USE STRICTLY IN ACCORDANCE WITH LABEL CAUTIONS; WARNINGS AND DIRECTIONS.

CAUTION:

Keep out of reach of children. Harmful if swallowed. Avoid contamination of feed and food stock. Avoid inhalation of dusts.

To avoid excessive residue at harvest, do not apply to Peaches, within 21 days of harvest; to Grapes within 14 days of harvest; to Apples, Cherries, Pears, Plums, and Beans within 7 days of harvest; to Strawberries, Raspberries, Peppers, Pumpkins, and Eggplant within 3 days of harvest; to Cucurbits, Tomatoes and Beans only when foliage is dry or drying conditions are good. Avoid applications when temperature is above 85°F. Injury may occur on Bosc pears, certain Ferns, and some species of stone crop (Crassula). Do not feed treated Bean vines to animals.

FOR CONTROL OF DISEASES, INSECTS AND MITES

DIRECTIONS FOR USE

FRUIT SPRAY is a wettable powder formulation and should be mixed with water before use. *Use 1 lb. per 12½ gals of water or 7 level tablespoonfuls per gallon.* Agitate the mixture frequently during use to keep the materials in suspension. Spray plants thoroughly, covering both upper and lower leaf surfaces. While relatively safe to handle and apply, one should read and follow all the caution statements that appear on this label.

FRUIT SPRAY is a combination of selected ingredients useful in controlling many common deseases and insect pests of the Home Gardens, Home Fruit Plantings, Home Flower Gardens, and Ornamental Shrubs as listed below.

FRUIT: For use on *Apples, Peaches, Pears, Cherries* and *Strawberries* to control diseases such as: Scab, Brook's Fruit Spot, Sooty Blotch Fly Speck, Bitter Rot, Black Rot, Brown Rot, Rhizopus Rot (Peaches only), Leaf Spot, and Botrytis Fruit Rot. For control of Botrytis Fruit Rot of Strawberries through the harvest period, application of *Captan 50W* sprays immediately after each picking is suggested. *Fruit Spray* may be used on *Apples, Peaches, Pears, Plums, Grapes, Raspberries,* and *Strawberries* to control Aphids, Mites, Plum Curculio, Codling Moth, Apple Maggot, Bud Moth, Red-Banded Leaf Roller, Fruit Tree Leaf Roller, Pear Psyllia, Cherry Fruitworm, Cherry Maggot, Oriental Fruit Moth, Leafhoppers, Japanese Beetle, Rose Chafer, Grape Berry Moth, Grape Leaf Skeletonizer, Spittlebug and Strawberry Weevil.

TIME OF APPLICATION: Begin applications when leaf or flower buds are opening and repeat at weekly intervals until the fruit is approaching harvest. (see cautions).

ORNAMENTALS: To control disease such as Black Spot, Rust Leafspot, and Flower Blight of Rose, Carnations, and Crysanthemums. FRUIT SPRAY may be used to control the following insects – Aphids, Mites, Rose Chafer, Japanese Beetle, Flea Beetle, Bagworm and other chewing and sucking insects on annual and perennial flowers deciduous and evergreen trees and shrubs.

TIME OF APPLICATION: Begin applications when pests first appear or conditions favor their development and repeat at weekly intervals or as necessary to maintain control.

VEGETABLES: DISEASES – Early Blight, Late Blight, Septoria, Anthracnose, Stemphylium, Angular Leaf Spot, Downy Mildew, Phomopsis, and Cercospora on Tomatoes, Potatoes, Cucurbits (Cucumbers, Squash, Melons), Eggplant, and Peppers. Insects and Mites – Aphids, Mites Leaf Miner, Thrips, Bean Leaf Beetle, Mexican Bean Beetle, Leafhoppers, Cucumber Beetles, Flea Beetles, Potato Beetles, Japanese Beetles, Fall Armyworm, Squash Vine Borer, and Corn Earworm on Beans, Cucurbits, Eggplant, Peppers, Potatoes, and Tomatoes.

TIME OF APPLICATION: For most pests mentioned, begin application soon after plants appear above ground or are set in the garden and repeat applications at weekly intervals as long as pests threaten. (See cautions).

STATEMENT OF LIABILITY: WE DO NOT MAKE ANY WARRANTY EXPRESSED OR IMPLIED, AND THE USER ASSUMES ALL RISK FROM ITS USE.

Reprinted from A Guide to Safe Pest Control Around the Home, Courtesy of the New York State College of Agriculture.

Manufactured by Marvel Chemical Company, Marvel, New York, U. S. A.

Products which are difficult to use or which might be harmful if improperly used must have detailed informative labels. Note the quantity of information in this example of a label that might be used on a pesticide container. Is there any other information that might have been included?

that must be reported on labels. Third, he should regard labels as an important source of selling points to use in presenting merchandise. Few customers read labels in detail at the time of purchase. Thus, it is a salesman's duty to report the facts that the label carries. To avoid customer dissatisfaction in the use of a product, the salesman should stress the care and assembly directions that may be given on the label.

CHECKING YOUR KNOWLEDGE

Vocabulary:

(1) packaging
(2) unit prepacks
(3) descriptive label
(4) informative label
(5) grade label

Review questions:

1. From the consumer's point of view, how does packaging add value to a product?
2. From the businessman's point of view, how does packaging add value to a product?
3. What are some important reasons for the increased use of packaging?
4. By whom may a package be designed for a manufacturer?
5. What information may properly be given on an informative label?

For discussion:

1. In what merchandise lines, other than food, is the package a major factor in customer choice?
2. Why is packaging a special phase of the "what to sell" problem?
3. Do you think packaging will become more or less important in the future? Justify your answer.

part D

sources of product information

A young salesman had been selling neckties for many months but really knew nothing about his product. His technique was to knot a tie, hold it up for the customer to see, and make such comments as "Isn't this a nice tie?" or "I think you'll like this color." Using this technique, his sales volume was only mediocre. One day a woman who happened to be an expert on ties stopped at his counter. The customer examined one tie and commented on its good construction. The salesman asked what feature she was referring to, and this led to a conversation in which the customer showed the salesman a number of interesting features in his merchandise. She showed him that good ties are cut on the bias to give elasticity, that fine ties are loosely stitched at the back by hand rather than by machine so they will hold their shapes better after repeated knotting, and that highly weighted silk ties look fine at first but are likely to crease badly and become flimsy after cleaning. The salesman decided to use this information in his sales talks; when he did, his sales volume increased tremendously.

This salesman drew his product knowledge from a single source: the customer. However, sources of merchandise information are everywhere—both inside and outside the selling firm—and with a little effort, any salesman can become an expert on any product. The most important sources of product knowledge will be discussed in the following paragraphs.

SOURCES WITHIN THE SELLING FIRM

A salesman can easily locate sources of merchandise information in the firm he is working for. The most important internal sources are (1) the merchandise itself, (2) customers, (3) supervisors and fellow salespeople, (4) specifications of his firm, and (5) merchandise manuals.

The Merchandise

Studying any article will reveal a great deal about its composition, construction, appearance, and uses. Its wearing qualities can often be determined by making some simple tests. For example, the wearing quality of a fabric can often be determined by rubbing and pulling it; and a sample can be washed to determine its colorfastness. A machine can be operated to see how it performs and what specific jobs it will do. In fact, salespeople should try to subject their products to the same uses that customers will give them.

Information on how to use and care for products and information on their construction can often be obtained from product labels attached by manufacturers. Informative labeling is becoming increasingly necessary, since both consumer groups and the federal government are insisting that more merchandise information be made available to the consumer. The salesman should study the information on merchandise labels, and so should consumers. A salesman should also call the customer's attention to printed instructions on how to operate and care for a product.

Customers

Other than the merchandise itself, customers may well be the salesman's chief source of product information. Since customers actually use the articles being sold, they often know more about the performance of a given product than the salesman does. Every salesman should listen carefully to his customers' comments and should ask about their product experiences.

The salesman's experiences as a consumer can also be a source of merchandise information. A salesman should use his own products as often as possible and study their performances carefully. It may not always be wise for a salesman to express his own product experiences to a prospective customer. He must be sure that he already has the customer's confidence; otherwise, the customer might take his remarks as an unwarranted intrusion.

Supervisors and Fellow Salespeople

On the retail level, salespeople often report to a store buyer, who must be a merchandise expert in order to assemble his assortment of goods. The buyer spends part of his time on the selling floor telling salespeople about new merchandise. When a buyer purchases for a group of stores, he may be unable to spend time on all the selling floors; and, in this case, he will send merchandise bulletins to the proper sales supervisors. Outside salesmen report to a sales manager. A major duty of a sales manager is to give his sales force all the facts about their products or services. This is often done at group meetings.

A new salesperson will find that experienced salespeople are an important source of merchandise information. Sometimes they may seem too busy to tell him all he would like to know; but if he is cooperative and shows his appreciation, they will probably go out of their way to help him.

Specifications of the Selling Firm

Manufacturers' salesmen get much merchandise information from their firms' product specifications. Many large retailers, such as Sears, Roebuck and Company, also draw up specifications for goods that are made especially for them. They want to make sure that the goods they sell under their private brands meet rigid performance standards. The fact that merchandise must measure up to these standards provides important selling points.

Merchandise Manuals

Many salespeople have access to merchandise manuals published for specific trades or specific selling firms. Trade papers and magazines, manufacturers and retailers, have prepared such manuals. Some large department stores prepare a manual for each department within the store. There are two types of merchandise manuals. One is quite general in content and gives information that would be valuable to any salesman. The other type is quite specific and describes in detail the goods that are stocked in a particular department or made by a certain manufacturer.

SOURCES OUTSIDE THE FIRM

A salesman can also find sources of merchandise information outside his firm. The most important external sources are (1) competitors, (2) producers, (3) testing bureaus, (4) special courses, and (5) publications.

Competitors

In a debate, thorough knowledge of an opponent's point of view allows a debater to present his own case more convincingly. Likewise, the selling points that a competitor makes for his product form a good source from which a salesman can gain product knowledge. Of special importance are those areas in which his product is superior to the competitor's product.

Producers

A manufacturer naturally has the most information about the materials from which his goods are made, the method of construction used, and other important product features. For middlemen, the producer is an important source of merchandise information. Most middlemen and retail salespeople rely on the producer's salesman for merchandise information, but there are other methods of obtaining information from the producer.

Sales Conferences. Manufacturers and middlemen find that contacts through organized meetings or conferences are helpful in selling. Selling firms periodically hold sales conferences at central points throughout the country. These gatherings are like special schools designed to train distributors and their salesmen to do a better job of serving the customer.

Advertising. The manufacturer may direct advertising to the middleman and to the ultimate consumer. Both types of advertising give useful product facts, and alert salespeople tie in their personal selling efforts with this advertising.

Outline for Merchandise Manual

I. Cover—Title should be indicative of article or line

II. Introduction
   - A. Purpose of manual
   - B. Importance of merchandise knowledge from viewpoint of
     1. Customer
     2. Salesperson
     3. Store

III. What your customer wants to know
   - A. What the article is
   - B. Who uses it
   - C. What it is used for
   - D. How it is used
   - E. What it will do for the user
   - F. Outstanding features
   - G. Colors, sizes, and styles available
   - H. How it can be used in combination with other goods

IV. Qualities the customer is looking for in the article
   - A. Beauty
   - B. Color
   - C. Cut and fit
   - D. Comfort
   - E. Durability
   - F. Design
   - G. Ease of care
   - H. Fabric
   - I. Fastness of color
   - J. Finish
   - K. Quality
   - L. Serviceability
   - M. Strength
   - N. Style
   - O. Workmanship

V. How to recognize such factors as
   - A. Strength
   - B. Durability
   - C. Quality
   - D. Fastness of color, etc.

VI. Steps in making a sale
   - A. Preapproach
   - B. Approach
   - C. Presentation
   - D. Meeting objections and answering questions
   - E. Securing conviction
   - F. Closing the sale
   - G. Suggestion selling

VII. Learning your article's language
   - A. Pronunciation of new or foreign words
   - B. Descriptive adjectives and terms
   - C. Glossary

VIII. Summary and general information
   - A. Features of the article
   - B. Highlights of manufacture
   - C. Rules to follow in selling
   - D. Common questions customers may ask and answers to these questions

IX. Bibliography

Descriptive Booklets and Films. A producer will often prepare a booklet describing such things as history of his product, methods of manufacturing it, and ways it can be used. Many producers also prepare motion pictures and sound-slide films. Booklets can generally be obtained free, and responsible stores or groups of salespeople can generally borrow films without charge.

Factory Visits. Many manufacturers give tours of their factories to their own salesmen and also to wholesale and retail buyers and their salespeople. The salesman should take advantage of every opportunity to visit a factory that produces the goods he sells. Seeing goods being made is more informative than reading about or even seeing a movie about the manufacturing process.

Direct Inquiry. Salespeople have a right to know all the facts about the goods they sell, and their employers have a right to insist that manufacturers provide the necessary information. Some manufacturers still deliver goods with no accompanying information. Government regulations require some manufacturers to give facts on the materials used in their products. Retailers follow up the receipt of this information by requesting that, in certain instances, manufacturers provide other facts of value both to salespeople and consumers.

Testing Bureaus

Laboratories that test products are very important sources of merchandise information. There are independent commercial laboratories that will make tests for anyone, and many manufacturers and some large retailers operate their own laboratories. They test products on both construction and performance and then draw up selling points for their salespeople.

A few organizations test goods solely for the benefit of subscribing consumers. One such organization is the Consumers Union of the United States, Inc., which publishes the monthly magazine, *Consumer Reports,* and the annual *Buying Guide*. The organization obtains product samples from dealers' stocks in different parts of the country and tests the products. Based on the test results, products are classified as "acceptable" and "not acceptable"; and enough details about the products are included to give the consumer some basis for choosing among the "acceptable" products. Often a "best buy" is indicated.

General Motors

Producers often maintain testing facilities for their own products, and results of these tests may provide valuable product information to salesmen. This is an aerial view of a proving ground where General Motors automobiles are put through rigid performance tests. This proving ground consumes almost 4,000 acres and has over 62 miles of level and hilly roads of different road surfaces. About 40,000 test miles are driven there every work day.

Special Courses

In many communities, schools offer courses on different kinds of merchandise; and some large selling firms conduct similar courses for their employees. Courses dealing with special groups of products, such as textiles, are very popular. One appliance retailer in Chicago requires his salesmen to attend classes for 2½ hours a week to become fully acquainted with their products.

Publications

Books on nearly every field of merchandise can be found in most large libraries. In addition, fashion magazines and trade journals are crammed with product information. Sellers of women's fashions often study *Glamour, Seventeen, Vogue, Harper's Bazaar,* and *Women's Wear Daily.* The first four publications are read by ultimate consumers as well as by sellers. *Women's Wear Daily* is a trade paper read primarily by sellers and extremely fashion-conscious women. Nearly every field of merchandise has its trade journal, such as *Chain Store Age, Textile World,* and *Progressive Grocer.*

CHECKING YOUR KNOWLEDGE

Review questions:

1. What are the most important internal sources of product information?
2. Describe the two types of merchandise manuals. Who produces such manuals?
3. What are the salesman's most important external sources of information?
4. In what ways do producers supply product information to their own salesmen and to the salesmen of their customers?
5. What are the functions of a testing bureau? How can salesmen make use of the findings of a testing bureau?

For discussion:

1. Which sources of product information discussed in this part might be used by a furniture salesman? Explain your answer.
2. Do you think customers place much value on the findings of testing bureaus in regard to products? Why or why not?

part E

communicating product information

"Build a better mousetrap," somebody once said, "and the world will beat a path to your door." There is some truth in this old expression, but any seller who follows it blindly will probably find himself out of business in a hurry. The Super-Duper mousetrap—even if it's the world's greatest mousetrap—will never sell unless it is placed in businesses where customers would expect to find it and unless a salesman tells customers why the Super-Duper mousetrap is better than the Excello mousetrap. Product information must be communicated to customers before the product can be sold.

THE SALESMAN AS A PRODUCT SPECIALIST

A good salesman must know much more about his product line or service than the customer knows. Otherwise, he will contribute little toward solving his customer's buying problems. The good salesman is a product specialist. Being a product specialist, though, is not enough; the salesman must also be a communications specialist. He must convey his product knowledge to the customer in terms the customer can understand and will accept. Product knowledge does the salesman no good unless he can select the bits of information most important to customers and can then clearly communicate this information to customers.

As you learned in Part A, a salesman must have three kinds of product information. He must know: (1) the physical features contained in the product; (2) the features in the product that reveal associations to the customer; and (3) the benefits that the product will give the customer. Of these three kinds, information about a product's benefits is likely to tie in best with the customer's buying motives. In communicating product information, therefore, the salesman should concentrate on the product's benefits. These benefits generally become the selling points for a particular item.

SELECTING AND DISCUSSING SELLING POINTS

A product's chances of customer acceptance are much better if it has a point of differentiation that sets it apart from all other similar products. The need for points of differentiation is especially important in today's market, partly because many similar products are available to consumers and partly because consumers are becoming increasingly selective in their buying. Every good product designer tries to include one or more distinguishing features in each product he creates. The salesman should find these distinguishing features and bring them to the customer's attention as selling points.

Consider the Customer's Buying Motives

Customers want to know what a product can do for them; so, in choosing selling points, the salesman must be aware of his customer's personal characteristics and of his buying motives. A student, for example, will generally be more interested in how a typewriter can help in preparing daily assignments than in how the typewriter is manufactured. A housewife would rather know about the versatility

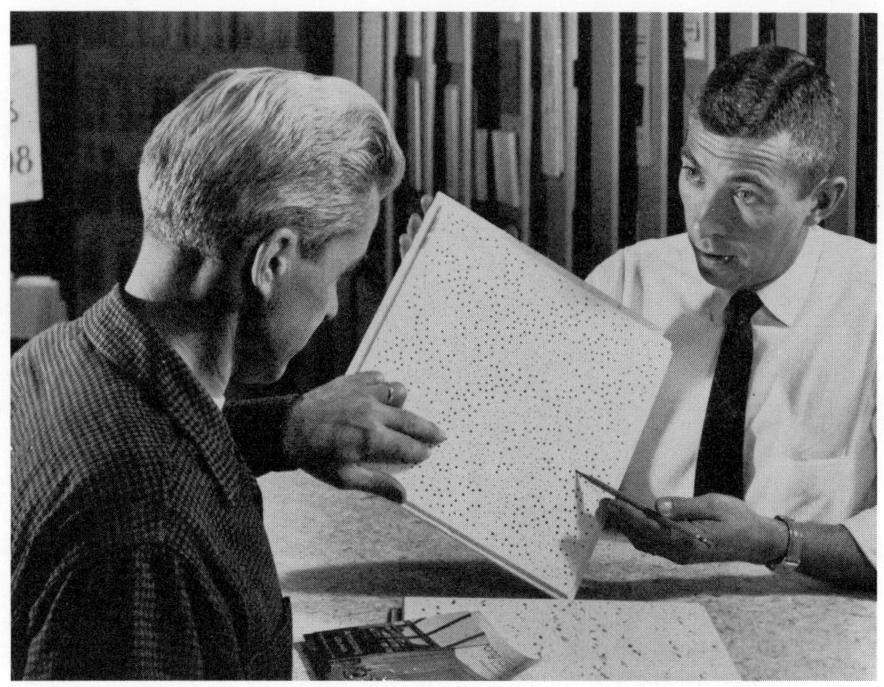

Armstrong Cork Company

When a salesman selects and discusses selling points for his product, he must consider his customer's needs, wants, and buying motives. This salesman is telling a building contractor about soundproof ceiling tile. Would he be likely to use different selling points if he were talking to a do-it-yourself homeowner?

of an electric skillet than about the metals from which the skillet is made. A farmer will be more interested in a tractor's durability than in the names of the manufacturing firm's executives.

In buying a service, too, customers are more interested in the value of the service to them than in the mechanics of the service. For example, a salesman is often employed by a hotel to sell its services as a convention site to trade and professional associations. The salesman must show customers that his hotel can meet the requirements of the customer's group, rather than stress the mechanics of how the hotel will do this.

This does not mean, however, that information concerning a product's inherent features and its associations should not be communicated. Sometimes, for instance, a customer will be just as interested in knowing whether a suit is made of all wool or of dacron and wool as he will be in knowing about the suit's all-season versatility. Through experience and through feedback from individual customers, a salesman will learn when he should introduce different kinds of product information.

Hold Product Information in Reserve

In communicating product information, a salesman should never feel it necessary to tell all that he knows about his product. If he does, he may find that his customer is either confused, overwhelmed, or bored. A sale is made by the salesman who drives home a few points clearly and forcefully rather than by the salesman who presents the most arguments. It is better to cover a few key selling points in detail than to hurry through all possible selling points. In discussing selling points, the salesman should not go on to another point until the one being discussed has been made clear and objections have been met.

Build Up Values

Discussing different selling points in a sales talk is intended to build up an article's value in the customer's mind until the value is at a level with the article's price. Such a build-up of values is necessary because, as you have learned, many product features and benefits are hidden. Suppose, for example, that a customer in a hardware store is looking at two pairs of grass trimmers. One pair sells for $3.50; the other pair sells for $5. They look very much alike; but the salesman knows that the second pair is made of better steel than the first pair, will not break as easily; is more rust resistant; and should hold its sharpness longer. Also, the performance of the second pair is guaranteed by the manufacturer; the performance of the first pair is not. By calling attention to the points of superiority of the first pair of trimmers, the salesman should be able to convince the customer that it is worthwhile to spend an extra $1.50 for the better pair of trimmers.

Follow the Customer's Lead

It is best for a salesman to follow the customer's lead in giving product information. In the sales talk, a salesman will first mention a number of product features and benefits that he thinks will arouse the customer's interest and create a desire for the product. If a selling point interests the customer, he will probably ask questions about it. The customer may raise objections, too; but this is a good indication. Few customers raise objections unless they are interested in the product and in what the salesman is saying. When a customer raises an objection, it usually indicates that the salesman should give more information. The customer may also show signs of interest by drawing closer to the article, by handling it, or even by suggesting some selling points in its favor. From these actions, the salesman can take his cue as to what

Harold M. Lambert Studios

In communicating product information, the salesman brings into proper relationship his merchandise or service and the customer's needs and wants. To do this, he must recognize the importance of the "you" attitude. A genuine "you" attitude exists when the salesman has a complete understanding of and respect for the prospect's interests, needs, and desires.

additional information should be given. If none of the initial selling points draws a favorable response, it may mean that the salesman is showing the wrong merchandise or presenting the wrong product information. For example, a customer looking at a pair of shoes may be interested in style and fashion, while the salesman is emphasizing durability and serviceability.

THE IMPORTANCE OF FEEDBACK

In communicating product information, feedback is essential. Feedback lets the salesman know whether he is presenting the right product information and whether or not the customer wants additional information. To create feedback, the salesman must encourage the customer to participate in the sales conversation and must learn how to be a good listener.

Getting the Customer to Talk

Before feedback can exist, of course, the salesman must encourage the customer to respond verbally to his sales talk and his product information. Communicating product information does not mean delivering a monologue. There are three important reasons for encouraging the customer to talk:

1. It makes the customer more attentive to what the salesman is saying.
2. It helps the salesman to understand the customer's requirements so that he can adjust his presentation and sometimes even his product or service to the customer's needs and wants.
3. When the customer talks, he is more likely to talk himself into acting on the buying proposition than into turning it down.

The Art of Listening

Listening is a courtesy which can build the customer's ego and make him more receptive to buying. Listening is also an important way for the salesman to learn the customer's needs and wants, opinions, and reactions to the merchandise and the sales talk. Half-listening to a customer's verbal responses can cause a salesman to miss an important excuse, objection, reason for buying, or even the moment when the customer has reached a favorable buying decision.

Salesmen can learn how to be good listeners by observing the following rules:

1. Be interested in what the prospective customer is saying.
2. Let the customer finish speaking before commenting on what he has said.
3. Avoid distractions.
4. Listen for ideas.
5. Participate mentally with the speaker.

Often, while thinking of what he will say next, a salesman loses part of the customer's message. Patient listening may clarify the salesman's thinking and help him to communicate more effectively. He will know almost automatically what to say next if he has been listening.

CHECKING YOUR KNOWLEDGE

Review questions:

1. Which of the three kinds of product information will be most important to customers?

2. Why must a product have at least one point of differentiation?

3. Explain the meaning of "building up values" and tell why this technique is important in selling.
4. Should the salesman follow the customer's lead in communicating product information? Why or why not?
5. Why is it important to encourage the customer to talk? How can the salesman learn to be a good listener?

For discussion:

1. It has been stated that salesmen should hold some product information in reserve. Do you think this advice applies to inexperienced salesmen? Explain your answer.
2. Is it more difficult to locate and discuss selling points for services than it is to locate and discuss selling points for merchandise? Explain.

BUILDING YOUR SKILLS

Improving your English:

On a separate sheet of paper, write the correct adverb or adjective to be used in each of the following sentences.

1. He gave a (good, well) demonstration of the blender and exhibited a great deal of product knowledge.
2. She was (quick, quickly) to point out quality differences in the fabrics.
3. The marketing manager has a (careful, carefully) prepared plan for launching the sales campaign.
4. Customers should always be greeted (cheerful, cheerfully) by salesmen.
5. The territory will be serviced (exclusive, exclusively) by Barton Truck Lines.
6. The monthly inventory reports are prepared (diligent, diligently) by Morris.
7. Color variations are evident when the fabric is examined (close, closely).
8. This is a (beautiful, beautifully) finished piece of art.
9. The final installment of the (current, currently) lecture series will be given this evening.
10. Market research data for product development are not obtained (easy, easily).

Improving your arithmetic:

Perform the following subtraction exercises.

1. A roofing contractor has used 23¾ feet from one roll of gutter tin and 35⅓ feet from another roll. If each roll formerly contained 50 feet, how many feet are now left on each roll?

2. DeVoe Construction Company ordered 92 yards of gravel for a housing project. The following quantities have been delivered: 7¾ yards, 14⅔ yards, and 12⅓ yards. How many yards of gravel are yet to be delivered?
3. The following amounts were sold from a tank containing 150 gallons of liquid fertilizer: 25½ gallons, 10¼ gallons, 15¾ gallons, and 10½ gallons. How many gallons are left in the tank? If fertilizer is reordered when the tank reaches ½ capacity, how many more gallons of fertilizer can be sold before reordering?
4. The Johnson Newsprint Company compresses into 500-pound bales its purchases of used newspapers. The following quantities have just been received: 75½ pounds, 24⅓ pounds, 14⅔ pounds, 89¼ pounds, 42¾ pounds, and 59½ pounds. How many pounds are still needed to produce a bale of paper?
5. The following quantities have been sold from a 175-foot roll of electrical wire: 17½ feet, 12¼ feet, 40⅔ feet, 21⅓ feet, and 40¼ feet. How many feet of wire are left in the roll?

Improving your research skills:

1. Salespeople should know many facts about the goods they sell. However, facts differ in importance, depending on the nature of the goods. In the first column below are listed eight different products. In the second column are listed eight different product features. For each product, select the product feature that you think will be of most importance to the salesperson selling the item. Give reasons for your selections.

Product	*Product Feature*
(a) Weed killer	(a) Construction
(b) Blanket	(b) How to use
(c) Woman's hat	(c) History or background
(d) Sewing machine	(d) Uses
(e) Mattress	(e) How to care for
(f) Refrigerator	(f) Material and composition
(g) Rose bush	(g) Performance
(h) Antique rocking chair	(h) Appearance

2. Conduct research to find out the branding policies of these companies: (a) Campbell Soup, (b) General Electric, (c) General Motors, (d) RCA, and (e) DuPont. In doing your research, consider as many as you can of the products made by each company. Write a report of your findings.
3. Visit a drugstore and obtain information on five articles that are packaged in two or more sizes. For each article, determine how much money is saved by buying the largest size. Ask the druggist which sizes are most popular. Find out the reasons for this popularity, and write a report of your findings.

APPLYING YOUR KNOWLEDGE

Case problems:

1. The Rival Manufacturing Company makes a new electric can opener with a cutting edge that can be removed for cleaning. This feature is clearly the can opener's point of superiority over other can openers, and Rival's advertising emphasizes this feature. In one community's leading department store, a customer saw a number of Rival can openers on display and asked a salesperson if they had the new removable blade. The salesperson had never heard about this feature and wasn't sure, from casual inspection, whether the blade was removable. She consulted the buyer, but he said he didn't know anything about how the can opener operated and that he didn't have time to investigate it. If you were the salesperson, what would you do now? If a buyer cannot be relied upon to supply the salesperson with product information, what other ways are there to assure that the salesperson has the proper information when he needs it?
2. Customers frequently ask salespeople for a certain kind of product but do not specify any particular brand. One supermarket stocks nine different brands of tomato juice, ranging in price from 15¢ to 39¢. Some cans contain 12 ounces, some contain 14, and one contains 20 ounces. Most of the labels give little product information beyond that which is required by law, and customers seldom stop to read the few labels that do give additional information. What information should the salesperson try to get about each brand so as to serve customers intelligently? Would one of the brands probably be best for all customers? From the store's point of view, might there be any objection to pushing the "best" brand?

Continuing project:

Prepare in your manual a section in which you analyze the most important features and benefits of your product and the most important sources of product information; describe the branding policies you would follow; and determine the methods of packaging and labeling you would use.

Extra credit:

Select a new product from one of these categories: branded foods, branded cosmetics, or branded electrical appliances. The product you select need not be an entirely new type; it may simply have a new feature or even a new, more functional package. For the product you select, determine the following information: (1) how it is being advertised (nationally, regionally, locally, or all three); (2) how it is being displayed (in store windows, inside the store, etc.); (3) what special devices are being used to promote it (coupons, premiums, special introductory prices, etc.); and (4) whether salespeople are trying to "push" it and whether they seem knowledgeable about it. Write a report of your findings, comparing the special selling methods used for this product with the methods used in selling established products.

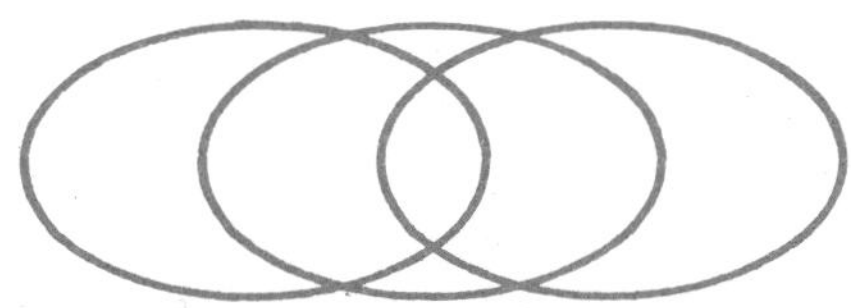

chapter 7

understanding the selling firm

KEY QUESTIONS

A What should the salesman know about the organization and management of his firm?

B What factors—both inside and outside the selling firm—affect the prices that will be set on the firm's products?

C Is the extension of credit a necessity in today's business world?

D Can good merchandise sell successfully if it is not accompanied by good service?

E As an employee, what can you do to assure good working relationships in your selling firm?

part A

organization policies

It is obvious that a salesman must know all he possibly can about the products or services he sells. It is not so obvious, however, that he can do a better selling job when he is fully equipped with a knowledge of his company and its policies. Information that would be valuable to a salesman concerns:

1. The image or central purpose of the firm.
2. History of the firm, including the date of founding, traditions, and growth and expansion.
3. Organization and management of the firm, including the type of organization, present officers, and number of stockholders.
4. Statistics on business operations, including the size of the plant or store, number of employees, and yearly sales.
5. Rules and regulations of the firm, including receiving procedures, advertising procedures, and rules for employee conduct.
6. Policies of the firm, including selling policies, customer service policies, and personnel policies.

Often a customer will be interested in such information. But even if the information is not communicated to the customer, simply knowing it can give the salesman confidence and can add depth to his sales talk.

THE IMPORTANCE OF POLICIES

A *policy* is a definite course of action established by management to govern relationships with the various "publics" with whom the firm deals. These "publics" include customers, employees, competitors, and suppliers. Salespeople do not generally determine company policies, but each salesperson has a duty to understand his firm's policies and to follow them. He is particularly responsible for knowing and implementing policies that govern customer relationships. From the salesman's point of view, the most important policies concern organization of the selling firm, buying and pricing, credit and collection, customer services, and personnel management. The rest of this chapter will be devoted to discussing these policies.

Many firms discuss their policies in training programs for their new salespeople. When a business does not offer such a program, a salesman is often furnished with a manual in which all the policy information is given. Although policies are adjusted periodically to keep up with changing conditions, new policies should not be adopted unless there is a fair chance that the firm will be following them for some time. Consistent policies are an important factor in establishing a reputation for fair dealing and in building goodwill.

ORGANIZING THE SELLING FIRM

As soon as possible after he accepts a job, the salesman should familiarize himself with his firm's organization structure. He should know the duties and responsibilities of each official and the work of each segment of the firm. Studying an organization chart can give him considerable information. An *organization chart* gives a graphic picture of the division of work in the business, indicates the flow of authority, and shows the people to whom employees are responsible. A careful study of the firm's organization chart will show the salesman how all segments of the business are interlocked and who is responsible for the proper functioning of each segment.

Characteristics of a Good Organization

There are two basic tasks in establishing an organization structure—assigning responsibility and delegating authority. *Responsibility* is the obligation to do an assigned task. *Authority* is the right to make decisions on work assignments and to require subordinates to perform assigned tasks in accordance with these decisions. In a good organization responsibility is assigned and authority is delegated so that each individual knows: (1) what his job is supposed to accomplish; (2) what his duties are; (3) what his authority is; (4) who he should report to; (5) who reports to him; and (6) what is considered satisfactory performance of his duties.

An extremely important characteristic of a good selling organization is high morale among salesmen and other employees. *Morale* is a state of mind that reflects a person's attitude toward his firm, his job, and his co-workers. The very nature of the salesman's job calls for great enthusiasm. This is sometimes difficult to maintain, especially if the salesman travels and is not in daily contact with his superiors. In such a situation, the sales manager may maintain high morale by phoning salesmen at regular intervals, by writing encouraging letters, and by showing respect for them when they visit headquarters. Sales incentive contests with worthwhile prizes, such as a vacation trip for the winner, also build loyalty and enthusiasm for the company.

Generally speaking, employees have high morale when the following conditions exist: (1) employees receive satisfaction from their jobs; (2) they take pride in the firm and in their jobs; (3) they cooperate with and respect their co-workers and their superiors; and (4) they are loyal to the firm and follow its rules and policies.

Types of Organization Structures

There are two basic kinds of organization structures that selling firms may have—the line organization and the line-and-staff organization.

Line Organization. With a *line organization,* authority and responsibility go in a direct line from the highest to the lowest administrative position. Suppose that in a manufacturing firm, the highest administrative office in selling is that of vice-president in charge of sales. In a direct line below him may be a general sales manager, then an assistant sales manager below the general sales manager, regional sales managers, and finally field salesmen.

The line organization can be very efficient if it is properly administered by capable personnel. Control of the business' operations is centralized, and decisions can be quickly made and put into practice. A line organization is usually used in fairly small businesses.

Line-and-Staff Organization. As a business grows, it often finds that a line organization is no longer practical. A line organization can lose its efficiency if there are many employees and if a business' operations are quite complex. Thus, most large businesses use a line-and-staff organization. A *line-and-staff organization* has the flow of authority and responsibility found in the line organization, but staff specialists in certain fields are added to the organization to give advice to line personnel. These staff specialists have no authority over line personnel; they can only advise.

Suppose that the manufacturing firm discussed above wanted to switch to a line-and-staff organization. The vice-president in charge of sales might add two specialists: a legal advisor and a marketing research consultant. These persons would act as advisors to the vice-president and to anyone else in the firm who needed advice in government and labor regulations or marketing research. They have no authority over other executives in the sales division.

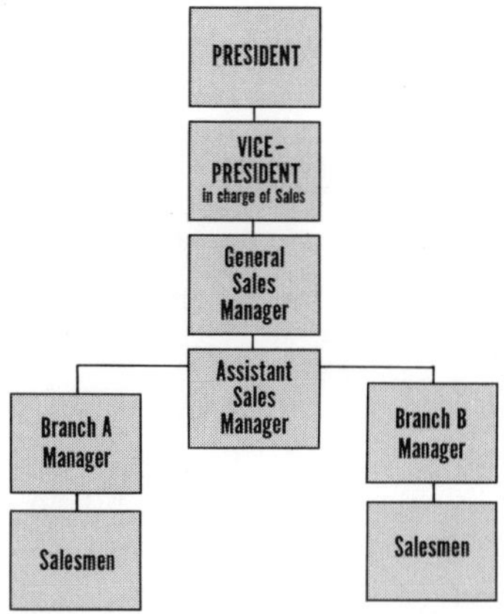

This chart shows the line organization of a sales division. Authority and responsibility flow in a direct line from the company's president to the salesmen. The line organization is the simplest type of organization structure, and in small businesses it is probably the most efficient type.

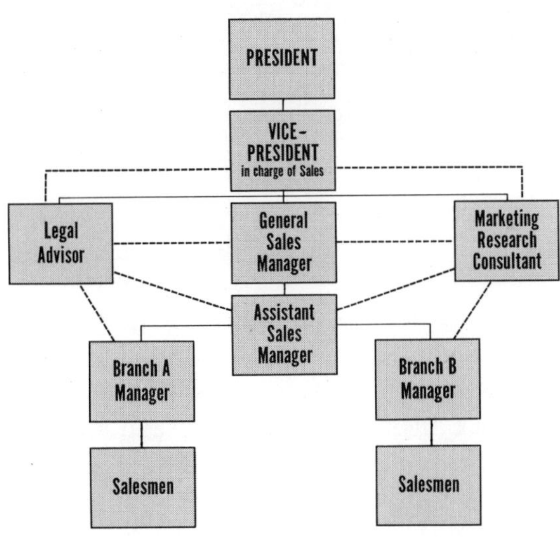

This chart of a line-and-staff organization is like the line organization chart above, but two staff specialists have been added to this chart. The dotted lines indicate that the legal advisor and marketing research consultant give advice to other persons in the sales division but have no authority over these persons. They only have authority over persons who may be beneath them, such as research interviewers.

Management Styles

In a selling firm—regardless of whether it uses a line or a line-and-staff organization—persons in supervisory positions may follow one of three management styles. These three styles are the paternalistic style, the bureaucratic style, and the participative style.

Paternalistic Management. Managers who believe in the paternalistic style of leadership try to develop the sales force into one big happy family. Seldom is anyone fired; many fringe benefits are provided; and promotions and salary increases depend more on seniority than on merit. Paternalistic management may attract and hold certain security-minded people, but it rarely builds a sales force of achievers. There is little motivation for persons to work hard; and with this lack of motivation, a sales force is often ineffective in meeting competition. Paternalistic management is rapidly becoming obsolete in selling firms.

Bureaucratic Management. Managers who practice bureaucratic management feel that there is one best way to prospect, to approach the customer, to present the product or service, to meet objections, and to close the sale. They try to determine what this one best way is for each selling activity, then they insist that salesmen follow that one best way "to the letter." Under bureaucratic management, the firm is quick to punish or even dismiss salesmen who do not get prompt results with the "proven" methods. Bureaucratic management is still used in sales supervision, but it stifles creativity and resourcefulness.

Participative Management. A third management style that is growing in importance is participative management. Here, managers act as both teachers and helpers to their salesmen. A sales manager will encourage his salesmen to make their own decisions, and salesmen are free to adjust their approaches to each selling situation. They help set their own sales goals and derive satisfaction from meeting these goals. Communication flows both from top to bottom and from bottom to top in the organization structure.

Although there are some areas in sales supervision where the paternalistic and bureaucratic styles can still be used, the varying nature of nearly every selling situation makes participative management the most effective style. It is the kind of management style to which intelligent and purposeful salesmen respond most favorably.

"If there is anything we don't want around here, it's yes men. Right, boys?"

Business Management

Sometimes the bureaucratic manager is the last person to admit he's a bureaucratic manager.

CHECKING YOUR KNOWLEDGE

Vocabulary:

(1) policy
(2) organization chart
(3) responsibility
(4) authority
(5) morale
(6) line organization
(7) line-and-staff organization

Review questions:

1. What information about the selling firm would be valuable to a salesman?
2. Name the two basic tasks in establishing an organization structure.
3. Under what conditions may high morale be said to exist in a firm?
4. What is the difference between a line organization and a line-and-staff organization?
5. Describe the three management styles that persons in supervisory positions may follow.

For discussion:

1. In what situations might a salesman fail because he was ignorant of company policies?
2. What might happen if a manager failed to delegate authority to his sales personnel?
3. Is it necessary for businesses to change their organization policies from time to time? Why or why not?

part B

pricing policies

Pricing products is an essential part of selling. Salesmen have little to do with actually setting prices, but they should understand their firms' pricing policies so that they can show the customer he is getting good value for his money. In this part, you will learn some basic principles of setting resale prices. Pricing policies vary considerably from seller to seller and are influenced by a number of factors: the type of selling organization, the type of product handled, the firm's customers, the firm's competitors, and the general economic environment. A salesman can learn about his firm's pricing policies by talking with the persons in the firm who are responsible for setting prices.

ESTABLISHING GENERAL PRICE LEVELS

Every seller must adopt a policy on the general level of his prices. If he is selling a standard or convenience-goods item, he will probably set his price at or near the *market price*. This is the price at which the product is currently being sold by competitors. Consumers will usually not buy a standard item for more than the market price.

A firm will hesitate to sell a standard item for less than the market price so long as it can get that price. If, however, the firm wants to increase its sales volume with the hope of reducing production costs, it may sell below the market price, or at *market minus*. The firm, of course, wants to stimulate customers to buy more of its products at the low prices. The firm that deals in goods of unusually fine quality or that offers extra customer services may set its prices above the market price, or at *market plus.* Most manufacturers of well-known standard goods tend to follow the price levels set by the largest manufacturer in their particular merchandise field.

CONSIDERATIONS IN SETTING INDIVIDUAL PRICES

Items must be priced so that consumers will buy them readily. Prices must also be set to cover the businessman's costs and expenses and provide him with a profit. The most important factor in pricing a certain item is the cost the businessman incurs in manufacturing the article or in buying it for resale. There are also three kinds of expenses that influence price—flat expenses, variable expenses, and overhead.

Flat expenses are about the same for each item handled, regardless of its cost or resale price. Storage and delivery expenses are generally flat expenses. *Variable expenses* are different for each item handled but have about the same percentage relationship to the resale price. Salespeople's salaries and advertising expenses are examples of variable expenses. *Overhead* refers to the costs of operating the business that do not vary with the number or value of items being sold. Rent and maintenance expenses are part of overhead. Selling organizations constantly use their knowledge of these costs and expenses in setting individual prices.

Granting Discounts

Manufacturers have the problem of establishing prices for a number of different customers—wholesalers, retailers, and ultimate consumers. One way of solving this problem is to grant different kinds and amounts of discounts to different customers. A *discount* is a reduction from a basic price that is granted to a customer when he meets certain buying conditions.

To his retail customers, a manufacturer may grant *trade discounts* which are equal to the usual markups taken by the retailers. An item may have a list price of $40, for example, and a trade discount of 40 percent. The retailer pays $24 for the item. To his wholesale customers, a manufacturer will grant a larger discount—called a *functional discount*—so that the wholesaler can realize a profit when he resells the goods to retailers. If the functional discount were 40 percent, 10 percent, the wholesaler would pay $21.60 for the $40 item just mentioned. You will learn more about how to calculate discounts in Chapter 11.

Two other discounts that are important in pricing are quantity and seasonal discounts. In many manufacturing concerns, large-volume production can help reduce operating costs. To encourage customers to buy in large quantities so that he can keep producing in large quantities, a manufacturer will grant *quantity discounts*. With a quantity discount, the customer can deduct from his payment a certain percentage of the total cost of the order—providing he places a large enough order.

In many merchandise lines, such as clothing, buying and selling are highly seasonal. Plants and personnel may be rushed at certain times of the year and almost idle at other times. To keep customer orders distributed evenly throughout the year, manufacturers often grant *seasonal discounts*. If the customer places his order during the off-season, he can deduct from his payment a certain percentage of the total cost of the order. The manufacturer can thus maintain an even production flow throughout the year.

Determining Markup

The retailer bases his selling price mainly upon (1) the average percentage of markup needed to make a reasonable profit and (2) what he believes customers will readily pay in view of their purchasing power and the prices competitors charge for similar goods. *Markup* is the difference between the cost of an article to the merchant and the price at which the article is sold. If an item costs a retailer $3 and is offered for sale at $5, the markup is $2. The *markup percentage* results from dividing the dollar markup by the retail price. Thus, if an article retails at $5 and its dollar markup is $2, the markup percentage is $2 divided by $5, or 40 percent.

Based on past selling experiences, the retailer should know what his average markup percentage must be in order to obtain a satisfactory profit. This does not mean, though, that this average markup will be applied to every article he sells. Suppose, for example, that a toolbox costs a retailer $3.50 and that when an average markup of 30 percent is applied, the resulting price is $5. He might feel that customers would buy the toolbox more readily if it were priced at $4.95 instead of $5. Or he might feel that the toolbox wouldn't sell for more than $4.50 because of competitors' prices. On the other hand, he might feel that the toolbox could be readily sold at $6 because of some unique construction feature. In pricing individual articles, the retailer may deviate from his average markup percentage, but this percentage is an important guide in setting prices.

Macy's

Retailers often set "psychological" prices. Setting a price several cents below an even price makes the item seem more like a bargain to the customer, although the price difference is insignificant. Many customers will buy at $1.98 who would not buy at $2.00. Likewise, an item priced at $2.49 will seem more like a bargain than the same item priced at $2.50.

One-Price Policies

As you have learned, a one-price policy means that at any given time, a merchant will charge all customers the same price for the same merchandise. Retailers should generally follow a one-price policy, but it is sometimes wise to allow price adjustments on large purchases. Such adjustments should be made available to all customers, however; there should be no discrimination.

For the sale of unusually large quantities, such as hotels and hospitals might buy, some retailers establish *contract departments* which quote prices considerably lower than the regular retail prices. This is, in effect, granting a quantity discount to certain types of customers. Another way of adjusting prices on large purchases without violating the one-price policy is through multiple pricing. With *multiple pricing,* the price of a group of articles is less than the price of the same number of articles bought separately. For example, if one pair of socks sells for 35¢, a retailer may multiple-price three pairs of the socks for $1.

Many manufacturers and wholesalers also have one-price policies, although there is more bargaining in wholesale than in retail transactions. Giving unfair price concessions to certain favored customers used to be common, but the federal government has now made it illegal for sellers—particularly manufacturers—to give some customers unfair price advantages. Price differences are allowed so long as they do not exceed the savings in the seller's expenses and costs that result from selling a large quantity.

Price Maintenance

Many manufacturers try to control the prices at which their products are resold. Contracts allowing the fixing of resale prices are legal in most states. These contracts allow manufacturers or distributors of branded goods to set the prices at which these goods can be resold by wholesalers or retailers. No merchant can legally sell below the established price if such a contract is in force.

Manufacturers of highly advertised, nonperishable, and widely distributed products usually want to set their resale prices. These products are often used as leaders or loss leaders. A *leader* is an item sold at a cut price—not to make a profit on the item but to attract to the store customers who will buy other goods at regular markups. When the item is sold at less than cost, including direct handling expenses, it is a *loss leader*.

When one distributor cuts the price of an item, competitors are generally forced to cut their prices on that item. If businesses find that this item is unprofitable, they will eventually stop carrying it; and the manufacturer loses sales. Also, retailers frequently try to sell customers profitable substitutes instead of the unprofitable leaders. This, too, can cause the manufacturer to lose sales.

The biggest disadvantage of resale price maintenance is that the price maintenance contracts are difficult to enforce. Manufacturers are generally reluctant to take legal action against their own customers who may violate the contracts. Also, recent court decisions limiting the manufacturer's right to stop selling to price-cutters have made enforcement difficult. Another disadvantage of resale price maintenance is that it may stimulate the development of private brands that can be sold profitably at lower prices than can the price-controlled national brands. Thus, price maintenance may bring new competition to the national brander and decrease the size of his potential market.

CHECKING YOUR KNOWLEDGE

Vocabulary:

(1) market price
(2) market minus
(3) market plus
(4) flat expenses
(5) variable expenses
(6) overhead
(7) discount
(8) trade discount
(9) functional discount
(10) quantity discount
(11) seasonal discount
(12) markup
(13) markup percentage
(14) contract department
(15) multiple pricing
(16) leader
(17) loss leader

Review questions:

1. What are the three alternatives from which sellers may choose in setting general price levels?
2. Name the most important factor in pricing a certain item. What other factors may influence the setting of a price?
3. What concessions are often made available to the buyer in the form of discounts?
4. How is markup calculated? How is markup percentage calculated, and of what value is it to retailers?
5. Why do certain manufacturers adopt price maintenance policies?

For discussion:

1. What effect does competition have upon a seller's pricing policies?
2. Would the perishability of a product have much of an effect on the price that is set on the product?
3. Many ultimate consumers object to price maintenance. What might be some reasons for their objections?

part C

credit policies

One of the most important functions that a business performs for its customers is the granting of credit—allowing customers to receive goods or services in return for a promise to pay later. Nearly all manufacturers and wholesalers sell on credit to business customers who can be relied upon to keep their promises. About one-third of all retail trade is conducted on credit. Credit extended by manufacturers and wholesalers is called *mercantile credit,* and credit extended by retailers is called *consumer credit.* Most ultimate consumers regard credit as a necessity, and they will patronize those stores that offer credit. As for wholesalers and retailers, they could not stay in business very long if their suppliers did not extend credit.

KINDS OF CREDIT

On both the mercantile credit level and the consumer credit level, there are great differences in credit policies. Some sellers, for example, assume a considerable risk of nonpayment by extending credit when they feel the buyer has a reasonably good chance of meeting his obligation. Other sellers extend credit only to buyers who are well established and who have shown good faith in past dealings. Sellers who take extra credit risks must set somewhat higher prices to cover their collection costs and expected losses.

Open Account Credit

Most credit is of the open account type. With *open account credit,* the seller agrees to extend credit to the customer for a short period of time, full payment is expected when the customer is billed, and there is no service charge. Title to the goods generally passes to the buyer when the goods are shipped or delivered. With consumer open account credit, goods bought in one month must usually be paid for in full during the following month, with no discount for early payment. If the buyer does not pay by the date specified in the terms of sale, the seller has legal means of trying to get payment. However, he does not have the right to *repossess* (take back) the goods he has sold.

Common terms for mercantile open account credit are net 30 days and net 60 days. These terms mean that credit is granted for either 30 or 60 days from the date of the invoice but that payment must be made before the 30 or 60 days are up. Invoices commonly are dated the day the goods are shipped. To encourage customers to pay their bills early, sellers sometimes grant cash discounts. If credit terms are 2/10, net 60 on a shipment made March 10, credit is granted up to May 9; but the buyer may deduct a 2 percent cash discount if he pays the bill within ten days, or by March 20. By encouraging customers to pay early, the seller can reduce the amount he has tied up in accounts due him and can reduce the risk of nonpayment.

Mercantile credit terms are expressed by the way a buyer's bill or invoice is dated, and you will learn more about special datings in Chapter 11.

Installment Credit

Under the *installment plan* of credit, the customer signs a contract requiring him to make partial payments—either weekly or monthly—on his purchase and to make these payments over a longer period of time than is feasible with open accounts. The seller makes sure he can repossess the goods in case of default on payment by: (1) entering into a *conditional sales contract* under which he holds title to the goods until payment is completed or (2) taking a *chattel mortgage* under which he can repossess the goods in case of nonpayment, even though title has passed to the buyer. There is a service charge for installment credit which covers not only the normal interest on a well-secured debt but also the costs of credit investigation, monthly billing, and risk of nonpayment.

On the mercantile credit level, the installment plan is commonly used to purchase furniture and equipment that the customer uses in his business operations. Installment credit is not usually available, however, to purchase for resale goods (inventory) that would not normally be in the buyer's possession at the time of a default in payment. However, when a buyer cannot pay for merchandise on open account, installment terms can often be worked out with the seller.

Revolving Credit

Use of the *revolving credit account* is growing rapidly on the consumer credit level. Under this plan, a credit limit is established, and the customer agrees to make monthly payments according to a prescribed schedule. As every payment is made, the customer's credit is restored in the amount of that payment. Thus, if a customer with a $200 credit limit and a $15 monthly payment buys $150 worth of merchandise during the month, he has a credit of $65 after the payment is made, since he then owes only $135 against a $200 credit limit. There is generally a monthly service charge on revolving credit accounts. Some firms carry insurance on the life of every revolving credit customer. The policy covers the amount that may be due at the time of the customer's death or disability. The customer's heirs, then, are not liable for the debt.

In department stores, open account credit is sometimes combined with revolving credit. Thus, if a customer pays for his purchases within 30 days of the billing date, he pays no service charge. If he pays none or only part of the bill in that period, his next bill will carry a service charge—commonly 1½ percent of the balance from the previous bill. He can continue to carry an outstanding balance if he makes the stated minimum monthly payments and pays the service charge on amounts not repaid in one month.

Other Credit Plans

For retail customers of limited means, variations of the open account have been devised. One variation, called the *junior account,* gives the customer a limited amount of credit—$60, for example—to be repaid in a few installments, such as $20 each month for three months. Sometimes the customer is sold on credit a book of coupons that may be used as cash in the store. The coupon book is paid for over a period of a few months. A service charge is generally made, but it may be waived if the customer pays for the book within a month or two.

On the mercantile credit level, a buyer may obtain credit by signing a *promissory note,* which is a written promise to repay the amount of his purchase plus interest by a specified date. Buyers can also purchase goods *on consignment.* This means that the manufacturer retains ownership of the goods and that the buyer simply acts as his agent in selling them. The buyer must resell at prices and terms set by the manufacturer, return all unsold goods, and pay promptly for what he has sold. Some sellers use this plan to control the distribution of their products. Others use it to induce hesitant buyers to take goods, since buyers run no risk of being forced to sell at a loss. On the other hand, this plan places a great risk upon the seller; and most established manufacturers will not sell on consignment.

WHO EXTENDS CREDIT?

Until rather recently, most credit was extended by the seller. Now, however, a considerable amount of credit is financed by institutions outside the selling firm. For example, since many sellers of expensive items such as cars have insufficient funds to extend installment credit, they generally arrange for a bank or finance company to lend money to the customer. The customer signs an installment purchase contract with the financing organization. The financing organization then collects

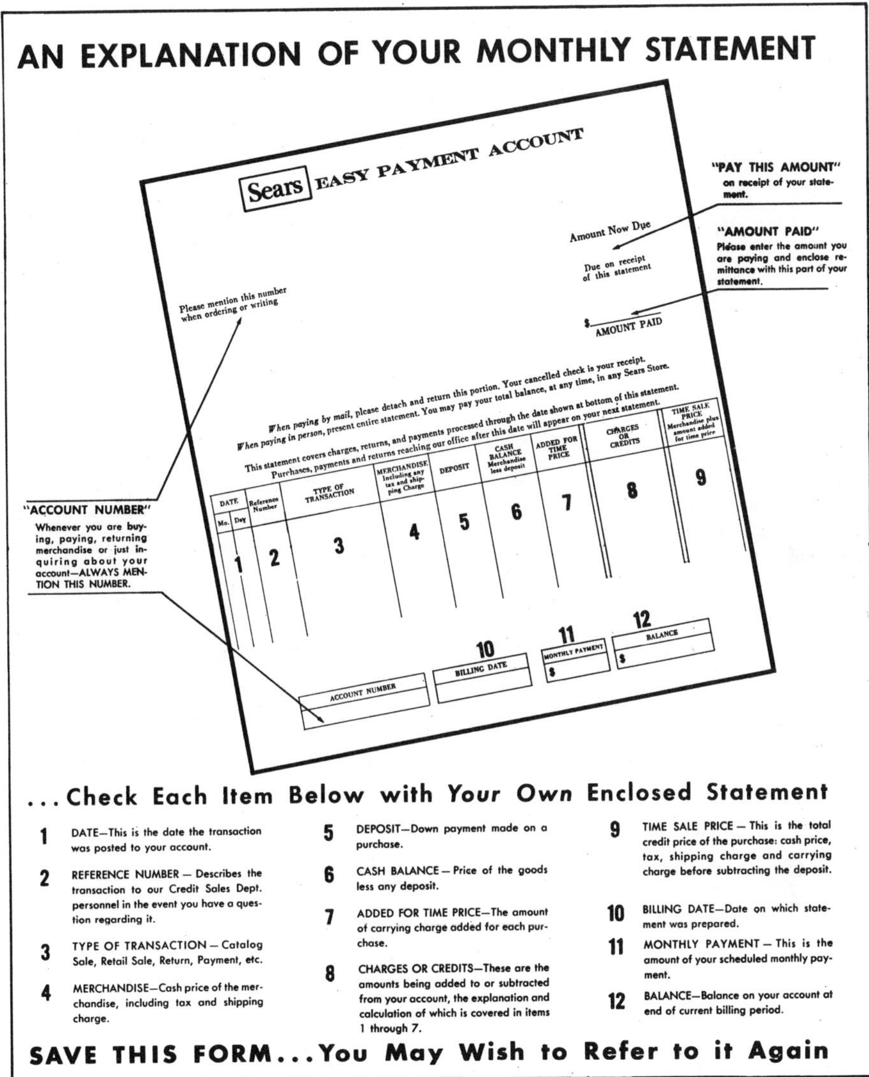

AN EXPLANATION OF YOUR MONTHLY STATEMENT

. . . Check Each Item Below with *Your Own* Enclosed Statement

1 DATE—This is the date the transaction was posted to your account.

2 REFERENCE NUMBER — Describes the transaction to our Credit Sales Dept. personnel in the event you have a question regarding it.

3 TYPE OF TRANSACTION — Catalog Sale, Retail Sale, Return, Payment, etc.

4 MERCHANDISE—Cash price of the merchandise, including tax and shipping charge.

5 DEPOSIT—Down payment made on a purchase.

6 CASH BALANCE — Price of the goods less any deposit.

7 ADDED FOR TIME PRICE—The amount of carrying charge added for each purchase.

8 CHARGES OR CREDITS—These are the amounts being added to or subtracted from your account, the explanation and calculation of which is covered in items 1 through 7.

9 TIME SALE PRICE — This is the total credit price of the purchase: cash price, tax, shipping charge and carrying charge before subtracting the deposit.

10 BILLING DATE—Date on which statement was prepared.

11 MONTHLY PAYMENT — This is the amount of your scheduled monthly payment.

12 BALANCE—Balance on your account at end of current billing period.

SAVE THIS FORM . . . You May Wish to Refer to it Again

Sears, Roebuck and Company

Sears, Roebuck is one selling firm that sends itemized monthly statements to its revolving credit customers. The information shown above was given to credit customers when Sears began sending itemized statements. It helps the customer understand the entries on his statement and allows him to compare his copies of sales checks, payment receipts, or credit receipts with the store's prepared statement.

the installments as they fall due and can repossess the goods if the customer fails to pay. If, at the time of repossession, the goods are not valuable enough to cover the balance of the debt, the customer can be held liable for the difference.

Banks do a considerable amount of credit extension. Under one plan, known as the *instant money* or *bank credit plan,* the customer is granted a certain amount of credit and allowed to write checks up to that amount. Customers can use the credit plan in any store that accepts the bank's checks. As the customer repays what he spends—plus a service charge on the unpaid balance—the money again becomes available for use.

There are also many cooperative bank-retailer plans in existence. A bank will issue credit cards to customers with good credit ratings, and the cards can be used to buy goods in any store that is part of the plan. When purchasing goods, the customer signs a sales check in the store. These sales checks are regularly turned over to the bank, and the bank credits the store's account for all sales checks received. The bank assumes all collection risks, and the store is charged a fee for the bank's services.

Some specialized credit organizations, such as the Diners' Club, American Express, and BankAmericard, may also take over the duties of extending credit. The customer qualifies for credit with the credit organization, not with individual stores. Businesses affiliated with such an organization honor its credit card and bill the organization for purchases the card holder makes. This kind of credit plan allows small businesses to extend credit without setting up elaborate credit departments and without tying up funds in accounts receivable.

SOURCES OF CREDIT INFORMATION

To determine a person's credit standing, sellers must have information on the three C's of credit—character, capacity, and capital. *Character* refers to the customer's honesty and probable willingness to pay. *Capacity* refers to the ability to earn. *Capital* refers to the tangible assets that a person or business owns which can be seized in case of default on payment. There are five main sources of mercantile and consumer credit information on these three C's: (1) the applicant himself; (2) credit agencies; (3) other businesses; (4) the applicant's bank, employer, or similar institutions and individuals; and (5) salesmen for the selling firm.

TAKEN BY:	REPORT	APPROVED BY	DATE	LIMIT	ACKNOW-LEDGE:	DUN O I	PLATE CODE

THE JOHN SHILLITO COMPANY
CINCINNATI, OHIO 45202

APPLICATION FOR FEW-PENNIES-A-DAY ACCOUNT

DATE OF APPLICATION
MONTH DAY YEAR

(PLEASE PRINT)

Your Name Mr. Mrs. Miss ______ First ______ Middle ______ Last ______ | Wife's First Name | Home Phone | Business Phone

Present Address ______ Number ______ Street ______ City ______ State ______ Zip Code | How Long Have You Lived there? Yrs.

Your Previous Address ______ Number ______ Street ______ City ______ State ______ Zip Code | How Long Did You Live there? Yrs.

Are You? ☐ Single ☐ Married ☐ Widowed ☐ Divorced ☐ Separated | Do You? ☐ Own your home ☐ Live with parents ☐ Rent ☐ Room ☐ Furnished ☐ Unfurnished | Your Age ______ | Number of Children ______

Husband's Employer:	Position:	How Long? Yrs.	Weekly Income
Husband's Previous Employer:	Position:	How Long? Yrs.	Weekly Income
Wife's Employer:	Position:	How Long? Yrs.	Weekly Income

Please list the firms with which you now have, or have had credit:
STORE, BANK, FINANCE CO., ETC.

1. ______
2. ______
3. ______

Give name, address and relationship of your closest relative other than husband or wife:
NAME ______
ADDRESS ______
______
HOW RELATED?

Name ______
In File ______ L.R. ______ No Card ☐
Address Same ☐ ______
Emp. Same ☐ ______ Ver. ☐

THIRTY DAY

Open	H.C.	Terms	Bal.	P.D.	Pays

REVOLVING

Open	H.C.	Terms	Bal.	P.D.	Pays

INSTALLMENT (CONTRACT)

Open	H.C.	Terms	Bal.	P.D.	Pays

CHATTELS
Date ______ Amt. ______ By ______
Date ______ Amt. ______ By ______
Date ______ Amt. ______ By ______
INQ. SINCE L.R. ______

OTHER INFO: ______

Information below heavy line on reverse side is given as a basis for obtaining credit, and is certified correct to the best of my knowledge. In consideration of credit to be extended to me or members of my family, I hereby agree to pay this account according to the terms of each individual purchase.

SIGNATURE ______

Shillito's, Cincinnati

For retailers, much credit information about an individual comes from the credit application. Each person desiring credit must fill out an application blank similar to this one, and the retailer studies the application carefully before deciding whether or not to offer credit.

Credit agencies are particularly important sources of credit information. Many retailers belong to a nationwide network of credit agencies, such as the National Retail Credit Association or the Associated Credit Bureaus of America. Credit agencies collect information on ultimate consumers and publish confidential reports for their subscribers. A retailer can request information on almost any consumer just by contacting his local credit agency.

Manufacturers and wholesalers may belong to a similar network, called the National Association of Credit Management. They may also obtain credit information through credit agencies operated by trade associations. An extremely important source of mercantile credit information is Dun and Bradstreet, Inc. This company publishes periodically a book of credit ratings which evaluates the financial strength of businesses throughout the country. Credit appraisals based on the investigations and opinions of Dun and Bradstreet agents are given in this book. Manufacturers and wholesalers can obtain credit reports on almost any business or professional man through the services of Dun and Bradstreet.

CHECKING YOUR KNOWLEDGE

Vocabulary:

(1) mercantile credit
(2) consumer credit
(3) open account credit
(4) repossess
(5) installment plan
(6) conditional sales contract
(7) chattel mortgage
(8) revolving credit account
(9) junior account
(10) promissory note
(11) on consignment
(12) instant money, or bank credit plan
(13) character
(14) capacity
(15) capital

Review questions:

1. Describe the open account type of credit. Can the seller repossess goods sold on open account?
2. For mercantile open account credit, common terms are net 30 days and net 60 days. What do these terms mean?
3. Under the installment plan, how may a seller assure himself of the right to repossess the goods in case of a default in payment?
4. Describe the credit plan in which features of open account credit are combined with features of revolving credit.
5. Who may extend credit outside the selling organization?
6. What are the five main sources of mercantile credit information?

For discussion:

1. Most consumers take the extension of credit as a matter of course. Do you think credit is a privilege? Why or why not?
2. Does the existence of replenished credit, as payments are made, constitute a strong temptation to overspend?
3. Why is it important that both business and ultimate consumers establish sound credit ratings?

part D

service policies

Goodwill is an asset for any business. It arises from the reputation of the business and its relations with its customers. *Goodwill* is the overall favorable attitude the public has toward the business. Both present and potential customers may hold this favorable attitude, since it results from the seller's considerate treatment of the general customer public. Goodwill generally induces customers not only to buy from the seller but also to recommend his product or service to friends and associates. Such a recommendation is often of greater value to the seller than is commercial advertising.

A seller can create or increase goodwill in three ways:

1. He can promote his organization so consistently through advertising and other such means that people will think of it as a business worthy of their patronage.
2. He can sell merchandise that satisfies customers in every respect.
3. He can provide good service that makes buying more convenient and pleasant or that contributes to community welfare.

Offering good service is particularly important in today's competitive marketplace. A business' reputation for service can often determine how successful the business will be in gaining customer goodwill.

KINDS OF SERVICES

It is an axiom of good business that a selling firm really sells two things—merchandise and service. Although retail businesses have made great advances toward self-service merchandising, many customers still want and expect good service when they are purchasing. Providing good service is equally important for manufacturers and wholesalers. Special services, such as cooperative advertising allowances, often have a great influence upon a customer's decision to buy from one particular manufacturer or wholesaler.

Delivery Services

Salesmen must frequently explain and perhaps justify their firms' delivery policies to customers. The manufacturer's delivery policies will determine who is to pay transportation charges for goods, and manufacturers may follow one or more of several delivery policies. For example, if a manufacturer sells goods on *FOB factory* terms, the buyer pays all transportation costs from the factory and owns the goods from the moment they are shipped. If the manufacturer sells on *FOB destination* terms, he pays transportation charges and holds title to the goods until they reach the customer. You will learn more about manufacturers' delivery policies in Chapter 11.

Generally, a local wholesaler is expected to deliver goods to retailers without charge. In most instances, he assumes the risk of getting the goods to the buyers.

The retailer bears the cost of wrapping packages for his customers' convenience and of packing merchandise for safe delivery. Delivery policies among retailers differ greatly. Most food, variety, and drugstores provide no delivery service, although some drugstores may make local deliveries of prescriptions. Department and specialty stores usually deliver free within their local trading areas, either using their own trucks or those of a *consolidated delivery service* that contracts to deliver on a fee-per-package basis. Many stores make a nominal charge for delivery service; some will not deliver merchandise valued at less than $3. Most stores encourage their salespeople to suggest that customers take goods with them when it is feasible to do so.

Returns and Adjustments

Some businesses have very liberal return and adjustment policies. Except when it is obvious that a complaining customer is trying to take advantage of the business, the adjustment will be made. Other businesses are noted for strict return and adjustment policies. Customers must shop extra carefully when they are patronizing such firms, because they may not be able to return unsatisfactory goods.

Most customers have legitimate complaints when they ask for adjustments, and every reputable seller stands behind his goods. He

United Parcel Service

The United Parcel Service is a well-known consolidated delivery service. Generally, packages picked up from a business in the afternoon are delivered to customers by the next day. Businesses using a consolidated delivery service have no investment in equipment, are reasonably assured of good service, and are relieved of transportation problems.

accepts returned goods if the merchandise is defective or is not what the customer ordered. For example, sometimes draperies may fade quickly, even though they were guaranteed to be fadeproof. Fabrics may shrink, even though they were properly washed. In such cases, the seller's policies should allow the goods to be returned and replaced or exchanged. This does not mean, of course, that a seller needs to make an adjustment on a product that was obviously misused. For example, if a television set is abused by children in the customer's home, the seller has no obligation to repair the set free of charge.

Salesmen can reduce the number of returns and adjustments by: (1) helping the customer select the right goods in the first place; (2) avoiding high-pressure selling methods; (3) being careful in filling orders and in recording names and addresses; and (4) making no unfulfillable promises concerning such things as service and merchandise quality and time of delivery.

Installation and Maintenance Services

With many products, such as wall-to-wall carpeting, air conditioning units, and furnaces, the seller will usually provide proper installation. He must also be certain that the person who will use the product is properly instructed in its care and use. Without instructions, the customer may quickly harm the product or become dissatisfied with it because he does not know how to use it correctly. A manufacturer of machinery, for example, is wise to train the purchaser's employees in operating the machinery he sells. This training may be provided by the manufacturer's salesmen or by a special serviceman.

Often retail salespeople must instruct purchasers on how to use their products. A salesman of vacuum cleaners, for instance, will show a woman how to operate the vacuum, attach the various accessories, and clean and store it. An automobile salesman will give the prospect a trial ride, show him the mechanical devices on the car, and let him operate them for himself.

A salesman must sell the available maintenance service when he sells merchandise. Few people today will buy an automobile, a television set, or office machinery without knowing exactly the kind of repair service they can expect from the seller. Many manufacturers permit goods to be returned to them for repair free of charge or for a nominal charge. With machinery, repair service is especially important. In large cities, major manufacturers maintain service facilities; in smaller towns and widespread sales territories, salesmen often make the service and repair calls.

Community Services

Businesses strive constantly to maintain or to improve their images with their various publics. Besides the policies concerning daily operations, most businesses set up definite policies regarding such things as donations to charities and contributions of advertising and display space to civic and cultural affairs. These activities are undertaken to indicate interest in the community. Through such community services, a business tries to be a real part of its community—not just an organization that exists to make money.

Many businessmen belong to service clubs that have a primary responsibility for developing high-level business relationships in their respective communities. These relationships involve dealings between buyer and seller as well as dealings among competitors. Most service clubs now have formal codes of ethics and committees on business relations whose duties are to educate members on the clubs' principles and goals. Some important service clubs are Sales Executives Clubs, Sales and Advertising Clubs, Rotary Clubs, Kiwanis Clubs, Exchange Clubs, and Lions Clubs.

Special Services for Ultimate Consumers

In today's highly competitive retail marketplace, many sellers try to attract customers by increasing their services. Retail stores now provide a great many conveniences that make shopping easier and more pleasant for customers. Among the more important extra services are: public telephones, escalators, banking and post office facilities, rest rooms and lounges, restaurants, theater ticket service, parcel checking, free parking, baby-sitters, beauty salons, personal shoppers, watch repair departments, bridal consultants, and knitting lessons.

Many large department stores frequently offer services that are only remotely related to the sale of goods. Such services tend to make the

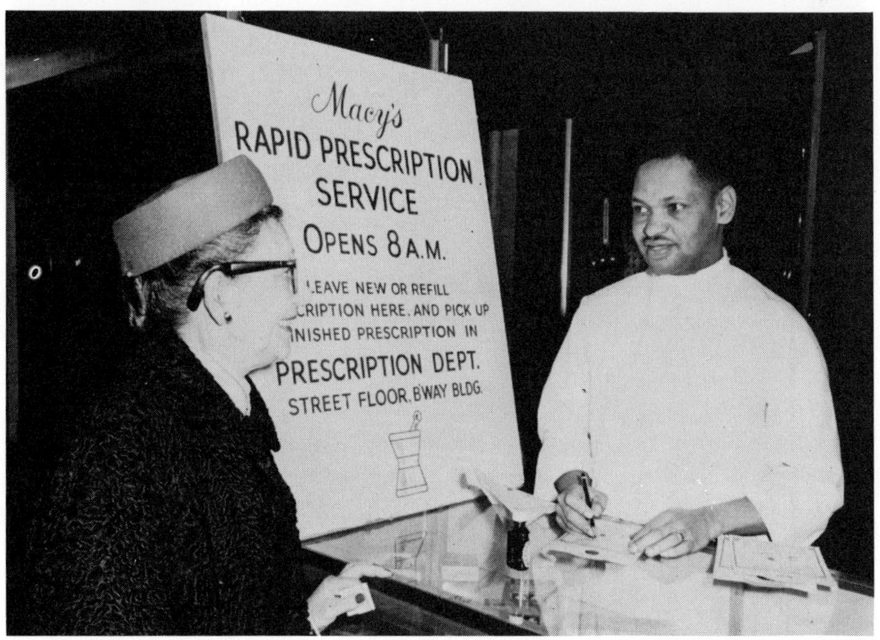

Macy's

Filling prescriptions is a special ultimate consumer service now offered by some department stores. Because the service must be adjusted to the needs of each buyer, trained pharmacists are needed to perform this service.

store a community center and to create goodwill. Examples of such services are lectures and concerts, art exhibits, travel agencies, and special classes in such activities as baby care, sewing, bridge, and golf.

Special Services for Business Consumers

Every dealer wants intelligent help in reselling his products, and he has a right to expect promotional services from his supplier. Two important services provided by manufacturers are cooperative advertising allowances and demonstrators. With *cooperative advertising,* the manufacturer agrees to pay part of the cost the retailer incurs in

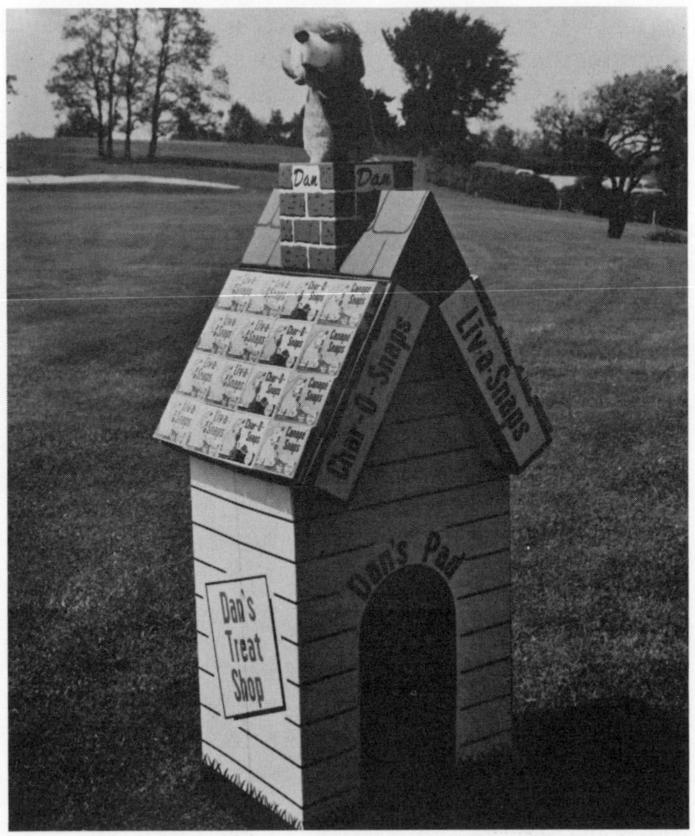

St. Regis Paper Company

Manufacturers and wholesalers frequently provide their customers with sales aids—generally advertising and display materials. Sales aids, or dealer aids, help promote the manufacturer's product in the retail store. Here is one such sales aid, designed for use as an interior display to stimulate the sale of pet snack foods.

advertising the manufacturer's product to the consumer. Retailers are sometimes reimbursed up to 50 percent of the amount they spend for advertising. The gross amount that a retailer may spend is usually determined by the volume of purchases made from the manufacturer.

Demonstrators, as you have learned, act as salesmen for the manufacturer's line. Sometimes the demonstrators are hired by the retail store, but most often the manufacturer supplies and trains demonstrators. If demonstrators are hired by the store, the manufacturer usually reimburses the store for the demonstrators' salaries. Demonstrators assure the manufacturer that his product will be well presented to the public, and the system keeps down the store's expenses for training and paying personnel.

Some manufacturers also provide management assistance to their customers. For some merchandise lines and types of retail businesses, model accounting and data processing systems have been developed. Automobile manufacturers, for instance, supply model accounting systems to their customers at a low cost. Occasionally a manufacturer may send an accountant to audit a dealer's books; and in some cases, manufacturers are prepared to answer dealers' questions regarding accounting procedures. Other manufacturers have worked out systems for handling merchandise control records, and still others have designed ideal store layouts which can be adjusted to the needs of a particular merchant.

CHECKING YOUR KNOWLEDGE

Vocabulary:

(1) goodwill
(2) FOB factory
(3) FOB destination
(4) consolidated delivery service
(5) cooperative advertising

Review questions:

1. What are three ways in which a seller can create or increase goodwill?
2. Should manufacturers and wholesalers be just as concerned about offering services to customers as retailers are? Why or why not?
3. How can salesmen reduce the number of returns and adjustments?
4. Why must salesmen "sell" maintenance service with certain kinds of products?
5. What are some important special services that retailers provide for their customers? What special services may manufacturers and wholesalers provide?

For discussion:

1. Sellers who offer many services to the ultimate consumer must charge higher prices for their products than do sellers who offer a minimum amount of services. In today's business world, which type of seller do you think will be more successful? Explain your answer.
2. What special services might be rendered by the following businesses? (a) fertilizer manufacturer, (b) radio manufacturer, (c) flour manufacturer, and (d) aspirin manufacturer.

part E

personnel policies

The personnel policies of most firms have become more liberal in recent years, and there are two main reasons why this has happened. The first reason is that federal, state, and local governments have passed important laws regulating employees' rights. The second reason is that management is coming to realize that it must give as much attention to the welfare of its employees as it does to the welfare of its customers. Even though a selling firm's merchandise and services are of high quality, the firm will never reach its maximum sales volume without contented, productive employees.

Before an employee can be happy on the job, he must understand and accept his employer's personnel policies. This is just as true for salesmen as for any other employees. Most retail salespeople work in a specific location each day, and the policies governing them tend to be fairly rigid. Manufacturers' and wholesalers' salesmen are generally moving from place to place, either in a large geographical area or in a smaller metropolitan area. They must be able to govern themselves conscientiously within their companies' personnel policies.

ACTIVITIES IN PERSONNEL MANAGEMENT

Personnel management is the segment of business management concerned with obtaining and effectively utilizing human resources. The areas of personnel management that are perhaps of most concern to salesmen are wages and salaries, working conditions, promotions and transfers, and training. Some businesses have personnel departments that formulate policies for all employees. In marketing businesses, personnel policies for salesmen are generally established by the sales manager or sales management division. Even if a selling firm has a separate personnel department, it does not establish personnel policies for salesmen without getting recommendations from the sales manager or sales management division.

The following discussion will cover some of the personnel policies which will be of most concern to the salesman. Because many of the activities in sales management involve establishing policies for sales personnel, additional discussion of personnel policies will be given in Chapter 15, "Activities in Sales Management."

Wage and Salary Policies

The salesman should, of course, understand his firm's wage payment policies so that he will know what to expect when he begins working for the firm and what he may expect to earn in the future. Does the firm pay the market wage and manage to obtain satisfactory personnel? Does it pay unusually high wages to attract the best people? If it pays less than the prevailing wage, are there compensating fringe benefits such as group insurance, paid holidays, and vacations?

The method of paying wages is also important. Does the firm pay a straight salary, straight commission, or base salary plus commission? Does it furnish a drawing account or expense account? Does it reward salesmen for exceptional performance through such devices as bonuses?

Working Conditions

Working conditions will naturally vary with the type of business and its location. Many firms have done much to reduce employee fatigue and to provide pleasant surroundings in the plant, store, or office. In many sections of the country, installation of year-round air conditioning has resulted in employee satisfaction and, ultimately, increased production. Giving coffee breaks is an almost universally accepted business practice, and employers usually provide lounges or rest areas where employees may spend their break periods. Large firms have cafeterias where employees may buy their lunches or eat lunches brought from home.

Hours of work are considered a part of working conditions. Some questions a salesman may have concerning hours of work are: Are the hours generally regular or irregular?; Is overtime paid?; What holidays are granted, and how much vacation time is earned in what length of time?

Promotion and Transfer Policies

Policies covering promotions to better jobs or larger salaries vary widely. Some firms believe in promoting largely from within; others look outside their organizations when they need personnel. Some firms have detailed plans for rating employees; others depend upon the general impressions that employees make on supervisors. In selling, the salesman who has the largest sales volume or has shown the largest sales increase in his territory is frequently considered for promotion.

Transferring an employee involves moving him from one job in the firm to another job. There can be many reasons for transfers, and employees should understand their firms' transfer policies. Sometimes salesmen who are destined to become sales managers will be transferred to different jobs in a firm to get an overall picture of the firm's operations. Or a salesman may be transferred from a traveling job to one in headquarters because he is unhappy with traveling.

Policies differ, too, in regard to discharging an employee. Some companies discharge only as a last resort. Others believe in quickly discharging an unproductive employee. They prefer to hire and train a new person rather than try to bring up to an acceptable level the unsatisfactory performance of the person already employed.

Training Policies

Most training in selling is *on-the-job-training*. A new salesman begins selling to customers immediately, but he generally works under the supervision of an experienced salesman until he can do the job by himself. In some firms—particularly manufacturing firms—training may consist partly of a period of study at the firm's headquarters. Here the new salesman learns about the firm's product line, company policies, and appropriate selling techniques. After this training, he becomes a junior salesman and may work under the direct supervision of an experienced salesman. It may be many months before he qualifies for his own territory and is recognized as a senior salesman.

BUILDING GOOD HUMAN RELATIONS

A first-class sales manager or other administrator of personnel policies wants his employees to feel important, to feel that they are essential to the organization. He wants to establish good human relations. *Human relations* refers to the interaction of people, and good human relations exists when people get along well together. An employer must establish good human relations if he wants his personnel policies to be effective.

The Manager's Role in Human Relations

The successful sales manager or personnel manager is concerned with each employee's interests, needs, and wants. He knows that all selling organizations must have a cooperative relationship between individuals before selling efforts can be successful. Managers find that their sales teams function better when each employee's feelings, attitudes, and emotions are considered.

In the last few years, dozens of books on human relations have been published. Seminars and conferences are being conducted everywhere to train employees in getting along with each other and to train managers in building good human relations. Some important rules for the manager to follow in building good human relations are:

1. Formulate fair personnel policies and enforce them without discrimination.
2. Give credit to employees for jobs they have done well and assume the blame for any mistake you have made.
3. Praise employees in public and criticize them in private.
4. Evaluate employees' performances periodically and let them know how they are doing.
5. Let employees take part, whenever possible, in decisions that may affect their futures.
6. Maintain good communications with employees so that they know what is going on in the firm.
7. Show respect for all employees.

The Employee's Role in Human Relations

Within the limits of his firm's personnel policies, a salesman can do much to establish good human relations with his co-workers. An important concept to understand is that every contact made with a human being can be either a plus contact, a minus contact, or a neutral contact. In a plus contact, both parties feel better because the contact took place. In a minus contact, some situation or attitude is worsened because of the contact. In a neutral contact, neither harm nor good results; the contact is merely a passing of time. There are few higher goals than to make every one of a day's contacts a plus contact. To do this, a person must assume that he is largely responsible for the response he elicits from another person. He must recognize that his duty is not simply to convey an idea but to evoke a favorable emotional response from the other person.

Bloomingdale's

Offering to help a fellow salesperson, even with a routine task such as stockkeeping, is one way of building good human relations. Cooperation among salespeople results in a more effective selling team, and everybody benefits.

The new employee, particularly, will find it hard to develop good human relations. Co-workers may take advantage of his youth and inexperience. If they think he is being trained for a higher position, they may try to discourage him by pointing out that they have worked hard for many years and have not been promoted. They may resent the new employee's efforts to be as productive as possible and his willingness to work late to finish a job. Meeting the resistance of co-workers and pleasing one's supervisor at the same time are seldom easy.

Here are some pointers an employee can follow to achieve good human relations:

1. Be loyal to your firm and to your co-workers.
2. Accept responsibility for all activities in your job and for other activities, if you are asked to perform them.
3. Be resourceful in handling your job and don't ask constantly for advice.
4. Show initiative. Stay after hours to finish a necessary job, take courses that will help you in your job, think of ways in which your firm's selling operations might be improved.

5. Show respect for the knowledge and skill of co-workers.
6. Avoid tension that makes you less productive.

Perhaps the best advice for the employee who wants to build good human relations is: Learn to see yourself as others see you. A person cannot be expected to influence and help other people unless they respond positively to him. Until one can see himself as others see him, he has no sound basis for knowing whether he is eliciting favorable responses from customers and co-workers.

CHECKING YOUR KNOWLEDGE

Vocabulary:

(1) personnel management
(2) on-the-job training
(3) human relations

Review questions:

1. Why have personnel policies of most business firms become more liberal in recent years?
2. Name the areas of personnel management that are probably of most concern to salesmen.
3. What have employers done to make working conditions more pleasant for their employees?
4. Describe the most common type of training in selling.
5. Name five things that a manager may do to build good human relations in selling. Name five things that an employee may do.

For discussion:

1. Can a salesman be held responsible in any way for the failure of his co-workers to be productive?
2. How important is communication in establishing and maintaining good human relations?
3. Is a large selling firm or a small selling firm more likely to have good human relations? Explain your answer.

BUILDING YOUR SKILLS

Improving your English:

On a separate sheet of paper, write the correct preposition to be used in each of the following sentences.

1. The stock clerk arranged the merchandise (on, with) the shelf.
2. Louise typed the order (for, with) the sales manager.

3. Experience is needed when selling wholesale goods (to, with) store owners.
4. Markup is directly related (to, with) the profits of a store.
5. The summary of changes agreed (with, to) our proposal.

Read both parts of each statement, decide upon a conjunction that you would use to complete the sentence, and write the conjunction on a separate sheet of paper.

6. Joe enjoys selling ______ his enthusiasm attracts many customers.
7. The price of the merchandise has been reduced ______ the inventory remains high.
8. The evaluation will be late ______ these changes must be made.
9. Bring the coupons when you shop ______ the regular price will be charged.
10. Several items have already been sold ______ we anticipate record sales this week.

Improving your arithmetic:

Perform the multiplication exercises given below.

1. If tomatoes are priced at 18¢ per pound, find the prices of the following quantities: (a) 4½ pounds; (b) 5⅓ pounds; (c) 7⅔ pounds; (d) 4⅓ pounds; and (e) 6½ pounds.
2. Find the total cost of the following items purchased by Frank Morton at a hardware store: 5½ pounds of finishing nails at 8¢ per pound; 24¼ feet of weatherstripping at 9¢ per foot; and 17¾ feet of chain at 15¢ per foot.
3. During one week, Sue Hill made the following purchases of meat: 3¾ pounds of sirloin tip roast at 99¢ per pound; 5¼ pounds of ground beef at 69¢ per pound; and 2½ pounds of chicken drumsticks at 59¢ per pound. Find the total cost of Sue's purchases.
4. Find the total cost of the following quantities of candy:

Quantity	*Price Per Pound*
3½ pounds caramels	49¢
2¼ pounds chocolate fudge	89¢
4¾ pounds divinity	69¢
2⅓ pounds peanut brittle	49¢

5. James Riley made the following purchase at Hank's Treat Shop:

Quantity	*Price Per Pound*
7¼ pounds English walnuts	39¢
8½ pounds black walnuts	22¢
5¼ pounds pecans	49¢
2⅓ pounds almonds	69¢

Find the total cost of James' purchase.

Improving your research skills:

1. Survey about 10 consumers to determine whether they like the protection of knowing that, no matter where they shop, the price of standard, nationally branded merchandise will be the same. Determine the conditions under which customers like to shop around for price savings on branded goods. Determine also the factors that may offset any possible advantage from resale price maintenance. Be prepared to report your findings to the class.
2. Listed below are ten different kinds of retail establishments. Visit five of these stores in your community and determine what types of credit plans these stores offer and what credit terms are available under the plans. Prepare a report of your findings and give reasons for the variations in credit policies from firm to firm.

(a) Chain grocery stores
(b) Independent grocers
(c) Furniture stores
(d) Drugstores
(e) Hardware stores
(f) Discount stores
(g) Service stations
(h) Laundries
(i) Men's clothing stores
(j) Restaurants

3. In order to set low retail prices, some stores may have separate charges for credit, delivery, alterations, installation, and repair. Ask five consumers whether they would prefer to have the cost of such services included in the established price for the goods or whether they would prefer to pay a separate charge for each kind of service. The class will then summarize the findings and discuss customer attitudes toward service charges.
4. Find in a recent periodical an article devoted to trends in personnel management and personnel policies. Read the article, prepare a summary of it, and write out your own reflections on what you have read.

APPLYING YOUR KNOWLEDGE

Case problem:

A particular women's clothing store operates at a very low markup by eliminating the usual customer services of delivery, credit, and alterations. Goods are openly displayed, and customers can buy most items without a salesperson's help. Customers take the merchandise of their choice to a wrapping desk where they pay for and obtain their packages. It is generally recognized that the store's prices are the lowest in the city.

An out-of-town customer has just selected an expensive coat from the store's stock. She has the cash to pay for it but is loaded down with suitcases and packages and cannot possibly take the coat with her. Therefore, she asks at the wrapping desk to have the coat sent by express or parcel post; and she offers to prepay the transportation charges. The store manager is called to the desk; and he courteously but firmly refuses to send the coat, saying that the store cannot deviate from an established policy which has been instrumental in making its low prices possible.

Do you think the manager was right in his decision? What effect would this decision probably have on the customer's attitude toward the store? If you were the manager, what would you say in an effort to retain the customer's goodwill?

Continuing project:

In your manual, describe briefly but as definitively as possible the policies you would adopt regarding organization of your firm, pricing of your product, credit, services, and personnel. Describe, too, the credit and service policies you would want from your suppliers.

Extra credit:

Collect as many examples as you can of how consumer preferences for certain merchandise and services in your town or city differ from consumer preferences in other geographical areas. To obtain such information, talk to a number of merchants—preferably those who have had selling experience in other parts of the country. If you can talk with a manufacturer's or wholesaler's sales representative, he can probably point out to you quickly how demand for his product line and services in your locality differs from the demand elsewhere. You can also compare local newspaper ads with ads in newspapers published in other cities.

After you have collected your examples, write a report telling how you obtained your information, the probable reasons for the variations in preferences, and the significance of such information in formulating selling policies.

Selling in the 1940's . . .

When the war button was pushed, marketing pocketed its ration card along with everyone else. Department stores expedited self-service, and Elmer Wheeler brought out a book, ***How Not To Sell, Gracefully.*** *The population bunched up around the middle, and by 1947, middle-class families had 43% of all disposable income, which carried them right to suburbia where discretionary dollars rule. "Convenience" became the marketable extra, and advertising found a new home: TV. In 1941, penicillin was developed. The biggest force in the postwar economy was the resurgence of private investment, which rose to $43 billion in 1947. Milk came in cartons, beer in cans, and everybody wanted a new home air conditioner. In 1948, the transistor had revolutionized the electronics industry. By the end of the decade, the U.S. was a nation on wheels, 50 million of them, while the GNP soared to $116 billion.*

(Reprinted by permission from *Sales Management, The Marketing Magazine* © Sales Management, Inc., 1968)

UNIT III

Personal Selling Techniques

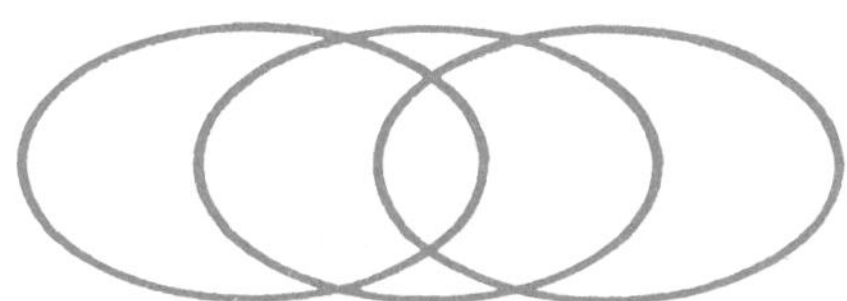

chapter 8

getting ready to sell

KEY QUESTIONS

A What are the advantages and disadvantages of cold canvassing, or door-to-door prospecting?

B From what sources may a seller secure names for a prospect list?

C How can retailers, wholesalers, and manufacturers prospect for customers through sales promotion?

D How does the preapproach of a retail salesman differ from the preapproach of a contact salesman?

E Is an appointment always necessary in making contact with a prospect?

part A

prospecting by cold canvassing

Many good products have failed to sell because the inventor didn't hunt for customers. Because he had faith in the excellence of his own creation, he thought that customers would somehow find him. The customers most likely to buy must be isolated from the total buying public before a product can be sold, and the job of hunting for and finding these potential customers is called *prospecting*. The salesperson selling automatic washers and dryers in a department store, the attendant selling gasoline in a service station, the farmer selling his produce from a roadside stand, the manufacturer's or wholesaler's salesman—each must make contact with customers before anything can be sold.

METHODS OF PROSPECTING

Many sources of prospects are available to the salesman. Three important methods of finding prospects are: by cold canvassing, by developing prospect lists, and by using sales promotion devices.

Prospecting by the *cold canvass* method means that no advance notice is given of the salesman's impending visit. In prospecting for ultimate consumers, the salesman may ring the doorbell of every home in a certain neighborhood. In prospecting for business consumers, the salesman may call on every businessman in a certain office building.

The second method of prospecting is to prepare prospect lists from various sources or to buy lists from a professional list supplier. Periodicals, newspaper stories, and trade directories are some sources of names of potential customers. This method of prospecting will be discussed in Part B.

Customers may also be found by making appeals through various means of sales promotion. Newspaper advertising, direct mail, display, and special feature publicity are some of the means that may be used. Appeals try to catch the interest of potential customers and induce them to get in touch with the seller. This method of prospecting will be discussed in Part C.

TECHNIQUES OF COLD CANVASSING

Cold canvassing is probably the oldest, simplest, and least scientific method of prospecting. For hundreds of years, peddlers used this method of finding customers. Selling firms use it to obtain both new business and repeat business. It is a unique method of prospecting because it not only searches for customers but also attempts to sell them products or services as soon as they are found. Persons generally associate cold canvassing with the sale of consumer goods, but it can also be used to sell goods to business consumers.

Cold Canvassing and Direct Selling

An important point that should be made is that cold canvassing is a form of direct selling but that all forms of direct selling are not cold canvassing. As you have learned, when a manufacturer sells his product directly to the consumer without going through a middleman, he is using direct marketing or direct selling. The four main methods of direct selling are route selling, selling by appointment, the party plan, and cold canvassing. The initial contact made in route selling may or may not represent cold canvassing. The names of prospects in a residential neighborhood, for example, may have been obtained from another source. Selling by appointment involves obtaining customer names through one of the other prospecting methods discussed later in this chapter and making arrangements to talk with customers. The party plan combines aspects of selling by appointment and selling by cold canvassing. Salespersons who handle Tupperware parties, for example, make an "appointment" to talk with women attending the Tupperware party. However, since the salesperson knows nothing about these women and since they may or may not be prospects for the product, some aspects of cold canvassing are involved.

Products Sold by Cold Canvassing

Even before the Revolutionary War, salesmen—peddlers—used the cold canvass method of prospecting and selling. This method, though, did not really come into its own until after World War II. Before then, only a few large companies—the most famous of which was Fuller Brush Company—were active. Today, some 3,000 companies prospect and sell door-to-door to ultimate consumers. Fuller Brush Company has been joined by such companies as Avon Products, Electrolux, and Amway.

Door-to-door selling was long used for such products as brushes, encyclopedias, and cosmetics; but now a tremendous variety of goods is sold by this method. Shoes, cameras, clothing, tableware, vacuum cleaners, stationery, and toys are some of them. Some sellers have found that they can get new products established on the market through cold canvassing and later sell the products through conventional retail outlets. Aluminum cookware, sterling silver, hosiery, sewing machines, and dishwashers are some products that have been marketed this way.

Depending on the product, two different means of delivery may be used once the prospect has been persuaded to buy the product. The product may be delivered immediately, as is done with certain inexpensive housewares; or an order may be taken and the product delivered later. Encyclopedias, vacuum cleaners, and cosmetics are sold by the latter method. Specialty salesmen who handle such products as office machines and equipment also take orders for later delivery.

Fuller Brush Company

Inexpensive household products, such as cleaners and brooms, can be sold profitably from door to door. The prices of Fuller Brush Company's products, for example, range from 39¢ for a child's toothbrush to $17 for a men's brush set.

Difficulties in Cold Canvassing

Cold canvassing requires a very special type of salesman. Because of the difficulties in this method, he must be able to interest the customer immediately in his product. He must be friendly, yet aggressive. He must be dominant, yet restrained. Perhaps most important, he must not become discouraged easily. It is probably easier for the customer to say "no" in cold canvassing than in any other method of selling. This is particularly true of business customers, many of whom resent being called upon by a salesman who has no appointment.

Preoccupied Customers. Since the prospective customer is called upon without advance notice, he or she may be preoccupied with business duties, household duties, or social activities that make him or her unwilling to listen to the salesman when he appears on the scene. This problem can be overcome, but it requires a great deal of finesse from the salesman. One way of minimizing it is to learn the hours that businessmen and housewives are most likely to resent being disturbed. Businessmen, for example, generally do not like to be disturbed early Monday morning when they are busy catching up on the weekend's correspondence.

Heavy Sales Resistance. Heavier sales resistance is encountered in cold canvassing than in selling in a store or direct selling by appointment. The customer who approaches a salesman in a store or who agrees to an appointment has already shown interest in the product or service and is ready to listen to the sales talk. The customer who is approached "cold" may have no interest. Or, even if he has a latent interest, he is likely to say "no" before he has really considered the proposition. His mental set may make him decide almost automatically that he doesn't want to listen.

Unavailability of the Prospect. With no predetermined arrangement for making contact with customers—whether house-to-house or business-to-business—the person the salesman wants to see may not be available. It is almost impossible to make a sale when no one with authority to purchase is at hand. This often happens in cold canvassing business customers. However, it is sometimes possible to interest someone at home or in the business who will arrange an appointment with the key prospect. If no one is at the home or business, a calling card may be left telling when the salesman will call again.

Difficulty of Supervising Salesmen. In cold canvassing ultimate consumers, the manufacturer or distributor has a problem controlling his

When your day consists of drying tears, making twelve peanut butter sandwiches, solving a new math problem, and a thousand other things, how do you find time for mascara?

Fortunately, you don't have to. Because Avon cosmetics are created just for women like you.

Frequently, one of Avon's neighborly Representatives will come to your door. She'll show you the latest things in makeup. She'll help you decide what's right for you.
Best of all, your Avon lady won't mind if you have to stop to warm a bottle. She may do the same thing herself when she isn't selling cosmetics.

So the next time she appears at your door, invite her in. After all, you deserve as much loving care as the house and kids.

ROCKEFELLER PLAZA, NEW YORK ©1969 AVON PRODUCTS, INC.

Avon Products, Inc.

The major companies in the door-to-door selling field are finding that there is less sales resistance to the cold canvasser if advertising paves the way for him. This ad appeared in a widely circulated women's magazine. Avon, a leader in this selling field, now spends about 3 to 4% of its total sales volume on advertising.

salesmen's actions. In their zeal to make a quick sale and move on to the next house, they are sometimes tempted to use unethical tactics. These tactics include gaining access to homes by pretending to be conducting a legitimate survey; misrepresenting the quality of their products; using high-pressure methods to prevail upon the customer to buy on the spot; and expressing willingness to accept small down payments, but with the customer agreeing to make payments for a long time and to be subject to severe penalties if payments are defaulted.

High Cost of Cold Canvassing. Cold canvassing is a costly method of prospecting and selling because many of the people contacted do not purchase. It is something like looking for a gold nugget in a sand dune, and there is a great deal of wasted selling effort. Usually the selling firm must pay the salesman a commission that represents a high percentage of the selling price. With cosmetics and household items, the commission may be 20 to 50 percent of the selling price.

Opportunities in Cold Canvassing

Despite the difficulties in cold canvassing, it is the most effective means of prospecting in some selling situations. With a product such as storm windows, for instance, the salesman can survey a house first and decide whether the homeowner might be interested in buying the windows. This survey gives him a better basis for his sales talk than if he were to approach customers randomly in a store. With cold canvassing, a salesman may be able to sell more aggressively than he otherwise could in a store. Also, if he can get the customer's attention immediately, he may be able to give a more effective demonstration than he otherwise could. There are fewer distractions in the home, for one thing, than there are in a store.

Cold canvassing is generally effective when a product requires very specialized selling techniques, when the selling firm wants to avoid a considerable amount of advertising, and when it may be difficult to convince wholesalers and retailers to stock a product.

EXAMPLE OF COLD CANVASSING

Here is how one salesman handled a cold-canvass contact. Study the dialogue carefully, because you will be asked to evaluate it later.

Gibbs calls at the Brooks home. When Mrs. Brooks answers the bell, he identifies himself by name and as a representative of the ABC Appliance Company.

GIBBS: May I step in to look at your refrigerator? I want to be sure it is in good working order.

MRS. BROOKS: Well, I guess it will be all right.

(Gibbs enters, is escorted to the kitchen, examines both the refrigerator and the stove, and finds both appliances modern and in good working order.)

GIBBS: While I'm here, will it be all right to look at your washing machine, too?

MRS. BROOKS: Yes, it's downstairs in the basement.

(Gibbs inspects the washing machine and returns to the kitchen.)

GIBBS: I see you still have one of those old-fashioned washers where you have to wring the clothes.

MRS. BROOKS: We've found it pretty satisfactory.

GIBBS: Let me show you an automatic washer and dryer I can recommend as being much superior. The dryer will spin dry your wash. (Shows illustrations.)

MRS. BROOKS: How much do they cost?

GIBBS: We have two sizes. If you'll tell me how large a laundry you usually have, I can recommend the best size and price for you.

MRS. BROOKS: It would be nice to have an automatic washer.

GIBBS: It would certainly be nice to be able to put the clothes in the machine, turn the switch, and forget all about them until they are all ready for ironing—and then to have an electric ironer to iron the flat work easily and quickly.

MRS. BROOKS: How much would the washer alone cost?

GIBBS: Let's figure on your weekly laundry requirements and work out the best size and price.

MRS. BROOKS: Yes, I guess we can figure on it; but I don't think we can afford one now. You'll have to see my husband about that.

(Gibbs and Mrs. Brooks discuss her needs in view of the size of her family and decide that a 12-gallon washer would be best. Gibbs leaves the necessary information about the machine for Mrs. Brooks to show her husband and finds out where he can telephone to speak to her husband.)

CHECKING YOUR KNOWLEDGE

Vocabulary:

(1) prospecting (2) cold canvass

Review questions:

1. Why is prospecting so important in selling? What are three main methods of prospecting?
2. Why is it said that cold canvassing is the oldest, simplest, and least scientific method of prospecting?
3. Name ten products sold by cold canvassing. How may these products be delivered?
4. Describe the difficulties a salesman might encounter in cold canvassing.
5. In what selling situations is cold canvassing generally effective?

For discussion:

1. Why is cold canvassing often the only way for a company to reach certain potential customers?
2. Many ultimate consumers distrust cold canvassers. Why do you think this is so? What could a reputable cold canvasser do to overcome this distrust? Give specific examples to support your answer.

part B

developing prospect lists

One of the best ways of prospecting is to develop a list of persons who are likely to be interested in your product or service and then to approach these persons by mail, telephone, or personal visit. Developing a prospect list is essential to the manufacturer and wholesaler and is useful to many retailers. It is usually better to use this method of prospecting than to go about knocking at strange doors.

The successful salesman must continually add to his prospect list. He cannot afford to ignore any lead, whether it is mentioned during a conversation with a friend, a customer, or another salesman, or whether it is mentioned in a newspaper or trade magazine. The successful salesman develops his own prospect list; he does not depend only on the list that his employer furnishes him. It is his business to find new customers. Some of the sources he can use to find these customers and develop a prospect list will be discussed in this part.

SOURCES OUTSIDE THE SELLING FIRM

The main sources of prospect names outside the selling firm are classified directories, organization membership lists, professional lists, tax lists, building permits, newspapers, and list brokers.

Classified Directories

City directories and telephone directories contain classified sections in which the salesman can find prospect names. A salesman of office equipment, such as calculators, might place on his list every business that has occasion to use such equipment. A salesman with an interstate trucking firm might list all firms that engage in interstate commerce. An insurance salesman might list all people whose occupations indicate that they can likely afford to carry large insurance policies.

In some large cities, the telephone company prepares a list of residential telephone users by address rather than by alphabetical arrangement. Thus, if a salesman wants to contact only customers in a well-to-do neighborhood, he can use such a list to select those persons who live on certain streets or in a certain housing development.

Organization Membership Lists

The salesman of an expensive article or service often finds excellent prospects on the membership lists of community service clubs and chambers of commerce. Many members of such clubs have fairly substantial incomes and probably can afford expensive products or services. Other organizations that furnish valuable membership lists are country clubs, golf clubs, sales and advertising clubs, and automobile clubs. These lists are valuable not only because they may include persons with substantial incomes but also because they reveal something of the prospects' interests. A member of a country club, for example, might be a good prospect for a variety of sporting goods and sportswear.

Professional Lists

The article or service that a salesman has to offer may appeal only to members of a certain profession. Thus, if he represents a manufacturer of medical supplies, he will use the membership list of the local medical association. If he sells law books, he will use the membership list of the county bar association. If he sells college textbooks, he may use a college catalog that lists faculty members and the subject areas in which they teach. Membership lists for practically every profession are available.

ARRIVAL OF BUYERS

A. M. C., 1440 BROADWAY

BOSTON. — WM. FILENE'S SONS CO.: M. Shapiro, aprons, uniforms, housedresses; R. Waters, misses' suits; C. Harris, misses', women's better coats.
CLEVELAND. — THE HIGBEE CO.; Len Carpenter, mdse. mgr., children's intimate apparel, piece goods; Charlotte Noe, girls' apparel, 3-6x; Jerry Rhinehalt, girls' dresses, coats, suits, 7-14; Leslie Rab, teens', dresses, sportswear, coats, suits.
PHILADELPHIA. — STRAWBRIDGE & CLOTHIER; Mrs. E. McCloy, girls' wear; Miss R. Dougherty, teens' wear; R. Moran, div. mdse. mgr.; Miss P. Thwaites, misses' better coats; Mrs. H. Porter, brides shop; Mrs. M. Strohecker, fashion coordinator.
PITTSBURGH. — JOSEPH HORNE CO.; J. Knight, furs.

ALLIED STORES CORP., 401 FIFTH AVE.

COLUMBUS. — THE FASHION; Mrs. E. Thewrer, aprons, housedresses, dresses; Miss N. Boyer, gloves, neckwear; Mrs. A. Stephen, leather goods, handbags; L. Miller, accessories, millinery.

JACK ANSTENDIG & SON-AMSTERDAN-LEHRER, 450 SEVENTH AVE.

AMHERST, N. Y. — PAMELA POST; Irwin Chertoff, knits, sportswear.
KINGSTON, N. Y. — LEVENTHAL; Mrs. Sylvia Leventhal, knit, dresses.
NEW ROCHELLE, N. Y. — TAFFYTOWN OF LARCHMONT, INC.; Bernie Alt, sportswear.

ATLAS BUYING CORP. 500 SEVENTH AVE.

CLEVELAND. — TOWER DISTRIBUTING CO.; Ed Ratner, mdse mgr. ready to wear.
DARBY, PA. — ABE FEINBERG & SONS CO.; H. Feinberg, ready to wear.
LONG BRANCH, N. J. — VOGEL'S; A. Vogel, ready to wear.
OLYPHANT, PA. — SULLUM'S; B. Abrams, lingerie, accessories.
PAWTUCKET, R. I. — NEW YORK LACE STORE; Jean Goldberg, dresses.

JACK BRAUNSTEIN, INC. 225 WEST 34TH ST.

ALLENTOWN. — JUNIOR COLONY; R. Hertz, ready to wear.
DETROIT. — FASHION; Alex Jacobson, ready to wear.
PARK FOREST, ILL. — JERI KAY; J. Kitzes, ready to wear.

HAROLD COHEN ASSOCIATES 505 EIGHTH AVE.

BALTIMORE.—LANNS OF BALTIMORE; Lillian Sobel, sportswear, lingerie, children's wear.
BROCKTON. — MAMMOTH MART; Allen Gross, children's wear; Howard Schecter, ready to wear, lingerie; Lenny Saks, sportswear, accessories.
CAMBRIDGE. — BARGAINS, INC.; Rita Craft, sportswear, ready to wear, lingerie, accessories, children's wear.
PHILADELPHIA. — JOY HOSIERY; Phil Rounick, sportswear.

Women's Wear Daily

In metropolitan areas, the published names of visiting store buyers are useful to manufacturers' and wholesalers' salesmen. New York trade papers carry daily announcements of arrivals of out-of-town buyers. Since each buyer is classified under the name of the buying office he patronizes, he can be easily contacted by salesmen.

Tax Lists

Tax lists are generally open to the public and often furnish the salesman with valuable information. These lists not only give an idea of the prospect's purchasing power but may also give his address. For example, a list of new homeowners in a suburban housing development would be valuable to a firm specializing in blacktopping driveways.

Building Permits

The salesman of building materials, shrubbery, or interior furnishings may compile his prospect list from published building permits. Announcements of these permits are published in daily newspapers or in special legal publications. Building reports, containing information on buildings being erected or to be erected, are sometimes published by private companies and may be purchased for a fairly small sum.

Newspapers

The newspaper—especially the small local paper—is a valuable source of prospects for such products as real estate, building materials, insurance, and household appliances. News items that furnish prospect names include announcements of engagements, marriages, births, political appointments, newcomers to a town, business promotions, business transfers, and real estate transfers. Although these news items are legitimate sources of prospect names, it is unethical to use news items about a disaster or personal tragedy to obtain prospect names. Unethical salesmen have been known to read obituary notices and then high-pressure widows into buying investments of dubious value.

List Brokers

Sellers who do not want to take the time to develop their own prospect lists may buy them from list brokers. Many sellers of insurance, membership in book and record clubs, and general merchandise such as luggage, pots and pans, and novelties, buy such lists. Lists of potential business customers are also purchased by industrial-goods sellers and by firms selling consumer goods to wholesalers and retailers. Some sellers exchange lists with other sellers. Thus, a person who has bought from a mail-order house specializing in gifts and novelties soon finds himself receiving catalogs from other similar firms.

List brokers furnish names and addresses of prospects for a given line of products or services. Usually, lists are purchased for a certain price per name or per thousand names. Obviously, the more selective the list, the higher the cost. The potential market that a seller hopes to reach must be assessed in terms of the selectivity desired. Otherwise, a too-selective mailing list may fail to produce the anticipated sales volume. Purchased prospect lists are reasonably accurate when they are supplied to the purchaser. However, there is no guarantee that they will remain so, for the population in this country is highly mobile.

There are two kinds of brokers—general-line brokers and limited-line brokers. A *general-line list broker* offers an extensive line of prospect lists. He will also compile special lists to the purchaser's order. A *limited-line list broker* supplies either national or local prospect lists for the product line in which he specializes. One such list might include all wholesale plumbing supply houses in eastern Ohio.

SOURCES INSIDE THE SELLING FIRM

The main sources of prospect names inside the selling firm are showroom and store contacts, recommendations and referrals, analysis of recent customers, and analysis of old prospect lists.

Showroom and Store Contacts

Salesmen of merchandise such as automobiles, refrigerators, ranges, washing machines, and furniture find prospects from among persons who visit the firm's showroom or store. Advertising and displays attract many prospects who do not buy on their first visit. However, the alert salesman will then make a follow-up telephone call to persuade the prospect to give further consideration to buying his product. Sometimes the salesman follows up the prospect's visit with a personal call at his home or place of business. Where good selling is taking place, every showroom or store contact is followed up in some way.

Recommendations and Referrals

A good way to prospect for new customers is to ask satisfied customers for the names of friends and acquaintances who might also be interested in the product or service. The customer may be willing to recommend the product or the salesman to his friends or to permit the salesman to use his name when he contacts these people. A recommendation or referral generally has considerable influence on a new prospect's decision to buy or at least listen to the sales talk.

Analysis of Recent Customers

Many manufacturers develop prospect lists from their records of past sales, and in retail stores the names of former customers generally make the best list for future sales promotion. Former customers, either cash or credit, represent an almost captive audience for future selling efforts. One national mail-order house, which also operates retail outlets, markets its encyclopedia by first preparing a prospect list from credit customers of its retail stores. The sale of children's merchandise on credit is an index of likely prospects for the encyclopedia.

When cash purchases are delivered, the names and addresses of customers can be obtained from sales checks. In some cash-and-carry clothing stores, salesmen ask customers for their names and addresses in order to develop a prospect list for future sales promotion.

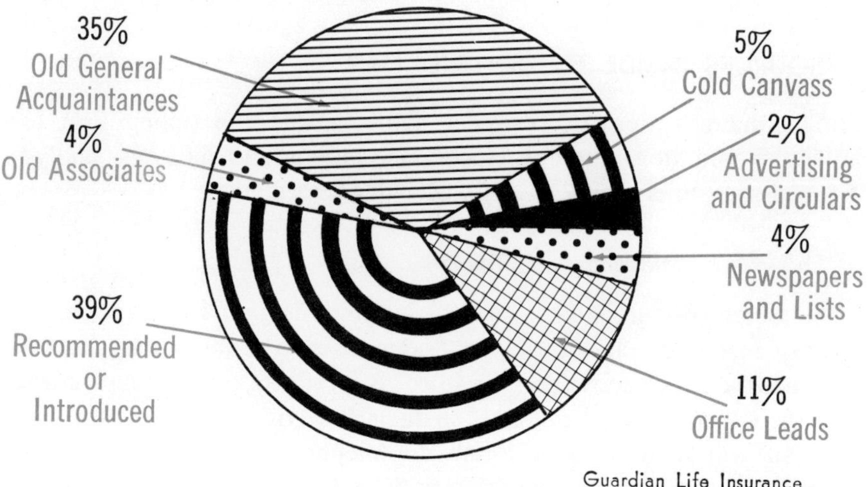

Guardian Life Insurance
Company of America

This chart shows where the salesmen for a leading insurance company find their prospects. Notice that in this particular area of selling, most prospects are found through recommendations from other policyholders.

Lists of credit customers are commonly classified as to the kind of goods customers formerly purchased, their financial status, the neighborhood they live in, and whether they buy for their families or for themselves only. A customer who has regularly bought low-priced dresses in a department store will be notified about a sale on household supplies but probably will not be solicited about buying an expensive oriental rug. A person living in the suburbs may be approached about buying garden supplies, and a mother may be notified of special sales on children's apparel.

Analysis of Old Prospect Lists

A person or company from whom an inquiry may have been received some time before or one who may have been a customer at some time in the past may be thought of as a new prospect. By going through his old prospect lists, a salesman may frequently make another approach by letter or phone. If he has a new product or service to offer, enough people are likely to respond favorably to make the effort worthwhile.

This does not mean, however, that prospect lists should never be discarded or revised. Prospect lists are of little value unless they are kept up-to-date. One insurance company gives this advice to its salesmen: "If and when any individual appears to be of little or no value to you as a source of profit, his name should be discarded from the prospect list. Do not permit your lists to become simply a collection of names. Bear in mind that eliminating undesirable names is important."

CHECKING YOUR KNOWLEDGE

Vocabulary:

(1) general-line list broker (2) limited-line list broker

Review questions:

1. What are the main sources of prospect names outside the selling firm?
2. Why are organization membership lists valuable to a seller?
3. What are the functions of a list broker?
4. List the main sources of prospect names inside the selling firm.
5. How may a business analyze its customers for prospecting purposes?

For discussion:

1. What organizations in your community might have membership lists that would be of interest to salesmen of (a) automobiles, (b) shrubbery, (c) dental supplies, and (d) children's encyclopedias?
2. What criticisms might be made regarding purchased prospect lists?
3. Is it wise to ask a satisfied customer to recommend you, a salesman, to a friend, or should you simply ask permission to refer to him when you contact his friend?

part C

prospecting through sales promotion

Using a variety of sales promotion media, retailers attract prospective customers to their stores. This is true whether the retailer operates a department store, a branch store in a shopping center, or some other establishment, such as a gift shop, service station, or restaurant. Manufacturers also locate some of their prospects by attracting customers to their showrooms or industrial exhibits. When prospects are located through sales promotion, there may be no personal solicitation of the prospect at his home or place of business.

METHODS OF SALES PROMOTION

Three of the most frequently used methods of attracting prospects to a seller's place of business are advertising, display, and special feature publicity. These nonpersonal methods are used both to locate prospects who will later be approached by salespeople and to make sales without the intervention of salespeople.

Advertising

Advertising involves purchasing media space or time to present product or service facts to the buying public. For most retailers, the newspaper is the most important advertising medium. The manufacturer depends upon newspapers, magazines, radio, television, direct mail, and other special media.

Most retail advertising is meant to attract prospects to a particular store, but some retail advertising is intended to stimulate product inquiries and orders by mail or phone. The manufacturer of consumer goods advertises not to attract consumers to his place of business but rather to his product, wherever it may be sold. Sellers of industrial goods use advertising both to attract prospects to their places of business and to stimulate inquiries and orders.

Inquiry Advertising. Much advertising in newspapers and magazines is intended to stimulate readers to write for more product or service information than is given in the ad. Inquiry advertisements usually include a coupon that the reader can fill out and mail in quickly. Pamphlets and brochures may be sent in response to an inquiry, or a salesman may phone and arrange a visit with the prospect. Sellers who solicit such inquiries must be sure that they are adequately staffed to handle the requests for more information. Recently one of the nation's largest health and accident insurance companies sponsored an advertising campaign that generated tremendous customer response. The inquiries were sent directly to the company's home office and were then distributed to district offices. The district office in an eastern city was at one point receiving 55 more inquiries weekly than it was equipped to handle. A great deal of potential business was lost, and considerable ill will was probably created because of the office's failure to follow up some of the inquiries.

Direct Mail. Both sales letters and business promotion letters are used to find prospects by direct mail. Each is a written sales talk; but sales letters try to interest prospects in a certain article or service,

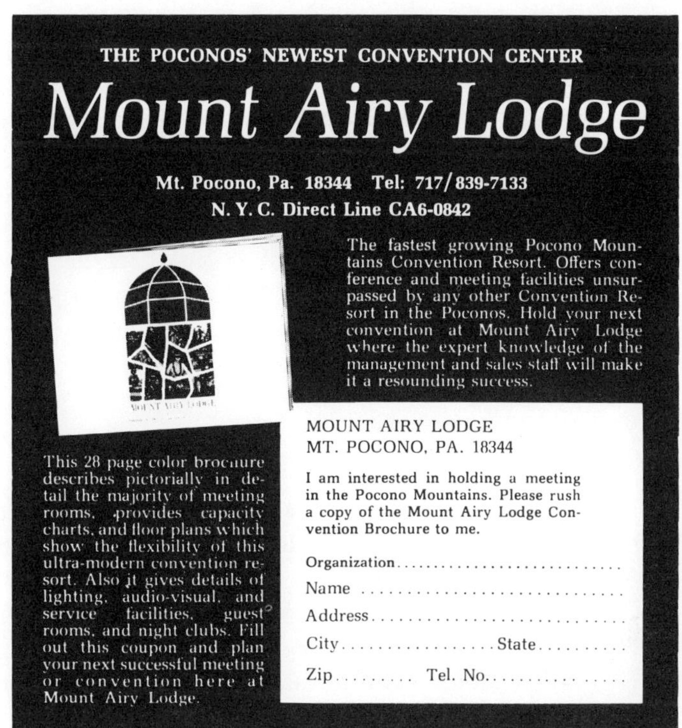

Mount Airy Lodge

Coupons are often included in inquiry advertisements because they make it easy for readers to obtain additional information without having to write letters of inquiry. Advertisements that solicit inquiries are commonly used by sellers of services, such as private schools, travel agencies, hotels, and insurance companies.

while business promotion letters try to interest prospects in a certain selling firm.

The chief requisites of successful sales letters are: (1) a reliable list of prospects, (2) an effective letter, and (3) a prompt follow-up. Generally, a short letter accompanied by a circular giving details of the product or service is more effective than a long letter attempting to give all the necessary information.

The business promotion letter may be used to secure prospects for practically every type of retail business. A prosperous bank in a North Carolina town sends a letter to all newcomers in the town, inviting them to become depositors. The list of newcomers is compiled from daily newspapers. The same bank sends a letter to every newly formed organization in the town—whether it is a large corporation or a small Sunday school class—inviting it to deposit its funds in the bank.

Business promotion letters frequently pave the way for personal visits by a salesman. Sometimes they merely break the ice by announcing when a salesman will call. Sometimes they include a postal card that the customer can return if he wants a salesman to call.

Dealers that sell primarily by mail or phone do their prospecting largely through mail-order catalogs, flyers, and letters with inserts. These are mailed to business or ultimate consumers in the areas in which the company has chosen to sell. Because of the waste that would result if such communications were sent out indiscriminately, the mailings are usually limited to prospects who have already shown some interest in buying.

Display

Many prospects are attracted to a store because of its excellent window displays, store fixtures, and interior displays. Most store managers feel it necessary to use window displays, even if they use no other form of sales promotion; exceptions are some suburban supermarkets and discount stores. These stores do not need window displays since they do not depend on attracting pedestrian traffic. Most people will make special trips to shop at these stores. Retailers catering to passing traffic increase their display space by recessing the fronts of their stores, by building fronts in the form of vestibules or arcades, and by building island display cases. Many stores keep their windows well lighted until late in the evening, thus adding to their value as a means of attracting prospects.

A strategic location for a store, a hotel or motel, an insurance agency, a real estate office, or a theater is in itself a form of display. If such a business is located where many people pass by, its chances of attracting prospects are increased.

Special Feature Publicity

Prospects are attracted to stores by several different forms of publicity. Special feature publicity may include the giving of newspaper publicity to store events without a direct charge for advertising. Generally, department stores and specialty shops that receive such publicity are regular advertisers in the newspaper; and usually this information appears in news columns rather than in advertisements. If a newspaper is to give free publicity to an event, the event must be something out of the ordinary; it must have news value. Such events include the showing of unusual merchandise; the holding of exhibits, fashion shows, lectures, and concerts; the sponsoring of contests; and the visiting of celebrities. The free newspaper publicity is, of course, supplemented by word-of-mouth publicity; and thus, many people are attracted to the store and may become regular customers.

Groups of manufacturers also attract wide attention to their products by holding style shows. Automobile and clothing manufacturers hold elaborate joint showings every year in various cities. These shows present the very latest models or styles made by the manufacturers sponsoring the show. Depending on the purpose of the show, orders may be placed on the spot or may be placed later with the manufacturer or dealer.

In large metropolitan areas, food stores sponsor exhibits to acquaint the public with new food products. Another popular exhibit is sponsored by manufacturers of boats and boating equipment. These promotions, used to attract attention to manufacturers' products, are undertaken on a cooperative basis with local retailers.

QUALIFYING PROSPECTS

Every name on a prospect list does not represent a potential customer. Some persons may not be interested in buying, even though it once seemed that they would be. Some lack purchasing power, and some may be unwilling or unable to settle their accounts. In selling to ultimate consumers, it may be desirable for the salesman to contact all prospects he has located; but the prospect list of business consumers must almost always be qualified. This means that the names of those prospects most likely to buy are separated from those less likely to buy.

Standards for Qualifying Business Prospects

Only those names on the prospect list that meet certain standards, from the seller's point of view, should be approached. The salesman should isolate from the entire list the names of those most likely to purchase or to purchase in quantities sufficient to justify the cost of selling. To isolate these names, the salesman should apply four general questions to each prospect name:

1. Is he a logical prospect for my line? The nature of his business, his location, and his class of customers will generally give the answer.
2. Will my merchandise or service help him solve a business problem with which he is faced? If I have nothing to offer him that he is not now receiving from his established sources of supply, he will not prove to be a worthwhile prospect.

Graler's Department Store
1066 Hastings Lane
Louisville, KY. 41506
613-891-6000

Largest department store in Louisville area. Best route - Kenwood Exit, I-71 N. Continue on Kenwood Road for 2 miles. Turn left at Emperor Circle. First right is Hastings Lane. Mr. Simms' office is lower level. Best time for appointment – 1 to 3 p.m. Monday, Tuesday, Thursday, Friday. Appliances - General Electric, Zenith, Norge, Philco, Whirlpool. Excellent Credit rating.

Buyer
George Simms
320 Greenhills Drive
Louisville, KY 41111
613-721-9306

Age-29; Birthday-July 4. Married to Amy Simms; one child, Larry, age 3. B.S. degree in Merchandising, University of Louisville, 1962. Membership in Kenwood Country Club and Rotary. Employed at Graler's for 6 years. Started as an assistant buyer. Became buyer in 1966. Knows his merchandise. Has full responsibility for purchasing appliances.

Prospect cards may be prepared in almost any form the salesman wishes, so long as they can be efficiently used. Each salesman will decide what information he wants to include on prospect cards. This is a sample of the form in which a prospect card might be prepared and the information it might contain.

3. Does he use or can he use enough of my line to make it worthwhile for me to call on him? This answer may be obtained by determining the size of the buyer's business and by analyzing the minimum order that it is profitable for the salesman's firm to handle.
4. Can he pay for what he buys? This information may be obtained from mercantile credit agencies and banks.

Preparing Prospect Cards

Once it has been determined that a person is a definite prospect, many salesmen prepare a prospect card for each person. This card may give business information about the prospect and also personal information about such things as hobbies, interests, and personal characteristics. Prospect cards are more frequently prepared for business consumers than for ultimate consumers. Salesmen who sell to business consumers contact the same persons regularly, while salesmen who sell to ultimate consumers may serve hundreds of different persons within a month or several months. Keeping prospect cards on each of these persons would be time-consuming and often impractical.

Before making a call, the manufacturer's or wholesaler's salesman can study the prospect card to refresh his memory regarding the prospect. He can then greet the prospect in a way that will show he has not forgotten his former visit or the prospect's interests. The salesman thus exhibits interest in the prospect and his business, and the customer is usually quick to recognize and appreciate this extra attention. Cards must, of course, be revised periodically to keep them up-to-date.

CHECKING YOUR KNOWLEDGE

Review questions:

1. Name three of the most frequently used methods for attracting prospects to a seller's place of business.
2. What is inquiry advertising?
3. What is the difference between a sales letter and a business promotion letter?
4. How is the strategic location of a business in itself a form of display?
5. What is meant by "qualifying prospects"? Name four standards for qualifying business prospects.

For discussion:

1. Why would a newspaper be willing to give free publicity to a fashion show in a retail store, whereas it would not give free publicity to an ordinary store sale?
2. Would sales letters or business promotion letters be more influential in attracting prospects to a business? Explain your answer.
3. Should a salesman with a poor sales record concentrate on qualifying his current prospect list more carefully or on building a larger list?

part D

the preapproach

Qualified prospects may be contacted by telephone, letter, or personal visit. No matter which method is used, the salesman should gather as much information about a prospect as he can before making the contact. The more information he has prior to actual customer contact, the better are his chances of making a good sales presentation. The securing of this information is known as the *preapproach.*

The salesman's preapproach is similar to a football coach's preparation for a game. The coach never starts a game without learning all he can about the opposing team. He knows the strengths and weaknesses of his opponents. He knows whether they are better on the offensive or on the defensive. He familiarizes himself as much as he can with the formations and plays they use. Then, based on this knowledge, he decides which of his men will play in the game and what plays they will use. The preapproach accomplishes much the same thing for the salesman.

PROSPECT KNOWLEDGE NEEDED

All prospects are different, and a sales presentation must be tailored to each prospect's personal characteristics. The close of the sale may be much the same for all customers, but the main portion of the presentation should be geared to the individual customer's needs and wants. To adjust the sales presentation to each customer, it is helpful to have advance information about the prospect. If the salesman cannot gather this information in his preapproach, he should at least analyze the customer during the sales interview so that he will know something about his characteristics the next time he sells to him. At the end of the sales conversation, the salesman may want to write notes or memos on the customer's likes and dislikes.

The Prospect's Name

A salesman should try to find out and use the prospect's name in the sales talk. This gets the sales interview off on firm ground because it helps show the salesman's interest in the prospect. In industrial and wholesale selling, it is essential that the salesman know the name of the proper person to see in an organization. He shouldn't just walk in and ask to see "the buyer." Many salesmen never see their key prospect because it is so easy for a secretary or receptionist to say that "the buyer" isn't in.

If the prospect list has been properly prepared by the manufacturer's or wholesaler's salesman, it should give the prospect's name. However, in retail selling there may be no way for the salesman to learn the prospect's name in the preapproach. In this case, he should try to learn the name during the initial contact so that he can use it in future selling situations. Here is how one seller—the owner of a barber shop—learned his customers' names. He decided to give away three bottles

H. Armstrong Roberts

Prior to calling on a customer, the salesman should refresh his memory on details concerning the customer's business, hobbies, and interests.

of after-shave lotion each week for three months. As each customer was about to leave the shop, the owner asked him to write his name on a slip of paper for a weekly drawing of a prize. The owner tried to associate each man's name with his face; and at the end of three months, he could call by name the majority of customers entering his shop.

Common Interests of Prospect and Salesman

Many orders are secured because of friendship between seller and customer. Friendship is based upon many things, and an important factor is the sharing of interests between salesmen and customers. Think of your own friends, and you will invariably find some common interests between you and them—you all attend the same school or church; you belong to the same fraternity or club; you are interested in the same sports; you are employed in the same office; or perhaps you live in the same neighborhood. The preapproach should indicate to the salesman the interests he shares with the prospect. This knowledge will give him some basis for starting his sales talk. It may also serve as the basis for building a lasting friendship and for securing future orders.

Here is how a knowledge of common interests can be used to make a sale. A real estate salesman, who was particularly interested in sports, had been trying to see a prominent doctor for several months; but every time he went to the doctor's office, he was told that the doctor was busy. The first two games of the World Series were to be played in a neighboring city, and he decided to go to one of the games. Knowing that the doctor was also a great baseball fan, the salesman bought two tickets. The day before the game, he called the doctor and asked if he had been able to buy a ticket. The doctor replied that he hadn't, so the salesman offered to sell him one of his tickets. The doctor said he would gladly buy the ticket and also accepted the salesman's offer to drive him to the city. Nothing was said about real estate during the ride to and from the game; but when the salesman called the next week, he was given a cordial reception. Eventually he sold the doctor a new home.

The Prospect's Buying Policies

A salesman will have a better chance of making a sale if he tries to discover, through the preapproach, something of his prospect's buying policies. A professional man, for instance, may prefer to buy all his clothing from one store; another may prefer to shop at a number of stores. One driver may insist on using a certain brand of gasoline and may go out of his way to get it; another may pay little attention to brands. Some business customers have a policy of buying from only one company. This is often due to reciprocity, which is the most difficult type of arrangement that a salesman must compete with. *Reciprocity* means simply this: a person gives his business to a particular firm because it directs business to him. Where reciprocity does not exist, a firm distributes orders to a number of companies.

There are other differences in buying policies from customer to customer. One prospect may buy in large quantities at long intervals; another may follow a hand-to-mouth policy and buy in small quantities at short intervals. If the buyer has a fixed policy, it may be futile to try to change it. It is better for the salesman to adjust himself and his presentation to suit the buyer.

The Prospect's Buying Problems

An important phase of the preapproach is learning something about the immediate buying problems the customer faces. If he is a business customer, the salesman might consider some of the following questions. Are his production costs too high? Is he seriously limited in space? Are his records cumbersome and incomplete? Is his product or service having difficulty competing? Does he need a new feature to give his product a point of superiority? Is his merchandise assortment inadequate to satisfy customers? Does his packaging lack customer appeal? Is he faced with too many customer complaints? Are his transportation charges eating up his profits? These are just a few of the problems which may be bothering the business prospect. The ultimate consumer has equally serious buying problems. The salesman should use his knowledge of customer needs, wants, and buying motives to determine, then demonstrate, how his product or service can help solve the prospect's buying problems.

THE PREAPPROACH IN RETAIL SELLING

Although the principle of the preapproach is sound, a salesman may conceivably waste time trying to learn all the personal characteristics of his prospects before calling on them. Personal judgment should determine how far to go in the preapproach. This is particularly true for the retail salesperson. The preapproach of the retail salesperson is somewhat different from the preapproach of the manufacturer's or wholesaler's salesman. It is desirable, but not always practical, to determine the prospect's name, common interests, buying policies, and buying problems. It is hard for the retail salesperson to gather such information before he contacts the customer; sometimes he must rely on knowing his merchandise thoroughly and knowing what it can do for all customers in a certain category. The alert retail salesperson tries to learn as much as possible about a customer during the initial contact so that he can better serve the customer in the future.

There are certain things concerning his merchandise and store that the retail salesman should learn to supplement his preapproach:

1. What types of articles are carried in the entire store. If he is working in a department store, he should know exactly which articles are carried in his department.
2. The location of all goods in the selling area to which he is assigned. A customer quickly loses confidence in a salesperson who must ask a fellow employee where a certain article is kept.
3. Some knowledge about the stock carried in selling areas other than his own so that he can direct customers quickly and accurately.
4. Whether extra supplies of articles sold in his department are in reserve in the stockroom and how to get stock from the reserve when it is needed. This is especially important in department stores which have adopted special forms and procedures to be used in getting stock from the reserve.

"I realize it's a big territory, Jones, but you'll have virtually no competition!"

Sales Management

As part of his preapproach, the contact salesman must gather all the information he needs to understand his territory fully.

5. How to care for the stock in the department. Some merchandise may need special care in handling or special protection from dampness, dust, heat, or light. No salesman knows his merchandise unless he knows the measures necessary to protect it.

THE PREAPPROACH IN INDUSTRIAL AND WHOLESALE SELLING

The manufacturer's or wholesaler's salesman, sometimes called a *contact salesman,* must consider more than the prospect's characteristics in his preapproach. Such a salesman is usually assigned a specific geographical territory to cover, and his first job is to study the economic and social forces operating in this territory and to anticipate their growth. He must estimate changes in such elements as population, incomes, and occupations. He must identify the expanding or deteriorating segments of his territory and the changes in their composition. Some segments, for instance, may be developing into business districts;

and others may be developing into better residential areas. He should try to forecast trends in the business community, trends such as the number of new businesses being attracted and the number of old businesses closing their local offices or plants. Through his preapproach the contact salesman tries to determine how his company's products or services can make a maximum contribution to a community's well-being.

From this planning, the salesman can make the most effective use of his working days. He may decide which of his present customers require considerable service and which can be handled quickly. He may decide to call on two new prospects out of every ten calls he makes, the other eight calls representing customers who already handle his products. Only about three hours of the contact salesman's day will be spent in face-to-face contact with prospects. Planning, traveling, waiting, preparing the presentation, and doing paper work will occupy the majority of his time. By good scheduling in the preapproach, he can make his three hours of direct contact time as productive as possible.

CHECKING YOUR KNOWLEDGE

Vocabulary:

(1) preapproach
(2) reciprocity
(3) contact salesman

Review questions:

1. How can the preparation of a football coach for a game be compared with a salesman's preparation for meeting a prospective customer?
2. Why is it important to know and pronounce correctly a prospect's name?
3. What are some different buying policies that a customer may have?
4. Name five kinds of information that the retail salesman should learn as part of his preapproach.
5. Other than the prospect's personal characteristics, what should a contact salesman consider in his preapproach?

For discussion:

1. Do you think the preapproach is more important for a contact salesman or for a retail salesman? Explain your answer.
2. "Reciprocity is an exchange of business that helps both firms." What is meant by this statement? Do you agree with it? What are the dangers of this practice?
3. What particular prospect information should be obtained in advance by the salesman of the following items? (a) accident insurance, (b) correspondence school courses, (c) expensive leather goods in wholesale lots, and (d) automatic washing machines.

part E

the appointment

"Mr. Madden, I have some new greeting cards that I've just received from the manufacturer. They're very attractive, and I think you might be interested in seeing them. Several merchants in town have made appointments to see these cards on Tuesday and Thursday afternoons. Aside from these hours, you could look them over any time. When would it be most convenient for me to stop by your store?"

In this excerpt from a telephone conversation, a wholesaler's salesman is doing the talking and is trying to make an appointment with a prospect. To secure an appointment, a salesman contacts his prospect by mail, telephone, or some other method and asks to set a definite time for a face-to-face sales conversation. In the retail store, the ultimate consumer generally approaches the salesman in person or by telephone; and no appointment is needed. Some business consumers also approach sellers instead of waiting for sellers to come to them. Making appointments, however, is necessary in so many selling situations that the salesman should know when and how to make an appointment.

IS AN APPOINTMENT NECESSARY?

Door-to-door salesmen generally do not make appointments. Many consumers would refuse to grant an appointment if they were contacted by mail or telephone, even though they might buy if the salesman just appeared at the door. In some situations, however, a door-to-door salesman may want to make an appointment. There may be no one at home during the day, or it may be important to talk to husband and wife together. In either case, an appointment minimizes waste of selling effort. Also, initial contacts are sometimes made with family members who have no authority to buy; and an appointment with the key prospect should be set up during the initial contact.

Manufacturers' and wholesalers' salesmen may find appointments unnecessary because some buyers have fixed hours for interviewing salesmen—from 9 to 12 in the morning, for example. Many buyers for department stores and chain stores and some manufacturers' purchasing agents insist that all salesmen who call during these fixed hours must be seen. Such firms realize that they cannot afford to overlook any product or service that can readily be resold or that will add to the firm's productivity.

Small-store proprietors are generally relatively easy to contact, but salesmen calling on them without appointments must expect many interruptions during an interview. The small retailer recognizes that it is good business for him to learn what the salesman has to sell, since it may be profitable to carry the salesman's product. The salesman should try to call on small retailers during what are likely to be their least busy hours of the day. In some cases, the salesman may have to rearrange his schedule to contact certain retailers at times convenient for them.

When a traveling salesman is visiting a number of cities and has plane schedules to meet, it is essential that he make appointments with the prospects he wants to see. Sometimes a contact salesman will call on an executive who does not devote all his time to buying. When this is the case, an appointment is also desirable.

METHODS OF MAKING AN APPOINTMENT

The salesman will often have to use his own judgment in deciding whether an appointment is needed. If there is any doubt in his mind, he should go ahead and make the appointment. The salesman who takes the time to make an appointment shows consideration for his customer. Appointments may be made by letter, telephone, preliminary visit, invitation, and by indirect methods.

The Letter

If the seller is from out of town, he may make an appointment with the customer by mail. The letter should not be a sales letter, however. The salesman should merely state enough of his business to (1) arouse the prospect's interest, (2) make him feel that it will be worthwhile to see the salesman, and (3) convince him that he should not buy from anyone else until he has interviewed the salesman. The letter should stress the importance of the proposed visit to the prospect rather than to the seller. An example of such a letter appears on page 286.

The Telephone

If, when arranging an appointment by telephone, the prospect asks why the salesman wants to see him, it is best to tell him the reason at once. The salesman should avoid a long discussion, though, since the

WILSON, NORTH CAROLINA 27893

July 1, 19--

Mr. Leslie Small, Sales Manager
Ohio Chemical Supply Company
1315 Weston Road
Cincinnati, OH 45223

Dear Mr. Small

You are undoubtedly preparing for the general increase in business which comes with the fall, and your plans probably include a considerable amount of direct-mail advertising.

Our representative, Mr. Samson, will be in Cincinnati all of next week and is planning to call on you on Tuesday morning. Mr. Samson will have a number of new ideas in direct-mail advertising, in which we know you will be interested. He has been working for several months on some clever features in sales letter writing and has also been making a study of what the most progressive wholesale firms of the country are doing along this line. The results of his study and investigation are at the service of our customers.

Mr. Samson will have a complete line of paper and envelopes to show you.

Sincerely yours

DRISCOLL & SMITH, INC.

Thomas B. Driscoll

Thomas B. Driscoll
General Manager

11

A letter such as this one can be effectively used to make an appointment and to pave the way for a salesman's visit.

call's purpose is to secure an interview and not to make a sale. If the salesman sells regularly to a buyer, he need do little more than greet the buyer cordially, announce that he is in the city or when he will be there, and ask for an appointment. It is often wise to suggest a time for the visit, to prevent the prospect from deliberating too long about the matter. In large organizations, the buyer's secretary generally answers the telephone. She can often arrange the interview, so it may not be necessary to speak to the buyer. The salesman should speak courteously to the secretary and clearly explain the reason for his visit.

Making appointments by telephone is often desirable if customers are to be contacted in their homes. The salesman who arranges by telephone to call on a housewife avoids wasting a visit when she is not at home or is busy with household duties. Moreover, the thoughtfulness of a telephone call may make the housewife more cordial to the salesman when he arrives.

The Preliminary Visit

When the salesman knows that it is difficult to get an appointment with a particular prospect, it may be helpful to call in person and ask for an appointment. Under these circumstances, the prospect may be less likely to refuse the request. If another customer has referred the salesman to this prospect, the customer's name should be mentioned at once to the prospect or his secretary. This will facilitate making a regular appointment. When the salesman calls to ask for the appointment, he may leave samples for the prospect to examine before the interview. Such samples will often arouse the prospect's interest in the salesman's product. Sometimes a prospect will decide to interview a salesman at once—just because the salesman is there—even though he might have refused to see him if the salesman had written a letter or telephoned. Of course, if the salesman is to have a reasonable chance of getting an unplanned interview, he should find out in advance the best hours during which to call.

In New York City, there are buying offices that represent retail stores in all parts of the country. In these buying offices, it is common practice for salesmen to arrange appointments by preliminary visits. Salesmen generally call at the offices from 9 to 11 a.m. and indicate on cards the visiting store buyers they want to see and the nature of their offerings. These cards are taken to the buyers, who check whether they will see the salesmen or not. Those they are willing to see must wait their turn for an interview. The interview itself is generally of a preliminary nature. It paves the way for a visit by the buyer to the seller's showrooms or for a visit by a traveling salesman to the store. When samples are shown, a sale may occasionally be made on the spot; but samples are usually shown just to help the buyer decide whether he wants to inspect the seller's full line.

The Invitation

In smaller cities where there are a number of likely prospects, the traveling salesman may set up a display of his entire line in a hotel or motel room. Almost all first-class hotels and motels have sample rooms where salesmen can display their wares. Store buyers are invited by letter, telephone, or telegram to call on the salesman at the hotel or motel where he has set up headquarters. Specific appointments are often made. Sometimes the salesman makes a presentation to the entire group of buyers, rather than making an individual presentation to each buyer.

Armstrong Cork Company

Contact salesmen often make preliminary personal visits to obtain appointments with consumers, dealers, and industrial users. Sometimes the prospect may decide to talk with the salesman on the spot instead of interviewing him at a later date, so the salesman should be prepared at all times to conduct his sales presentation.

Indirect Methods

There are some methods of securing an appointment that are more subtle than those we have just discussed. One method is for the salesman to interest the buyer's secretary in what he has to sell. A trusted secretary may virtually decide whom her boss will see, so it is just as important to influence her favorably as it is to influence her employer. Many a secretary has persuaded her boss to see a salesman because she believed he should know about the salesman's goods or services. It may also be possible to see an assistant if the buyer is inaccessible.

An offer to service an article will sometimes gain an interview when other methods fail. Suppose that, if an appointment for an interview is refused, the salesman says to the secretary: "I'm sorry I can't see Mr. Wessels today, for I would like to inspect his dictating equipment to make sure that it is in good working order." It is likely that he will be given an opportunity to examine the machine. Even if he does nothing more than clean it, he will probably be welcomed when he calls again. Some salesmen take a serviceman with them when they make difficult calls because of the goodwill that results.

One of the most successful indirect ways of making an appointment is to ask for permission to survey some portion of the prospect's establishment. The salesman of office or plant equipment, for instance, might survey office procedures, accounting methods, or procedures for handling raw materials. A salesman might survey any phase of the business in which he is knowledgeable because of the nature of the products he sells. Many businessmen appreciate the opportunity to have someone outside the firm make recommendations for improvements. Once permission is given, the salesman becomes thoroughly acquainted with the business' procedures and with key personnel. His recommendations are likely to include some of his own products and specialized services. Thus, his real selling attempt does not come until he presents his recommendations, often to a committee of key executives.

CHECKING YOUR KNOWLEDGE

Review questions:

1. Why is it necessary and wise to make an appointment for an interview with a prospect?
2. In making an appointment by letter, what should the salesman strive to accomplish?
3. Why is it desirable to make an appointment by telephone when an ultimate consumer is to be contacted in his home?

4. When is it good practice for a salesman to make an appointment by a preliminary visit?
5. How do traveling salesmen show samples of their products in small cities in which they have several potential customers?
6. Give several examples of indirect methods of securing an appointment.

For discussion:

1. If a manufacturer's salesman wanted to make an appointment with a wholesaler in his city, what would be the most effective method of making the appointment? Justify your answer.
2. Is there a danger of trying too hard to obtain an appointment for an interview?

BUILDING YOUR SKILLS

Improving your English:

On a separate sheet of paper, write the correct plural form of the word given in parentheses at the end of each sentence.

1. Grant's Melody Shop has a wide selection of ______ available. (piano)
2. Two ______ represented the defendant. (attorney)
3. The ______ of the new slacks have been hand tailored. (cuff)
4. These ______ were designed especially for cutting loosely woven fabrics. (scissors)
5. The assortment has been divided into ______ to avoid breakage in shipment. (half)
6. Most ______ of the western hemisphere were represented at the Arts Center display of Christmas trees. (country)
7. ______ had damaged the dress display window props. (Mouse)
8. ______ from two sides of the auditorium annoyed the band director. (Echo)
9. Paper and chemicals are the major ______ of this area. (industry)
10. Entertainment was provided for board members and their ______. (wife)

Improving your arithmetic:

Perform the following exercises involving aliquot parts—the fractional parts of 100.

1. A commission of 12½% is paid on all sales over $100,000. Sales last month were $164,000. Find the amount of commission paid. (12½% is an aliquot part of 100 because it is contained 8 times in 100.)
2. In a printing firm, 16⅔% of the 1,962 people employed are press operators. How many are press operators?
3. The Candle Shop's transportation expenses of $2,000 were 6¼% of August sales. How much were August sales?

4. A jewelry salesman determined that $9\frac{1}{9}\%$ of the 44 hours he worked last week were devoted to record keeping. How many hours did he devote to record keeping?
5. Accounts assigned to the salesmen below are contacted monthly. Percentages given for these salesmen indicate the proportion of accounts each salesman was able to contact last month. Compute the number of accounts contacted by each salesman.

Salesman	*Number of Accounts Assigned*	*Percent of Accounts Contacted*
John Berry	120	66⅔
Harry Masters	160	75
Phil Lackey	112	87½
Jim Wolfe	102	83⅓
Harvey Lamb	136	62½

Improving your research skills:

1. Cold canvassers may get involved in legal difficulties if they are not familiar with local regulations on door-to-door selling. Find out from your local authorities what regulations your community has regarding door-to-door selling. Prepare a short written report of your findings.
2. As a salesman for a printing firm, you have just been assigned to sell letterhead stationery to businesses. No prospect list is provided. Your firm has a portfolio of samples of all letterheads it has printed, and you are free to show prospects selections from this portfolio. Your territory covers a large metropolitan area. Write out a plan for locating prospects and for drawing attention to your offerings.
3. As the advertising manager for your school yearbook, you want to see a local retailer in order to sell him advertising space. Tell whether you would make an appointment by letter on school stationery, make an appointment by telephone, make an appointment by preliminary visit, or try to see him without an appointment. Prepare a written statement defending your choice. Include a summary of the personal information, if any, that you should find out about this retailer before calling him.

APPLYING YOUR KNOWLEDGE

Case problem:

Reread the dialogue given on page 264, then answer the following questions. Be sure to give reasons for your answers.

1. Would the average prospect have admitted Gibbs as readily as Mrs. Brooks did?
2. Did Gibbs do right in requesting permission to see the washer, too, even thought it was not in the kitchen?

3. Was Gibbs' comment about the washer a help or a hindrance to his sale?
4. Did Gibbs make a good move in recommending the automatic washer at this point?
5. Did Gibbs handle the first question of price well?
6. Was Gibbs' comment about the ease and comfort of an automatic washer likely to influence the average prospect favorably? Why or why not?
7. Was it good selling to ask the customer to help decide on the right size?
8. Will Gibbs probably sell the washer to this prospect?

Continuing project:

In your manual, describe the methods of prospecting for customers and the sources of prospect lists that you would use in selling your product. Then tell what prospect information you would hope to gather in your preapproach. Finally, decide whether you would probably make appointments with your prospective customers and describe the method you would use in making appointments.

Extra credit:

A representative of a television manufacturer is coming to your community to secure dealers to handle his line. First, list all the sources of information that he might use to secure the names of suitable prospects and tell why you think they are good sources of information. Then list the kinds of prospect information that the manufacturer's representative should try to get and tell why you think each kind of information would be valuable.

Suppose that the representative returns to your town a month later for another visit. His firm believes it would be advantageous to prepare the dealers for his visit by sending them a letter. Write the required letter, typing it if possible.

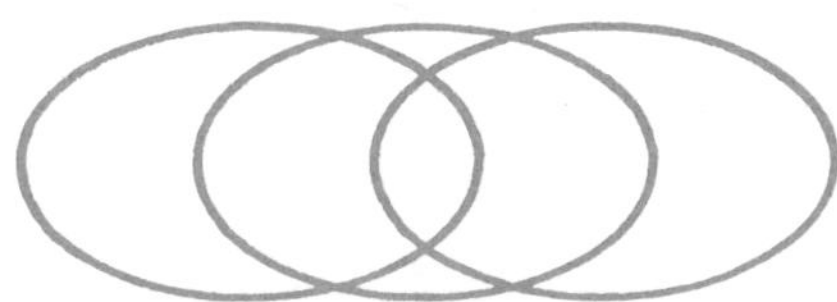

the approach and the presentation

KEY QUESTIONS

A Is the approach to a sale more important than the preapproach?

B What types of greetings may retail salespeople use in opening sales?

C In what way does interest differ from attention, and why must both be achieved in order to give an effective sales talk?

D Is there any type of merchandise that cannot be effectively demonstrated?

E What problems may the salesman encounter in serving the decided customer, the undecided customer, and the casual looker?

part A

elements of a successful approach

In any selling situation, 20 percent of the salesman's effort goes into making the presentation to the prospect and 80 percent goes into preparing for that presentation. In contact selling, preparation involves qualifying prospects, analyzing the needs of each prospect before confronting him, and deciding upon a strategy of approach and presentation. In retail selling, preparation involves determining the facts about each product in the assortment, analyzing the features and benefits of each, and figuring out the best way to present each item to the customer. In most retail selling situations, as you have learned, there is little opportunity to obtain advance knowledge about specific customers.

The *approach* is the second step in the selling process; it is the opening of the sale and a prelude to the presentation. Suppose that you walk into a store's handbag department and spend several moments looking over different summer handbags in a display. A salesperson walks up beside you and says: "These straw bags are lovely, aren't they? They're imported from Mexico, and we just received them yesterday." This is an approach. The salesperson wants to interest you in the handbags so that you will let her give a sales presentation.

In the approach, the salesman must interest the customer immediately in his product or service. Otherwise, he will not get the chance to go on to the presentation. There are three main elements in a successful approach: promptness, interest, and self-confidence.

THE IMPORTANCE OF PROMPTNESS

Promptness is essential in an approach because it helps to show that the salesperson has a sincere interest in customers and their buying problems. This characteristic of an approach is extremely valuable in attracting favorable customer attention.

Promptness in Contact Selling

In industrial and wholesale selling, promptness in keeping appointments is of the utmost importance. Business consumers have many demands on their time, and they resent being kept waiting. Suppose that a salesman has an appointment at 9 a.m. and another at 10:15 a.m. During the first sales interview, he realizes that there will probably be a half-hour delay in keeping the second appointment. Under these circumstances, the courteous and businesslike thing to do is to telephone the person who is to be seen at 10:15, explain that there will be a delay, and ask for a later appointment. When the salesman does this, it shows that he considers his customer's time to be important.

Promptness in Retail Selling

Being prompt is relatively easy for the contact salesman. Since he usually sells by appointment, all he has to do is be on time for the appointment. The retail salesperson, though, has a considerably different problem. He must be prompt but not too prompt; he has to learn just when to approach the customer.

When To Make the Approach. Promptness in retail selling doesn't mean that a salesman should pounce on the customer the moment he enters the selling area. Many customers like to look around before salespeople approach them, and in many stores they even prefer to wait on themselves. Under these circumstances, promptness means approaching the customer when he has shown some sign of needing assistance. If he has stopped to look at merchandise, if he seems to be uncertain of just which way to turn, or if he is clearly trying to get attention, he should be approached. But if he is just walking past a counter or looking casually at displays, he should be left alone. In some selling situations, a prompt approach is always desirable. In a restaurant, for example, even the unhurried customer appreciates having a glass of water and a menu handed to him soon after he sits down.

Reasons for Lack of Promptness. Why are retail salespeople occasionally slow in approaching customers? This lack of promptness may be caused by a number of factors:

1. *Carrying on conversations with other salespeople.* No personal conversations should be held within customer hearing, particularly one discussing another customer. Even business conversations should be suspended immediately when a customer is ready for assistance.
2. *Allowing friends to visit or telephone during working hours.* This is not common in all retail firms; but in stores where it does happen, customers are not getting the prompt attention they deserve.
3. *Indifference to customers who are waiting.* In some retail outlets where poor selling is being practiced, the indifference may range from the store manager or owner down to the salesperson.

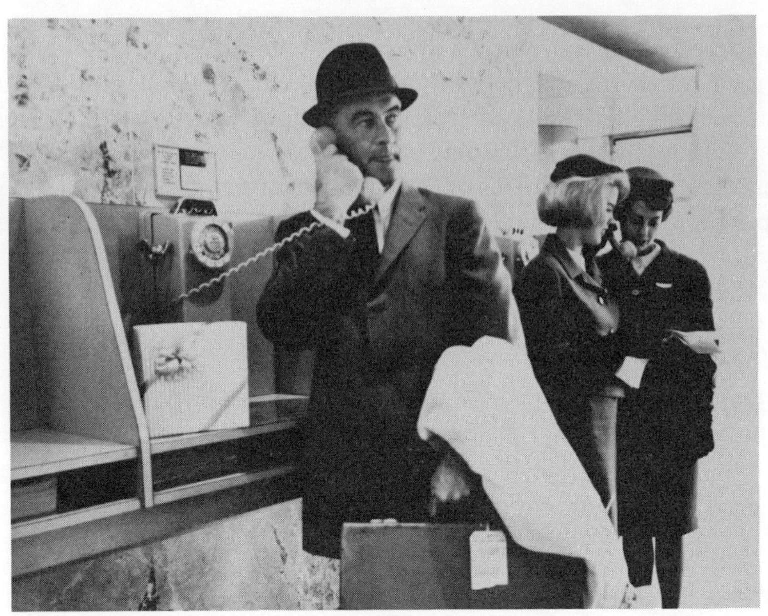

A T & T

Promptness in keeping appointments with business customers is essential; most businessmen resent being kept waiting by a salesman. If a contact salesman knows that he is going to be late for an appointment—because his plane was late, for instance—he should phone the businessman, explain the problem, and ask whether the businessman would prefer to set up another appointment.

4. *Becoming engrossed in other work and failing to notice customers.* Although retail salespeople must perform certain housekeeping duties in their selling areas, this work is always secondary to waiting on customers. Routine housekeeping and stockkeeping should be done early or late in the day when few customers are in the store.
5. *Being busy with other customers.* If the salesman is busy with a customer, he should greet the newcomer, then usually complete his sale with the first customer before helping the newcomer. In many stores, however, it is sometimes best to wait on a second customer after showing an assortment to the first—particularly when customers want to compare a number of styles before buying. The first customer always has prior rights. The salesman should never become so engrossed with the second customer's buying problem that he neglects the first when that customer is ready to buy or look at other merchandise.
6. *Fear of approaching a customer.* Some salespeople find it difficult to make the first personal contact in a sale. This should never happen when the salesman is selling a product or service that will benefit the customer. Salesmen who are afraid to approach customers need self-confidence.

IMPORTANCE OF INTEREST

A waitress in a Louisiana restaurant grows roses as a hobby. Each morning during their blooming season, she brings to work a large bowl of freshly cut rose buds. As she approaches men customers at her tables, she pins a rose bud on each man's coat lapel. Then she takes the food order. This waitress' interest in her customers is so genuine that she builds much goodwill for herself and for her employer.

A genuine interest in the customer and his buying problems is perhaps the most important feature of the approach. Some salespeople can be severely criticized because they show no real interest in the customer's problem; they act bored or preoccupied. If a salesperson does not immediately show interest in the customer, he will probably not be given a chance to continue the selling activity. The salesman who is truly interested in his customers shows this interest in his facial expression, his voice, and his actions.

Contact salesmen are more likely to exhibit sincere interest in their customers than are retail salespeople, mostly because they are responsible

General Electric

Some salespeople become so engrossed in stock work that they fail to approach customers promptly. Incidental stock work, such as replacing stock that was shown to a customer, can be done when there is no customer to be waited on.

for arranging meetings with prospects. Also, they meet the customer in his place of business—unlike retail selling in which the customer comes to the salesperson.

Showing interest in things important to the customer, even if they are not directly related to the sale, often facilitates the approach. A family picture, an unusual ashtray, or an athletic trophy in the customer's office may give some clue to the prospect's interests and personality. However, the salesman should not spend too much time talking about activities unrelated to the sale, particularly when he is making his first call on a prospect. New prospects are likely to think that the salesman is using the discussion of unrelated activities as a crutch and may even consider such a discussion an invasion of privacy.

The salesman who has a sincere interest in his customer and who shows this interest is said to have the "you" attitude. Frequently salespeople think that all they have to do to possess this attitude is to use the word "you" in the approach and presentation. However, using the word "you" or even repeating the customer's name throughout a sales talk does not necessarily mean that the salesperson has the proper "you" attitude. A genuine "you" attitude results from a complete understanding of and respect for the prospect's interests, needs, and desires. Without this "you" attitude, there is always the danger of spending too much time talking about oneself, the product, or the selling firm and never properly dealing with the most important problem: how the salesman can be of maximum service to the customer upon whom he is calling.

IMPORTANCE OF SELF-CONFIDENCE

Another element in a successful approach is self-confidence. Whenever a salesman hesitates or seems confused, the prospect is bound to react unfavorably. Good salesmen do not approach a prospect expecting to be turned away. Obviously, every contact does not end in a sale; but positive thinking can help eliminate selling failures.

One way to increase self-confidence is for the salesman to remember that he is rendering the customer a service by submitting quality goods for his consideration. As you have learned, the salesman's duties are essential in moving goods from producer to consumer; the marketing process could not function without him. The salesman shouldn't become condescending, though, because the prospect is also doing him a service by granting him an interview or permitting him to demonstrate his goods. A sales interview is mutually advantageous; so the salesman should approach the prospect with an attitude of self-confidence, tempered with respect and courtesy. This applies to all forms of selling.

Another way to help build self-confidence is for the salesman to know that he always presents a pleasing physical appearance. As you have learned, progressive business firms have dress and grooming regulations for sales personnel. This is true in industrial, wholesale, and retail selling. It is also true that good personal appearance is not so much a matter of an attractive face or figure as it is one of good taste and neatness. The salesman should conform to the standards of physical appearance discussed in Chapter 3, and he should check his appearance before approaching customers. Good taste in business dress, well-combed hair, well-pressed clothes, shined shoes, and clean hands and nails are some features to be checked. Anyone engaged in selling should make a great effort to have the best possible appearance because of the effect—either positive or negative—it has on the customer contacted.

CHECKING YOUR KNOWLEDGE

Vocabulary:

approach

Review questions:

1. What are the three main elements of a successful approach?
2. How may a retail salesperson know when the customer wants attention?
3. Name five reasons for lack of promptness in retail salespeople.
4. Why is interest in the customer perhaps the most important feature of a good approach?
5. How can the salesman increase his self-confidence?

For discussion:

1. When should a customer for a man's suit be approached in a popular-priced store or department? (a) when he first comes into the store or department; (b) when he first touches the suit as he browses around; (c) when he makes a second inspection of a suit after a casual inspection; (d) when he looks around for a salesman.
2. Is there a danger of trying too hard to look just right for a selling interview?
3. To what extent is management at fault for a salesperson's lack of promptness in approaching customers?

part B

opening the sale

In opening a sale, the main function of the salesman's remarks is to remove tension. Except with people who have dealt together for a long time, there is always tension between two persons about to engage in a business transaction. The customer is reserved and perhaps even resistant to the sales talk; and the salesman is probably wondering how he, his product or service, and his firm will be received. Both parties are on guard. The salesman should remove this tension as quickly as possible so that both can cooperate in solving the customer's buying problem. The greeting is designed to do this. The *greeting* includes both the words and physical actions the salesman uses in recognition of the meeting. What the salesman says in his greeting depends upon two things: (1) what he may have discovered in his preapproach and (2) how well he knows the customer.

OPENING REMARKS IN CONTACT SELLING

Most salesmen consider it more difficult to open a sale when they must call on the prospective customer, but this needn't be so if the salesman can make a relatively easy transition from the greeting to the purpose of his visit. If, through good planning, he knows the probable needs or interests of the prospect, there is a good chance of getting permission to give a complete sales presentation. When the salesman has been unable to get much information about the prospect before making the contact, he may ask questions to get further information.

Guidelines for Making Opening Remarks

The inexperienced contact salesman or the salesman paying a first visit to a prospect will find it easier to open the sale if he does certain things in his opening remarks:

1. Mention the customer's name in the salutation.
2. Mention his name and the firm he represents.
3. Thank the prospect for giving permission for the interview.
4. State the immediate purpose of the visit to turn attention from the salesman to the sales message.

5. Express interest in the customer's problem, mention a problem that he knows exists in the business, or ask a pertinent question.
6. Promise a benefit to the buyer early in the opening remarks.

A last-minute observation made while waiting for an interview or entering the prospect's office often suggests a suitable greeting to the salesman. A casual remark about the large number of people shopping in the store is welcomed by the owner or manager. A word of congratulation about the renovation of a store or factory is appreciated by the average businessman. Sometimes the salesman may be able to talk briefly about significant changes that have taken place in the community since his last call. These comments may relate to new businesses that have opened, shifts in the population, or a forthcoming business exhibit that may have a bearing on the buyer's sales.

Questions in Opening Remarks

In his opening remarks, the salesman may ask either verification or permissive questions. These questions may clarify the salesman's statement of purpose and reference to the customer's problem.

Verification questions are meant to determine whether information that the salesman has acquired in his preapproach is correct. He may have heard, for instance, that the prospect is planning to install an electronic computer. He may then say: "It's being said that you are planning to put an electronic data processing system into operation. Is this information correct?" Affirmative answers to such questions

Suggestions for Approaching a Customer

Find the proprietor and, calling him by name, say, "Mr. Blank, my name is Brown; I represent the National Cash Register Company." At this point you should have something different to say that will assure you of getting the merchant's attention.

Don't talk cash register when you first meet the merchant. You know he is not interested in this subject before you go into his store. Do not antagonize him by talking *your* proposition. Talk about *his* problems. There is nothing else in which he is so much interested as his own business.

The National Cash Register Company gives its salesmen these suggestions for approaching a customer. Do you think these suggestions could be applied to selling all types of merchandise?

make it easy for the salesman to state his purpose and proceed to the sales presentation. If the answers are negative, he can change his tactics and probe for the customer's real intentions or determine his actual policies. This probing should tell how his product or service can solve the customer's buying problem. Even if there is no sale at that time, the interview may build goodwill and pave the way for a later visit.

Permissive questions are meant to get the customer's assent for the salesman to go on with the presentation or even to ask some more questions. For example, the salesman of electronic data processing equipment might say: "May I take a few minutes of your time to show you this portfolio that illustrates the features of our computer?"

OPENING REMARKS IN RETAIL SELLING

Expressing courtesy and interest through voice and physical actions is more important than the type of greeting the retail salesperson uses. He should always bear in mind the importance of how things are said as well as what is said. In retail selling, there are a variety of suitable greetings. One is the formal salutation, such as "Good morning" or "How do you do?" These are appropriate when the customer obviously wants attention but has not shown interest in any particular merchandise. There are other more effective greetings, however, so the salesman should beware of using the formal salutation too often.

Service Greeting

A frequently used—perhaps overused—greeting is the *service greeting*. "Good morning, may I help you?" is a common example. The service greeting is intended to put the customer at ease, show the salesman's desire to help, and de-emphasize the salesman's desire to sell goods. This greeting is effective when there is some question as to whether the customer wants to be waited on or prefers to look around.

Some service greetings are decidedly bad: "Who's next?" "Do you want something?" "Something for you?" "Anything for you?" These greetings do not show proper consideration for the customer. Also, they may prove embarrassing to the customer who is just looking around. The question in the service greeting shouldn't require a major decision from the customer. "Do you want to buy a power lawn mower?" and "What price car can I show you, sir?" are premature questions. The customer is probably not yet ready to commit himself, and such questions in a greeting may actually drive him away.

Informal Greeting

An informal greeting is often used in service businesses with a regular customer clientele. For example, the salesperson in a dry-cleaning establishment might say: "How are you, Mr. Swanson? It's good that you brought these suits in today since we have a special on them this week." A service station attendant or owner can build goodwill by using greetings such as these: "It's good to see you, Dr. Barrett. Did you enjoy your vacation?" or "Well, how's the new car running?" Customers respond to being treated in a friendly manner; they like to feel that they are recognized and that their business is appreciated.

Merchandise Greeting

A particularly effective greeting is the *merchandise greeting*. It is usually the best one to use when a customer is looking at merchandise on display. The merchandise greeting refers directly to the goods the customer is looking at and perhaps handling. Thus, a saleswoman observing a customer examining a hosiery display might say: "Here's a new shade that goes well with the colors being worn this fall." Such a comment stimulates the customer's interest and is likely to trigger a response that will get the sales presentation under way.

Transferring Attention from the Salesman

When a salesman approaches a prospective customer, that customer's attention is probably directed first to the salesman. The salesman must, however, direct attention as soon as possible to the article or service being offered. Whatever impression of the salesman the prospect receives, favorable or unfavorable, it is likely to be transferred to the goods or services that are being presented.

In a retail store, it is fairly easy to turn attention to the goods. If the merchandise greeting is used, the customer's attention is focused on the goods immediately. If a question is used in the greeting, it should be directed to the customer's merchandise needs. If a formal greeting is used, a brief pause usually results during which the customer may express his needs.

THE INATTENTIVE CUSTOMER

Particularly during the opening of a sale, the customer's attention may wander. This is a normal situation and usually occurs because he

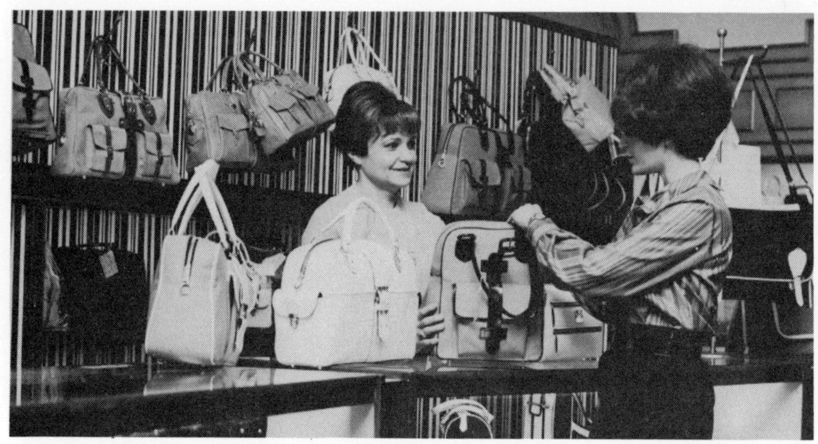

Franklin Simon

A merchandise greeting such as "This style of tote bag is very popular this fall" is likely to stimulate the customer's interest in the article.

is not interested enough in buying. Nearly every student can testify that his attention sometimes wanders even during a very interesting class hour. But just as a good teacher uses various techniques to recapture attention, the salesman should be able to switch the customer's attention back to his product or service.

Sometimes the customer's attention may be regained by asking a simple question or by summarizing what has been said up to that point. This at least consolidates the points the salesman has made and brings the prospect up-to-date so that the salesman can give his presentation. Sometimes the customer's attention can be retrieved by handing him an article, a model of the product, or an interesting piece of advertising literature dealing with the product. Generally, this will bring the customer's attention back to what the salesman has been talking about.

One of the best ways to hold the customer's attention is for the salesman to always look at the customer to show that the customer's needs have his undivided attention. Because speech is his number-one tool, he should become expert in it, following the guidelines given in Chapters 3 and 5. He should speak clearly in a well-modulated voice, always enunciating correctly and using language the listener understands. He should make sure that the technical aspects of his goods or services are made clear to the prospect. If the salesman tailors his opening remarks to each customer, he can get the sales interview off to a good start.

How To Attract and Hold the Customer's Attention

- The salesman momentarily attracts attention to himself through a pleasing physical appearance, well-modulated voice, courteous manner, and air of self-confidence.
- The salesman deliberately repeats the prime product features and benefits. He (1) tells his customer what he is going to tell him, (2) tells him, and (3) tells him what he has told him.
- The salesman employs the principle of contrast by varying the pace of his speech.
- The salesman employs movement. He sets up a simple display, demonstrates the goods, sketches a layout or writes down some figures, moves about, and gestures.
- The salesman isolates the product under discussion from other products so that the customer's attention will not be diverted to other products.
- The salesman may do something unusual to attract lagging attention, such as dropping a dish to show its strength or immersing a watch in water to show it is waterproof.

Before the salesman can give his sales talk, he must learn how to capture and hold the customer's attention. Here are some techniques for doing this.

GUIDELINES TO BEGINNING THE SALE

Here is a summary of points the salesman will want to follow in approaching customers and opening the sale:

1. Be sure your physical appearance is beyond reproach.
2. Be prompt in keeping appointments or in waiting on customers who are ready for your attention.
3. Be genuinely interested in the customer and his problems.
4. Have confidence in yourself and your product or service.
5. Greet the customer cordially with opening remarks suitable to the selling situation.
6. During the approach, try to sense the customer's mood and adjust your remarks to it.
7. Have your selling points organized so that your strongest ones can be used early.
8. When possible, give the prospect a sample of your product.
9. In opening a sale, appeal to as many senses as possible.
10. Place a value on the buyer's time as well as your own.

CHECKING YOUR KNOWLEDGE

Vocabulary:

(1) greeting
(2) verification questions
(3) permissive questions
(4) service greeting
(5) merchandise greeting

Review questions:

1. Upon what two things does a salesman's greeting depend?
2. What guidelines should generally be followed by the inexperienced contact salesman in greeting a customer?
3. Why do salesmen sometimes ask questions in their opening remarks?
4. What can the salesman do to recapture the attention of an inattentive customer?
5. List eight points to remember in beginning the sale.

For discussion:

1. Evaluate the effectiveness of the following greetings and describe the conditions under which each approach might be used: (a) Good morning!; (b) Good morning, I'm Mr. Chapman representing the Barto Corporation. May I speak with Mr. Edmonds?; (c) Good morning. May I help you?; (d) May I be of assistance to you?; (e) Find anything that interests you?
2. What is wrong with each of the following questions used as greetings? (a) Would you be interested in . . .?; (b) Is there anything for you?; (c) What purchase did you have in mind?; (d) Are you waiting for someone?; (e) Do you know the advantages of this. . . .?

part C

the sales talk

You have probably had an experience like this. You're walking down a business street, window shopping, when you suddenly notice an unusual window display. You look at the display briefly, then walk on because you aren't interested in the merchandise displayed there. Your attention was attracted, but you were not interested.

This can also happen in a sales transaction. The salesman may have all the background information he needs—information about customer behavior, his product, his firm—and still not make a sale. Often this failure is because he can't handle the transition from the approach to the second part of the sale: getting the customer interested in what he is selling.

Interest is really just sustained attention, but there is this significant difference: attention is largely involuntary, whereas interest is voluntary. Attention is affected by many factors outside the customer's control, but interest develops because the customer wants it to develop. A salesman may call attention to a particular product or show how this product will meet the customer's needs. If he can't do this skillfully, the customer's attention may be diverted by other merchandise, people passing by, or even the salesman's actions or mannerisms. Unless the customer's attention can be held and his interest aroused, there is little chance for continuing the sale.

GETTING THE CUSTOMER INTERESTED IN THE PRODUCT

The sales talk is intended to interest the customer in the product, and the talk may be divided into two parts: (1) the initial statement about the product or service and (2) a later, more detailed account of features and benefits. The second portion of the sales talk is usually given as the salesman demonstrates the product. Because of the great importance of demonstrating a product effectively, demonstration will be discussed separately in Part D.

The Opening Barrage

Brief initial statements that include a number of key product features are called the *opening barrage*. For example, in presenting a boy's shoe to the mother, a salesman may say: "This is a sturdy cowhide oxford with a scuffproof vinyl toe and skidproof rubber soles. It stays new-looking, even if your son drags his toes, and won't slip if he runs about in rainy weather." Note the elements in this opening barrage:

1. It names four features of the shoe: cowhide material, oxford style, vinyl toe covering, and rubber sole.
2. It relates these features to the customer's needs and wants: sturdy, scuffproof (retaining good appearance in rough use), and skidproof.
3. It is exact and interesting: "oxford" is used, for instance, instead of "shoe," which is obvious.
4. It is short: only 36 words, which will probably take no more than 20 seconds to utter.

This opening barrage is short enough to be used as a merchandise approach, if the customer were looking at the shoes when the salesman contacted her. It might also be used to determine the customer's exact wants or to start the sales talk after the salesman is reasonably sure he has found the most suitable merchandise.

In mentioning a number of product features and benefits, the salesman hopes that at least one will strike home and interest the customer in the shoes. The opening barrage should always include the product feature that makes it superior in at least one respect to competing products. For the shoe, it may be the vinyl-covered toe. If the customer shows interest in that feature, the salesman should go on to explain that even though vinyl is one of the strongest plastics, it doesn't detract from the appearance of the leather, that the toes will not scuff after rough wearing, and that they will look attractive with a minimum of care.

If none of the "shots" in the opening barrage draws a favorable response from the customer, it may mean that the salesman is presenting the wrong shoes.

Tested Selling Sentences

Contact salesmen are often taught a complete sales talk that covers each product, its features, and its benefits in the most compelling language the selling firm can devise. Some selling firms believe that this is the surest way to interest customers in their products. For a new salesman with one or a few products to sell, a "canned" talk is likely to create interest better than the impromptu talk he might otherwise make. But such precomposed talks are not suitable for the experienced salesman who knows how to adjust his talk to each customer and to interest the customer quickly in his product. Nor are they suitable for the retail salesperson who often has hundreds of different articles to sell. For such situations, a short opening barrage should be developed only for each key item in each line. Different statements should be tried out, and those that prove most effective may be called *tested selling sentences.*

A good deal of research has been done to determine the most effective selling sentences for various articles. Some of these sentences seem to have increased sales tremendously in certain selling situations. However, part of the success was undoubtedly due to the fact that during the test period, all salespeople were concentrating on certain products and were showing more interest and enthusiasm for these products than they normally would have shown.

A standard list of tested selling sentences shouldn't be relied upon solely, because each statement must be devised for a specific product and because merchandise features are constantly changing. Then, too, customers vary in their receptivity to various phrases and appeals. One of the best ways to determine what should be said in the opening barrage and how best to say it is to study current catalogs of the large mail-order companies. Their copywriters are expert in selling with words, since they cannot demonstrate the product nor obtain customer participation in the sales talk. What these experts write about each product can be readily converted into successful opening barrages and can also provide ammunition for the entire sales talk.

MAKING THE CUSTOMER WANT THE PRODUCT

Even if a customer is interested in a product, he will not necessarily buy it. Interest must be developed into a real desire for the product. To create desire, the salesman must effectively relate the article's features to the customer's needs and wants. Just talking about the goods and their technical features is not enough. The customer must be made to see how the goods or services will satisfy his needs. Simply stated, this is selling from the buyer's viewpoint. To create desire by means of the sales talk, the salesman must appeal to the customer's emotions, reason, or both.

Appealing to Emotions

Appealing to the emotions is most easily done by picturing an article in use. A vacation by automobile next summer, made possible by the purchase of a new car; the advantages of a college education for a son or daughter, made possible by an insurance policy or bank loan; the comforts of a cool home on a hot summer evening, realized through installation of central air conditioning—these are some ways in which desire may be created by appealing to the prospect's emotions.

In each of these examples, the prospect's emotions are reached through his imagination. The salesman's ability to appeal to the prospect's imagination depends partly upon the development of his own imagination and his enthusiasm. No salesman can make another see mental pictures that he does not see himself. Enthusiasm, too, is essential. A cold, indifferent sales talk—even though it gives all the advantages to be gained by using the article or service—will not secure an order. Of course, enthusiasm must be sincere; it should spring from knowledge of and belief in the article. The salesman who pretends to be enthusiastic about every article he sells or about the value of an article for every customer's needs, is probably insincere. His enthusiasm

A Sales Interview

Salesperson: Good morning. May I help you?

Mrs. Barton: I'm looking for a pair of gloves or mittens.

Salesperson: Are they for you?

Mrs. Barton: No, they're for my married daughter.

Salesperson: Will the gloves be for dress or everyday wear?

Mrs. Barton: For everyday wear. My daughter often takes her two little children to the park on cold days and spends a great deal of time in the cold while they play.

Salesperson: She would need warm gloves, then, and would probably like them to have leather palms so that she could handle packages or a stroller easily. (scans stock) Here's a mitten that we just received. It's made of Orlon acrylic fiber which is warm, sheds water, and doesn't shrink or mat when it's washed. It's easy to pull on and off (demonstrates) and is quite smart-looking. The price is only $4.95. I might mention, too, that no other store in the city stocks this mitten.

Mrs. Barton: (taking the mitten and examining it) Yes, it is very attractive.

Salesperson: (shows another article) Here's a slightly dressier glove which has pliable leather on both the back and palm. These knitted gussets between the fingers and at the sides are quite practical and attractive. This double-knitted wristband is very study, too. This glove costs $2 more than the mitten you're holding, and both the gloves and mittens come in different colors.

Mrs. Barton: I like the mitten. What sizes do you have? I'm afraid I've forgotten my daughter's size.

Salesperson: Both pairs come in small, medium, and large sizes. How does your daughter's hand compare with yours?

Mrs. Barton: About the same size, I guess, but she has longer arms and needs extra protection on cold days.

Salesperson: Then I'd recommend the large size. What color would you be interested in?

Mrs. Barton: My daughter's coat is gray.

Salesperson: (checking stock) Here's a pair of gray mittens that should blend well with almost any shade of gray.

Mrs. Barton: Good. I'll take this pair.

This salesperson's astuteness in correctly determining the customer's needs and wants and in showing exactly the right goods eventually resulted in the sale of five articles. Mrs. Barton liked the dressier gloves so much that she returned to the store the next day and bought a pair for herself. A few weeks later, she bought three more pairs of mittens to give as Christmas gifts.

is just on the surface, and it will ordinarily not create desire. Where genuine enthusiasm exists, it rubs off on persons the salesman contacts.

With many retail customers, an appeal to the emotions is more important than an appeal to reason. But this does not mean that appeals to reason should be omitted from the sales talk. People like to rationalize; they like to give logical reasons for doing what their emotions move them to do. They are somewhat reluctant to admit, even to themselves, that they act emotionally; and they may want logical reasons to justify their purchases to friends or associates. Often a person emotionally inclined to buy needs only what appears to be a valid reason as a final motive to make the purchase.

Appealing to Reason

There are a number of specific ways for the salesman to appeal to the prospect's reason in creating desire for his product. Some of these ways are by using facts and figures, by offering warranties, by presenting testimony, and by citing reports of testing bureaus.

Using Facts and Figures. Sales talks for many articles and services —especially machinery, insurance, and building materials—may be reinforced by facts and figures. Statistics may concern such things as past sales, uses, and performance of a product. Statistics should be presented in graph form wherever possible. The average person can grasp the meaning of statistics much more quickly when they are in graph form than when they are given as a table of figures. It makes sense to sit down with the prospect and figure out in black and white just how the sales proposition will work to his advantage.

Offering Warranties. A seller's promise that goods are of a certain quality or will perform in a specified manner is known as a *warranty*. When the selling firm warrants an article, this shows the firm's confidence in it. This in itself makes a good impression on the prospect. If warranties are really to impress the prospect, however, they must be specific. A statement such as, "We warrant this watch," has little meaning. The buyer does not know whether it is warranted as to material, durability, or workmanship. A much stronger statement is, "We warrant this watch not to gain or lose more than one minute a week." This statement is specific.

With such products as refrigerators, automatic washers, automobile tires, and television sets, reliable firms give printed warranties to customers. This paper may state that the article is warranted to be free of mechanical defects for a certain period of time or may state how a defective part is to be replaced and who is to pay transportation charges if the part must be sent back to the factory. Such a warranty makes a valuable selling point.

Presenting Testimony. Generally, testimony is valuable only when it is given by someone whose judgment is considered worthwhile. Testimonials, although widely used today for consumer products from razor blades to hair dressings, are intended mainly to keep a product's name

A Sales Interview

Salesperson: Can I show you something?

Mr. Clement: Do you handle air conditioners?

Salesperson: Yes, indeed. We carry both the CoolRoom and the Speed-Aire lines. Just follow me, please. This unit is the right size for the average house. How many rooms are there in yours?

Mr. Clement: Oh, we don't need that big a unit. But how much is it?

Salesperson: Let me show you . . .

Mr. Clement: How much does it cost?

Salesperson: The cost for electricity is very low, and you will have no upkeep expense. (demonstrates the features of the unit) See how conveniently this unit can be installed.

Mr. Clement: It is an improvement over my present air conditioner.

Salesperson: What kind do you have now?

Mr. Clement: I've got a small window unit, and are those electric bills ever high!

Salesperson: When you get this one, you'll make quite a savings each month on your power bills.

Mr. Clement: Well, my brother recently bought a new one, and his bills haven't . . .

Salesperson: Excuse me a moment. I want to show you a chart. Won't you try out the control switch while I look for it. (finds the chart in a moment or two) You can see from this chart how little current is consumed—only several cents' worth a day.

Mr. Clement: Even that will amount to a good deal more than my present electric bill. Thank you very much. I must be going.

Salesperson: But I do want to show you . . .

Mr. Clement: Sorry, I'm late now. I'll try to come in again.

How would you rate this sales talk—excellent, fair, or poor? Why? How could this talk have been improved?

before the public. People usually know that these testimonials are paid for, and the sales impact is often marginal. In using testimonials, the salesman shouldn't infer that the prospect cannot judge the worth of an article for himself. A testimonial regarding a piece of furniture would have little value, for the average woman would resent the idea that she couldn't tell whether a chair or table suited her needs. On the other hand, a testimonial regarding an electronic computer might be very effective. The experiences of others in using such equipment might be exceedingly important to a prospect whose knowledge of computers was limited.

Citing Reports of Testing Bureaus. A type of testimony that has great weight with customers is the reported result of tests conducted by an independent, reputable laboratory or testing bureau. Consumers Union of the United States, Inc., in its monthly magazine, *Consumer Reports,* gives results of extensive tests made on specific articles. Generally, manufacturers and distributors of consumer products are happy when their products are rated as a "best buy" in this magazine, since they know the reports are unbiased and based on careful research. Since the magazine carries no advertising, it is under no obligation to any seller.

In the sales talk, the salesman should not overstress the importance of a seal of approval that a magazine or commercial testing agency has placed on a product. Of course, approval by a medical authority—such as the American Medical Association—or by a trade-protective association—such as the Underwriters' Laboratory, Inc.—may well be stressed.

CHECKING YOUR KNOWLEDGE

Vocabulary:

(1) opening barrage
(2) tested selling sentences
(3) warranty

Review questions:

1. What are the two parts of a sales talk?
2. What should be included in the opening barrage?
3. Under what conditions may a "canned" sales talk be effectively used?
4. Explain the meaning of "selling from the buyer's viewpoint."
5. How may a salesman appeal to reason in creating a desire for his product?

For discussion:

1. What information on the uses of the following articles might be given in a sales talk? (a) ready-mix cement; (b) electric hair dryer; (c) endowment insurance; (d) floor wax.
2. What are four purchases that customers might tend to rationalize? What might be their reasons for doing so?
3. What kinds of facts and figures on the following articles might be given in a sales talk? (a) home freezer; (b) advertising space in a newspaper; (c) business law textbook; (d) automobile radio; (e) automatic overhead garage door; (f) color television set.

part D

demonstrating the product

Never just tell about a product when you can also demonstrate it. A salesman who is demonstrating a product makes a much more forceful impression upon the customer than does one who is just talking about a product. Demonstrations are designed to convince the customer that he should try the product. This is the point at which the customer mentally "tries on" the product or service and decides whether it is really what he wants. A good demonstration dramatizes how a product will fulfill a customer's needs.

The opportunities to demonstrate are limited only by the salesman's imagination and ingenuity. A furniture salesman may demonstrate a coffee table by setting it in front of a sofa in a living room display. This gives the customer a better idea of how the coffee table would look in her own home. A vacuum cleaner salesman may demonstrate his cleaner by placing dirt and lint on a rug and then vacuuming the rug using his cleaner. A salesman of transcontinental radio sets can demonstrate how the set performs by tuning in several programs coming from abroad. Virtually every product has some feature that lends itself to demonstration.

HOW TO DEMONSTRATE GOODS

In all forms of selling, it is important to differentiate between the demonstration and the display of goods. A demonstration involves activity by both salesman and customer, whereas a display may or may not involve activity by the salesman and not by the customer. You will learn about merchandise display in Chapter 14.

Effective demonstration occurs when the salesman shows how goods may be used, how they will look when worn, how they will appear in the home, how they will bring satisfaction to the customer, and even how they will sound, taste, or smell. Furniture, household appliances, office equipment, clothing, automobiles, musical instruments, and sometimes food and cosmetics—all must be demonstrated by the salesperson if he is to convince the prospect that the article will meet his needs.

Prepared Demonstrations

Many progressive business firms give their salespeople detailed instructions on how to demonstrate their goods. By establishing a pattern for all salespeople to follow, a refinement in demonstrating can be achieved over a period of time. Some automobile manufacturers develop step-by-step demonstrations to be used in the automobile showroom. By following these prepared demonstrations, salesmen make sure that omissions in the sales presentation do not occur. Important features of a new model and special features superior to those of other automobiles may be highlighted.

Demonstrating One Product Feature

Sometimes it is desirable to demonstrate just one feature of a product, rather than the entire article. In demonstrating a raincoat, water may be spilled on the fabric to show that it is waterproof. Plastic dishes may be knocked together or dropped on the floor to show that they are unbreakable. Or a customer may be asked to lie down on a mattress to prove that it is comfortable.

Acquiring Skill in Demonstrating

Regardless of what article a salesman sells, he can be sure of one thing: he will never be successful until he has gained skill in demonstrating. Skill requires practice. It is just as necessary for a salesman to practice demonstrating his product as it is for a football player to

Instructions for Demonstrating

The salesman should go through the demonstration time and time again so that he is sure he can perform the operations quickly and deftly. A bungled demonstration is worse than none at all, for the whole purpose of a physical demonstration is to show how neatly and easily a given operation can be performed. The salesman is naturally presumed to be perfectly familiar with his machine; if he is awkward and hesitant in a given operation, the prospect may be justified in concluding that any other operator will have the same difficulties and the whole force of the demonstration is lost.

To demonstrate an article properly, a salesman should be expert in using that article. That employers recognize this fact is shown by these instructions given to salesmen of one nationally known typewriter.

practice handling the ball. A typewriter salesman should be a reasonably skilled typist. The owner of a sporting-goods store should be adept at a variety of sports. Novices in such sports as skiing, for instance, not only need advice on what equipment to buy but also need minimal instructions in how to use it properly.

Site of the Demonstration

The salesman should take every precaution to see that conditions are right for the demonstration before it is begun. He cannot demonstrate successfully if he is situated where he will continually be interrupted. Many traveling salesmen realize this and therefore use a hotel or motel room for demonstration purposes. If a demonstration will take much time, a chair should be provided for the customer. Customers are usually asked to be seated while looking at floor coverings or wallpaper. Most stores provide chairs for women who are trying on gloves or hats.

Progressive retailers should install lighting that best simulates daylight. The manager of a retail store may question the effectiveness of his lighting system if customers have to step to a doorway or window to see the colors or designs in goods. The most important thing to remember in preparing the demonstration site is that the customer should be comfortable. If he is physically at ease, his attention is less likely to wander during the demonstration.

Handling Interruptions

The demonstration is sometimes interrupted, especially in contact selling. The most common interruption is a telephone call for the buyer, but the buyer's supervisor may drop in unexpectedly, or the buyer may have to leave his office for a moment to speak to someone outside. The salesman should never show resentment at an interruption. If the interruption is likely to be short, he should wait patiently for the buyer to finish. Then he should repeat his last statement before the interruption or summarize the discussion up to that point. This makes it easy for the buyer to get back on the right mental track. If the cause of the interruption seems confidential, the salesman should offer to step out of the room for a few minutes. If the interruption is likely to be a long one, he should suggest that he make a new appointment for a time when the buyer is not likely to be disturbed.

Interruptions also occur in the retail store and are generally caused by other customers demanding attention. The salesman should answer quickly specific questions asked by such customers and should offer to serve them as soon as possible. Occasionally he can wait on two customers at once if they are at different stages of the sale. Sometimes interruptions in retail stores are caused by a careless supervisor who demands a salesman's attention while he is demonstrating a product to a customer. This is a very poor management practice which top management should not condone.

Demonstrating Without Goods

Even the contact salesman, who is selling a large article that he cannot carry with him, can demonstrate. So can the seller of a service such as insurance. In demonstrating, these salesmen may use photographs or other illustrations along with exact specifications for the particular article or service. Obviously, a demonstration utilizing these substitutes is somewhat more difficult to give than if the article or a model of it were available. When a demonstration is to be given without the actual goods, it must be well organized and planned to meet the exact needs of the customer.

To eliminate the use of numerous large catalogs, descriptive booklets, and price lists, many manufacturers of machinery and other bulky articles prepare specification sheets. These are ring-bound portfolios which usually contain pages about the size of standard business letters. The sheets are usually tabbed and indexed at the side so that as the salesman gives his demonstration, he can refer to any particular page and place it before the customer to illustrate his selling point. Many companies have found that specification sheets printed in color lend more realism to the demonstration than do black and white illustrations. Many companies also furnish their salesmen with projectors and sound-slide films to use in demonstrating. The projector can be quickly set up, and the salesman can give a visual demonstration with sound.

SECURING CUSTOMER ACTIVITY

The child whose attention has been attracted by a new object immediately reaches for it. He wants to touch it, pick it up, play with it. It is instinctive for him to do so. It is likewise instinctive for a customer to want to touch or handle an article he is thinking of buying. In demonstrating, therefore, the salesman should encourage the customer to participate.

Creating Desire Through Customer Activity

Psychologists tell us that people remember only 10 percent of what they hear, 50 percent of what they see, and 90 percent of what they participate in. Gaining customer activity is a vital element in selling. When the salesman talks about merchandise, he appeals to the sense of hearing. When he demonstrates merchandise, he appeals to the sense of sight. When a customer handles merchandise, his sense of touch and sometimes senses of smell and taste augment the other senses. The salesman who appeals to all five senses in his presentation increases the likelihood of making a sale.

Actually handling an article stirs up a greater desire for the article than does merely looking at it or having another person demonstrate it—provided, of course, that the customer's handling of the article proves what the salesman has claimed. Allowing the customer to experience the satisfaction that would be his from owning and using the article is the surest way to arouse a desire to possess it. Let the customer try out a new motorboat that is being sold at a marina. Let the prospect write with the ballpoint pen, drive the car, taste the cheese, thumb through the book, try on the shoes, operate the typewriter. Whatever the article, the demonstration should be planned with the idea that the prospect will participate in it.

I. Howard Spivak

Customers are much more likely to buy if they are encouraged to handle the goods and participate in the demonstration. In selling clothing, the best way of securing customer activity is to have the customer try on the article he is looking at.

Asking Questions

You have already learned that it is important to encourage the customer to talk during the sales interview. One way to do this is to ask questions during the sales talk and demonstration.

The *developmental question* is designed to draw out comments from the prospect so that the salesman will know how he feels at each stage of the sales interview. It is often wise to ask how the prospect thinks others will react, not to ask bluntly what the prospect thinks of the sales proposition. "How do you think your board of directors will react to my proposal?" will probably reveal the prospect's own reaction much more accurately than will "What do you think of my proposal?" If a customer has personal doubts about buying, he is more likely to express them if he can attribute them to another person than if he alone must take the responsibility for them.

The *evaluative question* is intended to determine whether the customer fully understands the points the salesman has made. The salesman may say, "Have I made that point clear?" or "Would you like to study these figures further?" He should word his evaluative questions carefully. "Do you understand what I mean?" may be taken as a slight to the buyer's intelligence. The answer to an evaluative question may be "yes," "no," or simply a nod or an alert expression.

CHECKING YOUR KNOWLEDGE

Vocabulary:

(1) developmental question (2) evaluative question

Review questions:

1. What constitutes an effective demonstration?
2. Why do some selling firms prefer to develop prepared demonstrations for their salespeople?
3. How might the contact salesman handle interruptions in his demonstration?
4. Describe how contact salesmen may demonstrate without goods.
5. Why is it so important to stimulate customer participation in the sales talk and demonstration?

For discussion:

1. For each of the five senses, what are two products that can be demonstrated by an appeal to that sense?
2. Goods should ordinarily be handled with exceptional care by the salesman. Can you think of some articles which might be handled roughly on purpose to show appreciation of their quality?
3. If the demonstration is going to take a long time, making the customer comfortable is considered the right thing to do. What are some disadvantages to this practice, from the salesman's point of view?

part E

serving customers at various stages of decision

As you learned earlier, there are three general types of customers, classified according to their stage of buying decision at the time of the sales contact: the decided customer, the undecided customer, and the casual looker. The alert salesperson should be able to size up each prospect, determine his stage of buying readiness, and adjust the approach, sales talk, and demonstration to suit the customer's stage of buying readiness. In this part you will learn how to serve the decided customer, the undecided customer, and the casual looker.

SERVING THE DECIDED CUSTOMER

It is usually unnecessary to give a long, formal sales presentation to the decided customer. This customer wants prompt and accurate answers to questions, a sensible demonstration of the merchandise, and courteous treatment. He is interested not only in the merchandise but also in how to use and care for it.

A decided customer in a department store may make her wants clearly known: "I need three pairs of seamless nylon hosiery, size 9½, medium length, the $1.50 grade." A salesperson need only show her a few of the season's popular shades, and she will make a quick buying decision. If she had failed to mention the needed size, it would have been necessary to ask for it. Whether to ask about the price the customer wants to pay depends upon the salesperson's size-up of the customer. If she seems to be in a hurry or to have a definite article in mind, the price should be stated as the article is shown. But if it is likely that she would consider more than one grade, she should be shown both a popular-priced middle grade and a higher-priced grade. She should be encouraged to decide on price after inspection, not before. The salesperson thus has a better chance of selling the higher quality merchandise to the profit of the customer, himself, and the store.

Substitution Selling

Serving decided customers becomes a problem only if the store does not carry the article asked for or if it is out of stock of that article. When this happens, the salesman should work out a compromise and suggest that the customer accept the in-stock article that comes closest to meeting his needs. Suppose that a customer asks for a light gray hat to be worn with either a gray or navy overcoat. The salesman shouldn't say, "I'm sorry, sir, but we haven't a single one in stock," and show nothing. Instead he should study the customer and decide what neutral shades that are in stock could best be worn by the customer. The most suitable substitute should be brought out; and the salesman might say, "We haven't the exact shade that you requested in stock right now, but here's a hat that I think you will want to try on. This particular shade is very popular this season; and I'm sure it will look well on you, whether you wear gray or navy."

Brand Preference

If the customer insists on a certain brand not carried by the store, serving the decided customer is somewhat more difficult. Obviously, no store can afford to carry all brands in a particular class of products. One way to substitute a brand carried by the store is to ask about a particular feature of the brand originally requested. Suppose, for example, that the customer asked for a certain brand of steam iron. She may have been impressed with the advertising of this iron, which emphasized the variety of uses for the iron. The salesman should then show one of the store's brands that has the same features.

A salesman can better serve the customer if he understands the reasons behind a specific brand preference or brand insistence. The salesman should never knock the brand originally requested. This just makes the customer more insistent that he be sold the original brand and not a substitute.

Substituting a Different Product

Sometimes a salesperson can change a decided customer's mind so that he will purchase a different type of product. Suppose that a customer in a supermarket can't find the frozen strawberries and asks a salesperson for help. The salesperson might say, "Were you going to use them for shortcake?" If the customer says, "Yes," the salesperson may say, "I'm sorry, but we seem to be out of frozen strawberries right now. However, we do have some fine frozen blueberries, and I'm sure you'll find that they make a very tasty shortcake."

Such a suggestion is a service to the customer. It shows recognition of the customer's basic needs and attempts to satisfy those needs. Such suggestions can save the customer the trouble of visiting other stores, and a suggested substitute of a different type of product may even give greater customer satisfaction than the article originally requested.

Insistence on Unsuitable Goods

In retail stores, customers sometimes want to buy goods that are not properly suited to their needs. For example, a man may be shopping for a new suit and find one that he particularly likes but which is not his size. Although the salesman tells the customer that the suit is not a particularly good fit, the customer thinks that it can be altered to fit him. The salesman and the customer go to the fitting room, where the tailor refuses to alter the suit. The average customer will respect the store and its personnel if such a refusal takes place. It is obvious that the store's employees are giving prime consideration to the customer's long-run satisfaction with the suit, and it is possible that the customer will find another suit in the store that better meets his needs.

Ewing Galloway

Decided customers—particularly men—want most of all to complete the sales transaction quickly and be on their way. It is easy to serve the decided customer unless he asks for an article the store does not carry or which is temporarily out of stock. Then the salesperson must try to meet his needs with a similar item that the store carries.

SERVING THE UNDECIDED CUSTOMER

Most customers in grocery stores, stationery stores, drugstores, and service stations have decided what they want to buy, but the majority of customers in department stores and specialty shops are undecided. They know their needs, but they do not know exactly how to satisfy those needs. A woman may know that she wants a fur-trimmed winter coat; but when she visits a store, she has probably not decided on the kind of fur, the style, the material, the price, or perhaps even the color.

If a single product is to be shown to the undecided customer, it should be shown carefully. The features and points of superiority should be clearly explained and demonstrated. If the salesman has a number of articles to show, he shouldn't draw the customer's attention to too many at one time, or he will cause confusion. The salesman must try to analyze the customer's needs and then center the customer's attention on articles that will meet his requirements. The undecided customer is most in need of the salesman's assistance. Therefore, the salesman should assist him to make a wise selection rather than force him to buy.

Don't Ask Questions

Quizzing the undecided customer about price, color, material, type, and size before any merchandise has been shown forces the customer to make a decision before he has the necessary information on which to base that decision. Another undesirable result of asking questions is that in answering them the customer commits himself to a particular kind of article, an article that may not be in stock. No customer likes to be put in the position of sacrificing his expressed wants. As long as he has not stated a preference, he will be interested in a wider selection of articles; he may not have defined his preference even to himself.

There are two questions that may be asked in selling clothing and sometimes in selling home furnishings. The first is, "Is it for yourself or for someone else?" The second question concerns the use to which the article will be put. "Is the coat for sport, daytime, or evening wear?" "Is the hat to be for street or party wear?" "Is the rug for the living room, bedroom, or den?" Even the use to which an article is to be put can often be guessed.

How To Tell What To Show

If the salesman shouldn't ask questions, how is he to serve customers without bringing out a great deal of stock and wasting a great deal of time? Here are some rules for salesmen of men's suits that can be adapted readily to other merchandise:

1. Estimate the type of suit the customer would want, based on his general physical appearance.
2. Estimate his size. (With a little experience, this can be done easily.)
3. Show the materials that are popular at the time and suitable for the season.
4. Show three or four different styles in the customer's size that seem to be of the type, colors, and materials suitable to him.
5. Show him one higher-priced suit, along with one or two medium-priced ones.

Estimating Price

It is dangerous to estimate from his appearance what a customer will pay. Although a customer's clothes may help the clothing salesman decide which wearing apparel to demonstrate, other salesmen shouldn't be too hasty about judging a customer by his clothing. A person who wears inexpensive clothing may buy an expensive automobile, while a prospect who drives an inexpensive automobile may buy expensive clothing. It is in connection with price that sizing up the customer's wants is most difficult.

Asking what price the customer desires to pay may tie down both customer and salesman. An undecided customer knows what price he can afford; but if he sees a high-priced item that appeals to him, he will buy it even if he has to skimp on something else. Some people ask to see more expensive merchandise than they can afford just to impress the salesperson. The safest rule for the salesman to follow is to show medium-priced goods first, frequently showing a high-priced article at the same time to see which interests the customer. If even the medium-priced article seems to cause the customer to hesitate, a lower-priced article should be shown. It should never be shown, however, with an attitude of disdain.

Ewing Galloway

Customers are typically undecided when they are considering a large purchase. They have a general idea of what they want—a color television set, for instance—but they are not certain of the specific features they want in this article—size of screen, remote-control tuning, and so on. The undecided customer is most in need of a salesperson's assistance in order to make a wise buying decision.

SERVING THE CASUAL LOOKER

The casual looker does not intend to buy right away, but he is nevertheless a potential customer. The fact that he has enough interest to make an effort to look at merchandise shows that he has some desire to buy. He may, however, not need goods at the moment, may not have enough money, or may want to visit a number of selling firms before buying. The person who is "just looking around" is the most difficult customer to sell.

Business Customers Who Are Just Looking

Some businessmen upon whom a salesman calls may be classified as casual lookers. They are willing to look at what the salesman has to sell, but they must be persuaded to do something they had not intended to do when the salesman walked in. Such a businessman should be shown merchandise quickly and should be convinced that he has a need he had not previously recognized. Salesmen realize that no one buys anything until he feels at a disadvantage without it. Therefore, the business customer should not be hurried. It may take days or even weeks before he gets to the point of buying. At the time of the first call, the salesman may only be able to impress the prospect with the quality of his merchandise or service so that he will be given another chance to sell later.

Retail Customers Who Are Just Looking

Unless the looker in a retail store indicates that he wants to be waited on, it is usually best to leave him alone. Approaching him may make him overly cautious, and he will be less likely to buy. He may feel that the salesman is going to force him to buy against his will, so he puts up his defenses and resists all attempts at persuasion.

If the customer is looking at an article that should be demonstrated to be fully appreciated, the salesman may properly demonstrate it or at least say something about it. However, no attempt should be made to force the looker to buy. The salesman should try to gain the looker's goodwill so that he will come back to the store. If the salesman sells expensive merchandise in a large store, he may give his card to the looker so that the looker will return to that particular salesman when he is ready to buy. It should not be assumed that the looker will not buy at the time he is looking around. With the proper approach, many people who intended to defer buying will buy at once. If they find an article that suits them, they may decide that it is a waste of effort to look further.

CHECKING YOUR KNOWLEDGE

Review questions:

1. Why is it usually unnecessary to give a long, formal sales presentation to the decided customer?
2. When the salesman is serving a decided customer and the store does not carry the article specified, what can the salesman do?
3. How may the interest of a decided customer be switched to a brand not requested but which is carried by the store?
4. What two questions may be asked of the undecided customer in the selling of clothing and sometimes home furnishings?
5. How can the salesman deal with the casual looker?

For discussion:

1. Why is it a service to suggest some other article if a store does not have the specific article a customer requested?
2. One leading authority has defined retail salesmanship as the "art of making compromise easy." What is meant by this?
3. What would you say in order to suggest a substitute for a particular brand of each of the following articles, none of which brands are in stock? (a) bowling ball; (b) carbon paper; (c) garbage disposal; (d) perfume; (e) pizza mix; (f) canned ham; (g) steel filing cabinet; (h) cardigan sweater.

BUILDING YOUR SKILLS

Improving your English:

The words in parentheses at the end of each of the following sentences are similar in sound but different in meaning. On a separate sheet of paper, write the correct word to be used in each sentence.

1. The marketing manager should be able to ______ the speaking invitation. (accept, except)
2. The physical count of inventory will ______ any restocking of merchandise. (proceed, precede)
3. Winning the local sales campaign did not ______ his eligibility for the national contest. (affect, effect)
4. Fully lined skirts were ______ available only in the more expensive lines. (formally, formerly)
5. A local civic group recognized Charles for his ______ care of the injured puppy. (human, humane)
6. A ______ switch in the air conditioning unit made it hard to demonstrate the unit's automatic features. (loose, lose)
7. A wage increase of 20 cents per hour was given to all assembly line ______. (personal, personnel)

8. Elaine will ______ a slight modification of the work stations. (propose, purpose)
9. A ______ of many colors gives the desired effect to the window display. (complement, compliment)
10. Customers often ask informed salesmen for ______. (advice, advise)

Improving your arithmetic:

Calculate the percentages in the exercises that follow.

1. Last month, Mack's Department Store sold $12,000 worth of men's and women's clothing and shoes. Sales were divided as follows: men's suits, $1,200; men's shoes, $2,400; women's dresses and suits, $4,800; and women's shoes, $3,600. What percentage of the total sales was represented by each of these divisions?
2. Crank's Wholesale Drugs sold $8,400 worth of prescription drugs during a recent week. Sales to hospitals accounted for $2,100; sales to medical clinics, $3,300; and sale to retail druggists, $3,000. What percentage of the total sales was bought by each type of customer?
3. James Burke's total sales for last year were $225,000. He is paid a monthly salary of $700 plus a commission of 2% on all sales in excess of $125,000. What was his commission income last year? What was his total annual salary?
4. During one month, the $4,000 advertising expenditure of Bain's Department Store was distributed among the following departments: men's clothing, $1,000; women's fashions, $1,600; children's clothing, $600; home appliances, $400; and furniture, $400. Compute the percentage of the total that each department spent for advertising.
5. Credit sales accounted for $24,000 of the $60,000 total sales at Gibbons' Fashion Mart last month. Payments are now past due for $1,920 of the credit sales. What percentage of the total sales are represented by credit sales? What percentage of total credit sales are now past due?

Improving your research skills:

1. Prepare an opening barrage for a specific brand or model of each of the following products:

   (a) Tape recorder
   (b) Sports car
   (c) Banjo or guitar
   (d) Air conditioner
   (e) Man's hat
   (f) Battery-operated toy robot

2. In consultation with your instructor, select one of the following articles to be demonstrated by you:

   (a) Ballpoint pen
   (b) Typewriter
   (c) Necktie
   (d) Coat or sweater
   (e) Electric iron
   (f) Cosmetics
   (g) Raincoat
   (h) Musical instrument
   (i) Adding machine
   (j) Shoes
   (k) Tennis racket
   (l) Carbon paper

Do not attempt to give an entire sales talk; you are only to demonstrate the article. If possible, incorporate statements to encourage the customer to take part in the demonstration. You should practice the demonstration before coming to class so that you can conduct it without hesitation or awkwardness. Be sure you have a definite plan for the demonstration. Your demonstration will be criticized by your instructor, and you may be asked to repeat it in order to improve.

3. Ask five friends or acquaintances whether they know exactly what they want when they enter a store to buy the following articles or services: (a) canned peaches; (b) haircut; (c) winter coat; (d) candy bar; and (e) magazine. Summarize in writing the answers you receive. Does your investigation lead you to believe that some customers are always decided and others always undecided? Or are some customers decided about some articles and undecided about others? About what articles are most people decided, and about what articles are most people undecided?

APPLYING YOUR KNOWLEDGE

Case problems:

1. When a homemaker answered a knock on the front door, she found herself facing a young man carrying a briefcase in one hand and a small brass cylinder in the other. "This is a Preston Fire Extinguisher," the salesman said. Then he paused, apparently trying to decide what to say next. "Oh, but I have two fire extinguishers already, and that's enough," the homemaker replied, hoping to ward off a sales pitch for which she had little time. "You have?" said the salesman. He thanked the customer and left. What was wrong with the way this salesman opened the sale? How might a first-class salesman have opened it?
2. A customer wanted an inexpensive fur coat. The saleswoman showed her a coat that was priced at $175; but she handled it with the respect that might be given a $2,000 mink coat, and she "talked up" the proposition the same way. The customer bought the coat promptly, evidently believing she was getting a great bargain. Although the customer did get her money's worth, the coat was actually worth no more than could be expected at that low price. Was the salesperson wise in speaking so highly of a coat in the low-price range that the customer could afford?

Continuing project:

Perform the following activities in the next section of your manual:

1. Describe the approach you will use in contacting customers for your product or service, with special emphasis on greeting your customers.
2. Prepare a sales talk for your product, remembering to use techniques of getting the customer interested in the product and making the customer want to buy the product.

3. Prepare a demonstration for your product, whether it will be given with the goods or without the goods.
4. Tell whether customers for your product are likely to be decided customers, undecided customers, or casual lookers; and tell how you would best serve them.

Extra credit:

Listed below are 25 question-type greetings. Prepare a brief written evaluation of the suitability of each greeting. Tell whether each greeting could best be used in a department store, hardware store, or restaurant.

1. May I help you?
2. May I serve you?
3. May I be of service to you?
4. May I assist you?
5. May I wait on you?
6. May I direct you?
7. May I show you something?
8. How may I serve (help or assist) you?
9. How may I serve you today?
10. Is there something I can do for you?
11. Is there something I can show you?
12. Is someone waiting on you?
13. Have you been waited on?
14. Have you been taken care of?
15. Are there any questions I can answer for you?
16. May I show you the advantage of this . . .?
17. Isn't this a beautiful . . .?
18. Will you look at the lines of this . . .?
19. Have you one of these in your home?
20. Have you heard this latest . . .?
21. Have you seen this new . . .?
22. What may I do for you?
23. What is it for you?
24. In what way may I serve you?
25. What do you have in mind today?

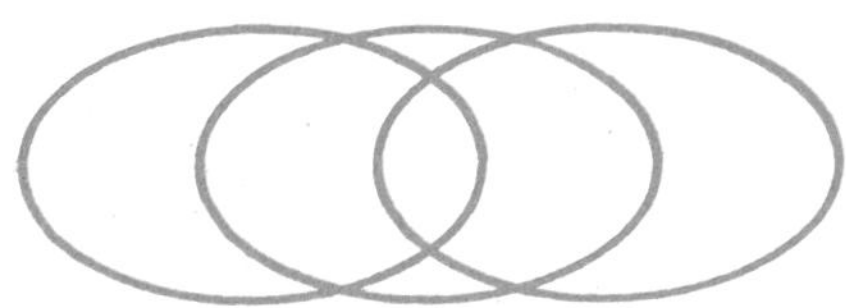

chapter 10

closing the sale

KEY QUESTIONS

A How can a salesman know when it is time to close the sale?

B How can a salesman bring the true objection to the surface so that he can handle it intelligently?

C What are the most common decision stimulators, and how effective are they in closing a sale?

D What activities are involved in the mechanics of closing?

E Why are the various techniques of plus selling so important to the salesman?

part A

preparing for the close

Experts in training salesmen say that one of the greatest mistakes in selling is failing to ask for the order, even after the customer has signalled his readiness to buy. Many salesmen either wait silently for the customer to act or make unnecessary remarks about the transaction. They are literally afraid to ask the customer to decide.

Bringing the customer to a buying decision should be no problem if the salesman has effectively handled his sales talk and demonstration. If the customer's wants have been properly determined and if the presentation has demonstrated that the product, its source, and its price suit these wants, the customer may need no help in making an affirmative decision.

CONVINCING CUSTOMERS TO BUY

Once conviction has been achieved, it is time for the salesman to begin closing the sale. Conviction means that a customer's desire for the product is no longer impeded by objections and resistances. Conviction normally requires that the customer voice his objections so that he and the salesman may weigh them together.

In making his sales presentation and in meeting objections, the salesman may use three techniques to convince his customers to buy: making a claim for the product, presenting evidence that a key point is true, or presenting proof through the customer's own experiences that an alleged fact is true.

Making a Claim for the Product

To convince a customer, salesmen often make claims about the quality of their products. In response to a question about colorfastness, for example, the salesman may assert that the color will withstand repeated washings. If he has had former satisfactory dealings with the customer and if the customer regards him as an authority, his unsupported claim may be enough. But few salesmen achieve such an enviable position in a customer's opinion, and an unsupported claim may only make the customer suspicious of the salesman's reliability.

Presenting Evidence

A more effective way to convince is to present evidence that a key point made in the presentation and perhaps questioned by the customer is true. This evidence should come from what is supposedly a more reliable source than the salesman himself. In connection with the colorfastness of a fabric, the salesman may refer to a label that verifies his claim. He may also show the customer written or printed evidence in the form of warranties, testimony of satisfied users, and reports from testing bureaus.

Presenting Proof

For skeptical and suspicious people, presenting evidence may not be enough. For some, conviction may be achieved only by proof that involves their own experience. In connection with colorfastness, it would be difficult to provide such proof since the product would have to be subjected to repeated washings or to strong sunlight. Offering a sample that the customer may test for himself or inviting the customer to visit the laboratory where the product has been tested may be enough to convince.

Many firms who sell by mail let the customer use the goods for a trial period, with the right to return the goods with no charge or penalty before the expiration of this period. In selling to businessmen, this technique is used a great deal. The salesman may leave samples that the buyer can offer for resale or test in his laboratory. Equipment is sometimes installed on an experimental basis to see how it will perform on the buyer's premises.

TECHNIQUES OF BUILDING UP TO THE CLOSE

To close the sale, the prospect should be fully convinced throughout the sales talk and demonstration that he can profitably use what is being sold. The salesman convinces him by proving the value of his product through a good demonstration. He substantiates claims he makes about it and provides evidence or proof as needed. He should always talk and demonstrate his product or service in terms of the prospect's interests and needs. When demonstrating, the salesman should point out product features related to such factors as utility, service, satisfaction, economy, and prestige. When demonstrating to dealers, he should talk about profits, fast turnover of goods, quality, consumer demand, and satisfied customers.

Narrowing the Choice

In selling merchandise for which details of design and fashion acceptance are important, narrowing the choice is a useful technique for building up to the close. A store buyer may inspect 50 different styles and select only five; a retail customer may try on six pairs of shoes and select one pair. A buying decision is greatly facilitated if the styles to which the customer reacts negatively are promptly put out of sight. This way, the customer is choosing one style out of two or three, not one out of six. The retail salesperson does this by showing not more than three styles at a time. If one or two are rejected by the customer, they are returned to stock; and one or two more styles are brought out for inspection. Similarly, the fashion manufacturer's salesman presents styles one at a time and places on a rack those in which the buyer expresses an interest. The other styles are removed. Those retained are then shown a second time.

Securing Customer Affirmation

An effective way of putting a customer in a buying frame of mind is to get his agreement on a series of comments made during the presentation. In presenting a television set, for example, the salesman might draw out a series of affirmations with these questions:

1. May I show you this new portable? ("Yes")
2. Isn't the picture unusually clear? ("Yes")
3. The case is very thin and smart-looking, don't you think? ("Yes")
4. Try lifting it; isn't it light? ("Yes")
5. Are you planning to buy soon? ("Yes")
6. At $119, doesn't the price seem like a bargain? ("Yes")
7. We think that our three-month payment plan with no carrying charge is very reasonable. Don't you agree? ("Yes")
8. Why don't you start enjoying this fine set right now?

The customer who has taken a positive position on a series of minor points is likely to make a positive buying decision. However, this technique can be dangerous in the hands of an unscrupulous salesperson. It should be used only when the salesperson is convinced that the purchase will be in the customer's best interests.

H. Armstrong Roberts

In closing the sales of many products, salesmen narrow the customer's choice to two styles that have been well received by the prospect. Rejected styles are returned to stock; thus, the salesman can help his customer reach a buying decision by concentrating on the merits of only two styles.

Reviewing Selling Points and Benefits

Another technique of building up to the close is to repeat the chief features of the product or service, to repeat the benefits that the buyer will derive through purchasing, and then to drive home the major benefit. These three devices have been called (1) touching all bases, (2) buttoning up the sale with benefits, and (3) locking the sale with the key issue. For example, after reviewing his product's chief features, a salesman of heating equipment may stress the equipment's contribution to health, to a reduction in house-cleaning efforts, to the prevention of freeze damage, and to a savings of $200 a year in fuel costs. If the customer responds most positively to the savings benefit, the salesman will concentrate on it as the key issue. He will present facts and figures on installations similar to the one he is proposing. If the evidence he presents is convincing, the sale will probably be made.

Helping Customers Make Their Decisions

With a well-organized sales presentation, most customers will make their own buying decisions without prodding. However, many times a customer must be helped to make a decision. The following kinds of customers commonly need help at the close of a sale:

1. Customers who have little money and who have carefully saved for their present shopping trip. The importance of a decision is magnified in their minds. They feel that if they make a mistake, they can never correct it.
2. Deliberate customers who want a long time to decide and who like to talk the matter over with others first.
3. Customers who have no faith in their own judgment. Unless they are accompanied by a trusted friend who will advise them, they hesitate to take action.
4. Customers who have in mind an ideal article that they may never find but who hesitate to accept a less attractive substitute.
5. Customers for whom making any sort of decision is a struggle.

These kinds of customers are found in both retail and contact selling. In each of these cases, the salesman must gain the customer's confidence. The customer must be made to feel that the salesman is not trying to take advantage of him, that the salesman wants to advise him correctly, and that the salesman is more interested in the customer's permanent satisfaction than in the immediate sale.

The Pros and Cons Close

In selling to businessmen and to consumers who are very logical in their thinking, a good technique is to list—sometimes on paper—the chief points in favor of the purchase and the chief doubts about the purchase. This is sometimes called the *balance sheet,* or *T-account close*. With the pros and cons clearly stated, the logical-minded person can weigh one against the other and hopefully conclude that the pros outweigh the cons.

TIMING THE CLOSE

Much has been said and written about the psychological moment for closing a sale. Some people believe that there is a particular moment during the sales talk when the prospect offers no sales resistance. They believe that the salesman should watch for that moment and then ask the prospect to buy. If such a moment really does exist, it is impractical to use it; such a technique may involve trickery. The right time to close the sale is when the prospect is so thoroughly sold on the article that a skillfully placed suggestion by the salesman or an indication of preference by the customer will secure the order.

To the alert salesman, the customer's comments, actions, and expressions are signals that it is time to close. Obvious interest is sometimes indicated by the customer's statements or questions: "I would have to have delivery on this electric range today." "My present television set has required considerable repair service recently." "What kind of guarantee do I get with this storage battery?" "Does this power mower require much service?"

The alert salesman realizes that such statements or questions indicate an interest in and possibly a desire for his product. When he has given satisfactory answers to the statements or questions, he should attempt a *trial close*. A trial close is like taking the customer's temperature. It might involve asking the customer which model he prefers. If he indicates which one, the sale may be closed at once. If he says that he has not decided or does not want either, the salesman can continue his presentation.

Contact salesmen use this technique a great deal. It is not always easy for them to tell when a prospect is ready to buy, yet it might be unwise to keep on discussing the proposition if he is ready to buy. Both salesman and customer would be wasting time, and the salesman might run the risk of talking himself out of the sale.

Statements for a Trial Close

- Will one box be enough?
- When might we deliver it?
- Will this be charge or cash?
- Do you want this gift wrapped?
- How would you like this shipped?
- How much do you want to pay down?
- Would you prefer the green or the blue?
- How would you like to handle the financing?
- Would you prefer the floor model or the table model?

Statements such as these might be used in a trial close. The salesman hopes to get the customer's commitment on one of these points, which means that the major buying decision has been made.

CHECKING YOUR KNOWLEDGE

Vocabulary:

(1) balance sheet, or T-account close (2) trial close

Review questions:

1. What three techniques may a salesman use in making his sales presentation and meeting objections?
2. What techniques may a salesman use to build up to the close?
3. With what kinds of merchandise is it especially important to narrow the choice in building up to the close?
4. What is meant by "touching all bases, buttoning up the sale with benefits, and locking the sale with the key issue"?
5. How can the salesman tell when it is time to close the sale?

For discussion:

1. Why is it impractical for a salesman to use the psychological moment for closing, even if such a moment does exist?
2. Have you ever seen a salesperson beg a customer to buy? What was your reaction to this behavior?

part B

handling objections

Objections do not mean that the sale is lost; the customer's objection really means, "Come on and help me make up my mind." Except perhaps for decided customers who know what they want before salespeople contact them, most customers raise some objection as part of the buying process. Even a decided customer may object to some feature of the article he asked to see. Thus, the salesman should regard objections as a normal part of selling and should be ready to meet them.

REAL OBJECTIONS VERSUS EXCUSES

There are two kinds of objections: real objections and excuses. The skillful salesman can turn real objections into reasons for buying instead of reasons for not buying. However, many objections are merely excuses to get out of a buying situation with as little embarrassment as possible. The store buyer who is not satisfied with a line of goods presented to him may say, "I'm sorry, but I can't exceed my planned order limit this month—management policy." The salesman must learn to tell excuses from real objections and to bring the real objection to the surface so that he may handle it intelligently. This can be done by:

1. Repeating—going over the selling points he has made to see if the customer seems suspicious of one of them.
2. Probing—asking questions to bring out the real objections.
3. Challenging—assuming an objection to be a real one and referring directly to it.

Even if the salesman thinks that an objection is really an excuse, he should treat it courteously. Ridiculing an objection or brushing it off as inconsequential is foolish. It simply antagonizes the customer.

KINDS OF REAL OBJECTIONS

The most common kinds of real objections concern (1) need, (2) product, (3) selling firm, (4) price, and (5) buying at the moment.

Objections Related to the Need

In the retail store, the customer stops to look at many things he does not need but that he may want if the salesman comments on the benefits they will provide. A customer who is buying varnish for a homemade stereo cabinet may not think he needs turpentine, sandpaper, and wood sealer. It is a service to him if the salesman spells out his true needs and shows how he can do a much nicer job if he has the proper materials.

The businessman's objection to the need is generally expressed in connection with a currently overstocked condition or a lack of customer demand for the product offered. If it is true that he is overstocked, it would be unethical to force more goods on him. A salesman must never try to persuade a customer to carry more stock than he should; but it is proper to point out to the customer (1) a situation in which a quantity purchase will reduce the unit-cost price and offset the additional inventory costs or (2) a situation in which a price increase is imminent and a large order at the moment will prove profitable in the long run. If the salesman's merchandise differs in some respects from the goods with which the dealer is overstocked, the salesman may demonstrate his product's features and suggest that he be given an appointment when the prospect is ready to buy later.

Objections to the Product

The retail customer's most common objections to the product concern style, type, color, size, design, suitability, comfort, or seasonableness of goods. There are four major ways of handling these objections:

1. Show more suitable goods.
2. Admit the validity of the objection, but show that some other feature more than offsets it.
3. Admit that the objection seems reasonable, then show that it doesn't really apply (the "yes, but" method).
4. Change the objection into a point in favor of the article.

The business customer's chief doubts about a product usually concern its general type, quality, and appearance. Retailers often say that there is no strong demand for the salesman's product. Instead of accepting this as a refusal to buy, the salesman should point out that by buying his product, the retailer can augment or fill out a line of current merchandise. If the product is new, the salesman must make newness a virtue, since business buyers are often cautious in buying new products. The salesman might discuss the results of product research, emphasize the reliability of his selling firm, show how the new product is better than the old one and how it compares with competing products.

Objections concerning quality are also raised, and the salesman must be ready to demonstrate quality by on-the-spot tests or by reference to laboratory tests. If a dealer states that a competitor has a product of better quality, the salesman shouldn't knock this product. If it does have certain superior features, he should readily admit them; but he should go on to emphasize the points of superiority in his own product.

When the buyer objects to the design and appearance of the goods, the salesman must either present evidence that customers are responding favorably to the current design or must listen carefully to the buyer's suggestions for changes. Then he should feed these suggestions back to his firm.

Objections to the Selling Firm

The retail customer who is already in the store is not likely to object to the firm; but the contact salesman encounters many customers whose objections are directed, not at his product or service, but at his firm.

"I Don't Like Your Company's Policies." The salesman should use extreme care in handling an objection to his company's policies. He shouldn't agree that a policy is wrong; he may lose the customer's

K Mart

The "yes, but" method is often used in handling customer objections. A customer may object to buying a certain refrigerator because she thinks it is too small, but the salesman knows that the model is usually quite adequate for the size of her family. The salesman can admit that the refrigerator looks small but then demonstrate how much food it can hold and point out the large size of its freezer compartment.

respect by doing so. He should show why company policies were formulated and try to get the prospect to see the situation from the company's viewpoint. Generally, a prospect will admire and respect a salesman who meets an objection of this kind with a thorough explanation.

"I Don't Know Anything About Your Company." When a businessman says he doesn't know anything about the salesman's firm, there is a temptation to deluge the prospect with facts and figures on the firm. Most prospects are not interested in this kind of information. They are more interested in the number of well-known dealers who have ordered the firm's product or in advertisements the firm is running in leading magazines and trade journals.

"I Will Have Nothing To Do with Your Company." A refusal to do business with the salesman's firm generally means that the customer has had a misunderstanding with another salesman from the firm.

Courtesy and tact should be shown, and the prospect should be encouraged to air his grievance. In the meantime, the salesman may help relieve tension by performing little acts of courtesy, such as passing along merchandising ideas he has observed in other businesses.

"I'm Satisfied with the Firm I'm Dealing with." Most business customers are not particularly anxious to change suppliers, especially if this involves substituting a new product for merchandise that is selling well. The salesman may be able to prove that his line can earn bigger profits through faster turnover. Or he might emphasize the promotional aids that his firm provides to dealers. He might recommend making a small initial order so that the customer can prove for himself what the salesman's line can do for his sales and profits. As you know, the salesman should never knock the competing supplier.

Objections to Price

Retail customers do not usually object to paying the price asked if they feel they are getting their money's worth. They object to price because they do not see the hidden values in the product. Such an objection indicates that the salesperson has not convinced the customer that the goods are worth the asking price. It may be necessary, therefore, for him to highlight the important selling points again to prove that the price is reasonable. If it seems that the retail customer really cannot afford the price asked, the salesperson should show less expensive merchandise. However, he should never show the merchandise so as to give the impression that it is cheap.

When a business customer says that the price is too high, he is usually trying to find out whether or not the goods are really worth the asking price. If the salesman's product has certain features that warrant charging a higher price than that charged for competing goods, he should stress these features. Often a price objection is based on careless observation by the prospect or is a trick to drive a hard bargain. The salesman should be thoroughly familiar with prices of his competitors so that he may handle this objection. Generally, a salesman knows that there is a lower price than his somewhere in the market. Most successful salesmen do not talk price only. Instead they talk about profits, value, quality, efficiency, customer demand, turnover, performance, satisfaction, service, economy, sales results, and prestige of the line. The salesman selling a quality line of products should not fear price competition and price objections.

A Sales Interview

Mr. Gray called on a furnace salesman to discuss the replacement of his old oil furnace. The salesman recommended a natural gas furnace. After he talked it up and demonstrated it, the following conversation took place.

Mr. Gray: No, I don't believe it is just what I want. I don't think I want to take a chance on a gas furnace.

Salesman: But let me show you again how well it operates. See how simple and foolproof it is—and the automatic feature eliminates so much bother and drudgery.

Mr. Gray: Yes, you told me that before.

Salesman: This furnace is in daily use in hundreds of homes. There is plenty of evidence that it is wholly reliable.

Mr. Gray: I don't care how many people use it; it is much too expensive.

Salesman: I'm glad you brought that up. Let's get down to facts and figures. Operating expenses are only . . .

Mr. Gray: That doesn't prove a thing. A friend of mine who has a gas furnace tells me it costs him much more than oil used to.

Salesman: You can't rely on a layman's opinion in a matter of this kind. I've made a scientific study of this problem and can assure you . . .

Mr. Gray: (interrupting) I'll think it over, but I'll probably stick to my oil furnace for awhile longer.

What did the salesman do wrong in handling Mr. Gray's objections? Do you think Mr. Gray's objections were real ones or only excuses to put off buying for the moment? What could the salesman have done to improve his sales talk?

Objections to Buying at the Moment

In contact selling, buyers commonly express an objection to buying at the moment by saying that they are too busy to listen to the sales talk. The salesman must exercise good judgment in deciding whether this is a valid objection or an excuse. If he believes it is valid, he should arrange for another appointment. Nothing is gained by discussing a product when the prospect really is pressed for time.

"I want to think it over" is a common objection of retail customers and of many indecisive purchasing agents. Many customers who raise this objection are not clear in their own minds as to their immediate needs. They may also feel that what the store has to offer will not suit them. In a few cases, this objection is raised by customers who are dissatisfied with the salesperson. Generally, the best way to meet this objection is to agree that the customer should look around or consult his friends but to invite him to look at additional merchandise before leaving the establishment. In contact selling, the salesman should give reasons why it is important to buy at the moment.

WHEN TO HANDLE OBJECTIONS

Generally, the time to handle an objection is at the moment it is raised. Sometimes the salesman may ask for a postponement of the objection until a later point in the sales interview. However, he should realize that the effectiveness of the presentation is greatly reduced until that objection is handled.

Sometimes it is wise to anticipate an objection before it is raised. This is called *forestalling the objection.* From past experience, the salesman may have found that many customers have the same objection to a specific product in his line; and he may have an excellent answer prepared for this objection. Bringing a common objection into the open is valuable even if it was not in the customer's mind. Nearly every customer quickly meets critics of his purchases. For the retail customer, the critics are his family and friends; for the dealer, his customers; and for the purchasing agent, the department managers of his firm. If objections that such critics are likely to make can be brought into the open during the sales talk, the customer can better defend his choice later.

CHECKING YOUR KNOWLEDGE

Vocabulary:

forestalling the objection

Review questions:

1. How can a salesman tell real objections from excuses?
2. What are the most common kinds of real objections?
3. Name four ways of handling a customer's objection to the product.
4. How may a business customer object to the salesman's firm?
5. When should an objection be handled?

For discussion:

1. "A successful salesman does not discuss price." Do you agree or disagree with this statement? Why or why not?

2. After the salesman has stated the price, the customer objects: "That's too much money. I can buy the same product at a much lower price at another store." How could this objection be handled?
3. How might a contact salesman meet this objection: "Your firm is too far away. I can get the same product here in town and get better service"?

part C

decision stimulators

To get the indecisive customer to act, certain techniques have been developed to bring the sale to a close. These techniques are known as *decision stimulators*. Some deserve frequent use; others should be used sparingly, if at all. They differ from the techniques of preparing for the close in that decision stimulators involve special devices to get the customer to buy when he is ready to take this step logically but still has an emotional resistance to committing himself.

COMMON DECISION STIMULATORS

The most common decision stimulators are the assumption close, the choice close, the action close, the premium close, the price-concession close, the impending close, the SRO (standing room only) close, and the you-owe-it-to-yourself close.

Assumption Close

With the *assumption close,* the salesman assumes that his presentation has convinced the customer to buy; and he takes the step that would logically follow the buying decision. He may start to write up the sales check or order, separate the goods for wrapping or delivery, call a tailor to determine what alterations are necessary, or state that delivery will be made on a certain day.

Choice Close

In the *choice close,* the customer is offered a choice between several articles with the belief that when his preference is stated, the major buying decision will also be made. Questions such as the following are commonly used in the choice close: "Which style do you prefer?" "Do you want the green or the blue?" "Shall we send it or will you take it with you?" "Is this cash or charge?" "Would you prefer to have the installation made in January or February?" This method may also be called "closing on a minor point." Once the choice is made, the assumption close follows. The same technique is used in the trial close.

Action Close

In the *action close,* the customer is specifically asked to buy. The salesman may say, "Let me take your order, since buying is clearly in your own best interest" or "I can have the merchandise ready for you tomorrow; will you call for it then?" This method is often successful in selling to business buyers. They do not resent this direct approach, since they know that the salesman is an advocate of the product line being offered. Retail customers, however, may expect salesmen to help them, not "push" them.

Premium Close

The *premium close* offers an "extra something" in addition to the goods sold at the regular price and terms. The premium may be a free gift or a free service such as monogramming or gift wrapping. There may be an offer of free delivery, extended payment terms, or the waiving of normal carrying charges.

The premium close is often effective and may not eat into profits if prices have been set high enough to make such concessions possible. On the other hand, this type of close may be costly to the seller and may undermine customer confidence in the seller's merchandise and prices. Normally, any premium offer should be incorporated into the sales presentation and should not be offered simply to persuade balky customers to buy.

Price-Concession Close

The *price-concession close* is one of the most common but most questionable decision stimulators used by small firms selling on both the retail and wholesale levels. It involves granting a special price concession to induce a customer to buy. For example, a customer may be well satisfied with a $35 jacket but says he cannot afford to pay more than $30 for it. The seller offers to "split the difference," and the sale is closed.

The seller may think it is better to move goods with some profit or at a minimum loss than to lose sales because of pricing inflexibilities. But, in the long run, the practice of giving price concessions is dangerous. First, the customer receiving the concession begins to wonder if he could have gotten the goods for even less and that maybe, even with the concession, he was overcharged. Second, the news gets around that the seller is tricky, that he asks too much for his goods initially, and that the only way to get good value is to bargain. Most American consumers do not like to haggle; they tend to stay away from a firm that does not have a one-price-to-all reputation.

Impending Close

In the *impending close,* the customer is reminded of the need for immediate action because of a coming event. Some retailing examples of impending closes are: "Mother's Day is tomorrow, and this is your last chance to get her something distinctive like this." "You'll want it for the opening of the fishing season Monday." "It takes two weeks for delivery. If you don't order now, you won't have it by Christmas."

In selling to businessmen, the impending close may take forms such as the following: "The Easter selling season starts in only two weeks, but I'll try to rush your order through." "My company has announced a price increase to take effect next Monday, but orders placed this week will be honored at the old prices."

SRO (Standing Room Only) Close

In the *SRO close,* the customer is reminded that "everybody wants this merchandise, and the supply is scarce." Some sellers limit their merchandise "one to a customer," which heightens the desire to be one of the few lucky buyers. Understandably, some unethical merchants have used this device to unload slow sellers.

You-Owe-It-to-Yourself Close

Many customers are moved by an emotional urge to splurge or to get personal recognition. In the *you-owe-it-to-yourself close,* the salesman appeals to this type of customer: "What if the hat does cost $20? It'll make you feel like a million dollars." "You'll feel like a corporation president when you wear this suit." The promise of such satisfaction, even though the customer knows realistically that such satisfaction may not result, is a potent force in overcoming negative buying factors. Such an appeal is often bolstered by following it with a rational

A Sales Interview

Mrs. Gordon tried on several pairs of shoes in a store but objected to the price of all over $12 and to the styles and quality of the less expensive ones. Finally, she found two pairs for $10.95 each that she seemed to like, but she could not decide between them. At the logical time to close the sale, she had one pair on and was holding the other pair.

Mrs. Gordon: They are both nice. I don't know which I want.

Salesperson: You won't make a mistake, whichever pair you buy.

Mrs. Gordon: I do want to be sure.

Salesperson: Why don't you take both? We have a "two for" plan by which we can sell you the two pairs together for $21 rather than $21.90.

Mrs. Gordon: Oh, I couldn't consider spending that much.

Salesperson: Well, then, try on again the pair you are holding and see which looks better on your feet.

Mrs. Gordon: (looking at her watch) I'm late already. Maybe my sister can come in with me tomorrow.

Salesperson: All right, but (handing her a card) be sure to ask for me so I can show you these two styles.

What are the positive features in the way the salesman handled this closing? What are the negative features? How could he have completed the sale successfully?

reason for the purchase. For example, the statement about the man's suit can be followed with "and it is selling right now in Bowmans' (the town's leading men's shop) for $15 more."

Even in selling to businessmen, the seller can often appeal to the buyer's pride. The buyer may want the most attractively furnished office in town or the most modern factory. Ostensibly, he wants these things to improve his production or sales, but his basic motive may be desire for recognition among his associates.

HOW NOT TO CLOSE

There are certain things to be avoided in closing the sale. One of the most common mistakes is the negative close. "You don't want this one, do you?" or "Won't you try a sample order?" deserves the answer "No." Sometimes negative statements that confuse the customer are used at the close. The statement that "This carpeting for your stairway will not wear so long as the other" gives the customer the idea that some of the store's carpeting is not of good quality. A much better impression is made by saying: "This carpeting at $8 a yard is unusually good for the price; but this carpeting, which sells for $10 a yard, will wear better." Here, the customer has been given the idea that both kinds of carpeting are good value for the money but that one is better than the other. Thus, he will not feel that he is buying something undesirable if he takes the less expensive carpeting.

Another mistake in closing is to frighten the customer with a contract. Retail salespeople are often required to fill out sales slips, and most specialty or wholesale salesmen use order blanks that require the purchaser's signature. These forms become contracts when they are signed. Most customers are, however, fearful of contracts or any other written papers that seem to bind them legally; and too often they have good reason for this fear. Some customers have unwittingly signed installment contracts that gave the seller the right to repossess the merchandise or to collect part of the customer's salary in case of default on payments. There may be nothing wrong with the installment contract, but the customer should know the terms under which he buys.

Retail customers are not particularly disturbed if the salesperson's sales book is in full view. In wholesale selling, the best practice is to keep the order blank in sight during the sales presentation. Thus, once the salesman begins to fill it out, the customer is not alarmed. The usual procedure is for the salesman to fill out the order for the customer and at the same time stress that the written order is simply a memorandum which helps to protect customers and prevent mistakes.

Another common error in closing is to "panic" the buyer with such statements as "There probably won't be any left if you delay" or "I have another customer interested in this apartment, and I expect he will close the deal this afternoon if you don't make a deposit now to bind the bargain." The appeal to fear should also be avoided: "The last fellow who didn't take my advice and install seat belts was killed in a horrible car accident last week."

Although these tactics sometimes work, buyers are more likely to regard them as "scare" techniques and will resist buying. Sometimes a salesman is justified in urging quick action in the customer's best interests. But only if he has been sincere in his previous dealings will his warning generally be heeded.

CHECKING YOUR KNOWLEDGE

Vocabulary:

(1) decision stimulators
(2) assumption close
(3) choice close
(4) action close
(5) premium close
(6) price-concession close
(7) impending close
(8) SRO close
(9) you-owe-it-to-yourself close

Review questions:

1. What activities may a salesman start to perform in the assumption close?
2. What are the advantages and disadvantages of the premium close?
3. Why is it said that a price-concession close is one of the most common but questionable decision stimulators?
4. Upon what buying motive or motives is the you-owe-it-to-yourself close based?
5. Name some mistakes that salesmen often make in closing a sale.

For discussion:

1. Of which of the decision stimulators discussed in this part do you approve? Of which do you disapprove?
2. How might the technique of closing on a minor point be used in selling each of the following articles? (a) waffle iron; (b) clock radio; (c) electric blanket; (d) fire extinguisher.

part D

the mechanics of closing

The basic decision a buyer must make, with the salesman's assistance, is whether or not to buy a product or service at a given price. But there are related decisions that the customer and salesman must make at the time of closing. These decisions may include how much to buy, how and when delivery is to be made, when the goods are to be paid for, and the services the seller is to provide along with the product. Good salesmen help customers make these decisions as well as the basic buying decision.

DECIDING ON THE RIGHT AMOUNT

Sometimes the most difficult problem in closing is deciding how much to sell the customer. Suppose that a wholesale salesman secures an order for ten dozen units of a certain article. During his next call, he finds that the retailer has been able to sell only three dozen units. Two bad effects result from such overselling. First, the retailer loses faith in the article. Three dozen units might represent an excellent rate of sale for the article; but because the merchant was oversold initially, he believes that the sales volume is poor. Second, a larger amount of capital than necessary is invested in stock; and this represents a loss to the retailer. He may lose faith in the product and also in the salesman because he recommended too large an order.

If the salesman had sold the retailer only four dozen units, the sales of three dozen would have represented a larger proportion of the purchased stock. On making his next call, the salesman would probably have found the retailer enthusiastic about the goods; and an additional order would likely have resulted. It is important that the salesman use good judgment in securing an order and that he be careful not to oversell. This is especially true in selling a line with which the retailer has had no previous experience, since he will be unable to judge his own needs. On the other hand, the salesman who advises the retailer to order less than he can probably use is showing poor judgment.

The retail salesperson also faces the problem of how much of a specific product a customer needs. It is not unusual for a hardware salesman to be asked, "How much fencing will I need to do the job?" or for a butcher to be asked "How many pounds should I buy to serve six people?" Such questions are encountered in all retail businesses, and the salesperson should be able to advise the customer correctly. He can give this advice if he has a complete knowledge of the goods he sells.

TERMS OF SALE

Choosing the terms of sale, such as delivery and method of payment, usually requires a separate decision after the customer has made the major decision to buy.

Delivery costs are high for most retail stores; thus, salespeople should try to keep customers from taking advantage of delivery services. To reduce delivery costs as much as possible, the retail salesperson should assume that the customer will carry all small packages. If a package is small, the salesman may say, "Will you take it with you?"

rather than, "Do you wish it sent?" The first question is more likely to result in the customer's carrying the package. If the customer is carrying several other packages, the salesperson can offer to wrap them in one package or furnish a shopping bag.

In wholesale selling, customers often haggle over terms and ask for larger discounts, advertising allowances, free delivery, immediate shipment, or extended payment terms. The wholesaler should have reasonable terms of sale that apply to all his customers. Nevertheless, since different buyers need different quantities of goods and different promotional aids, the seller's terms should be somewhat flexible—so long as he does not discriminate among buyers who purchase in like quantities and follow like methods of purchasing. Suppose that one buyer is located 2,000 miles from the seller's plant, and it takes two weeks for goods to reach him. The seller's regular terms may be 2/10, net 30; but requiring the buyer to pay within ten days of shipment to earn the cash discount would mean paying before the goods arrived and could be inspected. Under such conditions, it is fair to give this buyer ROG (receipt of goods) terms, permitting him to pay within ten days after receiving the goods and still earn the cash discount.

Sometimes a customer may want to buy a nationally advertised product without the national brand label. He feels that he can generate demand for the product through his own efforts without depending upon the manufacturer's national advertising. Since he is offering to buy the goods and not the established name, it is not unreasonable for him to ask for a concession. The salesman would seldom make the decision to grant such a request; rather, the matter would be referred to his superiors.

COMPLETING THE TRANSACTION

Salespeople go through certain routine steps in completing the sales transaction. These steps may involve ringing up the sale, writing out the order, wrapping the goods, or recording and following up on delivery instructions. The two requirements in this part of the sales transaction are accuracy and speed. Any error in recording the customer's name or address, any failure to send exactly what the customer selected, or any failure to keep delivery promises may lead to a cancellation of the sale and minimize the opportunity for future sales. Speed is important, too; once a customer has decided to buy, he is usually in a hurry to be on his way. Delay in locating a sales book or order blank and fumbling in recording the sale and wrapping merchandise simply irritate the

Montgomery Ward

Learning to operate the cash register quickly and efficiently is an important part of completing a retail sale. It is so important that many retailers conduct special training classes in cash register operation.

customer. Such delays may not result in a cancellation of the sale but reduce the likelihood of the customer's buying from that salesman again.

The contact salesman generally does not handle all phases of the mechanical close. He seldom handles the procurement, wrapping, and delivery of the goods. He books the order and turns it over to the production and shipping departments of his company. Nevertheless, he is responsible for the follow up to make sure that the goods are shipped as agreed. The buyer has a right to hold the salesman responsible if any delivery promises are not kept.

Every sale involves an exchange of goods or services for money. The quantity bought and the amount of money paid can only be expressed in numbers. Anyone going into selling, therefore, must have a working knowledge of arithmetic. Next to English, arithmetic is the salesman's most important tool, yet most employers report that young job applicants are weak in arithmetic.

Salesmen should have a thorough knowledge of addition, subtraction, multiplication, and division of integers, fractions, decimals, and percentages. Accuracy in performing calculations is more important than speed. Nothing is gained and much is lost by adding up a purchase quickly but incorrectly. Even if the mistake is in the customer's favor,

Procedures in Making Change

- State the amount of the purchase and the amount received in payment. "$2.15 out of $5."
- Leave the money and the printed receipt in sight while making change.
- Count up from the purchase price to the amount of payment, making change with as few coins and bills as possible and giving coins and bills to the customer one at a time. "$2.25 (giving the customer a dime), $2.50 (giving a quarter), $3 (giving a half dollar), $4 (giving a dollar bill), and $5 (giving a dollar bill)."
- Thank the customer.

Retail salespeople should know how to operate the cash register and to make change quickly and accurately. Here is a summary of basic procedures to follow in making change.

he loses confidence in the salesperson. Errors in arithmetic may drive away customers and result in financial loss to the business.

THE FAREWELL

After the salesman has secured his order and handled the mechanics of completing the sale, he should make his leave-taking as brief and cordial as possible. The sales transaction has probably already consumed considerable time, and his customer will be anxious to get back to other activities. One effective means of leave-taking is to call the customer's attention to some special service that the salesman or his firm renders and that has not been mentioned before. Above everything else, the salesman should thank the customer. Such phrases as "I'm sure you'll enjoy your purchase," "It was a pleasure to serve you," or "I hope we see you again," can be effectively used in many situations.

ANALYZING LOST SALES

If a sale is lost, the salesman should review the transaction and determine why he failed. In some cases, the sale may have been lost because of obstacles he couldn't overcome. For example, the salesman's firm may have been unable to provide just what the customer wanted at a price he was willing to pay. But most lost sales are caused by the salesman's blunders. By retracing the interview, step by step, he may find out his error and guard against it in the future.

A successful technique for contact salesmen is *curbstone training*. This means that when a salesman fails to make a sale, he takes the time to analyze the sales interview upon returning to his car. If he waits until the end of the day to analyze lost sales, he may forget information that might have cleared up the reasons behind his failure. As soon as possible after a lost sale, the salesman should ask himself the following questions:

1. What mistakes did I make in my greeting?
2. Did I have a warm and friendly smile?
3. Was I timid or overconfident in my approach?
4. Was my personal appearance all that it should have been?
5. Did I size up my customer correctly and show the right goods?
6. Did I use correct English, and was my language adapted to my prospect?
7. Was my talk coherent?
8. Did I talk too much and listen too little?
9. Did I clinch each point in the presentation as I went along?
10. Did I allow myself to become nervous and thus detract from the talk's effectiveness?
11. Did I overcome doubts, or was I flustered when they were raised?
12. In what way was my presentation effective, and in what way was it weak?
13. Was I in rapport with my customer, so that we exchanged ideas freely and explored the situation in depth?
14. Was any question raised regarding my goods or services that I could not answer?
15. Was any question raised regarding my firm and its policies that I could not answer?
16. Did I make the mistake of knocking my competitor or competing goods?
17. Was I discourteous at any time?
18. Where was I weak in my closing?

After analyzing the sale and determining the errors that he made, the average salesman is anxious to tackle another sale and overcome his weaknesses. Discovering and overcoming mistakes gives courage; the disheartening thing is to go along day after day, failing to make sales and not knowing the cause. An athlete becomes skilled when, through his own observations or through his coach's suggestions, he discovers the nature of his mistakes. So it is with salesmen.

CHECKING YOUR KNOWLEDGE

Vocabulary:

curbstone training

Review questions:

1. What are two bad effects that result from selling too much of one product to a customer?
2. Does a manufacturer or wholesaler ever adjust his terms of sale to suit different buyers? If so, under what conditions might he do this?
3. Why is a working knowledge of arithmetic so important to the salesman?
4. How should a salesman say farewell to a customer?
5. Why is it important to analyze lost sales? List at least eight questions that could be used in analyzing lost sales.

For discussion:

1. "The salesman must constantly make decisions throughout the sales interview." Explain this statement. What decisions must he make and why must he make them?
2. How can a salesman create customer goodwill in performing the mechanics of closing? How might he create ill will?
3. Should an employer check the arithmetic skills of potential salesmen before hiring them? If so, how?

part E

plus selling

Plus selling refers to the efforts to sell more goods to more customers by using special selling devices. These devices include suggestion selling, trading up, increasing the number of successful transactions, and following up sales. Because suggestion selling and trading up are perhaps most important in retail selling, they will be discussed separately in Chapter 12. Increasing the number of successful transactions and following up sales are important to all salesmen, however. In this part, you will learn how these techniques can be used. The various methods of plus selling, properly employed by salespeople, will encourage repeat sales and result in a satisfied clientele.

INCREASING THE NUMBER OF SUCCESSFUL TRANSACTIONS

Sales can be increased not only by selling more or better merchandise to customers but also by serving more customers successfully. There are two ways for a salesman to increase the number of successful sales transactions he handles: (1) by meeting more customers and (2) by selling to a larger proportion of those he meets.

Meeting More Customers

The traveling salesman or canvasser can call on more customers by working faster and longer and by routing his calls to save steps, much as a postman does. "Keep working" is the first rule of the outside salesman; every minute of his time should be put to good use. The retail merchant can contact more customers by attracting more prospects to his store through advertising, display, special feature publicity, and word-of-mouth recommendations from satisfied customers.

One way for the retail salesman to meet more customers is to handle more than one customer at a time. No retail store can employ enough salespeople to give every customer immediate attention during rush hours. Some salespeople, however, have learned to serve more than one customer at a time. Trying to wait on more than one customer at a time is like trying to juggle three balls at a time. Until a person is really skilled, there is a danger that he may drop one ball while trying to watch all three. But just as many people can throw and catch each ball separately, some salespeople can handle more than one customer at a time.

The secret is to have each customer at a different stage of the sale. A salesman should not greet two different customers at once. He should not try to determine the demands of each at the same time or try to show merchandise to both of them at once. After the first customer has been sized up and given an initial selection to examine, the salesman should excuse himself for a moment, approach the second customer, and determine his wants. The first customer may appreciate being left alone for a few minutes to consider the merchandise he has been shown. He will thus feel that no one is trying to force him to buy.

This plan for handling more than one customer at a time is not adaptable to selling all kinds of merchandise. If a salesman of meat products, for example, were to try to wait on two customers at once, both customers would probably buy elsewhere in the future.

Selling to More Customers Who Are Contacted

Salesmen can sell to a larger proportion of the customers they contact by (1) offering merchandise or service that is better suited to the prospect's needs than competing products and (2) by guiding the prospect skillfully through the sales interview to the basic buying decision.

H. Armstrong Roberts

During busy shopping periods, the salesman must know how to serve more than one customer at a time. When a salesperson is busy with a customer and another customer arrives, he should acknowledge the newcomer with a pleasant nod and a greeting, such as "Good morning, I'll be with you in just a moment." In certain stores, it is possible to wait on more than one customer at a time, so long as each is at a different stage of the sale.

A salesman must know his merchandise, show his merchandise, and tell about his merchandise before he can sell his merchandise. This applies to all kinds of salespeople.

Customers who fail to buy usually do so for one or more of the following reasons:

1. The salesman's indifference in waiting on customers.
2. The store's failure to stock the right merchandise.
3. The salesman's failure to analyze customer wants and offer appropriate goods.
4. The salesman's failure to demonstrate the merchandise effectively.
5. The salesman's inability to close the sale.
6. The failure to be served promptly.

Each of these negative causes can be eliminated if salesman and selling firm employ depth selling techniques. Earlier in this book you learned that depth selling explains both the "how" and "why" of salesmanship and that it accomplishes three major objectives of good selling:

(1) it helps the seller understand himself; (2) it helps him understand the needs and wants of others; and (3) it helps develop his skill as a decision maker and problem solver. Customers are more likely to respond favorably to depth selling techniques than to techniques of the stimulus-response theory, formula theory, and need-satisfaction theory. Let us study some examples to see how specific salesmen, by using depth selling, came to sell to a larger proportion of the customers they contacted.

Depth Selling in Retailing. A customer approached a department store's interior decorator for help in furnishing her new home; she had only some vague ideas of the final appearance she wanted. The decorator engaged in a series of conversations with the customer and members of her family. He visited the customer's present home to find out her family's tastes and living habits. He had no predetermined ideas on what furniture, rugs, draperies, lamps, mirrors, pictures, and accessories he would buy; but in his mind's eye, he had an image of the merchandise offered by his store and by the broader wholesale market.

The decorator devoted his talent and skill to creating the most attractive interior within the limits of the customer's budget. But the creation was not his alone; it was the joint effort of the customer and himself. The customer brought to the series of conversations her own private wants and ideas; the decorator contributed his knowledge of color, line, design, and of what was available in the marketplace.

Depth Techniques in Wholesale and Industrial Selling. The owner of an exclusive specialty shop approached a merchandise broker for help in selecting clothing that he could resell. They discussed the store's location, clientele, policies, and problems of operation. Then the broker suggested the particular manufacturers whom he believed could supply the clothing that would sell well in the shop. The broker went even further and helped the retailer select the particular style numbers that seemed most appropriate. The broker had no predetermined plan to sell any particular merchandise. He was a partner in a problem-solving experience.

Sales engineers do an outstanding job of depth selling. The sales engineer often spends many months trying to solve a potential customer's technical problem involving the class of products his firm makes. He holds many discussions with his clients and is always ready to create a new design or method of production that will achieve the buyer's goals. He offers his technical skill and that of his company. Since the final plan is a joint one, it does not have to be sold to the buyer. The

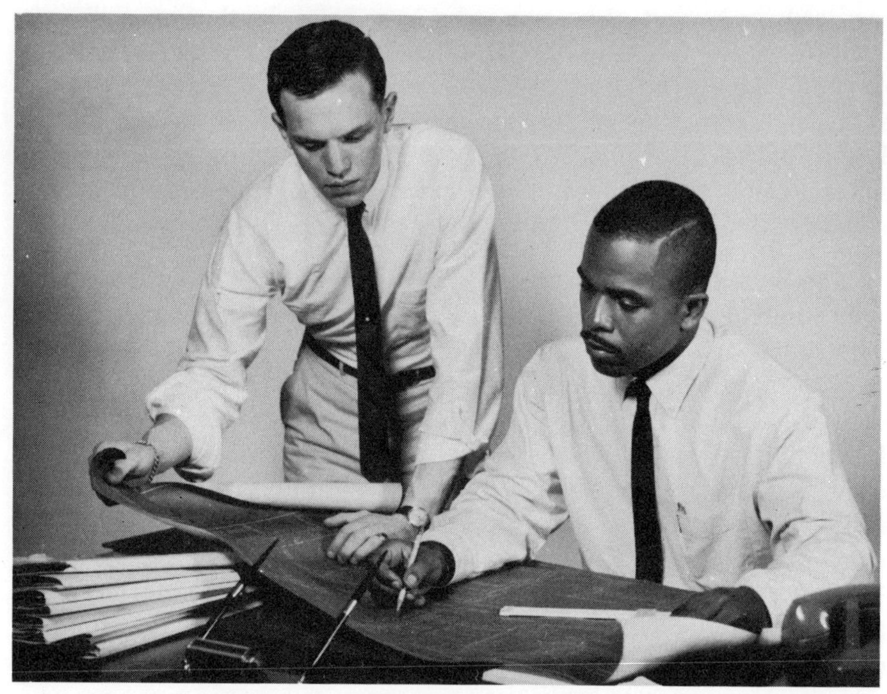

Harold M. Lambert

The sales engineer must constantly employ depth selling techniques. He may spend months working on the technical problems of a single client. His selling efforts are not a "one-way street" but rather a discussion in which two people with different information and attitudes concentrate on the problems of one of them and try to arrive at a solution that best meets this person's needs.

seller's remuneration comes when the customer finally places the order. The price agreed upon is partly for materials or equipment and partly for the time and effort that have gone into solving the problem. If the sales engineer does not arrive at a solution acceptable to the buyer, he gets no pay for his services.

Depth Selling of Services. In handling services, depth selling is essential, since services must frequently be tailored to each individual customer. The directors of a hospital decided to engage in a fund-raising campaign for the hospital. They were uncertain about how to conduct the campaign, so they approached a professional fund-raiser. He conducted lengthy interviews with the directors and employees of the hospital, estimated the amount of money that the organization could reasonably expect to raise, and drew up a tentative plan of operation. This was presented to the hospital's executive board. When it was approved, a contract was signed for the execution of the campaign by the fund-raiser. At the start of the investigation, the fund-raiser had no idea of what plan he would try to sell. The nature of his service and its ultimate cost were tailored as the client and the fund-raiser explored the nature of their mutual problem.

FOLLOWING UP SALES

Another important plus selling technique is that of following up sales. One furnace salesman keeps a record of every house in which one of his furnaces was installed. He includes a snapshot of the house, the kind and price of furnace and the date of installation. At the end of each winter, he calls on the homeowner to determine the heating costs and whether the furnace is working satisfactorily. The salesman feels that he accomplishes four things by doing this. First, he builds goodwill with past customers so that they recommend his furnace to their friends. Second, he forestalls development of ill will by correcting any failure of his product to give satisfaction. Third, he gathers valuable data on heating costs that provide him with facts and figures for future sales talks. Fourth, the practice endears him to contractors who know that, with him on the job, they will not be bothered by customers' furnace troubles.

When a mechanical device of some value has been purchased or when an article is likely to need periodic cleaning or repair, follow-up should be made as a matter of course. For example, pianos are generally tuned free of charge after delivery and are sometimes tuned a second time a little later. New automobiles may be given a 1,000-mile checkup by the dealer. Furriers make a practice of following up winter fur coat sales to sell customers on the idea of having coats cleaned and stored through the summer months.

It is not possible to follow up sales in every line. Certainly it could not be done in such firms as variety stores and most food stores. There are, however, many product lines in which salesmen do not commonly follow up sales but where the practice would pay dividends in goodwill. Vacuum cleaners, refrigerators, typewriters, and expensive clothing are articles whose sale might well include a follow-up. Even if there is little likelihood that the goods need attention, showing interest in the customer's satisfaction will do much to build future sales.

CHECKING YOUR KNOWLEDGE

Vocabulary:

plus selling

Review questions:

1. How may salesmen increase the number of successful sales transactions they handle?
2. Describe the technique of waiting on more than one customer at a time.
3. How may salesmen sell to a larger proportion of the customers they contact?
4. List five reasons why customers may fail to buy.
5. What is accomplished by following up sales?

For discussion:

1. Can the number of successful sales transactions be increased more effectively by meeting more customers or by selling to a larger proportion of those contacted?
2. In a busy drapery department, a woman asked a salesperson who was waiting on another customer to wait on her at once so that she would not be late for an appointment. What should the salesperson say or do?
3. Is depth selling more important in contact selling than in retail selling? Explain your answer.

BUILDING YOUR SKILLS

Improving your English:

On a separate sheet of paper, write the correct conjunction to be used in each of the following sentences.

1. Neither the customer (nor, or) the salesman noticed the reduced price.
2. Either the merchandise manager (nor, or) the advertising assistant prepared the ad copy.
3. No reports (nor, or) financial statements were available.
4. John read in the newspaper (where, that) the special prices had been discontinued.
5. The repairman had no sooner begun to check the range (until, than) the weird noise occurred again.
6. The customer wanted to know (whether, if) the manufacturer's warranty would cover last year's model.
7. The store will make the adjustment (provided that, providing that) the customer assumes responsibility for all transportation.
8. Modifications of the air conditioning system cannot be made (without, unless) the manager consults the engineer who submitted the bid.

9. The distributing firm cannot make Saturday deliveries (except, unless) previous arrangements have been made.
10. The design of the new package is just (like, as) the artist had suggested.

Improving your arithmetic:

Perform the required calculations in the exercises below.

1. Cost, $6; markup, $3. Find (a) retail price and (b) markup percent.
2. Retail, $15; markup, $5. Find (a) cost and (b) markup percent.
3. Cost, $7.50; retail, $10. Find (a) markup in dollars and (b) markup percent.
4. Retail, $3; markup, 30%. Find (a) cost price and (b) markup in dollars.
5. Cost, $7; markup, 30%. Find (a) retail price and (b) markup in dollars.

Improving your research skills:

1. Your instructor will assign another member of the class to work with you on this project. Call on the manager of, or an experienced salesman in, one of the following businesses: (a) men's clothing shop; (b) women's clothing shop; (c) interior decorating studio; (d) jewelry store; (e) insurance agency; (f) music shop. Explain that your salesmanship class is making a study of the main objections met by salespeople in your community. Inquire about the two chief objections met in the business. Then tell how you would meet these objections. Give your answer in writing.
2. In consultation with your instructor, select one of the following articles to be the subject of a complete sales talk:

(a) Hosiery	(g) Cheese
(b) Cosmetics	(h) Clock
(c) Toaster	(i) Shoes
(d) Typewriter ribbon	(j) Detergent
(e) Camera	(k) Dictionary
(f) Desk lamp	(l) Transistor radio

Another student will be assigned to play the part of the customer. This student should be instructed to raise objections and attempt to put off the close. The rest of the class should criticize the sales presentation.

3. In retail selling, one of the steps in completing the sale is to wrap the article that has just been sold. Although in many large stores the wrapping is done by a special wrapping clerk, in small stores the article is generally wrapped by the salesperson. Wrapping requires skill, and skill requires practice. In the classroom, you will now wrap two articles of different sizes and shapes provided by your teacher. You will be evaluated on the neatness of the wrapping and on the time it takes you to do the job.

APPLYING YOUR KNOWLEDGE

Case problems:

1. A purchasing agent said to a salesman: "I'm not interested in buying from your company; but if you can sell to me at one cent a pound cheaper than what I've been paying, I'll give you the order." How might the salesman answer him?
2. In checking over the records of the notions department, you find that one salesman has been consistently making small errors in ringing up sales on the cash register, adding totals for charge purchases, and giving change. What would you do in this situation?

Continuing project:

In your manual, describe how you would prepare for the close of a sale of your product, the techniques you would use to build up to the close, the objections you might encounter and the methods of handling them you would use, the decision stimulators that might be suitable for selling your product, and how you would handle the mechanics of closing. Then tell how you would use plus selling to increase the number of successful transactions you handle.

Extra credit:

On a separate sheet of paper, write out what you would say to the customer in making change for the following transactions:

1. Amount of sale, $15.35; amount of payment, $20.
2. Amount of sale, $1.21; amount of payment, $5.
3. Amount of sale, $8.39; amount of payment, $10.
4. Amount of sale, $.36; amount of payment, $1.
5. Amount of sale, $2.41; amount of payment, $5.
6. Amount of sale, $9.11; amount of payment, $10.
7. Amount of sale, $17.28; amount of payment, $20.
8. Amount of sale, $4.02; amount of payment, $5.
9. Amount of sale, $7.55; amount of payment, $20.
10. Amount of sale, $.65; amount of payment, $5.

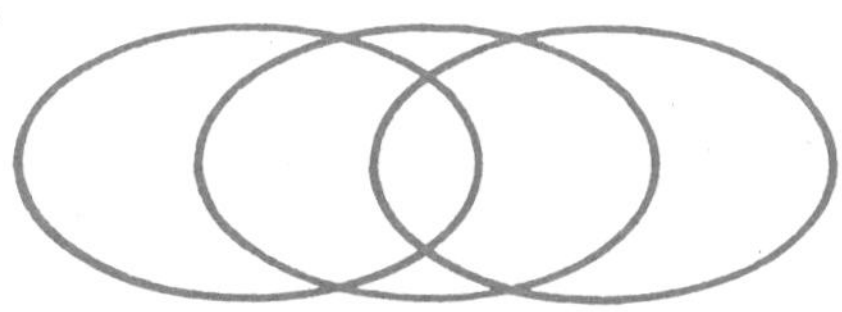

chapter 11

special skills in contact selling

KEY QUESTIONS

A Why should a contact salesman understand the discounts and datings his firm offers?

B Can a contact salesman perform a service to his customers by suggesting appropriate methods of transporting merchandise?

C Who absorbs the cost of cooperative advertising, point-of-purchase advertising, and premiums?

D Is the use of group selling likely to increase or decrease in the future?

E How does the average contact salesman spend an average working day?

part A

discounts and datings

Most ultimate consumers are reasonably familiar with the terms of sale that retailers offer. Thus, retail salespeople generally need to give only a minimum explanation of terms of sale. The same situation does not exist in industrial and wholesale selling, however. Terms of sale—particularly concerning such elements as discounts, datings, and transportation arrangements—differ from seller to seller. Since business customers obviously want to get the best possible goods at the lowest possible prices, they do a lot of shopping around to find the most favorable terms of sale.

The contact salesman must have a thorough knowledge of the discounts, datings, and transportation arrangements his firm offers. Generous terms of sale can be strong selling points for a product. This is particularly true in today's highly competitive marketplace, where many products of similar styles and quality are available. Often a liberal discount will mean the difference between getting an order and not getting an order. The salesman should, of course, be skilled in calculating various types of discounts and datings so that he can show customers the price advantages they gain by buying from his firm. Salesmen should also be able to explain to an objecting customer why a certain discount or dating is not offered.

KINDS OF DISCOUNTS

In Chapter 7, you learned the meaning of discounts, trade discounts, functional discounts, quantity discounts, and seasonal discounts. You may now want to turn back to pages 227 and 228 and read again the discussion of these discounts. The other discounts that are important to the contact salesman and his customers are chain, anticipation, and cash discounts.

Calculating Trade, Functional, and Chain Discounts

Discounts are calculated just as percentages are calculated, then are subtracted from the list price of an article or the gross amount of an invoice. Suppose that your wholesale firm offers a trade discount of 40 percent on an item with a list price of $1.50. Take 40 percent of

$1.50, which is 60¢, and subtract this 60¢ from $1.50. The resulting amount, 90¢, is what your retail customer would pay for the article.

Functional discounts, as you have learned, are larger than trade discounts and are granted by manufacturers to wholesalers. Suppose that your manufacturing firm offers a functional discount of 40 percent, 10 percent on an item with a list price of $5.00. Take 40 percent of $5.00, which is $2.00, and subtract this amount from $5.00. This gives an amount of $3.00. Then take 10 percent of $3.00, which gives 30¢, and subtract 30¢ from $3.00. The resulting amount, $2.70, is what your wholesale customer would pay for the article.

When manufacturers sell to other manufacturers, they may grant another functional discount. Thus, one manufacturer may grant another a discount of 40 percent, 10 percent, 5 percent. This may be called a *chain discount*. A chain discount is computed in the same way that a functional discount is computed, except that one more mathematical step—calculating the 5 percent discount—is added. With a chain discount of 40 percent, 10 percent, 5 percent, the manufacturer would pay $2.56 for an article with a list price of $5.00.

Calculating Anticipation Discounts

Some selling firms grant *anticipation discounts* to customers. This kind of discount means that a customer is rewarded for paying his bill before the date set for earning the cash discount. (The *cash discount* is granted by both manufacturers and wholesalers and is an allowance for paying promptly rather than letting a bill run for the credit period common in the trade.) For the number of days of prepayment, interest is deducted by the customer. This interest is usually at the rate of 6 percent a year. Suppose that on a purchase of $200, one of your customers can deduct a discount of 2 percent if he pays his bill by May 10. However, he chooses to pay the bill on April 10, a month in advance. The rate of interest for one month—based on a yearly rate of 6 percent—is ½ of 1 percent. Thus, your customer is entitled to an extra ½ of 1 percent of $200, or $1.00, for paying his bill a month ahead of time. He finally deducts a total of 2½ percent—2 percent cash discount and ½ percent anticipation discount—from the invoice. He pays your firm $195 for the merchandise he bought.

Calculating Cash, Quantity, and Seasonal Discounts

Cash discounts, quantity discounts, and seasonal discounts are figured just as a trade discount is figured. However, these three discounts are not calculated until all trade discounts, functional discounts, and/or chain discounts have been calculated. Quantity and seasonal discounts are figured on the remaining balance after any of the aforementioned discounts have been deducted. Cash discounts are figured on the net amount after all other discounts have been deducted. Of course, all of these discounts seldom apply to a single purchase.

Quantity discounts may be calculated on the dollar value of an order, on the number of units purchased, or on the size of package purchased. They may either be cumulative or noncumulative. A *cumulative quantity discount* is calculated on the amount a customer buys over a specified period of time, such as six months. This discount is intended to keep a customer reordering from one selling firm and to keep him from switching his patronage to another supplier. *Noncumulative quantity discounts* are calculated on single orders.

UNDERSTANDING DATINGS

Dating refers to the amount of time that a selling firm gives a customer to pay his bill. Like discounts, datings can provide good selling points for an article. The most common kinds of datings are COD, EOM, ROG, extra dating, and postdating.

COD (Cash on Delivery)

Members of your family have probably bought goods on COD terms at some time. *COD* means "cash on delivery"; goods must be paid for as soon as they arrive at the customer's home or place of business. COD terms are not often used in industrial and wholesale selling, since most businesses have sound enough credit ratings to warrant longer datings. With newly established businesses or with businesses that have poor credit ratings, however, goods may be handled COD.

EOM (End of Month)

With *EOM* terms, a customer's payment time is computed from the end of the month in which the goods were shipped. If goods are shipped on July 8, under terms of EOM, net 30, the customer does not have to pay his bill until August 30.

ROG (Receipt of Goods)

You have already learned that customers who are a considerable distance from the seller's place of business may be granted ROG terms.

A Buyer's Questions About Quantity Discounts

- ✓ Do I have enough money to buy the extra quantity?
- ✓ If I buy this quantity, will I be kept from buying other goods that I need?
- ✓ Do I have enough storage space for so large a quantity?
- ✓ Might the goods deteriorate in value before they can all be sold?
- ✓ Might the goods go out of style quickly and have to be sold at a loss?
- ✓ Is there any chance that the wholesale price might drop in the next few months and wipe out any savings from the quantity discount offered now?

Buyers do not always jump at the chance to take advantage of a quantity discount. They may mentally ask some of these questions before they decide. These questions may crop up as objections to buying, so the salesman should be prepared to answer them.

ROG means that the payment time is computed from the date the customer receives the goods. If goods were shipped under ROG, net 30 terms, and arrived at the customer's place of business on January 3, they would not have to be paid for until February 2. These terms are sometimes called AOG (arrival of goods) terms.

Extra Dating

Extra dating gives the buyer a longer-than-usual time in which to pay his bill. Perhaps the most common dating period is net 30; but with extra dating, the customer may be granted 60 extra days or a total of 90 days in which to pay his bill.

Postdating

With *postdating,* or *advance dating,* the payment time is computed from a particular date after the goods have been shipped. A bill for goods which were actually shipped on September 12 may be dated November 1. If they were sold with a regular 30-day dating, this means that the customer has until December 1 to pay his bill.

Postdating is something like a seasonal discount. It is intended to encourage buyers to place their orders early, in advance of the time they need the goods. If customers can be induced to order during dull periods, a manufacturer can schedule his production more evenly over the year.

CHECKING YOUR KNOWLEDGE

Vocabulary:

(1) chain discount
(2) anticipation discount
(3) cash discount
(4) cumulative quantity discount
(5) noncumulative quantity discount
(6) dating
(7) COD
(8) EOM
(9) ROG
(10) extra dating
(11) postdating, or advance dating

Review questions:

1. Explain briefly how a discount is calculated.
2. How does the calculation of cash, quantity, and seasonal discounts differ from the calculation of trade, functional, and chain discounts?
3. What purpose is served by the cumulative quantity discount?
4. Why are COD terms infrequently used in industrial and wholesale selling?
5. What is the purpose of advance dating terms?

For discussion:

1. How can the industrial or wholesale salesman effectively use the variety of discounts and datings offered by his company?
2. Do you think salesmen could improve their effectiveness if discounts and datings were eliminated so that the list price quoted would be the price paid by the customer? Why?

part B

transportation arrangements

An essential part of marketing is *physical distribution*—the activities involved in physically moving goods from producer to consumer. Most business customers make their own decisions on the method of physical distribution or transportation they will use. However, the contact salesman can often render a real service by advising customers of a more appropriate means of transportation than they have chosen. To do his selling job well, the contact salesman should be familiar with the available methods of transportation and should know which method is best suited to which kind of merchandise.

METHODS OF SHIPPING MERCHANDISE

For the business customer, the principal methods of shipping merchandise are by rail freight, motor freight, and air freight. There are other methods of transportation, but they are used only in special situations and not for the bulk of industrial and wholesale shipping. In choosing the best method of shipment, these factors should be considered: (1) speed, (2) convenience of pickup and delivery, (3) cost, (4) packing requirements for shipping, and (5) care in handling.

Rail Freight

Shipping by rail is probably the most widely used method of transportation. The railroad is especially well suited to handling bulky items and large quantities of goods. The advantages of shipping by rail are that virtually any product can be shipped; that many special types of cars, such as refrigerator cars, are available; and that the cost of shipping is quite low. Its main disadvantage is its slowness. Also, the destination of a shipment may not be conveniently located to a railroad line.

Shipping Rates. Charges for shipping by rail freight are based on (1) the class rate or commodity rate for the product and (2) whether or not the shipment fills an entire railroad car. A *class rate* applies to a related group of goods on which the same rate is charged. More than 25,000 different products are divided into classes, and each class has not only a special rate but also special rules in regard to shipping that product. A *commodity rate* is a special rate for a specific commodity, such as steel or coal. Sometimes a product will have both a class rate and a commodity rate. In such a case, it should be shipped under the commodity rate, since this rate is cheaper.

Goods may be shipped by carload freight (CL), less-than-carload freight (LCL), or express. When a shipment is large enough to fill an entire railroad car, it is shipped on *carload* terms at either a fixed rate for the car or fixed rate per 100 pounds. With *less-than-carload* terms, shipments from several sellers or shipments from a single seller bound for several different customers are placed in the same car. LCL rates are higher than CL rates, since more handling of goods is involved. Express rates are highest of all, since small shipments are sent by fast trains and there are sizable handling costs.

Special Rail Freight Services. To compete with other transportation agencies, many railroads have added special services to their basic shipping activities. One important service is *store-door delivery*. For an extra charge beyond the basic cost of shipping, railroads will pick up goods at the seller's place of business, deliver them to the railroad, load them, ship them, unload them at their destination, and deliver them directly to the customer's place of business.

Another special service is called *pool car service*. This means that if a seller has merchandise shipments going in the same direction to several customers, he can pack the goods in one car and be charged a carload rate until the car reaches the first point at which a shipment must be unloaded. After that, he is charged less-than-carload rates.

With *peddler car service,* different shippers can fill a car and have it stop at different points along the rail route so that goods can be unloaded and delivered to customers.

Another important service, particularly for sellers of perishable goods such as fruits and vegetables, is called *in transit privilege*. This means that the shipper may stop a car en route and either return it to his place of business, put the contents in storage, or change instructions for delivery.

Motor Freight

Motor freight is the most widely used method of transportation when goods are to be sent a relatively short distance and when shipments are too small to be handled economically by the railroad. Trucks are also used for shipping goods long distances, but they are generally most efficient and economical when used within a two- to three-hundred-mile radius. The main advantage of motor freight, as compared with rail freight, is that it is faster. Also, trucks can travel to any destination accessible by highway, can provide store-door delivery without any additional charge, and can easily handle shipments of varying sizes. Disadvantages are that trucks can be delayed by traffic congestion or mechanical breakdowns, that their size and capacity are necessarily limited, and that the cost of shipping by motor freight is higher than that for shipping by rail. It should be pointed out, however, that since deliveries are more prompt, since less loading and unloading time is needed, and since store-door delivery is part of the regular service, motor freight may be cheaper in the long run than rail freight.

Piggyback Service. A combination truck-rail service that is becoming increasingly important is called *piggyback service*. At the seller's place of business, goods are loaded into trailers. These trailers are driven to the railroad, removed from the truck cab, and put onto a flatcar. When the goods arrive at their destination, the trailers are moved, attached to cabs, and driven to the customer's place of business. This service actually combines the low cost of rail freight with the convenience of motor freight. When this method is used in shipping by water, it is called *fishyback*.

Containerization. A service similar to piggyback and fishyback is called *containerization*. The manufacturer packs goods into large containers similar to boxcars which can be carried on railroad flatcars, trucks, or ships. The containers can be transferred easily from one type of carrier to another, and loading and unloading of individual shipments is kept to a minimum.

Air Freight

Air freight is growing in popularity; but its cost is still very high, and it is limited as to the size of shipments that can be handled. Air freight is one of the fastest means of transportation; and it is well suited to handling goods that are small, expensive, perishable, or for which fast delivery is essential. Fashion goods such as clothing are often

Santa Fe Railway

This is one method of moving truck trailers onto flatcars for piggyback shipping. This mobile crane, the Travelift Crane, can straddle a trailer on a flatcar and lift 40-ton vans on or off flatcars in a matter of minutes.

shipped by air freight. Goods may also be shipped by air express, which is even faster than air freight and is also more expensive.

Other Methods of Transportation

Pipeline, water, REA express, and fourth-class mail are other means of transportation that industrial and wholesale sellers use less frequently than the means just discussed.

Moving products through a pipeline eliminates loading and unloading. Also, the cost is generally lower than costs for other methods of shipping. Obviously, there are only a few kinds of products that can be moved through pipelines. Oil, gas, and other liquid products used to be the only products moved through pipelines; but now such solid products as gravel are being mixed with water and moved through the pipeline.

Bulky items such as iron ore and coal may be shipped by water when there is no hurry about delivery. The cost of shipping by water is low, but considerable expense may be incurred because of special packing that shipments must receive.

Sometimes goods are shipped by REA Express. This agency used to ship only by high-speed trains, but now it uses both airplanes and trucks. The cost of express service is quite high, and shipments must be relatively small; but it can be used when speed of delivery is critical.

Few industrial firms use fourth-class mail as a means of physically distributing goods. Its two big advantages are that the cost is relatively low and that a shipment can be delivered to any place that has mail service. Its big disadvantages are that the sizes and weights of packages are strictly limited and that the delivery time is slow compared with such methods as air express or REA express.

SHIPPING TERMS

As you will recall from your reading of Chapter 7, under FOB factory shipping terms, the customer pays all transportation costs from the factory and owns the goods from the moment they are shipped. Under FOB destination terms, the manufacturer pays transportation charges and holds title to the goods until they reach the customer. Other commonly used shipping terms are FOB shipping point, FOB destination, charges reversed, and FOB factory, freight prepaid.

For goods shipped *FOB shipping point,* the seller pays transportation charges to the point at which goods are turned over to a transportation company. For goods shipped *FOB destination, charges reversed,* the seller owns the goods until they get to the buyer's place of business, but the buyer pays transportation charges. Under terms of *FOB factory, freight prepaid,* the customer owns the goods as soon as they are shipped, but the seller pays shipping charges.

Goods may also be shipped on consignment or on memorandum. As you learned in Chapter 7, when the manufacturer sells on consignment, he retains ownership of the goods and the buyer simply acts as the manufacturer's agent. When goods are sold *on memorandum,* the customer may return unsold goods to the supplier up to a certain date. The goods generally remain the seller's property.

Shipping terms are relatively standardized in many product lines. Women's clothing, for instance, is usually shipped under FOB factory terms. Giving more generous terms than the standard ones is actually a form of price concession. Sometimes contact salesmen encounter customers who demand more generous terms, and deciding whether or not to grant these terms is sometimes difficult. One purchasing agent who placed a small initial order with a selling firm stated flatly that he would not accept the goods unless they were shipped prepaid, even though the seller's terms were FOB factory. Since the shipping charges were relatively small, the salesman accepted the order so as to be sure of a new account. His firm noted the discrepancy but backed up the salesman and shipped the goods at its own expense. The buyer reordered again and again in ever larger quantities, always with the shipping charges prepaid. Since the first order was filled on these terms, the salesman and his firm postponed making an issue of the matter. Finally, the situation reached a point where the seller's profits were being eaten up by the transportation charges. The selling firm stopped paying the charges, and the customer immediately stopped using that firm as a source of supply.

Who is to pay transportation charges is actually a part of determining pricing policies. If a manufacturer intends to pay shipping charges, he must set the prices on his products high enough to cover these charges. Sometimes a nearby customer may feel discriminated against since the seller's actual delivery cost to him is much less than the average delivery cost to all customers. On the other hand, if faraway customers represent a larger proportion of total customers than the seller first expected, his prices might not be high enough to cover the shipping costs. If a seller refuses to absorb shipping costs, his business may be limited to nearby customers. He must consider all sides of the question before deciding which course to follow in regard to transportation charges.

CHECKING YOUR KNOWLEDGE

Vocabulary:

(1) physical distribution
(2) class rate
(3) commodity rate
(4) carload
(5) less-than-carload
(6) store-door delivery
(7) pool car service
(8) peddler car service
(9) in transit privilege
(10) piggyback service
(11) fishyback
(12) containerization
(13) FOB shipping point
(14) FOB destination, charges reversed
(15) FOB factory, freight prepaid
(16) on memorandum

Review questions:

1. Who is usually responsible for determining the method used to ship merchandise?
2. What are the principal methods of shipping merchandise?
3. When is motor freight the most widely used transportation method?
4. What one advantage to the customer is common to both piggyback and fishyback?
5. Are shipping terms ever considered a form of price concession? Why?

For discussion:

1. Do you think air freight will continue its growth in popularity as a method of shipping merchandise? Support your answer with examples.
2. Discuss the statement: "An effective contact salesman is familiar with available methods of transportation and can suggest the method best suited to each kind of merchandise." Give an example.

part C

dealer services

The more merchandise a business customer sells, the more merchandise a supplier can sell to that customer. This is a basic principle of contact selling. Every manufacturer or wholesaler wants to increase the sales volume of the dealer who stocks his product. Thus, most suppliers provide special dealer aids to help supplement their customers' own sales promotion efforts. Provision of dealer aids can be an important selling point for a firm's product, and the contact salesman should be familiar with the aids his firm offers.

There are many different kinds of dealer aids, from inexpensive window posters to full-page cooperative newspaper ads. Perhaps the three most important aids are cooperative advertising, point-of-purchase advertising, and premiums. They are probably the most widely offered dealer aids and the most effective aids in increasing dealer sales.

COOPERATIVE ADVERTISING

The *New York Times* estimates that over $2 billion is spent each year on cooperative advertising programs. As you have learned, cooperative advertising is an arrangement in which manufacturer and retailer share the costs of advertising the manufacturer's product in local media.

There are two basic arrangements for sharing the costs of cooperative advertising. Under the first arrangement, the manufacturer reimburses the dealer for all costs of advertising his product—so long as the costs do not exceed a certain percentage of the dealer's purchases from the manufacturer. The most common percentage is two to three percent; but for some products, it may run as high as ten percent. If the dealer's costs do not equal the stated percentage, the manufacturer reimburses him only for what he spends. If the dealer spends more than the stated percentage, he pays the extra costs himself.

The other arrangement, which is the most common, is for the manufacturer and retailer to share the advertising expenses equally. Sometimes a wholesaler will also participate in the cooperative advertising. Then the manufacturer may pay 25 percent of the cost; the wholesaler, 25 percent; and the retailer, 50 percent.

Advantages and Disadvantages to the Dealer

Dealers generally welcome cooperative advertising arrangements because they get more advertising money to spend than they would otherwise have. The dealer can run more ads in different media, and he can capitalize on a tie-in with the manufacturer's national advertising. Also, he gets professional help from the manufacturer in preparing ads.

Cooperative advertising's main disadvantage to the dealer is that the ads usually do not sufficiently emphasize the individual store. The manufacturer and his product get all the attention in the ad's headline and copy. The dealer's name may appear only in the "fine print" at the bottom of the ad. Cooperative advertising arrangements also involve more bookkeeping for the retailer. He must keep detailed records on when, where, how, and for how much he placed the cooperative ads.

Advantages and Disadvantages to the Supplier

For the manufacturer, cooperative advertising's major advantage is that it gives him more advertising coverage for his product. He could not get such widespread circulation with national advertising alone. Every local advertisement that a retailer runs helps to build customer demand for the manufacturer's product in a given community. The manufacturer also gets more mileage for his advertising dollar than he would with national advertising alone. Local advertising rates are considerably less than national rates. Since the retailer is billed according to local rates, the manufacturer actually gets more advertising space for his money. Also, cooperative advertising usually stimulates the dealer to give the product extra promotional effort inside the store.

The major disadvantage lies in the way the programs are administered. Some unethical retailers bill manufacturers for ads they never ran or for higher advertising rates than they actually paid. Sometimes the money spent for cooperative advertising is almost wasted; ads may be poorly timed, for example, or media may be poorly chosen. To solve these problems, manufacturers are becoming more strict about their dealers' cooperative advertising records. Now retailers must usually inform the manufacturer what kinds of ads are to be run, the media to be used, when the ads are to be run, proof that they were run, and the prices of advertising space.

POINT-OF-PURCHASE ADVERTISING

Point-of-purchase advertising includes all the devices—mostly temporary—placed near the point of sale to stimulate customers to buy. Such devices may be used either inside or directly outside the store. There are many different kinds of point-of-purchase aids; the Point-of-Purchase Advertising Institute, for instance, has listed 60 different kinds. The restaurant sign which bears the name "Coca-Cola" and also the restaurant's name is a form of point-of-purchase advertising. So is the cardboard display carton showing and dispensing Nabisco crackers. The point-of-purchase devices you will probably be most familiar with are display containers, posters, banners, counter cards, shelf strips, and signs.

Advantages of Point-of-Purchase Advertising

Point-of-purchase advertising is a stepchild of self-service merchandising. The main goal of point-of-purchase advertising is to encourage the customer to buy without the help of a salesperson. In fact, this advertising can actually take over many of a salesperson's duties. Some important advantages of point-of-purchase advertising are:

1. It can demonstrate the product effectively and can result in an immediate sale.
2. It can introduce a new product or new package effectively.
3. It can dispense samples of a product, coupons, premiums, or printed advertising materials.
4. It can point out features and uses of a product.
5. It can promote the sale of related items.
6. It can stimulate impulse buying.
7. It can give a product seasonal appeal or create new interest in an established product.

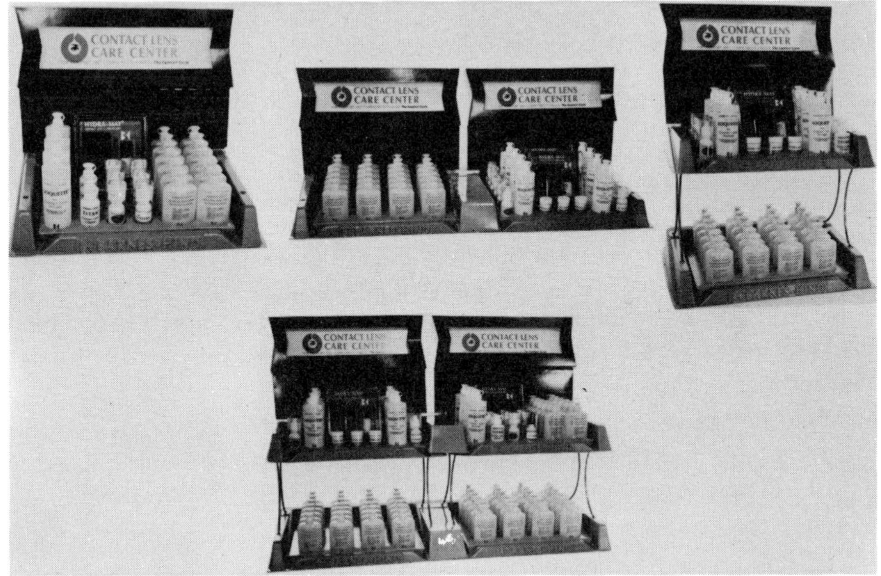

Barnes-Hind Ophthalmic Products

Dealers appreciate versatility in point-of-purchase devices. This modular contact lens care center can be made into a shelf, counter, or window display and can be added to horizontally or vertically. It comes with three separate platforms so that the pharmacist can select the best presentation of products for his store and a display card that can be changed as the need for a new promotional message occurs.

To the manufacturer, a significant advantage of point-of-purchase advertising is that its cost—in terms of the number of customers a single device can reach—is lower than for most other advertising media.

Requirements of Point-of-Purchase Advertising

To be effective, point-of-purchase devices (1) should display merchandise appropriately and attractively, (2) should be functional, (3) should contain space for imprinting the price, (4) should allow customers to handle the item being shown, (5) should be original, and (6) should be the right size for the store in which they are to be used.

Sometimes manufacturers will ship point-of-purchase devices along with the merchandise, since many of the devices (posters, for instance) are quite small and simple. Displays, though, are often set up by the salesman when he calls on the dealer. The manufacturer may even hire professional displaymen to set up elaborate displays. Manufacturers generally pay for the simpler point-of-purchase aids, although they may require dealers to share the cost of expensive aids such as overhead signs outside the store and special display fixtures.

PREMIUMS

A *premium* is something of value offered to encourage customers to buy a product or service. When you were a child and sent in a boxtop and a quarter for, say, a hand puppet, you were getting a premium. Even the simple toys in Crackerjack boxes are premiums.

Premiums are intended to increase the sales of a given product, because usually customers must buy one or more units of a product before they get the premium. This broad goal of increasing sales may include the supporting goals of getting people to try a new product, to meet price competition, to increase sales in an area where current sales are low, to encourage more frequent use of the product, or to increase the size of individual purchases.

Requirements of Effective Premiums

Not just any "free gift" can be an effective premium. First of all, premiums must suit the product being promoted. No smart seller will give a premium of a dish cloth with a purchase of men's shaving cream. Also, premiums must have some value to a customer, particularly if customers must go to the effort of sending away for the premium. Premiums should be reasonably easy to obtain, and the premiums that

The self-liquidating premium, such as the one shown above, is perhaps the most popular type of premium. Manufacturers buy the premium items in huge quantities at very low prices, and the small amount of money sent in by the customer generally covers all the expenses of offering the premium except for advertising costs.

a manufacturer offers should be changed periodically so that customers don't lose interest in the premiums.

Methods of Distributing Premiums

In deciding how to distribute his premiums, the manufacturer may choose from several methods. One of the most popular methods uses the *self-liquidating premium.* The customer is required to buy a certain product; send in a boxtop, label, or other proof of purchase; and pay a small price for the premium. This price is generally enough to cover the seller's low per-unit cost growing out of his quantity purchases. Premiums may also be given away with the product at the time of purchase. This method is effective, because the premium is free to the customer and because no extra effort is needed to get the premium. Bath towels packed inside detergent boxes are examples of giveaway premiums.

Another method of distributing premiums is the combination sale method, often used in introducing new products. One product is packed with an identical or related product and sold for a lower price than the two items would normally cost if bought separately. One cosmetics manufacturer offered a premium of a purse-size hair spray packaged with a regular-size can of hair spray and sold for the price of the regular-size container.

Perhaps the oldest kind of premium offer is that of exchanging coupons for gifts. The trading stamp represents a variation of this plan. Some manufacturers redeem coupons themselves, generally by mail. Trading stamps, however, are handled by premium distributing companies which exchange customers' stamps for gifts at redemption centers. Manufacturers bear the cost of coupons, but the dealer must pay for trading stamps himself.

CHECKING YOUR KNOWLEDGE

Vocabulary:

(1) point-of-purchase advertising
(2) premium
(3) self-liquidating premium

Review questions:

1. Name three of the most important dealer aids.
2. What are the advantages of cooperative advertising to the dealer and to the manufacturer?
3. What are the disadvantages of cooperative advertising to the dealer and to the manufacturer?
4. Who pays for point-of-purchase aids?
5. Name and explain three methods of distributing premiums.

For discussion:

1. Do you think that more effective cooperative advertising arrangements could be developed? Why?
2. Discuss the fallacies of the following statement: "Customers would continue to buy at the same rate if premiums were eliminated and the savings in the form of lower prices were passed on to the customer."

part D

group selling

High school students often take part in group meetings where they try to sell ideas to members of the group. Such group selling may be for the purposes of being elected to class offices, of promoting membership in school organizations, of soliciting subscriptions for a yearbook, or of getting greater support for a football or a basketball team. The contact salesman, too, is often involved in group selling. And although he sells a quite different item from that sold by the student, the basic principles of group selling are the same for both individuals.

THE TREND TOWARD GROUP SELLING

The majority of contact salesmen still make their sales presentations to one customer at a time. However, there is a growing business trend toward having purchasing committees make final buying decisions rather than placing the whole burden of decision making on one person. This practice is evolving as the number of large business units, such as chains, grows and the number of small business units decreases. For a large organization, purchasing means huge money outlays and substantial stock commitments. Top management in such organizations usually prefers to divide the decision-making responsibilities among a number of merchandising experts. It has been reported that about 80 percent of all food items are sold through group selling.

Group Buying

Under a plan known as *group buying,* salesmen present their firms' products to a group of buyers representing noncompeting stores from all over the country. Each member of the group votes on all the products shown and discussed and agrees to buy at least a minimum number of the products receiving a majority vote.

Central Buying

Most chain organizations follow a plan of *central buying.* One buyer purchases a merchandise line for all the units of a chain or associated group of stores. Thus, the salesman need not contact the individual store managers.

Since adding a new line or dropping an established one involves huge financial considerations, a committee of buying experts in a central office may make the final buying decision. Sometimes a single buyer will conduct most of the negotiations with various salesmen, but the final presentation is usually given to a committee.

Fashion Showings

A popular type of group selling today is the fashion show presented by a manufacturer, trade paper, and/or trade association for retail store buyers. Unlike group and central buying, no attempt is made to consummate sales during the fashion show. Sellers want to stimulate interest in their fashions so that buyers may consider purchasing their goods later. In the traditional show, models are introduced by a commentator, who is in a real sense a salesperson. He describes the major features of each garment and can be instrumental in creating excitement for the goods.

TECHNIQUES OF GROUP SELLING

Although group selling involves a unique form of sales presentation, the principles of personal selling discussed in Chapters 9 and 10 should still be followed. The salesman should determine the needs and wants of the group members, analyze his product's features and benefits that will meet these requirements, and present the features and benefits in a logical sales talk. There are, however, certain other guidelines that he should follow:

1. Try to keep the group fairly small, if he has any control over who is to attend the meeting.
2. Meet each individual in the group beforehand, if possible.
3. Prepare an agenda for the meeting, then stick to it.
4. Make every point clear and concise, and support it with facts.
5. Talk in a natural, conversational manner.
6. Use visual aids.
7. Review points frequently, draw conclusions, and ask for questions or comments.
8. Stick to a time limit, if there is one.

Planning the Group Sales Talk

The essence of a group sales talk is planning. The salesman gives basically a monologue; there are fewer chances for feedback than in

"Who called this meeting and for what purpose?"

Sales Management

Sometimes the salesman has no control over who will attend his group presentation. If he does have any control, he should try to limit the size of the group and to meet each person beforehand.

the normal one-customer-at-a-time contact, so the sales talk must be carefully prepared to be as perfect as possible. Most salesmen who sell to groups use standardized sales talks. In the past, standardized or "canned" sales talks have been looked down upon by experienced, competent salesmen. There is nothing wrong with a standardized sales talk, though, providing the salesman doesn't recite it as though he were a talking computer.

Group selling lends itself to using the standardized sales talk. The salesman will probably be talking to the same kinds of customers most of the time—buyers for a chain of food stores, for instance—and they will tend to have the same needs and wants. By preparing a good sales talk, rehearsing it, and refining it until it is as perfect as he can make it, he stands a better chance of selling his product than if he were to deliver an impromptu talk to each group he faced. The danger in using a standardized sales talk is that a salesman may lack flexibility in delivering it. A single question from a group member may interrupt the rigid delivery so that the salesman loses his composure and botches the rest of the presentation. Some salesmen think that once they have prepared a talk, this is all the selling effort needed to make a sale.

This is not true. A standardized sales talk is intended to provide a framework for the presentation, not necessarily to be all the presentation.

The Agenda and the Specification Sheet

Two important parts of planning the sales talk are preparing the agenda and the specification sheet. The *agenda* lists the points to be covered in the sales talk. It provides guidelines for the salesman to follow and helps assure that he will give a logical presentation. A copy of the agenda may or may not be circulated to the group members.

A *specification sheet* lists the product details most important to the group members, such as materials of construction, manufacturing methods, and so on. Specification sheets are circulated to group members so that they can study the product information before, during, and after the sales presentation.

Delivering the Group Sales Talk

A person who has made most of his sales presentations to one customer at a time may find it hard to hold the attention of a group. A single listener hesitates to let his attention noticeably wander, but it is easier for listening group members to let their attention wander. It helps if the salesman turns from one person to another as he speaks, so that each person feels he is being spoken to personally. The salesman should also keep calling for some response from the audience to keep the group members interested. He can ask for comments or questions on a particular point, or he may ask someone in the group to provide some additional information.

Using Visual Aids. A good way of developing interest is appealing to the eye as well as the ear. Many salesmen distribute product samples so that group members can study them while specific features are discussed in the talk. If a good sound-slide film or movie on the product is available, the salesman might use it as the basic part of the sales presentation and then follow it with a discussion period. He might also list the main points of his presentation on a chalkboard or on a series of posters that can be placed on an easel and flipped over as he talks.

If any charts or tables of figures are intended to accompany the sales talk, they should be printed and distributed to the group members. This is particularly wise for any complex figures or graphic material. The members can better understand the statistics involved and can study the information after the meeting if they want to.

In selling to groups, salesmen frequently supplement their talks with visual aids. Charts, such as this salesman is using, make it easier for group members to understand and remember the selling points that are made.

The Heart of the Talk. After arousing the group's interest, the speaker-salesman must try to create desire for the product so that members will take positive buying action. To do this, the salesman should first concentrate on the strongest selling point, then upon subordinate points, and finally should encourage group participation. Although a salesman may interest a group by covering a number of points, he is not likely to create desire unless he focuses the members' attention on the key selling points at the beginning of the presentation. Too many speakers ramble. This makes it almost impossible for the listener to understand the sales talk and to reach a decision. The salesman should list in advance the points he wants to make in the presentation and should avoid generalities. He may repeat certain points—preferably in different phraseology—for purposes of emphasis.

Closing the Sale. In pressing for positive buying action, salesmen address themselves to the person who seems to be the group leader. However, they also appeal to each member to share in a joint decision by pointing out that their firms can give better service if all responsible members of the customer's firm are in agreement and ready to cooperate. In selling to a group of business customers, buying action will generally not take place directly after the presentation. The salesman should thank the members for coming and will probably ask when he can hope to hear from them again.

SELLING TO GROUPS OF ULTIMATE CONSUMERS

A considerable amount of group selling is done before groups of ultimate consumers. This kind of selling uses the basic group selling principles used for business customers.

Retail representatives of stores or traveling manufacturers' representatives frequently address groups of women on such subjects as housewares, clothing, fashions, interior design, and good grooming. No attempt may be made to close sales at these meetings, but an interest in certain activities may be developed that will in turn create a desire for the seller's goods. In department stores where demonstrators talk to groups of ultimate consumers, there is an attempt to close the sale after the presentation.

Another form of group selling is the "house party" where a housewife invites friends to her home and the salesperson shows samples, gives demonstrations, and takes orders for the merchandise. The hostess is rewarded with premiums for her efforts.

USING TECHNIQUES OF GROUP SELLING

You should welcome the chance to apply the selling techniques you have learned in dealing with groups and individuals. Group presentations, in particular, help to develop poise and a forceful personality. The extracurricular activities found in every school offer a good training ground for tomorrow's businessman and businesswoman, whose jobs may be primarily selling ones. It is important that young people develop facility in appearing before and influencing groups. This is something that many people, even in high-level positions, have never been able to achieve.

CHECKING YOUR KNOWLEDGE

Vocabulary:

(1) group buying
(2) central buying
(3) agenda
(4) specification sheet

Review questions:

1. How do you account for the recent trend toward committee buying decisions?
2. How is the fashion show unlike group and central buying?

3. What precautions should be taken in delivering a standardized sales talk?
4. How can visual aids strengthen the group sales talk?
5. Explain briefly the procedures that should be followed in delivering the heart of the group sales presentation.

For discussion:

1. Some salesmen have a tendency to use only charts and graphs as the sales talk, and customers often react negatively to this kind of presentation. What do you think salesmen might do to prevent this reaction?
2. Do you think that an effective standardized sales talk will be received in the same manner by most groups? Why?

part E

time management

Recently the Research Institute of America surveyed some 3,000 contact salesmen to find out how they spent their working days. The results of the survey, as reported in *Sales Management,* showed that the average 8-hour working day for this kind of salesman was divided as follows: calling on customers, 2 hours and 45 minutes; telephoning, 41 minutes; traveling, 2 hours and 42 minutes; paper work, 26 minutes; meals, 40 minutes; entertaining customers, 21 minutes; personal matters, 13 minutes; miscellaneous matters, 8 minutes; and prospecting for new customers, 15 minutes.

What does all this mean to the contact salesman? Look again at the figures. Only 2 hours and 45 minutes, out of an 8-hour day, were spent calling on customers. Time, and what the salesman does with it, is one of the most important elements in contact selling. Every salesman should try to increase the time that he spends calling on customers and to decrease the time he spends on other duties, such as traveling.

THE NEED FOR TIME MANAGEMENT

Contact salesmen have more freedom in their selling activities than do most other types of salesmen. The retail salesman, for instance, is restricted in how he utilizes his time, since customers come to his firm and he must serve them as soon as they approach him. Manufacturing and wholesaling firms control such factors as the territory a salesman is to cover and the sales quota he must meet, but the salesman alone plans his activities for any given day or week.

The best reason for efficient time management is that it helps increase sales volume. The contact salesman's primary selling duty is the face-to-face sales presentation with the customer. By increasing the amount of time spent calling on customers, sales volume can be increased. Secondary selling duties include traveling, prospecting, paper work, waiting to see prospects, and handling complaints. These duties must be accomplished if the salesman is to do a thorough selling job, but he should try to minimize the time he spends on these secondary duties.

To manage his time effectively, the contact salesman must have self-discipline and a sense of responsibility to his employer. He must make a plan for his selling time and stick to it. Otherwise, declining sales volume will eventually reflect the fact that he is wasting valuable time.

TECHNIQUES OF TIME MANAGEMENT

As salesmen gain experience, they learn many shortcuts to save selling time. Some salesmen, for example, catch up on paper work while they are waiting to see customers. Two time-management devices that are used by both beginning and experienced salesmen are routing and scheduling.

Routing

Routing refers to the formal plan for covering a sales territory. In most selling firms, traveling contact salesmen establish their own routings. They are normally required to submit to headquarters their routings for a certain selling period, such as a week. This practice helps the firm's sales management division to know whether the salesman is effectively using his time. It also lets management know where a salesman will be on a certain date, in case they must get in touch with him.

Concentrating Sales Calls. To develop an effective routing plan, the salesman must know his territory thoroughly, including how long it takes to drive from one call to another. His goal is to conserve travel time, his firm's money, and his own energies. Thus, he should concentrate a maximum number of calls within a small geographical area. If the salesman covering a metropolitan area does his traveling by car, he may make one call on the north side of the city, drive to another appointment on the east side, then drive back to the north side. He may think that it is more trouble to route the calls together than it is to take a few extra minutes to drive back and forth. The minutes soon add up, though, and every minute spent traveling is another minute taken away from the primary selling duty.

A good routing plan depends upon making appointments with customers and then keeping them. Keeping appointments makes a routing plan somewhat strict, but it should be flexible enough so that secondary selling duties can be worked in.

Example of a Routing Plan. John Akin is a contact salesman who covers the territory of southwestern Ohio. His home is in Columbus. Here is his routing plan for the week of December 8:

1. Leave home early Monday morning. Make calls in Washington and Wilmington, working toward Cincinnati. Make calls in Cincinnati Monday afternoon. Stay in Cincinnati Monday night.
2. Make calls in Cincinnati on Tuesday and Wednesday. Drive to Dayton on Wednesday afternoon. Stay in Dayton Wednesday night.
3. Make calls in Dayton on Thursday. Stay in Dayton Thursday night.
4. Leave Dayton early Friday morning. Make calls in Fairborn, Springfield, and Urbana, working toward Columbus. Drive home Friday afternoon.

As you can see from the map on page 392, Akin planned his calls in a compact area so that he spent a minimum amount of time in traveling.

Scheduling

The *schedule* is a timetable of what the salesman is to do in a given day. Your school days are organized according to a schedule. You may have a class in typewriting at 9:00, a class in bookkeeping at 10:00, study hall at 11:00, and lunch from 12:00 to 12:30. The salesman may have an appointment with Mr. Casey at 9:30, an appointment with Mr. Meyer at 11:00, and plan to take Mr. Dunn to lunch at 12:30.

Selling firms do not require their salesmen to submit schedules, but most salesmen like to prepare them for their own personal use.

December 6 19--
Date

ROUTING OF MR. John Akin
Your name

for week beginning Monday, December 8, 19--
Date

MONDAY

Will make Washington, Wilmington, Cincinnati
Name Towns

Will call for mail at Stouffer's Inn, Cincinnati
Hotel or Motel

TUESDAY

Will make Cincinnati
Name Towns

Will call for mail at Stouffer's Inn, Cincinnati
Hotel or Motel

WEDNESDAY

Will make Cincinnati
Name Towns

Will call for mail at Holiday Inn, Dayton
Hotel or Motel

THURSDAY

Will make Dayton
Name Towns

Will call for mail at Holiday Inn, Dayton
Hotel or Motel

FRIDAY

Will make Fairborn, Springfield, Urbana
Name Towns

Will call for mail at Home
Hotel, Motel, or Home

SATURDAY

Will make Home
Name Towns

Will call for mail at Home
Hotel, Motel, or Home

SUNDAY

Home
Hotel or Motel City State

Send week end mail to Home - 221 Rolling Hills Lane
Columbus, Ohio

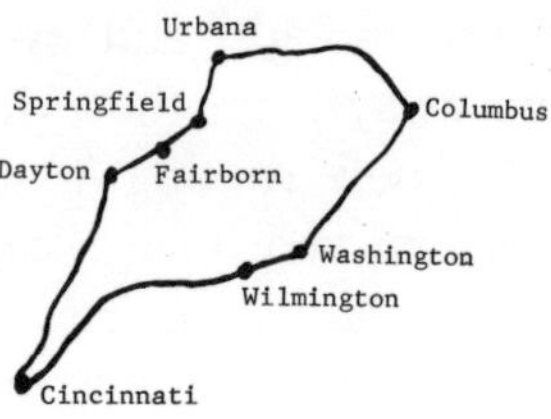

Much wasted selling time is due to unnecessary traveling. Here is an example of a good routing plan; it combines a maximum number of calls in a small geographical area. The form is typical of those used for salesmen to report their advance routing plans.

Tuesday: Cincinnati

8:30 a.m. Harrison Electric Supply (John Phillips, Mgr.)

10:00 a.m. Appointment with Frank Morris, Tri-State Building.

11:45 a.m. Lunch with Harry Reynolds B and B Electric (if Tri-State appointment does not conflict)

1:30 p.m. The Lite House (Susan Franklin, Mgr.)

3:00 p.m. Appointment with Harold Morgan, Craft Wholesale Supply.

4:30 p.m. Open. Check smaller accounts in Motel area.

Here is John Akin's schedule for one day in his week-long selling trip. Schedules should be flexible; they are intended only to guide a salesman's activities, not to bind them rigidly.

A schedule helps assure that a salesman accomplishes all the necessary activities for a certain day. Many salesmen like to make a rough schedule for an entire week, then make a more detailed schedule for each day on the night before.

Preparing the Schedule. A schedule is bound by the number of calls the salesman hopes to make in one day, the sales volume he hopes to attain, and the number of hours he plans to work. A good schedule depends greatly on the hours of work a salesman sets for himself. There should be a definite time for starting the day's activities. It is easy to sleep until 9 a.m., have a leisurely breakfast, and begin the day's calls at 10:30; but several hours of good selling time are lost. The salesman should set definite hours of work for himself—9 to 5, for instance—and start at the established time and stop no earlier than the established time.

Many salesmen fail to plan their most important calls for their best selling hours. Some people—salesmen and customers alike—lose energy and enthusiasm late in the afternoon. Thus, as much primary selling work as possible should be done early in the day. Secondary selling duties can be worked in around the important calls. Appointments should be scheduled for the customer's convenience, as much as possible. Enough time should be allowed for sales interviews to avoid making abrupt departures and being late for other appointments.

Most salesmen plan more work for a given day than they can accomplish. Sometimes appointments are unexpectedly cancelled, or an interview takes less time than the salesman had thought it would. If he doesn't plan enough activities in his schedule, he may waste valuable time. Many salesmen use the time available from a cancelled appointment to telephone prospects or to catch up on necessary paper work.

The Tickler File. An asset to scheduling is the *tickler file*. This is a file of reminders placed in chronological order. It "tickles" the salesman's memory and reminds him of things to be done on a certain date. Suppose that a salesman sold five electric typewriters to a publishing firm on July 9. Immediately after the sale, he made a note to follow up the sale in a month to see how the typewriters were operating. The card would be dated August 9 and filed in the "August" section of the tickler file. On the evening of August 8, the salesman would check through his file, pull the cards for August 9, and work into his schedule the follow-up call to the publishing firm.

March 4 (Tuesday) Submit bid to Tri-State Building Company (Jean Goodman, Receptionist)

Frank Morris, Manager attends Rotary on Wednesday Son in college; daughter in Junior High school

Good golfer likes to win

Dislikes our cycle billing

Ordinarily, cards in a tickler file contain only a limited amount of information, since they are intended to jog the salesman's memory about something he is to do on a given day. However, some salesmen like to add more detailed information, perhaps data on the customer they will contact on that particular day.

DETERMINING SALES PRODUCTIVITY

How can a salesman tell if he is managing his time successfully? The best way is to analyze sales volume, comparing it with his previous sales and the sales of his firm's other salesmen. Charts are effective in analyzing sales and making comparisons. Study the first chart on page 395. Along the horizontal axis, the number of weeks in the selling period are plotted. On the vertical axis, weekly sales are plotted. During the first week of the selling period, sales amounted to $900. Thus, a dot was placed where the first week's vertical line would intersect a $900 horizontal line. As dots for succeeding weeks are entered, they are joined by a heavy line, which provides a visual picture of the trend in weekly sales.

To compare his weekly sales with those of the company or of other salesmen in his region, the salesman can determine the approximate ratio of his sales to total sales. If his sales have, in the past, averaged about one tenth of total sales, he can add a total-sales scale at the right of his chart (see second chart). Here the plotted values are ten times as great as those given at the left. Plotting total sales in this way and joining the dots by a broken or different colored line enables the salesman to compare his performance with that of his firm or region. He could also chart a third line to compare his weekly sales of the current year with those of last year. If his sales are declining, it could mean that he is not managing his time as efficiently as he should.

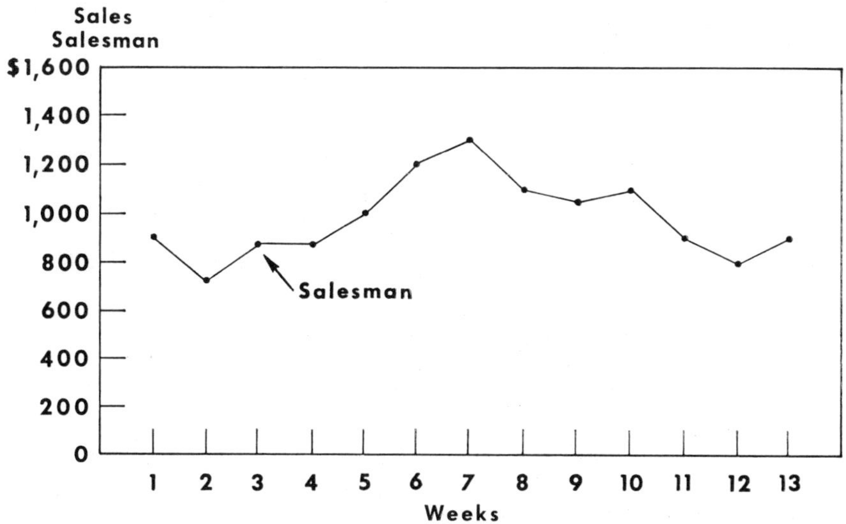

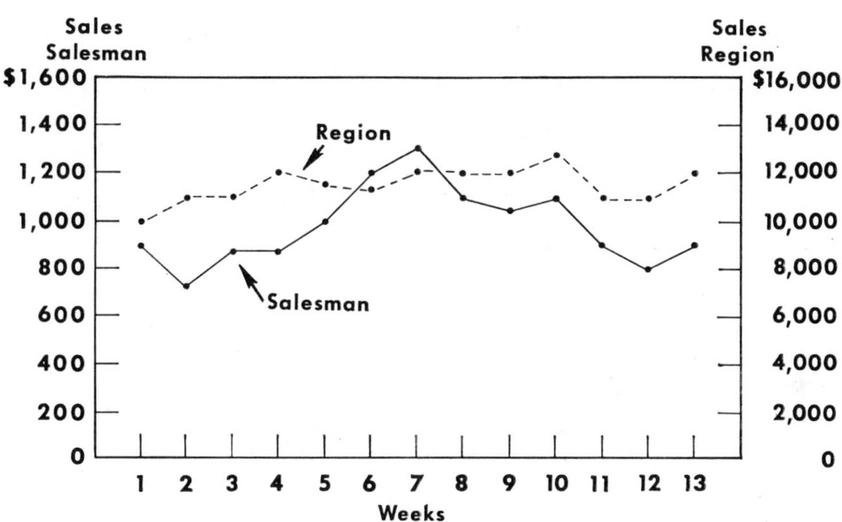

CHECKING YOUR KNOWLEDGE

Vocabulary:

(1) routing
(2) schedule
(3) tickler file

Review questions:

1. Why do contact salesmen have more freedom in their selling activities than do retail salesmen?

2. How can efficient time management increase sales volume?
3. What are the purposes of a routing plan?
4. How does a schedule improve a salesman's coverage of his territory?
5. What is the best way to determine whether a salesman is managing his time successfully?

For discussion:

1. Experienced salesmen sometimes feel that they should not be required to send a weekly routing plan to the sales manager. Do you think that experienced salesmen should be granted this privilege? Why?
2. Discuss the similarities and differences in time management plans for an industrial salesman covering selected accounts in the Midwest and a pharmaceutical salesman covering part of Chicago.

BUILDING YOUR SKILLS

Improving your English:

On a separate sheet of paper, write the correct verb to be used in each of the following sentences.

1. All the salesmen (was, were) able to meet their quotas.
2. Each of the stereos (was, were) designed for special sound effects.
3. Neither Hank nor Fred (was, were) available for the sales conference.
4. You (can, may) include cab fare in your expense report if you do not claim mileage.
5. The girls (has, have) reacted favorably to the suggested time schedule.
6. Both reports (is, are) as comprehensive as the manager suggested.
7. If I (was, were) planning the January sale, all lines would be marked down.
8. Mr. Cohn (sat, set) down so that the complete landscape would be visible.
9. The buyer (don't, doesn't) want a lengthy fashion showing.
10. There (is, are) two salesmen working the metropolitan area.

Improving your arithmetic:

Calculate the discounts in the following exercises.

1. Trade discounts of 20% and 15% are given on an invoice for $5,000. What is the net amount of the invoice?
2. A discount of 3% is given on an invoice for $750. Compute the amount of the discount and the net amount of the invoice.
3. A gas furnace is listed at $495, less trade discounts of 30% and 25%. Terms of the sale are 2/10, net 30. Compute the net amount of the invoice after all discounts have been taken.

4. Leonard's Hardware Store is short of cash but wants to take advantage of a 4% cash discount on a $925 invoice. The store borrows $888 at the bank for 15 days at a cost of $2.22. What is the amount of discount on the invoice? What is the net saving realized by borrowing to pay the invoice?
5. A paint supplies store is given discounts of 20%, 10%, and 5% on an invoice for $550. Compute the net amount of the invoice.

Improving your research skills:

1. Your instructor will appoint a committee to visit a drugstore, a hardware store, and a women's dress shop. Talk with the manager of each store to determine the importance he places on discounts and transportation arrangements in deciding to buy from a particular selling firm. Report your findings to the class.
2. Watch for cooperative advertising appearing in your daily newspaper this week. Visit the cooperating stores to see if point-of-purchase advertising is related to the store's cooperative advertising. Clip the cooperative ads from the newspaper and bring them to class, along with a report on the relationship of point-of-purchase and cooperative advertising.
3. Talk with a traveling salesman and a retail salesperson to determine the amount of time each spends in actual selling. Make a comparison of their daily activities and prepare a report of your findings.

APPLYING YOUR KNOWLEDGE

Case problem:

John Holmes, a salesman of industrial air conditioning systems for the Arctic Refrigeration Company, had prepared a comprehensive sales presentation to be given at the monthly board meeting of a local bakery. The board members had no technical knowledge of air conditioning, but they were eager to install a central air conditioning system in the bakery. The salesman for a competing air conditioning firm was to give his presentation after Holmes. Holmes gave a thorough and professional presentation of his firm's proposed air conditioning system. He did not involve any group members while he made his presentation, and very few questions were asked after he completed his talk. The salesman for the competing firm gave a less knowledgeable presentation. He involved the group in his sales talk and answered questions as they arose during his presentation. The group participated extensively in his presentation, even though he did not have the polish or superior product knowledge of John Holmes. The competing salesman eventually obtained the order. How did Holmes fail in his presentation? Simulate a sales talk that Holmes might have given and indicate the points at which he should have drawn out questions and discussion.

Continuing project:

Perform the following activities in your manual:

1. Try to find out the common discounts and datings given for your chosen product and tell how you would use this knowledge if your chosen sales occupation involved contact selling.
2. Describe the best transportation method for your product and the most common shipping terms for your product.
3. Tell whether dealer services such as cooperative advertising, point-of-purchase advertising, and premiums are commonly offered with your product. If such aids are commonly offered, tell how you would turn these aids into effective selling points for your product.
4. Tell whether you would have to sell your product to groups and, if so, outline procedures for preparing a group sales talk.
5. Outline a plan for effective management of your selling time.

Extra credit:

Select an item of merchandise that you could sell to group buyers. Give some description of the backgrounds of the buyers you would probably be contacting. Prepare a standardized sales talk, mentioning any audio-visual aids that might be used, for presenting this merchandise to the group buyers.

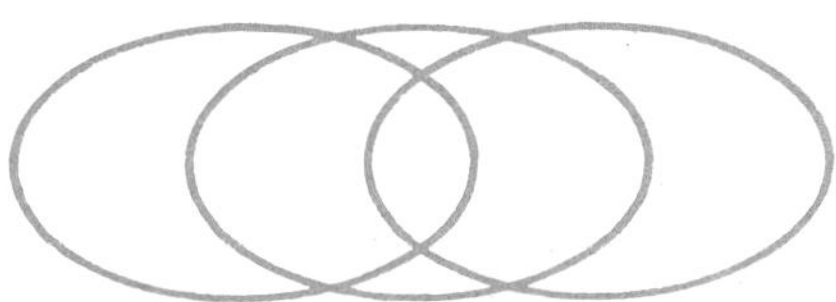

chapter 12

special skills in retail selling

KEY QUESTIONS

A How can a salesman use suggestion selling in an attempt to sell more goods than the customer had intended to buy?

B What rules should the salesman follow to maximize his chances of making a successful telephone sales presentation?

C In selling by telephone, what preparations should be made prior to placing the calls?

D What kinds of stock records may retail salesmen be required to maintain?

E Why is the retail salesman in a unique position to handle customer complaints and guard store security?

part A

suggestion selling and trading up

In Chapter 10 you learned that plus selling includes all attempts to increase sales beyond the basic sales presentation. You also learned about three methods of plus selling: increasing the number of customers contacted, increasing the number of successful sales transactions, and following up sales. In this part you will learn about two other plus selling techniques: suggestion selling and trading up. These techniques are perhaps best suited to retail selling because of the wide range of articles available in many retail stores. However, wholesale salesmen can often suggest to their customers additional goods, new goods, or goods that they feel will sell especially well in a particular community.

SUGGESTION SELLING

Suggestion selling is an attempt to sell more goods than the customer had intended to purchase by: (1) promoting a larger quantity of the goods selected; (2) promoting related goods; and (3) promoting additional but different goods, usually with a special price or seasonal appeal.

Selling Larger Quantities

Most customers have a tendency to buy only what they need at the time, even though they know they will soon need more of a certain product. A woman who finds that she has a run in her last pair of nylons feels a pressing need for a new pair. Because she wants to invest as little money as possible in hosiery, she is likely to buy just one pair—even though she knows she will have to buy more stockings before long. In such a case, the salesperson is performing a real service by suggesting the purchase of an additional pair or two. Even though the immediate investment will be higher than the customer first expected, the suggested purchase will save her time and shopping effort in the near future.

The salesperson must word the suggestion so as not to convey the idea that the main purpose is to sell more merchandise. The salesperson wants to increase his sales, of course; but he should have a real desire to be helpful to the customer, and that desire should be apparent. When a customer asks for hosiery and has decided on color, size, and weight, the saleswoman might suggest: "Would you like to take three pairs? You can buy the same color in all three pairs and stretch the life of the stockings by matching up single stockings when one of a pair gets a run."

Selling Related Goods

The fact that one article is always related in some way to some other article offers an excellent opportunity for suggestion selling. The customer who buys thread can probably use needles. The customer who buys a dress may need a hat or shoes to go with it. The buyer of a cartridge fountain pen needs refills. The buyer of vinyl tile needs a special adhesive to install the tile. Suggesting such related items is often a real service, because the salesman may save the customer a trip back to the store.

Ordinarily, the suggested item should be lower in price than the original purchase; it should be something that the customer can afford. The service station attendant may ask, "Shall I check your oil?" This is a perfect suggestion of a related article. The extra outlay is small, the checkup is a service to the customer, and the suggestion puts emphasis on being of service and not on the additional sale.

Occasionally, higher-priced merchandise can be suggested, particularly if the customer's wants are well known. For example, an art collector may like to be told about new art pieces that a gallery has for sale. In a sporting-goods store, a man who is examining fishing lures may appreciate being directed to a shipment of spinning rods that has just been received.

Selling Unrelated Goods

Goods unrelated to the original purchase can sometimes be sold through suggestion. If the suggested goods are low in price, new, and of an impulse nature, they are often acceptable to the customer. Some stores select each week an especially attractive item for suggestion selling. By means of various forms of advertising and by means of oral presentations, these suggested goods can be sold in quantity to customers who come into the store to buy something else.

The Components of Suggestion Selling

Suggestion selling should be thought of as "service selling" to customers.
Understand also the salesperson's effort that results in the sale of additional merchandise.
Generally people can be influenced by the power of suggestion.
Goods known as staples, necessities, impulse, and new merchandise items make good suggestions.
Easier to suggest items that are closely related to the first purchase.
Seventy-one percent of 2,000 customers surveyed recently liked to have the salesperson suggest merchandise.
Tact must be used in suggestion selling.
Interest in what the customer is to do with goods helps to suggest additional items.
Offer good reasons for recommending additional merchandise.
Not a good policy to force additional goods upon customer.

Suggest and show related merchandise.
Emphasize why it is worthwhile for customers to accept suggestions.
Let counter and store displays help in suggesting additional items.
Learn about related goods sold in other departments and suggest them.
Interest customers in additional merchandise through demonstrations and dramatizations.
Notice closely the reactions of customers during suggestion selling.
Goodwill for salesman and store can result when suggestion selling is regarded as a service.

Studying and using these components of suggestion selling can help a salesman succeed in his job. The possibilities of suggestion selling have not been fully realized; increased attention should be placed on this phase of selling in the future.

Rules for Suggestion Selling

Here are a few general rules to guide the retail salesman in making suggestions:

1. Remember that goods will suggest themselves if they are properly displayed; thus, display inexpensive and novelty merchandise prominently.
2. Suggest goods that will really benefit the customer. By studying past sales, determine which items are commonly bought together and suggest these combinations.

3. Do not suggest a long list of articles. Nothing is more irritating to a customer than to listen to a long list of suggested articles and have to say, "No, I don't need it," about each one.
4. Do not make suggestions indiscriminately to all customers. Some customers are in a hurry, and some will already own the article suggested.
5. Demonstrate the suggested goods whenever possible. For example, show how well a suggested tie looks with a shirt the customer has just selected.
6. Avoid negative suggestions such as: "Is there anything else?" "Do you want more than one can?" or "You don't want anything else, do you?" These suggest the answer, "No."
7. Make suggestions after the customer has made his major decision but before the sale has been written up or rung on the register. Suggestions made earlier than this take the customer's attention from his main purchase. Suggestions made later delay the customer when he is about to leave and may require recording an extra transaction.

TRADING UP

Trading up does not involve selling additional merchandise but rather emphasizing better quality than the customer would otherwise have purchased. Better quality is not always associated with higher price, but in any line the higher-priced merchandise is generally of better quality. It will wear longer; it will drape better; it will look better; it will be more comfortable; it will taste better; it will perform better. The old adage that "It pays in the long run to buy better quality" is generally true. As customers acquire more discretionary purchasing power, they do not look simply for more goods. They want better goods—goods that will not only satisfy basic needs but also provide the special satisfaction that only higher quality can bring.

In retail selling, trading up requires that management provide an adequate assortment of better merchandise in addition to currently popular goods and that the salesperson know when and how to suggest the better goods. For example, after showing some carpeting made of Orlon acrylic, a carpeting salesman might say: "You may find that you will like this durable all-wool carpeting better than that made of Orlon acrylic." The salesman has made no attempt to force all-wool carpeting on the customer, but the suggestion may result in the sale of the higher-priced product.

It is a good rule to show the customer a better article than he asked for to permit a comparison. When the customer sees the two articles side by side, he will frequently choose the better one of his own

I. Howard Spivak

How might this saleswoman in a cosmetics department use suggestion selling after the customer has decided to buy a lipstick? What opportunities might there be for trading up? Would it be more difficult to use these two selling techniques with cosmetics than with other merchandise, such as housewares?

accord. In attempting to sell better goods, the salesman must avoid unethical practices. For example, he should not belittle the article originally asked for. He must be equally careful not to insist that the better article be purchased. However, he may discuss which of the two would be more useful under certain circumstances.

An unethical practice followed by some dealers is to place a flashy but relatively poor-quality article in the display window, marked at what seems to be a very low price. When a customer enters and asks for the displayed article, the salesperson does everything he can to pressure the customer to buy a much higher-priced article by pointing out the shortcomings of the article requested. Customers should always be treated fairly and honestly and should be given good value for their money.

CHECKING YOUR KNOWLEDGE

Vocabulary:

(1) suggestion selling (2) trading up

Review questions:

1. Why are the techniques of suggestion selling and trading up best suited to retail selling?
2. How can the salesperson provide a service for the customer through suggesting the purchase of a larger quantity?
3. How does price affect the related goods suggested to the customer?
4. How are unrelated goods sold through suggestion selling?
5. Why is it a good rule to show the customer a better article than he asked for?

For discussion:

1. Do you think that suggestion selling generally improves the customer's relationship with the store? Why?
2. Some customers resent the idea of trading up. Should a salesperson usually attempt trading up with the customer? Why?

part B

techniques of telephone selling

There are about 80 million telephones in the United States—about 45 telephones for every 100 persons. The telephone is such a commonplace means of communication that its importance as a selling tool is sometimes overlooked. The telephone is used, of course, to locate prospects, to make appointments, and to follow up sales in both contact and retail selling; but many businesses have ignored the telephone as a means of giving a sales presentation. Convenience goods or items with a relatively low price tag can often be sold readily by phone. This kind of selling is a service to customers. If goods can be ordered over the phone and delivered to the customer's home, the customer is saved the time and effort of a shopping trip.

THE TELEPHONE IN RETAILING

Telephone selling is especially suited to retailing because of the products involved. Few business customers respond to a sales presentation by telephone alone because of the large money outlays that may be made on a single order. They want to talk to the salesman in person and evaluate his sales proposition carefully. Telephone selling to business customers is perhaps best suited to suggestion selling of new or related goods after the customer has placed an order. It can also be used to an extent in following up sales and selling additional items. One wholesaler of plumbing supplies, for example, acknowledges all mail orders by phone. He thanks the customer, describes the shipping arrangements for the goods, and is sometimes able to sell larger quantities of goods to the customer.

Using the telephone in retail selling is quick, convenient, economical, flexible, and productive. The salesman's customer is as close as the telephone at his selling station, and customers can be reached for a low cost per call. If one customer isn't available, the salesman can simply dial another number. Many large retail stores maintain an order department that takes customer orders by telephone. Customers may order merchandise that they have seen advertised in the newspaper and may ask that the goods be sent COD or charged to their credit accounts. Although salespeople in the order department may not normally initiate calls to customers, they have excellent opportunities for suggestion selling when the customer calls in his order.

Salespeople may often be employed to sell a product or service entirely by phone. Such a salesperson is given or prepares a prospect list, calls the customers on that list, and gives his sales presentations over the phone. Most salespeople, though, will sandwich telephone selling between other selling duties. They may call current customers to advise them of new merchandise that has come in or may call former customers whom they have not seen for some time. Making telephone sales calls during slow selling hours can result in good use of time that might otherwise be wasted.

RULES FOR TELEPHONE SELLING

There is a very definite difference between telephone selling and telephone order taking. When a customer calls to order merchandise, the salesman may only have to write down the necessary customer and merchandise information to make sure that the order is correctly filled and delivered. If the customer seems to be quite decided about what he wants, he may not even be a prospect for suggestion selling. Sometimes the salesperson will give the order to a special individual called an *order filler,* who performs the mechanics of assembling the goods for delivery. Generally, though, telephone selling requires a special sales

Handy-Boesser Photographers

These women are order takers in the telephone order department of a large retail store. The order taker's primary duty is to record accurately all information concerning the order. There may also be some opportunities for suggestion selling.

technique and personality. The salesman is working under a handicap from the start, since he cannot see the customer and the customer cannot see him. It is more difficult to project a good selling personality over the telephone than it is in a face-to-face contact.

To maximize the chances of making a good telephone sales presentation, the salesman should follow certain rules:

1. The merchandise or service must be of good quality, fairly priced, and have a good chance of being interesting to the prospect.
2. The prospects called must be carefully selected, and prospect lists must be reviewed and modified at frequent intervals.
3. Sales talks must be carefully worked out prior to calling the customer.
4. Salespeople must know their products well and know their firms' sales and service policies.
5. There should be a special reason for phoning—a new stock of an item previously bought by the customer, late models, new packages, or new services.
6. The call should be made at a time convenient to the customer.
7. The salesman must not make promises that cannot be kept by the selling firm.
8. The salesman must "put his best voice forward."

THE TELEPHONE PERSONALITY

Customers approached by telephone need special consideration, since neither the salesman nor the customer can see each other. The customer's impressions of the salesman and the selling firm are formed to a great extent by the salesman's voice and manner. As radio is to television, the telephone is to personal selling. Physical appearance and facial expression are blacked out, and many vital personality factors that affect people favorably must be projected through the voice alone. "Telephone personality" is really the sum of those actions which express orally the different characteristics of an individual.

To favorably express his personality over the telephone, a salesman should: (1) be courteous; (2) show personal interest and attention; (3) be sincere; and (4) indicate a spirit of helpfulness appropriate to the situation. The presence of these elements in a telephone sales contact gives a positive character to the sales talk.

Courtesy Is Important

The successful telephone salesman must conform to commonly accepted requirements of business etiquette, and one of these requirements is showing courtesy to the customer. To reflect friendliness and courtesy on the telephone, the salesman should: (1) identify himself; (2) acknowledge greetings, questions, and the closing appropriately; (3) listen attentively; (4) respond properly to conditions calling for expressions of sympathy or regret; and (5) keep all promises he makes.

Show Interest and Attention

Telephone etiquette requires that the salesman concentrate on what the customer is saying. To express personal interest and sincerity over the telephone, the salesman should: (1) be a good listener; (2) express appreciation of the customer's point of view; (3) display interest in what is said; and (4) let the customer tell his story completely and without interruption.

Express Helpfulness

Warmth, friendliness, and a desire to be helpful are invaluable assets to the telephone salesperson. The telephone salesperson must convey the impression that his firm genuinely wants to satisfy the customer's needs and wants. The spirit of helpfulness may be expressed in several ways: (1) by giving information; (2) by granting a request; (3) by arranging to investigate the customer's problem; (4) by suggesting alternatives; (5) by recognizing unusual buying circumstances; and (6) by explaining, if a request cannot be granted, why it cannot be granted.

DEVELOPING THE TELEPHONE PROSPECT LIST

Developing a list of prospects to call by telephone is just as important as developing a list of prospects to contact through advertising or in person. Many of the techniques you learned about in Chapter 8 can be used to develop the telephone prospect list.

Reviving Inactive Accounts

In developing a telephone prospect list, first attention should be given to current customers, former customers, or inactive credit accounts. Some of the seller's best prospects may be hiding right under his nose in the file marked "Inactive." Smart retailers, manufacturers, and wholesalers all analyze their customer accounts and pick out those they think should be active but that are not.

In trying to revive inactive accounts by telephone, the salesman should get all the information he can before calling. He will especially want to know the date of the customer's last purchase, the details of this last purchase, how long he has been a customer of the firm, the approximate amount that he has spent with the store, whether he has ever had any complaints about the business' operation, and any other pertinent details.

Analyzing the Prospect List

In small businesses, it is often practical to secure a list of customers maintained by other small local merchants such as druggists, grocers, service station owners, or insurance agents. The telephone book itself may be a source of prospects in small towns. Developing a good prospect list for telephone selling is a matter of individual tastes, interests, and industry on the part of the seller.

To analyze a prospect list, the salesman should have the following information about the people he is going to call:

1. Are they current customers? If so, what have they been buying? How often? How much? What items might they be interested in purchasing by telephone?

2. Are they former customers? If so, why did they stop buying from the firm? What were their former buying habits?
3. Are they new prospects? If so, what do you know about them? What might they know about your firm?

The more information the salesman has about his customers, the easier it is to select the proper opening remarks and use the best sales appeal in telephone selling.

CHECKING YOUR KNOWLEDGE

Vocabulary:

order filler

Review questions:

1. What kinds of retail goods are best suited to telephone selling?
2. Distinguish between telephone selling and telephone order taking.
3. Why is the telephone salesperson always working under a handicap?
4. How should a salesman favorably express his personality over the telephone?
5. Where should attention first be given when developing a telephone prospect list?

For discussion:

1. Many retailers in large cities do not use telephone selling but have large telephone order-taking departments. Discuss reasons that might account for this.
2. Suggest steps a retailer might follow in training a telephone sales force.

part C

the telephone sales talk

A haphazardly handled telephone call wastes the salesman's time, wastes the prospect's time, wastes the money paid for using the telephone, may lose customers permanently, and is seldom successful. In face-to-face selling, the salesman should plan his approach and sales appeals, then adapt them to his customers and to the product he is selling. Good planning will also help the telephone salesman meet the varying conditions in telephone selling.

Planning does not mean preparing a series of pat speeches that leave no room for individuality, personality, ingenuity, or imagination from the salesperson. Planning a telephone sales talk is merely a method of organizing ideas so that the salesman can complete a sale successfully. Too much selling takes place without proper planning. Selling points are often made incidentally, almost accidentally, by many salesmen. In telephone selling, the seller should write out his ideas step by step in advance. In doing this, he makes sure that no vital point is overlooked. Since few people talk as they write, materials that are written out should never be read or memorized for a verbatim presentation. Such a presentation lacks spontaneity and sincerity.

GETTING ATTENTION AND INTEREST

Using the prospect's name is important in all forms of selling. In telephone selling, the salesman should greet the prospect by name. This should be relatively simple, since he will be calling from a prospect list. However, this technique should not be overused in a telephone conversation. After greeting the prospect, the salesman should introduce himself. Usually a simple statement of his name and the firm's name is sufficient.

To attract attention, the salesman appeals to the prospect's self-interest or curiosity; in telephone selling, this should be done quickly. The following attention-getters may often be effectively used:

1. *Thank-you approach.* "Mr. Bernard, this is Ted Kash of the Midway Garden Store. Thank you for your order we received this morning. I thought I'd call you to see how many bags of fertilizer you have on hand and how long this supply will last you."
2. *Service approach.* "Mrs. Fanella, this is Bruce Carter of the Ace Appliance Company. A number of people in this section of the city have been surprised to learn that we handle service and repairs. Therefore, I'm calling a few of our neighbors to let them know about it."
3. *Inactive account approach.* "Good morning, Mr. Rich. This is Mr. Edmonds of Edmonds Meat Products. We haven't done any business with you for two months, and I thought I'd call you and find out why."
4. *Special-occasion approach.* "Good morning, Mr. Pryor. This is Mr. Saylor of The Jewel Box. Congratulations on your first wedding

anniversary next week. I was looking over my sales of a year ago and saw your name on my list. I suppose you're thinking about some sort of anniversary present for your wife. . . ."

5. *Demonstration approach.* "Good morning, Mrs. Glennon. This is John Strong of Hartag TV Sales and Service. We're calling a few of our neighbors to tell them about a special display of new models and a demonstration that we're having at our store."
6. *Special sale or bargain approach.* "Good morning, Mrs. Jones. This is Jane Frost of the Runnels Shop. We have just received a new shipment of beautiful sweaters that would be most suitable for your daughter. . . ."
7. *After-mailing approach.* "Good morning, Mr. Bechtold. This is Charles Thornton of the Equitable Life Insurance Company. I mailed you a letter last week about our new 'One-Package' insurance policy. What do you think of this as an insurance plan?"

CREATING DESIRE FOR THE PRODUCT

To make the customer want the product, the salesman must tell him about the product or service—what it is; why he needs it; what it will do for him; how, when, and where he can get it; and how much it will cost. Including these elements in the talk indicates good planning.

Ask Questions

By asking questions, the salesman may sometimes help the customer create his own need. The questions should be pertinent and not involve previously offered information. It is desirable to phrase questions so that a "yes" response will be given. By doing this, it is more difficult for the customer to say "no" later on. Telephone selling techniques can be improved by talking "with" the customer and not "at" him. The salesman should try to see things as the customer does and to speak the customer's language. He should also be alert to the hidden needs of his customers. An intelligent appraisal of the customer's problems, through tactful questioning, will show the salesman's interest and better help the customer to realize his needs.

Use "Sparkle"

"Sparkle" is of prime importance in telephone selling. Through a knowledge of his product, the salesman should know what appeal will bring the best response. He should express this appeal in "sparkling" terms so that the prospect can visualize product features and benefits from the spoken words. Three examples are: (1) instead of saying

"It's a good buy," say "This purchase will save you 90 cents every week"; (2) instead of saying "It's fine quality," say "This dress is made of long-wearing, easy-washing Orlon"; (3) instead of saying "We give good delivery service," say "Our deliveries are so regular you can almost set your watch by them."

Describe the Product Realistically

In telephone selling, products must be described realistically because the prospect cannot examine the product during the presentation. What is said over the telephone should be in terms that the prospect understands. Two good descriptions are: (1) "The compact is about the size and shape of a pack of cigarettes" and (2) "The bed, when folded, fits neatly into a space the size of an ordinary clothes closet."

Give All the Necessary Facts

Prospects who are being called on the telephone need all the necessary product facts. Statements of factual information are: (1) "This electric skillet is 12 inches wide"; (2) "The refrigerator has a freezer unit, an all-steel cabinet, space for various-sized bottles, and an ice-maker"; (3) "The dresses come in navy, black, and brown in junior sizes and half sizes." In telephone selling, it is sometimes possible to emphasize bargains. A real bargain appeals to customers. If the size of the order can be increased by offering a bargain, this obviously means a larger sale for the salesman and may well mean money in the customer's pocket. This may also be the time to point out the availability of new products, if they are related to the initial purchase.

CLOSING THE TELEPHONE SALE

Before the sale can be closed, objections must be answered sincerely, carefully, and completely. Business firms that do a good job of telephone selling take into consideration the most commonly raised objections and develop lists of "best answers" for objections. Such a list of objections and appropriate answers should be kept handy for easy reference. When objections are raised, the salesman should be careful not to antagonize the prospect; he might win the argument but lose the sale.

The salesman must be able to recognize the telephone customer's readiness to buy. Even the best planning can be destroyed by fumbling and an uncertain attitude, once the customer has decided to buy. It may

A Telephone Sale

Salesperson: Shopping Service, Miss Warren.

Customer: Yes. I'd like to order 4 unfitted sheets, double-bed size.

Salesperson: Surely. Double-bed size at what price?

Customer: I believe I saw them advertised in the paper at $2.69 a sheet.

Salesperson: That's correct. We also have some fine pillowcases on sale at 98 cents each.

Customer: You have? Well, give me six.

Salesperson: Surely. That will be four sheets at $2.69 each and six pillowcases at 98 cents each.

Customer: Yes.

Salesperson: Will that be charge or COD?

Customer: COD.

Salesperson: May I have your name, please?

Customer: Mrs. Arthur Daley.

Salesperson: "D" as in "David" A-L-E-Y.

Customer: Yes. The address is 329 73rd Street.

Salesperson: 3-2-9 73rd Street. That's Brooklyn, isn't it, Mrs. Daley?

Customer: Yes.

Salesperson: Thank you for your order, Mrs. Daley. The sheets and pillowcases will be delivered Wednesday.

Customer: Thank you. Goodbye.

Salesperson: Goodbye.

New York Telephone Company

This is a well-handled telephone sale. Notice that the salesperson rendered a service to the customer by suggesting the purchase of the pillowcases, that she verified the order, that she checked the spelling of the customer's name, and that she had the proper address for delivery purposes. Notice, too, that the salesperson kept the call brief and free of needless questions.

well be time for the salesman to say, "Fine, Mr. Phillips; let me arrange to have it sent to you" instead of "When you decide that you want one, Mr. Phillips, call us." In the latter statement, the salesman is actually suggesting that the prospect spend time mulling over whether or not he really needs the product.

Many lost sales are lost because the salesman neglects to ask for the order. He often assumes that after he has given all the reasons why a prospect should buy, he has done a good sales job. No one should be ashamed to ask for an order if he has a good product and has described it properly. One might frankly ask the prospect to purchase by saying: "Since you agree that my product (name it) will benefit you (briefly tell how), shall I arrange to send it out?" If this technique is used, the prospect will generally say "yes." Another positive approach in trying to close the sale is to ask the prospect "which" rather than "if." For example, a salesman might say: "May I call tonight, or would tomorrow be better?" The customer is placed in a position where he is to make a choice. If general agreement has been obtained up to that point, closing the sale should be relatively simple.

THE MECHANICS OF THE TELEPHONE SALES TALK

To make sure that a telephone customer's order is properly filled and delivered, certain information must be obtained. The salesman should record (1) the customer's name; (2) the name of the person to whom the goods are to be charged or sent COD; (3) the address to which the goods are to be sent; (4) the address to which goods are to be charged; (5) special delivery instructions; and (6) a description of the article, including quantity, price, brand, size, and quality.

Throughout the sales talk, the salesman should remember to choose his words correctly, use proper volume, and speak distinctly. Using variety and flexibility in the voice can help convey mood and attitude. These two qualities can be attained by using pitch, inflection, and emphasis. Pitch is the key in which one speaks; a low-pitched voice generally carries best over the phone. Inflection is a change in pitch or tone. It keeps speech from being monotonous and creates a feeling of interest and life in the voice. Emphasis or stress placed on certain words or groups of words may well change the meaning of what is said. All three of these elements should be used in making a successful sales presentation.

CHECKING YOUR KNOWLEDGE

Review questions:

1. What is involved in the planning of a telephone sales talk?
2. How are attention and interest gained in telephone selling?
3. What is the purpose of asking the customer questions during the telephone conversation?
4. Describe the importance of "sparkle" in telephone selling.
5. How do some businesses handle objections given during telephone selling?

For discussion:

1. Discuss the statement: "Good telephone selling involves the same basic principles used in contact selling."
2. Reactions to words spoken carelessly by the salesman in telephone conversation might cause the customer to react negatively, whereas a negative reaction to the same words might not arise during face-to-face selling. Why is this so?

part D

stockkeeping

A necessary duty for most retail salespeople is caring for the stock in their selling areas. In small stores, a salesman may be responsible for all stockkeeping duties from checking in merchandise shipments to taking inventory. In larger stores, he may only have to replenish stock in his selling area, maintain any required stock control records, and help at inventory time.

Performing stockkeeping duties offers several advantages to the salesperson and to the customer. A major advantage to the salesman is that stockkeeping helps him become familiar with the merchandise he is selling. A major advantage to the customer is that he can be served more promptly by the salesman who has a good knowledge of his stock.

DAILY STOCKKEEPING DUTIES

A salesman's daily stockkeeping duties may include covering the goods at the end of the selling day to keep dust from accumulating on them, removing the coverings in the morning and putting them away, arranging small display fixtures, replenishing stock, maintaining stock records for store management, and keeping the selling station neat and clean at all times.

Replenishing Stock

The salesman should check his stock toward the end of the selling day to see whether the supply is getting low. He can then make it a point to replenish the stock himself when he arrives at the store the next day or can prepare a reserve requisition and send it to the stockroom or warehouse so that stock can be delivered early the next day.

In replenishing stock, it is essential that fresh stock be placed beneath older stock so that the older goods will be sold first. If this practice were not followed, stores would eventually be faced with a considerable loss in shopworn merchandise. The salesman should also follow carefully the display methods set up by the store when he replenishes stock.

In some stores, stock clerks replenish stock after the salesman or buyer has notified them that stock is low. If the salesman is to replenish stock himself, he must understand his store's stockroom arrangement so that he can find promptly the goods he needs.

Types of Stock Arrangements

Depending on the type of store, one of several stock arrangements may be used. *Forward stock* is that stock which is found on the selling floor. In some stores or departments, such as stationery departments, some surplus stock is kept in or under the display fixtures on the selling floor. This is called *under-the-counter stock*. One of the most common arrangements of stock is to maintain a separate stockroom close to the selling floor. Merchandise stored in such an area is called *reserve stock*. This merchandise is usually arranged much as is the stock on the selling floor so that salespeople can find quickly the goods they are looking for.

Some stores use upper floors or the basement as reserve stockrooms. When this is done, salespeople usually do not go after merchandise themselves but rather fill out lists of requested stock (called *reserve requisitions*) to be delivered to their selling areas or else telephone directly to the stockroom when goods are needed. A comparable plan for large items such as furniture and appliances is to keep the reserve stock in a warehouse and to deliver the items from the warehouse directly to the customer.

Some stores build stock space around the perimeter of the selling area, with a partition separating the reserve stock area from the selling area. Other stores, such as discount stores, virtually do away with reserve stockrooms and try to place as much merchandise on the selling floor as they possibly can.

Maintaining Stock Records

You have already learned that many stores require their salespeople to maintain want slips, which are records of merchandise customers have asked for but which is not in stock. This is an important stock record, for it can help in determining what goods to buy in the future. Salesmen are also required to keep other stock records, particularly in large stores. Stock control is essential to good business operation. Buyers must maintain a good balance of stock at all times, and they must be able to get a prompt picture of their stock situation when they need it. When salesmen maintain the necessary stock records accurately and efficiently, they are making a real contribution to their firms' successful operations.

Never-Out List. One stock-control system is called the *checklist,* or *never-out list system.* On a form prepared by the store, all items to be stocked and the amount of each style to be stocked are listed. Periodically salespeople check this list against actual stock to see if it meets the specifications of the never-out list. If it does not, a merchandise order is placed. This system works well for goods such as groceries, drugs, and hardware supplies.

Perpetual Inventory Lists or Cards. Some goods, such as fashion items, must have an elaborate system of stock control. Buyers must know at all times just how many and what styles of such goods they have in stock. Salespeople may be required to prepare daily lists, based on copies of sales checks or price ticket stubs, of what they sell. This list is given to the store buyer, and he can get an accurate picture of his stock situation by studying the list along with his purchase records.

Perpetual inventory cards are maintained by salespeople or clerks. A card may be prepared for each merchandise style, and entries on the card may include the number of that style ordered on a certain date and the number received on a certain date. On the card for a given style, salespeople enter the number of that style sold each day and the balance remaining. Sometimes the "on hand" figures on the cards are checked by a physical count of the merchandise.

"Warehouse" Control Cards. When goods cannot be physically counted easily, when they are of high unit value, or when they are quite bulky, a *"warehouse" control system* may be used. Salespeople are then required to maintain control cards for each piece of merchandise. Each card tells when the item was received, its cost, original retail price and any markdowns taken. When the item is sold, the card is removed from the file. A quick glance at the file of these cards gives an accurate picture of the stock situation.

Reorder Slips. Many stores establish low and high limits for their stock. The low limit is the point at which merchandise should be reordered, and there are various ways of flagging the salesman's attention to this limit. Sometimes a piece of tape is attached to the item or group of items representing the minimum quantity. When the salesman sells down to the taped items, he knows that it is time to reorder. Sometimes a form is placed on top of the item that represents the low limit. This form is called a *reorder slip*. When the salesman reaches this slip, he should fill it out and give it to the buyer.

Slow-Selling Lists. Sometimes salespeople must prepare lists of slow-selling merchandise. They record the age of each item on hand, measured from the date of purchase. If there is a considerable amount of slow-selling merchandise, management may decide to make a special promotional effort to get rid of the stock.

TAKING INVENTORY

In stores or departments selling fast-moving items, salesmen may have to take a daily inventory. Some stores take weekly inventories, but a more common practice is to take inventories every six months or once a year. The salesman will be involved in taking a physical inventory and filling out various inventory records. The information he gathers

Flah and Company

What stockkeeping duties might this saleswoman have? What stock records would she be most likely to maintain?

will be used to determine future buying plans, to guide the store's future promotional efforts, and to calculate profit and loss.

Taking a Physical Inventory

With a *physical inventory,* the amount of stock on hand is determined by an actual count of the merchandise. Before taking inventory, stock may be reduced as much as possible through special sales, then the merchandise is sorted and put back into its proper place. Once this has been done, salespeople may use one of three listing methods to record the necessary information. With the first method, tags numbered in sequence are attached to each style or lot number of merchandise. The merchandise is counted, and the count is entered on each tag. With the second method, sheets are used instead of tags; and many lot numbers are entered on each sheet. With the third method, two salespeople work together. One person counts the merchandise and calls out the item and lot number. Then the second person enters the data in punched cards.

A *book inventory* may also be maintained, but this is usually not the salesman's responsibility. A book inventory is computed from purchase and sales records without a physical count of merchandise.

Understanding Price Tickets

In taking an inventory, salespeople must be able to understand the information on price tickets, particularly figures on the article's cost to the retailer. The information contained on a price ticket often includes the retail price, cost price, date the goods were received into stock, size and color, kind of material, manufacturer or vendor number, and store department and merchandise classification number.

Cost prices are expressed in a code on price tickets. Otherwise, customers might think that the difference between the retail price and the cost price represented the retailer's profit. This is not the case, because of the operating expenses the retailer incurs in addition to cost. There are many different kinds of cost codes; but perhaps the most common one is that code using a word or phrase of ten letters, each of which represents a consecutive digit. One such phrase might be:

M	O	N	E	Y	T	A	L	K	S
1	2	3	4	5	6	7	8	9	0

An item that costs $21.30 would bear on its price ticket the letters OMNS. An item that costs $16.50 would be written MTYS.

Wanamaker's

Taking inventory is nearly always a team effort involving two or more salespeople in a given selling area. Here are some inventory scenes in a large department store. Can you figure out what each inventory team is doing?

CHECKING YOUR KNOWLEDGE

Vocabulary:

(1) forward stock
(2) under-the-counter stock
(3) reserve stock
(4) reserve requisitions
(5) checklist, or never-out list system
(6) "warehouse" control system
(7) reorder slip
(8) physical inventory
(9) book inventory

Review questions:

1. What benefits do the salesman and the customer realize from the salesman's performance of stockkeeping duties?
2. Name the stockkeeping duties a salesman might be asked to perform.
3. Why is fresh stock always placed beneath older stock?
4. What is the primary reason for maintaining stock records?
5. Describe the procedures used in taking a physical inventory.

For discussion:

1. Do you think that all sales personnel should share equal stockkeeping responsibilities? Why?
2. Is it possible that the salesman's attention to stock and inventory records could affect store profits? Support your answer with examples.

part E

handling complaints and guarding store security

Because he is almost always on the selling floor, the retail salesman is in a unique position to handle two important aspects of retail store operation: dealing with customer complaints and guarding store security. His skill in handling customer complaints can help develop future goodwill for his store. His skill in guarding the store from employee pilferage and shoplifting by customers can help to maximize store profits. The salesman who can handle both of these duties efficiently is an asset to his selling firm.

HANDLING CUSTOMER COMPLAINTS

There is a difference between an objection and a complaint. An objection is raised in connection with a buying proposition during a salesman's sales presentation. A complaint is made after the sale, usually in relation to unsatisfactory merchandise, slow deliveries, or incorrect billing.

Complaints Are Inevitable

Every selling firm is going to encounter some customer complaints at some time. Contact salesmen get their share of complaints, but retail salesmen encounter more complaints because of the greater number of customers with whom they deal and also because ultimate consumers tend to buy less cautiously than do business customers. Many ultimate consumers buy in a hurry with the thought that they can always return merchandise if they are not satisfied with it. Business customers buy more carefully because large money outlays are involved in almost every buying and selling transaction.

While the merchandise complaints of business customers are not often caused by their own careless buying, they do often complain that they are shipped the wrong goods or quantity or that the goods received fail to measure up to quality standards. They also complain about slow deliveries or inconsiderate treatment from another salesman. The contact salesman should handle such complaints promptly and make sure that the situation is not repeated in the future. Once he corrects a complaint, he should find out if the adjustment was handled to the customer's satisfaction. In this way, the customer is subtly reminded of the salesman's efforts in his behalf.

The salesman should not treat a complaint as just an unfortunate occurrence. Rather, he should treat it as an excellent opportunity to build goodwill and ensure future business. When a customer makes a satisfactory purchase, he gives little thought to the salesman or to the desirability of buying from him again. But if he complains about the purchase and receives a sympathetic and prompt adjustment, he is generally favorably impressed and is likely to return to the firm again.

No selling firm can avoid getting some complaints, although skillful initial selling can reduce the number of complaining customers.

Methods of Handling Complaints

Retail customers generally take their complaints to the person who sold them the goods or to some other salesman on the selling floor. However, the salesman is not always the person who eventually makes the adjustment. Some stores use a centralized system for handling complaints. Under such a system, all complaints are referred to a centralized adjustment office. Other stores, particularly small ones, use a decentralized system. Persons on the selling floor handle all complaints and make all adjustments. Most stores use a combination of centralized and decentralized adjustment. For example, salesmen or department mangers may handle merchandise complaints on the selling floor, while complaints about deliveries or incorrect billings will be referred either to an adjustment office or to the department responsible for the error.

Rules for Handling Complaints

The primary rule for salesmen to follow in handling complaints is to let the customer get the grievance out of his system. The salesman should let the customer talk freely and make no attempt to interrupt or argue. Until proven otherwise, it should be assumed that the customer has a legitimate complaint. Some customers will take advantage of a liberal adjustment policy, but most customers honestly think they have legitimate complaints. Even if a complaint is not justified, they will not admit it until the salesman shows respect for their point of

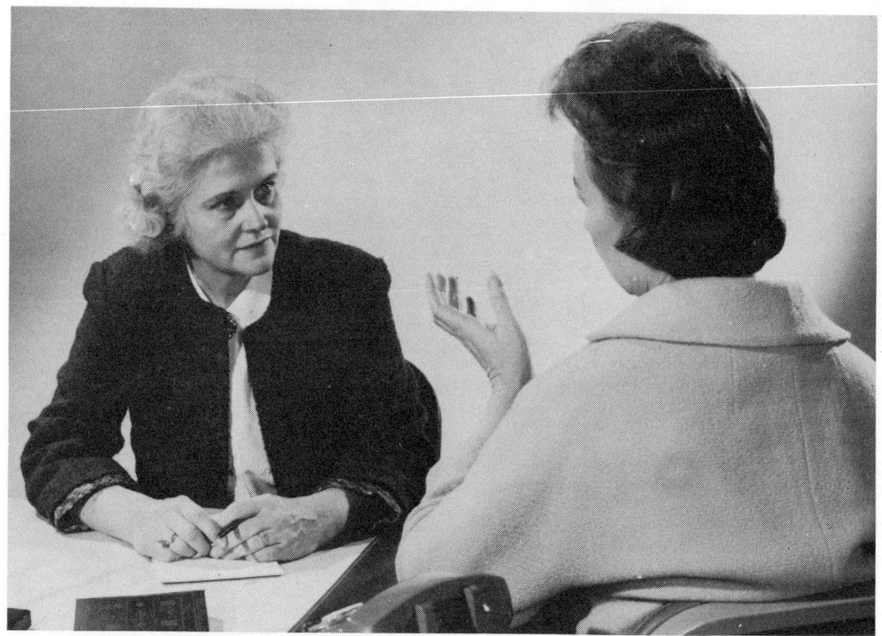

H. Armstrong Roberts

In many large stores, most or all customer complaints are handled in a centralized adjustment office. The persons who handle complaints in these offices must be especially skilled in dealing with people. Adjustments must be made to the satisfaction of both the customer and the store.

view. The few trouble-making customers who know they are in the wrong can generally be detected readily and can be treated with firmness.

The second rule for handling complaints is to get all the facts about the complaint and its cause. This can be done by tactfully asking questions or by examining the merchandise, if the cause of the complaint is unsatisfactory merchandise.

Making Adjustments

Salesmen do not always have the authority to make merchandise adjustments. Store procedures may require them to have their supervisor's approval before making the adjustment, although they may recommend an adjustment to the supervisor based on what they have learned about the complaint. In response to a complaint, a store may make a cash refund, a merchandise exchange, a credit to the customer's account, or a partial allowance on the purchase price. The kind of adjustment made is based on the cost of the item in question, the value of the customer to the store, how often the customer makes complaints, and who is responsible for the complaint. For example, most stores would exchange or refund money on a 59¢ item—even if there was some doubt that the customer's complaint was justified—because the price involved is too small to risk losing the customer's future business.

Returned Goods

When customers want to return merchandise and exchange it for other merchandise, the salesman must be familiar with his store's procedures. Some stores have a policy of not accepting returned goods that were sold during a special sale. Other stores require that the customer show his sales check when he wants to return merchandise. Since the retail salesman deals mainly with complaints about merchandise, complaints and returned goods are two problems that go hand in hand. Returned goods can represent a costly problem to the retailer. It usually costs as much to put returned goods back into stock as it costs to sell them in the first place; and they still must be sold a second time. Sometimes returned goods are soiled, damaged, or out of fashion and must be marked down in price in order to be sold. Salespeople can reduce the number of complaints and the amount of returned goods by making sure that the customer's needs and wants are correctly met before the initial transaction is completed.

GUARDING STORE SECURITY

It is estimated that in many retail stores, losses from theft of money and merchandise by employees and customers amount to about one and a half percent of total sales each year. Stores naturally want to do whatever they can to reduce pilferage by employees and shoplifting by customers. Many self-service stores have installed large mirrors above each aisle so that management can observe customers. Some stores have installed closed-circuit television sets which are monitored continuously by a member of the store's security force. The retail salesman, though, is still the store's best means of guarding security. He is almost always on the selling floor and has the best opportunity to observe customers and other employees carefully. Naturally, the salesman shouldn't make it appear that he distrusts everyone; but he should keep his eyes open for pilferers or shoplifters so that a dishonest person can be reported to management.

Theft by Employees

A few dishonest employees may steal money from cash register drawers or take merchandise from selling areas. The salesman who sees a fellow employee doing this should first point out to him that it is wrong. If this has no effect, it is the salesman's duty to report the employee to management. This is not "tattling"; it is part of the loyalty that a salesman owes his employer.

Shoplifting

Customers steal merchandise from stores for several reasons. Sometimes they steal merchandise that they need but are too poor to buy, such as food. Sometimes they do it for "kicks," sometimes because they are mentally disturbed and cannot control the urge to steal, and sometimes because they intend to resell the merchandise later. A person's reason for shoplifting, determined by questioning him after he has been apprehended, will influence the action that a store will take against him.

Recognizing Shoplifters. It is not always easy to recognize shoplifters, because some are professionals who know all the tricks of the trade. These persons may use such devices as specially designed coats which look, on the outside, like any other coat but have deep pockets inside to hold shoplifted merchandise. Amateur shoplifters may carry shopping bags or oversized purses to hold merchandise they have stolen.

Shoplifters tend to gravitate toward open displays near entrances and exits to the store. They hope to pick up merchandise and leave the store quickly without being noticed. Salespeople who have such displays in their selling areas should watch them closely. Shoplifters also tend to operate in crowds where there is less likelihood of being spotted. Obviously, it is impossible for the salesman to watch everyone in a crowd of shoppers and still serve his honest customers; but he should be watchful for shoplifters' tricks on days when the store is crowded—during special sales events or during the Christmas buying season, for instance.

Persons who sell clothing may find from experience that shoplifters try to get away with merchandise by wearing it out of the store. This usually happens during cold weather when customers are wearing heavy coats. The customer may take three or four garments into the fitting room, put one or two of the garments under the clothing he is already wearing, and walk right out of the store. Salespeople should make sure that customers come out of the fitting room with as many articles as they took in, and in most stores customers are allowed to take only one or two garments into the fitting room at one time.

What To Do with a Shoplifter. The one thing that a salesman shouldn't do with a shoplifter is to accuse him of being a shoplifter. Legal action usually cannot be taken until a person has been caught leaving the store with stolen goods. Professional shoplifters can often dispose of the merchandise quickly and then claim that they were falsely accused. A rash accusation of shoplifting could lead to a damage suit against the store.

When a salesman spots a shoplifter, he should discreetly notify the department manager, store owner, or someone from the store's security force. Many large stores have plain-clothes detectives who pretend to be shopping but who are really watching out for pilferers and shoplifters. The salesman should never try to search a suspected shoplifter nor physically try to prevent him from leaving the store.

A technique that some salesmen use to handle a shoplifter is to approach him and ask, "May I help you?" Amateur shoplifters are sometimes so flustered by this question that they bring out the concealed merchandise, make some explanation of why it was concealed, and ask that a sales check be written out or that the sale be rung up on the cash register. The salesman should go ahead and complete the sale. The customer will usually think that the salesman saw him take the merchandise, so the salesman need not say anything about the shoplifting.

The salesman should then report the incident to management. Generally, a person who has been caught shoplifting in a store—even if he was never formally accused—will not try shoplifting in that store again.

CHECKING YOUR KNOWLEDGE

Review questions:

1. What is the difference between an objection and a complaint?
2. Why do retail salesmen usually encounter more complaints than do contact salesmen?
3. Why should the salesman treat a complaint in a positive manner and not as an unfortunate incident?
4. What is the primary rule for salesmen to follow in handling complaints?
5. Under what circumstances may legal action be taken against a shoplifter?

For discussion:

1. It has been said that effective salesmanship can eliminate many customer complaints. Do you agree? Why?
2. How would you deal with a shoplifter who has been a good customer of your store in the past?

BUILDING YOUR SKILLS

Improving your English:

On a separate sheet of paper, complete each of the following sentences by writing the correct form of the irregular verb given in parentheses after each sentence.

1. The salesmen ______ prepared routings for next week. (has)
2. New name tags will be ______ by all demonstrators. (wear)
3. The district manager ______ the territory representative on Wednesday. (write)
4. The company's rules for preparing schedules are seldom ______. (break)
5. The customer ______ he would study competing units before making his decision. (say)
6. Several directions were ______ as the salesman asked for the location of Harper's. (gave)
7. He ______ to the regional meeting of power tool manufacturers. (go)
8. Carl ______ the model which the salesman recommended. (buy)
9. Bert ______ the district in sales last month. (lead)
10. Reserve stock was ______ from the customer's view. (hide)

Improving your arithmetic:

The problems below involve more than one step in obtaining their solution; show each step used.

1. Jim Clark, a salesman for the Federinko Clothing Store, had gross sales of $3,500 last week. Merchandise returned amounted to $280. Jim receives a salary of $75 per week plus a commission of 1½% of his net sales. Find (a) Jim's net sales for the week; (b) Jim's commission for the week; (c) the amount of commission lost due to returned merchandise; (d) what percent that merchandise returned is of gross sales; and (e) Jim's total income for the week.
2. As a door-to-door salesman for the Wunch Brush Company, your sales for one day are $120. You receive a 12% commission on sales in addition to a weekly salary of $40. If you continue to sell at the same rate, how long will it take you to earn $72 in commission alone? If you work 20 days this month, what will be your total income from salary and commission (assuming the same sales rate)?

Improving your research skills:

1. Visit two local retail stores and observe the kinds of merchandise that are sold through suggestion selling. Prepare a written report of your findings.
2. Review some of your family's recent purchases. Try to determine whether any trading up was done when the purchase was made. Your instructor will give you an opportunity to discuss your findings in class.
3. Talk with some of your friends or neighbors and determine their reactions to telephone selling. Try to obtain at least one good and one poor example of telephone selling. Review each of these in a written report based on what you have learned about telephone selling.
4. If you were manager of a furniture store, what stockkeeping duties would you assign to your salesmen? Why would these duties differ from those stockkeeping duties in a hardware store?

APPLYING YOUR KNOWLEDGE

Case problems:

1. A customer asked a salesperson in a men's clothing store for a tie and decided to purchase the one suggested by the salesperson. The salesperson then suggested that the customer consider a handkerchief to match. The customer agreed to look at one and seemed about ready to take both items when the salesperson mentioned the price of the two items together. The customer looked startled, said he would look elsewhere, and left without buying anything. Is there any way the salesperson could have suggested the related merchandise without jeopardizing the sale of the tie?

2. This is the salesperson's side of a telephone conversation:

"Hosiery Department. Miss Gardner speaking.
"No, Ma'am, no Bali nylon stockings in size 9 at $1.
"Yes, we usually have them, but we're out of them now.
"What?
"No, we have some nylons at 89¢.
"Oh, yes, they're good quality.
"Our next price? $1.19.
"All right.
"Well, of course, if you want to see them.
"Sorry. Good-bye."

What did the salesperson do wrong in handling this sale? What might she have done to complete the sale successfully?

Continuing project:

In your manual, perform the following activities:

1. Tell whether you could use suggestion selling effectively with your product and describe the techniques of suggestion selling that you might employ. Mention related or unrelated goods that you might suggest to a customer buying your product.
2. Tell how you would sell your product by telephone and outline a sales talk that you would use.
3. Explain the stockkeeping duties that you would probably be asked to perform in connection with your product.
4. Describe the complaints you would most likely encounter with your product and describe how you would handle them.

Extra credit:

Prepare a telephone sales talk to be used in selling an item you select. Indicate the variations in voice you would use to avoid a monotonous presentation.

Selling in the 1950's . . .

The modern world of U.S. enterprise began with the 1950's. The most spectacular gains were made by the high-technology industries, with electronics leading the way to total annual sales of $10 billion by 1959. Even Edison might have rubbed his eyes in amazement. After a post-Korean War spending spree, Americans started saving. Business, panicked into price-cutting at first, eventually responded with the successful "marketing concept." The 1950's saw the mass importation of foreign cars, a middle class that included just about everybody, and a baby boom. Besides Mickey Mantle, the decade introduced the solar battery, coast-to-coast color TV, and a thousand other famous firsts. Between 1946 and 1961, the GNP jumped to a phenomenal $521 billion.

(Reprinted by permission from *Sales Management, The Marketing Magazine* © Sales Management, Inc., 1968)

UNIT IV

Nonpersonal Selling

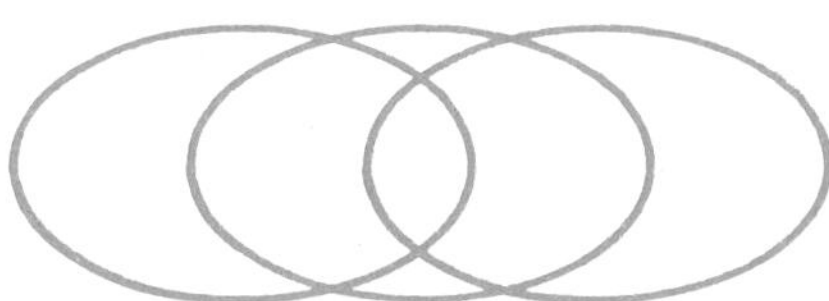

chapter 13

selling through printed advertising

KEY QUESTIONS

A What kinds of advertising media may a selling firm use to promote its product?

B What are the advantages of newspaper advertising that make this medium so popular?

C Do consumer magazines, class magazines, and trade, technical, and professional magazines carry ads for the same kinds of products?

D Is direct-mail advertising used more frequently than television advertising?

E Why is an individual sales letter more effective than a form letter?

part A

principles of advertising

Sales promotion includes all means of communicating with potential customers for the purpose of effecting sales. In this chapter and the following chapter, we shall discuss the two major nonpersonal selling methods: advertising and display. The principles that govern good selling also govern all kinds of advertising and display. To do the best advertising job, one must master the principles of salesmanship. Most advertising today is designed to attract the customer's attention and create interest and desire, with the closing of the sale left to the salesman. Some advertising, though, does result in customer buying action without a salesman's intervention.

ADVANTAGES AND DISADVANTAGES OF ADVERTISING

Advertising is an accepted, important part of our marketing system. It fills an economic need for informing and educating consumers so that they may choose more wisely from the unprecedented variety of goods and services now on the market. Advertising has certain inherent advantages in comparison with personal selling. First, advertising quickly gains attention. A prospect may refuse to talk to a salesman; but he is exposed to many forms of advertising in newspapers, magazines, direct mail, radio, and television. It is hard for him to ignore all forms of advertising. Second, advertising reaches individuals at a much lower cost per contact than is true in personal selling. Third, the content of advertising can be controlled by the selling firm. Businesses have difficulty, however, controlling the statements or actions of their salesmen.

Advertising also has certain disadvantages in comparison with personal selling. First, an advertisement is nonpersonal in nature. Therefore, it is less compelling than any personal contact by a salesman. Since it is projected to a mass audience, an advertisement cannot be adjusted to the specific needs of each prospect. Second, for many products, the advertisement cannot answer all the questions a potential customer might have. It may attempt to anticipate such questions and objections, but it cannot deal with each of them specifically.

OBJECTIVES OF ADVERTISING

For most businesses, the objectives of advertising are:

1. *To stimulate demand for specific products of specific sellers.* A toiletries manufacturer, for example, developed the brand name VO_5 for his products. Promoting this name through advertising built up brand preference and even brand insistence for the products.
2. *To stimulate demand for the services of specific sellers.* Often the advertiser is not the provider of the service but the seller of equipment that the service seller uses. For example, Boeing Aircraft advertises the comforts of its short-range, 737 twin-jet airplane in periodicals widely read by travelers. Boeing doesn't want to sell the jet to these readers; it wants them to book flights on these planes. If this advertising is successful, airlines will buy more of the jets.
3. *To attract attention and create interest.* Advertising can attract prospects' attention and create sufficient interest so that they will visit the seller's place of business, submit an inquiry by mail or telephone, or receive salesmen.
4. *To sell the advertised product directly.* Advertising can also create desire and secure action. This is especially true if, to place an order, the prospect must mail in a coupon that is part of the advertisement.
5. *To keep former customers satisfied.* A customer who has purchased a product must be satisfied that he made the right buying decision. When he sees the product widely advertised in various media, he is likely to pass along favorable word-of-mouth advertising about it.

Montgomery Ward

The preparation of advertisements is a team effort in most selling firms. Many people, including the copywriter and artist, are involved.

KINDS OF ADVERTISING

All advertising is designed to increase sales volume, but the immediate purposes of advertisements differ. Classified according to purpose, advertisements may be either institutional or promotional.

Institutional Advertising

Institutional advertising attempts to convince the customer that the advertiser is a good firm with which to do business because it has certain desirable standards for merchandise and service. Such advertising does not look for immediate sales results; it tries to build goodwill for the advertiser.

Promotional Advertising

Promotional advertising features particular products or services and is intended to solicit a prompt buying response. There are three kinds of promotional advertisements.

Pioneer advertisements educate customers about new products or services. They emphasize the desirability of buying from the broad class of goods to which the specific product belongs and also emphasize the specific product's points of superiority. New products that have required pioneer advertising are Corfam, a leather substitute, a watch operated by a tiny battery, and the self-cleaning oven.

Reminder advertisements simply try to keep the name of an established product or service in the customer's mind. This is done by frequently repeating the product's brand name through jingles or on signs and billboards.

Notice-of-sale advertisements stress the availability of goods for which customer demand already exists. The suggested reasons for buying may include seasonal or fashion-rightness of the offering, wide assortments from which to choose, quality, and price. Most retail ads are of this type. When a bargain is featured, these ads are called special-sales ads; when other demand factors are stressed, they are called regular merchandise ads.

REQUIREMENTS OF EFFECTIVE ADVERTISING

The five requirements of effective advertising are: (1) to advertise the right goods or services; (2) to advertise at the right time; (3) to advertise to the right market; (4) to advertise in the right media; and (5) to use the right advertising technique.

Valley Theatre Shop-In
7617 Reading Rd.
Phone 761-2400

CINCINNATI'S FINEST WOMEN'S STORE

A STATEMENT OF POLICY FROM CINCINNATI'S FINEST WOMEN'S STORE

At Rachele you will be promptly and courteously waited on. (If you're not, management wants to know.) Whether your purchase be from our daytime dresses starting at eighteen dollars, from our one of a kind couturier fashions to one thousand dollars, or from our sportswear or lingerie and accessory department, you will be treated with the dignity that you deserve and expect. Should you need an alteration you will be fitted by Irmgard Wedekind, Estelle Kopp, or Ann Elbert. These three ladies are known in Cincinnati to be the top specialists in their field. Your satisfaction is guaranteed or you will be properly compensated for any purchase at Rachele (provided we are notified within a reasonable period of time).

Why is Rachele Cincinnati's finest Women's store? Because here the customer is the most important article we have!

Rachele, Cincinnati

Promotional advertisements are far more often used than are institutional advertisements. However, institutional ads, such as this one, can be extremely effective in building goodwill for certain types of selling firms.

The Right Goods or Services

The very best advertising campaign will fail if the product is not worth being advertised. In the average retail store, only about 10 percent of the articles carried in stock are ever advertised. One firm insists that every advertised item must first be evaluated according to the following criteria:

1. Is it the right kind of product for current consumer needs?
2. Does it have popular appeal? Are the size, color, shape, and material in fashion?
3. Is it a good value for the money?
4. Is it priced so that many people can afford it?
5. Is it properly packaged?
6. Does it have a point of superiority over competing products?

The Right Time

It is important to advertise at the right time. Ski suits cannot be successfully advertised in the spring, nor swim suits in the fall. Home furnishings are most successfully advertised on Sunday for Monday and Tuesday selling, because on Sunday the whole family has a chance to consider the money outlay involved. The selection of the right time is not restricted to the right season of the year or day of the week. It also includes the point in time when a particular style may or may not be in fashion.

The Right Market

Products and services may be advertised to three broad groups of buyers: (1) ultimate consumers, (2) institutional users, and (3) dealers in a product line or business users of it. All groups may buy the same product, but the appeals to the three groups have to be different. A new producer of a single product may find consumer advertising too expensive. So, through trade papers and personal salesmanship, he may direct his promotion efforts to the dealer market. If his product has points of superiority over established items, dealers may be induced to buy it for resale. Large, established firms may advertise to the three different markets at the same time, using different advertising media for each market. In determining what the right market is, the tools of market segmentation are extremely important.

The Right Media

Selecting the right media grows out of the decision on which market to be reached. The media from which a seller may choose are:

1. Newspapers, including daily newspapers, shopping newspapers, and trade papers.
2. Magazines, including consumer magazines and trade journals.
3. Direct mail, including sales letters, pamphlets, and package inserts.
4. Outdoor advertising, including posters and electric signs.
5. Transportation advertising, including car cards and station posters.
6. Broadcast advertising, including public address systems, radio, and television.
7. Occasional publications, including programs and booklets devoted to a product or an industry.

A combination of media generally gives best results. Thus, a store with the newspaper as its chief advertising medium may also use television, direct mail, signs, posters, handouts, and package inserts.

The Right Technique

Advertising follows the basic principles of personal selling in that every advertisement must first attract attention, then create interest in and desire for the merchandise, then induce some sort of action.

Attention. In thumbing through a newspaper, the average reader devotes only a few seconds to a page. If his attention is not captured in that fleeting moment and heightened into interest, the ad is wasted. Advertising elements that secure quick attention include the size and type of ad, position of ad, pictures, color, headline, and miscellaneous devices, such as unusual type.

Interest. The "you" attitude, which arouses a prospect's interest in a sales talk, is equally effective in arousing a prospect's interest in an advertisement. The "you" attitude involves keeping the customer's interests and needs in mind while preparing an advertisement. This attitude may be expressed in an illustration or headline which not only attracts attention but also prolongs attention into interest because it relates in some way to the prospect's needs.

Desire. An advertisement may create desire by appealing to reason or emotion, just as in personal selling. Copy that appeals to the prospect's reason is called *reason-why copy*. The advertiser may use facts and figures about sales, demonstrations, warranties, testimony, and results of laboratory tests, and may even suggest how a customer can test a product for himself. Copy that appeals to a prospect's emotions is called *human interest copy*. Such advertisements depend almost as much on pictures as on written copy. The human interest element is common today in magazine and television advertising.

Action. If an advertisement's purpose is to sell as well as to pave the way for a sale, it must induce the prospect to buy. This may be done in any one of these ways:

1. *Urge the prospect to act.* Near the end of the ad, there may be a direct command such as: "Order a box today" or "Telephone 274-6000 for delivery within 24 hours."
2. *Make it easy for the reader to act.* Printed ads frequently contain coupons which the reader can cut out, fill out, and send in to receive the advertised article.
3. *Offer the prospect an inducement to act.* Promises to refund a customer's money if he is not satisfied with the product may induce a prospect to act. Sometimes a premium is offered for paying in advance for goods rather than having them sent on approval.

4. *Induce a customer to ask for more information.* The purpose of an ad may be to induce the prospect to visit a store or manufacturer's place of business or to write or telephone for more information. With institutional advertising, the desired action may be simply a decision to visit the store in question or to examine the manufacturer's line when next in the market for the goods or services advertised.

CHECKING YOUR KNOWLEDGE

Vocabulary:

(1) institutional advertising
(2) promotional advertising
(3) pioneer advertisements
(4) reminder advertisements
(5) notice-of-sale advertisements
(6) reason-why copy
(7) human interest copy

Review questions:

1. How are the principles of good selling related to advertising and display?
2. What are the advantages and disadvantages of advertising in comparison with personal selling?
3. What are the objectives of advertising?
4. Why do the immediate purposes of some advertisements differ?
5. List the five requirements of effective advertising.

For discussion:

1. It has been said that advertising is an economic waste, that the costs of advertising are passed on to consumers in higher prices. Discuss the implications of this statement.
2. Do you think it would be possible to eliminate salesmen for certain types of goods with an effective advertising program? Why?

part B

newspaper advertising

There are many media that a selling firm can use to get its sales message to the buying public, but a large number of advertisers rely mainly on printed messages. Particularly for small advertisers, the newspaper is the most important advertising medium. Newspaper advertising brings quick results. The ads do not have to be planned far ahead, and the medium is a relatively inexpensive one for reaching a local area. Most newspaper advertising is directed to ultimate consumers.

SOME CHARACTERISTICS OF NEWSPAPERS

There are about 9,900 daily newspapers and about 9,000 weekly newspapers published in the United States. Of the 150 daily papers with the largest circulations, slightly more than half are evening papers. There are also about 550 Sunday papers that are published regularly. Among these daily, weekly, and Sunday newspapers are some printed in foreign languages and others devoted to business and financial affairs.

Universal Readership

In the United States, about 50 million newspapers are sold each day; and more than 47.5 million copies of Sunday papers are sold each week. Many of the metropolitan daily and Sunday papers have enormous circulations, not only in their home cities but also in cities and towns for hundreds of miles around. Boston papers, for example, circulate in all parts of New England except southern and western Connecticut.

These circulation figures indicate how universally the newspaper is read. They also suggest the varied character of newspaper readers. Rich and poor, old and young, men and women—all read the newspaper. Because of the wide variety of reader interests, the newspaper is best suited to advertising those products which are in general use. When the product appeals to a limited number of people, there is likely to be a waste of advertising money because only a small percentage of the readers are possible buyers. Other advertising media will be more productive for goods that appeal only to special groups.

Range of Appeal

While newspapers have something of interest to everyone, they do differ in the kinds of customers they reach. Readership is determined to a certain extent by the way the paper presents the news and its editorials. The advertiser must consider whether the readers of a particular newspaper are prospects for his product. Papers featuring sensational news are naturally read by a group of people different from those who read more conservative papers. A house selling for $70,000, for example, might be advertised in a paper read by well-to-do customers, while one selling for $18,000 would be advertised in a paper read by the general public.

Adults 21 Years & Over Who Read A Daily Newspaper Yesterday

BY EMPLOYMENT

Professional	88%
Managerial	91%
Clerical, Sales	85%
Skilled Labor	80%
Other Manual	71%
Farm	70%
Unemployed	68%

Source: Opinion Research Corp.

Adults 21 Years & Over Who Read A Daily Newspaper Yesterday

BY SEX

ALL ADULTS	78%
Men	78%
Women	78%

Source: Opinion Research Corp.

Adults 21 & Over Who Read A Daily Newspaper Yesterday

TOTAL U.S.	78%
By Region:	
Northeast	88%
North Central	79%
South	68%
West	80%
By City Size:	
Metropolitan Areas	82%
500,000 & Over	79%
50,000-499,999	81%
Under 50,000	84%
Non-Metropolitan Areas	71%
2,500-49,999	80%
Under 2,500	67%

Source: Opinion Research Corp.

Adults & Teenagers Who Read A Daily Newspaper Yesterday

BY AGE

12-20	69%
21-34	75%
35-49	79%
50-64	83%
65 & Over	74%

Source: Opinion Research Corp.

Adults 21 Years & Over Who Read A Daily Newspaper Yesterday

BY INCOME

Under $3,000	59%
$3,000-$4,999	70%
$5,000-$7,999	79%
$8,000-$9,999	88%
$10,000 & Over	89%

Source: Opinion Research Corp.

Adults 21 Years & Over Who Read A Daily Newspaper Yesterday

BY EDUCATION

Grade School or Less	62%
Some High School	75%
High School Graduate	85%
Some College	87%
College Graduate	90%

Source: Opinion Research Corp.

Bureau of Advertising, ANPA

Here are some statistics about the individuals who read daily newspapers. For many selling firms, the newspaper is the most important advertising medium, although they may use other media in combination with the newspaper.

Short Life

The advertiser must plan his newspaper ad knowing that the paper will be read hastily and perhaps even discarded after only the headlines have been read. This is especially true of the morning paper. Evening papers are more likely to be read by the entire family, and for that reason they carry a larger share of retail store advertising than do morning papers. Retail stores place about 60 percent of their newspaper advertising in evening papers, 20 percent in morning papers, and 20 percent in Sunday papers.

There is so much copy in the paper that only a small part can be read thoroughly. The advertiser must realize that unless his ad uses especially attractive features, it will suffer in the competition for attention. His message must be told in a concise and appealing way that will make an impression even when the advertisement is merely scanned.

ADVANTAGES OF NEWSPAPER ADVERTISING

Newspaper advertising offers the following advantages to the selling firm:

1. The newspaper is universally read.
2. Its circulation is largely localized, so it is the natural medium for retail stores.
3. It is an excellent medium for test sales-promotion campaigns.
4. It is a medium for obtaining quick sales.
5. The sales appeal may be made very timely.
6. The copy may be changed daily.
7. Planning advertising far in advance is not necessary. Although the copy may be submitted late at night, the newspaper containing the advertisement will be on the breakfast table the next morning.
8. Many newspapers in large urban areas assist the small merchant in the preparation of layout, copy, and illustrations.

KINDS OF NEWSPAPER ADVERTISING

There are two distinct kinds of newspaper advertising: display advertising and classified advertising.

Display Advertising

Display advertising, which is scattered throughout the pages of the newspaper, is placed by both local and national advertisers. About two-thirds of the advertising in daily papers is made up of the display advertising of local retail stores and of classified advertising. National advertising is often placed by manufacturers and producers in conjunction with other forms of advertising.

Newspapers are adaptable to local advertising campaigns from which quick results are desired. The *Chicago Tribune* points out that advertising instituted in 13 metropolitan distributing centers of this country reaches a majority of the country's buyers. Localized sales campaigns can be organized in one or many of these districts to supplement the advertising. Quick results over a large territory are thus obtained.

Classified Advertising

Classified advertising is grouped in certain sections of the paper and is thus distinguished from display advertising. Such groupings as "Help Wanted" and "Real Estate" are often made. The rate charged for classified advertising is less than that charged for display advertising. Classified advertisements represent a convenience to the reader and a money savings to the advertiser. The reader who is interested in a particular type of advertisement finds all ads of that type grouped together for him. The advertiser may thus use a very small advertisement that would be lost if it were placed among larger advertisements in the paper. The reader approaches the classified ad in a different frame of mind from that in which he approaches other ads in the paper. Since his attention is voluntary, the advertiser does not need to rely a great deal on unusual type, layout, or headlines to get the reader's attention.

NEWSPAPER SPACE AND RATES

In general, the cost of advertising space depends on the newspaper's circulation—on the number and character of people whom the advertisement is likely to reach. Newspapers make available to advertisers reports on their circulation. Nearly all reputable publishers have their circulation data audited by the Audit Bureau of Circulations. The advertiser is thus assured that the publishers' claims concerning their circulations are true.

Restrictions on Advertising Space

Most newspaper pages are made up of eight columns. The width of the columns and the number of lines on a page may vary from one newspaper to another. The average page contains something over 2,300 lines. The *advertising rate card* gives the exact dimensions of a paper, its advertising rates, and any restrictions that there may be on the size of advertisements. Some papers refuse to accept an advertisement extending over two or more columns unless it contains at least a specified number of lines. For example, a paper may not accept an advertisement three columns wide unless it is at least 50 lines deep.

The Agate Line and the Milline Rate

All measurement of advertising space is based on agate type and the agate line. The advertising rates of newspapers are usually quoted per *agate line,* which is 1/14th of an inch deep by one column in width. The advertiser is interested, however, in knowing how much he will get for his money; that is, how many people will see his advertisement if he purchases space in a given newspaper. The relation between these two factors—rate per agate line and circulation—determines the actual cost of an ad. To arrive at a single cost figure that can be compared with similar figures for other newspapers, these two figures may be combined in a formula:

$$\text{Milline Rate} = \frac{\text{Line Rate} \times 1{,}000{,}000}{\text{Actual Circulation}}$$

Top 25 Newspaper Advertisers

1967 Rank		1967 Expenditure	1966 Rank	1966 Expenditure	Percent Change
1	General Motors Corp.	$46,039,401	1	$58,848,332	—21.8
2	Ford Motor Co.	24,191,929	2	26,619,940	— 9.1
3	National Dairy Products	15,997,362	5	12,932,138	+23.7
4	Chrysler Corp.	13,539,645	3	17,111,923	—20.9
5	Distillers Corp.-Seagrams	12,730,497	4	13,988,861	— 9.0
6	Radio Corp. of America	10,856,245	6	8,682,265	+25.0
7	General Foods Corp.	6,686,779	11	5,747,286	+16.3
8	Goodyear Tire & Rubber Co.	6,446,847	10	5,870,113	+ 9.8
9	National Distillers	5,636,222	8	6,498,774	—13.3
10	Hiram Walker-Gooderham	5,598,483	12	4,729,449	+18.4
11	American Tobacco Co.	5,586,434	7	7,088,630	—21.2
12	Standard Brands Inc.	5,145,653	16	4,099,967	+25.5
13	Firestone Tire & Rubber Co.	5,133,705	14	4,331,129	+18.5
14	Columbia Broadcasting System	4,387,021	23	3,733,670	+17.5
15	Delta Air Lines	4,376,153	22	3,767,748	+16.1
16	United Air Lines	4,328,163	20	3,834,439	+12.9
17	Doubleday & Co.	4,210,498	29	3,201,217	+31.5
18	R. J. Reynolds Tobacco Co.	4,197,988	35	2,579,138	+62.8
19	Eastern Air Lines	3,888,549	34	2,627,802	+48.0
20	General Electric Co.	3,848,556	13	4,398,459	—12.5
21	American Airlines	3,845,935	17	3,979,774	— 3.4
22	Trans World Airlines	3,826,531	24	3,623,946	+ 5.6
23	Pan American World Airways	3,678,081	25	3,592,479	+ 2.4
24	Spencer Gifts Inc.	3,308,683	41	2,233,797	+48.1
25	Heublein Inc.	3,162,650	15	4,151,082	—23.8

Bureau of Advertising, ANPA

These 25 selling firms spent the most money on newspaper advertising in 1967. For each firm, what makes its products or services particularly well suited to newspaper advertising?

The *milline rate* is the cost of a single agate line of space adjusted to a newspaper circulation of one million. The advertising rates of any paper can be converted to a common standard: the rate for one line per one million circulation.

Suppose that Newspaper A has a base rate of 80 cents a line and a circulation of 445,000. Newspaper B has a base rate of $1.50 and a circulation of 950,000. Computation shows that the milline rate for Newspaper A is about $1.80, while that for Newspaper B is about

$1.58. If the quality of circulation is disregarded, it is evident that the paper which charges the higher price per line is actually the less expensive medium.

Preferred Positions

When an advertisement is submitted with no stipulation as to where it is to be placed in the paper, it is given *run-of-paper (ROP)* position. There are certain positions in the paper, however, where advertisements are more likely to be seen than in other positions. Since these preferred positions are more valuable to advertisers, the publisher charges more for them. The additional charges for the various preferred positions differ greatly. For some positions, the cost is two or three times as much as the base rate. Some preferred positions are:

1. Outside pages.
2. Special news pages (page 2 or 3).
3. Sports page.
4. Women's page.
5. Amusements page.
6. Top of a column.
7. Top of a column next to reading matter.
8. Next to and/or following reading matter.

By developing certain special sections or pages, newspaper publishers have tried to assure the advertiser that his display ad will not be overlooked by the natural prospects for his product. Sports, household, financial, real estate, textile, and hardware pages have been made interesting by articles and news items in these special fields. Advertisements related to these subjects are likely to be seen by the desired class of readers when placed on these pages. Thus, the advertiser is willing to pay an extra price for the preferred positions.

CHECKING YOUR KNOWLEDGE

Vocabulary:

(1) display advertising
(2) classified advertising
(3) advertising rate card
(4) agate line
(5) milline rate
(6) run-of-paper (ROP)

Review questions:

1. Why do small advertisers rely on the newspaper as their primary advertising medium?

2. Why is the newspaper best suited to advertising those products which are in general use?
3. How does the short life of a newspaper affect the advertiser in preparing his ad?
4. Why is the rate charged for classified advertising less than that charged for display advertising?
5. What determines the cost of advertising in a newspaper?

For discussion:

1. The newspaper advertising rate charged to national advertisers is usually higher than that charged to local advertisers. What might explain this?
2. Special sales are often featured in an advertising supplement to the regular edition of a newspaper. What advantages does this kind of newspaper advertising have?

part C

magazine advertising

Advertising in magazines gives prestige to the advertiser and permits an effective use of color. Magazines have a longer reading life than newspapers and make a good medium for educating consumers about a product or service. Although magazine advertising is used mostly by manufacturers of quality products, retail chains with outlets all over the country may also use this medium.

A wide variety of magazines, catering to the different interests and tastes of individual groups, are published every month. There are three main kinds of magazines: consumer magazines; class magazines; and trade, technical, and professional magazines. Some of these magazines are published weekly; others are published every two weeks; others are published monthly; and a few are published quarterly. Most magazines are sold and delivered by mail on an annual subscription basis, but single copies may also be obtained at newsstands.

CONSUMER MAGAZINES

Consumer magazines contain articles of interest to most ultimate consumers. Some articles deal with rather technical subjects but are written in layman's terms. The kinds of articles indicate that these magazines are excellent media for advertising products which are in general demand or for which general demand may be stimulated. *Look, Life, Newsweek,* and *Time* are examples of general consumer magazines.

There are other consumer magazines that carry articles which appeal to particular groups of ultimate consumers. These special articles attract a selected group of readers and make such magazines excellent media for advertising products for which the readers are natural prospects. Women's magazines, such as *Good Housekeeping, Family Circle, Vogue,* and *Ladies' Home Journal,* fall into this group. *House Beautiful* and *Fortune* may also be classified as special-interest consumer magazines.

The present advertising trend in consumer magazines is to devote more space to art, photography, design, color, white space, and larger illustrations. Less area is being devoted to copy. Also, there is a trend toward the use of multiple-page advertisements. Double-page advertisements are common; four-page spreads are not uncommon; and even eight-page spreads may be found.

CLASS MAGAZINES

The *class magazine* reaches a very select group of prospects. Class magazines include sportsmen's magazines, religious papers, automobile journals, farm magazines, and so on. *Farm Journal, Christian Herald, Catholic Digest,* and *Sports Illustrated* are class magazines. Since this kind of magazine usually has the confidence of its particular readers, its prestige is shared by the advertiser.

Farm magazines are, by the very nature of their circulation, important advertising media for many products. The buying power of the rural population cannot be overlooked, and perhaps the surest way to reach a large part of this group is through farm publications. There are now more than 200 farm publications, many of which are loyally read from cover to cover.

TRADE, TECHNICAL, AND PROFESSIONAL MAGAZINES

Trade, technical, and professional magazines are those publications that appeal to special business and professional groups. These include magazines for distributors of wool, hardware, or dry goods; magazines for railroad men, plumbers, or engineers; and magazines for professional people such as doctors, teachers, or lawyers. *Dry Goods Economist,*

Hardware Age, Chain Store Age, Iron Age, Journal of Accountancy, and *Journal of the American Medical Association* are examples of such magazines. The price of advertising space in trade, technical, and professional magazines may seem high in relation to their circulation. However, there is so little waste that this kind of magazine may well be the most productive medium for the advertiser whose product appeals to a limited group of people.

PLANNING THE MAGAZINE ADVERTISEMENT

In planning the magazine ad and choosing the proper magazine for the ad, the selling firm will want to consider the magazine's circulation, advertising rates, where to place the ad, and whether or not to use a preferred position.

Analyzing Circulation

The magazine publisher will usually furnish a prospective advertiser with an analysis of his magazine's circulation, showing the number of copies circulated, the geographical distribution, and sometimes even the occupations of readers. It is important to know what portion of the circulation is made up of regular or paid subscriptions and what portion represents free or sample copies. The advertiser should expect only small results from a magazine that has a large free list. One magazine publisher gives the following analysis of his reading audience:

1. 58.5% are college-educated.
2. 38% earn more than $10,000 a year.
3. 48% of the household heads are professional, technical, or managerial people.
4. 89% own their own one- or two-family homes.
5. 33% own two or more cars.
6. 26% have children in private schools or colleges.
7. 24% traveled outside the United States last year.

Advertising Rates

One page of black-and-white advertising may cost from $25,000 to $50,000 in widely circulated magazines such as *This Week, Parade, Reader's Digest, Life, Look, McCall's,* and *Ladies' Home Journal.* The first two are magazine supplements to Sunday papers that have wide circulation. Do the sales returns warrant such large expenditures? The fact that the same business firms use magazine space year after year and

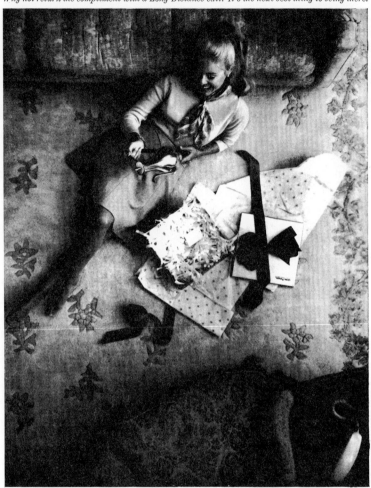

Why not return the compliment with a Long Distance call? It's the next best thing to being there.

A T & T

Some manufacturers advertise in all three kinds of magazines—consumer magazines, class magazines, and trade, technical, and professional magazines. This advertisement appeared in a consumer magazine, while the ad on the next page appeared in a class magazine directed to businessmen.

Stay on your toes and off your feet

(Selling by phone saves time, money, and shoe leather.)

With the Bell System network ready to work for you, there's less need to go gallivanting about the country. The calculated use of the telephone can make a super-salesman even more so. By phone, you can cover a broader market. Service small accounts. Trim travel time. Handle re-orders. And conserve time for business which actually requires your presence. A phone is just a phone until you learn how to use it.

A T & T

Study this ad in relation to the one on the opposite page. What similarities and differences do you notice in the sales messages of the two ads? What similarities and differences do you notice in the graphic appearance of the ads? How do you account for these differences?

sometimes must place their contracts two and a half years in advance to obtain a preferred position indicates that the expenditure is justified.

Two of the top three magazines in circulation are women's magazines. When one considers that household items make up a large percentage of the retail purchases in the country and that women buy most of these articles, it is evident that these specialized magazines are excellent advertising media. Through women's magazines, advertisers are able to reach a selected group of readers who are potential buyers of all types of household articles and clothing.

The true cost of any magazine advertisement depends on the number of persons exposed to the advertising copy. Assume that it costs $30,000 for one page of advertising in a popular magazine and that the magazine has a circulation of 6 million copies. When the cost of $30,000 a page is spread over 6 million copies, the unit cost to the advertiser is ½ cent for each subscriber or buyer of the magazine. Because most copies of a given magazine are read by more than one person, the cost per reader becomes even less.

Placing the Advertisement

Another important factor in determining advertising costs is the probability of the advertisement being seen. This probability depends on two things—circulation and position. The larger the circulation, other things being equal, the higher the advertising rate. Advertising has brought about a change in the arrangement and even in the size of many magazines. Formerly, most magazines contained fairly small pages divided into two columns, with advertisements grouped at the front and back of the magazine. Today, however, most of the popular magazines are printed on large pages, with three or four columns to the page. Since one or two columns of advertising appear on the same page with reading matter, the advertisements are brought near the reader's vision. This concession to the advertiser is not always pleasing to the reader, but it is justified because the advertiser pays the major cost of publishing the magazine. The advertisements, in turn, make it possible for the publisher to pay higher prices for manuscripts and thus obtain the services of better writers. Interest in these articles increases the total circulation of the magazine.

Preferred Positions

There are also certain preferred positions in magazines, for which higher rates are charged. Formerly, publishers classed the following as preferred positions: outside back cover, inside front cover, inside back cover, page facing the table of contents, page facing the inside front cover, and page facing the inside back cover. Since advertising is now distributed throughout magazines, the number of recognized preferred positions has been very much reduced. There are few magazines that now charge extra amounts for any page, except either of the back covers, the inside front cover, or an inserted page with color.

CHECKING YOUR KNOWLEDGE

Vocabulary:

(1) consumer magazine
(2) class magazine
(3) trade, technical, and professional magazines

Review questions:

1. What selling firms make the most use of magazine advertising?
2. What is the present advertising trend in consumer magazines?
3. Why is there little waste of the advertising dollar spent in trade, technical, and professional magazines?
4. Explain the factors that the true cost of magazine advertising depends upon.
5. Why is less emphasis now placed on preferred positions in magazine advertising?

For discussion:

1. The *Reader's Digest* carries a large amount of advertising, yet its page size is relatively small when compared with that of *Life* or *Look*. How do you account for advertisers' willingness to purchase space in *Reader's Digest* when considerable emphasis is placed on a large page size and much white space in modern magazine advertising?
2. Some advertisers buy space in a regional issue of a nationally circulated magazine. Such advertising appears only in the geographic region of the country in which that issue of the magazine is circulated. Do you think this is a good advertising practice? Why?

part D

direct-mail advertising

You or your parents probably receive some kind of direct-mail advertising every day. Enclosed with a department store's monthly charge account statement may be a separate notice of a furniture sale. This is direct-mail advertising. Or you might find in the mailbox a booklet inviting you to join a record club. This is also direct-mail advertising.

Direct mail is the third most important advertising medium, in terms of advertising expenditures. Newspapers are first, of course, then television. Direct-mail advertising includes all printed materials containing a sales message that are sent directly to selected prospects. The most commonly used kinds of direct-mail advertising are sales letters, folders, broadsides, booklets, mailing cards, catalogs, envelope stuffers, and brochures. Because the sales letter is such an important advertising medium, it will be discussed separately in Part E.

ADVANTAGES OF DIRECT MAIL

Almost every kind of selling firm—from the manufacturer of industrial air conditioners to the local beauty shop—can use direct-mail advertising. Direct mail can be sophisticated, or it can be nothing more than a mimeographed bulletin. Here are some of the reasons why selling firms like to use direct mail:

1. It can be directed more specifically to certain individuals or groups than can any other form of advertising.
2. It can be made as personal in appeal as the seller cares to make it.
3. It does not compete as directly with other selling messages for customer attention as is true with other media, such as television.
4. It has no limitations on size or length.
5. It can be timed to reach customers with more accuracy and less wasted effort than is true of most other media.
6. It can be followed up with related mailings if the first mailing does not produce results.
7. It is relatively inexpensive to produce.

Direct-mail advertising has so many advantages that too many businesses use it, and this has become its major disadvantage. The volume of direct mail has increased to such an extent during the last few years that, on the average, more than a million pieces are mailed every hour in the United States. Business and ultimate consumers are so accustomed to receiving "junk mail" that they often toss it into the wastebasket without opening the envelope. If a selling firm can make its direct-mail pieces original enough to attract customer attention, direct-mail advertising can be an extremely effective medium.

THE DIRECT-MAIL CAMPAIGN

Once a selling firm has decided to use direct mail, either alone or in combination with other media, there are certain basic decisions that must be made.

Preliminary Questions

The seller must set down some general policies when he is formulating his direct-mail campaign. Some questions he might ask to help establish these policies are:

1. How will the mailing list be prepared? What names will make up the list, or what groups will be represented? From what sources will it be compiled? How often should the list be revised?

Flowers make a woman feel special. And what makes a mother feel more special on her day than roses?
On Monday, Tuesday, and Wednesday (May 6, 7, and 8), you can buy a dozen of our regularly priced $12.50 long-stemmed roses for $9.50. Just call us at 331-6161 and place your order. We'll deliver our garden-fresh roses to your mother in time for Mother's Day.
Make your mother feel special.
KUCIA'S FLOWER BOX -- 2950 Hart Lane

Mailing cards are one of the least expensive forms of direct mail. They may be sent as self-mailers or enclosed in envelopes along with other sales-promotion materials or bills. Single cards measure 3 by 5 inches. Double cards measure 6 by 5 inches and are then folded to the 3-by-5-inch size.

2. How much should the campaign accomplish? Must it make direct sales or just locate prospects? Will it try to educate the prospect, to build prestige for the firm, or to seek acceptance of a product or service?
3. How much money will be spent on the campaign? What expenditure is needed to get the desired results successfully and profitably?
4. How many mailings will be needed? Does the sales problem call for one mailing, a group of mailings, or mailings sent out at intervals of three, four, or more weeks?
5. What sales appeal will be used? Is there a seasonal factor or other time element that may influence the presentation of the product or service?
6. How will the pieces be mailed? Will they be sent by first-class or third-class mail? Will they be sent in envelopes, or will they be self-mailers?
7. What kind of paper, printing, and design will be used?

The Mailing List

Earlier you learned about the need for a seller to keep his prospect list up-to-date. A *mailing list* is a form of prospect list. It is prepared by using some of the same prospect sources you learned about in Chapter 8. The mailing list must be kept current. If it is not, much money will be wasted in sending direct-mail pieces to people who have changed addresses, died, or, for other reasons, are no longer prospects.

Purchasing lists from list brokers is perhaps the most common way of obtaining mailing lists. Many list brokers sell copies of their lists on sheets, cards, or gummed stickers. Certain other brokers offer their lists on a one-time rental basis for "addressing only." Under such circumstances, the addressing of the individual direct-mail pieces is done by the list broker. The complete mailing is guaranteed by a receipt signed by the local postmaster when the list broker places the contracted number of pieces in the mail.

Scheduling the Mailing

Selling firms may choose from three general procedures for scheduling mailings. Sometimes they make a single mailing to a single list of prospects. A department store, for instance, may send a mailing card announcing a special sale of oriental rugs. The prospects who receive the card may be those persons who have recently made substantial furniture purchases in the store.

A second method of scheduling is to make four or five mailings designed to sell a single product or service. Magazine publishers often use this technique. They may want to encourage new prospects to subscribe, or they may want to stimulate current or former subscribers to renew their subscriptions. If the first mailing brings no results, other mailings are made. Each mailing will have a slightly different appearance and appeal from previous mailings, but its purpose will be the same.

Selling firms may also establish a series of mailings on a regularly scheduled basis. Grocery stores who send out folders every Wednesday or Thursday to promote their weekly specials are using this type of scheduling.

PREPARING DIRECT-MAIL ADVERTISING

Like other forms of advertising, direct-mail pieces employ many of the same techniques used in personal selling.

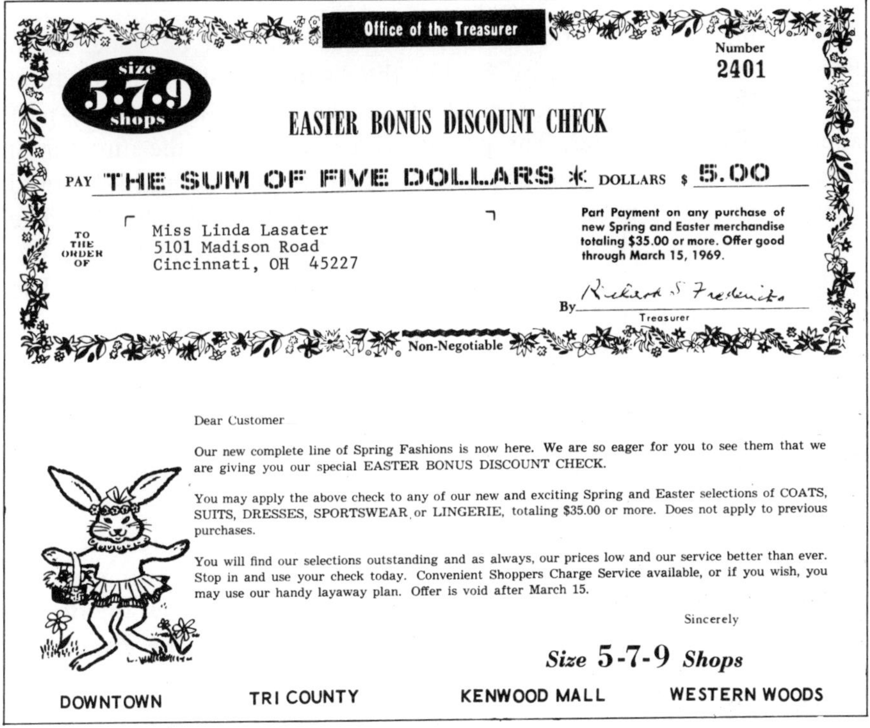

Office of the Treasurer

size 5•7•9 shops

Number 2401

EASTER BONUS DISCOUNT CHECK

PAY THE SUM OF FIVE DOLLARS ✱ DOLLARS $ 5.00

TO THE ORDER OF Miss Linda Lasater
5101 Madison Road
Cincinnati, OH 45227

Part Payment on any purchase of new Spring and Easter merchandise totaling $35.00 or more. Offer good through March 15, 1969.

By Richard S. Fredericks
Treasurer

Non-Negotiable

Dear Customer

Our new complete line of Spring Fashions is now here. We are so eager for you to see them that we are giving you our special EASTER BONUS DISCOUNT CHECK.

You may apply the above check to any of our new and exciting Spring and Easter selections of COATS, SUITS, DRESSES, SPORTSWEAR or LINGERIE, totaling $35.00 or more. Does not apply to previous purchases.

You will find our selections outstanding and as always, our prices low and our service better than ever. Stop in and use your check today. Convenient Shoppers Charge Service available, or if you wish, you may use our handy layaway plan. Offer is void after March 15.

Sincerely

Size 5-7-9 *Shops*

DOWNTOWN TRI COUNTY KENWOOD MALL WESTERN WOODS

Size 5 • 7 • 9 Shops, Cincinnati

This direct-mail piece represents a single mailing to a single list of prospects. It is actually a combination of a coupon mailing and a sales letter. Coupons are often used for single mailings. They can be quite effective, but the important thing to remember in using them is that the value of the coupons must be high enough to stimulate recipients to visit the selling firm.

Attracting Attention

The first thing that the direct-mail piece must do is attract the prospect's attention. If it cannot do this, it may be destined for the garbage can. High quality paper, high quality printing, and color are three important ways of attracting favorable attention. The direct-mail piece must look important. It must make the prospect think that it is worth his while to study it. Gimmicks are widely used to attract attention. Some sellers have pasted a couple of pennies onto the direct-mail piece so that the pennies show through a window in the envelope. These pieces are almost always opened and read. The gimmicks that can be used to attract attention are limited only by the imagination of the person preparing the direct-mail piece.

Arousing Interest

Arousing interest in the direct-mail piece can best be done, as in all other forms of selling, by having the "you" attitude. Information about the article or service must tie in with the interests or past experiences of the reader. The person who is preparing the direct-mail piece should know the general interests of his prospects, and he should structure the sales message so that it fits these general interests. The real "you" attitude is expressed, not through any special words, but rather through keeping the reader's interests constantly in mind. The writer must put himself and his firm in the background and put his readers' needs and wants in the foreground.

Creating Desire

As in personal selling, desire may be created by appealing to the prospect's reason or emotion. The first method of appealing to reason is to present facts and figures on the product. Statistics must be used carefully, though, because they are likely to be uninteresting to the reader. Once he sees them, he may skip over them or throw the direct-mail piece away unread. If a great many statistics are to be given, it is best to print them in a booklet separate from the main direct-mail piece.

The second method of appealing to a prospect's reason is to demonstrate the article. A paper supplier may enclose paper samples in his direct-mail piece, with instructions for testing the paper's strength. A seller of clothing may enclose cloth samples. There is obviously limited use of this method, since many articles cannot be demonstrated by mail. Direct-mail writers may also appeal to prospects' reason by offering warranties and testimonials from recognized authorities.

Ordinarily the writer can appeal to his readers' emotions by picturing the article in use. This requires imagination, and you can probably think of many instances in which direct-mail pieces have appealed to prospects' emotions. Social service agencies raising funds for philanthropic purposes use this kind of appeal.

Securing Action

To stimulate the reader to act—whether to order goods, visit a store, or request a salesman to call—several devices may be used:

1. *Urge the reader to act.* Sometimes prospects may be urged to act by commands given toward the end of the message: "Call our office while you think of it." Many people dislike being commanded, though, so writers generally make suggestions rather than commands: "Only ten days left to take advantage of the August sale."
2. *Make it easy for the reader to act.* If the writer wants the reader to place an order, a large card that merely requires a yes or no response, the affixing of a stamp, or the insertion of an enclosed token in the correct slot may be sent with the direct-mail piece. A business-reply envelope makes it easy for the prospect to take action. Sometimes an order blank will be enclosed.
3. *Offer inducements to act.* Writers of direct-mail pieces may offer an inducement to act, such as a promise to refund the reader's money if he is not satisfied with the article or calling his attention to the fact that the article will go up in price after a certain date. In their direct-mail pieces, banks may offer free gifts to all new customers who open accounts with a stipulated minimum amount.

CHECKING YOUR KNOWLEDGE

Vocabulary:

mailing list

Review questions:

1. What are the most commonly used kinds of direct-mail advertising?
2. Why is direct mail such a popular advertising medium?
3. What is the greatest disadvantage of direct mail?
4. Explain three methods of scheduling mailings.
5. How do direct-mail pieces employ many of the same techniques used in personal selling?

For discussion:

1. Do you think that gimmicks placed inside a direct-mail piece are generally effective in obtaining additional sales? Why?

2. Considering the relative advantages of direct mail and personal salesmanship, which would you advocate using in selling the following items? (a) electrical wiring to contractors; (b) overseas airplane trips to teachers; (c) air conditioning units to homeowners; and (d) photocopying equipment to office managers. Explain your answers.

part E

the sales letter

Sales letters are used at times by almost every type of selling firm. Ultimate consumers most commonly receive sales letters from: (1) retail stores; (2) mail-order houses, usually selling a narrow line of merchandise such as novelties; (3) investment institutions, offering recommendations on securities to be bought and sold; (4) accident and health insurance companies; (5) publishers of periodicals, soliciting subscriptions and renewals; and (6) social service agencies, requesting contributions to worthwhile causes. A sales letter may try to complete a sale without a salesman's intervention, or it may be designed just to make a favorable impression which will lead to a salesman-customer contact.

INDIVIDUAL LETTERS VERSUS FORM LETTERS

Sometimes a special sales letter may be written to each prospect, just as you would write a personal letter to a friend. The selling points and the language of individual letters can be adapted to the reader, and such letters are often extremely effective. Obviously, though, writing a special letter to each prospect when there are hundreds or even thousands of prospects is too difficult and too costly for selling firms. Especially in selling low-priced articles, businesses are more likely to send the same sales letter to all the people on the prospect list. This kind of letter is called a *form letter.*

Suppose that Byron Rogers is a prospect for an automobile. The most effective sales letter that could be written to him would be one based on a study of his interests, needs, and financial status and written to him personally. But suppose that Rogers is a physician. Then he could be sent a form letter prepared for all physicians in his city.

This letter would emphasize the features of the car that would meet the needs of physicians in general. This form letter would not be so effective as the first letter, since Rogers' needs are bound to be slightly different from those of other physicians. A form letter might also be prepared for all the people living in Rogers' suburb. This would be the least effective letter, for its sales message would have to be very general. It might not appeal to Rogers as an individual or as a physician, although it would probably appeal to some people who received it.

Individual sales letters are more difficult and costly to produce than are form letters, but they get better results because they appeal to the individual needs of readers.

PREPARING THE SALES LETTER

In writing the sales letter, there are certain general rules to follow:

1. Use attractive and appropriate stationery.
2. Set up the letter in a generally accepted business form.
3. Write with the "you" attitude.
4. Write as though you were talking to the reader face to face.
5. Suggest the action that the reader should take.
6. Be friendly in tone.
7. Use a postscript occasionally, to command attention for an important point.

The mechanics of a good letter must not be slighted: paper of good quality, a well-printed letterhead; clear and legible typing or printing; balance in the arrangement of the parts of the letter; liberal margins; and correct grammar. These elements should be combined so as to give the sales letter a personality that will bring the desired results.

The Envelope

Probably the first thing that a reader notices when he receives a sales letter is the quality of paper in the envelope and letter. The envelope should give the immediate impression that it contains an important personal letter. The reader's name and address should be neatly typed, carefully arranged, and correctly spelled. The selling firm's address should be printed in the envelope's upper left-hand corner.

The Letterhead

A reader's attention is further attracted by the letterhead of the sales letter. Some companies try to include too much information in their letterheads. A letterhead should contain only the information that

"I'd sure hate to be in our creditors' shoes *this* month!"

Cartoon from a magazine that, in other respects, is dead serious: **Consumer Reports,** the non-profit journal that's concerned exclusively with saving you money on everything you buy.
This letter offers you a rare chance to subscribe at considerable savings, and in the bargain, to acquire a valuable book, **FREE.**

Dear Consumer:

If you pride yourself on prudent management of household finances ... but if the first of the month, nevertheless, always seems darker than the other 29 or 30 days ... welcome to

CONSUMER REPORTS

... a unique magazine dedicated to helping you get the most out of every dollar you spend. A monthly magazine, timely as tomorrow's newest products. And a nonprofit magazine, beholden to no one.

Consumer Reports calls spades spades, names names, lets chips fall where they may (and do.) Anyone past the age of buying penny candy knows not to expect the picture on the package to be a replica of what's inside... not to depend on the number of servings described on the label...not to expect a bargain just because of a "cents off" claim on the package... not to count on finding anything really new in the package boasting "New!" in big type, or even "New! New!"

But it takes a lawyer, for example, to figure out what a guarantee really covers. A research chemist to determine whether "additives" make any difference. An automotive engineer to help you decide between those two handsome cars, Ford's Mustang and Chevrolet's Camaro. A mathematician

Consumer Reports

This is the first page of an effective form sales letter. It is effective partly because it attracts the customer's attention immediately with the cartoon. The "you" attitude is evidenced in the first paragraph, and the letter is written in a spritely, conversational style.

is necessary, just as specialty shops may display only one or two choice items in their store windows. The letterhead may include the firm's name, address, telephone number, and, in some cases, the name of the selling department. The content and style of a letterhead should reflect the personality of the firm using it.

Using the Prospect's Name

Many progressive businesses try to personalize correspondence even when they are sending out form letters. Machines are available that can print each recipient's name and address not only on the envelope and in the inside address but also in the salutation and body of the letter. Using the prospect's name attracts favorable attention that might not otherwise be attracted. It is seldom wise, though, to include the reader's name more than once in the body of a letter, for this would look like insincerity.

Opening Remarks

Just as the salesman attracts attention through the opening remarks of his sales talk, the sales letter writer attracts attention through the opening remarks of his letter. Such shopworn expressions as "Here is an opportunity to save money" or "May I have your attention for a few minutes?" will never stimulate interest. Here are some opening remarks that can effectively attract attention and stimulate interest:

1. A sentence that relates to the prospect's needs: "Now that you have nearly finished building your home, you are probably thinking of shrubbery to plant around it."
2. A question: "Does the approach of Christmas find you with enough money to buy gifts?"
3. A reference to a current event: "More than one-third of the property owners involved in last week's fire had insufficient insurance."
4. A testimonial: " 'The ten days spent at the LaPorte Hotel were ten days of rest, comfort, and recreation,' said one of our last year's patrons in making a reservation for this summer."
5. A sentence that condenses the whole thought of the letter: "A made-to-order shirt that combines comfort, style, and moderate price—that is what you get when you buy a Rand Custom shirt."

Length of Sentences and the Letter

The meaning of each sentence should be so clear that if the reader were to stop at any point, he would have an understanding of the sales message up to that point. Generally, sentences should not be more than

35 words long. In letters being sent to a cross-section of the general buying public, sentences should not be longer than 15 words.

A sales letter should seldom be more than one page long. The average reader's interest lags unless he quickly sees how the article or service offered can meet his needs. Technical or professional people will read longer letters if they recognize that the product or service will make their work easier or more profitable. Some firms selling exclusively by direct mail find that their customers will read long letters if they tell a story about the article offered.

The Signature

A personal signature at the end of a sales letter differentiates it from a mere announcement. A hand-written signature is, of course, essential for individual sales letters and highly desirable for form letters when a small mailing is to be made. If hundreds of letters are to be sent out, however, the writer can have an engraved plate of his signature prepared. This gives an imprint that is difficult to distinguish from an original signature.

Enclosures

Many writers try to give too many details in a sales letter. The reader receives a two- or three-page letter, glances at it, sees that it will take him some time to read it, and throws it away unread. A better plan is to keep the sales letter short and to give details about the article in a separate pamphlet.

EVALUATING THE SUCCESS OF SALES LETTERS

A sure way to build skill in preparing sales letters is to study those letters that have failed to produce sales results and those that have succeeded. After the reason for failure has been uncovered, the selling firm can avoid repeating that failure. If the success of a particular letter has been established, letters similar to it may be effectively used in the future.

Cameron McPherson, writing in *Printed Salesmanship,* gives the following five tests for letters that have failed:

1. Was the right appeal used? Do you really know, or do you just think you know?
2. Have you used the right approach? Did the opening paragraph of your letter "touch a nerve"? Or did it generalize about something

that might be very interesting to you but was of only minor interest to the person to whom you were trying to make a sale?

3. Was your "build-up" effective? In other words, did you set up your letter so that you would make the prospect want what you were selling before you asked him to buy? Having made him want it, did you make it easy for him to say "yes"?
4. Was the letter really convincing or, without giving supporting evidence, did you expect the prospect to believe what you said?
5. Did its appearance stamp the letter as important; or did a cheap envelope, a smudgy address, and indifferent spelling brand it as a poor circular letter?

CHECKING YOUR KNOWLEDGE

Vocabulary:

form letter

Review questions:

1. From what selling firms do ultimate consumers most often receive sales letters?
2. List the general rules that should be followed in writing the sales letter.
3. What are the first things a reader notices when he receives a sales letter?
4. What kinds of expressions should be avoided in the opening remarks of a sales letter?
5. How can selling firms evaluate the success of sales letters?

For discussion:

1. Do you think that enclosures strengthen the sales letter or weaken its effectiveness? Support your answer with examples.
2. What guides would you follow in restricting the length of sales letters?
3. "One should not tell everything in the sales letter; leave something to the reader's imagination." What part does this statement play in the writing of a sales letter? Give an example of how this could be done and tell why it is important.

BUILDING YOUR SKILLS

Improving your English:

On a separate sheet of paper, write the correct pronoun to be used in each of the following sentences.

1. (Who, Whom) was promoted to the position of sales manager?
2. Neither Mary nor (I, me) could foresee the response to the small ad.

3. New layouts were given to Ben and (I, me) this morning.
4. The new milline rate was discussed with (they, them) and the advertising assistants.
5. The Bruning account was given to (he, him) and Michael.
6. It was (he, him) who insisted that we advertise in the new trade magazine.
7. (She, Her) and John have prepared a sketch of the February window display.
8. The head cashier provided the necessary information for (we, us) early shoppers.
9. Promotional literature was mailed to (they, them) and the office managers.
10. The gift subscription for (she, her) and Allen was continued.

Improving your arithmetic:

The problems below involve more than one step in obtaining their solution; show each step used.

1. For his efforts in selling a data processing installation, a sales engineer received $960. This represented a 5% commission, based on the selling price of the installation. What was the selling price of the installation?
2. At Midwest College, the September enrollment of 2,820 students represented a decrease of 6% from the previous September's enrollment. What was the September enrollment of the previous year?
3. On January 2, 1969, Adele Jones deposited $2,000 in a savings account at First Federal Savings and Loan. First Federal pays interest at the rate of 5% per year on deposits of $2,000 or more. Interest is paid on the account each six months and is added to the current balance. On July 1, 1969, Adele deposited an additional $500. How much money did she have on deposit on January 2, 1970, if no withdrawals had been made during the year and no deposits had been made after July 1?

Improving your research skills:

1. For each of the items listed below, select an advertising medium that is especially well suited to promoting it. In a report, write your media selections and your reasons for selecting each medium.

(a) Movie	(f) Clock radio
(b) Fresh seafood	(g) Breakfast cereal
(c) Costume jewelry	(h) Furniture
(d) Automobile	(i) Fishing tackle
(e) Printing press	(j) Chemical equipment

2. Bring to class five newspaper or magazine advertisements. Be prepared to tell how each advertisement attracts attention, what kind of action it is trying to secure, and how it attempts to induce this action.

3. Prepare a newspaper advertisement based upon the merchandise information given on page 468. Assume that Trimbels Department Store is a large store selling popular-priced merchandise and that it has several suburban branches. Decide on the number and depth of columns the ad will consume. You do not have to draw an illustration of the swimming pool, but you should indicate where the illustration is to be placed on the advertising layout sheet. You may write your advertising copy on a separate sheet of paper, also indicating on the layout sheet where the copy is to be inserted.
4. Select one of the following articles: (a) residential humidifiers, (b) gift wrapping paper, (c) overhead garage doors, (d) college class rings, and (e) cat and dog food. Prepare a sales letter for the article you have chosen, keeping in mind the principles you learned in Part E.

APPLYING YOUR KNOWLEDGE

Case problems:

1. Assume that you are employed in the advertising department of the Sparky Electronic Company, manufacturers of radios, stereos, and television sets. You are told to prepare a 50-word advertisement for a new transistor radio soon to be put on the market. What type of advertisement would this be? What information would you include in such an advertisement?
2. Frances Barnett opened a small dress shop in a neighborhood shopping district of a large city. Window displays and word-of-mouth advertising failed to produce satisfactory sales, so she investigated the following advertising media available to her: metropolitan newspapers, neighborhood papers, handbills, direct mail, follow-up telephone calls to infrequent customers, low-cost form telegrams. What media should Miss Barnett use to increase the sales of her dress shop? Explain.

Continuing project:

In your manual, tell which advertising media would be most effective for your product. Evaluate all media carefully and give reasons for your selections. Rough out a newspaper advertisement for your product, including both copy and a rough sketch of any illustration. Prepare a form sales letter for your product and outline the direct-mail campaign you might employ.

Extra credit:

In the library, study the ads appearing in consumer magazines, class magazines, and trade, technical, and professional magazines. Write a report on the similarities and differences you find in these ads. Consider such things as selling appeals, the kind of action the ads are trying to induce, and the visual appearance of each.

TRIMBELS DEPARTMENT STORE
Merchandise Information for Advertising

Date of Ad. 6/7/ Dept. No. 123

Size of Ad. 600 agate lines (shape optional) Paper Times

DEPARTMENT NAME AND LOCATION: Adult Games - 6th Floor

STORES: New York, Westchester, Hempstead, Newark

Day Selling Is to Begin: June 7

On Sale Until: All summer long

Name of Merchandise: Swimming Pool

Most Important Benefit to Customer: Fun for family all summer long

OTHER SELLING POINTS:

2 G. E. filter pump--1,850 gallons per hour

3 Construction--heavy gauge vinyl liner, double ladder, diving platform, galvanized steel wall, 2-inch tubular supports, 1-inch tubular frame top and bottom

4 Size: 4 feet deep by 18 feet in diameter

5 Comes with four 6-foot air mattresses

Selling Price $199.99 Comparative Term and Price Requested None

Colors Wall is in colorful stripes--blue and green

Store Hours Fri. 10 A.M. - 9 P.M. Sat. 10. A.M. - 6 P.M.

Mail and Phone Yes ☒ No ☐ Coupon Yes ☐ No ☒
Credit Statement Yes ☒ No ☐

Art Information Show pool plus accessories

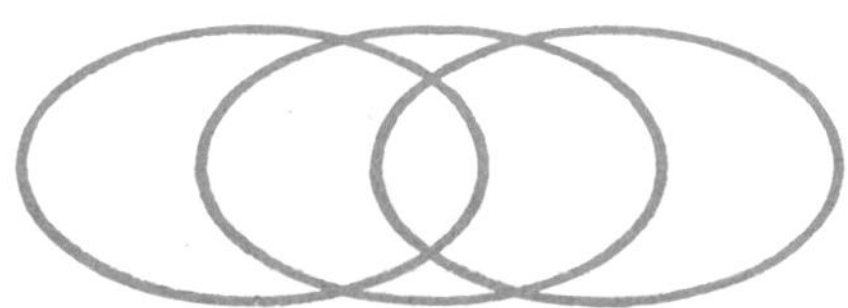

chapter 14

broadcast advertising and merchandise display

KEY QUESTIONS

A Why is television a more important advertising medium today than is radio?

B Are the principles of personal selling followed in preparing and evaluating a broadcast advertisement?

C What are the major considerations in scheduling broadcast advertising?

D In planning window and interior displays, what important factors should sellers consider?

E Does self-service merchandising in certain stores eliminate the need for personal customer attention by a salesman?

part A

status of the broadcast industry

The inventions that resulted in today's mass selling are radio and television. The techniques of transmitting speech and music over radio waves were developed early in this century, but radio did not become an important advertising medium until the 1930's. Television was not perfected in the laboratory until the 1930's, and sets were not marketed to the consumer until after World War II. Television's ability to carry a message to the eye as well as the ear and to reach many more people than even a newspaper can reach has made it a major advertising medium. In terms of expenditures, television surpassed radio advertising some years ago and is now second in usage only to newspapers.

THE STATUS OF RADIO

Ultimate consumers own nearly 200 million radios, including millions of transistor radios carried about in handbags and pockets. More than 65 million automobile radios are in use, and some 11 million radios are used in public places such as restaurants. There are more than 6,000 radio stations in this country; the number of TV stations is only about one-tenth as great. These statistics help to show that, in spite of the tremendous growth of television, radio is still an important advertising medium. Radio is listened to by millions of people who have neither the time nor the desire to watch television at certain times of the day. For many people, the radio is a companion that keeps them in touch with news and the kinds of music they enjoy. Radio advertising can be transmitted while the listener is doing other things. The housewife who listens to a musical program while doing household chores, the mechanic who follows a baseball game while working in the shop, the student who keeps up-to-date on the latest hit records while eating lunch—each is a potential customer that radio advertising can easily reach.

Radio advertising does not reach a selected consumer group; it reaches everyone who happens to have his set tuned to a particular station at a particular time. Thus, radio selling messages must be geared to the

Top 25 National-Regional Spot Radio Advertisers

1967 Rank	Company	Estimated Gross Time Expenditure, 1967 (in millions)	1963 Rank
1	General Motors	$19.3	1
2	Ford Motor Co.	12.8	3
3	Chrysler Corp.	11.7	2
4	Coca-Cola Co. Bottlers	9.2	5
5	Pepsico, Inc.	7.9	13
6	R. J. Reynolds Tobacco Co.	6.3	4
7	American Home Products Corp.	5.7	28
8	American Telephone & Telegraph Co.	5.0	9
9	American Oil Co.	4.6	10
10	Joseph Schlitz Brewing Co.	4.4	41
11	Anheuser-Busch	4.3	6
12	Campbell Soup Co.	4.0	18
13	Royal Crown Cola Co. & Bottlers	3.3	*
14	Pan American World Airways	3.3	*
15	Colgate-Palmolive Co.	3.2	*
16	Humble Oil & Refining Co.	3.2	17
17	P. Lorillard Co.	3.1	14
18	American Tobacco Co.	3.1	7
19	Falstaff Brewing Co.	2.9	38
20	General Foods Corp.	2.7	*
21	Sun Oil Co.	2.7	*
22	Canada Dry Corp. & Bottlers	2.5	*
23	Bristol-Myers Co.	2.5	40
24	Beneficial Finance Co.	2.4	23
25	Carling Brewing Co.	2.3	8

* Not included in top 50 advertisers in 1963

Advertising Age

Why do you think these selling firms find spot radio advertising so effective? How do you account for the changes in ranking from 1963 to 1967 and also for the fact that six of these top 25 advertisers were not even listed in the top 50 in 1963?

general interests of many diverse groups. The radio is well suited to advertising products for which a general demand exists, such as coffee. It is also well suited to short advertising announcements, especially of newsworthy events such as a special department-store sale. Firms selling services often use radio advertising because most services do not lend themselves to visual appeals. Radio advertising is not suitable for any product which must be seen to develop interest and create desire for the product.

THE STATUS OF TELEVISION

More than 94 percent of the homes in this country have one or more television sets. The firms which spend the most money on TV advertising are manufacturers of national brands, including soaps and cleansers, food products, tobacco products, drug products, beverage products, and automobiles. Local retailers have used TV advertising sparingly, giving it less than 10 percent of their average promotional dollar. Most of them cannot afford to spend huge sums to promote individual articles, as national advertisers can. However, some large retailers have found TV to be an effective medium. Sears, Roebuck, for example, increased the number of its weekly television ads more than 500 percent from 1964 to 1967. As many retail stores extend their trading areas, TV gives them a chance to reach more people than any other medium can reach and to do more dramatic things than any other medium can do.

Kinds of Television Programs

The kinds of TV programs currently provided by stations and networks are:

1. Adventure.
2. Children's shows.
3. Comedy, evening.
4. Comedy, daytime.
5. Documentary.
6. Drama, evening.
7. Drama, daytime.
8. Feature films.
9. Games, evening.
10. Games, daytime.
11. News, evening.
12. News, daytime.
13. Public affairs, evening.
14. Public affairs, daytime.
15. Religious.
16. Sports.
17. Variety, evening.
18. Variety, daytime.
19. Westerns.
20. One-time specials.

The currently most popular shows include feature films, evening variety shows, evening comedy shows, westerns, one-time specials, evening dramas, adventure, evening game shows, and sports events. Manufacturers of national brands can afford to sponsor these popular programs, but local sellers must depend mainly on the sponsorship of

Top 25 Television Advertisers

1967 Rank	Company	Estimated Gross Time Expenditure, 1967 (in millions)	1963 Rank
1	Procter & Gamble Co.	$192.1	1
2	General Foods Corp.	93.8	5
3	Bristol-Myers Co.	74.3	4
4	Colgate-Palmolive Co.	71.1	2
5	American Home Products Corp.	57.8	3
6	R. J. Reynolds Tobacco Co.	57.2	7
7	Lever Brothers Co.	56.0	6
8	American Tobacco Co.	45.8	16
9	Gillette Co.	43.1	11
10	General Mills, Inc.	42.6	9
11	Warner-Lambert Pharmaceutical Co.	42.5	18
12	General Motors	41.8	10
13	Coca-Cola Co. Bottlers	41.3	13
14	Sterling Drug, Inc.	39.0	23
15	Kellogg Co.	37.8	12
16	Philip Morris, Inc.	36.6	14
17	Liggett & Myers Tobacco Co.	33.8	19
18	P. Lorillard Co.	33.3	17
19	Brown & Williamson Tobacco Co.	33.2	22
20	Miles Laboratories, Inc.	30.8	15
21	Chrysler Corp.	28.4	34
22	Ford Motor Co.	27.6	25
23	Pepsico, Inc.	25.5	31
24	S. C. Johnson & Sons, Inc.	25.4	30
25	Quaker Oats Co.	25.1	*

* Not included in top 50 advertisers in 1963

Advertising Age

Compare this table with the one on page 471. Only one firm had the same ranking in both tables—the R. J. Reynolds Tobacco Company. The leader in television advertising expenditures is not even listed among the top 25 spot radio advertisers. Can you explain such variations in the two tables?

local news programs and on brief announcements between sponsored programs.

Criticisms of Television Advertising

Television sales messages have received a lot of public criticism in recent years. Commercials have been called everything from "corny" to "unbelievable." Some of the so-called proofs of product performance have been phony. The result is a fatigued viewer, who may not turn off his TV set during a commercial but who is oblivious to the sales message he sees and hears. Persons in the advertising trade call this reaction CEBUS—Confirmed Exposure But Unconscious. To overcome this reaction, television ad men are using all kinds of devices—satire, gags, skits, slapstick comedy—to catch attention and sustain interest. The real problem, though, is not getting the customer to look at the commercial but getting him to associate the commercial with a particular brand. Television can be a potent selling tool, but only if viewers pay attention to what they see and hear and then develop a favorable impression of the product or service being advertised. Honesty and sincerity must be combined with showmanship.

KINDS OF BROADCAST TIME

A selling firm may buy two basic kinds of radio or television time—sponsored programs and spot announcements. With a *sponsored program,* a selling firm buys time for the entire program and intersperses

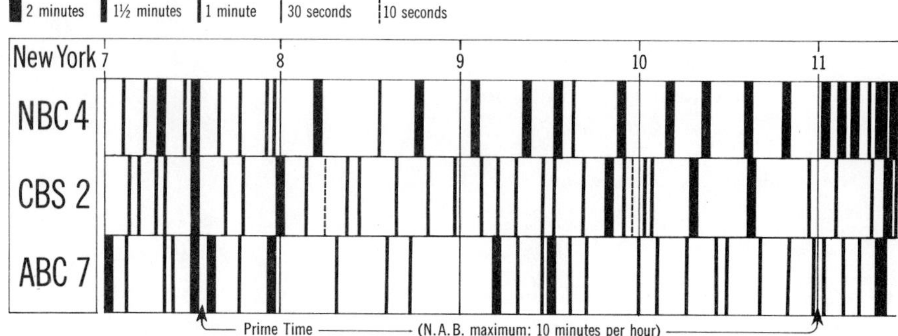

Between 7 a.m. and 1 a.m. each day, the three television networks devote about 3¾ hours to commercials—over 20 percent of total air time. This chart shows the amount of time given to commercials between 7 p.m. and just after 11 p.m. The width of the bars indicates the length of each commercial, running from 10 seconds to 2 minutes.

brief selling messages throughout the program. A *spot announcement* is a brief selling message delivered between sponsored programs. The advertiser pays only for the time his message consumes, whether it is 10 seconds or 60 seconds.

The kind of broadcast time that a seller uses will depend partly on his advertising objective. The main objectives of broadcast advertising are: (1) to sell a particular product or service; (2) to build goodwill for the business as a whole; and (3) to promote a particular department or division of a business. Some advertising may combine these objectives, but it is generally best to concentrate on one objective at a time.

Program Sponsorship

The advantage of program sponsorship is that the selling firm can make a stronger, more favorable impression than can usually be made with a spot announcement. If customers like the sponsored program, they will be more receptive to the selling message and more likely to buy the seller's product. Sponsored programs are intended mainly to build goodwill.

Types of Sponsored Programs. There are two general types of sponsored programs. First, there is the popular program that has no direct relation to the seller's product or service. Sometimes the seller presents no selling message during such a program; an announcer merely states at the beginning that the program is presented through the courtesy of, say, "The Weaver Company." Most often, though, the seller presents commercials throughout the program.

The second type of sponsored program is built around the seller's product or service. An entire program, for example, may be devoted to giving helpful information about the merchandise the sponsor sells. One large department store conducted a Consumers' Quiz program in which a group of women were quizzed each week about their merchandise knowledge. The show gave the master of ceremonies a chance to present facts about some of the merchandise available in the store.

Sharing Program Costs. A selling firm may choose to pay the entire cost of a sponsored program, or it may share costs with other noncompeting firms. With the high cost of broadcast advertising today, the number of single-sponsor programs is decreasing. One method of sharing sponsorship costs is called *dual sponsorship*. Two advertisers split the costs of the program and receive equal commercial time during that program. A second method is called *alternate sponsorship*. Every other week, one sponsor will pay for the program and receive commercial time; the next week, another advertiser will pay for the program and receive his commercial time. A third method is called *participating sponsorship*. Several noncompeting advertisers pay equal parts of the program's cost and receive equal commercial time during the program.

Spot Announcements

Spot announcements may consume 10 seconds, 20 seconds, 30 seconds, 40 seconds, or 1 minute. They are most often used to sell a particular product or service or to emphasize certain institutional features, such as broad assortments, low prices, quality merchandise, style leadership, exclusiveness, or excellence of personal service.

The main advantage of using spot announcements is that they allow greater repetition of the sales message. Since the advertiser pays only for the actual time that the selling message consumes, he can afford to scatter many selling messages throughout a broadcasting day or week for the same amount he would pay to sponsor a single program. This allows him to reach a variety of viewers and listeners because the messages are broadcast at different times.

Many spot announcements are delivered between halves of a sponsored program or between two different sponsored programs, during the station break. Such a spot announcement is known as either a *chain break* or an *I.D.* Sometimes a selling firm will give prepared commercials of less than 60-seconds' duration to a station and tell the station to use them whenever time is available. This kind of spot announcement is known as a *run-of-station (ROS) announcement*. Another spot announcement is known as an *in-program annoucement*. It is broadcast during station-sponsored programs, such as local feature presentations or reruns of old network film series.

CHECKING YOUR KNOWLEDGE

Vocabulary:

(1) sponsored program
(2) spot announcement
(3) dual sponsorship
(4) alternate sponsorship
(5) participating sponsorship
(6) chain break, or I.D.
(7) run-of-station (ROS) announcement
(8) in-program announcement

Review questions:

1. What is the status of radio today in terms of the number of radios in use and the number of people who listen?

2. For what kinds of products is radio advertising especially well suited? Why?
3. What are five of the currently most popular types of television programs? Who sponsors such programs?
4. Describe the two general types of sponsored programs.
5. In what selling situations are spot announcements frequently used? How much time is usually consumed by a spot announcement?

For discussion:

1. Is there any difference between listening to the radio for amusement and listening to it for companionship? In which mood is the listener more likely to respond favorably to a sales appeal?
2. Does the announcement that a particular seller is sponsoring a program affect you more favorably than seeing or hearing a spot announcement from a nonsponsor?
3. What types of programs are most popular on your local radio stations? Why do these types of programs differ from the types that are most popular on TV?

part B

preparing and evaluating broadcast advertising

How many commercials can you remember from watching television last night or listening to the radio this morning? Five, perhaps? Maybe none? If you do remember a certain commercial, can you remember the advertiser's name? Attracting attention, arousing interest, creating desire, and securing action are more difficult in broadcast selling than in personal selling because these steps must usually be performed in 10 to 60 seconds. As a seller prepares his broadcast messages, he must be sure that the messages will perform these steps quickly and effectively.

ATTRACTING ATTENTION

It has been estimated that ultimate consumers see or hear about 900 commercials every month. Obviously, every advertiser has quite a job to keep his selling message from being "tuned out." Many consumers are critical of so many breaks in their favorite programs, and sellers must find ways to make their selling messages truly interesting and informative—and brief.

There are five important ways of attracting attention to the selling message. First, the seller must select the station that will attract the largest proportion of potential buyers. A Cadillac dealer, for example, would probably not advertise on a radio station that played only country-western music since he wants to reach people in the upper-income brackets. Second, the seller can broadcast at a time when the proportion of potential buyers to total listeners will be greatest. In Part C, you will learn more about the best hours for radio and TV broadcasting. Third, he can repeat the selling message at intervals to catch those persons who might have missed the message the first time. Fourth, he can use other media to reinforce the broadcast message. For example, if the broadcast message is supplemented by window displays and newspaper ads, the combination will probably be more effective than the broadcast alone would have been. Fifth, the seller can place his message immediately before or after a popular program to catch that program's viewers. *Block programming* groups together programs with similar appeal to encourage the carryover of viewers from program to program. An ad incorporated into such a block is likely to get the attention of viewers who tuned in early. Saturday mornings, which are filled with children's programs, exemplify block programming.

AROUSING INTEREST

It is much more difficult to hold the interest of radio and TV audiences than it is to hold the interest of prospects met face to face. Listeners and viewers feel no sense of obligation to be interested. They don't feel it is rude to walk out of the room while a commercial is on, turn off the set, or tune in another station.

How effectively an advertiser arouses interest in his selling message depends on how original he can make that message. Think back to the TV commercials of several years ago, and you can see that commercials have become much more original, even "gimmicky." Out of every three or four commercials you see on television, several will rely on comedy or a short skit to attract attention and create interest.

Although the advertiser on a sponsored program must create interest in the program to create interest in his selling message, his purpose is to sell a product or service and not just to amuse the audience. Much broadcast advertising fails because it cannot transfer the listener's

There is a trend in television commercial production to use skits or brief human-interest situations in which the product is the star. However, many advertisers also try to encourage customers to buy their products by employing well-known public personalities to deliver commercials.

interest from the program to the commercial. Many commercials are heard but not registered in listeners' minds. Other commercials are so inappropriate or such exaggerations of the truth that they create ill will. The "you" attitude must be evident in broadcast messages before interest can be aroused.

CREATING DESIRE

To create desire for the product advertised in a broadcast message, the seller can follow five principles. First, he must select the right goods to be advertised. He must be sure that the product or service has popular appeal, that it is timely, that it is offered at the right price, and that it is a good value. Second, he should concentrate on one item or a few closely related items in the commercial. Like the trial lawyer who drives home one point at a time, the broadcaster should promote one item at a time so that the audience can grasp the details of what is being sold. Third, the commercial should relate the product to the listener's need.

Instead of saying, "Our expert craftsmen have fashioned a shoe that combines the utmost in comfort and style," the announcer should say, "You will enjoy new walking comfort and the knowledge that you are smartly dressed when you wear a shoe made by our expert craftsmen." Fourth, the commercial should be brief, since the listener's major interest is in the program. Fifth, the announcer should speak in a pleasing, sincere tone. People tend to have more confidence in what someone tells them orally than in what he tells them in writing. The seller must justify his listeners' confidence by not making statements over the air that he would hesitate to make to them in person. Some local advertisers have successfully acted as announcers for their own products. If the seller has a reasonably good voice, he can often inject his personality and enthusiasm more successfully into the commercial than can a hired announcer.

SECURING ACTION

As with all selling activities, the desire created by radio and television advertising must be turned into buying action. National and regional advertisers usually do this just by suggesting immediate action and by stressing repeatedly the product's brand name. Some people may be induced to act by being offered an attractive premium.

Local sellers should stress their own names and addresses rather than the product's brand name, unless the broadcast message is a cooperative one. Listeners may be urged to write down the advertiser's name and address. One successful plan is to stress the seller's phone number and to urge customers to call for a product sample or demonstration immediately after the broadcast.

EVALUATING BROADCAST ADVERTISING

In using any selling medium, the seller should check the sales results to find out whether the preparation efforts and expenditures have been worthwhile. This will tell him whether a particular presentation is effective or whether it should be improved. The local retailer can easily evaluate the effectiveness of broadcast messages by analyzing sales of a certain product without broadcast advertising and sales of the product with broadcast advertising—taking into account other factors that may have affected sales. It is much more difficult to evaluate the effectiveness of broadcast advertising intended to build goodwill.

Sampling

For scientific evaluation of broadcast advertising, sellers need information on both the quantity and quality of the audience. Quantity refers to the number of listeners or viewers; quality refers to the type of listener or viewer—children, men, housewives, and so on. The techniques used to get such information is called *sampling*. A small group of customers is selected at random from within a given broadcast area, then surveyed on their listening or viewing habits. Data obtained from the sample give a good picture of the total audience's listening or viewing activity.

In surveying the sample for information, sellers may use three different methods:

1. *Telephone method.* Persons whose names are chosen at random from the phone book are called and asked which program they are watching or listening to and who is watching or listening. They may also be asked about shows they have recently seen or heard. This method can determine the attraction power of a particular program but tells little about long-run audience viewing or listening habits.
2. *Diary method.* Consumers are invited to join a panel, and each panel member is required to keep a diary of his or his family's viewing or listening during certain time periods and who did the viewing or listening. One research organization using this method, the American Research Bureau, has a panel of more than 2,300 homes all over the United States and determines the response to network showings.
3. *Audimeter method.* A mechanical device, called an *audimeter,* is linked to TV and radio sets in the sampled homes. The audimeter records when, how long, and to what station the receiver is tuned at any particular time. It does not tell, though, who is viewing when the set is on. This method has been perfected by the Nielsen Company, and its reliability is widely accepted.

Continuing Nature of Broadcast Research

In the broadcast advertiser's interests, research is continually being conducted to determine the amount of listening done and the response to particular programs. Television research is considerably more extensive and complex than is radio research, but radio stations are conducting research in the hope that they can regain some of the consumers they have lost to television.

A number of radio stations support the All-Dimension Audience Research survey that samples some 17,500 homes and reports—on a quarter-hour basis—the size and listening frequency of the audience tuned into network programs. Some early results of this research

A. C. Nielsen Co.

This machine, the audimeter, provides the information that results in the famous Nielsen ratings. These ratings are widely used to evaluate the success of broadcast advertising. The audimeter records the percentage of homes equipped with an audimeter which were tuned to a particular broadcast at a particular time.

reveal that more than 19 million people are tuned to radio during the average quarter hour; that 95 percent of the population 12 years of age and older listens to the radio in the average week; that 6 out of 10 people listen to a network affiliate during the average week; and that 3 out of 4 adults and 4 out of 5 teenagers listen to radio during the average day.

Detailed analyses of TV viewing habits are available to advertisers. Information gathered by various research organizations is usually put in ranked order so that advertisers can compare sizes of audiences attracted to certain programs broadcast during certain test periods. The data may be broken down into such categories as homes reached by color transmissions; number of men, women, teenagers, children, heads of households, and housewives reached; education levels of the viewing heads of households; family sizes; and size of audience for the various types of programs. It is interesting to note the variations in the nature of an audience for a specific program. In one survey, "Bonanza" ranked second in the number of homes reached; but it ranked fifth in popularity among women and tenth in popularity among the heads of households with 13 or more years of formal education.

Such detailed information has great value for advertisers in evaluating the programs they are sponsoring or those programs surrounding their spot announcements. Such evaluation helps in deciding what sponsorship or scheduling to consider in planning future advertising.

CHECKING YOUR KNOWLEDGE

Vocabulary:

(1) block programming
(2) sampling
(3) audimeter

Review questions:

1. What are five ways of attracting attention to the broadcast selling message?
2. Why is it more difficult to arouse and hold the interest of radio and TV audiences than to arouse and hold the interest of prospects met face to face?
3. Name five principles of creating desire for the product advertised in a broadcast message.
4. How can a seller determine whether his radio and TV sales messages are meeting his needs?
5. Describe three methods for gathering information from a sample of radio listeners or TV viewers.

For discussion:

1. What is the proper length for a radio or TV commercial in relation to the length of the program?
2. What is the most important quality of a good announcer?
3. Do many of the TV spot announcements you see make attempts to get prompt action from viewers? Should they do more along this line?
4. Does it seem reasonable that a sample of less than one percent of all TV viewers will give a fairly accurate picture of the total audience's viewing habits? Explain your answer.

part C

scheduling broadcast advertising

Scheduling involves selecting the best time to broadcast a particular selling message. Obviously, good scheduling helps to assure that a broadcast message will successfully produce sales. To determine the best broadcast time, a seller must analyze his potential market. Among other things, he must know:

1. *Its working habits.* Housewives and night workers, for example, may view and listen at very different hours than does the majority of the population.
2. *Its age and sex.* More women than men view and listen at all hours; but the number of male viewers and listeners is high in the early morning and in the evening. Television viewing by children is at its peak between 5 p.m. and 8 p.m.
3. *Its place of residence.* In general, farm families listen or view for fewer hours than do city dwellers. However, farm families tend to listen more in the early morning hours and less in the afternoon and late evening.
4. *Other programs that are popular with the potential customers.* It is not ordinarily wise to time a program to compete with a very popular one, but it may be wise to precede or follow such a program to catch the attention of persons who are already tuned in.

CONSIDERATIONS IN SCHEDULING

The major considerations in scheduling are selecting the proper station, selecting the proper time of day, selecting the proper day of the week or season, and deciding when to repeat the sales message.

Selecting the Proper Station

A television or radio advertiser can broadcast his message over a local station whose waves reach only one city and its surrounding area, or he may arrange for a network showing. The network may cover a region or the whole country. The three national TV networks are NBC, CBS, and ABC; each is linked with enough stations to assure adequate reception over the whole country. Originally TV shows were predominantly network in character and were sponsored by large manufacturers of national brands. Today, however, about 50 percent of purchased television time is devoted to local presentations and is bought by local advertisers.

The kind of station that a seller should use depends upon how widely his merchandise or service is distributed. A national manufacturer with a product sold in virtually every city and town in the country would probably use a network. He might also find it effective to broadcast uniform programs over either regional or local stations, just as national manufacturers advertise in local newspapers as well as in national magazines. Certain department stores and specialty shops that serve a 50-100 mile trading area might economically use a large metropolitan TV station.

The local businessman might well be wasting his advertising money if he used either a regional network or even a large metropolitan station. He should usually confine his broadcasting to a local station that reaches the specific customers he is equipped to serve. A neighborhood merchant should probably not use broadcast advertising at all. He draws trade from only a small portion of his city, and advertising on even a local station would result in much waste circulation.

Selecting the Time of Day

In scheduling television advertising, a selling firm may choose from three types of viewing time. The first is called *prime time* and extends from 7:30 p.m. to 11 p.m. Eastern Standard time. The time just before and after prime time is called *fringe time*. This generally extends from 5 p.m. to 7:30 p.m. on weekdays and 11 p.m. to signoff time on all evenings. The rest of the broadcasting day is called *nonprime time*. Advertising rates are based in part upon these time periods. Prime time rates are most expensive, then fringe time rates, then nonprime time rates. It is estimated that television reaches about 30 million American homes from 6 a.m. to noon; about 38 million from noon to 6 p.m., and about 43 million from 6 p.m. to midnight.

There is a small radio listening audience at 6 a.m.; but from that time on, the number of listeners increases until it reaches a peak just after noon. Listening drops slightly in the afternoon and then rises to a higher peak at 9 p.m. It then drops off sharply, with very little listening between midnight and 6 a.m. Although listening reaches a peak at 9 p.m., that hour is not necessarily the best time to sell every product. It might be the best time to advertise a national brand of toothpaste, since almost every listener would be a likely prospect. However, a morning hour when most housewives are at home and interested in food problems would be a better time to advertise national brands of food products.

A local retailer who caters to persons going to work early may successfully advertise on an early-morning news program or weather report. One large retailer was successful with a program from 1 a.m. to 6 a.m., a period during which many odd-hour workers and insomniacs—all potential customers for his product—were awake. The late, late TV show attracts a similar audience.

Day of the Week or Season

The listening of different groups varies not only with the time of day but also with the day of the week and with the season. On Saturdays—

except late in the evening—there is less listening and viewing than on other days. Generally, people stay up later on Fridays and Saturdays than they do on other days. On Sunday morning there may be much less viewing and listening, since people go to church or sleep late. So far as the season is concerned, more attention is given to broadcasting in the winter than in the summer, since there are more outdoor activities in the summer.

Importance of Repetition

Retention of a sales message is increased by repetition. Persons who hear or see a commercial only once may not catch or may quickly lose the commercial's information. There are two ways to repeat a message. The first is to broadcast it at a number of different times during the day, hoping that prospects who are not listening or viewing at one time will catch the broadcast at another time.

The second way is to present a program at what seems to be the best time of day or week, then repeat the same commercial at intervals during the program. The seller should sponsor a program that prospects will look forward to. In his desire to gain attention by repetition, the seller shouldn't overlook the fact that listeners or viewers are irritated by an excessive number of commercials. A commercial that is repeated too often may gain attention, but it is unfavorable attention.

No seller can expect either radio or TV advertising to be successful unless he uses it regularly over a period of time. Most sellers who have found broadcast advertising successful have used it for at least a full year.

ADVERTISING RATES

An important part of scheduling is considering what the various time segments will cost. Obviously, the more desirable the time period in terms of the audience likely to be watching or listening, the more expensive is that time period. Rates may be quoted on units of one minute or less, five minutes, ten minutes, 15 minutes, 30 minutes, and 60 minutes. These rates may range from $6 a minute on a small local radio station to more than $70,000 a minute on a national TV network.

As you learned earlier, television rates are highest for prime time, are lower for fringe time, and are lowest for nonprime time. If the advertiser knows the nature of the audience at a given time, he may gain more potential buyers per dollar by contracting for nonprime time. For

Benton & Bowles

Part of scheduling is deciding on the best time of day to broadcast a commercial. Here, an advertising agency account executive and a television producer iron out last-minute details of scheduling before the taping of a commercial.

example, children who generate the buying of toys may be watching during the nonprime hours of 9 to 10 a.m. or 4 to 5 p.m.

Generally, radio and TV stations charge their advertisers a lower per-minute rate for long time segments and for frequent broadcasts. For example, advertisers who contract to buy spot announcements for use at planned intervals over a long period of time are given substantial discounts. Such advertisers are called *rateholders.*

Radio stations structure their rates differently from the rates of television stations, and the rates of different television stations vary considerably. All stations publish their rates on rate cards, which may mention—in addition to time costs—discounts, terms of sale, and station policies on programs, commercial length, and products that will not be accepted for advertising.

To determine the comparative costs of broadcast advertising, sellers can calculate the cost of reaching 1,000 listeners or viewers using a particular broadcast program. This is called the *cost-per-thousand.* For example, if a TV network show has 20 million viewers per minute and the cost for a 60-second spot is $40,000, the cost-per-thousand is $2. This means that it costs the advertiser $2 to reach every 1,000 persons in the audience.

GETTING THE COMMERCIAL READY FOR BROADCASTING

Obviously, radio commercials will involve only audio—someone's voice delivering the sales message. Television commercials may also be prepared in this manner; this technique is sometimes used for the chain-break type of commercial. The most common methods of preparing TV commercials are to use some kind of demonstration and narration or to use dramatization.

Commercials may be delivered live on the air or may be prerecorded on video tape or film. Radio commercials are generally given live; but few TV commercials, except perhaps on local stations, are given live. It is more common to prerecord the commercials for rebroadcast at a later time. This prerecording can be done at a time convenient for the advertiser, the station, and the performers in the commercial. Such a prerecorded program can be placed on the air whenever the sponsor buys time for it to be shown. Video tape is more expensive than film for prerecording commercials, but it is also more flexible. It does not have to be developed and can be viewed immediately after taping. Necessary changes can then be made to produce a polished, effective commercial. Also, video tape gives the appearance of a live presentation.

The creation of a television commercial is a complicated process involving the talents of many people—persons from the selling firm, the advertising agency, and the commercial production studio. The first step is to agree upon a script. Then a storyboard is prepared. This serves as a guide for preparing the actual commercial. It contains such elements as rough sketches of the visual action, description of the action, words to be spoken by the announcer and actors, and placement of background music. After any necessary changes have been made in the rough script, a final commercial is agreed upon, a shooting schedule prepared, and the actual filming accomplished. Raw film is edited until the commercial fits together well and runs for the precise number of seconds. Then it is ready for broadcasting.

CHECKING YOUR KNOWLEDGE

Vocabulary:

(1) prime time
(2) fringe time
(3) nonprime time
(4) rateholders
(5) cost-per-thousand

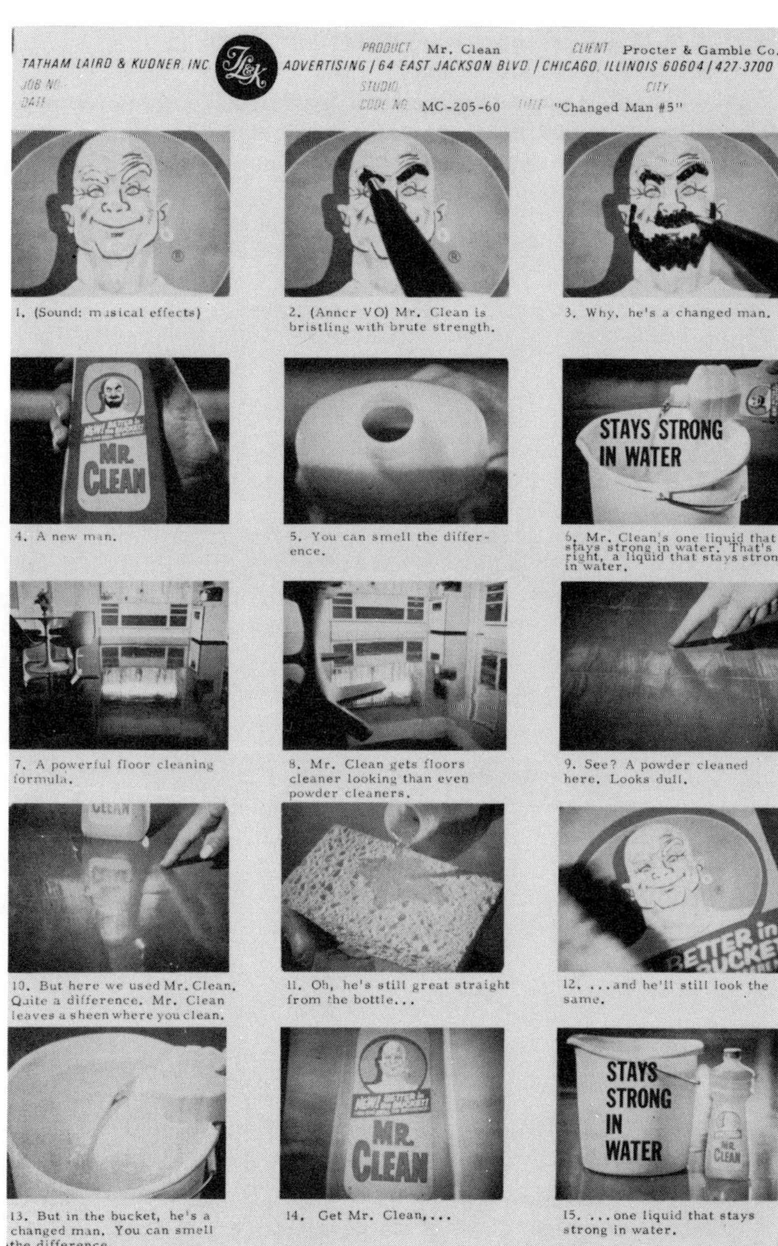

Procter & Gamble

This is a pictureboard. It resembles the storyboard which is used as a guide in preparing the television commercial, but the pictureboard is actually prepared from the finished film. It is kept as an easily viewed and stored record of the commercial.

Review questions:

1. What facts must the seller know about his potential customers in order to select the best broadcast time?
2. What kinds of stations may be used for broadcast messages? What is the major factor that influences the kind of station a seller will use?
3. Why are the advertising rates for prime time more expensive than the rates for fringe or nonprime time?
4. Describe the two methods of repeating sales messages.
5. Under what circumstances will broadcasters charge a per-minute rate lower than the basic rate?
6. Describe the production of a television commercial.

For discussion:

1. What groups of people are most likely to be listening to the radio at the following hours: 5 a.m.; 7:30 a.m.; noon; 3 p.m.; 5:15 p.m.; 9 p.m.; and 11 p.m.? What people are most likely to be watching television at these hours? Explain your answers.
2. Does a cost of $2 to reach 1,000 viewers seem high or low to you? What other factors should be considered in evaluating this cost figure?
3. Are there any advantages to a national advertiser in having a program prerecorded for use over local stations rather than using a national network?

part D

principles of display

Advertising is not the only form of nonpersonal selling. For many retailers, merchandise display is just as important. A display shows the merchandise itself, rather than giving information about it. An advertisement may show a picture of the goods, but this is not as effective as showing the actual goods.

A good merchandise display is a tremendous aid to personal selling. First, a window display contacts passersby—who cannot be contacted by personal salesmen—by gaining their attention. It may draw customers into a particular store or to a particular location in the store. It may stimulate them to ask for merchandise information. Second, displays create interest and desire by showing merchandise for the customer's consideration. Interest and desire are stimulated more by seeing products than by merely reading or hearing about them. Third, display is a kind of suggestion selling which may result in the customer purchasing related goods. Fourth, display may actually perform the entire selling process. It can result in the customer purchasing an article without a salesman's help.

Some rules to keep in mind when preparing both window and interior displays are:

1. Decorate from the customer's viewpoint.
2. Maintain unity throughout the display.
3. Keep the display fixtures and the merchandise clean.
4. Use background and lights to add to the display's effectiveness.
5. Make clever use of line and design.
6. Make original and pleasing use of color and harmony.
7. Where possible, show the merchandise as it would be used.
8. Make displays reflect the store's character.
9. Change displays often.

WINDOW DISPLAYS

There are two kinds of displays: window displays and interior displays. A window display is one of the best methods of contacting customers and gaining favorable attention, because the windows represent the store's first physical contact with the customer. Other external media may depict and describe the store's offerings, but the window display presents the merchandise itself.

Retailers are not the only sellers who use window displays. Wholesalers and manufacturers may use window displays to attract visiting buyers. If a whole building is devoted to the showrooms of manufacturers of one kind of goods, each manufacturer's showroom will have a window display facing the building's main corridor.

Kinds of Window Displays

There are three different kinds of display windows. A *closed background window* is completely separated from the store's interior by a full panel, or background; such a window is often seen in department stores. A *semiclosed background window* has a half-partition which allows customers to see into the store and also allows a display to be set up in front of the partition. Drugstores often use this type of window. The *open background window* is often seen in supermarkets. This window shows the whole interior of the store; the interior itself is actually the window display.

A number of different displays may be set up in these windows:

1. *Seasonal display*. Many department stores use special displays tied in with a season or holiday. Thus, there may be window displays for fall, Christmas holidays, or Easter. Such displays have great attention-getting power.
2. *Theme display*. In this kind of display, every piece of merchandise is tied into a general theme, such as back-to-school.
3. *Related merchandise display*. This type of display is similar to the theme display, except that there is no single theme tying the display together. A men's clothing store, for example, may display related articles of clothing in the window; but there may be no central theme.
4. *Sale display*. A window may contain merchandise that is offered in a special sale, and window banners and signs may emphasize the "sale" merchandise.
5. *Line-of-goods display*. Retailers who sell only one kind of goods, such as men's shoes, may use the line-of-goods display. Wholesalers also use this type of display. If a wholesaler handles the line of a well-known manufacturer, he may display in his showroom window all the items of that line which he handles.
6. *Feature display*. This is a kind of institutional display, intended mainly to build goodwill. It may or may not be directly connected with specific items the store sells. Many retailers develop feature displays around such events as their city's centennial celebration.
7. *Mass display*. The mass display is really just a quantity of merchandise arranged helter-skelter in the window. Few principles of good display design are used. Hardware stores and small discount stores often use this kind of display.

Planning the Window Display

The first step in planning the window display is deciding what merchandise to display. The seller should make sure that: (1) the merchandise chosen represents the entire line from which it was taken; (2) it is stocked in enough depth to meet the demand created by the display; (3) it creates a desire to enter the store and examine the goods more closely; and (4) it suggests related items to the customer. The chosen merchandise should have sales appeal, eye appeal, and time appeal.

The seller should also give considerable attention to selecting the display's components. These components include background materials, such as velvet or some other cloth used to drape the window backdrop; props, including functional props used to hold merchandise and decorative props used to accent the merchandise; accessories related to the major merchandise units; floor coverings; and show cards or price tickets. Each of these components has an important part in making the display successful.

Bloomingdale's

This window display presents a dramatic showing of women's accessories made from leopard skin, imitation leopard skin, or leopard-printed cloth. Do you think this could be called a theme display or a related merchandise display?

Another part of planning the window display is deciding which display windows to use. Most retailers have more than one display window, and large stores may have many windows. A substantial number of merchants place a percentage value on their various display windows. This value is determined partly by each window's location and the number of customers who can be expected to pass that window in a given time period. Merchants actually count the number of customers passing a certain window to get a good idea of average customer traffic. Obviously, the most appealing display or the one promoting the most profitable merchandise would be placed in the most valuable selling space. The windows in the front of the store are almost always the most valuable. More customers are likely to pass them than are likely to pass, say, side windows.

INTERIOR DISPLAY

An interior display, as its name indicates, is a merchandise display set up inside the store. Interior display is becoming more and more important in retailing because of the trend toward self-service merchandising. Many goods displayed in self-service stores—especially in supermarkets, discount stores, and variety stores—sell themselves. A cashier is needed only to wrap the goods and ring up the sale. In Part E, you will learn more about display in self-service businesses.

Such retailing firms as department stores, specialty shops, supermarkets, roadside stands, and automobile agencies use interior display constantly. Merchandise may be effectively displayed on counters, open tables, racks, ledges and walls, platforms, gondolas, enclosed cases, or, in the case of automobiles, directly on the selling floor.

Kinds of Interior Displays

There are five main kinds of interior displays:

1. *Open display.* In this kind of display, goods are placed on a counter or on open racks. This is an effective display, because the customer can actually handle the goods.
2. *Closed display.* Expensive or fragile goods may be displayed in showcases, wallcases, or windows facing the inside of the store or showroom. Customers can study but not handle them, so the goods are kept properly arranged and free from damage.
3. *Platform display.* This is usually comprised of one or more mannequins placed on a platform near elevators and entrances to departments. Several pieces of furniture may also be shown on platforms.
4. *Ledge and wall display.* Such a display allows the retailer to use space that would otherwise be wasted. Pegboards are sometimes used to hang or otherwise display merchandise items.
5. *Architectural display.* In this kind of display, goods are shown in a decorative setting. A model room, such as a kitchen or living room, may be completely outfitted. Or a store may display riding clothes in a shop resembling a stable. This is becoming the major method of displaying home furnishings in better department stores.

Planning the Interior Display

There are certain rules to follow in selecting merchandise for interior display. First, the goods should currently be selling well. Some slow-moving merchandise can be promoted through temporary displays; but, generally speaking, floor selling space is too valuable to use for unprofitable items. Second, all merchandise in interior displays should be

Franklin Simon

Ledge and wall displays are popular because they make good use of space that would otherwise be wasted. Sometimes the merchandise is simply hung from hooks on the wall. Such an arrangement is quite appropriate for these casual handbags.

coordinated with the merchandise in window displays. Third, it is best to feature goods which are being advertised nationally or locally. As you have learned, coordinating all forms of selling gives the most effective combination for encouraging the customer to buy.

In setting up interior displays, the seller should make sure that: (1) fixtures provide enough aisle space for customers to move freely about the store; (2) fixtures are low enough so that customers can see over them; (3) they are designed to show the merchandise to best advantage; (4) they are placed perpendicular to the main traffic aisle rather than parallel so that customers who want to examine goods will not be jostled by passing traffic; and (5) they allow customers to examine the goods closely.

The most valuable space for interior displays is the area just inside the front door. Goods to which the seller wants to give special promotional effort, such as seasonal merchandise, should be placed near the front. The least valuable space is near the back of the store, and items for which there is a heavy demand should be placed toward the rear

Burdine's

How many different kinds of interior displays can you identify in this photograph? How many different kinds of display props—garment stands, body forms, elevation units, and so on—can you spot?

of the store. Customers do not mind going out of their way to find these items. Also, while customers are walking toward the rear of the store, they are likely to pass other items and buy them on impulse. Other valuable locations for interior displays are to the right of the front door, at the ends of aisles, opposite service counters, at the checkout station, and near elevators and escalators.

CHECKING YOUR KNOWLEDGE

Vocabulary:

(1) closed background window
(2) semiclosed background window
(3) open background window

Review questions:

1. What are the advantages of merchandise display as an aid to personal selling?
2. List six rules to keep in mind when preparing window and interior displays.
3. Describe five different kinds of window displays.
4. Describe five different kinds of interior displays.
5. What are some valuable locations for interior displays?

For discussion:

1. Would it be best to select high-priced, medium-priced, or low-priced goods for a window display? Explain your answer.
2. What type of window and/or interior displays would you use with each of these items? (a) portable TV set; (b) china; (c) carpeting; (d) half-price shirt sale; (e) small kitchen utensils. Give reasons for your answers.
3. It has been stated that it is important to arrange displays attractively. Can you think of any instance when your attention was caught by a disorderly merchandise arrangement? How might a disarrayed display sometimes benefit the retailer?

part E

self-service merchandising

Retailing today is vastly different from retailing of twenty or thirty years ago. Merchants used to be almost jealous of their stock. They guarded it behind counters, in cases, in stockrooms. They believed that customers should be served personally—"waited on"—and not allowed to handle the merchandise. Around the 1930's, the revolution took place. In the grocery field, a few retailers reasoned that selling would be more efficient and less expensive if customers could serve themselves. Their reasoning was sound; and the idea, once implemented, spread rapidly throughout retailing. The merchant found that self-service had attractive advantages both for him and for the customer. Today the buying public is thoroughly conditioned to the privilege and responsibility of serving itself.

DISPLAY AND SELF-SERVICE MERCHANDISING

An essential part of self-service merchandising, of course, is good interior display. Most merchandise items lend themselves to open display and selection by the customer. For most convenience goods—such as well-known food, drug, and cosmetic products—display is all that is

Advantages of Self-Service Merchandising

To the Retailer

Allows the preparation of a bright, cheerful, attractive "salesroom" that invites people into the store and makes its buying appeal by display, convenience, and shopping ease.

Arrangement of fixtures and display equipment permits customers to circulate freely throughout the entire store.

Arrangement of merchandise enables customers to see, handle, and examine not only articles presold through advertising but also new or impulse items.

Conveniently located checkout stations allow selected articles to be handled quickly and accurately and assures the maintenance of proper records.

To the Customer

Makes shopping easier and faster.

Enables him to buy what he wants with no forced or hurried decisions.

Gives the opportunity to substitute items of his own choosing if the originally desired items are out of stock.

Eliminates any self-consciousness he may have about shopping in front of others.

Makes leisurely shopping possible, if that is desired.

Presents him with a mass of merchandise skillfully displayed for his convenient selection.

To the Salesman

Reduces the number of contacts with customers to permit giving better service to those who are contacted.

Eliminates stress and strain formerly experienced in trying to keep up with customer demands during peak periods.

Enables him to concentrate on more productive selling duties.

Places responsibility for handling sales transactions at the checkout station.

National Cash Register Co.

Almost everyone likes self-service merchandising for many selling situations. Here are some of the advantages of self-service merchandising to the retailer, customer, and salesman. Can you think of any disadvantages of self-service merchandising?

needed to make a sale. The customer is usually reasonably familiar with the features and benefits of the merchandise. And sellers know that desire is often most strongly created when the customer can make his own merchandise selection.

Self-service display is actually a kind of nonpersonal suggestion selling. In many supermarkets, variety stores, drugstores, department stores, and cafeterias, customers buy additional articles when the merchandise is displayed so that it can be readily seen and examined. Supermarket operations offer perhaps the finest examples of self-service display techniques, and some of these techniques will be discussed in the following paragraphs.

Distinguishing Between Demand and Impulse Items

A principle of self-service display and nonpersonal suggestion selling is to distinguish between demand items (those which most customers include in their shopping lists) and impulse goods (those which will be bought only if they happen to be seen). Demand items are displayed throughout the store so that to obtain them the customer must walk through every part of the store. Frozen goods, for example, may be found along one side of the store; fresh fruits and vegetables, along the other side; and meats, in the back of the store. Paper goods, soaps and detergents, and canned goods may be positioned along the aisles. Impulse goods will be scattered among these demand items. For example, a new cake mix—which would probably not appear on any shopping list—might be placed next to a five-pound bag of sugar, a major demand item.

Exposing Many Items on Shelves

Supermarkets try to stock many different items horizontally on display shelves so that the customer can view almost every item in stock. Vertical space is used for various sizes of the same product, with large containers placed on the lower shelves. Impulse items, particularly those with high markups, are placed at eye level so the customer will see them first and perhaps buy them.

Using "Ends"

Stock locations tend to remain constant for long periods of time. Customers get used to finding certain merchandise in certain places, and they are usually displeased with changes in the layout. However, displays of specially priced or seasonal merchandise can be put temporarily in key locations. Special displays called *ends* (because they are placed at the ends of aisles) are sure to be seen. Sometimes the merchandise displayed in "ends" can also be found in its regular stock location, but customers who fail to notice the merchandise in its regular location can hardly fail to notice the "end." Mass displays of special goods can also be set up temporarily near the store entrance so that customers entering and leaving the store are sure to see them.

Grouping Related Merchandise

Supermarkets tend to group together goods that are related in use. There are two plans for doing this. The first is to provide an assortment that will induce customers to select more than one item from the assortment. For example, all condiments may be displayed together so that the customer shopping for cinnamon will see cloves, sage, and allspice and buy them, too. The second plan is to set up special displays of items that are used together, such as all the items needed for a special dinner or all the ingredients needed to make a special dish. The regular stock of these items may be found in different parts of the store, but the special display makes a good "shopping list" of all the necessary items. Sometimes space may be available next to the display for a small stock of the key items.

Placement of Impulse Items

Small impulse items of a convenience nature are often placed near the checkout stations. As the customer waits in line, she is likely to add some of these items to her shopping cart. Items commonly displayed in such a location are chewing gum, cigarettes, candy bars, razor blades, magazines, cellophane tape, and pencils.

AUTOMATIC VENDING

An important kind of self-service, nonpersonal selling is carried on through automatic vending. It seems odd to think that machines can "sell," but automatic vending has a significant place in today's marketing network. Cigarettes, candy, fresh fruit, soft drinks, and postage stamps are only some of the products sold through vending machines. These machines now produce close to $3 billion in sales annually. Vending machines are best suited to selling standard, low-priced articles that are quickly consumed.

Persons selling through vending machines must use good selling techniques both in selecting the type of product to dispense and in

Federation of Migros Cooperatives, Zurich

Automatic vending is an international method of selling. Even gasoline is now sold through automatic pumps in this country and in Europe.

selecting locations for the machines. Since most vending machines are found in business establishments and public places, negotiations for the locations and their rentals demand salesmanship from the franchiser. Customer satisfaction depends on the quality of the goods and on proper maintenance of the machines.

SELF-SERVICE AND THE SALESMAN

Self-service merchandising has not eliminated the need for personal customer service. No store is completely self-service. Some merchandise will always need explanation and perhaps a formal sales presentation. Customers' questions, too, must still be answered by a salesman. A salesperson in a self-service store serves customers by directing them to merchandise, advising them on purchases, and sometimes convincing them to buy in their own best interests. He must generally do these things by interrupting his stock work and sales-related duties. At peak selling periods, all his efforts may be devoted to giving personal service and to suggestion selling.

Tips for the Self-Service Salesman

- Greet customers when possible. A friendly "Good morning" or "Good afternoon" will be appreciated and will indicate your availability.
- Approach customers to offer service only when they obviously need help.
- Open a service or sales contact with a greeting such as, "Are you finding what you want?" Be friendly. Smile. Never ask if you can wait on the customer.
- If possible, always direct a customer to merchandise rather than take him to it. He may see other things he wants on the way.
- Leading customers around the store establishes a customer-salesperson relationship that tends to stop customer selection of merchandise.
- Suggest related items after assisting a customer to find what he wants.
- End a sales contact by suggesting that the customer look at other items in other departments.
- Don't accept payment for merchandise on the selling floor if there is a central checkout station.
- Tactfully offer a customer a shopping cart or carrier if you see that his arms are getting full.
- Help in keeping carts or carriers at various locations throughout the store.
- Don't lead a customer with merchandise to the checkout station. This automatically stops him from buying other things in the store.
- Always see that shelves and display equipment are well-stocked, that merchandise is kept clean and dust-free, and that every item's price is clearly marked.
- Keep a constant surveillance of all customers shopping in self-service areas to discourage shoplifting and to give prompt attention to those customers indicating that they need help.

National Cash Register Co.

Principles of good selling are employed in self-service stores just as they are in personal service stores. There are, however, certain other principles unique to self-service selling. Here are some pointers for the self-service salesman to follow.

Be Alert To Give Service

Regardless of what the salesman is doing, he should always be on the alert to give service to customers who need it. When a customer does want service, it is usually obvious. The salesman should unobtrusively watch for the puzzled expression or "where can it be" look.

Once he sees a customer who appears to need help, he should quickly offer his assistance. Constant surveillance of all customers in the self-service area should not be noticeable; customers do not like to feel they are being watched.

Greet Customers

Many times, all a salesman must do is to indicate his availability by a friendly greeting. If the customer does not ask for help, he should do nothing else. He should allow the customer to continue shopping. The salesman remains free to serve others, while the customer is free to shop as long as he wants. Dozens of impulses-to-buy are imparted every minute that a customer is left free to associate with openly displayed merchandise.

Approach the Customer with a Suggestion for Service

In approaching the customer who appears to need help, the salesman may ask, "Did you find what you wanted?" or some other appropriate question. The customer's answer will indicate what further action is needed. If the desired article needs selling or explaining, the salesman should give that service. If the customer is just searching for a particular item, the salesman can direct him to it.

Help the Customer Make a Selection

When it is obvious that the customer is interested in an item that calls for selling help, the salesman should give all the information, advice, or selling effort that is needed. All the principles of salesmanship that you have learned in this book can be applied in self-service stores. The need for product knowledge and demonstration know-how is particularly important. The salesman in the self-service store should have time to study his product carefully and gain this knowledge.

Let the Customer Resume Shopping

Although the salesman may finish serving a customer, he should never terminate the shopping trip in the store. His objective is to leave the customer still exposed to the silent but most compelling sales force: the merchandise. After the customer has said he will take an article, the salesman might hand it to him or place it in a shopping cart, then indicate that the article may be paid for at the checkout station. This is a good time to employ suggestion selling, particularly in relation to specially advertised items in other areas of the store.

CHECKING YOUR KNOWLEDGE

Vocabulary:

ends

Review questions:

1. List eight different stores that use self-service merchandising to a considerable extent. What inherent factors of these stores' products make them adaptable to self-service merchandising?
2. What is the difference between demand items and impulse items? How do supermarkets display such items to maximize the sales of each kind?
3. Describe two plans for displaying related merchandise.
4. What kinds of products can be sold through automatic vending machines?
5. Name five pointers that the salesman in a primarily self-service store should follow.

For discussion:

1. Is it possible that self-service merchandising might eliminate the need for personal selling in the future? Explain your answer.
2. How many different products can you name that are sold through vending machines?
3. Which person has the more difficult job: the salesperson in a self-service store or the salesperson in a non-self-service store? Give reasons for your answer.

BUILDING YOUR SKILLS

Improving your English:

Complete each of the following sentences by writing on a separate sheet of paper the correct form of the adjective given in parentheses.

1. Browning's bid was the ______ of the five submitted. (high)
2. The color portrait is the ______ of the two. (pretty)
3. The view from Lookout Mountain was the ______ of all we had seen during the trip. (beautiful)
4. Field Services had the ______ accident rate of all the automobile leasing firms. (bad)
5. Studio audiences for the afternoon television shows are ______ than the morning audiences. (large)
6. Returns from the direct-mail campaign were ______ than he had expected. (bad)
7. "October Morn" was the ______ of the two landscape paintings. (beautiful)
8. The early morning radio show was the ______ of all daytime programs for promoting garden supplies. (good)

9. The viewing audience of the later afternoon children's show was the ______ of the two. (large)
10. Television advertising is the ______ of the two media we are using. (good)

Improving your arithmetic:

The problems below involve more than one step in obtaining their solution; show each step used.

1. A hardware dealer buys riding lawn mowers for $500, less discounts of 30% and 20%. Transportation charges are $20 on each mower. At what price must the dealer sell the lawn mowers in order to make a gross profit of 20% of the selling price?
2. Neal Tate bought 250 dresses for $12.50 each, less a 15% discount. He sold 200 of the dresses for a total of $3,863.64. At what price, to the nearest cent, must he sell each of the remaining dresses to realize a gross margin of 40% on the selling price of the entire group of dresses?

Improving your research skills:

1. Your instructor will appoint a committee to visit a radio or TV station. This committee should discuss with the manager the use of his station as a selling medium for both local and national advertisers. In particular, committee members should find out what the station does to help advertisers get maximum returns. They should also find out the station's charges for broadcast time and the conditions under which discounts are allowed. The committee's findings should be reported in class.
2. Based on the following information, prepare a radio spot announcement to be broadcast during a women's program:

   Flint Hollow-Ground Cutlery (Kitchen Set)

   Six different hollow-ground knives of chrome vanadium cutlery steel: paring knife, ham slicer, serrated vegetable knife, roast slicer, utility knife, and French cook's knife. Handles of imported polished hardwood. Polished hardwood holder to hang on the wall or fit into a drawer. Price, $15.95.
3. Prepare a television spot announcement for a product of your choice.
4. Ten different merchandise items are listed below. Survey stores in your community to find out which kinds of window and interior displays are used to promote these products. Give your findings in report form. Tell whether you think each display you observed was the most suitable for the particular item. Tell, too, whether or not window and interior displays were coordinated.

   (a) Men's topcoats
   (b) Mirrors
   (c) Watches
   (d) Refrigerator
   (e) New dress style
   (f) Canned vegetables
   (g) Power tools
   (h) Sportswear
   (i) Bathroom equipment
   (j) Meats

5. Prepare a sketch of a display (window or interior) that could be used to promote spring fashions for college coeds.

APPLYING YOUR KNOWLEDGE

Case problem:

A grocery chain has been sponsoring a 15-minute radio show every day at 9 a.m. The program includes store news of interest to housewives, menu hints, and short musical selections. The broadcast reaches only the metropolitan area of the large city in which the chain has its headquarters and its largest number of stores. The cost for the 15 minutes of time is $90 a day. The total cost to the chain is $125, since a person is employed to prepare the program and handle other advertising duties for the chain.

The program has been successful, and a substantial increase in the sales of many staple items seems partially attributable to the broadcasts. It has been proposed that the company sponsor a half-hour musical program in the evening, covering the entire area in which the chain operates. The total cost per broadcast would be about $2,500, or 20 times the present cost. If the evening program covered only the 50-mile radius covered by the present morning program, the cost of evening broadcast time would be $300 for one half-hour, compared with $90 for 15 minutes of morning broadcast time.

Do you think it would be wise for the chain to introduce the evening program? If so, should it replace or supplement the morning program? Why? If introduced, should it be presented daily or weekly? Why?

Continuing project:

Perform the following activities in your manual:

1. Tell whether your product or service is suited to promotion by radio or television. If it is suited to broadcast advertising, tell whether it should be associated with a program of entertainment or whether it should be promoted in a spot between programs. Discuss the best time of day for scheduling your broadcasts; and tell whether national, regional, or local coverage is desirable.
2. Prepare a script for a 45-second spot radio or TV announcement for your product or service and place this script in your manual.
3. Discuss the display techniques that could be used with your product.
4. Prepare sketches of possible window and interior displays of your product and enter these sketches in the manual.

Extra credit:

Visit a self-service store, then prepare a report explaining the kinds of selling aids the store used to make merchandise available for sale. Mention the various display fixtures used and the promotional devices used to attract customers' attention. Prepare a floor plan of the store and include it in your report.

Selling in the 1960's . . .

Laser beams, micro-miniskirts, astronauts, hippies, everything and anything psychedelic is making big news in the 1960's. But mergers have the business spotlight. Since 1960, as many as four or five in a single day are announced, and some 70 percent of these are of the "conglomerate" type, rapid acquisition companies with assets in any number of diversified fields. Whether these corporate marriages are bold, new economic ventures, or simply marriages of convenience (or inconvenience), only the decades ahead will tell, but some 3,500 are projected by the end of 1968 alone. And planning has the marketing spotlight. The decades ahead need communication between marketing and technology and have an even greater need for visionary thinkers who know how to plan ahead successfully.

UNIT V
Sales Management

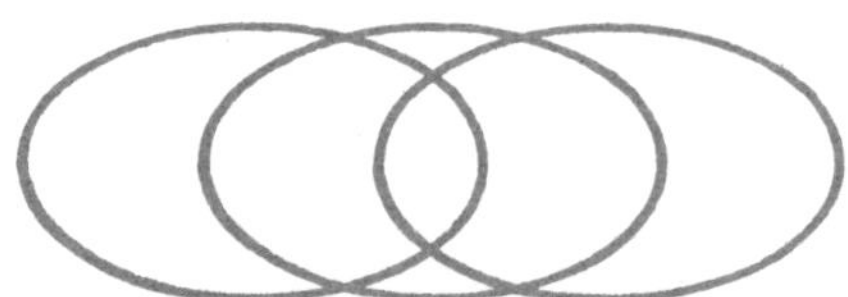

chapter 15

activities in sales management

KEY QUESTIONS

A With what important selling activities is sales management concerned?

B Why is it said that there is no foolproof technique for hiring salespeople and building the sales force?

C Can fringe benefits ever be as important as salary to encourage a salesman to do his best selling work?

D Why is it necessary to evaluate periodically the productivity of individual salesmen and the total sales force?

E What has made it necessary for selling firms to use faster and more accurate means of collecting, classifying, and analyzing sales data?

part A

responsibilities of the sales manager

Sales management is concerned with the planning, administration, and supervision of work assigned to a sales department or division. Most successful sales managers have come from the ranks of salesmen, but the sales manager's job is quite different from a salesman's job. The sales manager's job is an especially varied and demanding one that calls for a great deal of ability as a planner, organizer, and leader.

GENERAL DUTIES OF THE SALES MANAGER

The duties of the sales manager will differ somewhat with the size and organization of the selling firm. Duties will also differ depending upon whether the selling firm is a retailing business or a wholesaling or manufacturing business. Generally, a sales manager's duties will include the following:

1. Recruiting the sales force.
2. Training employees.
3. Devising financial and nonfinancial incentives.
4. Assigning territories and/or setting sales quotas.
5. Supervising job performance.

Recruiting the Sales Force

Company policies vary in regard to recruiting salesmen. In some companies, all recruiting activities are handled by the district sales manager's office. In other firms, the hiring decision is made by the sales manager after applicants have been screened by the personnel department. In some retailing firms, the hiring decision may be handled by the personnel department. You will learn more about techniques of building the sales force in Part B.

Training Employees

Training in many firms consists of study at sales headquarters where the salesman learns his product line, company policies, and appropriate

In retail stores, salespeople are often trained by the lecture or classroom method in special activities such as credit authorization. The store may employ a person known as a training supervisor who handles all special training activities for the store.

selling techniques. The new employee then becomes a junior salesman and may work under the direct supervision of an experienced salesman. It may be many months before the new employee qualifies for his own territory and is recognized as a senior salesman. In retailing, most salesmen are trained on the job and begin selling as soon as they report to the selling floor. There are commonly special introductory classes, though, in such things as cash register operation, credit authorization procedures, and store policies.

Devising Financial and Nonfinancial Incentives

One of the sales manager's chief responsibilities is to provide incentives that will encourage salesmen to do their best selling. There are two kinds of incentives—financial and nonfinancial. *Financial incentives* include all monetary rewards for doing a job well: salary, commissions, premium money, and so on. *Nonfinancial incentives* include fringe benefits and special devices other than money. A commonly used nonfinancial incentive is the sales contest, which gives awards such as a vacation trip to the winner. Winning a sales contest, with its publicity and recognition within the company, is often as much of a sales stimulus as a monetary reward.

Assigning Territories and Setting Sales Quotas

A contact salesman's territory is the geographic area he is assigned to cover; the sales quota indicates how much business the salesman should be able to obtain from his territory. Assigning territories and setting quotas involves considerable marketing research and statistical analysis. A territory must be large enough to provide a fair income for the salesman, yet small enough for one man to contact frequently the territory's potential buyers. Although retail salesmen do not have geographic territories assigned to them, they are generally given sales quotas which they must meet.

Supervising Job Performance

Salesmen need direction in the work they do in their assigned territories or departments. Group supervision is handled by conducting frequent meetings of salesmen. These meetings are devoted to discussing the changing product line, its prices, its terms of sale, techniques of presenting it, and successful ways of handling difficult sales situations. Individual supervision is handled by means of individual conferences at which each salesman's performance is reviewed. Contact salesmen are often expected to send the sales manager a written report of their field activities, and the sales manager replies with commendations or suggestions. Sometimes the sales manager may accompany a salesman on his rounds.

Once or twice a year, the sales manager rates every salesman under his supervision. These ratings are the basis for salary increases, transfers, or promotions.

RETAIL SALES MANAGEMENT

Retail sales management is different from sales management in manufacturing and wholesaling firms. Many retail stores are small, and the supervisor of salespeople is usually the owner or manager. Larger stores are departmentalized, and each department is usually supervised by a buyer who is really a department manager. Typically, the buyer is responsible for the selling activities as well as for planning the merchandise assortment. In many department stores, however, buyers become so involved in merchandise selection that the sales force in each department is placed under a section manager. The section manager, in turn, reports to a service superintendent.

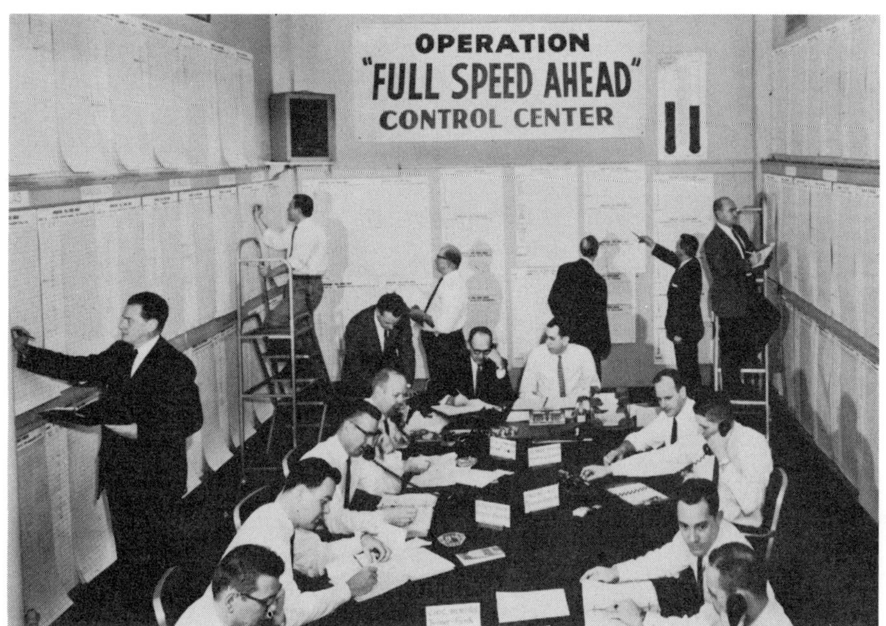

Sales/Marketing Today

To supervise sales performance during one manufacturer's major selling campaign, management required that each salesman and each district in the country report its up-to-the-minute sales to the control center. Any territory not measuring up to expectations or needing more assistance was immediately spotted.

An increasing number of stores are going to chain and branch-store systems. In such systems, the buyer's work is much more specialized. He relinquishes his responsibility for supervising the sales force, since he is fully engaged in buying for a number of selling units. With this plan, each selling department in each store unit is headed by a department sales manager. The department manager's duties include responsibilities for personnel, customer services, merchandise services, and general services.

Personnel Responsibilities

Among other personnel duties, the department manager must regulate attendance, timekeeping, and the assignment of work to salespeople. The department must be fully manned each day, and sometimes the manager will have to get additional help or different personnel. The manager assigns certain departmental duties, such as housekeeping, to employees so that they know what they are to accomplish each day in addition to their selling activities. Of course, the department manager must supervise his employees' selling techniques and take action to improve poor selling techniques. He also is responsible for maintaining the physical welfare of his employees and for maintaining good human relations among them.

Customer Service Responsibilities

As the department manager supervises employees' selling techniques, he will also be handling some of his customer service responsibilities. He should be fully aware of the need for prompt approaches to customers and of the need for courteous, efficient customer treatment. Sometimes he may have to serve customers by authorizing special credit and delivery transactions, and he may even have to handle sales transactions himself during peak periods when all salespeople are busy. Also, an initial complaint adjustment will usually be made through the department manager.

Merchandise Service Responsibilities

Maintaing a stock control system is another of the department sales manager's duties. Reporting selling trends and store conditions to management, supervising departmental displays, and protecting merchandise are other responsibilities. While the purchase of new goods is the responsibility of a central buyer, the departmental sales manager is increasingly being given the authority to reorder goods in the quantities he deems desirable. Even though he is not responsible for advertising, he must be ready to execute sales effort for the publicized selling event.

General Service Responsibilities

Opening and closing the department promptly are two general service duties of the department manager. He also has responsibility for the carrying out of routine but necessary duties, such as requisitioning supplies and housekeeping. He will sometimes have certain responsibilities for handling sick or injured persons, whether they are department personnel or customers.

PREPARATION FOR SALES MANAGEMENT

If a person wants to advance to a sales management position, he will normally need educational experiences beyond high school in addition to training and experience in selling. Statistics show that of those persons in sales management positions today, about one-third have had some college training. In the future, more formal education will be demanded of those persons moving to top-level sales management positions.

Individuals with high school training in distribution, coupled with good selling experience, may be able to attain middle-management positions. Even these positions, however, are being filled more and more by persons with college educations. Examples of middle-management positions are an assistant district sales manager, a sales supervisor of a group of showroom salesmen working at the wholesale level, a department sales manager in a large retail store, and a store manager supervising a unit in a chain system.

Participating in a cooperative work program while still in school is very worthwhile. One should make the most of every opportunity to develop leadership qualities while in school. These qualities may prove helpful when applying for a selling position with a company that selects its salesmen partly on their potential as sales managers. While he is still a salesman, an individual should be alert to the problems, policies, and decisions of sales management that come down to him through regular communication channels. Once he is in a sales management position, the experience of evaluating what he has observed in others will be most helpful.

The sales manager must be a good organizer and a natural leader. He must be skillful in selecting and training salesmen. He must have the confidence of his customers and the respect of his sales force. He must be able to work well with other persons in his firm. As our economy continues to grow, there will be a greater and greater need for good salesmen. There will also be a corresponding need for good sales managers. Success as a sales manager comes from intensive study, broad experience, and hard work.

CHECKING YOUR KNOWLEDGE

Vocabulary:

(1) financial incentives (2) nonfinancial incentives

Review questions:

1. What are the general duties of the sales manager?
2. Explain how individual and group supervision of salesmen is handled.
3. What are some ways in which retail sales management differs from sales management in manufacturing and wholesaling firms?

4. Name the primary areas of responsibility of the department sales manager.
5. What tools will the salesperson need to advance to a sales management position?

For discussion:

1. How can marketing research and statistical analysis be used in defining the territory assignments of contact salesmen?
2. It has been predicted that in the years ahead, more and more formal education will be required for top-level sales management positions. Why do you think this prediction has been made?

part B

building the sales force

Progressive companies try to hire the best sales personnel available. There is no foolproof technique for hiring salespeople; but many companies try to minimize the possibility of hiring unsuitable persons by requiring candidates to fill out application blanks, by thoroughly interviewing these persons, and by giving them psychological tests. If poor recruiting exists, employee turnover may be high. *Turnover* is the ratio between the number of separations from the sales force and the average number of persons in the sales force. When new men are carefully selected, are thoroughly trained before being placed in a selling job, and are intelligently supervised, turnover should be low.

RECRUITING SALESPEOPLE

Studies have shown that the cost of hiring a new salesman may range from a hundred dollars up to several thousand dollars. It is plain to see that a company cannot afford to make mistakes in hiring new employees.

Sources of Employees

The sales manager may use a number of sources in finding sales recruits. Some of the most important sources are newspaper advertising, other divisions of the selling firm, recommendations of other salesmen, applications currently on file, unsolicited applications, and employment agencies. The source used will depend largely upon the kind of selling to be done.

Some organizations that need specialty salesmen do their recruiting through vocational schools. Another recruiting technique is to visit colleges and universities that offer degrees in either business administration or liberal arts. If the sales manager has a degree in business administration, his recruiters will probably be most interested in graduates of such programs, particularly those with marketing majors. If the sales manager has a liberal arts background, he may want to hire liberal arts majors and train them for specific selling jobs in his company.

Inside Recruiting Versus Outside Recruiting

The firm that always looks outside its own ranks when it needs a salesman is being short-sighted. For example, the price that must be paid to woo a good salesman away from another firm is often exorbitant, and the salesman may have little loyalty to the new firm. Training young men and women for sales careers in a reputable firm is generally the best policy. The National Cash Register Company has a reputation for finding salesmen in the ranks of its servicemen. The servicemen are hired with the idea that they will ultimately become salesmen for the company.

It is not always wise, though, to develop salespeople only from within the firm. People with fresh ideas are necessary if a firm is to adjust successfully to change. Persons who have worked only for one firm and are thoroughly indoctrinated in its policies may not bring to their jobs the new point of view that is needed. A combination of company-trained people and creative people from outside the firm makes a winning selling team.

Making the Hiring Decision

In small companies, salesmen are often selected by the owner himself. In a medium-sized company, the hiring decision is usually made by the sales manager. In larger firms, someone in the personnel department will normally assist the sales manager with the recruiting and initial interviewing.

As part of the hiring process, many firms give psychological tests to all applicants. Various types of tests are used: intelligence tests, personality tests, aptitude tests, and interests tests. Usually, a battery

Ewing Galloway

Many large firms conduct two sets of interviews before making the hiring decision. In a preliminary interview, the applicant is asked a few questions and his appearance is evaluated to determine whether he should be given further consideration. This interview is designed to screen out obviously unsuitable candidates. Those who seem promising are asked to fill out application blanks and return for a final interview.

of tests is given, since one test may reveal a particular trait not revealed by other tests.

One way of gaining insight into an applicant's character is to classify human interests into four groups: people, things, figures, and ideas. A test or an interview may reveal that an applicant's major interest is in people. If this is true, he is likely to make a good salesman. He may also fit into teaching, social service, or personnel work. If his major interest is in handling things, he may have the makings of a mechanic, engineer, or natural scientist. If a person enjoys dealing with figures, he is likely to enjoy work in accounting, statistics, mathematics, or computer technology. The idea-oriented person may make a good journalist, political scientist, or advertising and sales promotion specialist.

The final decision on whether or not to hire an employee should probably not be made on test scores alone. The results of the interview with an experienced sales manager are of more importance. However, one internationally known company has a policy of not hiring a salesman if he fails a written aptitude test.

"Selling" the Selling Job

One of the most effective ways of finding the best possible salesmen is to "sell" the selling job to young people looking for career guidance. Local chapters of sales and marketing executive clubs have made time available to guide young people with the qualifications for selling and the desire to enter this field. The same organizations may sponsor clinics for persons who are already in sales work as well as for potential salesmen.

TRAINING AND EVALUATING SALESMEN

Two important aspects of building the sales force are training and evaluating salesmen. Large selling firms usually have planned training programs for their salesmen; smaller firms do not. Small firms rely mainly on on-the-job training, with advice and supervision from experienced salesmen. A formal training program is usually desirable in any firm, whether it is conducted through correspondence with field salesmen, lectures in a classroom, or conferences with a training supervisor, experienced salesman, or department manager. Training is especially desirable: (1) for all new men; (2) for older salesmen when their productivity is decreasing or when their selling duties are changed; and (3) for all men in the sales force when a new product or new sales promotion campaign is introduced, when new territories are assigned, when a new method of distribution is adopted, or when customer complaints are increasing.

A planned training program may include information on the company and its products and policies, on the product line, on selling techniques appropriate to the product, on the market structure for the product, and on nonselling duties related to the basic selling activity.

Salesmen's performances must be periodically evaluated by sales managers. As you have learned, such evaluations are the bases for promotions and transfers in the organization. Evaluations may be either objective or subjective. Objective evaluations involve an analysis of a salesman's sales volume in comparison with the sales volume of other salesmen, with the sales volume of the entire firm, or with the sales goals the salesman has set for himself. You will learn more about how such evaluations are made in Part D, "Determining Sales Productivity."

Subjective evaluations are based upon a supervisor's observation of the salesman at work. Department managers in retail firms commonly use subjective evaluations. They may rate the salesman on such points as his product and store knowledge; his approach, demonstration, and close; and his effectiveness in building customer goodwill. Salesmen may also be rated on their ability to get along with co-workers.

Some retail firms employ persons who pretend to be shoppers, actually buy some item from the salesman, then rate him later on how he handled the sales presentation. They may use a rating form similar to the one shown on page 521. This is actually a combination of an objective and subjective evaluation.

DEVELOPING A SELLING TEAM

Many sales managers could greatly improve the effectiveness of their sales forces if they would take a tip from managers of professional baseball teams. Each spring, teams are taken to training camps for several weeks of intensive training. Each manager gets to know the playing habits and special skills of each man, and he works to develop each man's physical and mental potential.

Many sales managers, especially at the retail level, don't maintain such a close working relationship with their salesmen. Frequently they learn of selling errors only through customer complaints. The sales manager's primary responsibility in building a sales force is to develop the relationship between himself and his salespeople. He must do everything he can to encourage, recognize, and stimulate his salesmen.

The human relations approaches of some sales managers have not been effective. They have tried to create a big happy family of workers, so quick to excuse each other's failings that sales productivity has suffered. Most personnel specialists now believe that the best way to get results from salesmen is to give them a maximum of responsibility and authority so that the job itself becomes the chief motivation to do well. Salesmen are stimulated to greater accomplishments—not only by praise and bonuses—but by being given more challenging tasks to perform. This may mean that a salesman will be given considerable authority in setting terms of sale and in applying various sales techniques. Once he feels that the job demands his utmost ingenuity and skill and that he can act as a responsible businessman, he will be much more successful.

PROMOTIONAL OPPORTUNITIES WITHIN THE SALES FORCE

Promotional opportunities differ from firm to firm. The new salesman can study his firm's organization chart to find out how he might

S. Q. B.

(Selling-Quotient-Builder)

S.Q. 62 %

Company Name Remrite Co.
Address Main Street
City Center City State Mass.

Quan.	Mdse. Purchased	Amt. Sale	Amt. Tend.
1	Handbag	4.98	
	Fed. Tax	1.00	
		5.98	5.98

Sample Copy

Date Nov. 6, 1958 Time 11:10 A.M. P.M.
Dept. Handbags Floor Main

DESCRIPTION OF SALESPERSON

Man ○ Woman ⊠ Sp's. No. or letter
Approximate Age 30 Build: Slender ○
Height 5' 2" Medium ⊠
Color of hair Auburn Heavy ○
Style of hair Bob Wearing glasses ○
Description of clothes Dressed in white blouse and blue skirt
Special marks of identification

A—APPROACH TO CUSTOMER (Yes | No)

1—Department Busy? ☐ | ⊠
2—Prompt Approach? ⊠ | ☐
3—If not prompt—
a. did sp. recognize you as waiting customer? ☐ | ☐3
b. You waited aprox .... min.
c. Reasonable delay ☐ | ☐3
4—Sp's expression pleasant on approaching ⊠ | ☐2
5—Quote greeting No verbal greeting
VALUE 8

B—SECURING ATTENTION

1—Was requested mdse. in stock? ⊠ | ☐
2—If not, did sp. attempt to fill your requirements? ☐ | ☐10
a. Suggested a substitute ○
b. Offered to order item ○
c. Directed you to another dept. ○
3—Name item not in stock
VALUE 10

Did you voluntarily select all mdse. from a display ☐ | ⊠
(If "Yes" do not answer Section "C")

C—ESTABLISHING INTEREST

1—Was sp. familiar with location of stock? ⊠ | ☐2
a. Familiar with prices? ⊠ | ☐2
2—Showed wide enough assortment of mdse. ⊠ | ☐3
3—Showed mdse. pleasingly ⊠ | ☐3
VALUE 10

Was there any need to create desire or induce decision on purchased mdse.? (Yes | No) ⊠ | ☐
(If "No", do not answer Section "D")

D—CREATING DESIRE FOR MDSE.

1—Gave details on good qualities of mdse.? ⊠ | ☐3
2—Stressed benefits you would enjoy from mdse. in use ⊠ | ☐3
3—Justified price of mdse. ⊠ | ☐2
4—Answered questions satisfactorily ⊠ | ☐3
VALUE 11

E—TRADING UP

No opportunity to trade up ○
1—Made effort to trade up on requested mdse.? ☐ | ⊠12
a. Offered larger size unit ○
b. Better quality mdse. ○
c. More than one of item ○
2—Actually showed this mdse. ☐ | ☐2
3—Stressed benefits to be enjoyed from more or better mdse. ☐ | ☐2
VALUE 12

F—SUGGESTION SELLING

No opportunity to suggest ○
1—Suggested additional mdse. other than that requested ☐ | ⊠12
2—Did sp. show this mdse.? ☐ | ☐2
3—Did sp. stress benefits of buying suggested mdse.? ☐ | ☐2
4—Quote suggestion
VALUE 12

G—APPEARANCE OF SALESPERSON (Yes | No)

1—Hair neat? ⊠ | ☐1
2—Clothing neat? ⊠ | ☐1
3—Fingernails clean? ⊠ | ☐1
4—Was salesperson—chewing gum— ○1
smoking on duty?— ○1
VALUE 5

H—APPEARANCE OF DEPARTMENT

1—Floor clean? ⊠ | ☐
2—Mdse. neatly arranged? ⊠ | ☐1
3—Dept. well lighted? ⊠ | ☐
4—Mdse. clean and fresh? ⊠ | ☐
VALUE 1

I—COMPLIANCE WITH STORE SYSTEM

1—System used—Register ⊠ Book ○ Cert. ○
2—If register used, was drawer Closed ⊠ Could not observe ○ Open | ○3
3—If system calls for receipt to customer—Was receipt given on above purchase? ☐ | ⊠8
4—Was merchandise given to you—After you paid ⊠ Before you paid ○6
5—Did salesperson call back—
Amt. sale ⊠ | ☐2
Amt. tend. ⊠ | ☐2
Change ☐ | ☐2
No change required ⊠
6—Did sp. give you mdse. and change without unusual delay? ⊠ | ☐2
VALUE 25

J—CLOSING OF SALE

1—What did sp. say at close?

Said nothing at close | ⊠6
VALUE 6

ADD NUMBERS LISTED BESIDE "NO" SQUARES AND CIRCLES IN WHICH X MARKS APPEAR. SUBTRACT TOTAL FROM 100, GIVING YOU THE S.Q. PERCENTAGE.

Remarks Handbags were price-ranged from $4.98 to $12.98, but salesperson limited her selling efforts to the $4.98 bags. She did not suggest I purchase additional merchandise, although there was a pre-holiday sale in the Glove Dept. I was not issued a receipt for the above purchase.

Willmark Service System, Inc.

Persons who pretend to be customers but who are actually employed by the store to rate salespeople's performances are called professional shoppers. This is a form frequently used by professional shoppers. Stores have found that scores above 80 percent are unusual.

advance in the company. Here is how a salesman might advance to the top management level in one manufacturing firm:

1. Salesman.
2. Sales supervisor or branch manager.
3. Assistant district sales manager.
4. District sales manager.
5. Regional sales manager.
6. Assistant general sales manager.
7. General sales manager in charge of all personal selling.
8. Vice-president in charge of marketing.

At the second level, the individual might be responsible for as few as three or four salesmen. The assistant district manager might supervise 10 to 15 salesmen. The regional sales manager is usually responsible for dealing with several district sales managers and may supervise 50 to 100 men, depending on the company, its size, and the nature of its business. The assistant general sales manager works closely with the general sales manager in overseeing the entire sales force. The position of vice-president in charge of marketing usually requires that the person have more general marketing responsibilities, rather than being restricted only to selling.

The top sales and marketing executive of any company has a tremendous amount of responsibility. He must keep his company's production high by marketing salable products and must also keep in mind the impact of his job upon the total economy. Studies show that about 100 factory workers and their dependents are directly affected by the results attained by each salesman. It is easy to understand why the person charged with sales management responsibilities must get the maximum results from his sales force.

CHECKING YOUR KNOWLEDGE

Vocabulary:

turnover

Review questions:

1. What is the relationship between recruiting and turnover?
2. What sources are used in recruiting sales employees? Why do these sources vary among selling firms?
3. What kinds of psychological tests may selling firms give their applicants?
4. When is it especially desirable to develop training programs for salesmen?

5. How are subjective evaluations of salesmen made?
6. Why have the human relations approaches of some sales managers not been effective? What do personnel specialists recommend that sales managers do to overcome this problem?

For discussion:

1. Do you think that expert salesmen are always the best candidates for a sales manager's position? Why?
2. Some employers give numerous tests to all sales applicants, while other employers give few, if any, tests. Do you think either policy is wise? Why? What do you think accounts for the varying importance placed on formal pre-employment testing programs?

part C

compensation of salesmen

As you learned in Part A, businesses offer financial and nonfinancial incentives to encourage salesmen to increase their sales volume and lower selling expenses. Deciding what incentives or compensation plans to offer is not easy, since selling jobs may differ considerably even within the same selling firm. Some sales engineers, for example, may spend many months on a single sales transaction. Even though the sale may eventually amount to many thousands of dollars, it is not fair for the sales engineer to be paid on a straight-commission basis. No amount of attractive nonfinancial incentives would make up for the fact that, for several months, he earned no money. In the paragraphs that follow, you will learn about the financial and nonfinancial compensation plans often found in selling.

FINANCIAL COMPENSATION PLANS

Four main types of financial compensation plans are the time wage plan (hourly wages or straight salary), straight commission plan, salary plus commission plan, and quota plan. Firms may also offer certain supplementary financial compensations in addition to these major plans.

Time Wages

Time wages are based on a definite time period, such as an hour, day, week, month, or year. Few selling firms pay their sales personnel hourly wages, except in the case of part-time retail salespeople. With a *straight salary*—also a kind of time wage—individuals are paid a flat rate per week or month. Many salesmen are paid by the straight salary plan, particularly in retailing.

Perhaps the chief advantage of time wages, for the selling firm, is that it is easy to determine what salary expenses will be for a given period. This amount can thus be provided for in the firm's budget. The major disadvantage of time wages is that they do not stimulate salespeople to put forth extra selling effort. Salespeople may do just enough work to get by, particularly if they see that other salespeople are doing less work than they are and receiving the same salary.

Straight Commission Plan

When a salesman is paid by the *straight commission plan,* he receives a definite percentage of his sales volume as his earnings. Outside retail salesmen, for example, may be paid at the rate of 5 percent of their net sales volume. They receive no set salary.

The major advantage of the straight-commission plan is that it stimulates salesmen to put forth their best selling efforts. The more they sell, the more they earn. Perhaps the major disadvantage is that the plan often encourages high-pressure selling. The salesman may be so concerned about making the maximum number of sales that he loses sight of his customer's needs and wants. This builds customer ill will and can mean the loss of future business.

In highly seasonal lines, the straight commission plan may mean that the salesman earns little during the off-season. This lack of a steady income may make it difficult for him to meet personal financial obligations. To overcome this problem, many firms provide *drawing accounts*. The drawing account allows money to be advanced to the salesman. His later earnings are credited against the withdrawn amounts. There is a possible danger with the drawing account, although it is a beneficial device to salespeople. If a salesman has a particularly bad selling season, he may find that he owes the company money at the end of the year. Withdrawals may exceed the total commissions he earned.

Salary and Commission Plan

The *salary and commission plan* eliminates most of the problems connected with the straight salary and straight commission plans. The salesman is paid a straight salary and also receives a commission on his net sales. If the commission rate is 2 percent and he sells $800 worth of goods during a week, he earns a commission of $16 in addition to his salary. Since the commission is calculated on net sales, the salesman should make allowances for probable merchandise returns when he is estimating his earnings.

Quota Plan

The *quota plan* is really a variation of the salary and commission plan. The salesman earns a straight salary and receives a commission on sales exceeding his quota. A salesman who earns a monthly salary of $500 may be given a 4 percent commission on all monthly sales over a quota of $4,000. If his sales during September amount to $6,200, his commission will be $88; and his total monthly earnings will be $588.

In setting sales goals or quotas, the sales manager may consider such factors as population in the trading area, incomes of families, volume of retail trade, and number of outlets carrying his type of goods. For example, the sales manager of a firm manufacturing automatic dishwashers may conclude that a certain territory has a potential for 1 percent of the total national sales of his merchandise. If his firm's national sales goal is $20 million a year, the territory will be given a quota of $200,000.

Back-to-School Merchandise	Estimated Aug.-Sept. Volume per 1,000 Families		No. of Families in Your Market (in Thousands)		Your Market's Total Potential
Girls' Wear – Age 2-15	$15,123	X		=	
16-17	4,142	X		=	
Girls' Footwear – 2-17	4,384	X		=	
Boys' Wear – Age 2-15	11,855	X		=	
16-17	2,658	X		=	
Boys' Footwear – 2-17	4,686	X		=	
Luggage, Briefcases, School Bags	1,276	X		=	
Portable Typewriters	435	X		=	
TOTAL					

Bureau of Advertising, ANPA

This table is based on U.S. Department of Commerce figures and shows the expenditures per 1,000 families for back-to-school items. When the retailer determines the number of families in his store's market area, he can combine the two sets of figures to set sales goals for his back-to-school campaign.

Supplementary Financial Incentive Plans

A supplementary financial incentive plan found in retailing is called *push money,* or *premium money.* A reward is given salesmen for "pushing" the sale of a certain article. The store may want to get a slow-moving item out of stock and will offer a reward of 75¢ for each of these items sold. Push money may also be offered by a manufacturer or wholesaler. For him to give push money to retail salespeople is likely to be found illegal unless the following conditions are met:

1. The retailer has consented to the payments.
2. No lottery is involved in making the payments.
3. The sales of competing products the store sells are not unduly hampered.
4. The device is available to salespeople in competing stores on proportionally equal terms.

Another common type of supplementary financial incentive is the bonus. The *bonus* is different from a commission because there is no predetermined relationship, such as a percentage, between the bonus and the salesman's performance. The bonus is similar to a commission, though, because it is given for above-average performance. Bonuses are flat sums given to salespeople for accomplishing certain tasks, such as increasing sales of the company's more profitable products, developing new accounts, or increasing the number of calls made in a given time period.

NONFINANCIAL COMPENSATION PLANS

Years ago, the major benefit that a salesman expected from his job was his salary or commission. Today, most firms provide many other supplementary advantages, called *fringe benefits.* Firms are required by law to provide some of these benefits; other benefits are provided voluntarily to build a satisfied, effective selling team.

Fringe Benefits Required by Law

According to the Social Security Act, businesses must provide Old-Age, Survivors, and Disability Insurance, health insurance, and unemployment insurance for their employees. *OASDI* gives pensions to retired employees, death benefits to survivors of employees, and benefits to disabled employees. Both the employee and his employer pay taxes to support this program. The health insurance program is commonly called

Medicare. One of its provisions is hospital insurance, which covers certain expenses an employee incurs if he is hospitalized. Employees and employers pay taxes to support hospital insurance. Medical insurance can also be obtained under the health insurance program. Employees pay small amounts for it, and their payments are matched by the federal government.

All states have *unemployment insurance plans* under which qualified individuals who are totally or partially unemployed receive weekly payments. Employers pay taxes to support these programs. All states also provide *workmen's compensation programs.* If employees are injured on the job, they are covered by insurance which pays medical expenses and benefits to them.

Fringe Benefits Not Required by Law

Fringe benefits not required by law vary considerably from firm to firm, but some of the most common are:

1. Group insurance plans, which enable employees to obtain life insurance at much lower rates than they could obtain if they were to buy it outside the firm. Sometimes the selling firm pays part or all of the premium.
2. Pension plans, which provide money for an employee after retirement.

Maccabees Mutual Life Insurance Co.

A fringe benefit that many selling firms voluntarily provide is a clean, attractive cafeteria. Many firms subsidize the cafeteria operation so that food is provided at a reasonable price to employees, and the firm itself makes no profit from the cafeteria operation.

3. Paid vacations and holidays.
4. Health and safety programs.
5. Stock purchase options, which allow the employee to have a certain amount of money deducted from his pay check to buy stock in the firm. Some companies match each employee's purchase with an equal amount of stock, which is given free to the employee.
6. Employee discounts, which allow the employee to obtain his firm's products at a certain percentage off the list price.

Additional Nonfinancial Incentive Plans

As you have learned, selling firms frequently sponsor sales contests and give prizes and awards to stimulate selling effort. Many firms give rewards for employee suggestions on business operations that the company adopts. Posting each salesman's standing in such areas as total sales, increase in sales compared with previous years, number of new customers obtained, and proportion of potential market reached is a strong stimulus to further achievement. In fact, management's public recognition of a salesman's accomplishments is one of the most important nonfinancial incentives.

CHECKING YOUR KNOWLEDGE

Vocabulary:

(1) time wages
(2) straight salary
(3) straight commission plan
(4) drawing accounts
(5) salary and commission plan
(6) quota plan
(7) push money, or premium money
(8) bonus
(9) fringe benefits
(10) OASDI
(11) Medicare
(12) unemployment insurance plans
(13) workmen's compensation programs

Review questions:

1. Why is it difficult for management to establish fair compensation plans for salesmen?
2. Give the advantages and disadvantages of the time wage and straight commission methods of compensation.
3. What factors might a sales manager consider when setting a sales quota for his salesmen?
4. What fringe benefits are required by law?
5. Name five fringe benefits not required by law but commonly provided by many firms.

For discussion:

1. Some salesmen refuse to work on anything but a straight commission plan. Others refuse to work on a straight commission plan. Do you think that either extreme reaction to the straight commission plan is justified? Why?
2. Since more fringe benefits are now required by law, do you think that employers will tend to increase or decrease the number of fringe benefits they voluntarily provide?

part D

determining sales productivity

Sales managers must periodically evaluate the performance of individual salesmen and of the entire sales force to find out whether sales productivity is as high as it should be. Analyses of sales productivity are used in planning and forecasting sales operations. If a sales manager finds that sales productivity is less than it should be, he can isolate the causes and take action to correct the problem.

ANALYZING THE SALESMAN'S PRODUCTIVITY

Some basic measures of a salesman's productivity are: (1) sales volume (by product and customer); (2) relationship of sales volume to quota; (3) gross margin (difference between total sales volume and total production costs or purchasing costs, not including operating or selling expenses); (4) size of orders; (5) ratio of number of transactions to sales volume; (6) ratio of selling expenses to sales volume; and (7) cost per sales call or transaction. The last three measures will be discussed in the following paragraphs.

Average Sale

The relationship of the number of transactions to the total sales volume for a given period is called the *average sale*. This figure is useful in comparing the productivity of different salesmen. The average sale is computed by dividing dollar sales by the number of transactions. Thus, if a retail salesman makes 500 sales during a month and his net sales for that period are $4,000, his average sale is $8.

In outside selling, the number of calls made on customers—rather than the number of transactions completed—may be used to figure the average sale. Suppose, for example, that two house-to-house salesmen selling similar articles each have sales of $500 during one week. One salesman made 50 calls; the other made 100 calls. The first salesman thus had an average sale of $10, and the second salesman had an average sale of $5. These figures show that the second salesman is not selling as efficiently as the first salesman. He had to make twice as many calls to sell the same amount of merchandise. He should learn how the first salesman sells $10 worth of goods in the average call. To obtain the larger average sale, the second salesman may have to reduce the number of calls he makes and concentrate upon selling more effectively to the persons he contacts.

Selling Cost Percentage

Dividing a salesperson's earnings and expenses by his net sales gives a figure called the *selling cost percentage*. In applying this formula to a traveling salesman, expenses for such things as travel and entertainment would be considered as part of his selling cost. In applying the formula to retail salesmen, management customarily considers only the salesman's earnings.

Many firms have found from past experience that selling costs tend to remain fairly constant or that one selling cost percentage is the maximum that the firm or department can have and still operate profitably. Thus, they settle upon a standard selling cost and use it in budgeting and planning. They may also use this standard selling cost figure as a means of comparison for the salesman's actual selling cost. If his selling cost is considerably higher than the standard cost, it decreases the firm's profits and productivity.

Suppose that a salesman is hired at a salary of $100 a week. If the firm considers 5 percent to be the standard selling cost of his department, it is easy to determine how much he should sell in a week for him to be considered satisfactorily productive. If 5% of his total sales equals $100 (his salary), 1% of his sales will equal $20. Thus, 100% (his total sales for the week) should be $2,000. If, after an adjustment period of a few weeks, this salesman does not sell an average of $2,000 worth of goods a week, he may be in danger of losing his job.

"Do you think it might help if we went back to the old unimproved product?"

Sales Management

Determining sales productivity has implications for virtually all areas of planning, including changes in the product line.

Cost Per Call or Transaction

A particularly important problem for today's sales manager is the rising selling cost per call or transaction. The cost per call or transaction can be determined by dividing the total selling expense—the salesman's earnings plus expenses for such things as travel and entertainment—by the total number of transactions or calls in a given time period. Selling firms obviously want to minimize the cost per call while still assuring that customers are adequately served.

An industrial selling survey revealed that the average cost of a single call is now about $43; it was less than $17 only 15 years ago. The cost per call is lower with large sales forces than with small ones. In firms whose sales forces are composed of more than 50 salesmen, the average cost per call is $29.60. In firms whose sales forces are composed of 10 to 25 salesmen, the cost is $44.95. Greater concentration on a smaller geographic area and better supervision probably account for the greater productivity of the large force.

In retail selling, it is difficult to keep records of all customer contacts, so the cost per completed transaction is calculated. In department stores, selling salaries alone amount to about 50 cents per transaction. However, the transactions average only about $6 each, compared with transactions of hundreds or thousands of dollars in contact selling.

ANALYZING THE SALES FORCE'S PRODUCTIVITY

It is helpful to analyze the productivity of the total sales force in relation to other aspects of the firm's operations. This gives an overall picture of the sales division's place in and contribution to the business. Three important measures that may be made are sales and expense comparisons, calculation of the break-even point, and calculation of net income.

Sales and Expense Comparisons

Suppose that a dairy farmer spends $10,000 a year to operate his business. This amount covers the hired man's salary and farm supplies. The amount of $10,000 in itself has no significance. It becomes important only when it is compared with something. It becomes important when it is compared with sales. Suppose that the sales of milk amount to only $10,000. The expenses and costs are thus 100% of sales. However, if sales are $20,000, the expenses and costs are 50% of sales, and the farmer has a 50% margin to repay him for the use of the farm, equipment, his labor, and his managerial skills.

From this simple example, you can see that a comparison of expenses, selling costs, and profits with sales volume is more significant if it is expressed in percentage form rather than in dollars. If a store's expenses amount to $15,000 a month and sales amount to $50,000, the expenses are 30 percent of sales. This is much more meaningful than saying that expenses were $35,000 less than sales.

Most firms will know the maximum percentage of sales their expenses can be and still have a profitable operation. Using this standard percentage as a means of comparison, they can determine whether sales should be increased or expenses reduced to maintain a desirable ratio. Sales and expense comparisons expressed in percentage form make it easy to compare one firm's sales with another firm's sales, even though the dollar figures are very different.

Calculating the Break-Even Point

The *break-even point* is that point at which the total costs of producing or purchasing and distributing a product just equal the revenue from the sale of that product. Calculating the break-even point is helpful in establishing sales quotas, because as sales increase beyond the break-even point, there will be a margin of profit. Firms obviously want to maximize this margin of profit.

Suppose that 60 percent of a company's sales volume for a product is equal to the cost of producing that product. This leaves 40 percent of the sales volume to cover all marketing expenses and give a margin of profit. Suppose also that salesmen are paid a straight-commission rate of 8 percent, that advertising accounts for about 3 percent of sales, and that merchandise handling costs are about 7 percent of sales. Other marketing expenses, such as administrative salaries and office expenses, are relatively fixed. This means that they do not vary much over the short run with changes in sales volume. Assume that these expenses amount to $66,000 for a given time period. Expenses of salaries, advertising, and merchandise handling amount to 18 percent of sales. This leaves 22 percent of sales to cover fixed expenses and give a profit. Just to break even, this 22 percent would equal the fixed expenses of $66,000. One percent of sales would equal $3,000, and 100 percent of sales would equal $300,000—the break-even point. The ability of the sales force to sell more than $300,000 will result in a profit.

Calculating Net Income

Another important measure of sales productivity and of the firm's overall operating efficiency is the calculation of net income. Every selling firm calculates net income at least once a year. An *income statement,* which shows the net income or loss of a firm over a given period of time, may be prepared in any one of several forms. Regardless of the exact form used, the statement will contain information similar to the following:

Sales during year		$20,000
Inventory at beginning of year	$ 6,000	
Merchandise purchased during year	15,000	
Goods available for sale during year	$21,000	
Inventory at end of year	8,000	
Cost of merchandise sold during year		13,000
Gross margin to pay expenses and provide profit		$ 7,000
Expenses		5,000
Net income		$ 2,000

Manufacturers prepare much more elaborate income statements than do retailers. This is partly because manufacturers buy materials rather than finished goods and must add the cost of labor used to manufacture the finished goods.

CHECKING YOUR KNOWLEDGE

Vocabulary:

(1) average sale
(2) selling cost percentage
(3) break-even point
(4) income statement

Review questions:

1. What are some basic measures of a salesman's productivity?
2. Of what value is knowledge of the ratio between number of transactions in a given selling period and total sales volume for that period?
3. Why do firms compute a standard selling cost percentage and use this percentage in planning?
4. Is it better to express sales and expense figures in percentage form or in dollar form? Why?
5. The break-even point is of particular significance to aggressive, cost-oriented businesses. Why is this so?
6. What important information may be contained in an income statement?

For discussion:

1. Some firms place considerable emphasis on each salesman's cost per call or transaction. Although this cost analysis is important, it does have some objectionable features. Can you identify some of these objectionable features?
2. Profits of some large companies are smaller today than they have been in recent years, although their sales are considerably higher. How do you account for this? Why is knowledge of the break-even point especially helpful to these firms in analyzing production and distribution costs?

part E

data processing in selling

Our economy's growth during the past 30 years has made it necessary for selling firms to use methods of collecting, classifying, and analyzing sales data that are faster and more accurate than the old manual methods. If a selling firm is to effectively evaluate its financial status, it must have the proper information available when it is needed.

It is no longer practical for a selling firm to wait several weeks while clerks compile the data to be used in analyzing a product's market performance. A delay in recognizing an unprofitable or slow-moving item can be costly.

IMPORTANCE OF AUTOMATED DATA PROCESSING

Suppose that a selling firm with yearly sales of $10 million wants to determine the sales volume of each of its 30 salesmen. If the average amount of an order were $500, clerks would have to sort through 20,000 separate orders to determine one person's sales volume. Today such sales data may be obtained quickly by using techniques of automated data processing. *Data processing* is a procedure or combination of procedures whereby the recorded information about transactions is manipulated by hand, mechanical, or electronic methods; and readable reports are prepared from the manipulated information. When this work is done by machine with a minimum amount of human effort, the process is called *automated data processing,* or *automation.* Modern data processing equipment makes it possible to rapidly collect, classify, analyze, and report information in readable form.

Businesses that have meaningful reports available for study at the proper time can compete more effectively. A manufacturer, wholesaler, or retailer must know what his market is, where it is located, and how he can best service it. He must be able to determine whether salesmen are covering the market satisfactorily and whether his sales promotion media are working successfully. He must know what his present sales are, what his past sales were, and what his potential sales are. With automated data processing, he can obtain this information quickly.

AUTOMATIC DATA PROCESSING

Automatic data processing (ADP)—a mechanical method of processing data—was introduced about 40 years ago to provide a more efficient method of reporting information. With this method, data are first transferred to punched cards from source documents such as salesmen's reports and orders. The punched cards are then sorted and tabulated, and reports are prepared. ADP equipment cannot store information for immediate recall and use. It merely processes the information as it is received. ADP was used extensively by businesses until the early 1950's, but now its use is limited mainly to small business operations.

"It says today is the tomorrow you worried about yesterday."

Sales Management

Some managers find it difficult to make effective decisions without the computer's help.

ELECTRONIC DATA PROCESSING

The need to obtain more kinds of information more quickly than ADP could provide resulted in business' adoption of the computer. The *computer* is an electronic device that receives data, stores it, performs arithmetic calculations with it, and produces reports that management can use. The first workable electronic computer was developed in 1946 at the University of Pennsylvania. It had only one purpose: preparing ballistic tables to reveal the motion of missiles in flight. Computers were first used in business in the early 1950's.

Processing data with the computer is known as *electronic data processing (EDP)*. A basic difference between ADP and EDP is that the computer can store information and recall it. Information can be retrieved in a fraction of a second and combined with other data to produce a report. EDP is much faster and more flexible than ADP.

Data Processing Service Bureaus

Many businesses cannot afford to buy or rent ADP or EDP equipment, but they can now take advantage of data processing by sending their data to a service bureau. The *data processing service bureau* is an

ADP or EDP installation that processes data for businesses on a fee basis. Reports are usually available within two or three days after the bureau receives the information. The bureau's charges for processing data are often less than the costs of processing data manually, and the variety of reports available from the bureau is greater than could be obtained by manual processing.

Computer Time-Sharing

One of the latest data-processing developments is *computer time-sharing*. Numerous businesses are linked by telephone lines to a high-speed computer. A device similar to a typewriter is located in the business, and data entered through this device are carried over the telephone line to the computer. The device in the business is also used to report in typed form the information transmitted from the computer. For reports involving many mathematical computations, computer time-sharing is particularly efficient. Subscribing businesses are charged only for the actual amount of time they use the computer.

Central Computer

Selling firms whose branch offices are scattered throughout the country frequently link all offices by telephone to a central computer in the home office. This computer receives all data direct from the branches and begins processing the information almost as soon as it is received. Other selling firms prefer that branch offices mail in their data, in the form of punched paper tape or punched cards, to avoid expensive telephone charges. The needs and size of the business will determine how it uses electronic data processing.

USING DATA PROCESSING IN SELLING

The data to be collected, classified, and analyzed will vary from selling firm to selling firm and even within a single firm. However, some applications are common to most businesses, both at the salesperson's level and the sales manager's level.

The Salesman and Data Processing

The salesman is often involved in collecting information for automated data processing. In most retail stores, for example, sales are recorded at the cash register. Newer cash registers enable the printed record of the day's sales transactions to be taken and converted instantly

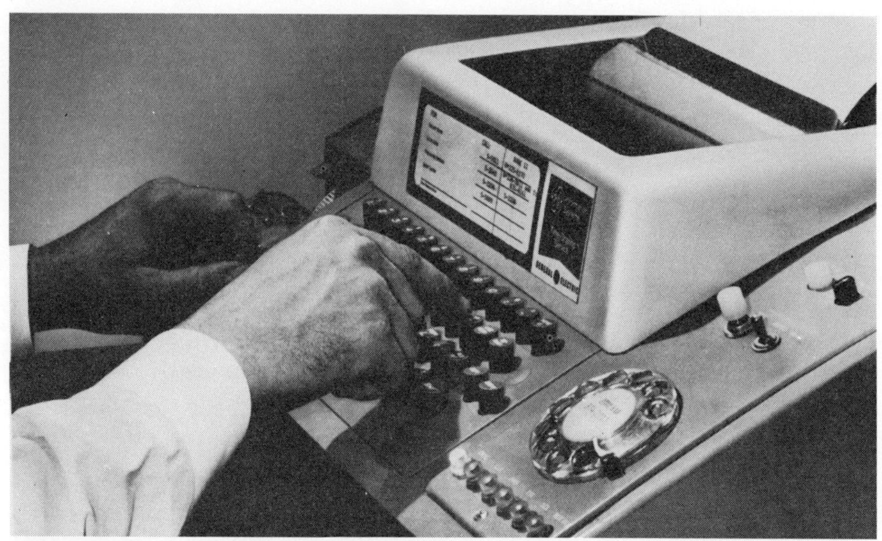

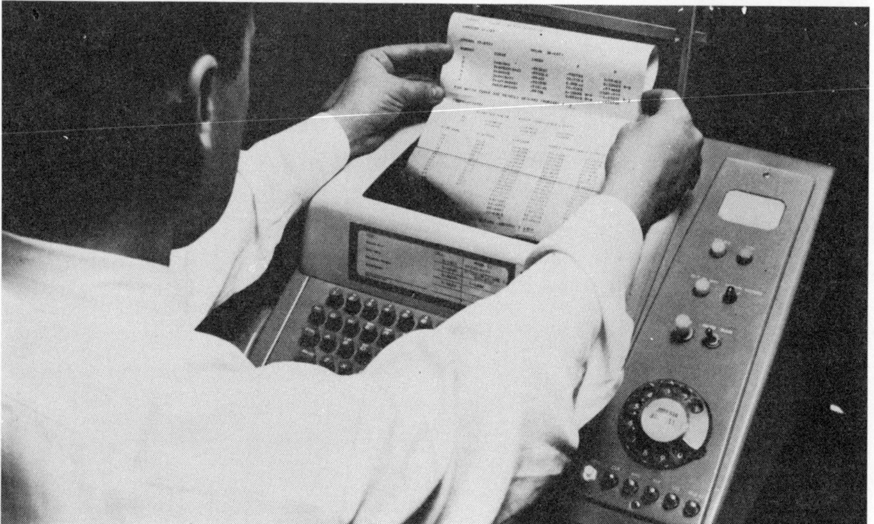

General Electric

These illustrations show the basic parts of a computer time-sharing installation in a business. The input device is connected by telephone lines to a computer, and data are entered through the keyboard and carried over the telephone lines to the computer. The sample report below illustrates the kind of information the business may receive from the central computer. Data for the report are conveyed back to the business through the telephone lines and typed out by the same device used to send the information to the computer.

into code form that can be used by EDP equipment. Some cash registers prepare optical font tape as a by-product of the checking operation. *Optical font tape* has printed characters that can be converted into electronic impulses for the computer by a device called an *optical scanner.* Some stores connect their cash registers to a central computer. As sales are rung on the register, data are transmitted directly to the computer. Sales are then automatically analyzed, inventories determined, and merchandise orders prepared when an item's stock reaches a designated low limit.

Some traveling salesmen prepare orders on *mark-sensed cards.* These cards are marked with electrically conductive pencil marks. A machine later converts the pencil marks into code form that can be interpreted by data processing equipment.

Data processing is also used in preparing and processing some types of price tickets. Information contained on price tickets may be recorded in punched cards that can later be sorted and analyzed by ADP or EDP. Other tickets are prepared like punch cards with tiny pinholes that indicate in code an item's price, merchandise classification, and other such information. These tickets can be processed by a machine that prepares regular full-size punched cards for every pinhole ticket. The punched cards can then be sorted and tabulated and the necessary reports prepared.

Computers are also used in authorizing retail credit purchases. Data about a customer's credit limit and current account balance may be stored in the computer. When a customer presents his credit card for a purchase, a cash register or other machine linked to the computer signals the computer to check the customer's credit standing. If the account is in good standing, the computer will give an affirmative response to the salesperson. If the account is not in good standing, the computer will indicate that the customer is to be referred to the credit department.

The Sales Manager and Data Processing

One of the first data processing applications that a sales manager makes is analyzing sales. A computer can quickly analyze the merchandise sold by a variety of classifications such as size and style and can analyze the sales volume produced by a single salesperson. With contact salesmen, a sales analysis in relation to the potential volume of a given territory may reveal some discrepancies in territory assignments. For example, a computer report may show that a normally productive

AT&T

With the equipment shown above, the salesperson can feed into a central computer information on the customer's account number, price of the goods, merchandise code, and her salesperson's number. The information recorded can then be used for sales analysis purposes. The computer can also use this information to check the customer's credit standing and authorize the transaction.

salesman is obtaining only 25 percent of the available business in his territory. An alert sales manager would then take steps to place additional salesmen in the territory so that a larger sales volume might be obtained.

The computer is also used to receive and direct customer orders. With the computer doing the paperwork, many firms can fill an order within 24 hours instead of four or five days. The same computer can determine the best shipping routes, prepare customer invoices, and even determine the cost and pricing of special orders. For example, a customer may need motors, drives, and gears that are not part of a manufacturer's regular inventory. The computer can calculate the cost of producing the items and the probable selling prices of them.

DECISION MAKING WITH THE COMPUTER

Planning data processing applications has forced management to become more analytical. To obtain the reports that will effectively direct total marketing effort, managers must think through each step of collecting, processing, and analyzing data. This forces them to look objectively at facts, and this objectivity results in more realistic directions from management. Subjective opinion alone cannot produce profits. Armed with a computer's comprehensive reports, managers can objectively interpret information on a given situation.

Future applications of data processing will probably involve a broader analysis of potential markets. Although analyzing current sales is extremely important, it is equally important to plan. Computer reports can give management greater insight into potential sales and profits and greater awareness of marketing problems. No application, though, is possible without human beings to develop and plan information for the computer. The computer cannot think; it can only act on the information given to it. Individuals with creativity and vision will always be needed to profitably use the computer in marketing decision making.

CHECKING YOUR KNOWLEDGE

Vocabulary:

(1) data processing
(2) automated data processing, or automation
(3) automatic data processing (ADP)
(4) computer
(5) electronic data processing (EDP)
(6) data processing service bureau
(7) computer time-sharing
(8) optical font tape
(9) optical scanner
(10) mark-sensed cards

Review questions:

1. Explain the steps followed in processing data by EDP techniques. How does EDP differ from ADP?
2. Why do many businesses use the services of data processing bureaus and computer time-sharing?
3. How is the salesman involved in collecting data for analysis by EDP equipment?
4. Describe the computer's activities in handling customer orders.
5. How have data processing applications forced management to become more analytical?

For discussion:

1. Is it possible to place undue emphasis on the computer's role in decision making? Why?
2. Some managers feel they are being given too much information, with the numerous data processing reports made available to them. Do you think this is possible? Why?

BUILDING YOUR SKILLS

Improving your English:

On a separate sheet of paper, write the correct adverb to be used in each of the following sentences.

1. The fashion model walks quite (graceful, gracefully).
2. The cars moved (slow, slowly) toward the expressway access ramp.
3. The shipment of dresses arrived (to, too) late.
4. (Most, Almost) every order had been processed by Jane Williams.
5. Of the many colors suggested, blue will be (more, most) appropriate for this background.
6. The advertising seminar was the (less, least) constructive activity of the three training sessions.
7. Richard had a (real, very) good understanding of the marketing problem.
8. The sales manager planned the conferences (good, well) so that each hour would be used effectively.
9. Susan is (real, quite) happy with the selection of office furniture.
10. Salesmen will (sure, surely) obtain additional orders if they convey adequate product knowledge to the customer.

Improving your arithmetic:

The problems below involve more than one step in obtaining their solution; show each step used.

1. Fred Way, a salesman for the Grant Manufacturing Company, is compensated for all travel expenses and is allowed a drawing account of $500 per month, which is charged against his commissions for the month. He receives monthly commissions of 2% on the first $25,000 of sales, 2½% on the next $15,000, and 3% on sales in excess of $40,000. What is the total amount due him for a month in which his drawings were $500 and his sales were $42,790?
2. When property that is insured by several companies is destroyed by fire, each company shares the loss in proportion to the percentage of the total insurance carried with that company. The Star Sports Shop was insured for $100,000. The American Insurance Company carried $65,000 of the insurance, and the Mutual Insurance Company carried the remainder. Fire damaged the store, and damage amounted to $75,000. How much will each insurance company have to pay?
3. Variable selling and merchandise handling expenses in a store are about 12% of sales, and fixed expenses are $46,000. The store operates at a gross margin of 35%. What is the store's break-even point?

Improving your research skills:

1. Select two selling positions from the list given on page 543. Through research in your school library or by talking with a sales manager whom you know, determine what recruiting methods and training and

supervision procedures might be used by sales managers of these salesmen. Identify also the promotional opportunities that might be available in each job. Present your answers in report form.

(a) Sales engineer for a steel supplier (sells steel for industrial building construction, highway programs, and government contracts).
(b) Manufacturer's representative for an automobile producer (calls on the manufacturer's dealers).
(c) Direct salesman (sells cosmetics by door-to-door canvassing).
(d) Combination detailer (represents a pharmaceutical manufacturer and calls on doctors, druggists, and wholesalers).
(e) Retail salesperson (sells small appliances in a department store).

2. Select three sales positions from the list of five given in Problem 1. Determine the compensation plan that you feel would be best for that kind of position. Be prepared to give to the class your answers and the reasons for your answers.
3. The costs of contact sales calls have increased rapidly in the past few years. Outline a program that a manufacturer might follow to reduce the cost of sales calls.
4. Bring to class a sample of a report or bill prepared by data processing equipment. Most bills from utility companies and major oil companies are prepared by data processing equipment. Identify the information contained in the samples you select and try to find out why each kind of information was included. See if you can find out how the arrangement of the data facilitates rapid handling of the data by data processing equipment.

APPLYING YOUR KNOWLEDGE

Case problem:

Timothy Griffin, sales manager for the Freemont Food Corporation, had been a contact salesman with the firm for ten years before recently being promoted. He was the company's outstanding salesman in total sales volume for most of his years in the field. Mr. Griffin is a very disciplined person and firmly believes that all sales personnel should utilize every moment with a customer to effect a sale. As sales manager, he accompanies salesmen regularly on their sales calls. Newer salesmen find it difficult to be at ease with customers when Mr. Griffin is along, since he frequently interrupts the salesman if the sales presentation is not going well. He gives the salesman a critical analysis of each sale as they travel to see the next customer. Several salesmen have indicated an inability to discuss sales-related problems with Mr. Griffin, since he always seems to have a ready-made answer for each situation.

What positive features can you identify in Mr. Griffin's supervision of his salesmen? What negative features do you see? Suggest ways in which he might be more effective in working with his salesmen.

Continuing project:

Assume that you have advanced to the position of sales manager in your chosen selling job and type of selling firm. In your manual, describe the recruiting, training, and supervisory policies you would establish for salesmen beneath you. Describe the compensation plan you would adopt for salesmen selling your product and the kinds of fringe benefits you would provide. Also, tell how you would analyze the productivity of your individual salesmen and of the sales force and tell whether you would be able to use data processing procedures in making your necessary analyses.

Extra credit:

Visit a store in your community that uses ADP or EDP procedures. Determine the kinds of ADP or EDP procedures used. Identify the kinds of reports made available to management and determine how these reports are used in guiding management decisions. Prepare a chart or poster depicting the flow of data from collection to the finished report prepared for management. Write a summary of your findings.

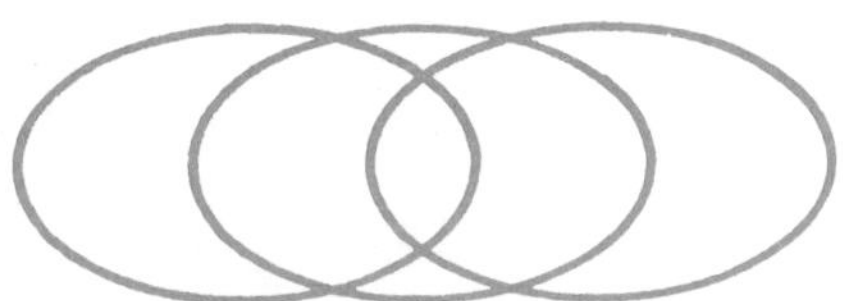

chapter 16

legal aspects of selling

KEY QUESTIONS

A Why is it important that the salesman have a working knowledge of business law?

B What is the difference between an employee, an independent agent, and an independent contractor?

C Have food and drug products always been subject to some type of grading and labeling regulation?

D What are some important nonfood items that come under federal labeling regulations?

E Why are there more rules and regulations to govern advertising statements than there are to govern oral statements made in personal selling?

part A

the laws of contract and sales

Standards governing selling conduct are set both by laws and regulations of public authorities and by codes of ethics developed by business itself. To do his job well, the salesman must have a working knowledge of business law. Laws have been enacted to guide the salesman in his dealings with other people. If the salesman does not understand the laws governing his sales, he may do serious injustice to himself, his firm, and his customers. Of particular importance to him are the laws of contract and sales.

THE LAW OF CONTRACT

A *contract* is an agreement between two or more competent parties which creates a binding legal obligation. This obligation is recognized and enforceable by law. If one of the parties does not fulfill his part of the agreement, the other party may take legal action to make him fulfill his obligation.

Example of a Contract

A contract may evolve from a face-to-face conversation, from an exchange of letters, or from a telephone conversation. Suppose that Jack Roberts telephoned the Hyde Park Building Products Company and ordered several pieces of wallboard to be delivered to his home the next day. The materials cost $47.63, which was to be charged to his account, payable in ten days. The result of this telephone conversation was a contract. If either party failed to fulfill his part of the contract, the other party would be able to enforce his rights in court as long as he could provide evidence that the agreement had been made. Although all contracts are based upon agreements, not all agreements are contracts. People often make agreements that are not expected to be enforceable in court. For example, Katie accepts an invitation to attend a dance with Bill, so an agreement has been made. However, if Katie later changes her mind and decides to accept a date with Tom, she is not breaking a contract.

Essential Elements of a Contract

For an agreement to be enforceable in a court of law, it must have these elements: competent parties, offer and acceptance (mutual assent), legal agreement, consideration, and proper legal form.

Competent Parties. To be recognized by law, a contract must be made by competent parties—those who are not prevented by law from making enforceable agreements. For example, under certain conditions one who is mentally ill or one who is intoxicated may not be competent to contract. In many cases, a minor—a person not of legal age—may not be competent to contract. Some sellers may ask the minor's parents to confirm a contract by agreeing in writing to pay if the minor does not. In department stores that offer charge accounts for minors, the parents may be asked to guarantee the agreement between the store and the minor.

Offer and Acceptance (Mutual Assent). For a contract to be legally binding, there must be an agreement to do or not to do a certain thing. For example, Ray Holmes offers to trim the shrubbery on Martha Blair's property for $30. Mrs. Blair accepts the offer, thus promising to pay the price asked. There was mutual agreement, called *mutual assent,* between the two parties. There is no contract, however, unless both parties have freely and intentionally agreed to the same thing.

Legal Agreement. If a contract is to be legally binding, the making and carrying out of it must be legal. A contract is illegal if its objective is socially harmful, criminal, injurious to others, or opposed to public policy. For example, an agreement to steal someone's car cannot be enforced because this contract is obviously illegal.

Consideration. An agreement to give something for nothing usually cannot be enforced. The person who makes the promise ordinarily must receive something for his promise. *Consideration* is something given in exchange for a promise to do something else. Consideration may take the form of money, goods, services, or another promise to do or not to do something he has a legal right to do.

Proper Legal Form. Many contracts are made merely by the exchange of a few words. Certain contracts, however, must be prepared in the written form specified by law to qualify as legal contracts. For example, contracts for the sale of real estate must be in writing to be enforceable in the courts.

Ewing Galloway

All contracts do not have to be prepared in written form in order to be legal. However, certain contracts—such as those for the purchase of real estate—must be prepared in the proper written form prescribed by law.

THE LAW OF SALES

The *sale of goods* involves the transfer of ownership from the seller to the buyer. There is a distinct difference between a sale and a contract to sell. In a sale, any loss following the transfer of ownership that is not caused by the seller is the buyer's responsibility. This is true even if the seller retains possession of the goods. For example, an appliance purchased and paid for at the agreed price but left in the dealer's warehouse to be picked up the following day would be the buyer's loss if it were destroyed by fire during the night. Ownership passed to the buyer at the time of sale.

In a *contract to sell,* ownership does not change until an agreed time has arrived and the agreed conditions have been met. The buyer usually does not suffer loss if the goods are damaged or destroyed unless he has agreed to assume the risk of loss. The appliance buyer would not have borne the loss in a contract to sell, since all conditions of the sale would not have been met. Ownership likely would not have been transferred until the dealer had received all payments for the appliance. Even if the buyer were to assume the risk of loss in this example, that risk would probably not begin until the appliance had been delivered to the buyer.

In an attempt to formulate uniform answers to questions and problems arising in different locations, the rules governing the buying and selling of goods have been brought together in the *Uniform Commercial Code*. The *Code* has been adopted in 49 of the 50 states.

Conditional Sales

A *conditional sale* is used primarily to protect the merchant or manufacturer who sells on credit. In a conditional sale, the buyer has possession of the goods, but the title is retained by the seller. When the entire purchase price is paid, title to the goods passes to the buyer. While the buyer has possession, he may make use of the goods. However, if he does not make his payments according to the contract's stipulations, the seller can repossess the goods.

As you have learned, some installment sales are handled under a chattel mortgage. A chattel mortgage is an agreement under which the purchaser pledges his personal property as security for the debt owed to the seller. Title to the goods passes to the buyer upon delivery, but he signs a mortgage in which he agrees that ownership shall revert to the seller in case the buyer defaults in making payments.

Bailments

A *bailment* exists whenever one person has possession of the goods that belong to another person. The person turning over possession of the goods is the bailor, and the one who receives possession of the goods is the *bailee*. The bailee is responsible for the physical security and protection of the goods to the extent that he may be negligent or fail to take reasonable care of them. The bailee agrees either to return the goods or to redeliver them in accordance with the contract.

Suppose that Jim Holt, a salesman, left a diamond necklace with a retail jeweler, Johnson. The necklace was stolen when Johnson left the store to perform an errand and did not lock the store. Johnson is legally obligated to pay for the necklace, even though no contract to purchase exists. He acted as a bailee in taking possession of the necklace and is responsible for carelessness in its safekeeping. If Johnson had been held up by an armed robber, he would not be obligated to pay for the necklace.

Consignment Selling

Consignment selling is a method of selling by which a person is given possession of property or merchandise and is expected to sell it. For

CONDITIONAL SALES CONTRACT

Account No. ____________

The undersigned seller hereby sells, and the undersigned purchaser hereby purchases, subject to the terms and conditions hereinafter set forth, the following property, delivery and acceptance of which in good order is hereby acknowledged by purchaser, viz.:

DESCRIPTION	SERIAL NO.	PURCHASE PRICE
		$
Salesman	Total	$

For a Total Time Price of .... $________

Payable in an amount on or before delivery of .... $________

Leaving a Deferred Balance of .... $________

Payable at the office of The Philip Stern Company in installments of .... $________

on the same day of each successive month, and commencing ________________ 19___

The final installment payable hereunder shall equal the amount of the deferred balance remaining due. Interest is due on installments after maturity at the highest lawful contract rate, and if this contract be placed with any attorney for collection, 15% of the amount due hereunder shall be paid by purchaser as attorney's fees, or if prohibited, the amount permitted by law.

The title in the property above described shall remain in the seller until the terms of this contract have been fully complied with. In case of any default in the performance of the terms and conditions hereof, the seller shall have the right to declare the full unpaid amount immediately due and payable and/or retake all the property. Buyer agrees not to move, sell, mortgage, encumber, pledge, or otherwise dispose of the property until paid for in full. Upon the performance by the buyer of all the conditions of this contract, title to the property is to vest in the buyer. It is mutually agreed that this instrument sets forth the entire contract.

Executed this ________________ day of ________________ 19___

____

(Purchaser's Signature) (Street) (Town) (State)

____

(Seller's Signature) (Street) (Town) (State)

________________________ ________________________

(Witness) (Witness)

Conditional sales agreements are set down in a legal form such as this. The form, properly filled out, signed, and witnessed, sets down the conditions of the contract and gives the seller the right to take legal action if the buyer does not meet the contract's conditions.

purposes of the sale, the consignment is a bailment. The owner, known as the *consignor,* retains ownership of the merchandise until it is sold. The person to whom the merchandise is shipped is known as the *consignee.*

As you have learned, merchandise is sometimes shipped on consignment by a manufacturer or distributor to a retailer. For example, a manufacturer of golf balls shipped three dozen packages of golf balls to the Perry Store to be sold at a specified price. The Perry Store was to sell the golf balls, deduct its selling commission and expenses, and remit the difference to the manufacturer.

Warranties

To complete a sale and encourage additional sales, a seller often makes certain guarantees of his product. The obligation the sellers incurs as a result of a guarantee is a warranty. The warranty may include a promise to repair or exchange the merchandise if defects are found to exist. There are two types of warranties: express and implied. If the article fails to operate as promised or to exist as represented, the contract is not void; however, the injured party has a right to make a claim for damages.

Information for a Warranty

- Who is making the warranty (manufacturer, wholesaler, or retailer).
- Whether the warranty applies to the entire product or only to parts of it.
- How the transaction of repair or replacement will be handled in case of unsatisfactory merchandise.
- Who is to pay for transportation and labor charges in replacing a part.
- Whether the replacement is to be valued at the price the customer paid for the product or at a higher replacement price (where the allowance under a warranty varies with the amount of use before failure, as with tires).

Express warranties should not simply be delivered orally; they should be printed on labels or leaflets accompanying the goods. Consumers Union recently set down these points as information that should be included in every warranty.

Express Warranty. An *express warranty* is a promise, representation, or assurance of some fact made by the seller to induce the purchase of his goods or services. For example, if a manufacturer states that a garment is sunfast, a buyer may bring action for damages if he purchases the goods and finds the statement to be false.

Implied Warranty. An *implied warranty* is an unstated assurance that is regarded as a characteristic of every contract to sell. Although the warranty is not made by the seller in words, it is implied by the law. Usually, the following implied warranties apply to sellers:

1. That the seller has a right to sell the goods.
2. That the buyer, upon receipt of the goods, shall not be troubled by the claims of others against the goods.

WARRANTY

THIS WARRANTY DOES NOT INCLUDE LABOR, SERVICE, OR TRANSPORTATION CHARGES

Zenith Radio Corporation warrants to the original consumer purchaser that it will replace Zenith parts, transistors and tubes (including color picture tube) in this Zenith color television receiver with new or rebuilt Zenith parts, transistors or tubes (including color picture tube) or at its option repair any such Zenith part, transistor or tubes (including color picture tube) in this receiver which, after regular installation and under normal use shall be found to have been defective and which is returned to an authorized Zenith dealer within one year (two years in case of color picture tube only) from the date of original consumer purchase of the receiver. Zenith approved replacement parts, transistors and tubes must be used and they will be covered for the unexpired portion of the applicable one or two year period. This warranty does not include labor in connection with the removal and/or installation of such repaired or replacement parts, transistors or tubes; nor does it include transportation or service charges.

Zenith Radio Corporation assumes no liability for failure to perform or delay in performing its obligations with respect to the above warranty if such failure or delay results, directly or indirectly, from any cause beyond its control including but not limited to acts of God, Acts of government, floods, fires, shortage of materials, and labor and/or transportation difficulties.

CONDITIONS AND EXCLUSIONS

This warranty is expressly in lieu of all other agreements and warranties, expressed or implied, including any implied WARRANTY OF MERCHANTABILITY OR FITNESS, and Zenith Radio Corporation does not assume any other obligation beyond the terms of this warranty.

The warranty herein extends only to the original consumer purchaser and is not assignable or transferable and shall not apply to any receiver or parts or transistors or tubes thereof which have been repaired or replaced by anyone else other than an authorized Zenith dealer, service contractor or distributor, or which have been subject to alteration, misuse, negligence or accident, or to the parts or transistors or tubes of any receiver which have had the serial number or name altered, defaced or removed.

Zenith Radio Corporation is under no obligation to extend this warranty to any receiver for which a Zenith warranty registration card has not been completed and mailed to the Corporation within fifteen (15) days after date of delivery.

ZENITH RADIO CORPORATION • CHICAGO, ILLINOIS 60639

MAIL THIS CARD TODAY

WHEN YOU MAIL THE REGISTRATION CARD BELOW THE WARRANTY ON YOUR

TELEVISION RECEIVER BECOMES EFFECTIVE

WARRANTY IS VOID UNLESS REGISTRATION CARD IS RETURNED TO US WITHIN 15 DAYS OF PURCHASE

IMPORTANT—PLEASE FILL IN BOTH SECTIONS OF CARD

MAIL THIS CARD TODAY

Zenith Corporation

This written warranty accompanied the purchase of a color television set. The customer was required to fill out and mail in a registration card before the warranty became valid. Note the information contained in this warranty.

3. That if the buyer makes known the particular purpose for which the goods are to be used and relies on the seller's skill and judgment, the goods shall be fit for that purpose.
4. That when the goods are sold by description, sample, or model, the goods shall conform to that description, sample, or model.
5. That when goods are sold by a manufacturer or a dealer who commonly handles such goods, the goods are or shall be salable.

One man bought a used car and soon thereafter suffered an accident that was caused by a defective steering mechanism. The court found that there was an implied warranty made both by the used-car dealer and by the manufacturer that the car was not defective. The court upheld the buyer's right to sue for damages.

CHECKING YOUR KNOWLEDGE

Vocabulary:

(1) contract
(2) mutual assent
(3) consideration
(4) sale of goods
(5) contract to sell
(6) conditional sale
(7) bailment
(8) bailee
(9) consignment selling
(10) consignor
(11) consignee
(12) express warranty
(13) implied warranty

Review questions:

1. In a contract, what may one of the parties do if the other party does not fulfill his part of the agreement? How may a contract evolve?
2. Name and explain the essential elements of a contract.
3. What is the difference between a sale and a contract to sell?
4. What responsibility does a bailee have for the goods that have been turned over to him?
5. Name five implied warranties that usually apply to sellers.

For discussion:

1. What are some examples of consideration? How might each of these examples apply to an actual contract?
2. Do you think that a salesman's responsibility also includes answering customers' questions about sales contracts? Why?
3. Suppose that you entered into an agreement to buy certain merchandise from the Jaeger Company, on the condition that the merchandise is delivered to you by the first Monday of next month. If the merchandise fails to arrive on the specified date, what recourse do you have?

part B

the law of agency

Anyone who does work for and is supervised by another person, such as a salesman of men's suits in a department store or a stock clerk in a discount store, is an employee. He is usually assigned regular working hours and must follow instructions on what he is to do and how he is to do it. In return, he is compensated according to the existing wage plan and receives the firm's various employee benefits.

Some workers carry out business transactions by making contracts for others whom they represent. A person who acts as a business representative for another is an *agent.* The person represented and authorizing the representation is the *principal.* Some workers are both employees and agents. A door-to-door salesman of encyclopedias is an agent in making contracts between the publisher and its customers, but he is an employee with respect to the job of soliciting orders.

CREATING AN AGENCY

Generally speaking, no one may act for another person unless he has authority to do so. When an agent is authorized to represent the principal in dealings with third persons, the relation of *agency* exists. The most common method of creating an agency is by appointment. The *appointment* defines the agent's duties and indicates the compensation or commission to be paid him. The appointment may be oral or written, formal or informal.

To understand the law of agency, you should know the difference between an employee and an independent agent or independent contractor. An employee, as distinguished from an independent agent, does not usually have the power to bind his employer in a contract. Also, he may not be hired to represent the firm in dealings with a third party. An *independent contractor* is hired to perform tasks for a specified fee but is independent of the control of the other party to the contract. The independent contractor may perform the job in any way he sees fit as long as he adheres to the contract's terms. Thus, a homeowner may either hire a gardener or make arrangements with an individual or company engaged in the lawn cutting and trimming business. The homeowner has many legal obligations to the gardener, who is an employee, that he does not have if the same job is done by an independent contractor.

Most professional salesmen are employees. Technically, in their selling negotiations they are inviting buyers to make offers which are accepted not by the salesmen themselves but by the firms they represent. Of course, the principals of many companies do the selling themselves and can complete contracts on the spot. Some salesmen are agents who agree to perform selling tasks for another in return for a fee or commission, not for a salary.

CLASSIFICATION OF AGENTS

Agents perform different kinds of duties, and their responsibilities vary. Agents are classified as general and special agents.

General Agent

A *general agent* is authorized to transact all of his principal's business of a particular type or all of his principal's business at a given place. The agent usually has the necessary power to conduct his principal's business. An example of a general agent is a purchasing agent. Unless limited by his principal, he has the power to purchase merchandise and may have the power to settle merchandise claims and to do all the other acts necessary to complete the purchasing duties.

Special Agent

A *special agent* is authorized to transact some specific act or acts of business. He has much less authority than the general agent. A retail employee who is authorized to buy goods is a special agent. Another kind of special agent is the commission merchant who sells property the principal delivers to him for that specific purpose. A broker is a special agent whose task is to bring buyer and seller together without taking possession of the goods. A manufacturer's agent is a special agent, since the prices and terms of sale are controlled by the principal and title passes from him directly to the agent's customers. An auctioneer is a special agent who sells property or goods to the highest bidder. He acts merely as the owner's representative in making the sale.

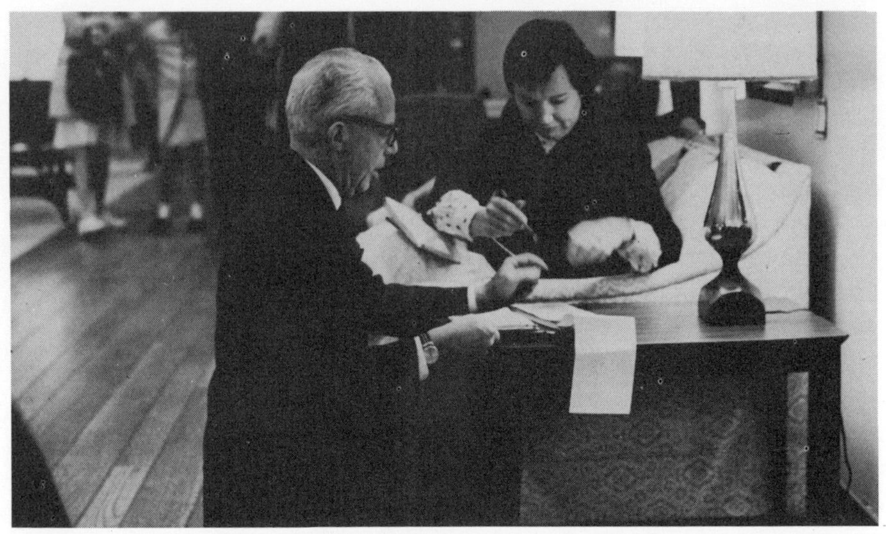

Macy's

This furniture salesman is explaining a conditional sales contract to a customer. Do you think that this salesman is an employee or an agent?

AUTHORITY OF AGENTS

The principal gives his agent certain *authority,* and it determines the extent of his power to act for the principal. The principal is bound by the agent's acts as long as the agent stays within this authority. The authority of agents may be classified as express, implied, or apparent.

Express Authority

When an agent is specifically appointed by a principal and given the right to act for him, the agent has *express authority*. For example, a distributor authorizes his agent to sell canned peas at $2.88 a case, so the agent has express authority to sell the peas at this price.

Implied Authority

When an agent has the authority to do anything necessary or customary to carry out the expressly authorized duties, he has *implied authority*. Suppose that Hendrickson, the principal, has authorized his agent, Robb, to purchase a farm tractor but has not given him funds to pay for the tractor. The agent thus has implied authority to purchase the tractor on credit.

Apparent Authority

An agent has *apparent authority* when the principal's words or actions reasonably lead a third party to believe that the agent has that authority. Wilkin bought a used car from Alden's Auto Company and left it on Alden's lot. Later, Hammer offered to buy Wilkin's car and Alden, without Wilkin's knowledge, sold it to him. Because Wilkin allowed Alden to retain possession of the car, he clothed Alden with apparent authority to sell the car. Wilkin could not recover the car from Hammer.

LIABILITY OF THE PRINCIPAL

The principal is liable to the third party for performing any contract made in his name as long as an agent acts within the authority given by his principal. If unauthorized acts of an agent are ratified, the principal is also liable. The principal is liable on authorized contracts made in his agent's name, except for certain negotiable contracts such as notes and checks. An agent authorized to purchase a new automobile would make his principal liable by signing the contract, "Foreman Construction Company, by John Hawkins, Agent." If Hawkins had omitted "Foreman Construction Company" and signed "John Hawkins, Agent," either he or the Foreman Construction Company would have been liable but not both.

If fraudulent acts are committed by an agent while performing his duties or if the acts are ratified, the principal is liable to third parties for these acts. If a commission merchant commits a fraud while selling something to a customer, the principal and the commission merchant are liable. A principal is also liable for any information the third party gives an agent, since knowledge or notice given to the agent is the same as knowledge or notice given to the principal.

LIABILITY OF THE AGENT TO THE THIRD PARTY

An agent may become personally liable to the third party in any one of several ways.

An agent may make himself personally liable for the breach of his principal's contract if he makes an express agreement with the third party. For example, an agent may promise delivery of goods by his company within 60 days. If the goods are not delivered within that time and his principal did not authorize the promise, the agent is liable.

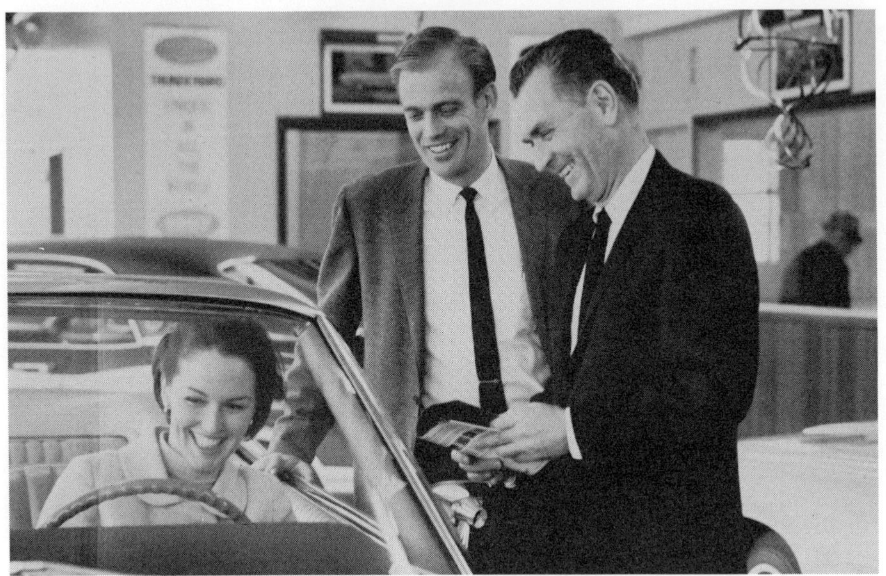

Ewing Galloway

Is an automobile salesman likely to be an agent? If so, is he likely to have express authority, implied authority, or apparent authority?

A person who acts as if he were the agent of another, without authority or by exceeding his authority, becomes liable to the person with whom he is dealing. Suppose that Jones claimed to be an agent of Smith and contracted with Thompson to sell a lawn mower belonging to Smith. Jones did not have authority to act for Smith, so Thompson could not hold Smith to the contract. However, Thompson could try to recover damages from Jones.

With a simple contract, if an agent conceals the existence or name of his principal, the third party can hold either the agent or the principal liable. With formal contracts, the agent alone is liable to the third party.

An agent is liable to a third person for money paid in error to the agent for his principal. An agent is not liable if the money has already been turned over to his principal in good faith.

Any wrongdoing committed within or outside the scope of an agent's employment makes him liable, even though he is acting as an agent of another. For example, a salesman for a farm machinery manufacturer made fraudulent statements in order to sell tractors to a dealer. The salesman was liable to the dealer for fraud, even though he was acting at the time as an agent. The salesman's principal was also liable.

RESPONSIBILITY OF THE PRINCIPAL TO HIS AGENT

Principals have the same obligations to their agents as employers have to their employees. An agent has the right to abandon his agreement if these obligations are not met. An agent is entitled to compensation if this has been agreed upon, although some agents may act without compensation from the principal. The principal is also obliged to reimburse the agent for expenses he incurs in performing his duties. The agent may not recover expenses made for illegal purposes or incurred through his own negligence. An agent can recover from his principal expense for any losses or damages he sustained in legally performing his duties. For example, an agent who innocently sold a bicycle belonging to a third party would be entitled to recover damages from his principal if the third party brought suit.

RESPONSIBILITY OF THE AGENT TO HIS PRINCIPAL

The agent has obligations to his principal because he derives certain authority from his principal. Greater confidence and trust are demanded of an agent than of an employee because an agent acts as a business representative of his principal. The agent must show good faith in all transactions for his principal. He owes his principal loyalty, and all his efforts must be for the principal's benefit. The agent is to obey his principal's instructions if they are legal and within the scope of his authority. An agent is required to exercise the degree of skill, care and diligence that a reasonably prudent man would use. An agent must account for all of the principal's money, merchandise, and equipment that are in the agent's possession; and he must keep his money and property separate from his principal's money and property.

TERMINATING AN AGENCY

An agency is terminated in accordance with the terms of the agreement, and either the principal or the agent may terminate an agency at any time. A principal terminates the relation by revoking his agent's authority; this is usually done at the principal's discretion. The power to revoke an agent's authority does not exist if the agent has a financial interest in the agency other than his commission or compensation. If a principal wrongfully revokes an agent's authority, he is liable for damages. If the agent wrongfully abandons the agency, the principal is entitled to damages.

CHECKING YOUR KNOWLEDGE

Vocabulary:

(1) agent
(2) principal
(3) agency
(4) appointment
(5) independent contractor
(6) general agent
(7) special agent
(8) authority
(9) express authority
(10) implied authority
(11) apparent authority

Review questions:

1. Explain the difference between an agent and an employee. Can a person be both an agent and an employee?
2. When is the principal liable to the third party for his agent's acts?
3. Under what conditions may an agent become personally liable to the third party?
4. What responsibilities does a principal have to his agent?
5. Why are greater confidence and greater trust demanded of an agent than of an employee?
6. How is an agency terminated?

For discussion:

1. Do you think that all salesmen would be more productive if they were agents rather than employees? Could all salesmen be agents rather than employees? Explain your answer.
2. Would a principal normally spend more time evaluating a prospective general agent with implied authority than he would a prospective employee who is to be closely supervised? Why?

part C

grading and labeling food and drugs

Warranty provisions of the law of sales give today's consumer some protection against buying unhealthful, unsafe, or unsuitable products. However, both consumer and government groups recognize that enforcing these provisions is not enough to protect the buyer. The sale of certain products must be approved or disapproved, and certain facts must be disclosed on labels and packages. Many sellers, in the interest of gaining repeat business, have voluntarily made such disclosures; but passing laws has been necessary to insure general compliance.

GRADING FOOD AND DRUG PRODUCTS

Grading is the process of separating a certain commodity into classes according to established standards. Standards to be met by food and drugs are established by two federal bodies, the Department of Agriculture and the Food and Drug Administration. The Department of Agriculture (USDA) inspects meat, butter, and eggs sold in interstate commerce and also makes sure that other foods are graded and inspected to insure their wholesomeness and quality. The Food and Drug Administration, which is responsible for administering the Food, Drug, and Cosmetic Act, has established standards for food and drug items to be shipped in interstate commerce. Goods are inspected to make sure they meet these standards.

Standards for Grading Foods

In cooperation with the USDA, food producers have developed standard grades for wholesome foods, such as A, B, C, and Off Grade. Off Grade products are safe for consumption but do not meet the requirements of the other grades. A USDA designation on a food item lets the consumer know the quality of the food she is buying. Canned tomatoes, for example, are graded using this scoring scale:

	Points
Drained weight (proportion of tomato solids to juice)	20
Wholeness (% of whole tomatoes)	20
Color	30
Absence of defects	30
	100

Tomatoes that score 90 points or more may be labeled grade A; and tomatoes with lower scores are labeled B, C, or Off Grade.

There is a direct relationship between grades and prices. It costs the producer more to meet the requirements of the higher grades. It may cost more to grow or procure better raw materials, and more care may be needed in sorting and packing.

In addition to the federal grading and inspection regulations, various states have their own regulations for foods sold in intrastate commerce. In New York, for instance, eggs must be graded by size, freshness, and appearance. The size grades are large, medium, small, and pullet (very small). The freshness and appearance grades are fancy grade, grade A, grade B, and grade C.

Grading and Inspecting Meats

Considerable attention is being given today to the grading and inspecting of fresh meat, poultry, and fish. The USDA requires that all meat sold and delivered across state lines be inspected to make sure it meets certain standards for wholesomeness. If the standards are met, the meat is stamped "USDA Inspected and Passed." Regulations now require that beef, veal, lamb, and mutton entering interstate commerce carry grade labels. The standard grades are Prime, Choice, Good, Standard, Commercial, and Utility. Most meats sold in supermarkets are of the Choice and Good grades, with Prime meat going mainly to high-class restaurants and dealers in meat specialties.

Food and Drug Administration

To make sure that food and drug products are safe for human consumption, the Food and Drug Administration does considerable testing of products before allowing them to be marketed.

Some states have been lax in their control of fresh meats, poultry, and fish; and some unhealthful products have been handled in intrastate commerce. The federal meat inspection laws are now being extended to meats sold in intrastate commerce to insure that only wholesome meat is available everywhere.

The Food, Drug, and Cosmetic Act

The Food and Drug Act of 1906 was the first major legislation designed to protect consumers from impure and misbranded foods and drugs. The act was amended in 1938 to include cosmetics. The amended act is known as the Federal Food, Drug, and Cosmetic Act and is enforced by the Food and Drug Administration. This law is concerned with protecting the consumer by insuring that foods are safe, pure, wholesome, and made under sanitary conditions.

The Food, Drug, and Cosmetic Act prohibits the manufacture or introduction into interstate commerce of any food that is adulterated. A product is *adulterated* if it does not meet minimum standards of purity and quality. The grading of foods is affected by provisions of the Food, Drug, and Cosmetic Act because no adulterated food could meet USDA standards. Generally speaking, a food is adulterated if any substance has been mixed with it so as to reduce its quality. This act also prohibits foods sold in interstate commerce from being prepared under unsanitary conditions. The Food Additives Amendments of 1958 and 1962 prevent the use of food additives that have not been adequately tested to establish their safety.

LABELING FOODS AND DRUGS

Labels on foods that meet acceptable standards must not be false or misleading. The Food, Drug, and Cosmetic Act has strict provisions for labeling food and drug items. Failure to state the required facts on the label is known as *misbranding,* and the firm guilty of misbranding is subject to a penalty.

Requisites for Labeling Foods

The chief requisites for labeling food products are:

1. *Standards of identity.* Foods labeled with certain names must measure up to certain standards. For example, the term "jam" may not be used unless the food contains at least 45 parts of fruit, by weight, to 55 parts of sweetening agent.

2. *Standards of quality.* Minimum standards of quality have been set up for many foods. For example, butter must be at least 80 percent butterfat to be labeled "butter." If a product does not measure up to the standard, it must be labeled "Below standard quality."
3. *Standards of fill of container.* Minimum standards of fill have been set up for many foods. For example, if canned tomatoes are not filled to at least 90 percent of capacity, they must be labeled "Below standard fill."
4. *Requirements for foods for which the FDA has not set standards.* The label must give the common name of the food—if there is one—and the ingredients—if the food contains two or more—named in the order of their prominence by weight.
5. *Foods sold for special dietary use.* If vitamin content is given, the label must also state the minimum daily requirements for the vitamin supplied by a specified amount of the food.
6. *Artificial coloring, flavoring, and chemical preservatives.* The presence of these elements must be stated on the label, except that artificial coloring does not have to be mentioned on labels for butter, cheese, and ice cream.
7. *Packaged foods.* Labels must state the name or place of business of the manufacturer, packer, or distributor, and the quantity of the contents in terms of weight, measure, or physical count.
8. *Processed foods.* Labels must state all the ingredients, except for freshly prepared foods such as baked goods.
9. *Imitation foods.* If the food is an imitation of another, it must bear on its label the word "imitation" (vanilla, for example).

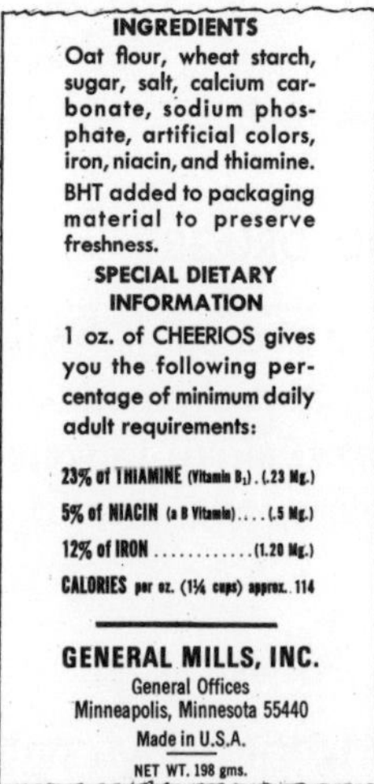

INGREDIENTS

Oat flour, wheat starch, sugar, salt, calcium carbonate, sodium phosphate, artificial colors, iron, niacin, and thiamine.

BHT added to packaging material to preserve freshness.

SPECIAL DIETARY INFORMATION

1 oz. of CHEERIOS gives you the following percentage of minimum daily adult requirements:

23% of THIAMINE (Vitamin B_1). (.23 Mg.)
5% of NIACIN (a B Vitamin) . . . . (.5 Mg.)
12% of IRON . . . . (1.20 Mg.)
CALORIES per oz. (1¼ cups) approx. 114

GENERAL MILLS, INC.
General Offices
Minneapolis, Minnesota 55440
Made in U.S.A.
NET WT. 198 gms.

General Mills

Study this portion of a label from a box of breakfast cereal. Does it conform to the chief requisites for labeling foods?

Requisites for Labeling Drugs

The chief requisites for labeling drug products are:

1. If a drug differs in strength, quality, or purity from the standards in the *U. S. Pharmacopoeia* or the *Homeopathic Pharmacopoeia* (publications containing standards developed by agencies of the federal government), the label must tell how it differs.
2. If a drug does not comply with the identity prescribed for it in one of the official publications, the name by which it is designated must differ clearly from the name in the publication.
3. Both the generic name and the drug must be stated on the label.
4. Packaged drugs must be labeled with the name and place of business of the manufacturer, packer, or distributor, and the quantity of the contents in terms of weight, measure, or numerical count.
5. If the drug contains any one of 17 narcotic or hypnotic drugs, its presence and proportions must be indicated. The label must also contain the statement: "Warning—May be Habit Forming."
6. If a drug is compounded of two or more ingredients, the label must state the name of each active ingredient; the quantity, kind, and proportion of any alcohol present; and the presence and quantity of any one of 18 drugs specified by law as dangerous to some people.
7. Labels must carry adequate warnings against use in pathological conditions or by children.
8. In labeling new drugs, possible side effects and inadvisable usages must be stated.

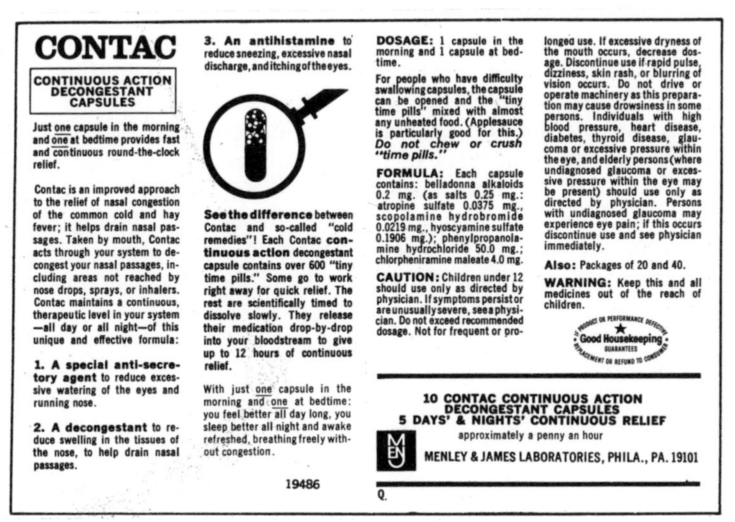

Menley & James Laboratories, Ltd.

This drug label gives detailed information to protect the safety of the consumer. Notice how it conforms to the above requisites for labeling drugs.

Fair Packaging and Labeling Bill

The Fair Packaging and Labeling Bill, passed in 1967, has important implications for the labeling of food items. The five general provisions of this piece of legislation are:

1. Containers must be labeled so that shoppers can easily see the weight or volume of the contents.
2. Meaningless or misleading designations such as "jumbo pound" cannot be used.
3. When a package promises to give a certain number of servings, it must state the weight per serving.
4. A certain ratio of air space between the top of the box and its contents must be maintained.
5. The use of "cents off" labels that indicate an item is being sold at a bargain price are regulated but not prohibited.

CHECKING YOUR KNOWLEDGE

Vocabulary:

(1) grading
(2) adulterated
(3) misbranding

Review questions:

1. Name the government agencies responsible for establishing food and drug standards. Briefly describe the activities of each.
2. What is the relationship between grades of foods and their prices?
3. Explain the basic purposes of the Food, Drug, and Cosmetic Act and the Food Additives Amendments of 1958 and 1962.
4. Name four important requisites for the labeling of food products and four important requisites for the labeling of drug products.
5. What are some important provisions of the Fair Packaging and Labeling Bill?

For discussion:

1. Do you think that government grading has resulted in more nutritious foods? Why?
2. Some meat and egg producers feel that their products should not be subject to federal regulations as long as these products are sold locally. Do you agree? Why?
3. Do customers pay much attention to the mandatory information that appears on labels? If not, is there any value in demanding that the information appear?

part D

labeling nonfood products

Various legislation regulates the labeling of many nonfood items. Some important nonfood items which come under such regulations are cosmetics, cigarettes, textile products, furs, shoes and slippers, and household products and appliances. As you learned in Chapter 6, it is the salesman's duty to (1) notify his employer if any articles he sells fail to carry the required labels; (2) acquaint himself with the significance of all ingredients that must be reported on labels; and (3) regard labels as an important source of selling points to use in presenting merchandise.

LABELING COSMETICS

The major provisions of the Food, Drug, and Cosmetic Act in regard to cosmetic labeling are:

1. The labels of packaged cosmetics must state the name and place of business of the manufacturer, packer, or distributor, and must give the net weight of the contents.
2. Labels of products made with coal-tar dyes must carry the following statement: "Caution: This product contains ingredients which may cause skin irritation on certain individuals, and a preliminary test according to accompanying directions should first be made. This product must not be used for dyeing the eyelashes or eyebrows. To do so may cause blindness."
3. Exaggerated claims of benefits from using the product must not be made.
4. If the name of a cosmetic suggests an ingredient, such as cucumber cream, then cucumber must be an important ingredient in the product.

The cosmetics themselves must be made of pure, fresh, and nonpoisonous substances and packed under sanitary conditions. Hair dyes are the only cosmetics that may contain coal-tar substances.

LABELING CIGARETTES

There is growing evidence of a causal relationship between cigarette smoking and cancer and certain respiratory diseases. This evidence led to the recent passage of the Federal Cigarette Labeling and Advertising Law. All cigarette packages must bear the warning statement, "Caution: Cigarette smoking may be hazardous to your health." This statement has had little or no effect on the consumption of cigarettes, however. The Federal Trade Commission—the government agency responsible for administering the law—would like to have another phrase added to cigarette packages: "and may cause death from cancer and other diseases." The Commission is also pushing for labeling laws to require disclosure of tar and nicotine content and laws to prohibit advertising of cigarettes on television.

LABELING TEXTILE PRODUCTS

Prodded by consumers and certain business groups, the federal government became convinced some years ago that dealers and ultimate consumers needed information about the fiber content of the textile products they were selling or purchasing. One law which was passed as a result of this movement was the Wool Products Labeling Act. It requires that, with a few exceptions, labels on wool products indicate the percentage of new wool, reprocessed wool, and reused wool in the product. The label must also give the name of the manufacturer or his registration number and the name of the reseller.

In 1958, a broad textile labeling law covering all fibers was enacted. This act, the Textile Fiber Products Identification Act, requires that textile products be labeled so as to reveal the fiber content. With fabrics made of several fibers, the percentage, by weight, of each fiber in the product must be stated.

To protect buyers and sellers of certain synthetic fibers that are dangerous when used in wearing apparel, the Flammable Fabrics Act was passed in 1953 and amended and revised in 1967. This act prohibits the manufacture and sale of any fabrics which are so highly flammable as to be dangerous when used in wearing apparel or home furnishings. Unfortunately, the standards of flammability are not stringent enough to eliminate all risk to the careless user.

LABELING FURS

The Fur Labeling Act requires that all fur products be labeled with the following information:

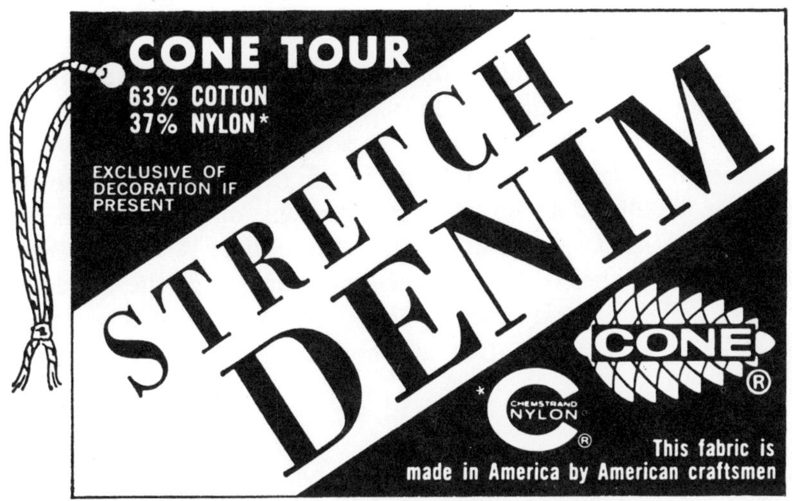

WASH AND WEAR
CARE INSTRUCTIONS

Wash by machine or hand using any good soap or detergent. Avoid the use of chlorine bleach. This garment can go through the full washing machine cycle. When home dryers are used, best results will be obtained by using the low temperature setting. If automatic dryer is not used, rewet the garment after washing cycle has been completed, then place on wooden hanger to drip dry. If touch up ironing is desired, use a steam or warm iron (low or synthetic setting) on dampened garment. If dry cleaned, make certain dry cleaner is advised of fiber content.

®CONE MILLS INC.
New York 18, N. Y.

A CONE® FABRIC

Printed in U.S.A.

L-1100-16

Does this textile product label conform to the basic requirements of the Textile Fiber Products Identification Act? What important selling points might this label give the salesman?

1. How the fur has been finished (natural, bleached, dyed, and so on).
2. The established name or names of the animal or animals that produced the fur.
3. The name of the country of origin, if any imported furs were used.
4. The name or registered identification number of the manufacturer or dealer.

LABELING SHOES AND SLIPPERS

The Federal Trade Commission has set down rules requiring the labeling of shoes and slippers made of nonleather materials that have the appearance of leather. These rules do not have the force of law, but the Commission can issue a complaint charging unfair competition if a manufacturer or seller does not have stamps, tags, or labels attached to these nonleather articles, indicating their composition. All-leather items do not have to be labeled; but they generally are, since the all-leather composition makes a good selling point. Retailers find it wise to ask their suppliers for assurance that all shoes and slippers are properly labeled.

LABELING HOUSEHOLD PRODUCTS AND APPLIANCES

Some household products, such as furniture polish, cleaning fluids, and metal polishes, contain substances which can cause illness or death if they are improperly used. The Federal Hazardous Substance Act requires that labels must warn consumers about the hazards of using products containing toxic substances. Also, the label must contain directions for precautionary measures and must describe antidotes or first-aid treatment to be given in case of accident.

With electric and gas appliances, labeling based on industry tests has proven practicable. For a small fee, the Underwriters Laboratories, Inc., will test and authorize the use of electrical appliances as being free from fire and shock hazards. This organization's seal of approval on an item is a protection to both the seller and the consumer. Gas appliances are similarly tested by the American Gas Association.

CHECKING YOUR KNOWLEDGE

Review questions:

1. What are the provisions of the Federal Cigarette Labeling and Advertising Law? Why was this law passed?
2. What are the general provisions of the Textile Fiber Products Identification Act?
3. Explain the basic provisions of the Fur Labeling Act.
4. What is the Federal Hazardous Substance Act?
5. How do the Underwriters Laboratories, Inc., and the American Gas Association contribute to improved household appliances?

For discussion:

1. Should the advertising of cigarettes on television be banned?
2. Do you think that increased use of man-made fibers will bring about less need for federal regulation of textile fiber identification? Why?

part E

regulation of advertising and pricing

Years ago, selling firms were guilty of unethical practices in advertising and pricing their goods. Sellers made statements about their goods that were either not true or were exaggerations of the truth. In pricing their products, some sellers discriminated among buyers and tried to drive competitors out of business by cutthroat pricing tactics. Some sellers are still guilty of such things as false advertising and price discrimination, but now there is a considerable amount of legislation to protect consumers from these unethical practices.

ADVERTISING REGULATIONS

There are many more rules and regulations to govern advertising statements than there are to govern oral statements made in personal selling. From an ethical point of view, the salesman should adhere to the same standards required for advertising and labeling when he makes his sales presentation.

In 1938, Congress passed the Wheeler-Lea Act. Before that time, the Federal Trade Commission could restrain the unethical advertising practices of selling firms only if injury to competition could be proved. But under the provisions of the Wheeler-Lea Act, it is necessary only to prove that customers are being misled and deceived. The bill gave the Commission specific jurisdiction over the advertising of foods, drugs, and cosmetics, with the power to issue temporary injunctions to stop misleading advertising. Formerly, such practices could not be stopped until extensive hearings had been held. Other laws extended the jurisdiction of the FTC.

False and Misleading Advertising

Under the broad provisions of federal laws, the FTC can take legal action against all firms engaged in interstate commerce whose advertising is false or is intended to be misleading. *Puffing,* however, is not illegal. This refers to a slight exaggeration of the truth that reflects the seller's enthusiastic opinion of his product. It is permissible to advertise a sewing machine as "almost human" but would be illegal to say that the machine "gives the housewife a tailor's skill."

Bait Advertising

Bait advertising tries to lure a customer to the seller's place of business where the seller will try to convince him not to buy the bait product but to buy another item whose sale is more profitable to the seller. Sometimes salesmen claim that the supply of the bait product has been exhausted, or they make disparaging remarks about the bait product while they promote the virtues of the more profitable article. These tactics are illegal for goods involved in interstate commerce and are also illegal under the laws of most states.

Advertising Disclosures

In connection with labeling laws, the FTC has the authority to set and enforce advertising standards for textiles and other products that must carry informative labels. In connection with textile fabrics, the chief rules are:

1. The generic name of the fibers used must appear in each advertisement unless an assortment of items with varying fiber content is advertised collectively with no reference to fiber contents.
2. With fabrics made of mixed fibers, the various fibers must be listed in descending order by weight but not necessarily in percentage form.
3. At least once in an advertisement for mixed goods, the generic fiber names must be disclosed in immediate conjunction with the fiber trademark and in the same size type.
4. Words or terms that imply the presence of a fur, hair, or fiber not contained in the product should not appear in the ad.

Misleading Guarantees

Some retailers make broad statements to guarantee something about their products, without spelling out just what the guarantee means. The

Prominence
to constituent fibers in mixed goods
CORRECT
rayon and linen
DRESSES
Correct without highlighting.
Reinforced with Nylon
made of cotton and 10% nylon
Correct as heading indicates "nylon" is a minor component, the % of same is given, and the full disclosure appears in bold type.
ARNEL* and cotton
DRESSES
Arnel Triacetate and Cotton
*Celanese trademark.
Fiber trademark of predominant fiber emphasized in headline with full disclosure made in body in equal size.
Cashmere blend
SWEATERS
made of cashmere and wool
Correct if cashmere is predominant by weight.
There's SILK
in the BLEND
Rayon, Acetate and
25% Silk Dresses
$15
Silk is not predominant fiber and heading does not indicate it is a minor fiber. Full disclosure and per cent of featured fiber is made in subhead.
INCORRECT
Every Fashion Angle says
WOOL
in a fabric of rayon, acetate and wool.
Improper emphasis on minor fiber with constituent fibers only mentioned in body copy. Headline also implies all wool.
Rayon and
Silk
CORD SUITS
Improper since silk in larger type, is minor fiber and a subhead giving % of same and full disclosure is nct used.

Here are some of the correct and incorrect ways of advertising fiber content of textile products. Can you find any instances in which textile advertising standards have been violated?

FTC regards guarantees as illegal unless there is an exact description of the guarantee and the action that a customer can take if the product fails to live up to the guarantee. To state "Guaranteed lowest price in town" is illegal unless there is a statement of the recourse available to the customer if he finds an equal or a lower price in town.

Advertising Comparative Prices

A retail advertising practice that has often been misleading to customers is the advertising of comparative prices. This is done to make customers think that the advertised goods are a great bargain when, in reality, the comparative price quoted may not be a truthful figure. In 1964, a number of rules for advertising comparative prices were passed. Three of the most important of these rules are:

1. If the comparison is made with a former price of the seller, the comparative price must be the actual price at which the article was offered to the public for a considerable period of time.
2. If the comparison refers to the price charged by other retailers, the seller must be reasonably certain that the higher price he advertises does not appreciably exceed the price at which substantial sales of the article are being made in his area.
3. If the comparison refers to retail or list prices suggested by the manufacturer, this price must be the actual one charged in the retail outlets that do not conduct their business on a discount basis.

Although these rules cover advertising whose circulation crosses state lines, the seller should also follow them as an ethical matter in his local use of signs and mailings. Salespeople should be careful not to make comparative claims that violate these rules.

PRICING REGULATIONS

The salesman usually has no direct control over the setting of prices. However, understanding the price regulations and restrictive agreements that are illegal makes it easier for him to resist undue pressure from buyers and to keep from participating in discussions with competitors aimed at keeping up prices or monopolizing the market. The kinds of pricing regulations with which every salesman should be acquainted are price discrimination laws, resale price maintenance laws, and antitrust laws.

Price Discrimination Laws

Price discrimination laws are designed to keep manufacturers and wholesalers from giving favored buyers price advantages that are not given to competing buyers who purchase goods of like quantity and quality. The principal law prohibiting price discrimination is the Robinson-Patman Act. It provides that any concessions in selling price must be justified, mainly on the basis that they do not exceed the seller's savings in production, sales, and delivery costs growing out of the quantity purchased by the buyer or out of his special purchasing methods. Concessions are also justified due to changes in market conditions and to the necessity of meeting a competitor's prices.

Buyers who knowingly or without reasonable investigation accept discriminatory prices are liable for penalties, just as sellers are. Salesmen should recognize that their firms have a responsibility to resist buyers' demands for unfair concessions. Negotiation with buyers in regard to price and terms is lawful, but the agreements reached must consider the rights of other buyers and be justifiable under the law.

Resale Price Maintenance Laws

There are two kinds of resale price maintenance laws: fair-trade laws and unfair-practices laws. Both kinds of laws are enacted by the states. *Fair-trade laws* permit manufacturers or distributors of trademarked or branded goods to set by contract with wholesalers and retailers the prices at which these goods will be resold. In some states, once a contract for a certain resale price has been signed with a single dealer in the state, the product cannot be sold for less than the stipulated price anywhere in the state. Fair-trade laws are intended to keep retailers from cutting prices on the manufacturer's product.

Unfair-practices laws keep dealers from selling merchandise below cost. Such laws are designed specifically to prevent the use of loss leaders. Unfair-practices laws help protect small merchants from cutthroat pricing policies of large merchants who can often buy for less because of their quantity purchases and can afford to sell a few items at a cut price to attract customers to their stores.

Antitrust Laws

The Sherman Antitrust Act of 1890 makes it illegal for a company to use its power to gain a position of monopoly, or control of an industry or service. This act declares that contracts, combinations, or conspiracies in restraint of trade are illegal. The Clayton Act of 1914 outlaws the sale and lease of merchandise on the condition that the buyer will not handle a competitor's products. While it is legal for a seller to restrict his sales to an exclusive agent in a sales territory, he may not insist that the buyer handle no competing lines or that the buyer restrict his selling wholly to a specified territory. The Federal Trade Commission Act of 1914, under which the Federal Trade Commission was created, has as its main objective the maintenance of a free enterprise system. The Antimerger Law of 1950 attempts to prevent the suppression of competition through the merger or consolidation of corporations, but many mergers are still permissible.

CHECKING YOUR KNOWLEDGE

Vocabulary:

(1) puffing
(2) bait advertising
(3) price discrimination laws
(4) fair-trade laws
(5) unfair-practices laws

Review questions:

1. What was the first law to give the Federal Trade Commission strong authority to regulate advertising practices?
2. What must a guarantee state in order to be legal?
3. List three of the most important rules for advertising comparative prices.
4. What is the principal law prohibiting price discrimination? What are its basic provisions?
5. Who enacts resale price maintenance laws?
6. Explain the unethical selling practice that is outlawed by the Clayton Act of 1914.

For discussion:

1. Are many customers really fooled by false or misleading advertising, or do they recognize the tendency of advertisers to exaggerate?
2. Would it be a good thing if all use of comparative prices in advertising were outlawed? Why?
3. Would you prefer to see sellers free to set any prices they wish rather than being subject to certain pricing restrictions? Explain.

BUILDING YOUR SKILLS

Improving your English:

Each of the following sentences contains one word that makes the sentence incorrect. On a separate sheet of paper, write the correct word to be used in each sentence.

1. The boy and girls has attended the pet show.
2. John gave the package to Mary and I.
3. Neither the principal or the school secretary was aware of Linda's illness.
4. The mantel clock is the largest of the two displayed.
5. Charles Ivey, of all the engineers, are quite familiar with the use of enzymes.
6. The chain link fence is the more durable of the three.
7. Dealer reaction to the new display case should be obtained easy by our salesmen.

8. The relation of agency did not exist between Raymond and he.
9. Food grading regulations are being followed in all Freedman stores accept Store 22.
10. The personnel manager has been unable to advice her because the newer regulations have not been announced.

Improving your arithmetic:

The problems below involve more than one step in obtaining their solution; show each step used.

1. Frank Lyons receives a monthly salary of $400 and is paid a commission on all sales. His total earnings last year were $9,460. If his sales for the year were $116,500, what was his rate of commission?
2. Joe Jones has purchased a new car for $3,200. His trade-in allowance for his old car was $600. He financed the car through a local bank at the rate of 5% on the original unpaid balance. How much will the monthly payment be on a 24-month contract?
3. Hanson, Carr, and Hobbs invested $10,000, $20,000, and $30,000, respectively, in a partnership. They have agreed that each will receive 6% interest on his investment each year and that the remaining profit will be divided equally. The profit for last year was $25,350. How much should each partner receive as his share of the profit?

Improving your research skills:

1. Contact at least two different retailers in your community who sell merchandise under conditional sales contracts. Secure the following information: (a) what type of merchandise is usually involved; (b) why the merchandise is sold under a conditional sales contract; (c) when the customer acquires possession of and title to the merchandise; (d) action that is taken if the customer defaults on payments; and (e) who suffers the loss if the merchandise is destroyed or stolen while the customer has possession of but not title to the merchandise.
2. Inspect five warranty statements attached to appliances. Do they provide the information recommended on page 551?
3. Through research, find out what you can about the scoring systems used in grading various food products. Give your findings in report form.
4. Study the labels on a food product, a drug product, and a cosmetic product. Do they all conform to the requisites for labeling given in the text? Give your findings in class.
5. Collect five newspaper or magazine advertisements containing statements that you think could be termed false or misleading. Rewrite these statements so that their claims are realistic.
6. Make a list of at least a dozen articles sold in your community whose prices are fixed by manufacturers and which are sold under the fair-trade laws.

APPLYING YOUR KNOWLEDGE

Case problems:

1. Assume that you are a licensed driver and that you borrow your father's car to run an errand. While you are running the errand, the car's fender is dented in a minor accident. Your father takes the car to a body shop for an estimate of the cost to repair the fender. He accepts the repairman's estimate as a fair charge and instructs the repairman to fix the fender. Upon completion of the repair job, the repairman says that he made a mistake in his estimate and that the charge is $10 more than originally agreed upon. Must your father pay the extra charge? Why or why not?
2. Assume that you enter a drugstore and ask the druggist for a preparation that will fight sleepiness. The druggist recommends a preparation called Wideawake and states that, "One Wideawake table will definitely rid you of your sleepy, drowsy feeling for at least three hours." After taking one Wideawake tablet on several different occasions, you find that it does not reduce your drowsy feeling at all. What type of warranty was extended to you by the druggist? What recourse, if any, do you have?

Continuing project:

In your manual, perform the following activities:

1. Tell how the laws of contract and sales and the law of agency will affect you in selling your product.
2. List the grading and labeling regulations, if any, that would apply to your product.
3. Describe the advertising and pricing regulations to which you would have to conform.

As the last chapter in your manual, show how you could use the manual (or at least the merchandise knowledge you have gained in preparing it) in obtaining a job selling your chosen product or service. Then edit your manual carefully, enclose it in an attractive cover, and submit it to your instructor.

Extra credit:

The Federal Trade Commission is now concerned over the widespread use of consumer games by supermarkets and service stations. These games increase distribution costs unless stores can increase sales volume five dollars for every dollar spent on games. Few stores now can realize such a sales-increase ratio. Besides the cost question, the FTC is also concerned with the following practices:

1. The prize-winning numbers are often made available to customers during the first weeks of the game, with all later numbers being

losing numbers. Yet, advertising gives the impression that players have an equal chance of winning any time during the game period.

2. Rather than distributing winning numbers at random, stores needing a special publicity boost are sometimes chosen in advance to receive the large prize-winning numbers.
3. Advertising gives the impression that the customer has a good chance of winning a substantial prize, but his chances of winning anything are remote.
4. Some dishonest dealers try to spot prize-winning numbers and keep them for themselves.
5. Dealers are sometimes coerced by their suppliers to participate in the game and share in the costs, even though the dealers would prefer not to do so.

Using these facts, research this subject in current newspapers and periodicals. In a report, tell what steps, if any, you think the FTC should take in regard to the regulation of such games.

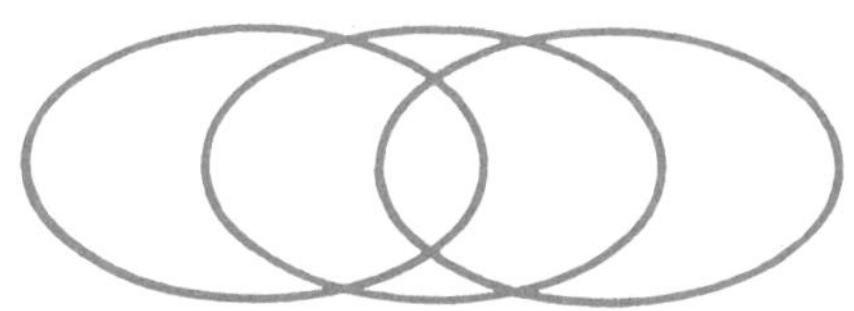

index

a

b

d

e

f

h

i

n

o

P

S

t

u

v

y